"At times a book comes along that subjects common rhetoric and typical tropes to a withering criticism, but rarely does that kind of critical study put in place an alternative that compels—but William Witt has done just that with this compendium on ordaining women. This will become the standard book for years to come. A rare achievement."
　　　　　　—SCOT McKNIGHT, *Professor of New Testament, Northern Seminary*

"Theologian, ethicist, and skilled reader of biblical texts, William Witt sets forth a refreshing, intentionally theological defense of the ordination of women. One might have thought this question settled. Indeed in many churches of the enclave of Protestant bodies it is, either yea or nay. But Witt steps back to examine the scene and delineates a number of positions, kinds of approaches, and types of arguments. Witt's ecumenical examination into the subject of the ordination of women is respectful, learned, and convincing. A creative step forward."
　　　　　　—KATHRYN GREENE-McCREIGHT, *author of* Feminist
　　　　　　Reconstructions of Christian Doctrine

"Should women be allowed to be ordained church leaders? While some may think the conversation has moved on and the question is settled, this is simply not the case for our diverse and global Church. In this wonderfully comprehensive and convincing new book, Witt provides us with the best single volume yet on the topic of women in church leadership. The book is theologically orthodox and biblically grounded in a way that should appeal to any thoughtful Christian. By taking on both Catholic and evangelical arguments in a scholarly yet readable style, he shows the weakness of the majority view that would bar women from priesthood or pastorate on the basis of their gender. Demonstrating a generous orthodoxy and biblical faithfulness, this book should be studied by thinking Christians of all kinds and places considering this question for the Church today."
　　　　　　—ALAN G. PADGETT, *Professor of Systematic Theology, Luther Seminary*

ICONS OF CHRIST

A Biblical and Systematic Theology for Women's Ordination

William G. Witt

BAYLOR UNIVERSITY PRESS

Cover and book design by Kasey McBeath
Cover image: St Justina, detail from the Holy Virgins Procession, mosaic, north wall,
lower level, Basilica of Sant'Apollinare Nuovo (UNESCO World Heritage List, 1996),
Ravenna, Emilia-Romagna. Italy, 6th century. © A. Dagli Orti / De Agostini Picture
Library / Bridgeman Images

First paperback printing in January 2021 under ISBN 978-1-4813-1319-3
First printed case printing in January 2021 under ISBN 978-1-4813-1666-8
The paperback and printed case printings include a new section entitled
"Postscript to chapter 3" (pp. 37–38). Pagination is unchanged from the
hardcover printing.

The Library of Congress has cataloged the hardcover as follows:

Names: Witt, William G., 1955- author.
Title: Icons of Christ : a biblical and systematic theology for women's
    ordination / William G. Witt.
Description: Waco : Baylor University Press, 2020. | Includes
    bibliographical references. | Summary: "Addresses traditional Catholic
    and Protestant arguments against women's ordination and mounts
    counterarguments from Scripture and tradition"-- Provided by publisher.
Identifiers: LCCN 2020024822 (print) | LCCN 2020024823 (ebook) | ISBN
    9781481313186 (hardcover) | ISBN 9781481313384 (pdf) |
    ISBN 9781481313209 (epub)
Subjects: LCSH: Ordination of women--Christianity. | Ordination of women.
Classification: LCC BV676 .W53 2020 (print) | LCC BV676 (ebook) | DDC
    262/.14082--dc23
LC record available at https://lccn.loc.gov/2020024822
LC ebook record available at https://lccn.loc.gov/2020024823

NATIONAL
ENDOWMENT
FOR THE
HUMANITIES

Icons of Christ has been made possible in part by a major grant from the National
Endowment for the Humanities: NEH CARES. Any views, findings, conclusions,
or recommendations expressed in this book do not necessarily represent those of
the National Endowment for the Humanities.

CONTENTS

Catholic Arguments

The Ministry of Women in the New Testament

PREFACE

HOW THIS BOOK CAME TO BE WRITTEN

A few years ago, my colleague the Rev. Dr. Martha Giltinan asked me to write some essays on women's ordination. I originally declined for the following reasons: (1) I am a man, and I thought that a woman should make this argument; (2) I am a lay person, and I thought that these essays should be written by someone who was ordained; (3) I wanted to encourage Martha to write more on this topic since it concerned her directly. Martha responded by pointing out that I had the theological background in historical and systematic theology that she did not, and she was not going to quit asking me until I wrote something. I finally gave in, and began writing what I thought would be a short series of essays, but turned into a book. Unfortunately, Martha became ill shortly after I began and did not live to see me finish this project.

I dedicate this book first to my dear friend the Rev. Dr. Martha Giltinan, a woman who lived out her vocation as an Anglican priest, who ministered to and was loved by literally thousands of people. No one who knew Martha was ever the same afterward. I have also known a number of orthodox ordained women clergy who are my friends, and whom I greatly admire, and at the seminary where I teach I have been privileged to have as students women who were among the best students, finest preachers, and some of the most promising theologians of any of my students. I think it would be a great tragedy for the church to deny these women the opportunity to use their gifts and pursue their callings, but also to be served by them. I wrote this book primarily for these women. May this book encourage you to follow your vocations, whether lay or ordained.

A NOTE ON BIBLE TRANSLATION AND "INCLUSIVE" LANGUAGE

One of the issues that had to be settled when I first began writing this book was which English translation of the Bible I should use. On the one hand, translations such as the New Revised Standard Version and the more recent New International Version have the advantage of using "inclusive language"; that is, inasmuch as possible they translate passages that refer to both men and women in a manner that avoids the use of language that could be read as referring only to males. Unfortunately, as a result, these translations sometimes lean toward paraphrase. The NRSV pluralizes Psalm 1 so that it begins, "Happy are those who do not follow the advice of the wicked" rather than the more literal earlier RSV, which makes clear that the Hebrew text refers to an individual: "Blessed is the man who walks not in the counsel of the wicked."

Because much of my argument depends on a careful reading of biblical texts, I have preferred a more literal translation, and so, unless indicated otherwise, all biblical references are to the English Standard Version, which, like the NRSV, is a revision of the RSV, but more faithfully follows the RSV's more literal "word for word" translation philosophy. Unfortunately, the translators of the ESV also tend toward a "complementarian" theology, and occasionally their translation inconsistently departs from a more literal approach to impose a complementarian reading on texts that is not in the original languages. For example, the NIV correctly translates 1 Corinthians 11:10 as, "it is for this reason that a woman ought to have authority over her own head, because of the angels." That is, the "authority" to which the apostle Paul refers is the woman's own authority. The ESV misleadingly translates this: "That is why a wife ought to have a symbol of authority on her head, because of the angels," implying that the authority is that of a husband over his wife. However, the words "symbol of" are not in the original Greek, and nothing in the context indicates that the woman is a wife. When the ESV translation is misleading, or, when necessary to clarify the meaning of the original texts, I have supplied my own translation or indicated alternative translations.

Introduction

1

Preliminaries

In this book, I intend to make a theological argument for the ordination of women to the ecclesial ministerial office of presbyter (New Testament *presbyteros*, πρεσβύτερος), usually referred to in Protestant churches as "pastors" and in Roman Catholic, Orthodox, and Anglican churches as "priests." There is a general ecumenical consensus that the primary role of the presbyter/pastor/priest is to lead the gathered congregation in worship, specifically in the preaching of the Word and in celebrating or presiding over the ministry of the sacraments.[1] For purposes of clarity, this office of Word and Sacrament needs to be distinguished from other forms of service or ministry in the church that might be designated as "charisms," but are examples of what could be called "lay ministries," and which might include some forms of teaching, preaching, or various ministries of service, such as ministering to the sick.[2]

The office of presbyter would be distinguished from such lay ministries by its permanent rather than occasional character, a certain sort of authority that pertains to office as opposed to other forms of service, presiding over the gathered worship of the community, and a designated setting aside by the greater church usually denoted by such sacramental gestures as the laying on of hands. This distinction between church office and lay ministries is important to make clear that the argument concerns not whether women can exercise some sort of ministries within the church, but specifically whether women can be set aside and ordained to the office of Word and Sacrament.

An actual argument needs to be made because the ordination of women to church office is (in terms of the entire expanse of church history) a relatively recent phenomenon, first occurring after the American Civil War in the late nineteenth century among churches connected with the abolition of slavery.[3] The first woman ordained as a priest in the Anglican communion was Asian, Florence Li Tim-Oi, ordained in Hong Kong in 1944. The ordination of women was gradually introduced into mainline Protestant churches in the mid-twentieth century, with perhaps the majority of Lutheran, Reformed, Anglican, and Methodist churches now ordaining women. Within the Roman Catholic Church, some called for the ordination of women following the Second Vatican Council. Among liberal Protestants, women's ordination is closely connected to the theological movement of "feminist theology."

At the same time, the practice of ordaining women continues to be controversial, especially among more conservative or "traditional" denominations. Within mainline Protestant denominations, there are still significant numbers of Lutherans, Reformed, Anglicans, and Methodists who oppose the practice of ordaining women. For Evangelicals, disagreement is marked by the differing positions of "complementarianism," opposing women's ordination (associated with "The Council on Biblical Manhood and Womanhood") and "egalitarianism," affirming women's ordination (associated with "Christians for Biblical Equality"). The magisterium of the Roman Catholic Church definitively stated its opposition to the ordination of women in Pope John Paul II's *Ordinatio Sacerdotalis* (1994), and the Eastern Orthodox Churches continue to oppose women's ordination. However, among Roman Catholics, there has been considerable disagreement with the official position, and there have even been some Orthodox advocates of women's ordination.

The ordination of women is related to other recent movements in social and cultural history following the industrial revolution connected with the changing nature of the family, changing roles between men and women, as well as modern movements for greater social freedom and equality. These include the abolition of slavery, the civil rights movement of the 1960s, movements for greater worker equality and practices such as labor unions in the work place, racial equality, changes in industry and economic structures leading to more women working outside the home. More recently there have been changes in sexual mores, such as rising divorce rates, greater acceptance of pre-marital and extra-marital sex, homosexuality and, even more recently, transgenderism.[4]

The historic churches (mainline and Evangelical Protestant, Catholic and Orthodox) have responded to these social changes with ambivalence. Generally, they have embraced the positive fruits of modern social change and the civil rights movement, endorsing racial equality as well as affirming the rights of workers in the workplace. Churches have often been at the forefront of movements to care for immigrants, the poor, and the homeless. All historic churches now affirm the equality of women in the family, the workplace, and in churches. At the same time, churches have resisted many of the negative and more controversial social corollaries of modern and postmodern culture; rising divorce rates, changing sexual mores, and, in particular, issues connected with homosexuality and sexual identity politics have become major sources of controversy and division.

The issue of women's ordination cannot be separated from these other cultural changes. It needs to be asked whether the ordination of women is a logical corollary of the equality of women in the church now recognized by all historic churches, whether it is rather a mistakenly drawn implication of the same, or, indeed, whether it is an aberration, one of the problematic consequences of postmodern culture, perhaps an example of the influence of modern unbelieving secularism in churches.[5]

THREE DIFFERENT KINDS OF ARGUMENTS AGAINST WOMEN'S ORDINATION

It is important to acknowledge that there are not simply two positions regarding women's ordination, a conservative or traditionalist position opposed and a liberal or progressive position in favor. Opposition to women's ordination can be found among both traditionalist Catholics and Protestants, but for very different reasons, as will be seen below. Among liberal theologians (both Protestant and Catholic), approval of the ordination of women has been associated with the theological movement of "feminist theology," often critical of historic orthodox Christianity as "patriarchal," "oppressive" toward women, and detrimental to their flourishing. Liberal feminist theology has often been associated with a "hermeneutic of suspicion," and with revisionist theologies characteristic of liberal Protestantism in general. Although opponents of women's ordination often focus on what are perceived to be the theological aberrations of progressivist feminist theology, orthodox Catholic and Protestant endorsement of the ordination of women associated with a position that could be designated as a "biblical feminism," or what has been designated (among Evangelicals) as "egalitarianism," needs to be distinguished from liberal feminist (Protestant and Catholic) advocacy of women's ordination. The number of orthodox Christians endorsing women's ordination is not a small or insignificant group. Reformed theologian T. F. Torrance, Methodists Richard Hays, Michael Gorman, and Alan Padgett, Anglican bishop and New Testament scholar N. T. Wright, the late Roman Catholic theologian Edward Kilmartin, and Eastern Orthodox writers Elisabeth Behr-Sigel and Bishop Kallistos Ware are just a few of the orthodox biblical scholars and theologians who have written in favor of gender equality or women's ordination, or both.

It also needs to be recognized that these four positions—(1) Evangelical Protestant opponents to women's ordination, (2) traditionalist Catholic opponents to women's ordination, (3) liberal feminist theologians, and (4) orthodox Evangelical and Catholic egalitarians—*all* represent *new* theological developments in response to cultural changes of the last couple of centuries. All four positions agree in acknowledging an equality and dignity of women in the churches that was lacking in previous centuries, and (whether acknowledged or not) is indeed a *new* development and a *new* theological stance. Later chapters will look at this in more detail.

Some have responded that, in light of this *new* recognition of the equality of women in the church, women should now be allowed to pursue the same vocation to ordained ministry that men had pursued in the past—the position endorsed in this book. At the same time, those who continue to oppose women's ordination have not simply preserved the historic tradition of the church. Because of the necessity of simultaneously acknowledging a *new* theology of women's equality that had not existed previously while persisting in resisting the ordination of women, both Protestant and Catholic opponents of women's ordination have had to develop *new* theological rationales in opposition to women's ordination.

As there is no single position either for or against women's ordination, neither are there any single arguments for or against it. There are basically three different kinds of arguments in opposition to the ordination of women. The first kind of argument is non-theological pragmatic. For example, women's ordination is part of a secular agenda; women's ordination was introduced into the church by liberal theologians, and its adoption will lead the church to theological liberalism. This argument is characterized by lack of properly theological substance.

More properly theological arguments tend to fall into two different kinds: Protestant arguments and Catholic arguments. By "Protestant," I mean Christian traditions that have their roots in the Reformation, affirm *sola scriptura*, do not allow much authority to church tradition or councils, with the exception perhaps of Augustine and the Reformers, and who tend to have a low (if not Zwinglian) view of the sacraments. Some in Reformation churches—such as Anglicans and Lutherans—would not necessarily fall into this category, but there are Anglicans and Lutherans who would. By "Catholic," I mean Christian traditions that, while affirming the significance of Scripture, also place a high value on church tradition and have a high view of the sacraments. Churches that fall into this category would include not only Roman Catholics, but also the Orthodox, and some (but not all) Anglicans and Lutherans.

Protestants and Catholics (in the specific sense in which I am using the terms) understand the purpose of ordination differently, and consequently use different theological arguments against women's ordination. While ecumenical agreement understands the ministry of ordained clergy to be one of both Word and Sacrament, Protestant and Catholic objections to women's ordination tend to focus on one or the other. Protestants tend to understand the purpose of ordination as having to do with authority, preaching, and teaching, and their arguments focus on the exegesis of Scripture. Accordingly, the kinds of anti-ordination arguments they use generally focus on three related issues in biblical interpretation: (1) hierarchical relations between men and women (men are in charge, and women are not); (2) whether women should preach in the pulpit; and (3) whether women should teach men. Protestant arguments tend to be exegetical, appealing to biblical passages that (1) seem to affirm a hierarchical understanding of the relation between men and women; (2) forbid women to speak in church; and (3) forbid women to teach.

Catholics understand the purpose of ordination as having primarily to do with celebrating the sacraments (particularly the Eucharist); they do not object in principle to women exercising authority in the church or to women preaching or teaching. Catholics tend not to be concerned as much with exegetical issues involving Scripture, but rather focus on the tradition of the church and arguments regarding sacramental theology. Their arguments generally focus on (1) the tradition of the church; (2) the conditions of valid sacramental ordination; (3) issues of biblical exegesis, including questions concerning the function of the Old Testament priesthood; the relation between Jesus and his apostles; the kinds of roles women exercised in the church both in the Bible and in the history of the church.

Different understandings of ordination and different concerns result in anomalous contrasts between the two positions. Protestants who believe that lay people can celebrate the Eucharist would presumably have no problem with women doing so, but would not allow the same women to preach or teach or exercise authority over men. Catholics might have no problem with women preaching, teaching theology, and even perhaps exercising some kind of pastoral leadership, so long as they do not celebrate the sacraments. Because of these differences, particular arguments of Protestants and Catholics have to be addressed separately. Arguments that impress Protestants often have no interest for Catholics, and vice versa.

It is also important to note that there is a crucial difference between Scripture and tradition, on the one hand, and hermeneutics on the other. This is the difference between understanding what the writers of Scripture taught, and what was taught in the traditions of the church (exegesis and church history), and how we address the same issues today in a different ecclesial and cultural setting (hermeneutics and systematic theology). It is the difference between "what did it mean?" and "what does it mean?" between what Scripture and tradition said then, and how we apply that today. Too many opponents of women's ordination seem to think that the question can be resolved by a simple appeal to Scripture or tradition. Protestants will appeal to Paul's prohibitions against women speaking in church or having authority over men, Catholics will appeal to the church's tradition of ordaining men, and both will assume that these appeals settle the question. But the question needs to be addressed theologically. Biblical or historical precedent alone is not a theological argument without addressing the theological reasons behind the precedent.

In a book on eucharistic theology, George Hunsinger has made a helpful distinction between three types of theology: "enclave theology," "academic liberal theology," and "ecumenical theology." "Enclave theology" is "based narrowly in a single tradition, and does not really seek to learn from other traditions." While expressing concerns about "enclave theology," Hunsinger acknowledges the possibility of "dogmatic" or "confessional" theologies that can advance the concerns of particular confessions in ways that are fruitful beyond their boundaries. "Academic liberal theology" lacks allegiance to "established confessional norms," and the "biblical view of reality" is seen as "just one more culturally conditioned artifact." Ecumenical theology "presupposes that every tradition in the church has something valuable to contribute"; ecumenical theology "searches for unseen convergences" and hopes for "ecumenical progress," while being committed to the authority of councils, creeds, and confessions, which "provide a normative framework for the ecumenical understanding of Holy Scripture."[6]

In terms of Hunsinger's categories, Protestant and Catholic opponents of women's ordination clearly fit into the categories of confessional theologies, if not necessarily as narrow as "enclave" theologies. (Also in terms of Hunsinger's categories, liberal feminist theologies fall rather neatly within what Hunsinger calls "academic liberal theology.") Addressing concerns about ordination in terms of the categories of either male authority over women or male sacramental representation reflect very specific Protestant and Catholic understandings of ordination respectively.

Because opposition to the ordination of women tends to focus rather narrowly on these two issues of male authority (for Protestant Evangelicals) or administering the sacraments (for Catholics), the theological arguments tend to be narrowly focused as well. Largely missing from Evangelical arguments are broader considerations of the doctrines of creation, theological anthropology, relations between men and women, or Christology and redemption (apart from the single issue of male authority over women). Similarly, because Catholic arguments tend to focus on the single issue of the role of the presiding minister in celebrating the sacrament, largely missing from this discussion is any broader consideration of a theology of liturgical worship or the nature of ordained ministry (again, apart from the symbolic role of the male priest in presiding at sacramental celebration).

In contrast to both the confessionally narrow approaches of Evangelical Protestant "complementarians" or Catholic "traditionalists," on the one side, and liberal "feminist" theologies, on the other, I intend to follow a theological approach in this book that would correspond to what Hunsinger designates "ecumenical theology," or what could also be designated as "Evangelical Catholic," "Catholic Evangelical," or "critically orthodox" theology. Because my goal is to be both comprehensive and ecumenical, I intend to address all three of the varieties of arguments that have been raised in recent decades against women's ordination: non-theological arguments, Protestant arguments, and Catholic arguments.

However, the question of the ordination of women touches on numerous topics besides the rather narrow issues of the authority of men over women or whether only a male priest can preside at the celebration of the sacraments. Accordingly, although I intend to address what have become the standard arguments *against* the ordination of women, both Protestant and Catholic, I also hope to present a more *positive* ecumenical argument that will address numerous theological topics and touch on related issues: theological hermeneutics, the doctrine of creation, relationships between men and women, Christology and discipleship, mutual submission in the family and the church, theologies of worship and liturgy, the role of ordained clergy in leading the church in worship, among others. Because the issue of women's ordination touches on so many other theological issues, the argument will address issues of biblical exegesis and biblical theology, historical theology, systematic theology, as well as liturgical theology. The theologies of ordination and the arguments used against women's ordination by Evangelicals and Catholics are so different that one might assume that there is no relationship whatsoever between the two approaches. My hope is that the following discussion will make a positive argument for an *ecumenical* theology of ordination to the presbyterate as an office of Word and Sacrament that justifiably is open to both men and women.

2

Non-theological Arguments against the Ordination of Women

There is a crisis of identity in mainline churches today that has focused primarily on issues of sexuality, but more fundamental theological issues are at stake. Unfortunately, what is really a theological crisis often has been interpreted in non-theological categories. The most frequently used analogy borrows terms derived from secular Western (particularly American) politics and from the politically driven "culture wars," adopting the political categories of "liberal" and "conservative," "left-wing" and "right-wing," "progressive" and "reactionary."[1] Alternatively, but in the same vein, "progressive" or liberal Protestant Christians have expressed fears about a "fundamentalist takeover" of the church.[2] A third assessment of the current crisis contrasts a theology of diversity and inclusion with a theology of monolithic exclusivity.[3] In attempting to address a theological crisis with non-theological categories, these interpretations are fundamentally inadequate.

Concerning women's ordination, there is an uncomfortable parallel between the kinds of arguments used by advocates of the new "inclusivist" theology in the mainline churches, and many of the arguments used by opponents of women's ordination; in both cases, the arguments are not properly theological. Many of the arguments used by opponents of women's ordination are reverse-mirror images of the kinds of arguments used by advocates of theological inclusivity or diversity.

What follows will address some of these non-theological arguments against women's ordination. The following are summaries of non-theological arguments against women's ordination that are used frequently enough as to be considered "standard" arguments.

(1) The "Liberal Theology" Argument: the ordination of women is inherently and irrevocably connected to a theologically liberal and secularist agenda; the practice of ordaining women was introduced into the church by liberal theologians. The ordination of women is part of this secularist egalitarian agenda, and those in favor of women's liberation share these secularist assumptions. So-called "orthodox" advocates for women's ordination "stand on the shoulders" of these radical liberals, and ultimately share the same questionable egalitarian assumptions.

There is also an inherent connection, the argument continues, between the ordination of women and the ordination of practicing homosexuals. Both are based on the same individualist assumptions; both use the same egalitarian arguments, and embracing one cause inevitably and logically leads to the other. So there should be no surprise that the ordination of women has been followed by the ordination of those in sexually active same-sex relationships.

A quick glance at the above argument reveals a kind of "funhouse mirror" reverse logic to the liberal arguments. If advocates of "inclusivism" argue that their opponents are part of a "right-wing" conspiracy, opponents of women's ordination argue that advocates are part of a "liberal secularist" conspiracy. If advocates of "inclusivism" argue that their opponents are part of a "fundamentalist takeover" of the church, opponents of women's ordination argue that advocates of women's ordination are part of a "liberal takeover" of the church. If advocates of "inclusivism" argue in favor of "diversity" against the "exclusiveness" of their opponents, opponents of women's ordination argue for "hierarchy" or different gender "roles" in contrast to the "egalitarianism" of their opponents. In each case, the arguments rather cancel each other out. How does one assess whether a "liberal conspiracy" is worse than a "right-wing" one, or vice versa, whether the real "takeover" is on the part of progressives or fundamentalists, whether inclusiveness and diversity are better than exclusiveness, or, rather, whether, traditional gender roles are better than egalitarianism?

Even if true, the argument that women's ordination was originally advocated by liberal Protestants is a *post hoc, propter hoc* fallacy. It does not follow that because many of the advocates of women's ordination in the 1970s were theological liberals, there is then an inherent connection between advocacy of women's ordination and liberal theology. As another example, many who argued for civil rights for racial minorities in the 1960s were also theological liberals, but it does not therefore follow that to be in favor of civil liberties for racial minorities will inevitably lead to liberal theology.

Moreover, the argument can be turned on its head. Martin Luther King Jr. wrote his famous "Letter from a Birmingham Jail" in response to a letter written by eight white Birmingham clergy (including two Episcopal bishops) calling for a cessation of civil rights demonstrations being led by "outsiders."[4] Presumably, these clergy who opposed King were "orthodox" in their theology. Would one want to draw the conclusion that there is an inherent connection between "orthodox" theology and opposition to civil rights?

Nor does it follow that the connection is a common commitment to a secular agenda of egalitarianism. Drawing such a simplistic connection shows a rather short-sided view of history. There is a connection between the ordination of women and a social movement for liberty and equality, but its roots lie further back. The first advocates of the ordination of women made their case not in the 1960s but a century earlier, immediately after the American Civil War. It is not a coincidence that the case for women's ordination was first made right after the emancipation of African slaves and that the first advocates of women's ordination had also been abolitionists.[5] It is also not a coincidence that many of the leaders of the women's suffrage movement were Christian women, and that women's suffrage followed in the aftermath of the liberation of the slaves. It is also not a coincidence that the modern case for women's ordination appeared immediately after the modern civil rights movement. They are connected, but the connection is not secularist, but specifically Christian.

Among Martin Luther's contributions to theology was his notion of Christian liberty.[6] Luther was appalled, however, when those involved in the Peasants' Revolt appealed to his ideas to argue for social implications of equality and social and economic freedom, and responded with his "Against the Murdering, Thieving Hordes of Peasants."[7] Against the peasants, Luther insisted that the freedom of a Christian was a spiritual matter, and had nothing to do with political or social liberty.

In the next few centuries, however, theologians embraced the social implications of Christian liberty that Luther refused. John Wesley made the argument in his "Thoughts on Slavery" that Christian freedom includes not only spiritual freedom, but freedom in one's person, and thus slavery is incompatible with Christian faith.[8] William Wilberforce was the Evangelical Anglican member of Parliament who led the campaign to abolish the British slave trade, and John Newton's hymn "Amazing Grace" was written by a former slave trader who, after his conversion, eventually became an abolitionist. The abolitionist movement in the United States was also led by Christians, both whites and blacks who were former slaves.

After slavery, Christian thinkers addressed the question of workers' rights. The Roman Catholic social encyclicals *Rerum Novarum*, *Quadragissimo Anno*, *Pacem in Terris*, as well as Vatican II's *Gaudium et Spes*, argued that the Christian gospel not only provides salvation to individual Christians, but also renews and advances culture, and promotes liberty and equality among all peoples.[9] Although the focus of the earlier encyclicals was on the rights of workers (in opposition to the errors of both socialism and capitalism), *Gaudium et Spes* went beyond this to speak of issues of war and peace, the arts, and the Christian family. Significantly, *Gaudium et*

Spes made a significant advance over previous Roman Catholic teaching by speaking of the equality of women in the same context in which it spoke of the equality of workers: "Where they have not yet won it, women claim for themselves an equity with men before the law and in fact."[10] *Gaudium et Spes* consistently writes of both men and women rather than simply men, and states: "Women now work in almost all spheres. It is fitting that they are able to assume their proper role in accordance with their own nature. It will belong to all to acknowledge and favor the proper and necessary participation of women in the cultural life."[11] This is a significant shift from earlier Catholic teaching.

In the light of these advances beyond the limitations of Luther's understanding of Christian liberty, it is evident that in the last several hundred years Christians have come to recognize that the notions of Christian liberty and equality have implications not only for salvation, but for social liberty as well, including freedom of one's person, freedom in the work place, racial equality, and, finally, equality between the sexes. It is this notion of Christian freedom and equality that is the impetus for a properly orthodox case for women's ordination, and not a secularist notion of egalitarianism.

Is there, then, an inherent connection between the ordination of women, the ordination of practicing homosexuals, and the collapse of orthodoxy in mainline churches? There is a connection in the sense that those liberal Protestants who have embraced both women's ordination and gay liberation view both as a further implication of the civil rights movement of the 1960s, and that these same people have succeeded in taking over the leadership of some of the mainline denominations. However, liberal Protestantism is not a new movement. It existed well before the issue of women's ordination. For example, Karl Barth and the Confessing Church resisted a German Christian Church that endorsed Nazism and was also a largely liberal Protestant Church, but which certainly did not embrace the ordination of women. Just as orthodox Christians can agree with liberal Protestants in embracing racial equality, while disagreeing with liberal Protestants about endorsing same-sex unions, so they can endorse women's ordination without endorsing same-sex unions.[12] And they can endorse the ordination of women while remaining orthodox Christians, indeed, not in spite of their orthodox faith, but because of it.

(2) The Argument from "Consequences": the ordination of women leads inevitably to the collapse of orthodox theology; the practice of ordaining women was the beginning of the collapse of orthodoxy in the mainline churches. A key question is whether women's ordination has caused more harm than good to the church. Wherever women have been ordained, theological compromise has followed.

The above observation is a misleading one. Certainly the ordination of women with liberal Protestant convictions has been one of the major factors in the collapse of orthodoxy in the mainline churches, especially since many of these women have been advocates of a theologically liberal feminist theology.[13] The problem here, however, is not the sex of the people holding the theology, but the theology itself. There have been numerous male theologians who have also embraced liberal Protestant theology, and their theology would be problematic even if it had not a single ordained woman advocate. The question should rather be addressed on a case-by-case basis. One could equally ask, has the admission of men to clerical status been a blessing or curse to the Christian community? Which men under which circumstances, at which period in history? Athanasius? Arius? Cyril? Nestorius? Innocent III? Martin Luther? Cardinal Wolsey? Thomas Cranmer? John Calvin? William Laud? Dietrich Bonhoeffer? The bishops of the *Deutsche Christe*? Michael Ramsey? Rowan Williams? Karl Barth? Rudolf Bultmann? John Spong? N. T. Wright? All were/are male. All were/are ordained.

A more helpful question would be: has the ordination of women of orthodox theological convictions been (on the whole) a blessing or curse for the church? Women with orthodox theological convictions would be those women who practice ministry in the church, proclaiming the Word and administering the sacraments, who teach at or are students at numerous seminaries, who gladly embrace every article of the Creed, and affirm without hesitation the authority of Scripture, but differ on the particular question of women's ordination. Equating such women with liberal Protestants is as unfair as equating a biblical scholar like N. T. Wright with Bishop John Spong.

(3) The Argument from "Rights": the demand for women's ordination assumes that ordination is a matter of justice, a "right" to be ordained. Ordination is not about "rights." No one has a "right" to be ordained. Those who advocate women's ordination are appealing to a language of individual "rights" that is incompatible with Christian orthodoxy.

The question of a "right" to ordination is a fallacy of ambiguity. Certainly, no individual as an individual has a "right" to ordination. However, this applies to men as well as women. The proper theological question has to do with whether the church should refuse ordination to a particular group of human beings as a class simply because they belong to that class. Arguments must be made as to whether women as a class cannot be properly ordained. Whether such arguments are valid is the crucial issue. Pointing out that no individual as an individual has a right to be ordained is a red herring.

The argument in favor of ordaining women is the same argument as the argument for ordaining men.

Premise: Some human beings should be ordained.

Minor premise: Women are human beings.

Conclusion: Therefore some women should be ordained.

To the contrary, argue the opponents of women's ordination, that is the wrong major premise. The argument should rather be:

Counter premise: Some *male* human beings should be ordained.

Minor premise: Women are not males.

Conclusion: Therefore no woman should be ordained.

Scripture (presumably) speaks of the ordination of males to the presbyterate.[14] However, it is not self-evident in the passages where it does so whether those males are ordained in virtue of their maleness or in virtue of their humanity. The initial plausibility is that they are ordained because of their humanity because the kinds of things that they are required to do are the kinds of things that human beings in general are capable of doing: for example, preaching, teaching, leading others, or (although not mentioned in Scripture), administering the sacraments. If an argument is to be made against the ordination of women, it needs to be an actual argument that makes the case that only male human beings can be ordained by virtue of something specifically significant to their being male, and that excludes women from being ordained by virtue of something specifically significant to their being female. The burden of proof is thus on those who oppose women's ordination.

It is indeed the case that no individual has a right to be ordained, but the question to be addressed is not about individuals but about a class of human beings. No individual male human being has the right to be ordained, but the advocates of male-only ordination certainly believe that males as a class have a "right" to be ordained in a way that women as a class do not. Should the church discriminate against a particular class of human beings as a class when it comes to ordination?

(4) The Argument from "Discrimination": the church rightly "discriminates" against certain classes of people in the matter of ordination. Unbelievers cannot be ordained. The mentally defective or the insane cannot be ordained. Practicing homosexuals cannot be ordained. Children cannot be ordained. That women as a class cannot be ordained is no more problematic than that these classes cannot be ordained.

To the contrary, none of these are cases of discrimination against a class of human beings simply because they belong to that particular class. In each case, the barrier to ordination is not against a class simply as a class, but against a defect in an individual that specifically prevents that individual from properly exercising the duties of ordination. These defects can be remedied, in which case the particular individual can be ordained. An unbeliever can become a Christian, in which case he can be ordained. If the mentally defective or the insane were restored to full mental capacity or functional mental health, they could be ordained. Children cannot be ordained because they are not of sufficient maturity to exercise adult responsibility, but once they become adults, they can be ordained. The prohibition against ordaining homosexuals is not a prohibition against a class, but against a behavior. The church does not ordain those who engage in same-sex sexual activity for the same reason it does not ordain adulterers, or single people who are not chaste. This refusal is not a discrimination against a class of human beings, but against behaviors that are deemed to be incompatible with Christian discipleship. Sexual orientation in itself is not (or at least should not be) a barrier to ordination.

And, again, historically, the argument against the ordination of women was just such an argument based on a perceived inherent defect: women could not be ordained because of a lack of intelligence, emotional instability, and susceptibility to (particularly sexual) temptation.[15] However, all mainline churches now insist that this is not their position concerning women's participation in the church.

The prohibition against the ordination of women would seem to be the only case in which the church discriminates against a particular class of people solely because they belong to that class. They are not discriminated against because of an incapacity. Women can preach. They can provide pastoral leadership. There is nothing either in their capacity to inform intentions or physical limitations that would prevent them from celebrating the sacraments. The presumption against women's ordination is not then based on a moral disqualification or physical impairment. It is a discrimination against women as a class simply because they belong to the class.

Any argument against women's ordination needs then to be a properly theological argument, and it needs to make the case that there is something in the very nature of women as a class that makes it inappropriate or inherently impossible to exercise ordained ministry.

Attempts at such theological arguments will be addressed in the next chapters.

POSTSCRIPT: "FREEDOM'S JUST ANOTHER WORD FOR NOTHIN' LEFT TO LOSE"

The above discussion makes an appeal to a "freedom in one's person," which arguably finds its roots in Martin Luther's notion of Christian liberty, and which was then expanded in modern Christian movements that advocated the abolition of slavery, workers' rights (freedom in the workplace), civil liberties, and the equality and freedom of women in the home, the workplace, and the church. There are Christian theologians and ethicists who challenge the modern emphasis on freedom insofar as it espouses an individualist autonomy not grounded in an ontological good or related to a social common good. For example, D. Stephen Long argues that modern philosophy has "failed by turning the quest for the good into a quest for freedom that ends in nihilism." Long argues instead for a Christian ethic that is grounded in goodness: the goodness of the Triune God, the goodness of God's creation, the goodness of Jesus Christ in the incarnation, and the goodness of the Holy Spirit in the life of the church.[16]

While in complete agreement with Long's criticism of modern autonomous individualism, one nonetheless would want to distinguish between several different understandings of freedom. First, there is the notion of freedom as indifference. This is the basic freedom to choose between options that most people understand by freedom. This is the innocuous freedom to choose between such options as whether to wear the blue shirt or the yellow shirt when getting dressed in the morning.

Second is moral freedom, the freedom to choose rightly. This freedom is the freedom to choose the good consistently. Augustine distinguished between moral freedom and freedom of indifference. While the latter freedom is always retained, the former was lost in the fall into sin and can only be restored through the redeeming work of Jesus Christ.[17] This would also be the freedom discussed in Luther's "Freedom of a Christian," and is the notion of Christian freedom being advocated by Long when he writes of Christian ethics as the repentance in which we learn to love God's goodness.

The third notion of freedom is the autonomous freedom of modern secularism that has no relation to the good, and to which Long and others rightly object.

In addition, however, there is the notion of Christian freedom rooted in the Christian doctrine of vocation, which Luther rightly emphasized, but whose social implications he failed to recognize. This is the "freedom in one's person" that Wesley and Wilberforce correctly perceived to demand the abolition of slavery, which the Catholic Social Encyclicals argued had implications for social equality in the home, the workplace, and the church, and that motivated many of the Christian participants (such as Martin Luther King Jr.) in the civil rights movement. This notion of Christian freedom as vocation has implications for the ordination of women. It is not, however, a demand for "equal rights" in the church, but rather a request to serve in the church, to fulfill a Christian vocation.[18] This latter notion of Christian freedom is not in antithesis to a notion of divine and created goodness, and of Christian ethics as repentance and learning to love God, but is an expression of how that goodness plays itself out in the life of the church.

3

The Argument "from Tradition" Is Not the "Traditional" Argument

This chapter begins with a story.

Back in the days when families still baked bread, a mother was teaching her daughter to bake bread using the recipe that had been passed down from her mother and her grandmother before her. After she had kneaded the dough and formed it into a loaf, she took a knife, cut off the end of the loaf, threw away the cut-off end, and proceeded to bake the remaining loaf that was left. Being a dutiful daughter, the young girl followed her mother's instructions, but one day she asked an innocent question: "Mom, why do we cut off the end of the loaf, and throw it away before we bake the bread?" Her mother responded, "I'm not really sure. That's just how my mother taught me to bake bread. We've always done it that way in my family. Let's telephone your grandmother, and ask her why we do that." So they telephoned the girl's grandmother, and asked her why she had taught her daughter always to cut off the end of the loaf of bread before she baked it. She replied as her daughter had. "I'm not really sure. That's just the way my mother taught me to do it, so that's how our family has always baked bread. Let's ask my mother." So they telephoned the girl's great grandmother, who was quite elderly but still baked her own bread, to find the reason for this ancient family tradition. The great grandmother laughed. "When you were a young girl, and I taught you to break bread," she told her daughter, "we only had one bread pan, and it was too small to hold the entire loaf from the recipe that my mother taught me to make, so I just cut off the extra. Years later, after you had grown up and were married, I bought a new bread pan, and I haven't cut off the end of the loaf in years."

This story is included to make a point. A tradition is only as good as the reasons behind it. The same tradition done for different reasons is not the same tradition, but a new tradition. After learning the actual reason why Great Grandmother had cut off the end of the loaf, the mother and daughter of the story might have decided to continue to cut off the end of the loaf when they baked bread—perhaps just as a way of honoring an old family tradition—but they would not have been keeping the old tradition, because they would not have been doing it for the traditional reasons. They would have been inventing a new tradition—the tradition of cutting off the end of the loaf "because we've always done it that way."

One of the most frequently used arguments against women's ordination is the argument from tradition: the contemporary church cannot ordain women because there is a universal tradition against it. The argument from tradition is primarily a Catholic argument; those who oppose women's ordination for "Catholic" reasons link ordination to a sacramental understanding of orders and the sacraments that is often connected to a particular understanding of apostolic succession. Contemporary ordinations are valid only if they can be traced through an unbroken chain all the way to the time of the apostles. On such a view of ordination, an unbroken tradition is necessarily important because if someone is ordained invalidly, the chain of apostolic tradition is broken.

At the same time, the argument from tradition, while not as important for a "Protestant" understanding of ordination—which bases its case more on biblical exegesis—still has weight because the argument can be made that ordaining women is an innovation, something that Christians have never done. Protestants who oppose women's ordination can argue that they are simply defending a position that all Christians held until recently because it is the self-evident teaching of the Bible, and it is the way that the Bible has always been interpreted.

However, traditions are always based on reasons, and traditions are only as valid as the reasons behind them. If one discovers that the reasons for which a tradition is practiced are bad reasons, yet one decides to preserve the tradition anyway, but now claims different reasons for the practice, one is not really preserving the tradition. Rather, one has either begun a brand-new tradition, or one has continued what is a bad tradition, but has come up with a new reason to rationalize what can no longer be justified based on the old reasons.

The argument against the ordination of women based on tradition is the argument that one cannot ordain women because there is a universal tradition against it. In the words of Roman Catholic author Sara Butler: "The Church does not have the authority to admit women to priestly ordination. This judgment, ordered by Pope John Paul II in 1994, simply confirms a tradition observed in practice from apostolic times." Butler also writes, "The tradition of reserving priestly ordination to men is unbroken and unanimous in the Catholic Church. If ever women were allowed to exercise priestly functions, this innovation was quickly denounced." However, Butler then qualifies, "This tradition has been so solid that it has never required an explicit formulation by the magisterium."[1] If the tradition is as solid as Butler states, then it should be easy enough to trace the tradition and the reasons for it in the history of the church. However, this means that it should also be easy to compare the historic reasons with the recent "explicit formulation" to discover if they are the same reasons. If they are not, then the practice may be the same, but the theology is actually a *new* tradition, not the preservation of an old one.

What is crucial to the argument from tradition is to address the reasons behind the tradition, and these are not difficult to trace. Historically, there is a single argument that was used in the church against the ordaining of women: women could not be ordained to the ministry (whether understood as Catholic priesthood or Protestant pastorate) because of an inherent *ontological* defect. Because of a lack of intelligence, or a tendency to irrationality or emotional instability, a greater susceptibility to temptation, or an inherent incapacity to lead, women were held to be inferior to men, and thus were not eligible for ordination. Moreover, this argument was used to exclude women not only from clerical ministry, but from all positions of leadership over men, and largely to confine women to the domestic sphere.

In making this point, there is no intention to embrace the kind of diatribe that one occasionally encounters in revisionist feminist scholarship that portrays the entire history of the church as nothing but an unmitigated practice of oppressive subjugation and patriarchal abuse of women. Such one-sided readings can find their counterparts in accounts of how Christianity remarkably improved the status of women in the pagan world, and was, on the whole, a remarkably good thing for women.[2] Nonetheless, it is not difficult to trace a consistent pattern in the history of the church that explains why the church has not ordained women. Some selective examples that are typical, but not exhaustive, follow.

THE TRADITION AGAINST ORDAINING WOMEN

Origen, quoting the apostle Paul, wrote that "'it is shameful for a woman to speak in church' [1 Cor. 14:35], whatever she says, even if she says something excellent or holy, because it comes from the mouth of a woman."[3] Tertullian is infamous for the following admonition to women:

And do you not know that you are (each) an Eve? The sentence of God on this sex of yours lives in this age: the guilt must of necessity live too. You are the devil's gateway: you are the unsealer of that (forbidden) tree: you are the first deserter of the divine law: you are she who persuaded him whom the devil was not valiant enough

to attack. You destroyed so easily God's image, man. On account of your desert—
that is, death—even the Son of God had to die.[4]

Three passages in John Chrysostom's writings are crucial for understanding the
logic behind traditional opposition to the ordination of women. First, Chrysostom
makes clear that women should confine themselves to domestic roles: "To woman
is assigned the presidency of the household; to man all the business of state, the
marketplace, the administration of government. . . . She cannot handle state business well, but she can raise children correctly." Chrysostom claimed that there is a
division of labor "determined by God" and divided into two spheres—public affairs
and private matters—which is rooted in a kind of ontology of the sexes. Domestic
affairs are assigned to women, while the business of state, of the marketplace, and of
the military, is assigned to men. These differences are rooted in a kind of ontological
superiority of men over women. It is the work of God's wisdom that the man who is
"skilled at greater things" is useless at "less important ones," and these less important tasks are assigned to women. God did not make men and women "equal," lest
"women in their contentiousness would deem themselves *deserving of the front-row
seats rather than the man.*"[5]

Second, Chrysostom insisted that women are forbidden to teach:

> Why not? Because she taught Adam once and for all, and taught him badly. . . . There-
> fore let her descend from the professor's chair! Those who know not how to teach, let
> them learn. . . . If they don't want to learn but rather want to teach, they destroy both
> themselves and those who learn from them. . . . [S]he is subjected to the man and
> that . . . subjection is because of sin.[6]

In this passage, Chrysostom claims that sin overthrew an original equality between
man and woman, consigning women to a place of "subordination" or "subjection"
to men. In particular, he cites the admonition of 1 Timothy 2:11-12 against women
teaching (a passage to be examined later) as a biblical warrant.

Finally, in warning males of the dangers of temptation, Chrysostom pointed out
that women have a great tendency to sin, but also to incite to temptation:

> For it is not possible for the Bishop, and one who is concerned with the whole flock,
> to have a care for the male portion of it, but to pass over the female, which needs more
> particular forethought, because of its propensity to sins. But the man who is appoint-
> ed to the administration of a Bishopric must have a care for the moral health of these,
> if not in a greater, at least in no less a degree than the others. For it is necessary to visit
> them when they are sick, to comfort them when they are sorrowful, and to reprove
> them when they are idle, and to help them when they are distressed; and in such cases
> the evil one would find many opportunities of approach, if a man did not fortify him-
> self with a very strict guard. For the eye, not only of the unchaste, but of the modest
> woman pierces and disturbs the mind.[7]

It is important to note that Chrysostom's is not an argument against women's ordination as such, but an argument against women exercising any non-domestic roles whatsoever, among which women's ordination would certainly be included. It is significant that the argument is grounded in historic divisions between the sexes in preindustrial societies which no longer obtain in postindustrial societies: women's roles in preindustrial societies are necessarily confined to the domestic sphere because of the biological connection to childbirth, child care, and breast-feeding; women have to work at home in order to watch over children.[8]

Second, insofar as Chrysostom's argument specifically bears on issues of women's ministry, he does not address sacramental concerns (the modern Catholic argument), but rather focuses instead on issues of women's authority. Women may not teach men, and this is not a matter of ontological equality but different gender roles (as in the modern Protestant Complementarian argument), and is a consequence of women's sinfulness leading to a loss of an original equality.

Finally, Chrysostom expresses concerns about women's susceptibility to temptation. These claims will become the warrant for the traditional argument against women's ordination: women cannot be ordained to church office because they are less intelligent, emotionally unstable, more susceptible to temptation, and therefore are necessarily subordinate to and may not exercise authority over men. Moreover, the restriction is not simply a restriction from church office, but a restriction of women exercising authority over men in any public sphere whatsoever.

Thomas Aquinas's teacher Albert the Great had this to say about the inherent inferiority of women in comparison to men:

> [G]enerally, proverbially, and commonly it is affirmed that women are more mendacious and fragile, more diffident, more shameless, more deceptively eloquent, and, in brief, a woman is nothing but a devil fashioned into a human appearance . . . Therefore there is no faithfulness in a woman. . . . Moreover, an indication of this is that wise men almost never disclose their plans and their doings with their wives. For a woman is a flawed male and in comparison to the male, has the nature of defect and privation, and this is why naturally she mistrusts herself. And this is why whatever she cannot acquire on her own she strives to acquire through mendacity and diabolical deceptions. Therefore, to speak briefly, one must be as mistrustful of every woman as of a venomous serpent and a horned devil . . . [T]he female is more prudent, that is, cleverer, than the male with respect to evil and perverse deeds, because the more nature departs from the one operation, the more it inclines to the other. In this way, the woman falls short in intellectual operations, which consist in the apprehension of the good and in knowledge of truth and flight from evil. . . . Therefore sense moves the female to every evil, just as intellect moves a man to every good.[9]

In contrast to the misogyny of his mentor, Thomas Aquinas's own position is somewhat ambiguous. Aquinas could speak in almost glowing terms of the relations between men and women. Asking whether woman should have been made of the rib of man, Aquinas responds with an illustration that points to the partnership and companionship of men and women, an adapted form of which has been used in countless wedding services:

> It was right for the woman to be made from a rib of man. First, to signify the social union of man and woman, for the woman should neither "use authority over man," and so she was not made from his head; nor was it right for her to be subject to man's contempt as his slave, and so she was not made from his feet. Secondly, for the sacramental signification; for from the side of Christ sleeping on the Cross the Sacraments flowed—namely, blood and water—on which the Church was established.[10]

Similarly, Aquinas argues that women share equally in the image of God with men, that Genesis 1:27 does not imply "that the image of God came through the distinction of sex, but that the image of God belongs to both sexes, since it is in the mind, wherein there is no sexual distinction."[11]

However, in answer to the question "Whether Woman Should Have Been Made in the First Production of Things," Aquinas responds that woman was made to be a "helpmate" to man primarily for the purposes of sexual reproduction, since a man can be more efficiently helped by another man in most matters. What Aquinas writes about women being created equally in the image of God needs to be read in light of what he also writes about the subordination of women to men, which seems to reflect a kind of inferiority of nature. Women are subject to men based on an economic subordination in which "the superior makes use of his subjects for their own benefit and good. . . . For good order would have been wanting in the human family if some were not governed by others wiser than themselves. So by such a kind of subjection woman is naturally subject to man, because in man the discretion of reason predominates."[12]

This ambiguity is reflected in Thomas's answer to the question "whether the female sex is an impediment to receiving Orders?" Aquinas acknowledges that the gift of prophecy is sometimes given to women (2 Kgs. 22:14), and that in some cases women can exercise temporal authority (e.g., abbesses or the Old Testament Judge Deborah) "even as now women may have temporal power."[13]

Nonetheless, Aquinas argues against the ordination of women, appealing to 1 Timothy 2:12, making clear that his concern is with ecclesial authority of men over women (the traditional argument), and not whether a female priest can represent a male Christ (the current "Catholic" argument). Aquinas makes a standard sacramental distinction between a sign and the reality of the sign. Women can sometimes prophecy (exercise a charismatic gift) because they have the reality—"since in matters pertaining to the soul, woman does not differ from man . . . [and] sometimes a woman is found to be better than many men as regards the soul"—but women cannot have the sign. What is the "sign"? Not resemblance to a male Christ, but authority: "Accordingly, since it is not possible in the female sex to signify eminence of degree, for a woman is in the state of subjection, it follows that she cannot receive the sacrament of Order."[14]

What then about Aquinas's references to "abbesses" and to the prophetess Deborah? Both cases make clear that Aquinas's concerns are about women exercising authority over men in the church (the traditional argument) and not about sacramental representation of a male Christ (the new argument). Concerning abbesses, Aquinas writes that their authority is "delegated . . . on account of the danger of men and women living together"; delegated, that is, from a superior male authority, who would be preferable if there were no dangers of sexual temptation. Aquinas does seem to acknowledge concerning Deborah that women can exercise "temporal," but not "priestly" power. This would indeed make his position different from those earlier writers like John Chrysostom or Thomas's teacher Albertus Magnus or (later) Richard Hooker and John Knox, who quite explicitly draw a connection between an inability to exercise temporal authority and an inability to exercise ecclesial authority. At the same time, Aquinas makes clear that his opposition to the ordination of women is nonetheless because "it is not possible in the female sex to signify eminence of degree," specifically because a "woman is in the state of subjection." Aquinas wrote this early in his career, but when he later wrote the *Summa Theologiae*, he made clear the reason for female subjection: "[W]oman is naturally subject to man, because in man the discretion of reason predominates."[15]

It is apparent then that Aquinas's reasons for opposition to the ordination of women are the traditional ones. How is this consistent with what Aquinas wrote about women (like Deborah) exercising temporal power? If the necessary subjection of women to men provides the reason why women cannot be ordained (and, as noted above, Aquinas states that it is), then this should apply not only in the case of priestly ordination, but in temporal power as well. If subjection of women to men is not sufficient grounds for denying temporal power to women, then it should not be grounds for denying ordination to women. Aquinas seems to be inconsistent here, not to say incoherent.

Key to theological interpretation of the role of women is the exegesis of Genesis 1–3. Significantly, traditional commentators focus much more on Genesis 2 and 3 than on Genesis 1. Although all affirmed woman's equality in redemption, nevertheless, they found more in support of subordination in Genesis than of equality.[16] Although all agreed that women were to be subordinate to men, an important question was whether this subordination was something that was intrinsic to creation or rather was a consequence of the fall into sin. The majority opinion is that woman was created subordinate to man, but the fall brought about a worse state of subjection.

Augustine's position was typical: "Even before her sin, woman had been made to be ruled by her husband and to be submissive and subject to him. But . . . the servitude meant in [Gen. 3:16] is that in which there is a condition similar to that of slavery rather than a bond of love."[17]

The Protestant Reformation continues in this general tradition. John Calvin notes that Eve "had previously been subject to her husband, but that was a liberal and gentle subjection. Now, however, she is cast into servitude." Heinrich Bullinger paraphrases Genesis 3:16: "He [the man] will dominate you [the woman], that is, you will decide nothing by your private inclination but will act in everything by the inclination of your husband." Bullinger went so far as to quote Tertullian's "You are the devil's gateway" with approval.[18]

It seems that Martin Luther may be an exception to the patristic and Medieval notion that women are inherently less rational and capable of leadership than men. In Luther's *Lectures on Genesis*, he emphasizes the full equality and partnership of man and woman before the fall. Luther interprets Genesis 1:26 to mean that both man and woman have a mandate to rule over creation. Luther explains the difference between man and woman as primarily lying in their different bodily characteristics as related to their roles in reproduction. Luther states, "If the woman had not been deceived by the serpent and had not sinned, she would have been the equal of Adam in all respects."[19] Both man and woman are created in the image of God; both man and woman possess the same mental powers, and could understand the word of God, and there was a perfect harmony of will between them. After the fall, this changed. There was no longer mutual relation between man and woman, but an inequality in which the woman is now subordinate to the man, who rules over her. Nonetheless, Luther insists, even in the fall, woman and man are not separate, and woman does not live in isolation from the man. The chief penalty the woman entails as a result of the fall is pain connected with child birth, but she is promised that her offspring will crush the serpent. The chief penalty of the man is that he must now support his family, and he now has the role of ruling over and teaching over a recalcitrant creation. Even after the fall, this inequality is not the entire story, however. Man and woman are still mutually interdependent. Both still have a mandate to rule creation together. The promise of redemption points to a restored harmony between the sexes, and (in contrast to the medieval tendency to downplay the role of the family in light of an exalted view of celibacy), Luther emphasizes the concrete good of marriage.[20]

Within Anglicanism, there are similar affirmations of woman's inherent subordination tied to a lesser rationality. There is the rather infamous quote from Samuel Johnson, responding to his friend James Boswell, in reference to a Quaker woman preaching: "I told him I had been that morning at a meeting of the people called

Quakers, where I had heard a woman preach. Johnson: 'Sir, a woman's preaching is like a dog's walking on his hinder legs. It is not done well; but you are surprized to find it done at all.'"[21]

The views of Richard Hooker, perhaps Anglicanism's foremost divine, on the role of women in the church are infrequently expressed but are not significantly different from the patristic and medieval Catholic tradition that had preceded the Reformation. Hooker mentions the status of women only three times in *The Laws of Ecclesiastical Polity*. In the preface, he recognizes that many women embrace the Puritan cause; he believes that this reflects an intellectual inferiority, as their "judgments are commonly weakest because of their sex."[22] The second question has to do with the emergency baptism of infants by women, which Puritans rejected, as had Calvin and Bullinger. Hooker defended the practice, but says that it does not imply that women can be "ministers in the Church of God": "To make women teachers in the house of God were a gross absurdity, seeing the Apostle hath said, 'I permit not a woman to teach.'"[23] Finally, in Hooker's discussion of marriage in book 5, he discusses the practice of the delivering up of the woman by her father, the reason for which he explains as follows:

> And for this cause they were in marriage delivered unto their husbands by others. Which custom retained hath still this use, that it putteth women in mind of a duty whereunto the very imbecility of their nature and sex doth bind them, namely to be always directed, guided and ordered by others.[24]

Hooker was a "traditionalist" for whom the subordination and intellectual inferiority of women is simply assumed.[25]

This somewhat lengthy list of citations concludes with the Scottish Reformer John Knox's notorious *First Blast of the Trumpet Against the Monstrous Regiment of Women*, often considered to be a prime example of male misogyny. Knox's book was written against the Catholic queens Mary of Guise of Scotland and Mary Tudor of England. Knox was opposed to the rule of women or of any female authority over men, basing his views on what he considered to be biblical revelation: "I am assured that God hath reuealed to some in this our age, that it is more than a monstre in nature that a woman shall reign and have empire above man."[26] Knox argued that the rule of women was contrary to nature:

> Nature I say, doth paynt them furthe to be weake, fraile, impacient, feble and foolishe: and experience hath declared them to be vnconstant, variable, cruell and lacking the spirit of counsel and regiment. And these notable faultes haue men in all ages espied in that kinde, for the whiche not onlie they haue remoued women from rule and authoritie, but also some haue thoght that men subiect to the counsel or empire of their wyues were vn worthie of all publike office.[27]

Knox appeals to St. Paul as an authority here:

> Of whiche words it is plaine that the Apostle meaneth, that woman in her greatest perfection shuld haue knowen, that man was Lord aboue her: and therfore that she shulde neuer haue pretended any kind of superioritie aboue him, no more then do the angels aboue God the creator, or aboue Christ Iesus their head. So, I say, that in her greatest perfection woman was created to be subiect to man.[28]

This inherent subjection of women to men is only increased by the fall into sin:

> Herebie may such as altogither be not blinded plainlie see, that God, by his sentence, hath deiected all woman frome empire and dominion aboue man. For two punish-mentes are laid vpon her, to witte, a dolor, anguishe and payn, as oft as euer she shal be mother; and a subiection of her selfe, her appetites and will, to her husband, and to his will.[29]

Knox builds on what he understands St. Paul's restrictions of ecclesial authori-ty to women to a general prohibition. If women are forbidden to have authority in church, they are the much more forbidden to have political authority:

> The apostle taketh power frome all woman to speake in the assemblie. Ergo he per-mitteth no woman to rule aboue man. The former parte is euident, whereupon doth the conclusion of necessitie folowe. For he that taketh from woman the least parte of authoritie, dominion or rule, will not permit vnto her that whiche is greatest: But greater it is to reigne aboue realmes and nations, to publish and to make lawes, and to commande men of all estates, and finallie to appoint iudges and ministers, then to speake in the congregation. For her iudgement, sentence, or opinion proposed in the congregation, may be iudged by all, may be corrected by the learned, and reformed by the godlie. But woman being promoted in souereine authoritie, her lawes must be obeyed, her opinion folowed, and her tyrannie mainteined: supposing that it be ex-preslie against God, and the prophet [profit] of the common welth, as to[o] manifest experience doth this day witnesse.[30]

Knox concludes with vehemence:

> And therfore yet againe I repete that, whiche before I haue affirmed: to witt, that a woman promoted to sit in the seate of God, that is, to teache, to iudge or to reigne aboue man, is a monstre in nature, contumelie to God, and a thing most repugnant to his will and ordinance.[31]

Needless to say, Knox's book did not endear him to Queen Elizabeth I of England when she succeeded her sister to the throne and reintroduced Reformation Angli-canism to England.

The point of this somewhat lengthy summary, including numerous quotations, is to provide documentation of the claim made earlier. It should be clear from the above that the church has indeed had a historic position against the ordination of women. From a variety of sources—eastern, western, patristic, medieval, Reforma-tion, Catholic and Protestant—the following has been the key argument: women cannot be ordained or indeed exercise any positions of leadership in the church because of an inherent ontological incapacity. Women were characterized as less intelligent, more sinful, more susceptible to temptation, emotionally unstable, incapable of exercising leadership. In addition, it needs to be recognized that (with the exception of Aquinas) this disqualification was not merely a disqualification from clerical ordination, but from any position of leadership or of exercising authority over men, whether in or out of the church. An extreme position, perhaps, but Knox's essay shows that male theologians were willing to expand the disqualification beyond the clerical sphere to the secular. A fortiori, if women could not exercise leadership in the church, they certainly could not do so elsewhere.

There has been a major shift from this position in recent decades. Somewhere around the mid-twentieth century, the historic claims about women's essential inferiority and intellectual incapacity for leadership simply disappeared. Instead, all mainline churches—Catholic, Orthodox, Protestant, and Anglican—recognized the essential equality between men and women, including fundamental intellectual and moral equality. The kinds of negative rhetoric about women's incapacities that is summarized above disappeared. Arguably, this is a good thing, and a real advance.

Following this shift, three new theological positions appeared in recognition of the equality of women. First, there have been those who recognized that, since the historic reason for refusing to ordain women (inequality) no longer held, it was permissible, indeed necessary, to admit women to ordination. However, there also have been those who, despite the shift from affirming the inequality to the equality of women and men, nonetheless, insisted that women still could not be ordained. There were both Protestant and Catholic versions of this refusal.

In current rhetoric, there is a tendency to speak of those in favor of ordaining women as representing a new position, a shift against the church's historic position. However, it is important to recognize that both the decision to ordain women and the two positions that refuse to ordain women are *new* theological positions. All three positions are responses to the new recognition of the equality of women. None of these three positions represent the traditional position because all of them reject the historic arguments rooted in inequality. Indeed, the advocates of both the new Catholic position against the ordination of women and the new Protestant position are emphatic that they endorse the essential equality of men and women, and that their opposition to women's ordination is not based on any belief or claim that women are inherently inferior to men, or have an intellectual or moral incapacity that would make them incapable of ordination. In making this concession, however, those who still refuse to ordain women are admitting (whether they acknowledge it or not) that their reasons for refusing to ordain women are departures from the historic tradition of the church, just as much as is the decision to ordain women.

THE NEW CATHOLIC POSITION

Sara Butler, one of the more articulate defenders of the new Catholic position against the ordination of women, basically recognizes that a shift has taken place. The first appearance of the "new position" in Catholic circles appeared in Pope Paul VI's reply to the Anglican Archbishop Donald Coggan of Canterbury, expressing concerns about women's ordination among Anglicans. Butler notes that "the 'fundamental reasons' [the pope] supplied were not those commonly understood to explain the position of the Catholic Church."[32]

In response to the assumption of feminist theologians that the [Roman Catholic] Church's opposition to women's ordination was based on defective "anthropology," Butler acknowledges that "until quite recently Catholic theologians generally *did* explain the Church's practice, at least in part, by appealing to the difference and the 'hierarchical' ordering of the sexes. They appealed as well to the Pauline texts that prohibited women's public teaching in the Church and their exercise of authority over men." Furthermore, "Many Catholic theologians relied on the teaching of Saint Thomas Aquinas."[33]

However, notes Butler, "Because the contemporary magisterium has abandoned the view that women are unilaterally subject to men, it obviously does not supply this as the reason women cannot be priests."[34] Indeed, Butler is emphatic that contemporary Roman Catholicism affirms women's "equal rights," both in society and in the church, devoting an entire chapter to make this point. Women can (and do) exercise positions of leadership both in society and in the church, but they cannot be ordained.[35]

Instead, contemporary Catholics adopt different reasons for the inability of the church to ordain women based on arguments from sacramentality, specifically having to do with Jesus' choosing of twelve male apostles, and of the necessary resemblance of a male priest to a male Christ when celebrating the Eucharist. Butler notes that "the fact that Jesus did not choose any women to belong to the Twelve, and that the apostles followed his example by handing on the apostolic church only to men, was seen to be the 'fundamental reason.'"[36] This new position first appeared in the Congregation for the Doctrine of the Faith's *Inter Insigniores*, in 1977. The new position is followed by John Paul II in *Ordinatio sacerdotalis*, *Mulieris dignitatem*, and *Ordinatio Sacredotalis*. Although first formulated by Roman Catholic popes, the new reasons for refusing ordination to women then began to be appealed to in the years following by Orthodox theologians and Anglo-Catholics who opposed women's ordination.

Butler justifies the claim that what is clearly a new position is "not a new doctrine," but a "teaching preserved by the constant and universal tradition of the Church" (citing John Paul II) by distinguishing between "arguments" and "reasons."[37] Some of the "reasons" that were given against women's ordination in the past were "theological arguments" that have had to be abandoned, but these are not the [Roman Catholic] Church's "fundamental reasons" for not ordaining women. The single "fundamental reason" why the Church cannot ordain women is the "fact" of Jesus having chosen twelve male disciples.[38]

To the contrary, however, "facts" do not speak on their own, apart from interpretations of their significance. The argument that women cannot be ordained because Jesus chose only male apostles is just as much an argument as the abandoned argument that women cannot be ordained because of an ontological inferiority. It is just a new argument, and must stand or fall on its merits as an argument. The very distinction between "arguments" and "reasons" is a recognition that a genuine shift has taken place. It is, accordingly, misleading to affirm, as Butler does, that the church has an "unbroken tradition" of not ordaining women without being clear that there is no connection whatsoever between the "reasons" (or as Butler would say, "arguments") that theologians would have given for their unwillingness to ordain women in the past and the new "reasons" that the Roman Catholic Church would give today.

A significant difference between the traditional position and the modern one is that church fathers and medieval figures such as Albert the Great and Thomas Aquinas do not tie questions of the ordination of women to sacramental integrity, but to capacities for morality, leadership, rationality, teaching, and authority. Even when patristic writers note that Jesus chose only male apostles, the concern is about authority to teach and have authority over men, not about sacramental integrity, and again, they base their opposition on the ontological inferiority of women.

For example, Butler appeals to the fourth-century bishop Epiphanius of Salamis, the "first undisputed witness of patristic opposition to the priestly ordination of women," whom she recognizes as "arguably the most important piece of patristic testimony."[39] Epiphanius appeals to the biblical tradition that "Never at any time has a woman been a priest." Eve was not a priest; nor was the Virgin Mary. Epiphanius writes, "If it were ordained by God that women should be priests or have any canonical function in the church, Mary herself, if anyone, should have functioned as a priest in the New Testament."[40] As Butler correctly notes, Epiphanius also appeals to the masculinity of the twelve apostles: "Successors of the episcopate and presbyterate in the household of God were appointed by this bishop [James] and these apostles, and nowhere was a woman appointed." The daughters of Philip the evangelist prophesied, but they were not priests.[41]

However, Epiphanius is simply appealing to tradition here. He makes no *theological* argument. At no point does he draw an inherent connection between male priests or apostles and a sacramental argument concerning the apostles resembling a male Jesus Christ; nor does he attach any significance to the role of male apostles in celebrating the Eucharist. He does, however, provide a kind of warrant for his rejection of women's ordination in the section just preceding, when he refers to the women in the sect against which he is arguing: "And who but women are the teachers of this? Women are unstable, prone to error, and mean-spirited."[42] He goes on to write: "[H]ere the devil has seen fit to disgorge ridiculous teachings from the mouth of women."[43] He precedes the discussion about male priests and apostles to which Butler appeals by stating:

> Now, then, servants of God, let us adopt a *manly* frame of mind and dispel the *madness of these women*. The speculation is *entirely feminine*, and the malady of the *deluded Eve* all over again. . . . [W]e shall have reason to suppose that the *minds of these women* which have been *ensnared by the pride* of that snake, are like the ideas of the deceiver. . . . Once again he is bringing *death on that sex*.[44]

It is only then that Epiphanius continues: "Never at any time has a woman been a priest."[45] Epiphanius' estimate of women is, then, the one seen already. Women are irrational, emotionally unstable, and subject to temptation.

The *Didascalia apostolorum* also appeals to a male apostolate; however, the argument does not concern sacramental theology, but rather male authority:

> It is neither right nor necessary that women should be teachers, and especially concerning the name of Christ and the redemption of his passion. . . . For he the Lord God, Jesus Christ our teacher sent us the Twelve to instruct the people and the gentiles, and there were with us women disciples, Mary Magdalene and Mary the daughter of James and the other Mary; but he did not send them to instruct the people with us. For if it were required that women should teach, our Master would have commended these to give instruction with us.[46]

Again, the *Didascalia*'s appeal to a male apostolate is unhelpful because the contemporary Catholic Church's objection to women's ordination is not to women teaching, but to presiding at the celebration of the Eucharist.

Similarly, the *Apostolic Constitutions* forbids women to baptize, calling it "wicked and impious":

> But if in the foregoing constitutions we have not permitted them to teach, how will any one allow them, contrary to nature, to perform the office of a priest? For this is one of the ignorant practices of the Gentile atheism, to ordain women priests to the female deities, not one of the constitutions of Christ. For if baptism were to be administered by women, certainly our Lord would have been baptized by His own mother, and not by John; or when He sent us to baptize, He would have sent along with us women also for this purpose.[47]

It is clear that the concern has to do with the authority of men over women and a hierarchy rooted in ontological difference, not with administration of the sacraments:

For if the "man be the head of the woman," and he be originally ordained for the priesthood, it is not just to abrogate the order of the creation, and leave the principal to come to the extreme part of the body. For the woman is the body of the man, taken from his side, and *subject to him,* from whom she was separated for the procreation of children. For says He, "He shall *rule over* thee."[48]

And earlier:

We do not permit our "women to teach in the Church," but only to pray and hear those that teach; for our Master and Lord, Jesus Himself, when He sent us the twelve to make disciples of the people and of the nations, did nowhere send out women to preach, although He did not want such. For there were with us the mother of our Lord and His sisters; also Mary Magdalene, and Mary the mother of James, and Martha and Mary the sisters of Lazarus; Salome, and certain others. For, had it been necessary for women to teach, He Himself had first commanded these also to instruct the people with us. For "if the head of the wife be the man," it is *not reasonable* that the rest of the body should *govern* the head.[49]

Accordingly, the distinction between arguments and reasons does not hold because there is no logical correlation whatsoever between the two. There is no logical way to get from an intellectual incapacity indicating an *inequality* that demonstrates an inability to teach or exercise leadership to an intellectual and ontological *equality* that now allows teaching and leadership, but nonetheless does not allow celebration of the sacraments. If the "arguments" are so different from the "reasons" as that, then the current "reasons" represent the equivalent of an entirely new theological position. The claim simply to be representing the church's unchanging tradition collapses.

THE NEW PROTESTANT POSITION

If the current Catholic position against the ordination of women represents a new position, so does the Protestant position. In the last few decades, a position designated as "complementarianism" has been advocated by some Evangelicals. The influence of this perspective can largely be traced to a collection of essays edited by John Piper and Wayne Grudem that appeared in 1991.[50] As with the new Catholic approach, complementarianism departs from the earlier tradition in recognizing the ontological equality of men and women. What makes the position distinctive is that it argues that, while men and women are equal in being, they nonetheless have distinct *roles* to play. It is the role of men to lead and to direct; it is the role of women to submit to the leadership of men. While using the language of equality and complementarity, the position is essentially hierarchical; in contrast to the new Catholic position, Protestant complementarians prohibit not only the ordination of women, but any situation in which women might have authority over or exercise leadership over men.

Although complementarians claim (as do those advocating the new Catholic position) that they are simply affirming the church's historic stance over against the innovations of a *new* Evangelical feminism, complementarianism is as novel a position as the new Catholic position. Methodist theologian Alan Padgett points out:

> [W]e should notice that this view is no older on the historical evidence than about 1975. Though it makes a number of claims to be the true expression of historical Christian teachings, the historical evidence tells us otherwise. Complementarian theology is just as revisionist, just as influenced by modern thought, as the egalitarian view it paints as new and unbiblical.[51]

A comparison of the new Catholic and Protestant positions rejecting women's ordination reveals some inherent tensions between them. Where the new Catholic position has abandoned any arguments based on the traditional interpretation of Paul's writings in favor of a hierarchical understanding of the relationship between men and women, it is precisely such a hierarchical position that is at the heart of complementarianism. Where the new Catholic position defends itself against critics by pointing out that the equality of women means that they can teach and exercise various kinds of secular and ministerial leadership with the single exception of celebrating the sacraments, the complementarians argue that these are precisely the kinds of things that women must not do.

Both positions are also in tension with the previous traditional arguments against women's ordination. The more the new positions emphasize the ontological equality of men and women, the more they are in discontinuity with the arguments of the earlier tradition. The more they emphasize hierarchy, the more they are in continuity with the previous tradition, but the more they must struggle with logical incoherence in simultaneously speaking of "equality in being," but "difference of roles." The new Catholic position is more in harmony with the equality of women, but less in continuity with tradition in emphasizing that women can exercise leadership and authority, just not ordination to the priesthood. The new complementarian Protestant position, because it is hierarchical, is more compatible with the arguments of tradition, but less coherent in that it embraces the hierarchical stance of the tradition while rejecting its historic reasons.

Another interesting anomaly is that Christology plays a key role in each position, but for opposite reasons. The new Catholic position argues that women cannot be ordained because they do not resemble Christ, and only a male priest can resemble Christ. The new Protestant position uses an analogy based on a subordinationist understanding of the Trinity to argue that women cannot be ordained because they do resemble Christ insofar as Christ is equal to but subordinate to the Father in the same way that women are equal to but subordinate to men.[52] Whether these two sets of Christological arguments are mutually coherent, it is important to note that in both cases, these are *new* arguments against the ordination of women. One does not find arguments in historic Christian tradition that women cannot be ordained because they do not resemble Christ. One does not find arguments against women's ordination in the tradition based on analogies with the Son's subordination in the Trinity.

This lack of historical precedent makes clear that in both cases, the arguments against ordination "from tradition" are not the "traditional arguments." In both cases, the recent Catholic opposition to women's ordination and the recent Protestant opposition represent new theological positions, unknown to previous Christian tradition. It is all to the good that Catholics and Protestants have embraced the inherent ontological equality of men and women and no longer argue against women's ordination based on an inherent inferiority, irrationality, or sinfulness of women. However, in so doing, they can no longer argue that they are simply adhering to the church's historic stance against the ordination of women.

In affirming the equality of women, the church has abandoned the historic reasons that women were not ordained. In that light, the church needs to address the question of whether it should continue a practice that was based on a faulty anthropology. Rather than abandon the practice, however, current opponents of women's ordination have discovered new arguments (or reasons) to explain why women cannot be ordained. Later chapters will address these arguments.

POSTSCRIPT: WHAT ABOUT THE VIRGIN MARY?

One possible response to the above argument is simply to deny that the church's historic opposition to the ordination of women could be based on an ontological inferiority. Orthodox theologian Thomas Hopko summarizes a similar argument to that raised above: "Another possible explanation for the absence of women bishops and priests in Orthodox [and other churches] is that cultural conditions of the past, including philosophical and biological understandings, forbade the inclusion of women in these ministries on the basis of their natural inferiority to men." Hopko cannot bring himself to believe that this is the historic reason for opposition: "I believe . . . it impossible to think that women were excluded from the Church's episcopal and presbyterial ministries for reasons of sin, ignorance, convenience or custom."[53] As a counterargument, Hopko appeals to the church's historically positive estimate of women as

> canonized saints . . . women prophets, martyrs, missionaries, monastics, ascetics, elders . . . all of whom are glorified for exactly the same activities and accomplishments as men. . . . But we find no women bishops or priests. This can hardly be attributed,

in my view, to evil or ignorance. It appears much more likely that there must be good reasons.[54]

Later Hopko refers to the most honored Orthodox saint: "The Church's lives of saints are filled with stories of holy men and women who, except for biology, have all but wholly died to this age and attained remarkable progress in divine perfection and holiness. First among these saints, for the Orthodox, is Christ's mother Mary."[55]

In response, the claim here is not that the tradition of the church is an unmitigated history of the oppression of women. One-sided portrayals of the oppression of women can be encountered by offsetting views of the church as having been largely a blessing and an improvement to the status of women. Having said that, the only way to assess the historical reasons for the opposition of the church to the ordination of women is to examine the texts themselves. They repeatedly return to a single argument: that women cannot be ordained because they are less intelligent than men, emotionally unstable, and more subject to temptation. Sara Butler, one of the more able defenders of the new Catholic argument against the ordination of women, recognizes that the prevalent historic argument against the ordination of women was an appeal to female inferiority. Hopko's own argument is a combination of the complementarian appeal to male headship with a sacramental appeal to the bishop/presbyter acting as a representative of the male Christ.[56] Again, however, these are new theological arguments; they do not appear before the mid-twentieth century.

Moreover, appeals to the examples of women saints, and especially to that of the Virgin Mary, are mixed blessings at best, exceptions that rather prove the rule. New Testament scholar Ben Witherington III points to a heightened emphasis on asceticism, celibacy, and virginity that arose in the patristic period following the New Testament, and that led to a devaluing of marriage. This meant that women in the church could either serve in the celibate ministries of deaconesses, virgins, or widows, or they could marry, in which case, their role was restricted to that of wife and mother. The consequence was that the sexual identity of women as women was devalued.[57] The canonized women saints to whom theologians such as Hopko appeal as examples of the church's positive estimate of women were typically celibate and cloistered, not examples for most contemporary women who might be pursuing a call to ordained ministry. Moreover, the Virgin Mary sets what is literally an impossible example for contemporary women to emulate. Mary, as both mother and virgin, combines roles that are mutually exclusive for every other woman. Moreover, in both Catholic and Orthodox theology, Mary is sinless, again in contrast to every other woman. Thus, historically, it has been quite possible to combine a high estimate of the Virgin Mary (mother but not sexual, the perfect sinless example of the church's receptive faith) with a low estimate of women in general. The church father Epiphanius provides a prime example. He was able to appeal to the Virgin Mary as a *negative* example for other women—if God had intended for women to be priests, the Virgin Mary would have been a priest—while simultaneously denigrating those other women: "Women are unstable, prone to error, and mean-spirited."[58] Thus, the argument that the church has had a high evaluation of *some* women is not in itself a counterargument to the claim that the church's historic argument against ordaining women was based on an assumption of ontological inferiority.

A later chapter will address the question of the use of masculine and feminine symbolism as it applies to the question of the ordination of women. However, as it relates to the place of ordinary women in the church, it is difficult not to see the high value that some male theologians have placed on the Virgin Mary as primarily a reflection of their own self-identity as males. In the drama of salvation, the male Jesus Christ necessarily plays the primary active role, while the female Mary necessarily plays a subordinate and passive role. Moreover, the role that Mary plays is precisely that of being a mother. In this theology, while males can also be fathers, they play their primary role in terms of active accomplishment. Conversely, the primary role of the woman is that of motherhood, exemplifying passive receptivity.[59] As Paul K. Jewett wrote in one of the earliest books addressing issues of women's equality in the church: "It is difficult beyond measure for this writer to escape the suspicion that such an approach, in the last analysis, is simply an erudite statement of the man's understanding of himself as being like the Creator and of the woman as being like the creature."[60]

POSTSCRIPT TO CHAPTER 3

In the original hardcover printing of this book, I made the claim that the Catholic objection against ordaining women based on sacramental representation first appears in the Sacred Congregation for the Faith's Declaration *Inter Insigniores*. A reader has since drawn to my attention that Sara Butler makes a single reference to Bonaventure in her book *The Catholic Priesthood and Women*, which I had marked in my first reading but missed when I went back to write the chapter on the topic of the representative role of Christ as acting *in persona Christi*. The reference to Bonaventure comes on pp. 81–82 in a sentence at the end of the paragraph, followed by a quotation:

> The declaration [*Inter Insigniores*] follows instead [of Aquinas] Saint Bonaventure, who argued that priestly ordination is reserved to men because only a man can be the sign of Christ, who is male. According to Bonaventure,
>
>> In this sacrament the ordained person is the sign of Christ the Mediator; since the Mediator belongs only to the male sex, he can only be represented by the male sex; therefore, the capacity for receiving Orders belongs only to males who alone can represent him by nature and, having received the character, can effectively bear the sign [of Christ].

The footnote citation on p. 82 adds a significant qualification: "St. Bonaventure, In IV sent. d. 25, a.2, q.1, conclusion. Any appeal to Bonaventure must be a 'critical retrieval,' because his line of argument is *not free of ideas prejudicial to women.* Bonaventure also notes the objection that a woman cannot be advanced to the episcopate because she is not 'the bridegroom of the Church'" (emphasis added).

A footnote 9 in *Inter Insigniores* cites the Bonaventure reference, although no explicit discussion of Bonaventure's position appears in the document. There would then be a paragraph in *Bonaventure's Commentary on the Sentences* that claims that women cannot be ordained because of an inability to represent a male Christ. Bonaventure may have anticipated a position that would be adopted as the definitive Roman Catholic position several hundred years later in the twentieth century, but this quotation would seem to be a kind of lonely outlier of things to come.

Protestant Arguments

4

Hierarchy and Hermeneutics

Previous chapters have identified two very different groups who are opposed to women's ordination—referred to as "Protestant" and "Catholic"—and have noticed that their reasons for opposition are very different from one another. For the "Protestants," the opposition is based on a hierarchical understanding of authority: women are subordinate to men, and should never exercise authority over men. For the "Catholics," the opposition is twofold: (1) the tradition of the church: traditionally, the church has ordained only males; and (2) a sacramental understanding of ordination: women cannot be ordained because the priesthood is in succession to the apostolate, and Jesus chose only male apostles; in presiding at the Eucharist, the presbyter represents Christ (*in persona Christi*), and a woman cannot represent Christ.

The chapters that follow will address the theological rationales behind these new positions for opposing women's ordination. Whether one begins with the "Protestant" opposition or the "Catholic" is a somewhat arbitrary decision, but the Protestant position is addressed first because its opposition is primarily based on what its advocates claim to be biblical grounds. Discussion of what Scripture actually says about men and women will provide helpful theological background for discussion of not only Protestant, but also Catholic opposition to the ordination of women.

COMPLEMENTARIANISM

Although there are many Protestants who are opposed to women's ordination— entire denominations (such as the Southern Baptists and the Missouri Synod Lutherans, the Orthodox Presbyterian Church), their related seminaries (Southern Baptist Seminary, Concordia Seminary, Westminster Seminary), and several parachurch organizations (Campus Crusade for Christ, Focus on the Family,

Promise Keepers)—Wayne Grudem is the single individual who is most identified with the cause of opposition to women's ordination among North American Evangelical Protestants. In 1991, Grudem and John Piper edited *Recovering
Biblical Manhood and Womanhood: A Response to Evangelical Feminism*, a series
of essays that marked the beginning of the theology of "complementarianism,"
and the formation of a group called "The Council on Biblical Manhood and
Womanhood."[1]

Since then, Grudem has become the chief spokesperson for complementarianism, publishing several subsequent books and articles, most notably in recent years,
*Evangelical Feminism and Biblical Truth: An Analysis of More than One Hundred Dis-
puted Questions*, an eight-hundred-page book responding to Evangelical advocates
of women's ordination.[2] Grudem has also written a *Systematic Theology* in which
he articulates a Calvinist soteriology, verbal plenary inspiration and inerrancy of
Scripture, as well as his complementarian views.[3] Most recently, Grudem has written *Politics for the Bible: A Comprehensive Resource for Understanding Modern Political
Issues in Light of Scripture*, in which he argues for political positions that are basically
in line with the "conservative" Republican movement in American politics, that is,
lower tax rates, a strong military, a free market approach to health care, opposition to
gun control, and skepticism about global warming.[4] While Grudem's opposition to
women's ordination is not necessarily a direct consequence of his other theological
and political views, those positions do make clear that he stands within the broad
spectrum of the theological and political "Evangelical Right."

How prominent is Grudem's position? Grudem writes as if he is simply defending the church's historic theological position. He certainly has had an influence far
beyond his significance as a single theological writer and there are, as noted above,
entire denominations, parachurch organizations, and seminaries where "complementarian" theology would be normative. At the same time, Grudem is a single individual, and he represents a position that is not embraced by many (perhaps most?)
Evangelical Protestants these days. In his book, *Evangelical Feminism: A New Path
to Liberalism*, Grudem has a chapter in which he laments "Places Where Evangelical Feminism Already Has Much Influence."[5] In this chapter, he worries that what
he calls the "evangelical feminist position" is the "dominant position" at such standard Evangelical institutions as Wheaton College, Azusa Pacific University, Denver
Seminary, Fuller Seminary, Gordon-Conwell Seminary, Bethel Seminary, Asbury
Seminary, Regent College-Vancouver, InterVarsity Press, Baker Books, *Christianity
Today*, InterVarsity Christian Fellowship, and the Lausanne Committee on World
Evangelism, among other organizations. The "Christians for Biblical Equality" web-
site has endorsements from numerous Evangelical theologians and church leaders,
and, of course, such prominent orthodox biblical scholars as N. T. Wright have

made theological statements supporting women's ordination.[6] Is it more likely (as Grudem claims) that all of these people are part of a "new path to liberalism" among Evangelical Christians who have rejected the authority of Scripture, or, rather, that his position represents only one position, and a position that many (in some places a majority of) Evangelical Christians do not hold?

What is "complementarianism"? Grudem provides a definition in *Evangelical Feminism and Biblical Truth*. Complementarianism is the position that (1) "men and women are equal in value and dignity," but (2) "men and women have different roles in marriage as part of the created order."[7] At first read, few would disagree with this. All mainstream contemporary Christians believe that men and women are equal in value and dignity. And certainly, men and women have different roles in marriage. After all, only a man can be a husband and father. Only a woman can be a wife and mother. But Grudem means more than this. By "different roles," Grudem means that there is a permanent hierarchy within marriage. As part of the creation order, men always have a role of "headship," by which Grudem means "authority over" women. Within marriage, this means that the primary responsibility of the husband is to "to provide for, to protect, and to lead his family." The primary responsibility of the wife is "to respect her husband and serve as his helper." Again, the "man's responsibility [is] to provide for and protect, and the woman's responsibility [is] to care for the home and to nurture children."[8] These roles cannot be reversed.

Essentially, this translates to a permanent hierarchical relation between men and women. Men lead, teach, and exercise authority. Women follow, learn, and submit to male authority. In addition, this hierarchical subordination translates outside the sphere of marriage as well, particularly in the area of the church, where men (and men only) exercise all functions of *public* leadership and authority. Women are allowed to exercise some forms of ministry within the church, but never in areas of public leadership or speaking, and never in ways that might involve exercising authority over men. Grudem provides a detailed list of positions that must be restricted to men: president of a denomination, senior pastor in a local church, preaching in the pulpit to the whole church, teaching Bible or theology in a seminary or Christian college, leading a home Bible study that includes both men and women. At the same time, Grudem suggests that both men and women can do the following: be director of Christian education, Sunday school superintendent, choir director, administrative assistant to senior pastor, or church secretary, teach a high school Sunday school class, write a book on Bible doctrines or a commentary on a book of the Bible, teach a women's Sunday school class or Bible study group, teach Vacation Bible School, teach as a Bible professor at a secular(!) university, be an evangelistic missionary, perform a baptism, help serve the Lord's Supper, sing in the choir, give a testimony at a church service.

Several observations follow:

Although Grudem insists that men and women are "equal in dignity and value," but merely have "different roles" within the church, the difference in roles applies to only one sex. While women are excluded from certain roles in the church simply because they are women, men are excluded from no roles simply because they are men.

The above pattern of permissible church roles for women has a striking resemblance to the kinds of roles that women regularly would have played in American Protestant churches in the 1950s, the time during which Grudem grew up: church secretary, choir director, singing in the choir, teaching children. Even the one area where Grudem allows a woman to exercise a form of public ministry—as an evangelistic missionary—was an area where women were traditionally allowed a certain freedom among American Protestants before the rise of the modern women's movement. One wonders whether "complementarianism" does not represent so much a concern for biblical authority as a nostalgia for a kind of Evangelical Protestant era that no longer exists.

How does complementarianism differ from the historic reasons for church opposition to women's ordination? As argued in the previous chapter, historic opposition to women's ordination was rooted in a notion of ontological inequality—that women could not exercise positions of leadership because they were less intelligent, emotionally unstable, and more subject to temptation. In contrast to this earlier position, complementarians insist that they affirm the essential equality of women and men. At the same time, insofar as they depart from the earlier rationale, the logic of opposition to women's roles of leadership is the more difficult to justify. If women are not inferior to men in terms of intelligence, emotional stability, or susceptibility to temptation, what is that essential difference that makes men capable of exercising leadership and authority, but not women?[9]

The claim of a distinction between roles also makes less sense when it is noted that the distinction works only one way. Within the church, men are inherently capable of exercising roles that are reserved exclusively to men, but also to exercise all roles that women can fulfill. Within the church, it is only women who have exclusive roles, and specifically the role of being excluded from any position of public speaking, teaching, or exercising authority over men. In addition, there are some odd exceptions. Women may not teach the Bible publicly to men in the church, but they may write books or commentaries on the Bible, which men certainly might read. They cannot minister or preach in a church, but they can preach or teach the Bible to non-Christians in a missionary setting. If their male hearers were to convert to Christianity, however, would these women missionaries now need to submit to the authority of these new converts and no longer be allowed to preach to or teach them? Women cannot teach theology or the Bible in a seminary, but they may do so in a secular university setting. But what if some of the students in the secular university were Christian men? Would a female professor be able to teach a male student in a university setting, but not be able to teach the same male student in a Bible study that she could lead in her local church?

How does the new complementarian position differ from the new Catholic position in opposition to the ordination of women? In the most fundamental way. The new Catholic position no longer bases opposition to women's ordination in any way on perceived differences in freedom to preach, teach, or exercise authority over men. In particular, the biblical passages to which complementarians appeal to support the subordination of women to men are simply no longer considered relevant for Catholic opposition to women's ordination. Pope John Paul II, in his *Theology of the Body*, interpreted Genesis 1–3 to mean that men and women are fundamentally equal in marriage. It is only as a result of the fall that women have found themselves subordinate to men. John Paul II regarded Paul's assertion in Galatians 3:28 that there is "no male and female" in Christ to imply a fundamental equality between men and women within the family and the church. He interpreted Ephesians 5—a classic complementarian proof text—to teach a mutual submission in light of verse 21. If wives are to submit to their husbands (v. 22), then husbands also are to submit to their wives. The Pope stated: "All the reasons in favor of the 'subjection' of woman to man in marriage must be understood in the sense of a 'mutual subjection' of both 'out of reverence for Christ.'"[10] Roman Catholic author Sara Butler notes that "[t]his applies not just to husbands and wives but to all relations between men and women in the community of the redeemed."[11]

Accordingly, defenders of Catholic opposition to women's ordination are nonetheless emphatic that recognition of the equality of women implies that women can fulfill precisely the kinds of roles that complementarians would deny them. Butler notes the differences between the 1917 and the 1983 Code of Catholic Canon Law. In 1917, Catholic married women were considered to be "subject" to their husbands. Women were to be seated separately at liturgical services, excluded from the choir and various church societies. Women "religious" were required to travel in pairs. Women were not allowed to participate in such activities as diocesan synods. In the 1983 Code of Canon Law, "women now have essentially the same juridical status as men in the Catholic Church." Non-ordained women may now participate in diocesan synods, be members of parish councils, serve as diocesan chancellors, teach theology, philosophy, and canon law in seminaries. They can, if necessary, fulfill numerous tasks traditionally done by the ordained: they can preach, baptize, officiate at weddings, assist in pastoral care. Butler writes: "In principle, if not in practice, the equal access of women and men to the non-ordained ministries—apart from installation as lector and acolyte—has now been secured."[12] In other words, for Catholics, women can now perform all of those tasks that complementarians would regard as prohibited because of the differences between men's and women's "roles." For Catholics, the single ecclesial responsibility still reserved exclusively to ordained males is celebration of the sacraments.

A central issue for the discussion of the biblical texts to which complementarians appeal is the recognition that the crucial issues of disagreement are primarily hermeneutical, not simply exegetical. There are disagreements about exegetical issues, of course. For example, what did Paul mean by his metaphorical use of the word "head" in 1 Corinthians and Ephesians? Was Junia a female apostle? However, while such issues are important, the key issue has to do with hermeneutics: How does the church apply what we find written in the Bible to our contemporary situation? The larger hermeneutical concerns center around what the significance of certain biblical texts was during the times when Scripture was written, and what their implications are for today.

The complementarian position is that the subordination of women to men is rooted in creation; God's intention in creating humanity is that men should be in authority, and should teach, and that women should be subject to male authority, and should not teach or exercise authority over men. The position of Evangelical egalitarians is rather that the subordination of women in the Bible (particularly in the Old Testament) reflects the setting of Near Eastern patriarchal culture, but is no more a permanent divine intention than are other aspects of that Near Eastern environment. Concerning the New Testament, egalitarians tend to argue that the several controversial New Testament passages are either addressing specific situations that do not have universal significance, or that they have been misinterpreted as advocating hierarchy.

While Grudem himself insists that the differences in interpretation amount to a clear choice between an acceptance of biblical authority (his own position) and a rejection of it (the egalitarian position, or what he insists on calling "evangelical feminism"), his own position involves just as much hermeneutical interpretation and application as that to which he is opposed.[13] For example, Grudem interprets Paul's statement that "the women should be silent in the churches. For they are not permitted to speak" (1 Cor. 14:34) to mean that women should not engage in *public* preaching or *public* teaching of men or exercise of leadership over men. But this goes beyond what Paul says. A literal reading of Paul's words would be that women should be absolutely silent and never speak a word in a church setting. This seems to defy common sense, and to be in conflict with what Paul says elsewhere, so Grudem engages in a process of speculative hermeneutical interpretation; he does not subscribe to the literal meaning of what Paul actually wrote, but interprets this in light of what he thinks that Paul must have meant, and then arrives at suggestions at how this might be applied today. For example, Grudem allows women to sing in choirs, to give public testimonies in a church service, and to teach Sunday school classes to children, none of which Paul actually mentions, and all of which would be in violation of a literal reading that "women should be *silent* in the churches."

There is also a fundamental theological disagreement at the heart of the issue. Complementarians insist that male-female hierarchy is rooted in creation itself, and represents God's intentions for humanity for all times and all places. The fall into sin has aggravated and distorted dimensions of the essential difference between men and women, but the fundamental subordination of women to men is not the result of sin. To the contrary, egalitarians agree that there are fundamental differences between men and women, and that men and women are indeed complementary to one another in various ways; however, the fundamental subordination of men to women is the result of sin, not God's intention for humanity in creation.[14]

Despite Grudem's claims, such fundamental theological differences cannot be resolved by a straightforward literal reading of the handful of biblical texts to which he appeals. For example, Grudem insists that female subordination was intended in the original creation, apart from the fall; yet the first mention of female subordination does not occur in Scripture until Genesis 3:16, in which God tells Eve after the first sin that "your desire shall be for your husband, and he shall rule over you." A plain-sense reading of the text would suggest that female subordination was a consequence of sin, but Grudem provides a series of arguments to make the case that female subordination can be inferred in Genesis 1 and 2 even though it is not explicitly mentioned.[15] However, the very need for inference demonstrates that the complementarian position does not derive from a straightforward literal reading of Scripture.

In addition, other key New Testament passages on which Grudem's argument depends (1 Cor. 11; 1 Tim. 2:11-15) are notoriously difficult to interpret. What is the discussion of head coverings in 1 Corinthians 11 actually about? If this passage is teaching that women are supposed to be in subordination to men, then why does the actual Greek of verse 10 say that a "woman ought to have authority (ἐξουσία, *exousia*) over her head" (that is, it is the woman's own authority), precisely the opposite of the misleading English translations that imply that a woman's head covering represents her husband's authority over her head? What is the social setting that Paul is addressing in his discussion of Adam and Eve in 1 Timothy, and what could he possibly mean when he says that "women will be saved through childbirth"? A careful reading of the original Greek of Ephesians 5 casts doubt on the complementarian interpretation, misleadingly encouraged by standard English translations that it is wives (alone) who are being asked to submit to their husbands. Numerous exegetes agree that Paul is teaching mutual submission. Grudem places a tremendous amount of weight on the interpretation of the metaphor of "headship" that Paul uses in 1 Corinthians and Ephesians, insisting that the Greek word κεφαλή (*kephalē*) when used as a metaphor in these passages can only mean "have authority over," but numerous competent New Testament scholars have argued in recent years that, while this is a normal understanding of the metaphor in modern English, it was not necessarily the case for the understanding of the Greek usage of the metaphor at the time that Paul wrote. The above are just some of the problems with the complementarian insistence that advocates of women's ordination are willfully rejecting the plain teaching of Scripture.

As Methodist theologian Alan Padgett has noted, "Careful biblical exegesis is an essential and happy obligation, but it is not enough. The Bible is the word of God and contains all things necessary for salvation. But the Bible does not always answer our contemporary questions."[16] Padgett reminds us that exegesis is necessary, but exegesis alone will not give rise to Christian ethics.

There is a kind of historical parallel to the debate between complementarians and advocates of women's equality and ordination in an earlier disagreement in church history. In the debate between Puritans and Anglicans in the sixteenth century, disagreement settled around a basic question of biblical hermeneutics. Puritans advocated a *regulative* principle of biblical interpretation: whatever was not specifically commanded in Scripture was absolutely forbidden. To the contrary, in his *The Laws of Ecclesiastical Polity*, Anglican Divine Richard Hooker advocated a permissive hermeneutic for interpreting Scripture: whatever was not specifically forbidden was permitted. But even more, the Puritans seemed to have a simplistic understanding of how to read the Bible—one that assumed that it was only necessary to read a biblical text to understand not only what it meant at the time it was written, but also how it might be applied in the church at a later time. Against this, Hooker established principles of interpretation based on differences between natural law, revealed law, and positive law. According to Hooker, although Scripture contains many examples of divine precepts and laws, not everything that is either recorded or taught in Scripture is intended to be normative and valid for all time. What Hooker calls "positive law" may have had an application for a particular time and place in the history of revelation and salvation, but does not necessarily have permanent validity. Of significance for contemporary application, merely historical statements recorded in Scripture cannot be presumed to provide permanent warrants for later Christian practice. Hooker asked: "When that which the word of God doth but deliver historically, we counter without any warrant as if it were legally meant, and so urge it further than we can prove it was intended, do we not add to the laws of God, and make them in number seem more than they are?"[17] Accordingly, in applying the teaching of Scripture to contemporary settings, the church has to exercise reason—what we would today call "hermeneutics"—to determine which parts of Scripture have permanent validity for contemporary Christian practice, which have continuing relevance, and in what manner, and which simply are not for practice in the church today. This is not placing the authority of the contemporary church over the authority of Scripture. It is to take the authority of Scripture seriously by recognizing that not everything in Scripture has a direct contemporary application.

In recent years, several writers have addressed how to read Scripture in such a way as to respect its original historical setting, and how to make the attempt to apply the teaching of Scripture to a very different contemporary setting, and to do so in such a way that Scripture retains its authority. In one contemporary parallel to Hooker's hermeneutical recognition that not everything in Scripture is intended as an admonition to be followed for all time, New Testament scholar Ben Witherington III distinguishes between those things that Scripture "teaches," and those things that it merely "touches on."[18] Witherington suggests various hermeneutical principles for reading and applying Scripture in a contemporary setting, and notes that making the transition between two very different cultures in different historical periods is not a simple task: "The basic rule of thumb is that while principles remain the same, practices often do and should change with the differing cultural situations."[19] Other examples include the hermeneutical principles that Richard Hays suggests in his now standard textbook *The Moral Vision of the New Testament*,[20] the series of essays contained in *The Art of Reading Scripture*[21] and *Knowing the Triune God: The Work of the Spirit in the Practices of the Church*,[22] the canonical approach of Brevard Childs,[23] John Webster's *Holy Scripture*,[24] or, recently, N. T. Wright's *Scripture and the Authority of God: How to Read the Bible Today*.[25] Such approaches do not compromise the authority of Scripture. They do recognize that there is a difference between what Scripture teaches, what a modern interpreter understands it to have taught, and how contemporary Christians might apply that teaching today. They also are clear that contemporary application of the teaching of Scripture is not a direct move from "women were subordinate to men in various places in the Bible" to "women must be subordinate to men at all times and in all places."

5

Beginning with Genesis

The doctrine of creation is crucial to a number of related theological issues, and theologians have appealed to it when addressing numerous issues. Often theologians have engaged in a speculative exercise in which they distinguish between a created and a fallen world to address issues that initially might not seem directly related to the doctrine of creation. For example, theologians interested in the relation between Christian faith and politics have sometimes speculated about whether there would have been government if there had been no sin. Augustinians (and Lutherans) have tended to understand government as primarily concerned with justice, and, in particular, with restraining and punishing evildoers in a fallen world. So, they have argued, there would have been no need for government if there had been no fall. To the contrary, Thomists (and some Calvinists) have suggested rather that the purpose of government is to promote the common good, and even in an unfallen world, government would have existed. For example, even in an unfallen world, if people drove automobiles, there would need to be some way of deciding whether drivers should drive on the left or the right side of the road. How one answers this question will largely determine whether one sees the present function of government as a necessary evil, and, accordingly, limited largely to military and police functions, or, rather, whether one sees executing justice as only one of government's functions, which would also include numerous public goods as well: highways, national parks, promoting the arts, public education, economic assistance to the poor, having a positive role in promoting a healthy economy, and publicly funded health care.

Similarly the distinction between "natural law," "ceremonial law," and "civil law" that one finds in theologians and theological traditions as diverse as Thomas Aquinas, Richard Hooker, John Calvin, and the Lutheran Confessions presupposes a distinction between the kinds of laws that are rooted in the nature of creation itself, and the laws that would exist only in a sinful world. Thomas Aquinas argues, for example, that there would have been no private property and no need for laws against theft if there had been no sin.[1] Contemporary discussions about sexuality, particularly the question of whether Christians should approve of same-sex sexual activity, ultimately must address this question of "natural law"; that is, what was God's original intention in creating human beings as male and female, and what bearing does this have on sexual ethics?

For similar reasons, the doctrine of creation is important for assessing concerns about women's ordination. The interpretation of Genesis 1–3 has played a major role in the discussion of women's place, not only in marriage, but in the church and culture as well. The crucial question has to do with the interpretation of Genesis 3:16b: "Your desire shall be for your husband, and he shall rule over you." Is this verse a command, a curse, or a description? Is it a command that is a furthering of a subordination that was nonetheless part of God's intention in creation, or rather a punishment or curse in response to sin, or neither part of God's intention for creation or a curse, but simply a description of the way things are in a fallen world, and thus a departure from God's intention in creation? To be specific, if human beings had never sinned, would women be subordinate to men? Moreover, even if subordination is only a consequence of the fall, is that subordination something willed by God or something to be overcome as much as possible?

As pointed out in a previous chapter, historically many theologians have assumed that an essential subordination of women to men is rooted in an ontological inferiority rooted in creation: women are less rational, more emotional, and more subject to temptation than men.[2] There have been some exceptions. In his exegesis of Genesis, Martin Luther suggested that, apart from the fall, women would not have been subordinate to men.[3] John Chrysostom, in his commentary on 1 Corinthians, stated that the subjection of women to men is a direct consequence of the fall:

> Wherefore you see, she was not subjected as soon as she was made; nor, when He brought her to the man, did either she hear any such thing from God, nor did the man say any such word to her: he said indeed that she was "bone of his bone, and flesh of his flesh" (Gen. 2:23), but of rule or subjection he nowhere made mention unto her. But when she made an ill use of her privilege and she who had been made a helper was found to be an ensnarer and ruined all, then she is justly told for the future, "thy turning shall be to thy husband." (Gen. 3:16)[4]

There are a number of issues that might be addressed in a discussion of Genesis 1–3. For example, what is the relation between Genesis and issues raised by modern science: the age of the earth, the evolutionary origins of humanity, the connection between the first human beings described in Genesis and the various hominids known about from the fossil record (*Homo erectus*, Neanderthals) and possible pre-human ancestors of humanity such as *Australopithecus*? There are questions concerning Genesis and ecology: what does it mean for human beings to "have dominion" over nature? (Gen. 1:28)? There are questions concerning Genesis' account of the rise of humanity and civilization and modern archaeological and historical attempts at reconstruction, for example, the account of the rise of multiple languages and nationalities in Genesis 10 and modern linguistic theories. What should we make of the Genesis account of a global flood? Of the relation between the "primordial history" of the earliest chapters of Genesis and possible parallels in the mythology and folklore of other ancient Near Eastern peoples?[5] However, this chapter will focus on only one question: What does Genesis 1–3 teach about the relation between men and women? Does Genesis teach that the subordination of women that was presupposed in the ancient Near East and in all historical cultures until the rise of the modern era is part of God's intention for humanity in creation, or, rather, is such subordination a consequence of human sin?

GENESIS 1

The book of Genesis contains two different accounts of creation with different orders of events and different emphases. Modern source critics have seen this as evidence of two different sources lying behind the text. More recent readings have tended to focus on the canonical unity of the texts, noting that while each account has its own focus, they also share many of the same themes. The first account in Genesis 1 tends to be more cosmic in its focus, while the account in Genesis 2 and 3 focuses specifically on humanity.

For the purposes of this discussion, the key text in the first creation account is Genesis 1:26-28:

> God created *ha'adam* in his image;
> in the image of God he created him.
> Male and female he created them.

The Hebrew word הָאָדָם, transliterated here as *ha'adam*, has a multivalence that is not captured by the standard English translations. In its broadest sense, *ha'adam* simply refers to "humanity" or "humankind." However, the word is also used to refer to the first "human being" created in Genesis 2. Finally, it can also be a proper name, "Adam." The first unambiguous use of *'adam* (אָדָם) as a proper name (without the article) occurs in Genesis 4:25, although 4:1 is also a possibility.

English translations often translate *ha'adam* as "man" in Genesis 1:26, "the man" elsewhere, and "Adam" in 4:1. However, it needs to be understood that *ha'adam* is the generic name for "human" or "human being," and is not equivalent to the modern English "man" meaning "male human being."[6] Hebrew has no word for "humanity" other than 'adam, and this was common to Semitic usage before Genesis 1–3 was written. It is also important to distinguish between grammatical gender and physical sexual differences. Hebrew has only two genders, masculine and feminine, with no neuter, and the choice of genders for a noun is unpredictable. While Old English had gender, modern English does not, which gives English-speaking students endless headaches when first trying to make sense of a gendered language: What makes a French table (*la table*) "feminine"? Why does a Latin farmer (*agricola*) have a first declension ending (which should be female), but corresponding masculine adjectives? The point of this short digression about grammar is to be clear that *ha'adam* simply means "humanity," "humankind," or "human being," and, in itself, has no connotations of specifically male sexuality. Male grammatical gender does not necessarily mean male sexuality. For that reason, some variation of "human" or "human being" will appear as the proper translation for *ha'adam* in what follows rather than "man."[7]

The first question that arises from the above passage is what it means for humanity to be created "in the image of God." Classical interpreters have identified the *imago dei* with rationality, with a typological anticipation of Jesus Christ as the perfect image of God, or with the Trinitarian persons. Modern interpretations tend to move in two directions. Beginning with Karl Barth, some have identified the *imago* with sexual differentiation itself based on the Hebrew parallelism between "in the image of God he created him" and "male and female he created them."[8] The image thus points to personalism, that human beings by their bodily construction as "male and female" are inherently oriented toward one another and are incomplete without community.[9] More recent interpreters have tended not to follow Barth, but to focus on the specific blessing given by God in verse 28, to "be fruitful and multiply," and to "have dominion" over the earth. The image "mirror[s] God to the world"; human beings are an extension of God's governing of and care for creation.[10]

At the least, the creation account in Genesis 1 has the following implications:

(1) There is a fundamental equality between men and women, male and female as created in the image of God. The female is created in the image of God just as much as the male, and there is no humanity apart from the distinction between man and woman; to be a human being is fundamentally to be either male or female. Men and women are fundamentally alike as human beings, are made for each other, and are incomplete without one another.[11]

(2) There is a personalist dimension to the divine image. The inner-divine communication—"Let us make humanity in our image" (Gen. 1:26)—is echoed in God's address to the human beings created in his image. Both male and female are addressed equally in God's first speaking to them, and their task echoes divine providence over creation. God does not exercise power over creation on his own, but shares his governance of creation with human beings.[12]

(3) The task (or rather "blessing") of bringing forth children and of stewardship over the earth that is given to humanity is a common task for both men and women as created in the image of God. There are no "gender roles" or gender-specific responsibilities in the passage. Men as well as women are expected to nurture children; women as well as men are expected to exercise stewardship over creation. Neither male nor female exercises power or authority over the other; both are given equal power, authority, and responsibility.[13]

In short, Genesis 1 describes man and woman as created equally in the image of God, and equally given a responsibility by God to exercise stewardship over creation. There is nothing in the passage to imply any gender-specific roles or any hierarchy of unequal relationships of authority between the two.

GENESIS 2

While Genesis 1 describes a single creation of humanity (ha'adam), both male and female in the image of God, Genesis 2 tells the story of creation in a slightly different way, describing first the creation of a single human creature (ha'adam) and only later the creation of a female creature, after which the two are distinguished as man (male) and woman (female). It is also in the narrative beginning with Genesis 2 that a clear distinction is made between three uses of the Hebrew 'adam: as humanity in general, as the single human being who is created from the dust of the earth, and, finally, as the proper name "Adam," which, again, simply means "human being." Throughout Genesis 2, ha'adam occurs with the definite article, "the human being." The proper name 'adam (without the article) appears first in Genesis 4.[14]

In Genesis 2:7, ha'adam (the human being) is created from ha'adamah (הָאֲדָמָה, the ground). There is in Hebrew a deliberate pun that connects the human being who later cultivates the earth with the earth from which he is created.[15] Although it becomes clear in verse 23 with the creation of woman that the human being is male, at this point there is not yet any sexual differentiation implied in the text. The human being is simply ha'adam, the "human being." English translations frequently render this as "the man," but if "man" is understood to mean "male human being," it is misleading. Sexuality is not introduced into the text until the creation of woman. This does not mean that the first human being is an androgyne, as some commentators have suggested, but that sexuality does not yet exist as a reality until both sexes exist: there are no men without women, and vice versa. The best translation, then, is either "the human being," or, as some writers have suggested, based on the pun between ha'adam and ha'adamah, the "earth creature."[16]

For the first time in Genesis 2:18, something is described as being "not good." In contrast to the repeated judgments of chapter 1 after each act of creation that "God saw that it was good," and the statement in Genesis 1:31 at the conclusion of creation that "God saw everything that he had made, and behold, it was very good," the reader is now told that God said: "It is not good that the human being (ha'adam) should be alone. I will make a companion corresponding to (כְּנֶגְדּוֹ׃ עֵזֶר, 'ezer kenegdo) him." The expression here translated "companion corresponding to" ('ezer kenegdo) is misleadingly translated as "helper" in English translations. In English, "helper" implies a subordinate or inferior, an assistant. The Hebrew 'ezer has no connotations of inferiority or subordination. There are many places in the Bible where God is the 'ezer to Israel or to individuals who need assistance: "Such examples leave no doubt that 'ezer can refer to anyone who provides assistance, whatever their relationship to the one whom they aid."[17]

In an attempt to find the human being a suitable companion, God first brings him the animals, each of whom the human names. This does not solve the problem, however: "But for the human being there was not found a companion corresponding to him" (v. 20). God then puts the human to sleep and performs a bit of surgery, creating a fellow human being (the woman) out of a rib taken from the human being's side. This is an interesting difference. Where the first human being (ha'adam) had been taken from the earth (ha'adamah), this new human being is taken not from the earth, but from the side of ha'adam. The first human being now functions as the earth had functioned in his own creation; a new human creature is taken from him (ha'adam) as he was taken from the earth (ha'adamah). This new creature is thus a perfect match for him because she is taken directly from him.[18]

God brings this new human being to the first human being to see how he will respond. The purpose of bringing the animals to the human being, resulting in his dissatisfaction, was to accentuate his loneliness, and his need for one who is like himself. The purpose of the woman's "help" is companionship, to end his loneliness. The woman is not a subordinate, an assistant, but someone like the human, someone "corresponding" to him.[19]

With the introduction of the woman, the human being finally has a companion corresponding to himself, and greets her with the exclamation: "This at last is bone of my bones and flesh of my flesh; she shall be called Woman (אִשָּׁה, 'issa) because she was taken out of Man (אִישׁ, 'is)" (v. 23). Again, the focus here is on equality, not on hierarchy or subordination. This is demonstrated in the following ways.

First, it is only here that the text at last introduces sexuality, when the first human being recognizes himself as "man" ('is) and his corresponding companion as "woman" ('issa). For the first time, the Hebrew word for "man" (male human being) is introduced rather than the generic ha'adam. The terms 'is and 'issa emphasize the likeness of the man and the woman. The only difference is the corresponding feminine ending for the word 'issa. The woman is the same as the man, but a female version. Significantly, the man does not call the woman ha'adamah, the feminine version of the word ha'adam, because that word means "earth," a word already used in describing the human being (*ha'adam*) as having been taken from the earth (*ha'adamah*). As there had earlier been a wordplay between "earth" and "human being"—the *ha'adam* is a human being because taken from *ha'adamah*—so now there is a wordplay on man and woman; the woman is a woman (*'issa*) because she was taken from the man (*'is*).[20]

Second, the cry of recognition—"This at last is bone of my bones and flesh of my flesh"—points to equality and companionship, not to hierarchy or subordination. The woman is one who is like the man because she is taken from his own body.[21]

Third, the man does not "name" the woman, but recognizes her as one like himself. Authors disagree about whether the naming of the animals in verse 20 implies power or authority over or subordination of animals to the human being.[22] What is clear, however, is that the man's recognition of the woman is not a "naming," but an exclamation of recognition. He does not "name" the woman, but "calls" her. As Phyllis Trible points out:

> The verb *call* by itself does not mean naming; only when joined to the noun *name* does it become part of a naming formula. . . . The earth creature exclaims, "This shall be called *'issa*." The noun *name* is strikingly absent from the poetry. Hence, in calling the woman, the man is not establishing power over her but rejoicing in their mutuality.[23]

Moreover, "woman" (*'issa*) is not a "name," but simply a recognition that the woman is like the man (*'is*) and so is called the same, except for the feminine ending of the noun.[24]

Finally, Genesis 2 ends with the classic definition of marriage that is repeated in countless wedding ceremonies: "Therefore a man shall leave his father and mother and hold fast to his wife, and they shall become one flesh." That the man leaves his father and mother and "holds fast to" (clings to) his wife confirms the reading of the rest of the passage that the woman was created to satisfy the man's need for companionship. Genesis 2:24 brings back together that which God had separated by taking the woman from the human being's side. What was two has now again become one. Significantly, the passage does not say that the woman leaves her parents to "cling to" her husband, which we might expect if the hierarchical reading were correct, but that the man leaves his parents to cling to his wife.[25]

Genesis 2 ends with a situation of harmony, where the woman is the "corresponding companion" to the man, where there is mutual equality between them, and there is no hint of subordination or hierarchy. In Genesis 1, God told both man and woman to fill the earth and to exercise stewardship over it. In a corresponding passage in Genesis 2:15, *ha'adam* is told to cultivate the earth, and the human being is commanded not to eat of the fruit of the tree of the knowledge of good and evil (vv. 16-17)—the woman does not yet exist, so she cannot receive either command at this point—but nowhere is the man given authority over the woman; nor is he commanded to exercise authority over her or she to obey him. At the end of the passage, the two who had come to exist because God had taken the woman from the man are now "one flesh." The unity of "one flesh" points to both equality and completeness. There is no hint of hierarchy of any kind, let alone gender-hierarchy, in either Genesis 1 or 2.[26]

GENESIS 3

If Genesis 2 describes a setting of mutuality and harmony between man and woman, Genesis 3 is about the undoing of this harmony as a result of sin. The themes of equality, mutual harmony, and companionship were introduced in Genesis 2 to prepare for what follows in Genesis 3, where the introduction of sin disrupts the original harmony of creation, and, as it were, turns everything upside down. Where there was mutuality, cooperation, and the fruitfulness of a garden, there now comes to exist competition, distrust, and conflict between the man and the woman, subordination of the woman to the man, and the struggle of both to survive a world that now produces thorns.[27]

Although there are numerous theological issues raised by this passage concerning the origin of suffering and evil, the doctrines of the fall and original sin, the following will focus only on those issues specifically correlated to hierarchical relationships between men and women, and, specifically, on the issue of the subordination of women to men.

The first point to be noted is that subordination does appear for the first time in the texts, and it is specifically mentioned as a consequence of the fall into sin. The woman is told, "Your desire shall be for your husband and he shall rule over you" (Gen. 3:16). It is significant that this is a reversal of the situation originally described in Genesis 2, where it was the man whose loneliness needed to be filled by the introduction of the woman, where the relationships between the man and the woman had been described as harmonious, and where the man had greeted the woman as "bone of my bones and flesh of my flesh." The woman still yearns for the original unity of creation, but there is now a hierarchy of division, and, rather than living together in harmony, the man "rules over" the woman. The lost harmony occasioned by the fall into sin produces a disruption of relationships. Where human beings were originally supposed to cultivate the earth and act as stewards of God's providential order over creation, the earth now must be cultivated with pain and hard labor. Where human beings were originally commanded to be fruitful and multiply, now the woman's labor will also be increased, and she will bring forth children in pain. The original command to be fruitful and multiply is now more difficult. Where the human being had come from the earth, now he must till the earth with hard labor, struggling against thorns and thistles, working to make bread by "the sweat of your face," and returning to the earth at death (Gen. 3:16-19). It is only at this point, after the first sin, that the man now gives the woman a name: "Eve" (*havvah*), the mother of all living (*hay*).[28]

It is significant that the judgments on the man and the woman are not curses. The snake and the ground are cursed because of humanity's sin, but the man and woman are not.[29] Neither, however, should they be understood as punishments. Instead, they simply describe the situation in which men and women find themselves in a fallen world. They represent the undoing of the harmony that existed as God's original intention for humanity, but not a new order that—having come into existence because of sin—is supposed to be preserved. The beauty of creation has been damaged and, to some extent, destroyed by sin, but the sufferings listed in Genesis 3 are not part of God's intention for creation, but rather its undoing. They should not be understood as God's will for the world, or as if trying to correct them would in some way be a sin or the violation of a divine command. The use of medicine or painkillers to aid in the alleviation of illness or to ease the suffering of death should not be understood as a sin any more than the use of weed killers or fertilizer or tractors to make harvesting easier.[30]

Similarly, there is no reason to believe that the subordination of women to men described in Genesis 3:16 is anything more than a description of the sinful relations between men and women in a fallen world. The equality and harmony depicted in Genesis 1 and 2 are now depicted as having been disrupted because of human sin. Both the supremacy of the man over the woman and the subordination of the woman to the man are the consequences of shared disobedience to God's will, but not God's intentions for how redeemed lives should be lived. Genesis 3 does speak of a hierarchy of men over women and a subordination of women to men, but only in consequence of human sin. The writer of Genesis recognized that the patriarchal rule of the man over the woman was as much a judgment on the man as the woman.[31]

In short, Genesis 1 and 2 depict a relation of equality and harmony between man and woman. Both are equal partners in their *humanity*; both share God's image; both are made for one another; both are stewards of God's creation. In consequence of sin, this original harmony was broken, not only between man and woman, but also between humanity and creation. In consequence, disrupted harmony between humanity and the natural world means that human beings live out their life in a struggle of "sweat and tears" to eke out a living in a hostile environment. Broken relations between human beings means that the harmonious "one flesh" relationship intended by God for men and women in marriage is disrupted as women yearn for the restoration of an original harmony that no longer exists, and men forget the original purpose of woman as a "suitable companion," and instead tend rather to "rule over" women. The end result is dysfunctional relationships for both men and women. In conclusion, a straightforward reading of Genesis 1–3 does not teach that the subordination of men to women is part of God's original intention in creation; rather, Genesis teaches an essential unity and harmony between men and women with no mention of hierarchy or subordination before the introduction of sin into the world. Neither does Genesis 1–3 mention any gender-specific roles for men and women. Both men and women are commanded equally to be fruitful and multiply—of course, only "Eve," as a woman, can give birth to children, and is thus the "mother of all living"; both men and women are commanded to exercise God's stewardship over creation. The first mention of any subordination of women to men occurs in Genesis 3:16 when the man is said to "rule over" the woman as a consequence of sin. There is no divinely given authority in Genesis of husbands over wives or of men (in general) over women (in general) that is grounded in a creation order.

A "COMPLEMENTARIAN" READING OF GENESIS

One might think that the above reading would settle the question of whether Genesis 1-3 teaches that there is a fundamental hierarchy between men and women that is established in the very order of creation. A plain-sense reading provides no ground for a theory of inherent subordination of women to men. There is no explicit mention of hierarchy until Genesis 3:16, and it is in direct conflict with what the text says about God's intentions for the creation of man and woman in Genesis 1 and 2. The "rule" of man over woman is portrayed as a consequence of sin, and it is a disruption of the harmony that is portrayed in Genesis 1 and 2.

Because the texts say nothing explicitly about subordination before the introduction of sin, complementarians must use indirect arguments to claim that Genesis 1 and 2 imply a gender hierarchy. Wayne Grudem, the foremost advocate of complementarianism, lists ten such "arguments showing male headship in marriage before the fall."[32] The first seven will be addressed in turn. The last three deal specifically with the New Testament, and will be addressed in subsequent chapters.

1. The Order: Adam Was Created First, Then Eve

As should be clear from the above, this is a misreading of the text. "Adam," as a proper name, does not appear until Genesis 4. "Adam" is simply the Hebrew "human being" (*'adam*) used as a proper name (without the article). What Genesis indicates was created first was *ha'adam*, the "human being," understood as "humankind" in Genesis 1 and as an individual human being in Genesis 2. Moreover, *ha'adam* is a pun that points to the human being's creation from the earth (*ha'adamah*). It is not until Genesis 2:23 that sexuality first appears when both the "man" (*'is*) and "woman" (*'issa*) appear together.

Moreover, even if we grant that the "human being" of Genesis 2 is a male human being (not an androgyne), the order of creation has no particular significance for hierarchy. Richard Hess points out that in the Mesopotamian creation story of Atrahasis, which dates from the same culture and time as the laws of Hammurabi, and includes parallels to the Genesis references to a primeval paradise, a subsequent rebellion, and a flood, the woman is created first. Moreover, whenever men and women are mentioned, the woman is mentioned first. Nonetheless, ancient Mesopotamia was a highly patriarchal culture, even more so than ancient Israel. Hess concludes: "This indicates that the *sequence* of man's and woman's creation has no significance for implications of the society's view of or assumption regarding hierarchy."[33] Hess suggests that the man and woman are created sequentially in Genesis 2 in order to demonstrate their mutual need for each other after the man (i.e., the "human being") had failed to find an appropriate companion in the animals that God had brought to him. The reason for the sequenced order lies in the narrative flow of the text, not as an affirmation of hierarchy.[34]

2. The Representation: Adam, Not Eve, Had a Special Role in Representing the Human Race

Here Grudem points to the New Testament parallels between Adam and Jesus Christ. 1 Corinthians 15:22 states: "For as in Adam all die, so in Christ all will be made alive." In Romans 5, Paul makes a parallel between Adam and Christ, where Christ is portrayed as a "second Adam": "For as by the one man's disobedience the many were made sinners, so by the one man's obedience the many will be made righteous" (Rom. 5:19). Grudem suggests that, since Eve sinned first, Paul might have said that "in Eve all die." That Paul speaks of Adam instead indicates that Adam (as male) has a representative role.

The argument seems to miss the point of how typology functions in Paul's writings. Paul is quite capable of using female types to make a point. So, for example, in Galatians 4, Paul uses the female figures of Hagar and Sarah as types representing the two covenants of Sinai, the old covenant ("present Jerusalem") and the new covenant ("Jerusalem above"). Nothing in the typology suggests that either Hagar or Sarah are "representative" because of their sex.

Similarly, nothing in the Adam/Christ typology suggests that Adam is "representative" because of his sex. Rather, it makes sense that in making a typological comparison pointing to Jesus Christ, Paul would have used the male figure of Adam to prefigure Jesus, since Jesus was himself a male. Moreover, it also makes sense to draw a parallel between Adam (whose name "Adam" means "human being") as the first human being through whom sin originated, and Jesus Christ as the new creation of God (the second Adam or human being) through whom sin is destroyed. Note that throughout Romans 5, Paul uses the Greek word ἄνθρωπος (anthrōpos), properly translated "human being," rather than ἀνήρ (anēr), properly translated "male human being" (or, in modern English, "man") to describe both Adam and Christ. So, "sin entered the world through one human being (δι᾽ ἑνὸς ἀνθρώπου, di henos anthrōpou) . . . and death spread to all human beings (εἰς πάντας ἀνθρώπους, eis pantas anthrōpous)" (v. 12); "For if the many died by the trespass of the one, how much more did God's grace and the gift that came by the grace of the one human being Jesus Christ (τοῦ ἑνὸς ἀνθρώπου Ἰησοῦ Χριστοῦ, tou henos anthrōpou Iēsou Christou), overflow to the many!" (v. 15); "For just as through the disobedience of the one human being (οὗ ἑνὸς ἀνθρώπου, ou henos anthrōpou) the many were made sinners, so also through the obedience of the one, the many will be made righteous" (v. 19).

3. The Naming of Woman: Adam Names Eve

According to Grudem, just as God demonstrates his authority over creation by naming it, and Adam demonstrates his authority over the animals by naming them, so Adam demonstrates his authority over the woman by naming her. To the contrary, as noted above, the man's ('is) calling of the woman ('issa) is not a naming, but a recognition. The man simply recognizes the woman as someone like himself, a companion fitting for himself. Their equality is emphasized by the similarity in the nouns 'is and 'issa. Moreover, the man does not exercise authority over the woman, but recognizes her as one who relieves his loneliness. Again, as noted above, the text does not use the "naming formula" for woman that is used in reference to the animals. The man "calls" the woman, but does not name her. "Woman" ('issa), unlike "Eve," is not a name, but an exclamation of recognition.

4. The Naming of the Human Race: God Named the Human Race "Man," Not "Woman"

It is hard to account for this claim except as based on the ambiguity of modern English usage, leading to corresponding confusion in translations. As noted above, Hebrew makes a clear distinction between "humanity" (ha'adam), on the one hand, and "man" ('is) and "woman" ('issa) on the other. In Genesis, God does not name the human race "man" ('is), but rather "humanity" (ha'adam). 'Adam also functions as the proper name of the first human being, but this is based on a pun reflecting the human being's function. Adam ('adam) is the human being (ha'adam) because he is taken from the earth (ha'adamah) and cultivates it. In the same way, Eve is named for her function as the mother of all living.

The long and short of it is that the Hebrew of Genesis does not name the human race "man" ('is), but rather "humanity" (ha'adam). The generic "humanity" (ha'adam) has nothing to do with Adam's male sexuality, and the male gender of the word is a matter of grammatical gender, not human sexuality.

5. The Primary Accountability: God Spoke to Adam First after the Fall

This argument would seem to be a misreading of what is going on in the literary structure of the text. God addresses the man first because he was the first one that God had told not to eat of the fruit of the tree, and he was the last one who ate. More significant is a common Hebrew literary structure. The text introduces a chiasm. As the snake, the woman, and the man are introduced in that order in Genesis chapter 3, so they are referred to in reverse order in what follows: the man is addressed, who blames the woman; the woman is addressed, who blames the snake; finally, there is a return to the original order as, first, judgment is pronounced on the snake, then on the woman, and, last, on the man. The narrative structure of the text is thus as follows: (ABC) snake, woman, man; (CBA) man, woman, snake; (ABC) snake, woman, man.[35]

6. The Purpose: Eve Was Created as a Helper for Adam, Not Adam as a Helper for Eve

As pointed out above, Hebrew 'ezer does not mean a subordinate or an inferior partner, but someone who can provide genuine assistance. In the Old Testament, God is often portrayed as an 'ezer. Moreover, the way in which the woman serves as a helper to the man is made clear. The woman (unlike the animals) relieves the man's loneliness. She is a companion like himself, one who is fit for him. She is a female version ('issa) of what he is ('is). Moreover, in that the relationship between the man and the woman is one of complementarity and mutuality, the man is indeed as much a companion for the woman as she is for the man. Together they become "one flesh." Insofar as the text portrays the man as being the one who is lonely, it is he, if anyone, who is in a position of subordination here. It is the man who needs companionship in Genesis 3, since the woman had not yet been created.

7. The Conflict: The Curse Brought a Distortion of Previous Roles, not the Introduction of New Roles

Grudem claims here that there are three "roles" assigned to the man and woman in creation. The curse brings about pain in the area of each of these roles or "areas of particular responsibility." The man's "area of responsibility" is to raise food from the ground, and the ground is now cursed and will bring forth weeds and thorns. The woman's "area of responsibility" is the bearing of children, and she will now bring forth children in pain. The third area that the curse effects is to introduce pain and conflict into the relationship between the man and the woman. Grudem states:

> Prior to their sin, they had lived in the Garden of Eden in perfect harmony, yet with a leadership role belonging to Adam as the head of his family. But after the Fall, God introduced conflict in that Eve would have an inward urging and impulse to oppose Adam, *to resist Adam's leadership* . . . "Your impulse, desire, will be *against* your husband."

According to Grudem, Adam's response to this aggressive attempt to resist Adam's role will be an aggressive "rule that was forceful and at times harsh." Grudem goes on to claim that Genesis 3:16 shows that "the Fall brought about a *distortion* of previous roles, not the introduction of new roles. The distortion was that Eve would now rebel against her husband's authority and Adam would misuse that authority to rule forcefully and even harshly over Eve."[36]

The argument is an example of the fallacy of begging the question (*petitio principii*). As pointed out above, there is nothing in Genesis 1 and 2 about gender-specific "roles." Grudem attempts to introduce the complementarian notion of gender-specific roles into the text by drawing a parallel between the tasks that the man and woman fulfill in Genesis 2 and 3 and a "role" of male leadership and authority over the woman, but there is no such "role" given to the man in either Genesis 1 or 2, and Grudem's indirect arguments to make a case for such a role fail to succeed.

Rather, what Genesis 3 introduces is not a "curse" (Grudem's word) against the man and the woman (the snake and the ground are cursed, not the man and the woman), but a description of a breakdown in two kinds of previously harmonious relationships, those between human beings and the realm of nature, and those between the man and the woman. In the realm of nature, the man (*ha'adam*), who came from the earth, and who was to till the earth, will now discover that the earth will bring forth thorns, and that he will have to work by the sweat of his brow. The woman (Eve), the "mother of all living," will now discover that her labor and childbearing will be increased (or possibly that she will bring forth children in greater pain). In the realm of relationships, where the man's desire was for his wife—before the creation of woman, the man could find no companion suitable for him; after the creation of woman, the man will leave his parents and "cling to" his wife—now, instead, the desire of the woman is *for* (not "against") her husband, but instead of a harmonious relationship, the man now rules over his wife, domineering her rather than living in harmony with her.[37] The woman might well resist such domineering, but there is nothing in the text to suggest that the man exercised any kind of authority over the woman before the entrance of sin. Rather, such a domineering of man over woman is a result of the breakdown of the harmony between man and woman that existed before sin.

WOMAN IN THE OLD TESTAMENT

What then of the place of women in the rest of the Old Testament, and what implications might that have today? Two books in particular address these questions helpfully.

Jewish writer Tikva Frymer-Kensky addresses a central question in her book *In the Wake of the Goddesses*: "[W]hat happens in the Bible to central ideas of polytheism, and to the functions and roles once played by goddesses [after Israel embraces a monotheistic religion]?"[38] The tendency of many feminist critics of Judaism and Christianity has been to characterize the God of the Bible as a patriarchal male deity, but Frymer-Kensky points out that the masculinity of the biblical God has to do with "social male-gender characteristics." God is a king, to whom male pronouns are applied, but God is not sexually male: "God is not imagined below the waist. . . . God does not behave in sexual ways." God is Israel's husband, but he does not express physical affection for Israel, and there is no erotic dimension to the biblical God.[39]

The key difference between Israel and the pagan nations is not that Israel's God is male, but that God is One. The books of the Bible echo in many ways the cultural context of the Ancient Near East in which the Bible was written: the language and style of biblical poetry has Canaanite parallels; the wisdom literature is similar to that of Egypt or Mesopotamia; Israelite ideas about justice, society, and religion have Mesopotamian counterparts. "Ultimately, however, Israel developed a religious system essentially different from any of the great ancient Near Eastern systems, a system which proclaimed the importance of only one God and the irrelevance or nonexistence of all other divine powers. This biblical system, known only as monotheism, is the central feature of the Western religions."[40]

In consequence, the One God absorbs many of the attributes of the female goddesses, but, interestingly, not all, and the way in which Israel's God claims some of the attributes of female deities and not others "causes major changes in the way the Bible—compared with the ancient texts—looks at humanity, society, and nature."[41] In ancient religions, nature is governed by interaction, and sometimes conflict, between different divine powers. As the single God of Israel absorbed the functions of the goddesses, this interaction between the gods disappears. The one God of Israel has sole mastery over all of nature. Since God alone is Creator and controls fertility, there is no need for human beings to attempt to engage in religious rituals to help the earth to be fertile; God has created it to be that way. Because God is the sole power who is sovereign over the universe, he can be counted on to deliver the promises he gives to Israel at Sinai.[42]

However, that God is the sole divine power does not mean that God is the only power in the universe. The absence of competing divine powers results in new dignity and importance for human beings. In the absence of interaction between competing gods and/or goddesses, human beings are now raised to a level of partnership and interaction with the one God, and their actions, both good and evil, can influence the kinds of things that God will do.

> God's actions toward nature depend on human activity. . . . In effect, humans determine what God does, not by prayers and manipulation, but by their behavior. In this way, humanity mediates between God and nature. The ultimate responsibility for what happens to the natural world rests on the behavior of human beings towards nature, towards God, and towards each other.[43]

Specifically, human sin can bring judgment.

At the same time, although the biblical God absorbs all of the natural functions associated with male polytheist deities, there is one function that he does not absorb—the cultural arts associated with female goddesses. In the Bible, the cultural arts of learning, song, poetry, the arts, building cities—elsewhere associated with goddesses—are entirely a human activity. In consequence, human beings gain in significance because of the absence of goddesses.[44]

Another area in which the Biblical world differs from polytheism is in its portrayal of women. In pagan religions, stories about gods and goddesses provide the ideal models for how people should be related. In particular, stories about goddesses provide examples for the gendered-structured order of society. Human women are subordinate because female goddesses are subordinate to male gods. To the contrary, "[i]n the Bible, ideas about women and gender are conveyed in stories about human women."[45]

In the Bible, we see a situation in which women are indeed subordinate to men in the household. In contrast, some men in the Bible have power over some other men and women; women do not have such power. This imbalance of power is not uniquely biblical, but reflects the social structures of the ancient Near East, which was a preindustrial agricultural society: "The social system reflected in the Bible did not originate in Israel, nor is it substantially different in the Bible than elsewhere in the ancient Near East."[46] The preindustrial agricultural society of the Near East was divided along gender lines; the public sphere was the sphere of men; women primarily lived and worked in the domestic sphere. The social distinctions between king and subject, master and slave, male and female, were simply assumed. The laws of the Old Testament attempt to correct abuses of power in these relationships, and they minimize the harshness of division by defining proper boundaries. However, the Bible (i.e., what Christians call the Old Testament) never challenges this social structure. The prophets are often critical of social injustice, but they do not question the basic social system.

Despite the recognition of the subordination of women to men in Hebrew society, it is significant that the Hebrew Bible/Old Testament does not portray women as in any way significantly different from men. Women of the Bible are portrayed within the sphere of the home, with family-oriented goals, which is hardly surprising. At the same time, "there is no real 'woman question' in the Bible. The biblical image of women is consistently the same as that of men. . . . This biblical idea that the desires and actions of men and women are similar is tantamount to a radically new concept of gender."[47] There are no goals that women have that are distinctively "female" goals. Women are portrayed as capable of exercising rationality, and they provide wise counsel, as do men. There is no inherent conflict between men and women as such in the Old Testament. Women are portrayed as loving and supporting their husbands. The Old Testament recognizes the subordination of women to men, but does not justify it in any way by pointing to female inferiority or duplicity. Neither are women expected to or required to acquiesce in subordination or submission. The Old Testament assumes the social structures that were common in the ancient Near East, but nowhere justifies them or considers them of divine origin.[48]

Frymer-Kensky finds this "essential sameness" of men and women in the Bible to be a significant contrast to other ancient cultures, both Near Eastern and Hellenistic, and suggests that this was a direct consequence of biblical monotheism:

> This view of the essential sameness of men and women is most appropriate to monotheism. There are no goddesses to represent "womanhood" or a female principle in the cosmos; there is no conscious sense that there even exists a "feminine." Whenever radical monotheism came to biblical Israel, the consideration of one God influenced and underscored the biblical image of women.[49]

At the same time, the "Bible's gender-free concept of humanity contrasted sharply with the Israelite reality," which was hierarchical and structured along gender lines. The gender division of ancient Israel (as in other agricultural societies) originated in basic socioeconomic realities. The household was the basic unit of production, and men's and women's roles were determined by the biological reality that women bore and nursed children and men did not.[50]

A similar observation is a central theme in Carrie Miles's book, *The Redemption of Love*. Miles's approach differs from most standard discussions of men's and women's roles in the Bible insofar as she addresses the specifically socioeconomic factors that lie behind not only traditional preindustrial cultures, but also the differences in those factors that have arisen because of the industrial revolution. In traditional agricultural societies, family institutions were based on the need of farmers for labor, a need primarily provided by families with many children. In traditional rural economies before the industrial revolution, most necessities of life were produced at home, and families were largely self-sustaining. Children were a more reliable source of labor than servants because the loyalty of servants is unpredictable. Without a social system to provide for retirement income, children were also a necessary support in parents' old age. Miles relies on economist Gary S. Becker, who traces the traditional "sexual division of labor" in premodern cultures to the basic biological reality that women give birth to children and produce breast milk, and men do not. The need for many children to produce labor, combined with the necessity that women need to be near infants in order to feed them, meant that the kinds of work that women could do was restricted to work that could be done in a domestic setting: spinning, clothing construction, cooking, nursing the sick and the aged, being involved in household businesses. Men's work was the work that could be done in the absence of children. Accordingly, any work that needed to be done outside the household was necessarily restricted to men—the realms of politics, war, and finance; men were the hunters, farmers, blacksmiths, traders, sailors, soldiers. One could not do these kinds of things with children in tow.[51]

It is this biologically based division of labor that accounts for the historic subordination of women in traditional cultures. Men's greater competitive value in the workplace arose from their ability to marry women who could produce children. Women were largely confined to the domestic sphere because of their need to be close to children, which limited their social effectiveness outside the home. Because of the basic biological limitations created by pregnancy and the dangers of miscarriages, jobs that were heavy, dirty, or dangerous were necessarily done by men.[52]

Not only children, but servants are necessary in such a culture. "Many hands make light work," and many hands were necessary to grow and harvest crops in a preindustrial world without electricity or machinery, in which power was supplied mostly by the muscles of humans or animals. Accordingly, a power structure arose in which a handful exercised power and authority over the majority. Historically, patriarchy is not the rule of men over women, but the rule of some men over everyone else: men, women, and servants or slaves. "In ancient history, there were only a few patriarchs, but a great many slaves."[53]

Miles notes how closely this division of labor corresponds to the description of the fallen world given in Genesis 3:

> What is remarkable about Genesis 3 is how accurately it describes the economic and in turn the social, emotional, and spiritual consequences of living in a world in which the ground is cursed. An economic analysis of the effect of scarcity on male-female behavior predicts exactly the same results as those described in Genesis 3:14-19: masculine drive for power and control, feminine subordination, and a hardening of hearts between them.[54]

However, apart from the basic biological difference of producing children, and the economic consequences that follow from such a division in a preindustrial world, there is no inherent difference in the very nature of masculinity or femininity that would demand such a division of labor:

> From a theoretical point of view, this historic subordination is natural, because it follows from the one absolute difference between men and women: women's ability to bear children. But it is not *innate*, being instead shaped by the material, economic demands of living in an agrarian world of scarce resources.[55]

It should not be surprising, then, that as the industrial revolution changed the basic economic realities by which food was produced and which made large numbers of children necessary for survival, there have been corresponding changes in the culture, including historic gender roles. The first noticeable change took place in the numbers of children families produced. In the United States and in Western Europe, the number of children produced by the average family has dropped from over seven to less than two. Farming, which was once the occupation of most people, is now done by few, and most people now live in towns or cities where they work away from home. Many of the household tasks that used to be the role of women have now been industrialized and taken outside the home: sewing, spinning, food production, and medical care. Electricity and household appliances have meant that the traditional tasks of women are less time-consuming. At the same time, as many of the household tasks done by men have been replaced by automation as well, men have been pushed more and more outside the home to find work. Servants are no longer an economic necessity, but are rather a luxury few can afford. The practice of sending older children away from the home for schooling means that it is no longer economically necessary for women to be confined to the home, and as women give birth to fewer children, less of their time is occupied in caring for infants and breast-feeding. Moreover, in modern industrial cultures, children are no longer an economic asset, but rather an economic cost. They are not additional sources of economic labor, but they do need to be fed and clothed until they can reach adult independence. At the same time, as fewer and fewer economic goods are produced in the home, greater financial resources are needed to purchase the goods that are made outside the home.[56]

All of this provides both greater economic opportunities and greater economic motivation for both men and women to work outside the home. In addition, the kinds of work that are now available outside the home are largely the kinds of work that both sexes can do. With some exceptions, the work that is available outside the home does not necessarily require greater strength or is more dangerous than work done inside the home. It is not surprising, then, that postindustrial women exercise more economic independence and no longer find themselves confined to the domestic sphere: "No longer tied to the household, women are less dependent on men and suddenly not so subordinate anymore. Social change has thus made it apparent that there was nothing innate about women's once limited role in society, church, and family."[57]

At the same time, Miles recognizes that social mobility and more economic freedom for both men and women have been accompanied by some negative consequences. Modern people not only have more social and economic freedom, enjoying the advantages of greater mobility and wealth, freedom from the precariousness of the existence of the traditional preindustrial farmer, and more social and economic opportunities. The new postindustrial situation has also brought with it larger numbers of single people as marriage is no longer an economic necessity, but is perceived as a mixed blessing. The modern world also experiences higher divorce rates as marriage has fewer economic advantages and becomes tied almost exclusively to the emotional commitment of "being in love." Sexual liberation has been an almost inevitable consequence of the disconnection between marriage and the economic need for children, as well as the rise of the availability of artificial birth control. When virginity no longer has an economic value, freedom of sexual expression becomes almost a cultural requirement.[58]

In light of these changes, Miles points out correctly that it is not the "collapse of family values" that has created the new sexual morality with its corresponding chaos. Rather, it is the disappearance of the economic factors that lay behind the social structures of the traditional preindustrial family that have led to the "collapse of family values." People in preindustrial societies were not more "moral" than our contemporaries. The moral institutions of a previous era were only loosely based on "Christian principles."[59]

How should the church respond to the new situation that has resulted from new economic circumstances? Both Frymer-Kensky and Miles point out that the negative reaction of traditionalists is unhelpful. The "conservative" message that marital problems stem from a "breakdown" in traditional gender hierarchy is unhelpful because traditional gender hierarchy was itself based on economic and social structures that no longer exist in the industrialized world, and are more and more ceasing to exist in the "developing" world.[60] It is unlikely that even those who are most nostalgic for a time when men exercised authority over women, and women willingly accepted such subordination, would wish to return to the kind of preindustrial society that produced a necessary subordination of women to men. But regardless of one's wishes, it is not remotely likely that the social and economic changes that have created modern society with its radical changes in the social demands placed on men and women are going to be reversed.

An alternative response is to endorse the contemporary "liberal" alternative that embraces more and more "freedom" and accommodates to the new social changes.

This, however, is simply to capitulate to the new social situation with all of its attending problems, including the breakdown of marriage, high divorce rates, new kinds of inequalities between men and women, sexual promiscuity, and superficial social and sexual relationships. Both Frymer-Kensky and Miles suggest a third alternative that looks back to Genesis: the biblical concept of an equality and companionship of men and women who genuinely need and are partners of one another. Frymer-Kensky writes: "The biblical concept of an essential unity of males and females makes sense in our more egalitarian world."[61] Miles points out that the Bible does not use fear to motivate good behavior, but instead appeals to love. The Bible tells us that God has created men and women for one another. The creation accounts of Genesis portray men and women coming together to become "one flesh": "Ultimately, this positive message of what God intended us to be to each other when he made us both male and female is the only effective weapon we have in the battle to save marriage and the family."[62]

CONCLUSION

In a book concerning the ordination of women, it might seem odd to devote an entire chapter to discussing the exegesis of the first three chapters of Genesis. After all, ordination to Christian ministry is mentioned nowhere in the Old Testament, and certainly not in the first chapters of Genesis. However, as noted at the beginning of this discussion, questions concerning the nature of humanity's place in creation have been crucial for a number of theological issues. Particularly, a crucial question in disagreements about the ordination of women has been whether the historical subordination of women to men is based on some kind of essential ontological difference that is rooted in creation. As argued in a previous chapter, insofar as the question of whether women should be ordained arose at all, it was regularly assumed that women were inherently inferior to men in rationality, emotional stability, and spiritual capacity. Such differences would necessarily be rooted in creation.

In recent decades, all mainstream Christian churches have moved away from this position to affirm the ontological equality of women, and some churches have, accordingly, ceased their historical opposition to women's ordination. In contrast, Evangelical Protestant complementarians have continued to base their opposition on a theology of women's necessary subordination to men. Complementarians no longer speak in terms of inferiority; however, while affirming that men and women are ontologically equal, they nonetheless affirm that different male and female "roles" are rooted in creation. These roles have significant parallels to the historic male and female roles in preindustrial agricultural societies. The primary "role" of men is to work in the public sphere; the primary "role" of women is that of the household. Ordained ministry is a type of work that is done in the public sphere, and, accordingly, there is a kind of logical consistency to the complementarian opposition to the ordination of women.

Complementarians insist that the subordination of women is supported by the clear teaching of Scripture, and is based on a "headship" of men over women that is grounded in creation itself. In other words, to address the question raised at the beginning of this chapter, even if there had been no sin, it would still have been God's intention that women would be subordinate to men, and so should not be ordained. To the contrary, the argument of this chapter is that the complementarian position reads something into the first chapters of Genesis that is not in the texts. Genesis teaches that men and women were equally created in the image of God, were intended by God to be mutual companions to one another, and were equally intended by God to exercise stewardship over creation, and to raise and nurture children. There are certainly "role" differences based in basic biology; only men can be fathers; only women can give birth to and provide breast milk for children. And certainly, these biological differences account for some differences in how men and women will be partners and parents even in a postindustrial age.

At the same time, while Genesis 3 recognizes the subordination of women to men, the text presents this not as part of God's intention for humanity in creation, but as a symptom of the disharmony in human relationships that exists in a sinful world. The rest of the Old Testament certainly acknowledges the subordination of women to men that existed everywhere in preindustrial rural societies. It does not challenge this arrangement any more than it challenges other aspects of ancient Near Eastern culture; neither, however, does the Old Testament sanction the subordination of women to men or claim that it is part of God's intention for humanity rooted in creation. The laws of the Old Testament as well as the writings of the prophets take steps to mitigate some of the worst aspects of this inequality, and the prophets in particular speak out against injustice against women, children, the poor, and those on the bottom rungs of a hierarchical society. Significantly, the writers of the Old Testament portray women in the same ways as they portray men, as having the same motivations, and as engaging in the same kinds of actions as men. Aside from their biological role in giving birth to and being mothers of children, the Old Testament does not understand women to be inherently different from men, and so gives no theological basis for a division of "gender roles."

With the rise of modern technology in the postindustrial world, the social structures that laid the groundwork for the traditional "roles" assumed by men and women in traditional cultures have largely ceased to exist, and more economic mobility has meant, in many ways, more equality between men and women. No longer confined by both biology and economics to the domestic sphere, many women have now taken on "roles" once reserved to men, including the practice of ordained ministry. How should those in the Christian churches respond to this? In light of a more careful reading of the first chapters of Genesis, it is clear that this is entirely in accord with what it means for both men and women to have been created "in the image of God." God created men and women to be partners with one another, to be stewards together in order to "mirror" God's sovereignty over the created world. God intended men and women both to be parents and both to nurture children. Since one of the ways human beings can be stewards of God's creation is by exercising ordained ministry in the Christian church, this would be a crucial way in which both men and women serving together can demonstrate the partnership intended by God.

6

Disciples of Jesus

Previous chapters have identified two basic theological rationales endorsed by two different groups who oppose women's ordination, a Protestant approach and a Catholic approach. Both approaches appeal to Jesus, but do so for contrary reasons. The Catholic position emphasizes that both Jesus and his twelve apostles were all males. Since, it is argued, the ordained clergy represent Christ when they administer the sacraments—the ordained presbyter/priest acts as a representative of or "in the person of" Christ (*in persona Christi*)—a woman cannot be ordained because a female presbyter cannot represent a male Christ. Conversely, the Protestant position has recently stressed an argument drawn from a novel interpretation of the doctrine of the Trinity. Protestant opponents of the ordination of woman have argued for a parallel between the eternal relations of the divine persons of the Trinity and the relations between men and women. It is argued that, although all three persons of the Trinity are ontologically equal, from eternity the Son has a "role" of subordination to the Father, and the Father has a "role" of authority over the Son. From all eternity, the Father commands and the Son obeys. Similarly, it is argued, there is a parallel relation between men and women. Men and women are ontologically equal, yet, just as with the Father and the Son, there is always a subordination of "roles" between men and women. Men always exercise authority over women, and women are always subordinate to men.

The Catholic and Protestant positions thus provide contrary reasons for not ordaining women to church office. For the Catholic position, women cannot be ordained because they do not resemble a male Christ. For the Protestant position, women cannot be ordained because they do resemble Christ; in the same way, it is claimed, that the Son always submits to the Father, women must always be in submission to male authority. At the same time, insofar as these ironically contrary reasons for not ordaining women appeal to Christology for their opposition to women's ordination, they share a common characteristic. Both positions use highly abstract arguments that are somewhat removed from the actual narratives about Jesus in the gospels or the specific focus of the teaching about Jesus in the epistles. The Catholic argument presupposes a specific understanding of the role of ordained clergy in celebrating the Eucharist that was formulated first in the medieval period, and then attaches to that theological understanding a reflection on its significance for women that first appeared in 1976 in *Inter Insigniores,* a document produced by the Sacred Congregation for Doctrine of the Faith with the approval of Pope Paul VI.[1] The Protestant argument makes highly questionable assumptions about the eternal relations of the divine persons of the Trinity, insisting that the "economic" obedience of Jesus to his Father that appears in the gospels (an obedience of the Son in his "mission" as God-become-*human*) is a direct parallel to an eternal subordination of authority and obedience in the "immanent" Trinity itself, and, furthermore, that this eternal obedience of the Son to the Father is directly parallel to a permanent role of obedience of women to men.[2]

Neither of these arguments reflects a careful exegetical reading of what the New Testament actually says about Jesus. There are no New Testament discussions whatsoever about the role of ordained clergy in celebrating the Eucharist, let alone what the theological implications might be for the ordination of women. Nowhere in the New Testament is there a parallel drawn between the highly speculative theory about an eternal obedience of the Son to the Father in the immanent Trinity and a permanent subordination of women to men.[3]

At the same time, both positions are correct that a discussion of ordination and the relation between men and women rightly needs to focus on Jesus, and that what the New Testament teaches about Jesus is finally normative for what the church believes about the relations between men and women, and, ultimately for the question of whether women can be ordained to church office.

What follows will examine the relationship between what the gospels teach about Jesus and that teaching's significance for the relations between men and women, and particularly for the question of subordination. Does the New Testament teach a permanent subordination of women to men, and does it do so based on the example of Jesus? In addition, in contrast to the highly abstract Christological arguments endorsed by both Protestants and Catholics, this chapter will focus on the specific concrete teaching of the New Testament gospels, particularly the implications of their narrative and symbolic logic. The chapter will prioritize responding to Protestant rationales for opposition to the ordination of women; the Catholic sacramental argument that a female presbyter cannot represent a male Christ is addressed in later chapters.

CHRISTOLOGICAL SUBVERSION

Why narrative and symbol? In the last several decades, theologians have focused on the theological implications of the fact that much of the Bible is written in the genre of narrative. In the earlier decades of the twentieth century, almost as much focus was placed on the significance of "symbol" and "metaphor" in the language of Scripture. In *The Moral Vision of the New Testament*, Richard Hays lists four different "modes of appeal to the text in ethical argument": rules ("direct commandments or prohibitions"); principles ("general frameworks of moral considerations"); paradigms ("stories or summary accounts of characters who model exemplary conduct"); and, finally, symbolic world ("creates the perceptual categories through which we interpret reality").[4] Especially since the Reformation, much traditional theology and Christian ethics have focused on the specific "rules" or "principles" found in a "literal reading" of Scripture as well as using historical examples to provide precedents for contemporary behaviors. While the Bible does contain rules and principles that can apply to contemporary situations, not every historical incident mentioned in Scripture should be read as demanding a straightforward application.[5] At the same time, the narrative and symbolic aspects of Scripture have to be read in an entirely different way from "rules" or "principles," or "historical precedents," yet are just as significant for Christian theology and ethics. As Hays points out:

> To be sure, the Gospels—especially Matthew—do contain stories that represent Jesus as a moral teacher, but the moral meaning of the Gospels cannot be limited to these explicitly didactic passages. Stories form our values and moral sensibilities in more direct and complex ways, teaching us how to see the world, what to fear, and what to hope for; stories offer us nuanced models of behavior, both wise and foolish, courageous and cowardly, faithful and faithless.[6]

Accordingly, Hays insists, "the ethical significance of each Gospel must be discerned from the shape of the story as a whole." In order to grasp the ethical and theological significance of the New Testament, "we must ask how Jesus' life and ministry are portrayed in the story and how his call to discipleship reshapes the lives of the other characters."[7]

A crucial hermeneutical implication that follows from the centrality of symbol (or metaphor) and narrative in the language of Scripture is what could be called the principle of "Christological subversion."[8] What is meant by Christological subversion? Christological subversion is a special use of irony or paradox that we find in many New Testament passages. Irony and paradox are literary devices that use words in ways that seem to mean the opposite of their original meaning or seem self-contradictory but actually, when we think about them, have a deeper meaning. Martin Luther was very fond of this kind of paradox: the power of God is hidden in the weakness of the cross of Jesus; the believing Christian is simultaneously just and sinner. The reason for the use of the term "Christological subversion" is that throughout the New Testament the person or actions of Jesus take our normal conceptions of what should be the case and turn them upside down. So Jesus, the crucified peasant from Nazareth, is the King of the Jews. The Jesus who was declared guilty and crucified by the religious and political authorities of his time turns out to be the divine judge who pardons rather than condemns the guilty. Through his resurrection, the death of Jesus brings life.

The principle of Christological subversion is found in the way that the narrative structures of the four gospels each develop a Christology that is subversive of "common sense" and turns our world upside down.[9]

In Mark's Gospel, Jesus is identified at both the beginning and the end as the Son of God (1:1, 15:39). Although the reader knows this, the participants in the narrative do not, and, throughout the gospel, even Jesus' close disciples do not understand correctly who he is or the nature of his identity as Son of God or Messiah. In addition, Mark subverts the "common sense" understanding of what it would mean to be the Son of God or the Messiah. For Mark, to be the Son of God means to be the crucified Messiah (8:31), and messiahship is redefined in terms of Isaiah's image of the Suffering Servant (Isa. 53). To be a disciple of Jesus means to be called to suffering, to follow a crucified Messiah.

For Matthew, Jesus fulfills Moses' role as a deliverer and lawgiver. He is the authoritative teacher of the kingdom of God (as revealed especially in the Sermon on the Mount). At the same time, although Jesus' teaching is in continuity with the Torah, he radicalizes its demands. He calls for a radical righteousness of the "heart" that goes beyond the literal teaching of the Torah. Jesus' disciples are to love even their enemies, not resisting evil. They are forbidden not only to commit adultery, but even to lust. At the same time, Jesus' rigorism ("be perfect as your heavenly Father is perfect"; Matt. 5:48) is accompanied by an equally extreme demand for mercy to those who fail to live it out ("forgive seventy times seven"; Matt. 18:22).

In Luke, Jesus is portrayed as the Spirit-empowered servant of God who creates a restored Israel in which justice and compassion for the poor prevail. Luke's gospel upsets conventions by standing in tension with the established social order. In particular, in Luke we find an "eschatological reversal" that overturns the fortunes of the powerful in favor of the poor and the oppressed. Luke portrays women as having key roles in salvation history. Jesus' parables in Luke subvert normal standards of righteousness as the God who is the Father of Jesus seeks out and shows his favor to "lost sinners" rather than those who are normally considered "righteous" (the Good Samaritan, the tax collector and the pharisee, the Prodigal Son, the lost sheep, the lost coin; Luke 10:25-37; 18:9-14; 15:1-32).

Finally, the principle of Christological subversion can be found in the Gospel of John's use of the metaphor of "glory." In the Old Testament, glory is ascribed to God because of his mighty deeds (Exod. 14:4). God's power and wisdom are reflected in the created world (Ps. 19:1), the giving of the ten commandments (Exod. 24:16), and God's presence in the tabernacle (Exod. 40:34-35). In the Old Testament, glory is used as a way of distinguishing the divine majesty and power from everything else in creation: "I am the LORD; that is my name; my glory I give to no other" (Isa. 42:8).

However, in John's Gospel, as a prism focuses and refracts light, God's glory is refracted and focused in Jesus, the Jew from Nazareth, who is also the "Word become flesh." As the Old Testament indicates that God's glory dwelt in the temple, so John deliberately uses the same imagery to say that God's glory dwells in Jesus (1:14). As the Old Testament spoke of God's glory being shown in his mighty deeds, so Jesus' miracles also show the divine glory (John 2:11). John's most shocking use of Christological subversion occurs in Jesus' High Priestly Prayer: "Father, the hour has come; glorify your Son that the Son may glorify you" (17:1). The "hour" to which Jesus refers is the hour of his crucifixion. In John's Gospel, glory is found not in fame, greatness, recognition, or what the world thinks of as success, but in the Word who became flesh, who came to his own but was not recognized (1:11), who sought his Father's glory, not his own, and who finally was crucified. Glory is found in the self-abasement and crucifixion of the incarnate Word of God.

The basic narrative structure of the four Gospels demonstrates the way in which the principle of Christological subversion affects the relation between metaphor and narrative in Scripture. A careful reading makes clear that the metaphors of Scripture cannot be read in the gospel narratives with a kind of flat-footed literalness. Rather, through the principle of Christological subversion, the narrative accounts of Jesus' incarnation, life, death, and resurrection provide a context that gives meaning to the symbols and metaphors and in the light of which the meaning of the symbols and metaphors is redefined. The writers of the gospel narratives use the principle of Christological subversion to undermine straightforward and "literal" usages of ordinary language. Consequently, to allow a normative value to the metaphors and symbols of Scripture does not provide license to decide that we know ahead of time what those metaphors mean. Rather, it is by entering into the narrative logic of the canonical Scriptures that we discover the meaning of the metaphors and symbols, a narrative logic that subverts simplistic literalism. Theologically, the narratives themselves must be read in light of the incarnation, crucifixion, and resurrection of Jesus, but at the same time, it is the narratives that provide the proper interpretation to the meaning of such theological terms as incarnation, redemption, and Christology.

The Reformed theologian Karl Barth illustrates the principle of Christological subversion in his discussion of the way in which Jesus related to and interacted with the social structures of his own time: the religious structures, particularly the Jewish temple; the political structures, namely, the rule of the Roman empire; economic structures, and, finally, the family. At one level, Barth suggests that Jesus' stance can be described as a "passive conservatism": "Rather curiously, Jesus accepts and allows many things which we imagine He ought to have attacked and set aside both in principle and practice and which the community in which the Gospels arose had to a very large extent overgrown."[10] Barth notes that "Jesus was not in any sense a reformer championing new orders against the old ones, contesting the latter in order to replace them by the former."[11] Jesus did not align himself and his disciples with any religious or political parties. Jesus accepted that the temple was the house of God, and stated that the Jewish leaders "sat in Moses' seat." He insisted he had not come to destroy the law and the prophets. Jesus did not challenge the rule of the Roman empire, and he did not align himself with subversive groups such as the Zealots who wished to overthrow it. Jesus accepted that Pilate had authority over him, and forbade Peter to resist his arrest. Jesus did not challenge the economic system of the time, including the institution of slavery. Jesus' parables accept the existence of masters and servants, and of employees dependent on the good will of employers. He stated that the poor will always be with us. He accepted the existence of judges and prisons, that some will rule over others. He acknowledged the existence of the family.[12]

At the same time, however, Jesus' stance toward these social orders is marked by what Barth calls the "freedom of the kingdom of God." Although Jesus did not oppose any of these systems in principle,

> He simply revealed the limit and frontier of these things—the freedom of the kingdom of God. He simply existed in this freedom and summoned to it. He simply made use of this freedom to cut right across all these systems both in His own case and in that of His disciples, interpreting and accepting them in His own way and in His own sense, in the light shed upon them all from that frontier.[13]

This sovereign freedom of Jesus in relation to the social structures of his time meant that he inevitably clashed with these orders in a manner that displayed their "provisional" and "relative" character.

For example, although Jesus accepted that the temple was the "house of God," and paid the temple tax, he also made it clear that he was not subject to the authority of the tax (Matt. 17:24-27). Jesus insisted that something "greater than the temple" was present in his person (Matt. 12:6), and that the temple would be destroyed (Mark 13:2). At his trial, Jesus was accused of having claimed that he would destroy the temple and replace it with one not made with human hands. The event that precipitated his arrest was his driving of money changers from the temple, insisting that they had turned the house of God into a den of thieves. Jesus' attitude to the Sabbath, one of the most sacred Jewish institutions, is illustrated in his healings on the Sabbath as well as his claim that "the Son of man is Lord of the Sabbath" (Mark 2:28).

In the realm of political order, the center of Jesus' message was a call to repentance because the Kingdom of God was at hand. At the same time, God's kingdom does not appear through political revolution. Jesus called his disciples not to resist evil, to go the second mile, to give their cloak to those who asked, to forgive their enemies. Nonetheless, Jesus did not hesitate to refer to King Herod as "that fox" (Luke 13:32), and responded to the Pharisees' question of whether it was permissible to pay taxes with the statement: "Render to Caesar the things that are Caesar's, and to God the things that are God's" (Mark 12:13-17). In his Palm Sunday entrance into Jerusalem, Jesus allowed the crowds to proclaim him as the "Son of David" (Matt. 21:9), and the inscription over his cross—"Jesus of Nazareth, King of the Jews" (Mark 15:26; John 19:19)—makes clear that Jesus was crucified as a political pretender.

While not explicitly challenging the economic order, Jesus radically called it into question because neither he nor his disciples took any part in the acquiring or holding of possessions. In the Sermon on the Mount, Jesus told his disciples, "Lay not up for yourself treasures upon earth . . . take no thought for tomorrow" (Matt. 6:25). To the rich man who asked what he needed to inherit eternal life, Jesus replied, "You lack one thing: go, sell all that you have and give to the poor, and you will have treasure in heaven; and come, follow me" (Mark 10:21). When his disciples responded with astonishment at this demand, Jesus responded: "It is easier for a camel to go through the eye of a needle than for a rich person to enter the kingdom of God" (Mark 10:25).

Finally, Jesus even challenged the ultimacy of the order of the family. Jesus himself remained unmarried, something foreign to Jewish culture. In Mark 3:31-35, he asked, "Who are my mother and my brothers?" and answered, "whoever does the will of God, he is my brother and sister and mother." To the man who asked permission to bury his father before following Jesus, Jesus replied: "Let the dead bury their dead" (Luke 9:59-60). In perhaps one of his most shocking statements, Jesus said: "For I have come to set a man against his father, and a daughter against her mother, and a daughter-in-law against her mother-in-law. And a person's enemies will be those of his own household. Whoever loves father or mother more than me is not worthy of me, and whoever loves son or daughter more than me is not worthy of me" (Matt. 10:34-37).

Barth's final assessment is that Jesus called into question every human order. All human institutions are to the kingdom of God which Jesus proclaimed as an old cloth to which one cannot merely apply a new patch or an old bottle into which one cannot put new wine: "For Jesus, and as seen in the light of Jesus, there can be no doubt that all human orders are this old garment or old bottles, which are in the last resort quite incompatible with the new cloth and the new wine of the kingdom of God."[14]

The notion of Christological subversion makes clear the radical nature of Jesus' call to discipleship. On the one hand, Jesus simply accepted and did not challenge the existing social orders of religion, politics, economics, and family. On the other, the freedom of God's kingdom so transcends all of these orders as radically to call them into question, and this radical challenge to existing order is what eventually led to Jesus' crucifixion as a religious and political subversive.

THE SOCIAL WORLD OF THE NEW TESTAMENT

Before addressing the question of how Jesus' practice of Christological subversion might be relevant in a contemporary setting, it would be helpful first to look at the social situation in the world in which Jesus lived. An ahistorical approach to biblical hermeneutics assumes that honoring biblical authority is a straightforward matter of exegesis, determining the literal meaning of the biblical texts, and then applying that meaning in a "one-to-one correspondence" to a contemporary setting. However, contemporary Western culture is sufficiently different from first-century culture that a simple "one-to-one correspondence" is problematic. First-century Near Eastern and Mediterranean culture differed from contemporary Western individualist, postindustrial democratic cultures in a number of ways.

The first-century world was an "honor culture," in which honor and shame (or dishonor) were fundamental values.[15] This honor culture had some of the following characteristics:

In contrast to contemporary individualism, first-century culture was "group-oriented." "The focus of ancient people on honor and dishonor or shame means that they were particularly oriented toward the approval and disapproval of others." People were motivated to pursue the qualities and engage in the behaviors that were valued by the particular group of which they were members, and to avoid qualities or behaviors of which that group disapproved.[16]

Families were particularly important as the family was perhaps the central group to which one belonged. Any behavior that tended to bring shame or dishonor on the family would be met by pressure to conform, and possible ostracism for failure to do so.[17]

First-century culture was also very hierarchical. The husband/master exercised almost absolute authority over subordinate members of the family: wives, children, slaves. The submission of wives to husbands was a standard feature of first-century culture, both pagan and Jewish. Silence was considered an important virtue for women. Roman law gave husbands "binding authority" over wives and daughters. The Greek writer Plutarch stated that it is proper for a man to rule his wife. The Jewish writer Philo suggested that a wife's duty to her husband is like that of a slave.[18] In Judaism, laws of inheritance, betrothal, and divorce were to the advantage of the male. There was general agreement among both pagans and Jews that the domestic sphere was the proper place for women, rather than public places. The primary duties of Jewish women were domestic: "grinding flour, baking bread, washing clothes, breast-feeding the children for eighteen to twenty-four months, making the beds, working with wool, preparing her husband's cup, and washing his face, hands, and feet."[19] Women were also skilled in crafts that could be sold in shops that were attached to the house or could be sold in the market.

While the culture of the Old Testament was patriarchal, with female subordination to males, in the New Testament period this seems to have become exaggerated, perhaps under the influence of Hellenistic culture. Rabbinic Judaism advocated a strict separation of the sexes, and there was a strict separation of men and women in synagogue worship, a separation that did not seem to have existed in the Old Testament period. Jewish literature of the time frequently contained negative evaluations of women. Educational opportunities for women were also generally restricted. Plutarch stated that education was only for "free men." Jewish writers are not consistent about the extent to which women should be educated. While some rabbis forbade teaching Torah to women, others taught that both boys and girls should be given a knowledge of Scripture. The role of women in Jewish temple worship was restricted because of the regular problem of ceremonial uncleanness (Lev. 15:19-33). Josephus stated that the testimony of women was not to be accepted in court.[20] Of course, there were exceptions to the general exclusion of women from authority, financial independence, or education in first-century culture. There were some highly educated upper-class women. Women did attend synagogue, and there were some women who learned the law. At the same time, it is important to recognize that these women are significant precisely because they were exceptions.[21]

First-century culture was also a slave culture. One in five Romans was a slave, and the percentage was higher elsewhere. A master had complete control over a slave's family life, and slaves could not contract legal marriages.[22]

Finally, the relation between children and parents differed in significant ways from contemporary individualist culture. In the modern world, it is presumed that at some point after adulthood, grown children will achieve independence of their parents and are no longer under their authority. This was not the case in the ancient world, in which adult children were expected to remain under the authority of their parents well into adulthood.[23]

Focus on honor and shame had numerous consequences. Not only the family, but larger social groupings were also of major significance, reflected in the New Testament tensions between Jews and Gentiles. Public "shaming" was a chief means of social control. Examples include the "challenge-riposte," in which one gains honor at another's expense through posing a challenge that cannot be answered: "The gospels are full of these exchanges, mainly posed by Pharisees, Sadducees or other religious officials at Jesus, whom they regarded as an upstart threatening to steal their place in the esteem of the people."[24] Public challenges to honor were expected to be responded to in kind; failure to preserve one's honor was shameful. The public crucifixion of Jesus was a particularly dishonorable example of public shaming; crucifixion was meant to publicly humiliate criminals, and to remind observers of the shameful end of those who strayed from the culture's values.[25]

JESUS AND THE HONOR CULTURE

How then might the principle of Christological subversion address the question of the relation between men and women, and more specifically the question of whether there is an inherent subordination of women to men rooted in creation itself? What follows will examine first how Jesus subverted the traditional honor culture, and, then how Jesus' actions undermined the honor culture's treatment of women.

Family

Jesus did not simply repudiate the traditional family structure, nor, given what we have already seen about the principle of Christological subversion, would we expect him to. Rather, as Ben Witherington III points out, "Jesus not only accepted but also strengthened the physical family's bond in some respects."[26] For instance, Jesus affirmed the Old Testament teaching about honoring one's parents (Mark 10:19). Jesus challenged a tradition that allowed the setting aside of property that should have gone to one's parents by vowing to give it to God instead (Mark 7:9-13).

At the same time, Jesus subverted the way in which the family had been used as a means to uphold the traditional honor system. Jesus insisted that following him could disrupt traditional family ties and that loyalty to him superseded loyalty to family (Matt. 10:21, 34-37). By designating God as "Father," Jesus provided an alternative "fictive kinship" system.[27] Jesus identified his family not with his mother and brothers, but with "whoever does the will of my Father in heaven" (Matt. 12:46-50). In designating God as Father, Jesus also undermined traditional patriarchal understandings of what it means to be a father. Fatherhood is not to be defined by the expected actions of typical fathers, but by the character of the God whom Jesus called Father. Jesus' parable of the "prodigal son" provides the challenging paradigm. The younger son in the parable acts in a way that is entirely disrespectful and unacceptable in first-century culture: he is breaking all ties with his family, and, in effect, wishing his father were dead.[28] After receiving his inheritance, the son behaves in ways scandalous in Jewish culture: moving to a Gentile country ("a far land"), squandering his money on "debauchery," and, finally, working for a Gentile herding unclean swine. When the son repents and returns to his father, which would have had the effect of disgracing the family in front of the entire village, the father acts in a manner entirely contrary to the traditional honor code. The father is waiting for the son to return, runs to greet him, and publicly receives him back into the home as his son.[29] It is the older brother who abides by the traditional honor code, refusing to recognize the brother as kindred. Yet the father persists, addressing both the older brother as "son," and celebrating that the younger son, who in effect had "wished him dead," has himself returned from death to life (Luke 15:32). As N. T. Wright notes, "This tale subverts the telling of the story which one might expect from mainstream first-century Jews."[30]

The State

Jesus' proclamation of the kingdom of God subverted not only Roman rule and the delegated authority of Jewish leaders under the Romans, but also Jewish political movements such as the Zealots who wished to overthrow such rule. Two examples particularly illustrate this.

In Jesus' triumphal entry into Jerusalem riding on a donkey, during which he was greeted as the Davidic king, Jesus engaged in a symbolic action which, with its allusions to Zechariah 9:9-10, was "clearly messianic."[31] At the same time, the symbolic referent to Zechariah's prophecy of a king who rides on a donkey rather than a warhorse points to a king who reigns from a cross rather than a throne.[32]

Jesus' trial before Pontius Pilate focuses on this theme of the paradoxical nature of Jesus' kingship. In all four gospels, Pilate asks Jesus some variation of the question, "Are you the king of the Jews?" to which Jesus replies ambiguously: "You have said so." John's Gospel plays up the paradoxical nature of the encounter. To Pilate's statement that Jesus' own leaders have delivered him for trial, Jesus replies, "My kingdom is not of this world" (John 18:35-36). To Pilate's threatening question, "Do you not know that I have authority to release you and authority to crucify you?" Jesus replies, "You would have no authority over me at all unless it had been given you from above" (19:11). David Bentley Hart writes of how "shatteringly subversive" Christianity was of the certitudes of the ancient world, and points to this scene as a particular example. Because the gospel is written in light of the resurrection, the meaning of the scene is reversed: "If God's truth is in fact to be found where Christ stands, the mockery visited on him rebounds instead upon the emperor, all of whose regal finery, when set beside the majesty of the servile shape in which God reveals himself, shows itself to be just so many rags and briars."[33]

The Honor Challenge

Jesus' command to forgive subverted the dynamics of the "honor challenge." Rather than respond to the challenge to one's honor with an equal response of insult or perhaps violence, Jesus commanded his followers to respond to such challenges in a manner that reflected the alternative values of those whose God is the Father of Jesus by not resisting evil, turning the other cheek, and going the extra mile (Matt. 5:38-41). Potential accusers must be reconciled; those who make unreasonable demands must be met with generosity; enemies must be loved and prayed for.[34]

Crossing Boundaries

There are several areas in which Jesus' actions "crossed boundaries," subverting traditional Jewish distinctions between "clean and unclean," and between those "insiders" and "outsiders" within the Jewish version of the honor system. First, although Jesus' mission was primarily directed to fellow Jews (Matt. 10:5-7; 15:24), on more than one occasion Jesus ministered to Gentiles or non-Jews. In the case of both the curing of the Gentile centurion's servant (Matt. 8:5-13; Luke 7:1-10; John 4:46-54) and a Samaritan leper (Luke 17:11-19), Jesus commended the faith of non-Jews in contrast to the lack of response to his mission among his own people (Matt 8:10; Luke 7:9; Luke 17:18-19).

In the story of the parable of the Good Samaritan, a lawyer challenged Jesus' honor by asking him a question that was intended as a "test" or "temptation" (Luke 10:25-38). The lawyer's question about what one must do to inherit eternal life was, in essence, an attempt to get Jesus to identify the proper members of God's covenant people. Jesus responded to this "honor challenge" with his own question that, in effect, challenged the lawyer's honor: "What is written in the law?" That is, as a lawyer who was an expert in the Jewish law, Jesus' questioner already should have known the answer to this question. The honor challenge continues as the lawyer asks Jesus, "Who is my neighbor?" Maintaining boundaries between men, women, and Gentiles was essential to maintaining order, and identifying the neighbor was crucial to establishing the boundaries. Jesus' parable of the Good Samaritan shatters the boundaries. The man who has been beaten needs a neighbor, someone who will help him, and anyone will do. That a despised Samaritan is the one who turns out to be the neighbor rather than a priest, a Levite, or even an ordinary Jew challenges the traditional hostility between Jews and Samaritans and subverts the honor culture.[35]

Again, many of those whom Jesus healed belonged to categories of those who were excluded from full membership in the covenant people of Israel: lepers, the blind and deaf, and demoniacs. Jesus shared meals with notorious sinners, specifically tax collectors and prostitutes. In all of these ways, Jesus crossed "acceptable boundaries" and subverted the contemporary honor system. The effect of these cures was a sign that these who had been excluded from Israel were now included in the people of God. This association with and inclusion of outsiders was not only "deeply symbolic," but also controversial and subversive.[36]

Return to Creation

Finally, Jesus' assurance to his disciples that they do not need to worry about their economic needs, what they will eat and what they will wear, because they can trust their heavenly Father to provide for their needs (Matt. 6:25-34; 7:7-11; Luke 12:4-7) indicated that he saw in the dawning of the kingdom of God a return to the original creation order that reflected a pre-fallen world without care or anxiety. Jesus' call to trust in God as Father challenged the curse of a fallen world in which working by the sweat of one's brow had resulted from the fall into sin (Gen. 3:18-19).[37]

JESUS AND WOMEN

How is the principle of Christological subversion illustrated in Jesus' relationships with women? Parallel examples can be found to each of the ways in which Jesus, in his relations with women, subverted the honor culture.

Crossing Boundaries

Jesus' relationships with women challenged the honor system by "crossing acceptable boundaries." The story about Jesus and the Samaritan woman at Jacob's well (John 4) shows him not only associating with non-Jews, but also associating with a woman in a way that was contrary to accepted practice. In the story, Jesus and his disciples first went through Samaria on their way to Galilee. This in itself was unusual, given that Samaritans and Jews were historical enemies; in fact, Jews would normally have taken the "long way round" in order to avoid passing through Samaria. Second, Jesus broke a social taboo by talking to a woman in a place with no witnesses. Jewish men did not initiate conversations with unknown women. Rabbis did not converse with women even in public places. In addition, the woman Jesus talked to turns out to be a "sinful woman"; that she came to a well alone in the heat of midday indicates either that she was a social outcast or that she wanted to make contact with travelers who might be passing through. Further conversation reveals that she has been married five times, and is currently living with a man who is not her husband. There are other surprising turns in the story. By asking the woman for water, Jesus placed himself in a position of need, and humbled himself to be served. This gave dignity to the woman by allowing her to use her resources to help a stranger. In the subsequent conversation, Jesus engaged the woman's concerns in a manner that shows that he took her seriously. Jesus did not condemn the woman for her presumed immorality. In consequence, this Samaritan woman became the first missionary or witness to Jesus in John's Gospel, despite the traditional position that the witness of women is not reliable.[38]

Other gospel narratives include some of the same themes as this story of the Samaritan woman. The story of Jesus and the Syrophoenician woman whose daughter he healed once again depicts Jesus ministering to a woman who is not only a non-Jew, but a member of a group that is an historical enemy of the Jewish people, a "Canaanite," a descendent of the original non-Hebrew inhabitants of Palestine (Mark 7: 24-30; Matt. 15:21-28). The story is one of the "problem passages" in the gospel insofar as Jesus at first refuses the request of the woman because she is not a Jew, and only heals her daughter after she endures a humiliating exchange. Some recent interpreters have read the story as a case in which the woman changed Jesus' mind, and his views expanded as the woman helped him overcome prejudices against Gentiles. This interpretation seems unlikely in light of other incidents (such as the healing of the centurion's servant and the story of the Samaritan woman already mentioned). A more plausible interpretation is that Jesus had two audiences in mind, both the woman whose faith was tested and confirmed by the healing of her daughter, and also the disciples who begged Jesus to send her away. By healing the woman's child and pronouncing the blessing, "O woman, great is your faith!" Jesus not only crossed a gender and cultural barrier, but also exposed and challenged the prejudices of his disciples, who did not believe that his ministry should extend to Canaanites.[39]

Other incidents in which Jesus challenged current assumptions about "sinful women" include the story in which a "sinful" woman (presumably a prostitute) anointed Jesus' feet with perfume in the home of the pharisee Simon (Luke 7:36-50), as well as the incident of the woman who was caught in adultery (John 7:53–8:11). In both cases, Jesus challenged current expectations by offering forgiveness rather than condemnation.

A final pair of incidents deserving mention is the combined pair of stories in which Jesus both raised the daughter of Jairus from the dead, and also cured a woman suffering from a long-term hemorrhage who anonymously touched him in a crowd (Mark 5:25-34; Matt. 9:20-23; Luke 8:42-48). Under Jewish law, Jesus should have been made ceremonially unclean both by his touching a corpse and by being touched by a menstruating woman. Instead, by raising the dead girl to life and by healing the anonymous woman, rather than being contaminated by ceremonial uncleanness, Jesus extended the realm of holiness by raising the dead to life and by making the ceremonially unclean to be clean through an act of healing. Although it is not spelled out explicitly, Jesus' actions have implications for issues of women's discipleship. In Jewish culture, rules about ritual uncleanness effectively cut women off from taking an active part in public religious practice. In his act of healing, Jesus made clear that women are not defiled or defiling and thus made it possible for women to participate fully as his disciples.[40]

Returning to Creation

In Jesus' challenge of contemporary Jewish practice concerning divorce, there is a parallel to what we have already seen concerning Jesus' teachings about wealth and poverty and the "return to creation." In another of the many examples of the "honor challenge" that occur in the gospels, a group of Pharisees challenged Jesus over whether it was lawful for a man to divorce his wife, appealing to biblical precedent (Matt. 19:3-9; Mark 10:2-12; cf. Deut. 24:1-4). Significantly, Jesus responded (as with the issue of wealth and poverty) by appealing to the original creation account. Mosaic law allowed divorce as a concession to human sinfulness as a consequence of the fall. However, Jesus claimed (appealing to the creation accounts of Gen. 1:27, 2:24), that God's original intent in creation was that, in marriage, the man and woman created in God's image should be joined together as husband and wife so that the two should become "one flesh." Jesus concluded that anyone who introduces a third party into this relationship (through adultery) breaks the unity not only of the two parties, but also of God who has brought about the unity. By appealing to the original intention of creation, Jesus again reversed the curse brought about as a consequence of sin, but also spoke in a way that is liberating especially to women. Jesus assumed that it is men who are initiating the divorce, and that, by divorcing his wife, a man in essence forces her to commit adultery by forcing her into remarriage. The net effect is that Jesus rejected the traditional "double standard" concerning male and female sexuality and challenged stereotypes about women as temptresses, but he also gave women greater security in marriage.[41] Note also that in his appeal to creation, Jesus focused on the unity and likeness between men and women (as does the original Genesis account).[42] He says nothing about an inherent hierarchy or ontological ordering by which men are created to lead or exercise authority over women.

Women as Disciples of Jesus

It is significant that Jesus had women disciples. Kenneth Bailey notes four significant texts.[43]

First, in Acts 9:36, Tabitha (Dorcas) is called a "disciple" (μαθήτρια, *mathētria*, Gk. feminine).

Second, in Matthew's Gospel, when Jesus' family attempted to approach him through a crowd, he addressed the crowd: "'Who is my mother, and who are my brothers?' And stretching out his hand toward his disciples, he said, 'Here are my mother and my brothers. For whoever does the will of my Father in heaven is my brother and sister and mother'" (Matt. 12:48-50). As Bailey points out, the text makes clear that Jesus is addressing his "disciples," whom he identifies as brothers and sisters—that is, both men and women.

Third, in Luke 8:1-3, we read: "Soon afterward he went on through cities and villages, proclaiming the good news of the kingdom of God. And the twelve were with him, and also some women who had been healed of evil spirits and infirmities: Mary called Magdalene ... and Joanna ... and Susanna, and many others, who provided from them out of their means." The text indicates that Jesus was traveling with a group of men and *women* who were his disciples. This would imply that they were spending nights in strange villages. Bailey notes that this is a practice that would not be allowed even in contemporary Middle Eastern culture, where women are allowed to travel with men, but must spend nights with their relatives.

Mary and Martha

Fourth, the principle of "Christological subversion" is illustrated throughout the story concerning Mary and Martha (Luke 10:38-42). The immediate context for the story is the same as that of the Good Samaritan, which just precedes it in Luke's gospel. Both Mary and the Good Samaritan model what it means to be a disciple of Jesus in ways that challenge first-century Jewish culture: a Samaritan was not supposed to be a model of what it means to be a neighbor; a woman was not supposed to sit at the feet of men as a disciple.[44] When Mary sits at the feet of Jesus, she is, in effect, taking on the role of a disciple of Jesus (Luke 8:35; Acts 22:3). She is not simply sitting at Jesus' feet during a meal. Commentators consistently make the case that "to sit at the feet of" is a technical formula meaning "to be a disciple of."[45] This was highly unusual in first-century Jewish culture. As Ben Witherington III points out, women could attend synagogue, learn, and even be educated if their husbands were rabbis, but "for a rabbi to come into a woman's house and teach her specifically is unheard of."[46] Mary's sister Martha asked Jesus to rebuke her because she was, in effect, acting like a male, neglecting her duty to her sister to assist in the preparation of the meal, and bringing shame to her house by crossing a clear social boundary.[47] Jesus' response to Martha is not a rejection of her desire to serve, but a reversal of the notion of service. It is Jesus who has come to serve. He is the host, and Mary and Martha are his guests. The "one thing" that is important is not performing the typical domestic tasks that would have been expected of women in first-century culture, but listening to and becoming a disciple of Jesus.[48]

This key point of the story is so important—that Jesus accepted women as disciples in a manner contrary to the society expectations of the time—that it is necessary to respond to some objections raised by "complementarian" Wayne Grudem, who seems intent on deliberately de-radicalizing the implications of the story. Against the reading of scholars such as those noted above, Grudem insists to the contrary that there is nothing unusual going on in the story. Grudem claims that "everybody in Jewish society learned from the rabbis, so it is not clear that this citation proves anything special about Mary." He also claims that "people commonly sat at the feet of those who were teaching," so assertions about Mary's discipleship claim more than the text supports. Grudem also writes that Jesus was simply commending Mary for listening to him, not making a case for women's theological education.[49]

Grudem's counterargument flies in the face of the significance of "sitting at the feet of" as a technical formula, and also that rabbis did not go to the homes of women who "sat at their feet." While women did indeed learn in the synagogue, it would have been unheard of for a rabbi to enter into the home of a woman to whom he was not married and teach her as a disciple—as Witherington points out in the quote above. Moreover, Grudem's statement that Jesus did not make a case for women's theological training rather misses the point of the kinds of symbolic actions in which Jesus regularly engaged. Jesus did not set out to overthrow Roman rule, but when he rode a donkey into Jerusalem that was a symbolic action—a fulfillment of a prophecy in Zechariah—which was clearly understood as a threat to the political order and a Messianic claim. When Jesus cleansed the temple, he did not overturn temple corruption, but he did engage in a symbolic action that passed judgment on temple corruption. When Jesus called twelve apostles, that was a symbolic action; the number twelve indicated that the apostles were representatives of a new Israel, since the nation of Israel were the descendants of the twelve sons of Jacob. Similarly, when Jesus taught a woman who "sat at his feet," this was a symbolic action. Mary is extolled as a model disciple of the rabbi Jesus, a symbolic action that was subversive of the understandings of the permissible roles for women at that time.

Women as Witnesses

Given the low value that was attached to the testimony of women in the first-century Mediterranean world, another example of the principle of Christological subversion is the emphasis that the gospels place on the testimony of women. We have already seen the example of the testimony of the Samaritan woman in John's Gospel. She provides a parallel to another unlikely witness: the demoniac from whom Jesus cast out a "legion" of demons (Mark 5:1-20). It is in the events surrounding Jesus' crucifixion and resurrection that the gospels bring the testimony of women to the fore. As Ben Witherington III states, "Perhaps the most surprising reversal [of male-female expectations] was that Jesus' women friends and traveling companions, not the Twelve or even the Three [Peter, James, and John], became the primary witnesses to the crucial final events in Jesus' earthly career—the events surrounding His death."[50]

With the exception of the "beloved disciple" (John 19:26-27), all of Jesus' male disciples are portrayed in a negative manner during the events of his crucifixion. Judas, one of the twelve, betrays him. Peter denies him three times. The rest of the twelve flee. It is women who stay with Jesus at the cross. The only males who are portrayed positively in the crucifixion scene are the Gentile centurion, who recognizes Jesus as the Son of God, and one of the thieves crucified with him. After his crucifixion, it is women who are the first to visit his tomb and women who provide the first and primary witnesses to Jesus' resurrection. While the women believe immediately, the male apostles are portrayed as both doubting the testimony of the women as to his resurrection, and hiding out of fear during the time of his first post-resurrection appearance to them. In the gospels, it is women who are portrayed as Jesus' most faithful disciples during the time of his passion, and women who are the first witnesses concerning the truth of his resurrection from the dead. It is women whom the gospels portray as the church's first evangelists.

Servanthood and Submission

Finally, Christological subversion is evident in what Jesus teaches about servanthood and submission. Alan Padgett helpfully distinguishes between two different understandings of "submission" in the New Testament. The Greek words translated "submit" or "submission" in the New Testament are usually ὑποταγη (hypotagē) or ὑποτάσσω (hypotassō). Generally, the words simply mean the ordering of one thing under another. Sometimes the words mean what "submission" normally means in English, the involuntary obedience to an external authority. In this sense, the terms can be used in a military or political setting. While such obedience may be voluntary and willing, the key thing to remember is that it requires obedience to an external authority. Padgett refers to this as "Type I submission." Advocates of complementarianism write as if this is how the term is always used in Scripture.[51]

However, when used with the middle voice (which has to do with actions that one does to oneself), the term can take on the sense of a voluntary submission to another person out of love, humility, or compassion. Padgett calls this "Type II submission," a form of mutual submission, the taking up of a voluntary role of a servant or slave in relation to another.[52] This notion will be discussed in more depth when examining the apostle Paul's discussion of the relation between men and women in Ephesians 5, but, for now, it should be noted that this notion finds its roots in the teaching of Jesus and the way in which "Type II submission" subverts and undermines the logic of "Type I submission."

The prime example of someone taking up such a role of servanthood toward others is Jesus, who taught a model of leadership as servanthood to others.[53] There are three key passages in the gospels where Jesus makes clear his own understanding of what it means to exercise leadership among his disciples.

In Mark 9:35, Jesus responds to the question that his disciples had been asking among themselves about which one of them was the greatest by telling them, "If anyone would be first of all, he must be last of all and servant of all." In the parallel version in Matthew's Gospel, Jesus responds to the question, "Who is the greatest in the kingdom of heaven?" by giving the example of a child: "Whoever humbles himself like this child, he is the greatest in the kingdom of heaven" (Matt. 18:4). Jesus thus reverses normal understandings of leadership and authority. Those who wish to be great in God's kingdom must become humble, like children.

In Mark 10:35-45, Jesus responds to the request of James and John that they would be honored with prestigious positions in his kingdom by pointing them to suffering and, eventually, to the cross. Unlike the Gentiles, who lord it over one another, and who rule by exercising authority, Jesus' disciples are voluntarily to take on the role of slaves in their relations with one another: "But whoever would be great among you must be your servant, and whoever would be first among you must be slave of all." Jesus points to his own example and eventually to the cross to explain what it means to be his disciples: "For even the Son of Man came not to be served but to serve, and to give his life as a ransom for many" (Mark 10:44-45).

Finally, in John's Gospel, in the story of Jesus' washing of the disciples' feet during his last meal with them, we find another example of Jesus' subversion of the honor system. By washing his disciples' feet, Jesus deliberately took on a task that only a slave would have done. Peter's adamant initial refusal to allow Jesus to wash his feet illustrates the discomfort this produced. By taking on the role of a slave, Jesus engaged in humiliating and shameful behavior, which in turn led to a lowering of Peter's own status.[54] Again, Jesus spelled out the clear meaning of his actions: "For I have given you an example that you also should do as I have done to you. Truly, truly, I say to you, a servant is not greater than his master; nor is he who is sent greater than he who has sent him" (John 13:16).

More will be said about the role and significance of apostleship later (and specifically the significance of Jesus' choice of twelve *male* apostles), but, given what Jesus says about identifying leadership in terms of taking on the role of a servant to another, it is also important what Jesus does and does not say about authority in regard to his apostles. It is noteworthy that the authority that Jesus gave to his apostles was authority over demons and unclean spirits, as well as over illness and death (Matt. 10:1, 8; Mark 3:14-15, 6:7-30; Luke 9:1). When the gospels use the word ἐξουσία (*exousia*, "authority") in reference to the apostles, it is always in reference to their authority over nonhuman enemies of the gospel, never to human beings. Even in the case of Jesus giving to Peter the "keys" to "loose" or "bind," the authority has to do with the proclamation of forgiveness of sins, not with teaching, preaching, or power over others (Matt. 16:19, 18:18). When Jesus forbids his disciples to rule as the Gentiles do (Matt. 20:25), the words used to describe the forbidden behavior—κατεξουσιάζω (*katexousiazō*, a verbal form of *exousia*) and κατακυριεύω (*katakyrieuō*)—mean to "have control" or "bring into subjection."[55] What does it say that the kind of authority of men over women that complementarians insist is essential to the gospel seems to be the kind of authority of one person over another that Jesus explicitly forbids to his disciples?

These three stories make clear that Jesus repudiated the notion of authority as a simple hierarchical top-down structure in which some exercise authority over others whose responsibility is simply to submit. There are indeed leaders within the Christian community, as there must be leaders in all communities, but leadership in the Christian community is interpreted in terms of self-denial and service to those whom they lead, not in terms of authority over or control of others. Jesus' understanding of servant leadership in terms of what Padgett calls Type II submission is incompatible with and in direct contrast to Type I submission.

As Carrie Miles points out, this is another example of an undoing of the curse occasioned by the fall into sin by a call to return to the original creation. In a fallen world, anxiety about material well-being leads to an obsession for control, power over others, and status, especially for men. Jesus' teaching about servanthood repudiates this need for control since Jesus' followers can trust the God who is their Father, who clothes the lilies of the field, and numbers the very hairs of their heads. This does not mean that there are no positions of leadership in the Christian community. It does mean, however, that Jesus' followers must treat one another as true equals, not inferiors, without considerations of such things as status, or wealth, ethnic differences, or, indeed, gender. All Christians are called to serve each other mutually and to abandon the fallen quest to pursue status and power by attempting to control or exercise power over others.[56]

CONCLUSION

The purpose of this chapter has been to address the relevance of the person and teaching of Jesus for the question of the ordination of women. Both Catholic sacramentalists and Protestant complementarians are correct that Christology is crucial for a theology of ordination. However, in contrast to the highly abstract theories of eucharistic representation or eternal Trinitarian subordination, this has been a more concrete approach, a reading of the relevant material in the gospels to discover what Jesus actually taught and how he actually interacted with women, and, more specifically, whether one can look to the example of Jesus either to exclude women from ordained ministry or to find precedent for the notion that women should always be subordinate to male authority.

In addition, two specific hermeneutic tools—a narrative reading of the gospel texts and the principle of "Christological subversion"—shed light on how Jesus' teaching and mission challenged the hierarchical "honor system" of first-century Middle Eastern and Mediterranean culture. Narrative interpretation provides guidance in interpreting the symbols and metaphors of the gospels. We find out what such terms as "kingdom of God" or "Fatherhood of God" mean not by examining abstract general notions of "monarchy" or "paternity" in general culture, whether of the past or the present, but by how the gospel narratives redefine those terms by giving them a new meaning.

The principle of Christological subversion shows that, while Jesus did not set out to overthrow the first-century honor culture, his teachings and actions undermined it. Jesus did not join the Zealots in a political revolution to overthrow Roman rule, but his proclamation of the "kingdom of God" more radically undermined the claims of Caesar than did the Zealot embrace of political revolution because it made all political claims subservient to the absolute demands of God's rule and sovereignty. Jesus did not overthrow the hierarchical structure of the patriarchal family of the first century with its absolute rule of the *paterfamilias* over wives, children, and slaves, and the confining of women largely to the domestic sphere. Instead, by identifying God as "Father," Jesus offered an alternative "fictive kinship system" in which the God who is the Father of Jesus redefined what it means to be "Father," a Father who both welcomes the returning prodigal and demands a loyalty that transcends that of the biological and social family.

The principle of Christological subversion is clearly evident in Jesus' relationship to women. First, Jesus treated women as human beings, not hesitating to cross cultural barriers in order to engage women equally as men, and equally capable of being his disciples. Jesus' association with outcasts, "sinful women" such as the Samaritan woman at the well or the woman who anointed his feet, the Gentile Canaanite woman, as well as his curing of a woman whose illness made her ritually unclean, removed barriers that prevented these women from full participation in religious life.

Second, Jesus actually had women disciples. Women provided Jesus with financial support, and accompanied Jesus on his travels. Jesus taught women (such as Mary and Martha) and expected them to learn from him in a manner that evokes the teaching of a Jewish rabbi of male students. These women disciples of Jesus were among the first public witnesses to Jesus, and, when Jesus' male apostles deserted at his crucifixion, stayed by him in his death and were the first to witness to and proclaim his resurrection. When the male apostles failed, the women were faithful disciples.

Jesus' teachings had specific relevance to the question of the status of women in relation to men. Over against the honor culture, with its concerns for hierarchy, power and control, and economic security, Jesus appealed beyond the fallen world characterized by the curses of Genesis 3 to advocate a return to the original creation. Jesus identified the Torah's permissibility of divorce as a concession to human sinfulness, and instead appealed to the creation accounts of Genesis 1 and 2 to affirm the status of marriage as a permanent partnership between a man and a woman. This teaching elevated the status of women in first-century culture, contrary to rabbinic teaching that permitted polygamy and the divorce of wives by husbands, both practices that put women at an economic disadvantage. Significantly, by doing so Jesus emphasized the equality of husband and wife while saying nothing about "roles" of male rule or female subordination.

It is noteworthy that in Jesus' teaching in general, there are no examples of specific teaching addressed to men as males or to women as females. While Jesus used women as figures in many of his parables, Jesus' teachings are such as can be followed by any disciple, whether male or female. There is no evidence that Jesus ever gave specific instruction to women or to men about specific gender roles or responsibilities. When a woman called out to Jesus, "Blessed is the womb that bore you, and the breasts at which you nursed!" he replied "Blessed rather are those who hear the word of God and keep it!" (Luke 11:27-28).

Finally, Jesus' teaching about submission and servanthood further undermines any notion of a permanent subordination of women to men. The one area where Jesus' teaching might be expected to address traditional gender roles would have been in the area of submission and servanthood, given that in the hierarchical structure of first-century honor culture, one might expect that a rabbi would remind subordinates like wives and slaves of their responsibilities to submit to their superiors. To the contrary, Jesus' teaching about servanthood was addressed not to subordinates but to those who strive for positions of authority and leadership, instructing them that the leadership he expected of his disciples is a reversal of the temptations of the "honor culture" to strive for status and control of others. To the contrary, "greatness" among Jesus' disciples is identified with voluntarily being a slave to others. The distinction that Alan Padgett makes between "Type I submission" and "Type II submission" is a further example of the principle of Christological subversion. One discovers the meaning of "submission" for followers of Jesus not by turning to a standard lexicon to discover how the term was used by pagan contemporaries, but rather to the gospels themselves to discover that Jesus radically redefined the concept of leadership and submission by turning its usual meaning upside down. Jesus defined submission and servanthood not from the top down, but from the bottom up. Those who wish to be disciples of Jesus should remember that he gave instructions about submission not to subordinates but to those "in charge."

It is arguably anachronistic to look to the teaching and mission of Jesus to assess whether women in the twenty-first century can be ordained to church office. Jesus did not ordain anyone, and discussion of church offices (the roles of bishop, presbyter and deacon) appear in the New Testament only in the later epistles, describing a situation decades after Jesus' earthly mission. At the same time, however, the manner in which Jesus' teaching and mission subverted first-century assumptions about the proper cultural roles of men and women, as well as the way in which he related to women, both strangers and disciples, is relevant to the question of women's ordination, specifically to the question of whether there is anything about Jesus' teaching and mission that might count against the practice. The implication of this chapter is that there is not. Nothing in Jesus' teaching or relations with women implies a permanent subordination of women to men, grounded in a creation order. To the contrary, what he taught about the equality of man and woman in creation would seem to affirm the opposite, and what he taught about servanthood challenges traditional cultural assumptions about authority and power over others rather than affirms them. That Jesus had women as disciples in a manner quite at odds with first-century Jewish culture points in the direction of a challenge to those who would restrict the roles of women disciples of Jesus rather than those who would affirm them.

7

Mutual Submission

Previous chapters in this discussion have focused on the objections of those who designate their position as "complementarian," allowing that women and men are equal in status, but who nonetheless insist that they exercise different complementary "roles." The focus has been on the Bible, specifically the creation narratives in Genesis and the teaching and deeds of Jesus and his interactions with women, because the doctrines of creation and Christology are crucial to the debate. The argument is that both Genesis and the Gospels actually count against the complementarian position. Nothing in either Genesis or the Gospels teaches or implies an essential ontological subordination of women to men.

However, although complementarians appeal to Genesis and the Gospels to argue for female subordination, the primary complementarian arguments against women's ordination come from the epistles of the apostle Paul. Paul has no extended discussion of a theology of the relations between men and women. Instead Paul's views on men and women and how they relate to one another occur in places in Paul's occasional theology in which he writes about men and women in the context of some other issue: household management, worship in the church, or whether the single should marry. It is this handful of occasional texts in Paul's letters that have become central to the debate.

Complementarians appeal to two kinds of texts to support their position: (1) texts advocating for the submission of women to men; and (2) texts restricting women's activity in worship, either in speaking or teaching. In addition, in two letters, 1 Corinthians and Ephesians, Paul uses the word κεφαλή (kephalē), the Greek word translated "head" in English, to describe the relation between men and women. This single word kephalē is so central to the complementarian position that complementarians regularly use the term "headship" to describe their position, even when discussing passages where the word *kephalē* does not appear. For example, Wayne Grudem refers to "male headship" in his discussion of Genesis 1–3 although the Hebrew word for "head" that would have been translated *kephalē* in the Greek Septuagint appears nowhere in the creation narratives. George Knight III entitles the two main chapters of his book *The Role Relationship of Men and Women* "Submission and Headship in Marriage" and "Submission and Headship in the Church."[1]

Readers of Paul have responded to this handful of Pauline texts in different ways. Complementarians have appealed to them as the definitive linchpin in support of their position. Secular and liberal Protestant feminists have instead treated these passages as an excuse to dismiss Paul as an irremediable sexist. Other Christians, who recognize the canonical status of Paul's writings and appreciate Paul's crucial significance for Christian theology, especially his account of redeeming grace centered in the cross and resurrection of Christ, the Christian liberty that is a characteristic implication of his theology of grace (Gal. 5:1), and his affirmation of the fundamental equality of men and women in their unity in Christ (Gal. 3:28), read these passages with a kind of discomfort, perhaps wishing that Paul had not written them, or, in some cases, relieved that he did not.[2]

In recent decades, however, there have been numerous biblical scholars who have argued that a more careful reading of these passages does not support the subordinationist reading. What Paul writes is not inconsistent with the egalitarian position of Genesis or the Gospels, and Paul should neither be appealed to as an advocate of male hierarchy nor dismissed as a sexist. The next several chapters will look again at these controversial passages in Paul's epistles. This chapter will examine Paul's discussion of the relationship between husbands and wives in Ephesians 5 because it is the key New Testament passage laying out Paul's understanding of the relationship between men and women. Other passages need to be understood in the light of this passage.[3]

Looking at Paul's theology as a whole rather than focusing exclusively on the handful of problematic passages that have been central to the women's "roles" discussion shows the same themes discussed in the last chapter. Christology is central for Paul's theology, and he articulates the themes of Christological subversion and mutual submission through the category of "cruciformity." Pauline spirituality focuses on the cross. As Michael Gorman writes: "Paul's chief way of 'expounding' his theology of Christ crucified was to show the correspondence between Christ's death and the believing community's life."[4] Paul uses several "narrative patterns" to reflect on the meaning of Christ's death for the Christian community: (1) Obedience/righteousness/faithfulness: Christ's death was "an act of obedience, righteousness, and faithfulness"; (2) Love: Christ's death was an example of divine love; (3) Grace: Christ's death was an "act of unmerited generosity" by both God and Christ; (4)

Self-giving: Christ's death was an act of self-giving and self-surrender, a divine gift; (5) Voluntary self-humbling: Christ's death was an act of voluntary self-abasement, a "descent in status"; (6) Paradoxical power and wisdom: In Christ's death, power is shown in weakness, wisdom in apparent folly.[5]

The "master story" for Paul's cruciform spirituality is Philippians 2:6-11. In this passage, Paul identifies the love of Christ with a renouncing of status, a "self-emptying" (*kenosis* from κενόω, *kenoō*, Phil. 2:7) that prefers others over self, being humbled even to the point of death. In the incarnation, Christ submits himself to a fallen creation by taking on the form of a servant. This "master story" of Christ's self-emptying serves as a paradigm for Christian service. According to Gorman:

> Paul's . . . chief aim [in narrating the story of the cross] is to form individuals, and especially communities according to these narrative patterns. That is, his goal is formative, not informative; it is spiritual and behavioral, not theological (narrowly understood as convictional). . . . Paul's ultimate concern in narrating the love of Christ is to interpret his own life as a manifestation of that kind of love, on the one hand, and to urge his communities to embody it as well, on the other.[6]

Love, for Paul, has a "two-dimensional character." On the one hand, it does not seek its own advantage. It is characterized by self-renunciation. On the other, it seeks the good of others, pursuing their welfare rather than seeking one's own self-interest.[7]

As Jesus told his disciples that leadership was characterized by voluntarily taking up the position of a slave in respect to others, so Paul echoes the same themes throughout his epistles. Although Paul does not explicitly use the word "submission" in Philippians 2, Paul is clearly advocating what Padgett has called "Type II submission." Christians are not expected to take up Christ's self-emptying and exaltation in its fullest sense. After all, only Jesus is the unique Son of God; only the preincarnate Christ existed "in the form of God," only the incarnate Christ died for the sins of the world, and only the risen Christ is exalted to God's right hand to "receive a name that is above every name." But Paul does expect Christians to imitate the pattern of Christ's self-abasement: "Do nothing from selfish ambition or conceit, but in humility count others more significant than yourselves. Let each of you look not only to his own interests, but also to the interests of others. Have this mind among yourselves, which is yours in Christ Jesus" (Phil. 2:3-5).[8]

This pattern of voluntary mutual submission, modeled on Christ's "cruciform love," appears throughout Paul's writings. In Galatians 5:13, Paul exhorts Christians: "Through love serve [i.e., be slaves to] one another." This is also the model that Paul uses for his own ministry: "I try to please everyone in everything I do, not seeking my own advantage, but that of many, that they may be saved" (1 Cor. 10:33). Paul describes the mission of an apostle as "proclaim[ing] not ourselves, but Jesus Christ as Lord, with ourselves as your servants for Jesus' sake" (2 Cor. 4:5). Paul understood himself as a servant of Christ who imitates Christ's cruciform self-emptying on behalf of those to whom he ministered:

> But we have this treasure in jars of clay, to show that the surpassing power belongs to God and not to us. We are afflicted in every way, but not crushed; perplexed, but not driven to despair; persecuted, but not forsaken; struck down, but not destroyed; always carrying in the body the death of Jesus, so that the life of Jesus may also be manifested in our bodies. For we who live are always being given over to death for Jesus' sake, so that the life of Jesus also may be manifested in our mortal flesh. So death is at work in us, but life in you. (2 Cor. 4:7-12)

As Paul imitates Christ in becoming a slave to those to whom he ministers, so he expects those to whom he ministers voluntarily to become slaves to one another. It is in this context of seeking the advantage of others rather than the self that Paul counseled: "Be imitators of me, as I am of Christ" (1 Cor. 10:33–11:1). Padgett writes: "Type II submission is a central ethical teaching in the New Testament, and it is typically mutual—that is, it applies to every member of the body of Christ."[9]

EPHESIANS 5: STANDARD INTERPRETATIONS

With this background of Type II submission in mind, voluntarily taking on the role of a servant in relation to others that is patterned on Christ's own kenotic self-abasement, the discussion turns now to Ephesians 5. Why Ephesians 5? Ephesians 5 has been crucial to the discussion about relations between men and women, first, because of verses 22-23, which standard English translations typically translate like the English Standard Version: "Wives, submit to your own husbands, as to the Lord. For the husband is the head of the wife even as Christ is the head of the church, his body, and is himself its Savior. Now as the church submits to Christ, so also wives should submit in everything to their husbands." In what would seem to be a straight-forward reading of the passage, Paul commands that wives should "submit in everything to their husbands." This would seem to give husbands absolute authority over their wives. What else could "in everything" mean? Moreover, Paul says that husbands are "heads" over their wives, and draws a parallel between this "headship" and Christ's own "headship" over the church. As Christ as "head" has absolute authority over the church, so the husband as "head" has absolute authority over his wife. Moreover, at the end of the passage (v. 31), Paul echoes Genesis 2:24: "Therefore a man shall leave his mother and father and hold fast to his wife, and the two shall become one flesh." Accordingly, the passage has been read as teaching a hierarchical subordination between husbands and wives that is absolute (wives are to submit "in everything"), parallels the absolute authority that Christ as "head" has over the church as his body, and is grounded in creation itself (Gen. 2:24).

Is this a correct reading of the passage? What follows will argue that it is not. The passage is not best interpreted in such a straightforward manner as might first appear from standard English translations. The passage has been interpreted in at least five different ways, not just one:

(1) The "patriarchal" interpretation sees the wife as being subordinate to the husband and affirms this subordination. This is the interpretation of complementarians such as Wayne Grudem.[10]

(2) The "radical" view agrees that the text affirms a hierarchical subordination of wives to husbands, but rejects the text as patriarchal and oppressive. This would be the view of many self-identified feminist theologians.

(3) A third view reads the text as advocating a "qualified patriarchy" or "love patriarchy." The passage reinforces the patriarchal hierarchical understanding of marriage, but, at the same time, hierarchy is challenged by Paul's appeal to Christ's love as the paradigm for the husband's behavior toward the wife.

(4) A fourth view interprets the passage in terms of "revolutionary subordination." While the subordinate persons in the hierarchy (wives, children, slaves) are called to "submit," the submission is voluntary, and the dominant member of the hierarchy is challenged to submit to subordinates as well, in effect undermining the hierarchical structure without overthrowing it.

(5) A fifth view argues that Paul is actually affirming an egalitarian relationship between husband and wife.[11]

What follows will focus on the last two readings ("revolutionary subordination" and "egalitarian") as getting closest to what Paul was actually saying. In this light, the first two readings are simply misreadings. While the third reading ("love patriarchy") is moving in the right direction, it does not take seriously enough just how radically Paul challenged the hierarchical and patriarchal structures of first-century Mediterranean culture.

HOUSEHOLD CODES

Most Christian exegetes in recent decades discuss Paul's exhortations in Ephesians 5 in the light of the so-called "household codes" of antiquity (*Haustafeln*).[12] Such codes occur in Aristotle, among other pagan writers, and also among Jewish writers. In Aristotle, they address the same three relationships found in Ephesians: those between husbands and wives, fathers and children, masters and slaves.

Aristotle wrote:

The parts of household management correspond to the persons who compose the household, and a complete household consists of slaves and freemen. . . . [T]he first and fewest parts of a family are master and slave, husband and wife, father and children. We have therefore to consider what each of these three relations is and ought to be: I mean the relation of master and servant, the marriage relation (the conjunction of man and wife has no name of its own), and thirdly, the procreative relation (this also has no proper name).[13]

Concerning masters and slaves, Aristotle wrote:

[I]n the arrangement of the family, a slave is a living possession.... The master is only the master of the slave; he does not belong to him, whereas the slave is not only the slave of his master, but wholly belongs to him.[14]

Concerning the roles of husband and father, Aristotle wrote:

A husband and father ... rules over wife and children, both free, but the rule differs, the rule over his children being a royal, over his wife a constitutional rule. For although there may be exceptions to the order of nature, the male is by nature fitter for command than the female, just as the elder and full-grown is superior to the younger and more immature.... [Concerning] the relation of the male to the female ... the inequality is permanent.[15]

Aristotle believed that the rule of the master over slaves, the husbands over wives, and fathers over children is rooted in inherent qualitative differences:

[T]he freeman rules over the slave after another manner from that in which the male rules over the female, or the man over the child; although the parts of the soul are present in all of them, they are present in different degrees. For the slave has no deliberative faculty at all; the woman has, but it is without authority, and the child has, but it is immature.[16]

Typically, the purpose of these codes is to instruct the master of the household (the male husband, father, slave owner) in his duties toward those subordinate to him, as seen in Aristotle above. Note that Aristotle addresses no instructions to subordinates, but only to masters. He says nothing about the master's duties to his subordinates, but only of the master's responsibility to rule over the subordinates. The master is "to rule his slaves like a despot, his children like a king, and his wife treating her as a rational being but one without inherent authority."[17] Insofar as the household codes are concerned with subordinates at all, they are concerned with the exclusive obligations of the subordinates to submit to those in positions of authority over them.

What is unusual about Paul's discussion of household codes is not that he includes a discussion that has similarities to pagan and Jewish material, but the way in which he subverts the logic of the traditional codes. The previous chapter on Jesus and the gospels discussed the principle of "Christological subversion," seen here in Paul as well. First, the purpose of the codes in Paul is not about how the male master of the household is to act authoritatively toward his subordinates. To the contrary, Paul's entire discussion subverts that understanding. Specifically, there are the following differences between Paul and pagan household codes. First, Paul addresses the subordinates in the household first, treating them as responsible moral agents. In contrast, typical household codes addressed the master of the house, instructing him in his duties to order the behavior of his subordinates. Second, when Paul addresses the male of the household (the husband, father, and slave owner), he challenges the male figure who is more powerful in the relationship to act with gentleness and kindness toward the traditional subordinates in the household. While Paul in Ephesians addresses each one of the traditional subordinates only once, he addresses the traditional patriarch or *paterfamilias* three times, each time exhorting the more powerful figure in the family to act with love and consideration toward traditional subordinates. Finally, in each case, the commandments of the code are given a theological warrant that, in effect, transforms them in the light of the gospel.[18] In comparing what Paul writes in Ephesians to the pagan household codes, Ben Witherington III uses the language of "social engineering," and suggests "a significant equalizing of relationships within Christian marriage, altering the usual character and direction of a patriarchal marriage situation." Witherington states: "[I]f anything is the primary purpose of this code, it is to both ameliorate the harsher effects of patriarchy and to guide the head [*sic*] of the household into a new conception of roles that Christianizes his conduct in various ways and so turns marriage into more of a partnership and household management more into a matter of actualizing biblical principles about love of neighbor and honoring others."[19] Richard Hays states that "the exalted ecclesiology of Ephesians must deconstruct static patriarchal notions of marriage."[20] Far then from upholding the traditional understanding of the authority of the *paterfamilias* in ancient Mediterranean culture, Paul rather undermines it. In the words of Carrie Miles: "[I]f Paul paralleled any Greco-Roman household code, it was in order to stand it on its head. Far from advocating the status quo of patriarchy, Paul, like Jesus, sought to overturn it."[21]

REVOLUTIONARY SUBORDINATION

Recognizing the significant difference that Paul's transformation of the household codes makes for understanding the logic of Ephesians 5, there have been two slightly different approaches to reading Paul here. The first is the reading of "self-sacrificial love" or "revolutionary subordination." The term "revolutionary subordination" seems first to have been used by Mennonite theologian John Howard Yoder in his book *The Politics of Jesus*, but this reading is characteristic of a number of New Testament scholars: Markus Barth, Craig Keener, Richard Hays, I. Howard Marshall, David deSilva, and Ben Witherington III, among others.[22] Advocates of "revolutionary subordination" tend to make the following arguments.

First, Paul's own approach is contrasted to that of the "household codes," emphasizing how Paul both transforms and challenges the cultural values of ancient Mediterranean culture. As noted above, subordinates are addressed first as those who exercise responsibility. The subordinate person is thus treated as a moral agent, as someone who has the freedom to choose how to respond. The fact that subordinates are addressed as moral agents presumed that the content of the Christian message included an understanding that challenged their subjection. In contrast, the traditional household codes addressed only the householder, with the focus being on his responsibility to enforce obedience on his subordinates.[23]

Second, there is a mutual reciprocity between householders and subordinates. Only after subordinates are addressed is the master addressed. The dominant partner in the relationship is the one who is primarily addressed, and addressed in such a way as to challenge the household codes; the master is expected to change by becoming the servant of his servants. The husband is called to loving self-sacrifice toward his wife, with Christ as his model. The father is called not to anger his children. The slave owner is to recognize himself as a fellow slave with his slaves. This contrasts considerably with the pagan notion of the father as the *paterfamilias* who exercises a monarchical role over the household. The householder "is here cast as a patient pedagogue, a servant of the household educating the children."[24] As Witherington notes:

> [T]he Greco-Roman discussion is about how the master of the house should manage and exercise authority in his household—he is to rule his slaves like a despot, his children like a king, and his wife treating her as a rational being but one without inherent authority. . . . But the Christian household codes "are not about how *he* should act authoritatively." . . . In short, the Christian code is about everyone in the household and treats everyone as moral agents, even the children. It is not all about the head of the household any more.[25]

Third, it is pointed out that the commands are not general commands indicating a hierarchical relationship between men and women as such, but are specifically related to the household. Women are not called to submit to men in general, but only to their husbands.[26]

Fourth, the order of the household rule is modified by reference to Christ. All motivations for both subordinates and householders are related to Christ. Moreover, Christ is chosen as example precisely in his decision voluntarily to take on the role of servant. The wife submits as submitting to Christ (5:22-23). Children obey their parents "in the Lord" (6:1). Slaves obey their masters "with sincere heart, as you would Christ . . . as servants of Christ" (6:5-7). Thus, for subordinates,

> the meaning of [the household roles] was changed in substance by the stance of servanthood derived from the example and teaching of Jesus himself. His motto of

revolutionary subordination, of willing servanthood in the place of domination, enables the person in a subordinate position in society to accept and live within that status without resentment.[27]

Similarly, the householder's role is also challenged by Christ's servanthood. The notion of "headship" is transformed by the model of Christ's self-sacrificial death: "Husbands, love your wives as Christ loved the church and gave himself up for her." The husband is head of his wife only in the same way that Christ is head, as one who loves, provides for, nourishes, and sacrifices himself for her.[28] The husband is "head" as one who "'go[es] ahead' by loving his wife and by paying gladly whatever the appropriate price."[29] Although the household hierarchy may not be eliminated, the instructions to husbands make it clear that it is lived out in terms of servanthood as modeled by Christ. The husband is not told to command his wife, but to love and serve her. The model for this loving is the self-sacrificial love of Christ.[30]

Finally, advocates of "revolutionary subordination" speak of a "trajectory" when it comes to interpreting what Paul is doing in Ephesians. This trajectory is seen in two ways. First, as we have seen, a comparison of Paul's modification of the household codes to the usual way that they functioned in antiquity points toward an undermining of their hierarchical aspect, and a move in the direction of equality. Ben Witherington III writes:

> [T]he trajectory and contextualizing of the argument here are as important as the details of what Paul says. What we see here is an attempt to provide a significant equalizing of relationships within Christian marriage, altering the usual character and direction of a patriarchal marriage situation.
>
> [T]he emphasis on the modified behavior required of the head of the household (who receives the bulk of the exhortations, as husband, parent, and master), especially in loving and acting in a Christian manner with family members, has the rhetorical effect of setting up a trajectory or momentum in a direction of a more egalitarian approach to the marital situation.[31]

Richard Hays embraces a similar position. Paul's model of marriage as parallel to the relation between Christ and the church deconstructs patriarchal notions of marriage:

> [I]f marriage is a metaphor for the relationship between Christ and the church, the exalted ecclesiology of Ephesians must deconstruct static patriarchal notions of marriage. The church, in Ephesians, is not dominated by Christ; rather, in unity with Christ, it is nurtured into full maturity, into "the measure of the full stature of Christ" (4:13). What, then, must the *telos* of marriage be?[32]

The second way in which a trajectory is seen in this passage is by a comparison between what Paul says about marriage and what he says about slavery. Craig Keener notes both similarities and differences between Paul's admonitions to wives and his admonitions to both children and slaves, although unlike children and slaves, wives are not told to "obey." Given the evident parallels, however, Keener notes an uncomfortable dilemma for those who argue for contemporary subordination of wives to husbands: "Modern writers who argue that Paul's charge to wives to submit to their husbands 'as to Christ' is binding in all cultures must come to grips with the fact that Paul even more plainly tells slaves to 'obey' their masters 'as they would Christ' (6:5). If one is binding in all cultures, so is the other."[33] During the abolitionist debates of the nineteenth century, there were those who argued for the continuing existence of slavery as a Christian institution, and appealed to Paul's writings for support.[34]

Keener points out that, as a missionary, Paul's intent was to change the world where he could by demanding that Christians should love and respect one another as themselves. Although Paul did not call for the overthrow of slavery, the moral principles that Paul lays down "ultimately challenge the moral right of structures such as slavery to exist. . . . By saying that slaves and masters are equal before God, *and* that masters should keep this in mind, Paul is saying that slavery is not part of God's purpose."[35] Moreover, in Philemon, "Paul has begun to deconstruct the very notion of brothers or sisters being kept as slaves."[36] The parallel with the patriarchal hierarchy of ancient Mediterranean culture is evident. Although Paul did not explicitly call for the abolition of patriarchy any more than he did the abolition of slavery, the implications of the manner in which he transforms the household codes is evident: "Those who today will admit that slavery is wrong but still maintain that husbands must have authority over their wives are inconsistent."[37]

AN EGALITARIAN READING

What the "revolutionary subordination" reading says about Paul's subversive transformation of ancient household codes is persuasive. However, it would seem that "subversive transformation" or "revolutionary subordination" does not go far enough toward understanding what Paul is doing in Ephesians. A good case can be made that only an egalitarian reading of Paul is adequate to account for what he is doing in Ephesians 5 and 6. The reasons for this are as follows.

First, a reading of the Greek text makes clear that the usual English translations of the text misleadingly suggest that Paul is advocating a one-sided top-down subordination of husbands to wives. As noted above, the ESV translation is typical: "Wives, submit to your own husbands, as to the Lord. For the husband is the head of the wife even as Christ is the head of the church, his body, and is himself its Savior. Now as the church submits to Christ, so also wives should submit in everything to their husbands" (Eph. 5:22-24). Such English translations begin with a new sentence at verse 22, but the verse is actually a continuation of verse 21. This is necessary because there is *no verb* in verse 22. The verb "submit" that the ESV supplies as an imperative in verse 22 ("Wives, *submit* to your own husbands") does not occur in 21 at all, but is actually a continuation of a participial phrase in verse 21, "being subject to one another," or "submitting to one another."[38] Moreover, grammatically, verse 21 is a continuation of verse 18. Paul's thought thus follows a logical progression: "Be filled with the Spirit . . . by being subject to one another in the respect of Christ— wives to your husbands."[39] My own very literal translation follows:

> Be imitators of God, as beloved children, and walk in love, as also Christ loved (ἠγάπησεν, *ēgapēsen*) you and gave himself up on our behalf, a sacrifice to God as a sweet-smelling offering . . . [B]e filled with the Spirit, by (1) *speaking to yourselves* in psalms and hymns and spiritual songs, singing and psalming with your heart to the Lord, (2) *giving thanks* always for all things in the name of our Lord Jesus Christ to God the Father, (3) *being subject/subjecting yourselves* to one another in the reverence (φόβῳ, *phobō*) of Christ, (3a) wives to their own husbands as to the Lord, because a husband is head of the wife in the same way that Christ is also head of the church, himself Savior of the body. But as the church is subject to Christ, so in the same manner, wives to their husbands in everything. (3b) Husbands, love (ἀγαπᾶτε, *agapate*) your wives as also Christ loved (ἠγάπησεν, *ēgapēsen*) the church and gave himself up on behalf of it . . . Each of you [husbands] must love (ἀγαπάτω, *agapatō*) his wife even as he loves himself, and the wife should respect (φοβῆται, *phobētai*) her husband.[40]

Barth's and Gorman's own translations make clear that submission in this context is not something that is being asked uniquely of wives to husbands, but is rather an example of a mutual submission that is expected of all Christians one to another. Gorman's participial translation makes this particularly clear. All Christians are to be filled with the Spirit (1) by singing psalms and hymns and spiritual songs, (2) by giving thanks to God the Father, and (3) by being subject to one another. Wives are not uniquely to submit to husbands any more than only some Christians should sing psalms and hymns or give thanks to God the Father. The submission that is asked for in verse 21 is a mutual submission of all Christians. As Gorman writes, "It is as if the responsibility of wives to their husbands is presented as the first example of the meaning of mutual submission within the believing community. . . . The wife's marital responsibility may have particular manifestations, but it is essentially the same obligation that she has to all members of the community."[41] The subordination is mutual—not simply of wives to husbands, children to fathers, and slaves to masters, but of husbands to wives, of fathers to children, of masters to slaves. Similarly, Barth writes:

> [T]he call to mutual subordination seems to relativize, if not blur and destroy, any clear notion of authority and subservience. . . . [T]he subordination of wives is an example

of the same mutual subordination which is also shown by the husband's love, the children's obedience, the parents' responsibility for their offspring, the slaves' and master's attitude to one another.[42]

The two key words in verse 21 are ὑποτασσόμενοι ἀλλήλοις (*hypotassomenoi allēlois*, "submitting yourselves to one another"). The root word ὑποτάσσομαι (*hypotassomai*) is in the middle voice. It literally means "to place oneself under."[43] Complementarian exegetes argue that the verb "always implies a relationship of submission to an authority." They write that Ephesians 5:21 "does not teach mutual submission at all, but rather teaches that we should be subject to those whom God has put in authority over us—such as husbands, parents, or employers."[44] Padgett's distinction between "Type I submission" and "Type II submission" is, again, helpful here. Context determines meaning. The verb can mean involuntary submission to an authority—what Padgett calls "Type I submission." However, the context of Ephesians is quite different from the military or political context associated with "Type I submission." The entire context of the passage understands submission as the voluntary taking up the role of a servant that Padgett identifies as "Type II submission."[45] The model for such submission is the cruciform love of Christ himself (more on this below). *Hypotassomai* does not mean "obey" and it is neither in the active voice (a command given) nor in the passive (a command received). Paul is not urging Christians to exercise power over other Christians or asking Christians to submit to those in power. Rather, he is calling for them voluntarily to subject themselves to one another, to "opt out of the power struggle."[46]

The second key word is the pronoun ἀλλήλους (*allēlous*, "one another"), which means not that some Christians submit to others, but that all Christians submit to one another. Paul uses the word in Ephesians 4:2 ("bearing with one another in love"), 4:25 ("we are members of one another"), and 4:32 ("be kind to one another") as well. In each case, context makes clear that the behavior is mutual, and that the context is the "servant love" and "mutual submission" that all Christians exercise for one another, and which is modeled on Christ's own self-sacrificial giving of himself for the church.[47] It is clear then that Paul is asking not for a submission of some Christians to others, but of all Christians to one another. Paul is deliberately challenging the traditional top-down hierarchy of the ancient "household codes."[48]

Second, as Gorman points out, the principle verbs addressed to husbands and wives are drawn from the general imperatives addressed to all believers in the passage. They are not specific duties addressed to husbands and wives.[49] The following comparison is taken directly from Gorman.

Wives

5:21   All must be subject to one another in the respect (fear) of Christ (ἐν φόβῳ Χριστοῦ, *in phobo Christou*).

5:22, 24   Wives, [being subject] to your husbands as to the Lord. . . . Just as the church is subject to Christ, so also wives [are to be subject] to their husbands in all things.

5:33   [A] wife should respect (φοβῆται, *phobētai*) her husband.

Husbands

5:2   All must walk in love (περιπατεῖτε ἐν ἀγάπῃ, *peripateite in agapē*) as Christ loved us and gave himself up for us.

5:25   Husbands must love (ἀγαπᾶτε, *agapate*) their wives as Christ loved the church by giving himself up for it.

In each case, the responsibilities of husbands and wives to one another are no different from the responsibilities of all Christians to one another: "[W]ives and husbands alike are being called to act out in marriage the same type of self-sacrificing, respectful, submissive love they would in any and all relationships within the believing community."[50]

Third, there is a Christological moral model that is provided as the paradigm for each of the members of the household addressed, and the model is not that of Christ in glory (*Christos Pantokrator*), but the self-abasement of the crucified Christ who voluntarily took on the role of a servant, who loved the church and gave himself up for it. Ephesians 5:2 provides the warrant for everything else that follows: "And walk in love, as Christ loved us and gave himself for us." This verse makes clear that mutual submission and love are used as synonyms for the kind of self-abasement that characterized Jesus' own servanthood, a servanthood that is expected of all his followers.[51] So all Christians are urged to "submit themselves to one another," taking on the same role of servanthood that Christ assumed himself. Wives, in particular, are encouraged to imitate Christ's servanthood in relation to their husbands. Husbands are encouraged to love their wives as "Christ loved the church," by giving himself up to death. Children are called to obey their parents "in the Lord," and the counsel of fathers to "not provoke their children" and bring them up in the "discipline and instruction of the Lord" places fathers in the role of servants even to their children.[52] Slaves are encouraged to obey their masters "as servants of Christ," and masters are called to recognize that they too are servants who share a common master with their slaves. The paradigm for all Christians in their relationship to one another is that of the mutual "self-submission" of voluntary servanthood characterized by Gorman as "cruciformity" and by Padgett as "Type II submission." The moral model of Christ as servant undermines any notion of one-sided hierarchy where some always give orders and others always obey.

HEADSHIP

This notion of cruciform mutual submission brings us to the famous analogy that Paul uses comparing the relationship between husband and wife to that of Christ and the church. Crucial for the discussion is the meaning of the word "head" (κεφαλή, *kephalē*). The reason for the wife's submission to her husband—what is here argued is an example of the mutual submission of all Christians to one another and of both husbands and wives to each other—is that "a husband/man is head (*kephalē*) of the wife/woman as also Christ [is] head (*kephalē*) of the church, himself Savior of the body. But as the church is subject to Christ, so also wives to their husbands in everything" (5:24, author's literal translation).

In the Greek of Paul's time, as in modern English, "head" was used as a metaphor. The key exegetical question is: what did Paul mean by this metaphor when he wrote that the husband is "head" of the wife? In modern English, "head" used metaphorically often means authority, as the CEO is the "head" of the company or the commanding officer is the "head" of the platoon. Complementarian exegetes assume that "head" in Paul means "authority," and, as has been noted above, complementarians regularly identify the relationship between men and women as that of "headship."

However, it is not exegetically sound to assume that the use of a metaphor in modern English necessarily corresponds to its meaning in another language in another culture and time. There have been numerous studies in recent decades reassessing Paul's use of *kephalē* as a metaphor and challenging the meaning of "authority." The key discussion concerns Paul's use of *kephalē* in 1 Corinthians 11, and the next chapter will treat the modern discussion of *kephalē* in more detail. What follows will summarize a few key points that will be developed to argue that *kephalē* does not mean "authority" in Paul's discussion of marriage in Ephesians.

Much of the discussion has centered around the LXX translation of the Hebrew Old Testament and examples of the use of "head" metaphors in ancient culture. Numerous scholars point out that when the LXX translators translated the Hebrew word for "head" (*rosh*) where it is used literally, they regularly used the Greek word *kephalē*; however, when used as a metaphor for "leader," they rarely did so, and used the word ἄρχων (*archōn*) instead, implying that native Greek speakers did not normally understand the metaphor "head" to mean "leader" or "authority."[53]

Crucial for the discussion in Ephesians, however, is not how the metaphor might or might not have been used in military or political settings—which are not the context here—but how it was used in reference to the family, and how it is used in reference to Christ. Significantly, scholars know of only one use of "head" in a family context prior to the New Testament.[54] Aristotle wrote: "The rule of a household is a monarchy, for every house is under one head."[55] The context here is not referring to the relationship between husbands and wives, however, but between masters and slaves. Aristotle goes on to refer to a "science for the master and a science for the slave." The relationship is not necessarily one of gender, since female masters could rule over male slaves.

Paul's usage here is unique. He is the first to use headship language for marriage. He is the first to suggest that the husband is "head" of his wife, and the "wife" is his body.[56] Paul is also the first to make a comparison between husband and wife and Christ and the church. The only way to understand what Paul means by "headship" is to examine the context in which he himself uses the metaphor.

There are numerous places where Paul uses the metaphor of "head" in relationship to Christ. Interestingly, although Paul certainly understood the risen Lord Jesus Christ to have authority over the church and over all creation (Phil. 2:10), he tends not to use language of authority or lordship when using the metaphor of "headship."

For Paul, "head" (*kephalē*) and "origin" (ἀρχή, *archē*) seem largely equivalent. Christ is the beginning or source of the church as its body, and also the one from whom it receives its nourishment. In Colossians 1:18, Paul writes that Christ is the "head (*kephalē*) of the body, the church; he is the beginning (*archē*), the firstborn from the dead, that in everything he might be preeminent." In Colossians 2:19, Paul speaks of those who do not hold fast to the "head" (*kephalē*), "from whom the whole body, nourished and knit together through its joints and ligaments, grows together with a growth that is from God." This is parallel to the way that Paul speaks of Christ's headship of the church as his body in Ephesians 4:15; Paul states that "we are to grow up in every way into him who is the head (*kephalē*), into Christ, from whom the whole body, joined and held together by every joint with which it is equipped, when each part is working properly, makes the body grow so that it builds itself up in love." In the one passage in which Paul does associate Christ's "headship" with authority, he contrasts Christ's relationship with his body, the church, with those over whom he exercises authority: "And [God the Father] put all things under his feet and gave him as head (*kephalē*) over all things to the church, which is his body, the fullness of him who fills all in all" (Eph. 1:22). "Head" in reference to those who are "under [Christ's] feet" contrasts with "head" in reference to the church, his body, which is not, under his feet, but whom he "fills all in all."[57]

This notion of "headship" as giving life to the body, and as a source of nourishment, seems to be the key to Paul's understanding of Christ as "head" in 5:23: "Christ [is] head of the church, himself Savior of the body." "Savior" and "head" are in apposition, and thus identify what Paul means by "head." The context is not a notion of "authority over" or a top-down giving of orders, but of mutual love and care, nourishment and protection. The head and body language focuses on the one-flesh union between Christ and the church as his body and the one-flesh union between the husband and wife (5:31). In the immediate context, Christ acts as head of the church by nurturing the church. Christ also unites the church, and brings it together. Finally, Christ gives himself sacrificially to the church. The husband is being asked to be the "head" over his wife in exactly the same way that Paul is describing Christ's headship over the church, in terms of sacrificial love: "In the same way, husbands should love their wives as their own bodies. He who loves his wife loves himself. For no one ever hated his own flesh, but nourishes and cherishes it, just as Christ does the church, because we are members of his own body" (5:28-30).[58] The passage is not about authority of husbands over wives, but about self-sacrificing love of husbands for their wives.[59] At no point are husbands told to command their wives, or wives told to obey their husbands. Paul does not use such words as "authority" (ἐξουσία, exousia) or "lord" (κύριος, kurios) when describing the relationship between husband and wife, but "head," and the context makes clear that the model of the husband's "headship" is Christ's self-abasement and self-sacrificial cruciform love by which he gave himself up for the church.[60]

In short, Paul's discussion of the relations between husbands and wives, fathers and children, and master and slaves in Ephesians 5–6 is an example of "Christological subversion." Paul does not directly overthrow the *paterfamilias* patriarchal structure of the first-century Mediterranean family. He does not explicitly tell Christians to free their slaves. He does not explicitly advocate egalitarianism between men and women. But he modifies the ancient "household codes" (*Haustafeln*) in such a way that the implications are subversive. The *paterfamilias* is addressed more than anyone, and in each case, he is called not to exercise authority, but to give sacrificially, to love his wife as Christ loved the church, and to become a servant to his servants. The subordinates are addressed in light of the story of redemption. They are not commanded to "give in," but voluntarily to "submit themselves," that is, to opt out of the power struggle.[61] All are called to live lives of cruciform love, voluntarily submitting to one another, following the model given them by the Lord who emptied himself to become a servant by dying for them. Far from endorsing top-down understandings of hierarchical authority of husbands over wives, of domineering parents over children, and masters over slaves, Paul undermines them. Christians are not masters demanding obedience from one another, but servants of one another who voluntarily yield to one another out of love.

OBJECTIONS

Complementarians have raised a number of objections against the kind of egalitarian interpretation of Paul's teaching given above, and some of these will now be addressed.

(1) Are egalitarians inconsistent by reading Ephesians in terms of both mutual submission and as not explicitly rejecting patriarchy?

Wayne Grudem criticizes Craig Keener for what he considers to be an inconsistent argument concerning "mutual submission" in Ephesians. Keener's position is slightly different from the one advocated here, in that he upholds a variation of the fourth position, identified as "revolutionary subordination." Keener argues that Paul taught "mutual subordination" in Ephesians 5, but also suggests that Christian adaptation of "household codes" served an apologetic purpose—"to show that Christians were good members of society who did not seek to radically overturn Roman social structures."[62] Grudem complains: "But if Keener thinks Ephesians 5:21 teaches mutual submission in a way that nullifies a husband's authority in the marriage then he no longer can argue that Paul's teaching is meant to gain the approval of pagan Roman men who wanted to preserve authority over their wives."[63]

Whether Grudem's complaint is an accurate assessment of what Keener argues is questionable. Keener certainly does not argue that Paul "nullifies a husband's authority in marriage," which rather begs the question of whether Paul believed that a husband had the kind of authority in marriage that Grudem wants him to have. Grudem misses the point of what is here called "Christological subversion."[64] First-century Mediterranean culture—both Jewish and pagan—was an "honor culture," in which status, authority, and group identity were paramount. Jesus challenged this culture not by rebelling against it or by overtly challenging it but by advocating an alternative form of honor, one which depended on one's status before God, and one's membership in the new community of the church. One's status in this culture was tied to a new path of servanthood rather than self-seeking, what Padgett has referred to as "Type II submission," voluntarily taking on the role of a servant rather than "Type I submission," forcefully imposing authority on others in order to enhance one's own status. As argued in this chapter, Paul's theology echoes Jesus' understanding of servanthood in promoting a spirituality of "cruciformity." Like Jesus, Paul did not deliberately seek to overturn the structures of Mediterranean culture, whether Jewish or pagan. For example, although Paul argued against Gentile converts accepting circumcision in Galatians, he himself practiced the Jewish law when visiting Jerusalem in order not to give offense to Jews (Acts 21:21-26).

Similarly, Paul does not advocate the overthrow of slavery in Ephesians 6. Yet his reinterpretation of the relationship between slaves and masters by reminding masters that they too are servants of a common Master undermines the logic of slavery. In Philemon, Paul provides evidence of how he dealt with the concrete problem of slavery among Christians. Paul returns a runaway slave to his master; Paul does not command Philemon to liberate Onesimus, but one does not have to read too much between the lines to understand what he is requesting: "I preferred to do nothing without your consent in order that your goodness might not be by compulsion but of your own free will ... that you might have him back forever, *no longer as a slave* but more than a slave, as a beloved brother. ... Confident of your obedience, I write to you, knowing that *you will do even more than I say*" (Phil. 1:16, 21; emphasis added).

As with slavery, what Paul writes about marriage can mean more than he explicitly says. Paul does not explicitly advocate for the overthrowing of the patriarchal structure of first-century marriage. His transformation of the household codes follows the traditional order found in Aristotle: husbands, wives, children, and slaves. Yet Paul's *transformation* of the household codes is indeed a transformation; a close reading indicates that Paul is engaging in "Christological subversion." Paul's call for "mutual submission" subverts first-century assumptions about the authority of the *paterfamilias*, and implies an egalitarian understanding of Christian marriage.

(2) What about slavery? Do egalitarians wrongly draw a comparison between the abolition of slavery and a "trajectory" that implies equality in marriage?

As noted above, Paul argues that masters are also slaves, and so must "serve" their slaves. In time, the implicit logic of Paul's argument led to the abolition of slavery in the modern Western world, and Christian abolitionists were leaders of this antislavery movement. Grudem and other complementarians argue that the comparison between slavery and hierarchical marriage is not apt. Grudem states that "[s]lavery is very different from marriage and from the church. Marriage was part of God's original creation, but slavery was not. The church is a wonderful Creation of God, but slavery was not."[65]

One can only agree with Grudem when he asserts that the New Testament never commanded slavery, but merely provided principles to regulate it. However, one can find passages in the New Testament where slaves are commanded to obey their masters, as in Ephesians 6:5. It is the overall thrust of Paul's discussion that subverts the logic of slavery by challenging masters to understand themselves as fellow slaves, redeemed by Christ.[66]

At the same time, the question is not whether marriage is a creation order, but whether hierarchical dominance of men over women is a creation order. Keener had already addressed Grudem's objection in addressing a similar objection by George Knight III: "Knight is quite right that marriage and slavery differ in this regard [whether marriage is God-ordained], but his observation simply begs the actual question. The issue is not whether marriage itself is God-ordained, but whether a wife's submission to her husband is a permanently God-ordained part of marriage."[67]

(3) What about 1 Peter 3:1-7 and the Pastoral Epistles?

In 1 Peter 3:1-7 and Titus 2:4, admonitions are given to wives and slaves that are very different from those found in Ephesians 5–6. 1 Peter 2:13 begins with a general command to "be subject for the Lord's sake to every human institution, whether it be to the emperor as supreme, or to governors." In 2:18, slaves are told: "Servants, be subject to your masters with all respect, not only to the good and gentle but also to the unjust." Finally, 3:1 reads: "Likewise, wives, be subject to your own husbands, so that even if some do not obey the word, they may be won without a word by the conduct of their wives—when they see your respectful and pure conduct" (1 Pet. 3:1-2). There is little of the mutuality of Ephesians here. Generally, the corresponding balancing address to husbands is missing, although 3:7 states, "Likewise, husbands, live with your wives in an understanding way, showing honor to the woman as the weaker vessel, since they are heirs with you of the grace of life, so that your prayers may not be hindered." There is no mention of mutual submission, and the theological moral motivation rooted in Christ's self-giving cruciformity is less evident—although slaves are told to follow the example of Jesus "because Christ also suffered for you, leaving you an example, so that you might follow in his steps" (2:21).

Similarly, Titus 2:4-5 suggests that "young women [are] to love their husbands and children, to be self-controlled, pure, working at home, kind and submissive to their own husbands, that the word of God may not be reviled." Corresponding advice to slaves is found in verse 9: "Slaves are to be subject to their own masters in everything; they are to be well-pleasing, not argumentative . . . so that in everything they may adorn the doctrine of God our Savior." Again, the commands are one-sided. There are no corresponding instructions for husbands and masters. The self-sacrificial cruciform example of Christ is strikingly absent.

What is going on here? Alan Padgett suggests that what appears to be a one-sided Type I submission in contrast to the Type II submission of the gospels and Ephesians can largely be explained by a different social setting. 1 Peter, in particular, is a letter written to a persecuted church undergoing suffering. Where Ephesians is an "in-house" document, addressed entirely to Christians without concern for outsiders, the motivation in 1 Peter is largely concerned with the way that the church comes across in its dealings with outsiders. Under persecution, the concern to submit to political authorities is "not so much political as it is evangelical and apologetic."[68] The author writes, "For this is the will of God, that by doing good you should put to silence the ignorance of foolish people" (1 Pet. 2:15).

Masters are not addressed here because presumably the masters who are causing their slaves to "suffer unjustly" (2:18-19) are not Christian masters. The Christian slave who serves an unjust master is encouraged to follow the example of Christ. Finally, the premise of wives' subjection to their husbands presumes an apologetic motive—"be subject to your own husbands, so that even if some do not obey the word, they may be won without a word by the conduct of their wives—when they see your respectful and pure conduct" (3:1). Although there is an admonition to husbands that has some resemblance to what Paul says to husbands in Ephesians, the general focus is on Christian wives submitting to non-Christian husbands. It is this vastly different political context that explains the one-sided submission described in 1 Peter.

Similarly, the exhortations in the Pastoral Epistles seem primarily concerned about the church's stance toward outsiders. Concerning slavery, 1 Timothy 6:1 states, "Let all who are under a yoke as slaves regard their own masters as worthy of all honor, *so that* the name of God and the teaching may not be reviled." Titus 2 suggests that young women should be submissive to their husbands "*so that* the word of God may not be reviled" (v. 5). Young men are to be "self-controlled . . . models of good works . . . *so that* an opponent may be put to shame, having nothing evil to say about us" (vv. 6-8). Finally, slaves are to be submissive to their masters "*so that* in everything they may adorn the doctrine of God our Savior" (v. 10).

As Padgett points out, this appearance of one-sided submission reflects a particular social situation in a church under persecution at a time when it was a small movement and frequently slandered. These specific responses to a specific situation "do not lead to a universal call to *external submission* for either slaves or wives."[69]

Wayne Grudem complains that such a reading is an example of "the ultimate 'bait and switch' sales technique." Grudem suggests that, on this reading, "first-century evangelism was a deceptive maneuver in which the Word of God told people to use a morally deficient pattern of behavior simply to win unbelievers."[70] Grudem's comment ignores the actual textual differences between Ephesians and 1 Peter. Ephesians does speak of "mutual submission" in a way that 1 Peter does not. Ephesians is addressed to Christian households in which the householder who is simultaneously husband, father, and slave owner is presumed to be a disciple of Jesus who is called to recognize himself as a fellow servant of Christ. 1 Peter presumes that the husbands and slave owners of the text are *not* Christians. A comparative reading of the two texts indicates different concerns. At the same time, 1 Peter is also an example of "Type II submission" operating in a different cultural situation. Christian slaves and wives are called to submit themselves willingly in order to witness to non-Christian slaveholders and husbands. Contrary to Grudem, this is not an example of "bait and switch," but of Christological subversion, taking on the form of a servant to win others to Christ.

(4) What about trajectory hermeneutics?

The expressions "trajectory hermeneutic" or "redemptive-movement hermeneutic" are most associated with the work of William Webb.[71] Webb's basic argument is that there is a parallel between the example of slavery in the Scriptures and the hierarchical subordination of women. Slavery as a practice existed in both the Old and New Testaments, and was never explicitly condemned. At the same time, there are places in the Bible in which the evils of slavery are ameliorated. In comparison to other Near Eastern cultures, the biblical practice of slavery was more humane, both in the Old Testament and in the New (e.g., Paul's modifying of the traditional "household codes"). Similarly, Webb argues that in both the Old and New Testaments, as with slavery, there was a modifying of ancient patriarchy that led to more rights and freedom for women than in surrounding cultures. As with slavery, Paul's transformation of the "household codes" leads to a greater freedom for women. Webb argues that this modification of both slavery and patriarchy points to a trajectory that does not yet find its fulfillment in the New Testament, but anticipates eventual emancipation for slaves and egalitarianism for women. What Webb calls a "Redemptive-Movement" hermeneutic interprets Scripture with an eye to its contemporary application that, to a certain extent, goes beyond the literal text of Scripture to the redemptive direction in which it is pointing. While not in agreement with every detail of Webb's argument, there are similarities between his position and the fourth position described above, "revolutionary subordination." As noted, writers such as Ben Witherington III and Craig Keener use the language of "trajectory" in their interpretations of Ephesians 5 and make similar comparisons between the eventual liberation of slaves and full equality for women.

Grudem has two primary objections against the "trajectory" hermeneutic: first, that it locates authority not in the teaching of the New Testament, but the goal to which it thinks the New Testament is moving; second, that moral discernment in a "trajectory" hermeneutic is "a subjective and indeterminate process that will lead to ethical chaos among Christians."[72]

Grudem's first objection is fundamentally an objection against the hermeneutical process itself. Since contemporary Christians do not live in the first-century Mediterranean world, any attempt to apply Scripture in our own current situation necessarily engages in a process of imaginative construal where we have to ask how what the Bible meant in its own time and culture speaks to our own very different situation. Standard contemporary discussions of hermeneutics make this point.[73] But it was also a point made by traditional theologians such as Martin Luther in *The Freedom of a Christian* and Richard Hooker in his *Laws of Ecclesiastical Polity*. Traditional hermeneutical distinctions between moral, ritual, and civil law presume that not everything in Scripture is permanently binding for all times and in all situations. Grudem's objection could equally have been raised against those Christians of the nineteenth century who argued for the abolition of slavery.

Second, a "redemptive hermeneutic" is not "subjective" in that what is being argued about the equality of men and women is based on the explicit teaching of Scripture. The basic argument is that one of the goals of redemption is to restore men and women to God's original intentions for them in creation—that the subordination of women to men is not part of God's intention in creation, but a result of the fall into sin, that Jesus' treatment of women as equals and his calling of women to be his disciples is an initial sign of this redemption, and that Paul's cruciform spirituality points to a mutual self-giving service that frees both men and women to be loving servants of one another as equals in Christ. Far from being "subjective" and "indeterminate," a redemptive hermeneutic involves seriously listening to the internal logic of Scripture rather than simply endorsing either the "shame culture" of the first-century Mediterranean world or the male-centered values of much Western culture and then reading those values back into the Bible.

Finally, the basic argument of an egalitarian or redemptive trajectory hermeneutic is that women in Christ enjoy the same freedom as men in Christ. This does not mean that there are no "gender differences" between men and women. Only men can be husbands, fathers, sons, and brothers. Only women can be wives, mothers, daughters, and sisters. Neither is it denied that there are legitimate places for authorities. Parents have authority over children in a way that children do not have over parents. Teachers have authority over students in a way that students do not have over teachers. Government officials have authority over the governed in a way that is not reversed. And, of course, there is an inherent difference between clergy and laity, and there is a certain kind of authority attached to ordination. But there are no gender-specific hierarchical roles in the sense that certain individuals alone always exercise authority over other individuals, and those roles are never reversed. Moreover, the gospels and the epistles challenge what it means to be an authority. The leadership demanded of Christians in the New Testament is a "servant-leadership" that is countercultural to the traditional notions of leadership in "shame cultures." Those in authority lead by voluntarily becoming servants of those who follow. Those who follow voluntarily "submit" without succumbing to coercion. And, of course, roles of servant-leadership are not gender-specific. It is not the case that men always command and women always obey. Given the presumed complementarian acknowledgment that women are neither less intelligent nor less emotionally stable than men, it is puzzling that complementarians make the assertion that women exercising the same kind of freedom that men have always exercised will lead to moral chaos.

8

Women in Worship and "Headship"

There are four key passages in the Pauline epistles to which complementarians appeal to argue against women's ordination or church leadership, based on an inherent subordination of women to male leadership and authority. The first is Ephesians 5:22-33 (discussed in the last chapter), in which Paul exhorts women to "submit" to their husbands, drawing a parallel between Christ as the "head" of the church and husbands as the "heads" of their wives. Ephesians 5 is distinguished from the other three passages in that the subject matter of the passage concerns household relations, and so does not touch directly on the place of women in the context of church worship.

To the contrary, 1 Corinthians 11:1-16 focuses on problems concerning worship, and is one of three Pauline passages that are the linchpins of the complementarian argument excluding women from participation in church office. The other two are 1 Corinthians 14:34-35 and 1 Timothy 2:9-15. While complementarians appeal to other passages of Scripture to argue for female subordination—the creation narratives of Genesis 1 and 2, the role of women in the Old Testament, Jesus' relationship to the apostles and to women in the gospels, Ephesians 5—it is only these three passages that provide specific references to the status of women in the context of worship in the churches of the New Testament. What immediately follows will discuss 1 Corinthians 11; the other two passages are examined in the next chapter.

PRELIMINARIES

1 Corinthians 11:1-16 is not only very difficult to interpret; it is also one of the passages most discussed by New Testament scholars. Anthony Thiselton's bibliography in his commentary on 1 Corinthians published in 2000 refers to eighty publications

on this passage.[1] More have appeared since. The following is a list of controversial issues in the passage:

(1) What is the issue of concern in the passage? Hairstyles (long or short hair, hair arrangements)? Head coverings of some sort (hats or scarves)? Veils?

(2) What is the meaning of κεφαλή (*kephalē*), the Greek word translated "head"?

(3) What does Paul mean by drawing a parallel between God as the head of Christ, Christ as the head of man, and man as the head of woman?

(4) Do "man" and "woman" in the passage refer to men and women in general or to husbands and wives?

(5) What does Paul mean in saying that man is the glory of God, but woman is the glory of man?

(6) What does Paul mean when he writes that a woman is to have "authority" over her head?

(7) What is the meaning of the reference to angels? Are they "messengers" or supernatural beings?

(8) What does one make of Paul's statement that "nature teaches" that men should not have long hair?

(9) When Paul states that "we have no such practice," to what practice is he referring?

There is no single agreement on the answer to any one of these questions. Indeed, numerous suggestions have been proposed; despite a lack of clarity on so many questions, the passage has become key to the discussion about women's "roles" in the church for complementarians.

The previous chapter on Ephesians 5 noted five distinct hermeneutical approaches to the passage: hierarchical, radical feminist, "love patriarchy," "revolutionary subordination," and egalitarian. Commentators on this passage in 1 Corinthians follow several general approaches:

(1) Hierarchical: This is the approach associated with complementarians. The primary concern in the passage is that, in worship, women have been engaging in practices in regard to head coverings or hair arrangement that "abandons the order that God has ordained."[2] Paul's intention is to re-establish proper order by reminding women of their subordination to men. The passage is interpreted hierarchically, with Paul's use of "head" language understood to mean that men exercise authority over women in the same way that God (as "head") exercises authority over Christ, Christ (as "head") exercises authority over the church, and man (as "head") exercises authority over woman. At the same time, this authority of men over women does not imply inequality. Headship is not "derogatory"; in the same way that Christ's

"subordination" to God does not challenge his ontological equality with God, so women's subordination to men does not demean them or imply their inferiority, but merely indicates that men and women exercise different roles.

(2) Paradoxical: A second position argues that Paul is inconsistent. In the first half of the passage, he teaches that women are subordinate to men; however, in the second half, he backtracks and corrects himself, arguing that men and women are interdependent on one another.[3]

(3) Egalitarian: The egalitarian position argues that Paul is not talking about hierarchy, but order in worship, and maintaining proper gender distinctions between men and women. "Head" does not mean "authority over," but is usually understood to mean "source." Paul's entire argument is that men and women are distinct but mutually interdependent, just as God and Christ are. The passage is not about authority of men over women at all, or of men having prominence over women. Indeed, Paul's only reference to "authority" is to women having their own authority over their own heads.

(4) Revolutionary subordination/Christological subversion: This position is similar to one already discussed in the previous chapter on Ephesians 5. While conceding that *kephalē* might possibly mean "authority," or, more likely, "topmost" or "preeminent," the argument is that the "total perspective" of the passage undermines any notion of permanent hierarchy. Rather, "freedom" and "knowledge" are both challenged by love. Paul insists on gender distinctions, but any competition about "authority" is challenged in light of a reciprocity and mutuality of relationships.[4] Paul's concerns about "head coverings" reflect his desire to promote appropriate public behavior within a specific culture, but the specific imperatives do not have transcultural permanence. Paul's major concern is to prevent conflict and promote harmony within the church. As in Ephesians, where the context is that of "mutual submission," so in 1 Corinthians the focus is on "mutual dependence."[5] An advocate of this approach suggests that *kephalē* in reference to man be understood as "honorable" or "prominent . . . in terms of the patriarchal structure of Paul's day." However, "Paul then redefines this 'honored' position not in terms of Christ's *Lordship* over the church, but his *kephalē* that is manifest in his love and servant-self-giving and other-nurturing and promoting aspects of his relationship to the church."[6]

(5) Modified egalitarian: A final position argues that the passage has been badly misinterpreted. Paul is not advocating a position in favor of head coverings, but is responding to a demand of the Corinthians in favor of head coverings. This position is held by Alan Padgett, and has received little support from other scholars, but is worth considering because Padgett's argument makes clear that there are genuine ambiguities in the original Greek text that lead to cautions about traditional readings.[7]

Two pieces of background information help to shed light on the context of Paul's discussion in 1 Corinthians. The first has to do with the role of women in Paul's ministry. The Book of Acts makes clear that women exercised significant roles in the churches to which Paul ministered. A number of the respondents to Paul's preaching were women (Acts 16:14; 17:4, 12, 34). Lydia was a leader in the church at Philippi, which met in her home (Acts 16:11-15). After Paul's release from prison in Philippi, Acts tells us that Paul visited Lydia, and also "the brothers" (Acts 16:40). Lydia's significance in the church is indicated in that she is the only person named, and the male members are simply referred to as "the brothers." Phoebe, the leader of the church at Cenchreae (a port of Corinth), is referred to in Romans 16:1 as a "deacon" (διάκονον, *diakonon*, mas.) and a "patron/leader" (προστάτις, *prostatis*).[8] While living in Corinth for two years, Paul stayed with Priscilla and Aquilla (Acts 18:1-4). Priscilla, along with her husband, is credited with teaching Apollos, mentioned in 1 Corinthians 1:12 as a significant leader in the church. Also called "Prisca," she is mentioned several times in Paul's letters (Rom. 16:3; 1 Cor. 16:19; 2 Tim. 4:19), and is mentioned as being with Paul when he wrote the letter to the Corinthians. Significantly, in four of the six New Testament references to Priscilla, her name is mentioned before her husband. Clearly women exercised significant roles in Paul's ministries, and the recipients of Paul's letter would have remembered Priscilla and Aquila as the couple with whom Paul lived during the two years that he worked with their church.[9]

Second, the overall context of Paul's discussion in 1 Corinthians is that of worship in the church. In order, he treats of problems of men and women leading worship (1 Cor. 11:2-16); problems concerning the Eucharist or Lord's Supper (11:17-34); problems concerning charismatic gifts (12:1-30; 14:1-25); problems concerning women and men participating in (but not leading) worship. In the center of this discussion, he places his famous hymn to love (1 Corinthians 13).

Two aspects of this discussion are significant for the discussion in 11:2-16. First, women were involved in leading worship in the Corinthian church, including public speaking ("prophesying") and were doing it on the same level as men. Paul does not discourage this practice, but encourages it. Second, the "hymn to love" at the center of the discussion provides a helpful context to the entire series of issues that Paul addresses.[10] Paul is correcting disorder in worship that is characterized by a lack of love and respect for fellow Christians. This provides an important clue as to the context of Paul's concerns in his discussion about "head coverings."

HEAD COVERINGS?

The first area of puzzlement in the passage has to do with the nature of the controversy that Paul was addressing. Scholars agree that Paul was addressing an issue of disorderly worship, but the specific cause for his concern remains unclear. The basic problem concerns the meaning of the Greek expressions κατὰ κεφαλῆς ἔχων (*kata kephalēs echōn*, "down from the head"; v. 4) and ἀκατακαλύπτῳ τῇ κεφαλῇ (*akatakaluptō tē kephalē*, "uncovered head"; v. 5). The two basic options are that Paul is either talking about some sort of head covering, headgear (a shawl, hood, tunic or veil), or, alternatively, about hair styles (either long or unbound hair).[11] Ultimately, the issue is undecidable. Both Paul and his hearers knew things we do not know. Regardless of the specific practice that initiated the debate, the primary issue seems to be "that which distracts attention from God or Christ in public worship by generating a discordant, semiotic clothing code or hairstyle code which inevitably draws attention to the self in a way which makes the person's head a source of shame for his or her own self-respect, the respect of congregation, and the honor of the Lord who in public worship should be the central focus of thought and attention." Thiselton summarizes: "[I]t constitutes attention-seeking behavior which thereby dishonor[s] God and shames the self."[12]

The overall context indicates that there were some within the Corinthian congregation who had concluded that Christian liberty entailed freedom from wearing in worship some traditional gender-marker distinguishing women from men, associated with either some kind of head covering or with some manner of wearing the hair. This practice had led to public scandal of some kind, and this is the issue that Paul is addressing. As Kenneth Bailey notes, "From the outset, it is clear that the issue is gender *distinction*, not gender *subordination*."[13]

HEADSHIP

Key to the theological issue in Paul's discussion is the meaning of "head" (κεφαλή, *kephalē*) in verse 3: "But I wish you to know that the head of every man is Christ, the head of woman is the man, and the head of Christ is God" (author translation). Paul here uses two analogies based on a comparison between a woman's literal head (part of her body) and her metaphorical head ("man" or "the man") and a comparison between an artificial "head covering" (whether an object of clothing or a hair style) and her natural head covering (her hair).[14] Paul is using a word play on the notion of "head," which is not only a part of a woman's body, but also, metaphorically, "the man," and part of the woman's body whose covering or hair style is in dispute.

As in the English "head," the normal and most usual meaning of the Greek word *kephalē* refers to that physical part of the human body at its topmost extreme above the neck, and which contains the eyes, ears, mouth, nose, and hair. The crucial question is, what does Paul mean by the metaphorical use of *kephalē* when he refers to the man as the woman's "head"? In modern English, "head" is used metaphorically to mean one who is an authority over, a master over subordinates, a "boss," someone who is "in charge." Was this how the metaphor of "head" would have been understood by native Greek speakers in the Mediterranean world in which Paul wrote 1 Corinthians? When Paul wrote that the man is "head" of the woman, are we to understand his point to be that the male of the human species is supposed to have authority over and exercise a position of superiority to the female, who is always supposed to be subordinate to the male?

In recent years, numerous authors have questioned whether this would have been the natural understanding of the metaphor by Paul's readers, and there has been a lengthy discussion. Alan Johnson notes, "From at least the middle of the twentieth century there has been an ongoing, sometimes acrimonious debate over the meaning of the metaphor 'head' (Greek, *kephalē*) in Paul's letters, especially his use in male-female contexts."[15] Gordon Fee states, "Paul's metaphorical use of 'head' in verse 3 has set off an unfortunate, but massive, debate that has often produced as much heat as light."[16] Similarly, Anthony Thiselton writes, "The history of claims about the meaning of κεφαλή is immense and daunting."[17] The literature suggests three possible meanings of the metaphor: (1) authority over; (2) source; or (3) preeminent or foremost, metaphorically drawn from the physiological head as the foremost part of the body.[18] Each one of the three possible meanings has been argued for respectively, identified above as the (1) hierarchical, (3) egalitarian, and (4) "Revolutionary subordination/Christological subversion" readings. What follows will discuss the arguments for each reading of the metaphor.

HIERARCHICAL

Complementarian Wayne Grudem is the single individual who has exerted the most effort to argue that "head" in 1 Corinthians 11:3 means "authority over." Grudem has written several studies arguing for this view.[19] Grudem's primary argument is based on citations from Greek lexicons[20] and comparisons with the use of *kephalē* in (primarily) non-biblical Greek examples. For example, Grudem complains that Thiselton "advances a meaning for κεφαλή that is found in no Greek Lexicon at all."[21] Grudem's key claim is that in ancient Greek literature, *kephalē* normally means "authority over/ruler." He claims that "no examples have ever been found where person A is called the 'head' of person B and person A is not in a position of authority over person B."[22] His primary examples include military and political examples of authority from the LXX translation of the Old Testament (these will be discussed later), the handful of controversial passages from the New Testament, military and political examples from pagan and Jewish extrabiblical Greek literature, and, more recently, passages in patristic literature in which he argues that "authority over" or "rule" is the best interpretation of the metaphor for "head."[23]

The complementarian position has not essentially changed since its original presentation in George W. Knight III's, *The Role Relationship of Men and Women.* The basic argument is as follows. First, Paul establishes a "hierarchy of authority" based on the "role relationship" of men and women. Knight argued that Paul establishes "the role relationship of men and women by placing it in the hierarchy of headships (*kephalē*)." As Christ is the "authority of every man," so there is a "chain of subordination" between man and woman. This notion of "authority over" or "headship" is the primary meaning of man being the "head" of woman.[24]

Second, Paul establishes this hierarchy by describing a parallel between the "headship" of man over woman, and the "headship" of God over Christ. Thomas Schreiner claims: "Paul is saying that Christ is the authority over every man, man is the authority over woman, and God is the authority over Christ. Since Paul appeals to the relation between members of the Trinity, it is clear that he does not view the relations described here as merely cultural, or the result of the fall." As Christ's subordination to the authority of the Father does not imply an inequality between God (the Father) and Christ (the Son), so the subordination of women to male authority does not imply an inequality between men and women.[25]

Third, there is an appeal to the order of creation. Knight suggests that Paul's appeal in verses 8-10 to the order of creation in Genesis 2:18-25—"For man was not made from woman but woman from man. Neither was man created for woman, but woman for man"—establishes the "determined role relationship." Woman was created to be a "helper" for man. Man was not created to help woman. Schreiner also argues for a difference of "role relationships" on the basis of Paul's appeal to the creation narratives: "Paul obviously interpreted Genesis 2 as revealing a distinction in roles between men and women."[26] Schreiner has moved from a distinction between the sexes as male and female—which is in the texts, both Paul and Genesis—to a distinction of authority and subordination in roles, something mentioned nowhere in either text.

Finally, complementarians appeal to Paul's reference to "head covering" in verse 10 as evidence that Paul wants women to wear head coverings as a symbol of male authority over women: "A woman who does not wear a head covering both disgraces herself and brings dishonor on her authority, who is man." Complementarian scholars assert that the word ἐξουσία (*exousia*, "authority") in verse 10 refers to the woman's head covering as a sign of *male authority* over woman: "Paul wants women to wear a head covering in order to show that they are submissive to male headship."[27]

DOES "HEAD" MEAN AUTHORITY?

Is it correct to understand Paul's use of the metaphor of *kephalē* ("head") in this passage to mean "one who has authority over," and the wearing of a head covering by a woman in worship as a symbol of male authority over her as complementarians claim? Significant numbers of modern New Testament scholars disagree. The following arguments show that "head" in 1 Corinthians 11 almost certainly does not mean "authority over."

First, as noted in the previous chapter, in the Old Testament the Hebrew word for "head" (*rosh*) is used literally and, when used metaphorically, often does refer to one in authority. When the LXX translators of the Old Testament into Greek translated literal uses of *rosh* referring to the physical head, they naturally tended to use the Greek word *kephalē*. However, as numerous scholars point out, when the LXX translators translated *rosh* used as a metaphor meaning "ruler," they almost never translated it simply as "head" (*kephalē*), but rather used a Greek word that literally meant "ruler," such as ἄρχων (*archōn*). This implies that the LXX translators did not consider the Greek word *kephalē* normally to have been understood to mean one in authority. Although Grudem's main argument for "authority" is an appeal to those handful of verses in the LXX, as Gordon Fee points out, "The few instances (six in all) where they do not do this . . . are simply exceptions that prove the rule."[28]

Philip Payne argues that the use of *kephalē* referring to someone in authority first appears in the LXX, and is best explained in terms of Hebrew influence.[29] It is significant that in Grudem's most recent list of fifty examples of "head" meaning authority in ancient literature, all of the examples are from the LXX until he lists Josephus, Philo, and Plutarch (all first or second century). Apart from references to the New Testament, which are controverted, the rest of Grudem's references are to the second century or later. This means that (apart from the LXX and Philo), Grudem does not provide a single example in ancient Greek literature here prior to Paul in which "head" means authority.[30]

This leads to what was referred to above as the "battle of the lexicons." Contrary to Grudem, Payne argues that "authority" is *not* a common meaning in Greek lexicons. As mentioned above, Grudem listed six lexicons where "authority" appears as a meaning for *kephalē*. Payne lists nineteen where it does not so appear.[31] Experts in the field can decide for themselves whose appeal to which lexicons carries more weight.

It should be noted that, contrary to Grudem, it is not the case that when "head" is used metaphorically of persons in ancient literature, it always refers to those who exercise authority over others. Payne lists several examples where such a reading would be impossible, since the person referred to as "head" was long dead, and so could not exercise authority over those of whom he was listed as "head." In these cases, at least, a better translation than authority would be "progenitor" or "ancestor."[32]

Second, Paul is unique in the ancient world in using *kephalē* as an example of a relationship between man and woman.[33] Accordingly, Grudem's examples based on political or military uses of the metaphor of "headship" are beside the point. Moreover, the political examples on which Grudem draws are always examples of a "one to many" correspondence, of a single person who is "head" over many. Paul certainly does not understand the relationship between men and women to be like that between a single military commander and numerous soldiers or a single ruler and numerous followers. Both the use of the metaphor in a gender relationship and as a "one to one" correspondence thus mark significant differences between Paul's usage and Grudem's examples. Accordingly, modern exegetes argue that Paul is using what is called a "live metaphor." Rather than simply appropriating a "dead metaphor" already in use ("leader" and "followers"), Paul is creating a new metaphor by his analogy. The meaning of the metaphor must then be found in the context of Paul's own argument, not by looking to outside sources. Grudem's chief error (as well as that of some of his opponents) is to presume that the key to Paul's use of the metaphor "head" in this passage is to be found in how the metaphor is used in the LXX, and in pagan sources outside of Paul's own argument.[34] Since there are no examples outside of Paul to use "head" to describe the relationship between man and woman, it is only Paul's own context that can determine what he means.

Apart from the use of the metaphor "head" itself, there is absolutely nothing in the passage to indicate that Paul is concerned with issues of hierarchy. If Paul had meant to say that men are in authority over women, he had Greek terms he could have used: ἐξουσία (*exousia*, authority), ἄρχων (*archōn*, ruler), or κύριος (*kurios*, lord). Paul uses *exousia* (authority) only once in the passage, and it is in reference to the woman's own authority, not to the authority of others over her (v. 10). This verse has been misleadingly translated to read that the woman should have a "symbol of authority over her head," but "symbol of" is supplied by English translators. The Greek simply states that the woman herself should have authority over her own head, the exact opposite of what some English translations misleadingly suggest. Accordingly, those who read the passage hierarchically as implying that it is about the authority of men over women are reading things into the passage that are simply not there.[35]

If then the passage is not about the authority of men over women, what might be the point that Paul is arguing here? What follows will summarize several readings of Paul's argument in 1 Corinthians 11, beginning with the "egalitarian" argument that when Paul uses the metaphor of "head" in this passage, he means not "authority" but "source."

EGALITARIAN READINGS

Egalitarian biblical scholars argue that there are numerous precedents for the metaphor "head" being used to mean "source" in ancient literature. In Hebrew, *Rosh Hashanah* means the "head of the year." The first day of the year does not have authority over the rest of the year, but is the day from which the rest of the year follows. According to Psalm 111:10, "The fear of the Lord is the *head* [*rosh*] of wisdom." Modern English translations translate this as: "The fear of the Lord is the *beginning* of wisdom."[36] Philip Payne states that "In contrast [to 'authority'], 'source' is an established meaning for κεφαλή listed from the earliest Greek lexicons to the present."[37] Payne lists several references to rivers as "sources," but also a reference to Philo, where Esau is described as the progenitor or "head" of the clan; Philo identifies "the virtuous one" as the "head" of the human race from whom they draw their life. For Philo, the Ten Commandments are the "heads" (κεφάλαια), the "roots," the "sources" (αρχαί) the perennial fountains of ordinances. The *Apocalypse of Moses* says that lust is the "head" of every sin. According to the *Orphic Fragment*, "Zeus is the head, the middle, and from Zeus all things exist." Several manuscripts have *archē* (source) instead of *kephalē* ("head") for this saying.[38]

The above does not prove that Paul understood *kephalē* to mean "source" in 1 Corinthians 11, but it demonstrates that this was at least a possible or likely meaning. Given that Paul's own use of the metaphor in the passage is the most likely clue to discern his meaning, verses 8-9 and 12 would serve to corroborate "source" as a likely meaning. Verse 8 focuses on the creation account in which the woman was made from the man's side, and the woman created as man's partner or helper "fit for him" (cf. Gen. 2:20-23). Verse 12 continues with the theme of origins, noting that man is now born of woman, and "all things (or all persons) come from God." Assuming that "source" or "origin of" is the correct understanding of "head" in verse three, Paul's meaning would be: (1) The origin of every man is Christ, that is, Christ is the origin of creation; compare 8:6: There is "one Lord Jesus Christ, through whom are all things and through whom we exist." (2) The origin of woman is man. That is, woman (*'issa*) is taken out of man (*'is*) (Gen. 2:23). (3) The origin of Christ is God. God the Father is the agent of the incarnation. Payne notes that in each of the statements, the second member is highlighted with an article. Since in the other two cases, the article identifies a specific entity ("Christ," "God"), it would follow that "the man" is not a generic reference to "man in general"—the head (authority) of (every) woman is (every) man— but rather, the head (source/origin) of woman is "the man," that is, the first man, Adam, from whom the first woman was taken.[39]

What is the point of Paul's listing of the figures in the specific order in which he lists them: head of man = Christ; head of woman = man; head of Christ = God?

Grudem argues that the order reflects a hierarchy of relationships: "Paul is here referring to a relationship of authority between God the Father and God the Son, and he is making a parallel between the relationship in the Trinity and the relationship between the husband and wife in marriage."[40] To the contrary, as Fee and Payne point out, the order simply reflects the chronology of salvation history: all things were created through Christ; the man is the "source" of the woman's being; God [the Father] is the source of Christ's incarnation.[41]

What is the point of verse 7: "For a man ought not to cover his head, since he is the image and glory of God, but woman is the glory of man"? On a first reading, Paul seems to be at odds with the plain sense of Genesis 1:27 that the image of God consists in being created "male and female." Is Paul suggesting that only men (male human beings) are created in the image of God? Not even Grudem, despite his affirmation of female subordination, is willing to read Paul this way.[42] Schreiner argues that the point of the verse is twofold: (1) woman should honor man because he is her source; (2) the woman was created to help man in his tasks. No egalitarian would likely disagree with these two affirmations, but Schreiner goes on to conclude that Paul is interpreting Genesis 2 "as revealing a distinction in roles between men and women." Schreiner claims that the purpose of this distinction of roles becomes clear when we remember that "Paul means 'authority' by the word *head* in verse 3." Of course, this is the real issue of disagreement, and it has been argued above that Paul does *not* mean "authority" in his use of the "head" metaphor in verse 3.

Everything depends here on whether Genesis 2 teaches subordination of woman to man in creation itself and not as a consequence of the fall, and whether Paul himself interpreted Genesis 2 to teach such a subordination.[43] Fee suggests that Paul is reflecting the Genesis text in that the man by himself is not complete. The animals are not adequate and man needs a companion who is like him, but also different: "She is thus man's glory because she 'came from man' and was created 'for him.' She is not thereby subordinate to him, but *necessary* for him. She exists to his honor as the one who having come from man is the one companion suitable for him, so that he might be complete and that together they might form humanity."[44] Fee notes that there is no use of "glory" anywhere in the Bible to suggest that "glory" implies subordination. The context has to do not with authority and subordination, but with "shame" and "glory." The woman who is intended to be the man's glory is behaving in such a way as to bring "shame" on him.[45]

Note that complementarians and egalitarians are not in disagreement about the basic meaning of the passage here. Both agree that Paul is teaching that woman came from man, that she is intended as man's glory, and that she is man's companion and helper. Disagreement arises about the implications of this, and arguments to interpret the notion of "glory" in terms of authority and subordination or equality and companionship arise from prior assumptions about both the meaning of the Genesis accounts of creation and Paul's own argument earlier in this passage.

WHOSE AUTHORITY?

In a text full of difficulties, certainly one of the most difficult sections has been verse 10. This is the only place in the text where the Greek word for authority (ἐξουσία, *exousia*) is actually used. A literal translation of the passage would be: "Therefore the woman ought to have authority (ἐξουσίαν ἔχειν, *exousian echein*) over her head because of the angels." The straightforward sense of the text is that it is speaking of the woman's own authority, not of someone else's authority over her, but translators have been reluctant to translate the text this way. The KJV reads: "For this cause ought the woman to have power on *her* head because of the angels." This is not a bad literal translation, but what does it mean for a woman to have "power" on her head? The RSV reads: "That is why a woman ought to have a veil on her head, because of the angels." But *exousia* simply does not mean "veil" or "head covering." The ESV (as well as the NASB and the NKJ), reflecting the complementarian assumptions of many of the translators, reads: "That is why a wife ought to have a symbol of authority on her head, because of the angels." But the words "symbol of" are found nowhere in the Greek text, and make the text say the opposite of what it actually says by implying that the "authority" in the text is not that of the woman herself, but of someone else over her. The *New Living Translation*, admittedly a paraphrase, goes furthest in reading something into the text that is not there: "For this reason, and because the angels are watching, a woman should wear a covering on her head to show she is under authority." The most recent version of the NIV, which is often understood to be somewhat of a paraphrase rather than a literal translation, actually gets it right: "It is for this reason that a woman ought to have authority over her own head, because of the angels."

Schreiner claims that the verse should be translated "symbol of authority" based on context: "[T]he issue is a woman's proper role relationship to a man," and, since Schreiner has already insisted that this role relationship is one of submission to male authority, the verse can only be interpreted in a way that confirms this authority.[46] But this is question-begging. To the contrary, Fee asserts: "This construction (subject, the verb *echein* ['has/have'] with *exousia* as the object followed by the preposition *epi*) would be read in the only way it is known to occur in the language: the subject has the authority 'over' the object of the preposition."[47]

Assuming then that the passage means what a straightforward reading suggests that it means—that a woman is to exercise authority over her own head—what might this mean in the context of Paul's argument? And what does this authority have to do with "the angels?" Fee suggests that Paul is affirming that women do indeed have authority. Nevertheless, in light of what he has already written, they should exercise that authority in the correct way—by wearing a head covering.[48] Bailey suggests that a clue can be found in the use of the Greek word διά (*dia*) throughout verses 8-11, sometimes translated "for" and sometimes translated "because of." "For man was not created *for* [*dia*] woman, but woman *for* [*dia*] man. *Because of* [*dia*] this, the woman should have authority on the head *because of* [*dia*] the angels." Bailey suggests that *dia* should be translated "because of" in all four instances. Verse 9 refers to the creation story. Woman is created as a "helper" (Hebrew *'ezer*) to man not as someone who is weak and a servant, but rather as someone who comes to the man's rescue because he is alone and insufficient in himself. The key focus here is on mutuality and interdependence. The *this* in verse 10 ("because of this") refers back to the creation story where the woman is created to be the companion and partner of man. The woman should therefore have a sign of authority on her head when she prophesies in the worshiping congregation: "[T]he head covering [is] a visible symbol of [her own] authority to proclaim a prophetic word to the congregation."[49]

What about the angels? Payne points to biblical passages referring to the presence of angels in worship; Bailey suggests that "because of this" may refer to the presence of angels at creation. As the angels rejoiced at the new creation, so they are now rejoicing in the presence of Christian worship, and women should worship in such a manner that the focus is on God, not on themselves, so that the angels can again rejoice.[50] The reference is mysterious, but these at least are plausible suggestions.

INTERDEPENDENCE

Verses 11 and 12 mark the conclusion of Paul's argument; verses 13 to 16 are arguably supplementary, but do not add anything substantial to the theological argument itself. The word πλήν (*plēn*), translated "nonetheless" in verse 11, indicates that Paul is introducing something new into the argument while at the same time connecting what he is now writing to what has come before.[51] The passage is connected with what immediately precedes. The sequence "woman/man"—"Nonetheless, in the Lord woman is not independent of man"—makes clear that the authority in the preceding verse 10 must refer to the woman's own authority. If verse 10 were referring to the man's authority over the woman, Paul would have written, "Nonetheless, in the Lord man is not independent of woman."[52]

Crucial to the logic of Paul's argument is the parallel that he draws between verses 8-9 and verses 11-12. The following outline, adapted from Fee and Bailey, but drawing from other sources as well, demonstrates the parallelism:[53]

A	Not is man from [ἐκ, *ek*] woman,	a
	but . . . woman from [ἐκ, *ek*] man (v. 8; cf. Gen. 2:21-22)	b
B	Not was created man for the sake/because of [διὰ, *dia*] the woman,	a
	but . . . woman for the sake of/because of [διὰ, *dia*] the man (v. 9; cf. Gen 2:18)	b

Because of [διὰ, *dia*] this, the woman should have authority over her head, because of [διὰ, *dia*] the angels. (v. 10)

Nonetheless [πλὴν, *plēn*]

B'	Neither woman without [χωρὶς, *chōris*] man,	b
	nor . . . man without [χωρὶς, *chōris*] woman,	a
	in the Lord; (v. 11)	
A'	*For* just as the woman from [ἐκ, *ek*] the man,	b
	so also the man through [διὰ, *dia*] the woman	a
	and all (people) [πάντα, *panta*] from [ἐκ, *ek*] God (v. 12)	

Cf. 1 Cor. 8:6:

For us there is one God the Father, from [ἐκ, *ek*] whom are all (things) [πάντα, *panta*] and we in him, and one Lord Jesus Christ, through [δι᾽, *di*] whom are all (things) [πάντα, *panta*] and we through [δι᾽, *di*] him.

In this passage, "Paul is the first writer known to draw theological significance from the fact that every man is born through [*dia*] woman."[54] A comparison of 8-9 and 11-12 shows that Paul deliberately uses parallel constructions and the same prepositions (*ek* and *dia*) in both passages.[55] A comparison with 1 Corinthians 8:6 shows a parallel structure, and, once again, the same propositions as well as the same use of *panta* (all things or all people). Paul is reflecting on the role of men and women through a reading of the Genesis creation texts, but also reinterpreting creation through a Christocentric lens. "In the Lord," women are not without/separated from men, just as all men and all women have been created by God through Christ. This is parallel to verse 3; Christ is the "head" (creative source) of man, as man is the "head" (instrumental source) of woman, and the "head" (source) of Christ's incarnation is God the Father.

Note the parallels between verses 9 and 12. Man was not created because of [*dia*] the woman. However, man is born through [*dia*] the woman. Verses 11-12 repeat the terminology of 8-9 to show that the temporal priority of man in creation as the "source" of woman is balanced by the order of nature (natural birth) in which woman is the source of all men. Paul's juxtaposition here thus undermines any notion of subordination based on temporal order.[56]

The context indicates that *panta* should likely be translated "all people."[57] Woman originally came from man in creation. Man now comes from woman through childbirth. All people come from God in creation. "In the Lord" men and women are not separate, but interdependent.

What then is the meaning of *chōris* ("separate from/without")? Paul's statement about woman having authority over her own head might have led women to assert their independence. Instead, Paul is affirming that in Christ, men and women are equal and interdependent. He further justifies this by noting their interdependence in origin.

> To summarize, the normal meaning of χωρὶς [*chōris*] virtually demands that this statement be understood as an affirmation that in Christ there is no separation between woman and man. The introductory "however" shows that this is a new perspective, one that Paul regards as essential. "In the Lord" shows that it is something established in Christ, not something that was already established in society apart from Christ. . . . It does this [affirms the equality of man and woman in the Lord] by pointing out that every man's source in woman balances woman's source in Adam and by asserting that all this comes from God. Thus, the equal standing of woman and man in Christ is rooted in creation and biology and has its source in God. . . . Paul clearly does not want his specific instructions regarding the "head covering" issues raised by the Corinthian church to support any subordination of woman to man in Christ.[58]

Paul is thus defending here the equality of the sexes in Christ. Both men and women are called upon to lead and to speak ("prophesy") in the worship assembly. While it is true that woman was created for man's glory (v. 9), this does not imply that woman was created as man's subordinate, but as his helper, one who is both different from and like him. God has arranged things "in the Lord" in such a manner that men and women are interdependent and need one another.[59]

The above summarizes both the hierarchical/complementarian and egalitarian readings of 1 Corinthians 11. What immediately follows will examine two more recent readings that do not part company with the egalitarian reading, but bring into account slightly different emphases or readings of the text.

REVOLUTIONARY SUBORDINATION/CHRISTOLOGICAL SUBVERSION

The previous chapter on Ephesians 5 and "mutual subordination" identified a reading of Paul's argument as "revolutionary subordination" or "Christological subversion." In recent years, a similar reading of Paul's argument in 1 Corinthians 11 has appeared. Judith M. Gundry-Volf wrote an article on "Gender and Creation in 1 Corinthians 11:12-16" which explored a different interpretation from that of either the hierarchical/complementarian or egalitarian readings. This article influenced Anthony Thiselton's reading in his monumental commentary *The First Epistle to the Corinthians*, and, more recently, Alan F. Johnson in his own commentary. What follows will primarily focus on Johnson's own reading, as influenced by Gundry-Volf.[60]

Gundry-Volf makes the argument that Paul's concern is to correct a worship practice that, by bringing social shame on both men and women, was bringing shame on the church. Both men and women were involved in the practice, which blurred gender distinctions between men and women. Paul's concern was that men and women were bringing shame on their respective "heads," but also that the practice hurt the church's witness to prospective outsiders. Paul was arguing for a worship practice in respect to hairstyles that symbolized mutual respect, while acknowledging clear gender identity distinctions. He refers to the creation accounts in Genesis 1 and 2 to argue not only for gender differentiation, but also for a gender hierarchy concerning places of honor and respect. Thus, Paul affirms identical roles for men and women in worship while also maintaining gender distinction with some traces of patriarchal hierarchy.[61]

At the same time, Paul provides a second reading of creation in light of redemption in Christ. In verses 11-12, Paul argues that there is an interdependence of man and woman based on equality in Christ. Both men and women are mutually the source of one another's existence, the man the source of the woman through creation, and the woman the source of the man through childbirth. Gender distinctions are thus upheld but are relativized in Christ, "resulting in an egalitarian community patterned according to the redeemed creation, or new creation relationships, rather than according to fallen cultural norms."[62]

Johnson acknowledges that, on this reading, there is a "clear tension" between verses 2-10 and 11-16. Gundry-Volf suggests that Paul was maintaining a practice in which women and men were equally allowed to engage in public worship by praying and prophesying; however, by respecting the patriarchal social patterns of sexual distinctions in the surrounding culture, the church's mission to the world could be preserved.[63]

Johnson largely follows Gundry-Volf's reading, with some exceptions. He agrees that the context for Paul's discussion is social shame and not the sexual temptation of men, the subordination of women to men, or homosexuality. Paul's concern in the passage is mission to outsiders.[64] Johnson also agrees with Gundry-Volf (in a reading also followed by Thiselton) that the best understanding of Paul's "head" (*kephalē*) metaphor is not "'authority over' ... since there is no reference to submission (*hypotassō*) ... and no strict hierarchy ... beginning with God, then Christ, then man, then woman." Instead, he suggests, there is an "honor order of pairs." Man honors Christ;

woman honors man, Christ honors God. In each case, "head" is the "honored member" or "archetype" of the other. Johnson suggests a combination of "preeminent" or "honored" with "source." The "head" is the "honored source" of the pair: "[I]f there are any patriarchal tones in Paul's honored person pairs, it is muted and does not figure significantly in the passage in any specific way."[65]

Johnson suggests that in 7-9, Paul is drawing on the creation narratives to echo motifs resonant in the "shame/honor" culture of the Mediterranean world: glory, honor, and shame. Paul follows rabbinic exegesis, focusing on the man as the "glory of God" to suggest that the man should bring "glory" to God rather than the "shame" of a non-masculine hairstyle. Conversely, the woman is the "glory" of man, and so should not wear her hair in a manner that brings shame on the man, according to the cultural standards of the dominant culture. At the same time, the woman is the man's "glory" in that she is created from man, but is also his "helper" as a "partner," a companion who overcomes his loneliness. She should not then shame her partner by rejecting the cultural symbol of her womanhood.[66]

At the same time, Johnson acknowledges that "authority over" (ἐξουσία ἐπί, *exousia epi*; v. 10) refers to the woman's own authority over her head, not the man's authority over her. He considers two possibilities as equally likely—either that the woman has authority or control over her own head, or that she has the authority to lead in worship by prophesying. He acknowledges that there is no satisfactory interpretation for "because of the angels," but suggests that this is referring in some sense to the angels' presence during the church's worship. He concludes, "In any event it is clear that the text does not support the idea of male authority over the woman actually or symbolically."[67]

Johnson suggests that the *plēn* ("however") of verse 11 suggests a contrast to what had gone before, which is indicated by comparisons with verses 7-9. Instead of divergences ("man is not . . . but woman is") there are now similarities and parallels ("neither woman . . . nor man," "just as woman . . . so also man"). The priority of the man is now replaced with interdependence: "neither man without woman," . . . "man is through the woman." Paul indicates a new rationale for this new interpretation of the relation between man and woman: "in the Lord."[68]

In verses 11-12, Paul once again looks at origins. The woman's origin from man in creation is compared with man's origin from woman—every man is born through (*dia*) woman: "This seems to point in the direction of Paul's actually inverting the hierarchical relationship between the sexes and breaking out of the strictly patriarchal system for constructing gender identity and roles."[69]

How should one assess this new interpretation of Paul? It reads not so much as a rejection of the egalitarian reading as a qualifying or tweaking of it. By focusing on the issue of "honor" and "shame," the new reading pushes the passage more in the direction of "revolutionary subordination" or "Christological subversion." Rather than dwelling exclusively on the setting of Christian worship, this reading suggests that another audience must be kept in mind as well—that Paul is concerned at least as much about how the church will come across to outsiders as he is to the church's own internal order. Interpreting the "head" metaphor in terms of "honor" fits in with this shift, but does not significantly depart from understanding "head" in terms of "source." As Johnson reads *kephalē*, "honored source" is the best reading.

Where the reading might be problematic is in its assumption that there is a "tension" between what Paul writes in verses 2-9 and 11-12. Rather than reading these parts of Paul's argument as parallel ways of saying the same thing (as in egalitarian readings), 11-12 is seen in some sense as in contrast to, or perhaps even as a corrective of the earlier verses. This is similar to the view that Paul apparently contradicted himself, identified as the "paradoxical" reading above. Is it plausible that Paul would not have seen as in tension what so clearly seems to be a tension to the contemporary reader? Here is where the egalitarian reading seems preferable. Paul is not correcting what he wrote in the earlier verses so much as preventing incorrect interpretations that some might draw from what he had written. That the woman is derived from the man in creation does not imply a subordination, but rather an equality of partnership, and verses 11-12 make this emphatically clear.

MODIFIED EGALITARIAN: READING "FROM THE BOTTOM UP"

Perhaps the most provocative reading of 1 Corinthians 11 is that of Alan Padgett.[70] Padgett argues that, as in other cases, Paul's argument is best understood if read "from the bottom up." That is, the logic behind Paul's sometimes meandering argument is often best understood if one first reads his conclusion. Padgett suggests that the best clue as to the practice that Paul is addressing is found in verses 13-15, which, he argues, have been seriously misinterpreted. In verse 15, Paul writes: "For hair is given to her [by nature] instead of (ἀντὶ, *anti*) a covering." In verse 16, Paul appeals to the custom of the churches, and in verses 13 to 15, he provides an argument from nature. The controversial custom becomes clear in verse 13: "Judge for yourselves; is it proper for an uncovered woman to pray to God?" Given that there is no punctuation in the original Greek, Padgett suggests that this could as easily be read as a statement, "Judge for yourselves; it is proper for an uncovered woman to pray to God." He argues that verses 14-15 should only be properly read as a statement, not a question: "But nature itself has not taught you that if a man has long hair it is a shame while if a woman has long hair it is her glory; for hair is given to her instead of a covering." Modern translations and most interpreters treat 14-15 as a question—"Does not nature itself teach you that if a man wears long hair it is a disgrace for him, but if a woman has long hair, it is her glory?"—and commentators treat Paul's use of the word "nature" as referring to "social custom."[71] But Padgett argues that Paul is rather arguing against social custom, and instead is appealing behind custom to nature itself: there is no shame for a man to have long hair, and nature gives women long hair instead of the coverings that are placed on women's heads for social reasons. This is the natural reading of the passage, and Padgett notes that the Latin Vulgate correctly translates the verse as a statement, not a question. The custom that Paul was arguing *against* was the Corinthian social custom that it was shameful for men to have long hair, and for women to pray uncovered.[72] Thus, Padgett suggests that the position concerning women's head coverings in verses 4-7 is not Paul's own, but a quotation from the Corinthians whom he is correcting. Similarly, most scholars consider Paul's statement in 1 Corinthians 7:1—"It is good for a man not to touch a woman"—to be a quotation from his Corinthian audience, not his own views. Padgett suggests that when Paul uses the phrase "I want you to know" (11:3) in 1 Corinthians, he is correcting a mistaken Corinthian view (cf. 10:1, 12:1).[73]

Returning then to Padgett's "bottom up" reading, verses 11-12 provide a corrective to the Corinthian custom. "In the Lord," Paul argues, even though there is a temporal priority of man before woman in the creation story, men are now born of women. This balance between men and women is further emphasized in Paul's assertion that "all people come from God." The balance between men and women is based on the same Christological principle that Paul used in Galatians to argue for the breaking down of the division between Jew and Gentile, and the overcoming of the cultural mark of circumcision. The implication of Paul's argument in verses 11-12 is along the same lines: "In the Lord, these differences of dress are of no importance. Social customs of dress, which distinguish male and female, should not inhibit a woman or man from praying or prophesying in the worship of the Lord."[74]

This argument is further illustrated by verse 10 in which Paul writes that "a woman ought to have authority over her own head." Padgett points to the acknowledgment of New Testament scholars that the passage refers to a woman's own authority, but to their confusion about what this might mean. To the contrary, "What Paul says is simple enough: women ought to have freedom to wear their hair however they want to in church."[75]

Padgett's conclusion then, is that, in this passage, Paul was actually arguing for the opposite of what many have assumed. Paul was arguing for more liberty for men and women in Christ. He was only concerned with hairstyles or head coverings because of a Corinthian theology that was based on a false understanding of the relation between men and women. Paul was arguing against the notion that men alone were the glory of God by arguing that woman is the glory of man and thus should have freedom over her own head.[76]

Padgett's reading is intriguing, and it seems to solve a lot of the problems that arise from conventional readings of the passage. Padgett is convincing when he suggests that it would seem to be inconsistent with Paul's theology expressed elsewhere to insist that a social practice like wearing head coverings was indispensable. After all, in Paul's discussion of circumcision, he had argued vigorously against just such a social practice that was firmly entrenched in Jewish culture, and explicitly endorsed in the Old Testament. In addition, a reading of verse 14 as a statement rather than a question just makes sense. Nature does not teach that it is a disgrace for men to have long hair. Views about the propriety of hair length are social constructions and, for that reason, New Testament scholars who interpret Paul's statement here as a question understand Paul to be referring to a social construction, although he speaks of "nature." Finally, the plain sense reading of verse 10 is that a woman should have authority over her own head. That is, it should be her own decision whether she wears a head covering or has a particular hairstyle.

As inviting as Padgett's reading might be, the main problem with it is in making the case that the position that Paul describes in the first half of the chapter is actually the Corinthian position that Paul is opposing rather than the position that Paul himself is endorsing. Payne suggests that Paul's "I want you to know" is evidence that the Corinthians had not been opposing Paul, but simply needed new instruction. He writes that nothing in the passage indicates that what follows verse 3 is a quotation from Paul's opponents.[77] Fee refers to Padgett's "improbable suggestion";[78] Thiselton notes that when Paul cites a slogan from the Corinthians elsewhere, his citation is succinct, unlike the supposed citation in the first part of chapter 11.[79] While Padgett's proposal is intriguing, it is not one that has been endorsed by a significant number of New Testament scholars.

CONCLUSION

The purpose of the above discussion has been to argue that there is nothing in Paul's discussion of worship in 1 Corinthians 11:1-16 to suggest that he is advocating for a subordination of women to men, or restricting the permission of women to lead worship and to speak publicly (prophesy) in the assembly. The complementarian reading that suggests that Paul is advocating a hierarchical "headship" of the authority of men over women or is postulating different "role relationships" is simply not in the passage. Much about the passage is difficult to understand, and it should not be surprising that New Testament scholars have offered several different suggestions about what the problem was that Paul was addressing, and about the details of his solution. Nonetheless, despite disagreements about detail, the above readings point to a consensus about the main themes of Paul's argument. What conclusions might then be drawn from the passage?

First, both men and women are to engage equally in the practice of leading in worship and speaking in the public assembly. Paul's concern in the passage is not to restrict the public role of one sex or another in worship, but to stipulate that worship should be conducted in a manner that does not create public scandal.[80]

Second, "in the Lord" man and woman are not separate from or independent from another, but interdependent on one another. Paul's use of "head" language has nothing to do with a hierarchy of men over women, or with "role relationships" of authority of men over women.

Third, if man is the source of woman in the Genesis creation narrative, he is only the instrumental source. Woman is the instrumental source of man through childbirth, and God is the ultimate source of both man and woman, who equalizes their standing in Christ.

Fourth, that woman is man's glory does not mean that she was created for his purposes or utilitarian ends, but that men and women both need and are mutually dependent on one another.

Finally, even in the new age of redemption in Christ, sexual and gender distinctions are maintained; however, that does not mean that one sex is subordinate to the other, but that both are interdependent on and need one another.[81]

POSTSCRIPT: SUBORDINATION AND THE TRINITY

The theme of God's authority over Christ has become a central issue in this debate. In his earlier essay, Schreiner argued only for an "economic subordination" of the Son to the Father,[82] but Grudem has more recently insisted not only on an "economic subordination," but on an eternal subordination within the immanent or ontological Trinity itself. Grudem states:

> The differences in authority among Father, Son, and Holy Spirit are the only interpersonal differences that the Bible indicates exist eternally among the members of the Godhead. . . . [F]or all eternity there has been a difference in authority, whereby the Father has authority over the Son that the Son does not have over the Father. . . . These differences, in which there is authority and submission to authority, seem to be the means by which Father, Son and Holy Spirit differ from one another and can be differentiated from one another.

Grudem continues: "If we did not have such differences in authority in the relationships among the members of the Trinity, then we would not know of any differences at all, and it would be unclear whether there *are* any differences among the persons of the Trinity."[83] Grudem rejects the "egalitarian claim" that had earlier been affirmed by his fellow complementarian Schreiner of a merely economic subordination of the Son to the Father: "[T]he egalitarian claim that the Son's subordination to the Father was only for his time on earth is surely incorrect."[84]

Grudem draws on 1 Corinthians 11:3 as the key passage to support his argument:

> In this verse, "head" refers to one who is in a position of authority over the other, as this Greek word (*kephalē*) uniformly does whenever it is used in ancient literature to say that one person is "head of" another person or group. So Paul is here referring to a relationship of authority between God the Father and God the Son, and he is making

a parallel between the relationship in the Trinity and the relationship between the husband and wife in marriage.[85]

It was argued above that Grudem is mistaken both in his reading of 1 Corinthians as arguing for an authority-subordination relationship, but also in his claims that *kephalē* always means "authority" in ancient literature. Moreover, the context of Paul's discussion in 1 Corinthians 11 says nothing about husbands and wives. Paul is discussing men and women in the context of Christian worship, not husbands and wives in the context of marriage.

Grudem goes on to claim a "role relationship" between man and woman parallel to an eternal authority relationship between the Father and the Son:

> Just as the Father and Son are equal in deity and equal in all their attributes, but different in role, so husband and wife are equal in personhood and value, but they are different in the roles God has given them. Just as God the Son is eternally subject to the authority of God the Father, so God has planned that wives be subject to the authority of their husbands.[86]

Again, Grudem is emphatic that this authority relationship between Father and Son is eternal, inherent to the immanent Trinity:

> The Father has eternally had a leadership role, an authority to initiate and direct, that the Son does not have. . . . Authority and submission between the Father and the Son, and between Father and Son and the Holy Spirit, is a fundamental difference (or probably *the* fundamental difference) between the persons of the Trinity.[87]

This argument concerning the eternal subordination of the Son to the Father has become increasingly controversial in recent Evangelical theology, with numerous Evangelical theologians arguing that Grudem's notion of an "eternal subordination" and obedience of the Father to the Son is a departure from Nicene orthodoxy, and a reversion to a "subordinationist" theology rejected at Nicaea.[88]

Questions about the relationship between the immanent Trinity and the economic subordination of the incarnate Son are peripheral to the question of the relationships between men and women. Paul is making an analogy in 1 Corinthians 11:3, not engaging in sophisticated metaphysical arguments about the eternal relations between the three members of the Trinity. However, it is crucial to distinguish an economic subordination of the incarnate Jesus Christ (as human) from an eternal subordination of the Son within the immanent Trinity. Certainly the entire catholic tradition affirms that the incarnate Son (as human) is subordinate to the Father (as God) in terms of his economic mission. In context, 1 Corinthians 11:3 certainly refers to this economy of salvation; it is not that the eternal Father is the "head" (authority) of the pre-existent Son, but that "God" (the Father) is the "head" (likely "source," not "authority") of "Christ" (the incarnate Son). To read the passage as referring to the immanent Trinity is a misreading.

At the same time, Grudem's affirmation that the only basis for any eternal differentiation between the members of the Trinity would lie in differences of authority is historically mistaken. The traditional understanding of the Trinity is that the differentiations between persons in the immanent ontological Trinity arise from relations of origins. In the Eastern Cappadocian model, the Father is the *fons divinitatis* (fountain of deity); the Father eternally begets the Son, and the Spirit eternally proceeds from the Father. In the Western model, as formulated first by Augustine, and definitively by Thomas Aquinas, the Son is the *Logos* or Word whom the Father eternally begets, and the Holy Spirit is the mutual love who eternally proceeds from the Father and the Son.[89] Far from the Trinitarian relations being relations of authority, they are relations of mutual love. Moreover, given the historically orthodox notion that God is three eternal divine persons with a single divine nature, and that will is assigned to nature, not persons, it likely makes no sense that the Father would eternally command the Son, and the Son would eternally obey, since the Triune God has a single undivided will. On the Thomist/Augustinian model, at least, the "faculty" to which the Son (as Word) corresponds is intellect, with the Spirit (as Love) corresponding to "will." Moreover, the doctrine of *pericherosis* or *circumcessio* implies that what the three persons will, they will as one. To say that one divine person eternally exercises authority over or commands another divine person and that the second divine person eternally obeys and submits likely implies some version of tritheism, not Trinitarian orthodoxy.

It is significant in this discussion that Grudem indicates that the only possible relationship that he can imagine between more than one person is one that is based on the authority of one over the other, rather than a relationship of genuine equality based on mutual love, which is the historical understanding of the Trinity. The logical implication of Grudem's claim that the only ground to distinguish between the persons of the Trinity would be in terms of authority and obedience would imply that authority and obedience is also the only ground to distinguish between any two human persons as well, that in any case in which two human persons come into relationship to one another, that relationship must be fundamentally based on a hierarchy of obedience in which one of those persons has authority over the other, and the other obeys. It seems not to have occurred to Grudem that mutuality and equality based on love would not only be just as adequate a manner of differentiating between persons, but a superior one. This would seem to indicate that there is a more fundamental difference between complementarians and egalitarians than basic disagreements about exegesis. At stake seems to be a fundamental difference of understanding of how persons relate to one another, a difference rooted in divergent understandings of the nature of the triune God, the incarnation, and human beings. In the end, the disagreement may well lie in different theologies of soteriology and grace.

9

Speaking and Teaching

The previous two chapters in this discussion have focused on the two lengthiest passages in the writings of the apostle Paul to which complementarians regularly appeal to justify their position that women should always be subordinate to men and should not exercise authority over men in the church: Ephesians 5:21-33, in which Paul discusses the relationship between husbands and wives, and 1 Corinthians 11:3-16, in which Paul talks about disorderly practices connected with the ways in which men and women were leading church worship. The discussion now turns to address two much shorter passages in Paul's writing which, in the end, provide the strongest biblical warrants to which complementarians appeal, the "last resort" to which appeal is made if all else fails: 1 Corinthians 14:33b-36 and 1 Timothy 2:11-15. Indeed, these two passages are often the *first* resort in less formal settings. At first glance, a straightforward reading of English translations of the passages, especially when select verses are read out of context, makes it seem as if Paul intended to forbid any public role to women in worship: "As in all the churches of the saints, the women should keep silent in the churches" (1 Cor. 14:34b-35); "I do not permit a woman to teach or exercise authority over a man; rather, she is to remain quiet" (1 Tim. 2:12).

Complementarians themselves recognize that these are the crucial passages for their position in the light of which they then read other passages. George W. Knight III states that these two passages are "clearly the didactic passages on the subject [of 'headship'], while 1 Corinthians 11 only mentions the subject incidentally. Therefore, our interpretation of 1 Corinthians 14 and 1 Timothy 2 ought to govern our interpretation of 1 Corinthians 11, not vice versa."[1]

These are also the passages to which those arguing for a subordination of women to men in the history of church tradition have regularly appealed. Origen wrote, quoting Paul, "'It is shameful for a woman to speak in church' [1 Cor. 14:35], whatever she says, even if she says something excellent or holy, because it comes from the mouth of a woman."[2] The *Apostolic Constitutions* states: "If we did not allow [women] to teach, how can we assent to their being priests, which is contrary to nature?"[3] Thomas Aquinas stated that a woman should not exercise authority over a man.[4] Richard Hooker wrote: "To make women teachers in the house of God were a gross absurdity, seeing the Apostle hath said, 'I permit not a woman to teach.'"[5] John Knox wrote: "The apostle taketh power frome all woman to speake in the assemblie. Ergo he permitteth no woman to rule aboue man."[6] At the same time, it should be noted that, unlike the repeated complementarian assertions that subordination of women to men does not rest on any inequality, these earlier writers understood the subordination of women to men to rest on an inherent ontological defect. Women were considered to be less rational, more gullible, and more susceptible to temptation, and thus were restricted not only from church office, but from any position of authority over any men in any sphere whatsoever. It is these two passages that are often referenced by feminists as evidence that the apostle Paul was an irremediable sexist.

As with Paul's teaching about "head coverings" in 1 Corinthians 11, it needs to be acknowledged up front that these are two of the most difficult passages in Paul's writings to interpret. On a straightforward reading, 1 Corinthians 14:35 would seem to demand absolute silence of all women in church, and would forbid such activities as women singing in choirs or teaching Sunday School classes, activities women engage in even in complementarian churches. Moreover, if the passage demanded absolute silence of women in church, it would be in direct contradiction to 1 Corinthians 11, in which the context of Paul's discussion about whether women should wear head coverings when prophesying presumes that women are indeed speaking publicly in church, and in the same manner as men. Accordingly, whatever Paul is prohibiting in the passage, the statement that women should "keep silent" is clearly referring to some particular women in some particular context, not to all women at all times and in all places. Correct interpretation of the passage rests on discovering to which women Paul was referring in this passage, in what context, and under what circumstances.[7] Similarly, Paul's statement in 1 Timothy 2:14 that Adam was not deceived, but Eve was, might logically seem to imply that he is forbidding women to teach because women are inherently more susceptible to deception than men; whatever previous Christian tradition might have affirmed, complementarians do not want to draw this conclusion![8] Accordingly, a more careful reading of these two passages is in order.

1 CORINTHIANS 14:33B-36

As with Paul's discussion about "head coverings" in 1 Corinthians 11:3-16, 1 Corinthians 14:33b-36 is difficult to interpret because Paul assumes that he and his readers in Corinth have a common knowledge of things that we ourselves cannot possibly know. The contemporary reader is in the position of listening in on and trying to understand the gist of someone else's conversation when he or she has not heard the beginning. As with the earlier passage, any contemporary reader has no choice but to engage in a certain amount of speculation as to the actual problem that Paul is addressing, the context of the situation in Corinth that led to Paul writing these three verses, the reasons for Paul's prohibitions and, assuming that Paul is not deliberately contradicting what he had written in 1 Corinthians 11, the specific kind of silence that Paul is enjoining. Accordingly, any attempt to understand the passage is necessarily tentative, and that is as true for complementarian interpretations as for egalitarians. A certain humility is required. As Alan F. Johnson writes, "Frankly, it is much easier to cite views and dismiss them for various reasons than to offer a completely satisfying alternative."[9] The following is a summary of the various alternative interpretations offered by scholars.

PAULINE AUTHORSHIP?

A number of contemporary biblical scholars argue that the text is an interpolation, and was not written by Paul at all.[10] Scholars give several reasons to doubt the passage's authenticity.

(1) Gordon Fee points out that the Western manuscript tradition places 1 Corinthians 14:34-35 after verse 40, while no non-Western manuscript does so. There are two possible explanations for this difference. First, the verses were in Paul's original text, but very early in its transmission, a copyist, for unknown reasons, moved the verses to a different place. Alternatively, the verses were not originally in Paul's text, but a copyist wrote them in the margin. At a later date, two later copyists moved the gloss into the text, one after verse 33, one after verse 40. Fee argues on principles of "transcriptional probability" that the latter is more likely the case.[11] It is easier to explain the differences in the textual tradition by the assumption of a common origin in a gloss than to account for why a later scribe would have moved the verses from where Paul had originally put them.

(2) The verses read as an interruption to Paul's argument, and the passage not only makes perfect sense without them, but better sense if they are omitted.

(3) The linguistic ties to language used in the rest of the passage ("speaking," "silence," "submission") are used in such different ways from what had just preceded as to make them suspect.[12]

(4) The verses are in "obvious contradiction" to 11:2-16, which assume that women are praying and prophesying in public worship. To the contrary, the prohibition against speaking is absolute in these verses, and scholars must engage in numerous arguments to "get around" their literal meaning.

(5) The verses contain language that is contrary to Paul's usual manner, specifically the phrase "even as the Law says." When Paul appeals to the law, he always cites the text, and Paul never appeals to the law in an absolute sense to justify behavior. Quite the contrary! Also, there is no such text in the Old Testament law to which Paul could be appealing.[13] Finally, the expression "the churches of the saints" is contrary to Paul's language and the flow of the argument. Why would Paul suddenly switch to language about "the churches" when his immediate concern is the church at Corinth?

Likely the strongest textual argument that the passage is an interpolation occurs in a recent essay by Philip B. Payne, who examines the bar-shaped and two-dot symbols (technically known as "distigme") which mark the location of textual variants in the codex Vaticanus B (dated 325–350).[14] According to Payne, Vaticanus contains approximately 121 bar-shaped "obeloi" in the LXX translation of the Old Testament, which mark texts not in the Hebrew Old Testament.[15] Vaticanus indicates three times in Isaiah that "the [lines] marked with an obelos contain [text] not in [the] Hebrew text" (Payne's translation of the Greek). Thus, "Scribe B marked added text in the LXX prophets with obeloi and explanations that text was added."[16]

Payne examines eight New Testament passages in Vaticanus that he argues indicate textual variants: Matthew 13:51; Matthew 18:11; Mark 5:40; Luke 1:28-29, 14:24-25; Acts 2:47, 6:10; and 1 Corinthians 14:34-35. As in the LXX obeloi, these passages are also the work of "Scribe B" (as indicated by color of ink), are adjacent to two-dot symbols (distigme), and are distinguished by a bar that extends almost twice as far into the margin as other bars marking "paragraphoi." In addition, with the exception of one text indicating a different scribe (Acts 6:10), Scribe B leaves a gap either in the middle or end of the line of text exactly at the location of an acknowledged block of added text—a multi-word variant of at least three added words. Given that "manuscript evidence indicates a block of added text at the gap after every other Scribe B distigme-obelos," Payne concludes: "Since manuscripts confirm the accuracy of every other one of Scribe B's distigme-obelos critical judgments, one ought to assume that Scribe B also had manuscript evidence that 1 Cor 14:34-5 is added text."[17]

If the verses were not actually written by Paul, then there is no problem of interpretation to be addressed, at least for those who take seriously issues of apostolic authority. The "interpolation" argument is not accepted universally, however. Other New Testament scholars argue in favor of Pauline authenticity on the following grounds:

(1) The verses appear in all New Testament manuscripts we possess. Given that there are no manuscripts that lack the verses, it would have to have been inserted at an extremely early date.

(2) Verses 34-35 take up a significant amount of vocabulary from the preceding verses ("speaking," "silence," "order"). The concern about Paul's use of "the law" is surprising, but not inexplicable.

(3) The assumption that 1 Corinthians 14:33b contradicts 1 Corinthians 11 depends on whether one understands the passage as an absolute restriction on speech. If the contradiction were that obvious, then why did the supposed interpolator not notice it?[18]

A strong argument can be made that the text is an interpolation, but given that numerous scholars presume that the text was indeed written by Paul, what are the possible explanations for how it might best be understood? In particular, how do scholars address the tension between Paul's permission of women to speak in chapter 11 with the apparent prohibition in chapter 14?

A first possible suggestion is not very different from the interpolation option. Some scholars have argued that the words are not Paul's at all, but that Paul is quoting a position of the Corinthians, which he is actually rejecting. Against this suggestion is that, in previous examples of such quotations, Paul not only states the view to which he is opposed, but also provides a refutation. Again, the words in the passage that echo earlier words in the immediate context count against this suggestion.[19]

Assuming that the words actually are Paul's, and that he did not contradict what he had written previously, scholars argue that Paul's admonition is not about an absolute silencing of women, but about silencing some kind of disruptive speech in the context of ordered worship. The entire context of the passage in 1 Corinthians is about proper order in worship. In 1 Corinthians 11:2-16, Paul discusses issues of both men and women who are leading worship, and the appropriate attire when doing so. In 11:17-34, he discusses issues of disorder concerning the Eucharist. In 12:1-30, 14:12-33, he discusses the proper order of worship and disorder in the use of charismatic gifts. Paul's hymn to love in 12:31-14:1 provides a centering device in the middle of this discussion, focusing on love as the proper context in which worship should be conducted. Finally, in 14:33b-40, he discusses disorder among men and women in the congregation responding to those who are leading worship.[20] The issue that Paul is addressing is not then whether women should speak at all, but the issue of disorder in the midst of worship.[21] Paul's introductory statement to the passage makes this clear: "For God is not the author of confusion, but of peace, as in all the churches of the saints" (1 Cor. 14:33, KJV).[22]

Paul's exhortation to silence is consistent with what he has written in the previous paragraph. He tells three specific groups who were speaking in the church to be silent. In each case, he identifies the group, they are told to be silent, and a reason is given for the silence. In 14:28, he writes that if there is no interpreter present, the person speaking in tongues should "be silent in the church." In 30-31, he writes that if someone receives a prophetic word, the first person should "be silent" to let the other person speak. In both cases, the concern is about order and edification: "For you can all prophesy one by one, so that all may learn and all be encouraged" (1 Cor. 14:31). Finally, Paul addresses a third group, women, and asks them also to "keep silence." The overall context makes clear that Paul is not asking all women to be silent all the time any more than he was asking all tongue-speakers or all prophets to be silent at all times. Rather, Paul is clearly asking certain women to be quiet under certain circumstances because something about their manner of speaking must have been disruptive to the order of the service.[23]

What was the nature of the disruption that Paul was addressing? As with the question of "head coverings" in 1 Corinthians 11, there can be no absolute certainty because we do not share information to which both Paul and his readers were privy. The following scenarios have been suggested.

Scenario 1: Chatting in Church

Kenneth Bailey makes the case that what Paul was addressing was the disruptive practice of "chatting in church." Drawing on both history and his own experience living in the Middle East, Bailey suggests the following scenario: Corinth was Greece's largest ancient city, populated by people of numerous cultures and languages who communicated in the common language of Greek. The ability of non-native Greek speakers to understand Greek would have varied. The ancient Mediterranean was also predominantly an oral culture in which perhaps ten percent of the population could read. In oral cultures, the attention span of non-literate people for extended discourse is limited, and it is not uncommon for side conversations to take place in which chatting and discussion begin as listeners ask one another, "What did he say? What does he mean?" In addition, in an era before the invention of microphones and amplified sound, not only could the speaker be difficult to hear, but the conversation of listeners could itself contribute to distraction. Bailey notes that in ancient cultures, women would have been even less likely to be literate than men, and thus would be prime offenders in the disruptive conversations. Thus Paul's reference to saving the questions to ask husbands later.[24]

Paul was not then restricting women's speech in *leading* worship. Paul had been clear in what he wrote in 1 Corinthians 11 that this was allowed. He was, however, restricting the speech of those in the congregation who were supposed to be listening. His advice to these women, as to the tongue-speakers and prophets, is to be quiet so that others may be heard. They are to "submit" to those who are leading the worship. Paul is asking for quietness on the part of those who are listening so that they can hear and learn.[25]

Scenario 2: Asking Questions

The second scenario is a variation on the first scenario. Picking up on Paul's reference in verse 35—"If there is anything they desire to learn, let them ask their husbands at home"—some scholars suggest that the disruptive speech in which women were engaged is asking questions that disrupt the worship service. Craig Keener suggests that Paul is not addressing the question of women *teaching* in church—to be discussed below—but *learning* in church: "put more accurately, he opposes them *learning* too loudly in public." Keener notes that "the only kind of speaking *specifically* addressed in 14:34 35 is that the wife should ask her husband questions at home, rather than continuing what she is doing."[26] Keener refers to Plutarch's essay *On Lectures* for social background.[27] It was common practice in ancient Mediterranean culture, both non-Jewish and Jewish, for hearers to interrupt lectures with questions. There was an etiquette to these questions; the questioner was not to be rude or ask irrelevant questions. At the same time, cultural "shame" was associated in Mediterranean culture with women addressing unrelated men: "social convention particularly respected women who were socially retiring and did not talk much with men outside their household."[28] In addition, there would have been a contrast between the level of education among men and women in ancient culture. While some women would have been educated, their numbers, in relation to men, would have been small. And, as noted above, the level of literacy would have been low in general. If ten percent of the population were literate, the numbers would have been lower for women. Few women would have studied philosophy, for instance, and, among Jews (with some exceptions), women were discouraged to study the Torah.[29]

Paul's concern in the passage is then two-fold. On the one hand, he was trying to deal with a question of social disorder within worship by asking the lesser educated women who were disrupting worship with irrelevant questions to save these questions for later. Presumably, their husbands, being more educated, could answer these questions for them later. Second, in the semi-public setting of early Christian worship, Paul is concerned to avoid public "shaming" in the eyes of outsiders, in a culture in which women were expected to be decorous in public:

> The point is . . . that preserving church order (14:40) means preserving the common good by not scandalizing the culture. It was "shameful" or "disgraceful" for a woman to interrupt the service with her questions (14:34) the same way that it was "shameful" or "disgraceful" for a woman to have her head uncovered or hair cropped short (11:6); it offended the cultural sensitivities of those whom the church wanted to reach with the gospel.[30]

While such a proposal might seem sexist by contemporary cultural standards, in Paul's own setting it would have not only preserved the order of worship by challenging disruptive behavior, but also respected women by assuming that they were

indeed capable of learning, and encouraging them to do so—something not characteristic of ancient Mediterranean culture as a whole—just at the appropriate time in
the appropriate setting.[31]

Against this interpretation, complementarian Wayne Grudem complains that
Keener's references to Graeco-Roman and Jewish settings do not address the situation at Corinth: "Not one of them mentions women in the Corinthian church,
or in any first-century church for that matter. Proving that Greeks and Romans and
Jews had concerns for order in public assemblies does not prove that women in the
church at Corinth were being disruptive or disorderly!"[32] Grudem is correct, but,
at the same time, we should not expect to find material outside the New Testament
directly addressing the questions Paul was addressing in the church at Corinth. No
such material exists. This does not mean that scholars should not examine contemporary Jewish and Greco-Roman culture to provide clues for issues that Paul was
addressing. Similarly, there are no extra-biblical materials that discuss the problem
of "head coverings" in the Corinthian church (1 Cor. 11), but scholars do not hesitate to look outside the New Testament to find clues as to the issue that Paul was
addressing, such as ancient practices concerning women's head coverings or hair
arrangements. Grudem himself does not hesitate to appeal to Jewish and pagan
sources to help him decide the meaning of kephalē ("head") in 1 Corinthians 11, although none of these sources mentions the wearing of head coverings in the church
at Corinth.[33]

Grudem also complains that there is no "hard evidence" for Keener's assumption that verse 35 provides the clue to the issue that Paul was addressing: "[T]hat
does not prove that they were already asking disruptive questions, or any questions
at all, during the worship service."[34] Again, Grudem's assertion is beside the point.
Grudem's own suggestion is that Paul was requiring women to be silent with respect
to judging prophecies (discussed later), but there is even less evidence for this position than there is for Keener's suggestion.[35] Paul writes nothing whatsoever in these
verses about "judging prophecy," but he actually does mention asking questions.
Any suggestion for the disruptive behavior that Paul is addressing in this passage is
necessarily inferential because Paul is not specific. The "asking questions" scenario
has the advantage that it depends on something that Paul does mention in the text
itself.

Scenario 3: Judging Prophecy

The last scenario suggests that the silence to which Paul is referring is that of "judging prophecy." There are both egalitarian and non-egalitarian versions of this scenario. The egalitarian scenario builds on the notion that Paul is concerned with disruptive questions by suggesting that the specific kinds of questions being asked have

to do with standing in judgment over prophets (v. 29).[36] The scenario would be the following: (1) certain women believed that they were prophetesses who had the gift of weighing prophecy; (2) the prophecies that they were weighing were either those of their husbands or of other men in the congregation; (3) the wives were asking leading questions in such a manner as to interrogate or cross-examine their husbands; (4) this embarrassing humiliation by a close relative or wife brought disgrace rather than honor on the husband or other male relative. In the shame-honor culture of the first-century Mediterranean world, this behavior was particularly troubling. The result was chaos in the worship service. Paul's solution is to forbid such questioning during the worship service, and to suggest that the women should save these kinds of questions for when they are home: "Worship was not to be turned into a question-and-answer session."[37] Why were the women in particular being singled out? Because they were the ones who were causing this particular problem. Of special importance, however, is the connection between verse 33 ("For God is not a God of confusion but of peace, as in all the churches") and verse 36 ("Or was it from you that that the word of God came? Or are you the only ones it has reached?"). By focusing on order in the church, Paul's goal is to get the Corinthian church to follow the practice of all the other churches rather than "doing their own thing." The problems he addresses are not simply those of women, but of disorderly worship in the congregation as a whole.[38]

It is significant that the "judging prophecy" scenario has also been embraced by complementarians. In so doing, they recognize that Paul is not simply restricting the speech of women in worship, but a particular kind of worship. At the same time, they reject the reading that Paul was addressing problems of disruption or disorderly worship. Against the notion that Paul was addressing a local problem at Corinth is his assertion that women are to be silent "in all the churches."[39] Rather, a distinction is made between prophecy and teaching. Prophecy in the New Testament period was a spontaneous revelation of God to the prophet. Teaching, however, was the explaining of and applying of Scripture or the teaching of the apostles. In Corinthians 11, Paul does indeed allow that women can prophesy; however, in 1 Corinthians 14:34, Paul is asking women to be silent in reference to the judging of prophecy because the judging of prophecy involves the same kind of authority as teaching, and Paul forbids women to teach or exercise authority over men (1 Tim. 2:12).[40] Accordingly, Paul states, "[Women] are not permitted to speak, but should be in submission, as the law says" (1 Cor. 14:34). The "submission" referred to is submission to the authority of male leadership in the church. Paul's reference to "the law" without a specified passage probably refers to the creation order in Genesis 2, with its understanding of the principle of male leadership. Paul's statement about women asking questions of their husbands at home is meant to prevent any attempt by women to evade his teaching by asking questions that were really just a circuitous attempt to judge prophecy.[41]

What to make of these two variations on the scenario that Paul was addressing the issue of women judging prophecies in the church? If Scenario 2 builds on Scenario 1 by suggesting that the specific kind of disruptive speech that Paul was addressing was interrupting worship by the asking of questions, Scenario 3 builds on Scenario 2 by suggesting those questions concerned the evaluation of prophecy. While Scenario 3 raises a genuine possibility for interpretation of the passage, it is subject to the criticism noted above by Keener that "there is little reason to associate 'asking questions' here with challenging prophecies."[42] While Paul specifically mentions "asking questions" with reference to women, and also specifically mentions the weighing of prophetic speech (v. 29), he does not connect the two in any way. Moreover, as Keener also points out, judging prophecy is probably equivalent to the gift of "discernment of spirits" (12:10), and nothing in the discussion of spiritual gifts in chapter 12 suggests that only men exercised this gift. First Corinthians 14:29 suggests to the contrary that the weighing of prophecy was something expected of all who exercised the gift of prophecy, both men and women. Nonetheless, all interpretations of the issue that Paul is addressing are necessarily speculative, and this suggestion, while perhaps more so, is a plausible explanation.

Less plausible, however, is the complementarian interpretation. Grudem and other complementarians agree with egalitarian advocates of Scenario 3 that the issue concerns judging of prophetic speech (a connection not specifically made by Paul), yet reject the suggestion that women were engaged in disruptive speech or that women were raising questions—something Paul specifically mentions! While recognizing a distinction between prophecy and teaching is not unique to complementarians, complementarians make a leap considerably beyond the evidence in suggesting not only that the issue of concern was judging prophecy, but, more specifically, that women were not allowed to judge prophecy because this would be a form of teaching which would imply that women were exercising illegitimate authority over men.[43] Grudem and others appeal to 1 Timothy 2:12, yet 1 Timothy had not yet been written, so the Corinthians could not have been familiar with it, and nothing in the text whatsoever mentions either teaching or male authority.[44] Grudem's appeal to Paul's reference to "submission" and to "the law" are problematic simply because Paul provides no specific content for either. Paul does not say that the women are to submit to some person. Rather, submission (ὑποτάσσω, hypotassō, v. 34) is without a personal object. To assume that it means that wives should submit to their husbands is reading something into the text that is not there. A more plausible reading is that it refers to submitting to the "principle of order in the worship service." Again, Paul does not cite a specific text for "the law." Some (including complementarians) have suggested that Paul is thinking of the order of creation (cf. 11:8-9), but this provides no basis whatsoever to draw a connection to 1 Timothy 2:12. A more plausible suggestion in the context is that Paul is thinking of the Old Testament's repeated emphasis on order and purpose.[45] Thiselton suggests that *hypotassō* and "law" come together to form a common context of order. He suggests a plausible translation: "they should keep their ordered place." The order to which the women are being asked to "submit" is that of the order of the service. As the God of Genesis brought order out of chaos in creation, so the Holy Spirit brings order within the context of Christian worship.[46]

The above three scenarios all offer plausible suggestions as to the concern that Paul was addressing in his exhortation to women's silence in the Corinthian church. Paul does not provide many details in his discussion in this passage since he and his readers would probably be aware of them. Thus, all three of these positions involve a certain amount of speculation on our part. Nonetheless, a sufficiently common interpretation emerges. Assuming that Paul did indeed write the words of 1 Corinthians 11:14:33b-36, he was neither demanding absolute silence of women in church, nor affirming a principle of male hierarchy and female subordination. Rather, the entire context of 1 Corinthians 11–14 is dealing with questions of disorder in worship. In this passage in particular, Paul is not dealing with questions of "creation order" but "church order." He corrects an abuse of disruptive speaking caused by some women within the congregation not by forbidding them to speak at all, but by restricting the particular form of abuse, and redirecting their questions to the appropriate time and place.[47]

FIRST TIMOTHY 2:11-15

The single passage in the New Testament that is most critical to the complementarian argument is 1 Timothy 2:11-15. It is the only passage in the entire Bible that on a literal reading might seem to exclude women from teaching or having authority over men. Moreover, as those who advocate a hierarchical understanding of male/female relationships are quick to point out, the passage appears to be transcultural in that it grounds its argument in the order of creation itself. Because Adam was created first, women are not allowed to teach or have authority over men.[48] If the passage is crucial for advocates of women's subordination to men, it is equally troubling for those who affirm the full participation of women in the church:

> Few if any texts are more painful to modern sensibilities. The portrayal of women as effectively gagged in church, forbidden to exercise authority over men, and restricted to the role of childbearers, modest dressers, and doers of good deeds is about as remote from most twenty-first century evaluations of women's roles in Western society, as one could imagine. What does one do with a text like this?[49]

As with the other Pauline passages examined so far, this passage is also difficult to interpret, and raises a number of problematic issues. The meaning of almost every word in the passage is subject to debate and disagreement.

The first issue is that of authorship. Although 1 Timothy begins "Paul, an apostle of Christ Jesus . . . to Timothy" (1:1), most biblical scholars believe that the Pastoral Epistles of 1 and 2 Timothy and Titus are pseudepigraphal. That is, they were not written by Paul, but by a successor or disciple of Paul from a later period writing in his name. Differences from the authentically recognized Pauline epistles include: (1) a distinctive vocabulary and style; (2) a different understanding of "faith" as a body of content (what is believed) rather than an act of trust.[50] (3) different threats to the gospel: the Judaizers of Galatians and Romans, for example, have taken a back seat to new heresies; (4) church structures are more formalized, with distinct offices of bishop and deacon, and references to presbyters; (5) there is far more concern to conform to the culture. A focus on good order and the household is concerned largely about how the church will come across to the outside world.[51]

Concerning relationships between men and women, there is a curious lack of mutuality. In discussing the relationships between husbands and wives in Ephesians 5, Paul addresses both men and women, calling for mutual submission. In the exhortations to subordinates in Titus 2:1-10, this mutuality is missing. Those in subordinate positions (women, children and slaves) are addressed, but the householder is not.[52] In 1 Corinthians 11, when Paul discusses the order of creation, he balances what he says about the first woman being made from man by saying that now all men come from women in childbirth. This reciprocity is missing in 1 Timothy 2:13. In Romans 5:12, Paul is clear that sin came into the world through Adam, but in 1 Timothy 2:14, he seems to place the blame entirely on Eve: "Adam was not deceived, but the woman was deceived and became a transgressor." The cumulative weight of all of these differences has led most biblical scholars to question whether the same author could have written the recognized Pauline epistles and the Pastorals.

On the other hand, there are numerous characteristics of the Pastorals that suggest Pauline authorship, especially the numerous personal references, which are difficult to account for apart from some form of genuine Pauline tradition. Why would someone other than Paul go to the trouble of creating so many historical details?[53] Those who argue for Pauline authorship suggest that the differences can be explained by changes in historical circumstances and that there are enough continuities and similarities to support Paul as author. Three solutions have been proposed. First, Paul himself wrote the Pastorals, although changes of circumstance and other concerns account for the differences with Paul's other letters. Second, Paul did not write the Pastorals; they were written at a later period by someone who was familiar with Paul's writings, and perhaps incorporated some authentically Pauline material in the letters. Third, Paul wrote the letters using an amanuensis to whom he gave considerable liberty in composition. This would explain both the personal references and the differences from Paul's usual manner of writing.[54]

Although many of those who deny Pauline authorship tend to devalue the Pastoral letters or treat them as of having less authority than those recognized as authentic, theologically, the important point to recognize is that they are canonical Scripture, and have been recognized as such by the Christian church throughout its history. The authority of the Pastorals as Scripture does not depend on their authorship but on their bearing witness to the subject matter of Christian faith either as reflections of Paul himself under changed circumstances, or of churches who were influenced by Paul and saw themselves as continuing his heritage.[55] What follows will not attempt to resolve the issue of Pauline authorship, but will throughout refer to the author as "Paul." If Paul himself wrote the Pastorals, then "Paul" refers to the apostle. If Paul did not, then "Paul" refers to either his amanuensis or a later writer who wrote in his name, perhaps incorporating significant material from Paul's own hand.

EXEGETICAL BACKGROUND

A major theme of the Pastorals is a concern with both conflict in the church and false teaching. 1 Timothy 2:8 refers to "anger and quarreling" among men; 1 Timothy 5:13-15 mentions women who are "busy bodies," and some who have "strayed after Satan"; 2 Timothy 3:6-7 refers to women who are being led astray by false teachers, while Titus 1:10-11 refers to "empty talkers and deceivers" who "must be silenced." It is this conflict with false teaching that provides the context for the Pastorals, even more so than the concern for order which interpreters often emphasize.[56]

The immediate context of the passage suggests that Paul is addressing an issue of disorderly public worship that concerns both men and women. That men are requested to pray "without anger and quarreling" (1 Tim. 2:8) suggests that there were some men who were engaging in angry and quarrelsome behavior. The reference to women adorning themselves modestly and with self-control rather than with "braided hair and gold or pearls or costly apparel" (v. 9) indicates that there were wealthy women in the church who were attending worship dressed in a manner that was intended to draw attention to themselves.[57] The word "similarly" (ὡσαύτως, hōsautōs, v. 9), along with the lack of a verb (indicating that the verb must be supplied from verse 8), makes clear that Paul is addressing a problem caused by both men and women.[58] While the immediate context suggests issues of disorderly worship that concerned both men and women, the immediately following verses that speak only of women are the crucial verses for the complementarian argument that women cannot exercise church office because they cannot exercise authority over or teach men in the church.

Paul's instruction in verse 11 ("Let a woman learn quietly with all submissiveness") has been used as a warrant by complementarians to argue that women should be in submission to male authority.[59] There is nothing in the context that indicates that this would be the case, however. Women are being asked to learn quietly with submissiveness. This is neither a demand for silence, nor for submission to male authority. Rather, this is the kind of standard advice that would have been given to students in the ancient world. That Paul assumes that women should be learning is itself of significance, since this contrasts with both Gentile and rabbinic discouragement of women students at the time. The situation is, again, similar to 1 Corinthians 14:34. Paul is suggesting that women should listen to what is going on in the worship service rather than interrupting it with disruptive speech. There is also a possible parallel here to 1 Timothy 5:13, in which Paul refers to women who are "saying things they ought not." Note the parallel to the false teachers of 1 Titus 1:11, who "teach things they ought not." In its immediate context, the "submission" being asked for is not submission to a person (such as a husband or male authority), but to what is being learned.[60]

"I DO NOT PERMIT ..."

The crucial verse for the entire discussion of the permissible roles of women in church for complementarians is 1 Timothy 2:12, "I do not permit a woman to teach or to exercise authority over a man; rather she is to remain quiet." The last chapter referred to the lengthy debate about the significance of the word *kephalē* as the "battle of the lexicons."[61] The discussion about the meaning of a few key words in verse 12 has become equally contentious, and could reasonably be called the "battle of the Greek grammars and databases." The first key question has to do with whether the word ἐπιτρέπω (*epitrepō*) should be translated "I do not permit" or "I am not permitting." Complementarian Douglas Moo states that the meaning is indefinite:

> The fact is, however, that nothing definite can be concluded from the word. . . . As far as the present tense of the verb goes, this allows us to conclude only that Paul was *at the time of writing* insisting on these prohibitions. . . . It certainly is *not* correct to say that the present tense in and of itself shows that the command is temporary; it does not.[62]

Wayne Grudem goes further than Moo, and insists to the contrary that Paul's command must be understand to have permanent effect or it will undermine the authority of Scripture itself:

> Appealing to the present tense or to Paul's use of first person, "I do not permit," cannot be used to argue that this is a temporary command. Such a claim misunderstands the force of the Greek present in Paul's commands. . . . Christians who believe Scripture to be the Word of God have rightly understood these to be *commands that are applicable for all Christians for all times.*[63]

While rhetorically effective, Grudem's claim overreaches. Numerous scholars point out that the verb *epitrepō* should be translated "I am not permitting." Paul neither uses a possible rabbinic formula "it is not permitted" (1 Cor. 14:34), nor the future "I will not permit."[64] Payne points out that when Paul uses the first person present active indicative he indicates his personal advice for a situation that is not universal.[65] Paul tends to use imperatives when he is making universal exhortations. Moreover, all examples of *epitrepō* in the Greek LXX translation of the Old Testament refer to specific situations, as do the majority of New Testament occurrences. Jesus' reply to his opponents on the question of divorce (Mark 10:4; Matt. 19:8) makes it clear that he did not understand the Mosaic permission (ἐπέτρεψεν, *epetreupen*) to divorce to be permanent. The evidence suggests that Paul's use of *epitrepō* is temporally limited, and thus, the prohibition is neither universal nor for all time.[66]

The second issue of debate has to do with the meaning of αὐθεντεῖν (*authentein*), translated "to exercise authority over" in translations such as the ESV. Does it mean the neutral "have authority over" (as complementarians insist) or does it rather mean the more negative "to domineer," "to dominate," or "to assume or usurp authority," as suggested by a number of earlier translations?[67] Egalitarian scholars note that the pre-New Testament use of the word is rare, and that if Paul had simply meant "to exercise authority," he had numerous Greek words from which to choose that he regularly used elsewhere—for example, some variation of ἔχει ἐξουσίαν (*exei exousian*).[68] As with *kephalē*, this has been discussed at length. H. Scott Baldwin has produced an examination of eighty-two examples of ancient uses of αὐθεντέω (*authenteō*) to make the case that the word was understood neutrally as "to exercise authority," which Grudem has reproduced as an appendix in his *Evangelical Feminism and Biblical Truth.*[69] The problem with Baldwin's list (as with Grudem's word studies on *kephalē*) is that the vast majority of his references occur centuries after the New Testament period, and thus are of no use in assessing the meaning of the word when 1 Timothy was written.[70] What seems to be established is that the use of the word is rare in the period before the New Testament, that "there are no established instances with this meaning ['to exercise authority'] until centuries after Paul," and that, in earlier periods, it was understood to have primarily negative connotations of domineering or usurping authority. Ben Witherington III writes, "I conclude that the author means that women are not permitted to 'rule over,' master,' or 'play the despot' over men." Payne suggests "to assume authority" as the "best-supported meaning."[71]

Another debated issue in the discussion is whether the conjunction οὐδὲ (*oude*) separates two different prohibitions—women should not teach *or* assume/exercise authority—or rather whether this should be understood as a single prohibition— to teach *so as* to assume authority. Grudem argues that those who argue for a single prohibition have "misunderstood Greek grammar."[72] Payne argues at length for a single prohibition.[73] Belleville argues that the infinitives ("to teach," *authentein*) function as direct object nouns restricting the direct object "woman." The two infinitives are not synonyms or closely related ideas but rather combine to form a single purpose or goal: "I do not permit a woman to teach so as to gain mastery over a man" or "I do not permit a woman to teach with a view to dominating a man."[74] Those with the patience for detailed discussions of Greek grammar can pursue this discussion for themselves. However, assuming that Paul's prohibition is a temporary one, this discussion, while interesting, is not of deciding significance.

GENTLEMEN FIRST . . .

Whether these issues of Greek vocabulary and grammar can be resolved, the crucial issue for Paul's prohibition is found in verse 13, where he provides the warrant for the prohibition: "For Adam was formed first, then Eve; and Adam was not deceived, but the woman was deceived and became a transgressor." The complementarian interpretation of this passage focuses on Paul's appeal to creation order (Adam was formed first, then Eve) to argue that Paul is arguing for a hierarchical relationship between men and women based in the original pre-fall creation as the reason why women may not teach or have authority over men: "Paul emphasizes that the man was created 'first, then' Eve. . . . Both the logic of this passage and the parallel in 1 Corinthians 11:3-10 make this clear: for Paul, the man's priority in the order of creation is indicative of the headship that man is to have over woman."[75] Similarly, Grudem states: "Paul gives the reason for his command, and it is the creation order . . . not any false teaching by women. . . . Paul's reason is the Creation order: '*For Adam was formed first, then Eve.*'"[76]

There are two key problems with the complementarian approach. First, it assumes that Paul uses "because" (γάρ, *gar*) as a warrant in the sense of cause rather than a warrant in the sense of example. Grudem insists that this is the only meaning the text can have:

> The main problem is that it [the interpretation that says creation order does not have to do with authority] says that Paul is wrong. . . . But Paul's "for" (Greek *gar*) shows that that is exactly what he did. He used "Adam was formed first, then Eve" as a *reason* why he does not permit a woman to teach or have authority over a man in the assembled church.[77]

The Greek word *gar* can be used as a statement of causation ("because"); it can also be a simple connecting conjunction. However, it can also be used in the sense of an example. Witherington states: "What follows, then, is intended to be an historical example or precedent that explains the consequences of a woman being deceived and attempting to assume or assert an authority not given to her. The point of the example is to teach women not to emulate Eve."[78]

The use of Adam and Eve as examples would be consistent with Paul's typological usage of Old Testament imagery elsewhere. In 1 Corinthians 10:1-13, Paul uses the imagery of the Old Testament exodus, including crossing through the Red Sea, manna, the cloud that followed the Israelites, and the rock from which water flowed, to argue a typological interpretation in which the sea corresponds to baptism and the spiritual food and drink point to Christ: "[A]ll were baptized into Moses in the cloud and in the sea, and all ate the same spiritual food, and all drank the same spiritual drink. For they drank from the spiritual rock that followed them, and the rock was Christ" (1 Cor. 10:2-4). Paul writes: "Now these things took place as examples (τύποι, *typoi*) for us" (v. 6). Similarly, in Galatians, Paul interprets the Old Testament story of Sarah and Hagar typologically to contrast the old covenant of law and the new covenant of grace: "Now this may be interpreted allegorically: these women are two covenants" (Gal. 4:24).[79]

With the single exception of Luke 3:38, the New Testament always uses Adam and Eve as typological figures, who cast light on current situations at the time of the writer. In 2 Corinthians 11:3-4, Paul draws a parallel between the serpent who deceived Eve and the danger of deception for Christians that parallels the passage in 1 Timothy: "But I am afraid that as the serpent deceived Eve by his cunning thoughts, your thoughts will be led astray from a sincere and pure devotion to Christ" (v. 3). In Romans 5:12-21, Paul draws a typological parallel between Adam and Christ to argue that, as sin came into the world through Adam, so justification comes through

Christ. In Romans 16:20, Paul echoes Gen. 3:15: "The God of peace will soon crush Satan under your feet."[80]

To interpret the passage typologically is consistent with what Paul does elsewhere in his writings, and makes sense in the context. As in 2 Corinthians 11:3-4, Paul is using the example of Eve's deception to warn of the dangers of deception for Christian women at Ephesus. To argue that the passage should be interpreted as a causal explanation creates serious problems. Grudem and other complementarians argue that the key issue of the text concerns creation order. Women cannot teach or exercise authority over men because man was created first, and woman second. This is to misread Paul's argument selectively, however. Paul does not simply mention creation order, but draws a deliberate connection between creation order and deception: "For Adam was created first, then Eve; and Adam was not deceived, but the woman was deceived and became a transgressor" (1 Tim. 2:13-14). Numerous scholars write as if Paul were providing two separate reasons, but the most straightforward reading is that he rather provides a single reason that follows a kind of logical progression, and provides the warrant for Paul's prohibition in verse 12:

> The man was created first → The woman was deceived.

> The man was not deceived → Women should not teach or exercise authority over men.

Paul is clearly drawing a connection between the order of creation and the deception of the woman, and a connection between the woman's deception and women at Ephesus not exercising authority over men. If Paul's argument is causal and focused on creation order (as Grudem and other complementarians claim), then Paul is necessarily assuming that Eve was susceptible to deception because Adam was created first—and contemporary women should not teach, not only because Adam was created first (creation order), but because women are inherently more subject to deception than men. Numerous scholars recognize this as the necessary import of a causal interpretation of Paul's argument.[81] Such an argument would indeed be "lame" (as Hays suggests), not only because it gets Adam off the hook (contrary to Rom. 5:12), but also because it is simply not the case that women are inherently more subject to deception than men.[82]

That women were inherently more subject to deception than men was a key reason that theologians historically argued for the subordination of women, and some complementarians seem to have embraced this position. However, the official complementarian position is that women are not inherently inferior to men, but simply have different roles assigned them by God. Complementarians cannot then consistently appeal to the argument of deception.[83] Moo suggests that the point of the reference to deception is to remind the women at Ephesus that Eve was deceived by the serpent . . . precisely in taking the initiative over the man whom God had given to be with her and to care for her. In the same way, if the women at the church at Ephesus proclaim their independence from the men of the church . . . seeking roles that have been given to men in the church (verse 12), they will make the same mistake Eve made and bring similar destruction on themselves and the church.[84]

This is to read something into the text that is not there. Nothing in either the Genesis account or in Paul's argument suggests that the woman was deceived by taking initiative over the man or that God had forbidden her to take such initiative.[85]

Grudem's own reading resists any suggestion that Paul's prohibition against women teaching had anything to do with women teaching false doctrine or being deceived, and focuses exclusively on the argument from creation order:

Paul makes no reference to his culture or to women being susceptible to deception in the first century. Paul is talking about Adam and Eve, and he says that another reason women should not "teach" or "exercise authority over a man" is that "Adam was not deceived, but the woman was deceived and became a transgressor . . ." However we understand that passage, it is evident that Paul is saying that something is true of Eve in relationship to Adam that has *transcultural significance for women and men generally in the New Testament church*.[86]

Although he seems reluctant to draw this conclusion, the logical implication of Grudem's statement is that women should not teach because they are inherently subject to deception. Paul does not give Eve's deception as *another* reason. It is *the* reason, and it has an inherent connection to the reference to creation order. Eve was deceived because Adam was created first. Women should not teach in the situation Paul was addressing either (a) because the Ephesian women, like Eve, have been deceived; or (b) because of a reason of "transcultural significance," all women (like Eve) are inherently subject to deception. These are the only two possible options.

If Paul is using the story of Eve's deception typologically, as an example and not a causative explanation, then the argument changes. Paul is not saying that all women everywhere and at all times are inherently more subject to deception than men. Given a typological interpretation, what would be the point of the connection that Paul draws between creation order and Eve's deception? The most plausible suggestion would seem to be a reference made by Craig S. Keener to a rabbinic interpretation of the passage that Paul could have adapted. Because Eve, not having yet been created, was not present in Genesis 2:16-17 when God gave the commandment not to eat of the tree of the knowledge of good and evil, she was not directly informed by God, but indirectly informed by Adam, and therefore subject to deception.[87] On this typological interpretation, Paul would be suggesting that, like Eve, the women at Ephesus are not well-informed, and thus are subject to deception. They should not teach, but rather learn quietly in submission to the subject matter so that they will be better informed and no longer deceived. Presumably, once they had learned, they could teach.[88]

Are there other examples where Paul uses a similar kind of reasoning in the Pastoral Epistles? There is just such a similar parallel in Paul's discussion in Titus 1:10, where he again uses the language of deception, along with similar references to subordination and dangers of false teaching, and a solution that silences the troublemakers: "For there are many who are insubordinate, empty talkers and deceivers, especially those of the circumcision party. They must be silenced, since they are upsetting whole families by teaching for shameful gain what they ought not to teach." As in 1 Timothy, Paul then provides a warrant, and while it does not mention Scripture, it does make an absolute statement without exceptions: "One of the Cretans, a prophet of their own, said 'Cretans are always liars, evil beasts, lazy gluttons.' This testimony is true" (Titus 1:12-13). Moreover, Paul goes on to describe these Cretans as "defiled and unbelieving," having "defiled consciences," as "detestable, disobedient, and unfit for any good work" (vv. 15-16).

This is an example of what is sometimes called the liar's paradox. If a Cretan has made the true statement that Cretans are always liars, then when the Cretan made the statement, he must himself have been lying. But if he was lying when he said that Cretans are always liars, then he was not in fact telling the truth, in which case it is not a true statement. Leaving aside the logical conundrum, if someone were to read Paul's statement using the hermeneutical principles of complementarians, then he or she would have to presume that under no circumstances could Cretans ever exercise church leadership. If Paul is arguing causally and without restriction (as it is said that he is in 1 Tim. 2:13), then "Cretans are always liars" would have "transcultural significance," and would necessarily imply that no Cretan could ever be trusted with authority. Yet Paul makes clear in the previous chapter (Titus 1:5) that Titus is to appoint Cretan elders who are to hold firmly to the word they are taught, so that they can give instruction in sound doctrine (v. 9). Paul is not silencing all Cretans (even though "Cretans are always liars") but only those who are deceivers (1:10-11). Those who hold fast to what they are taught can later become teachers themselves. Concerning those who are subject to deception, Paul exhorts Titus to "rebuke them sharply, that they may be sound in the faith" (1:13). The parallel to 1 Timothy 2 is illuminating. Presumably, even though Eve was deceived, Paul's statement that he "is not permitting a woman to teach or exercise authority over a man" would not imply a permanent prohibition any more than Paul's warnings about Cretans would imply a permanent injunction to silence (Titus 1:10-11). Rather, like the Cretans, who after having held fast to the trustworthy word they are taught are then able to give instruction in sound doctrine (Titus 1:9), the women at Ephesus, who like Eve were in danger of deception, could "learn quietly with all submissiveness" (1 Tim. 2:11), after which, like the Cretans, they also could presumably give instruction in sound doctrine.

A point not often enough addressed is that the crucial issue in addressing Paul's prohibition of women teaching or exercising authority in 1 Timothy is primarily hermeneutical, not exegetical. That is, the concern is not so much what Paul wrote to address his own situation in Ephesus, but how we appropriate what he wrote then to address a very different situation today. In the passage, Paul does not provide an imperative –"Do not allow women to teach or exercise authority over a man"—but an indicative—"I am not allowing women to teach or exercise authority [probably better, "domineer" or "assume authority"] over a man." Paul is describing a particular historical situation and his response to it, and the reason he gives is not a timeless warrant, but an example. Because certain women had been deceived at Ephesus, Paul suggests they should not teach, but rather should learn. Nothing in his statement or his example presumes that his indicative is intended to be permanent.

The disagreement about what to do with this text in our own setting has similarities to the earlier disagreement between Anglican Divine Richard Hooker and his Puritan opponents, discussed in a previous chapter.[89] In contrast to the Puritan assumption that it was only necessary to read a biblical text to understand not only what it meant at the time it was written, but also how it might be applied in the church at a later time, Hooker insisted that merely historical statements recorded in Scripture cannot be presumed to provide permanent warrants for later Christian practice.[90] Complementarians who read this passage seem to be making the same error that the Puritans made, presuming that an historical example dealing with a specific situation provides a permanent warrant for the church to follow at all times.

CONCLUSION

This last chapter examining Protestant objections to the ordination of women— those focusing on issues of male authority over women and a hierarchical subordination of women to men—has focused on the two passages in Paul's writings to which complementarians regularly appeal because the passages speak explicitly about women not speaking in public worship or not teaching or exercising authority over men. As with the previous passages in Paul's writings to which complementarians appeal, these two passages are beset with interpretive difficulties because we do not know the particular details of the situation that Paul was trying to address. As noted several times in this discussion, all attempts to understand such passages rely on a certain amount of speculation in which interpreters necessarily must attempt to fill in the missing details.

Assuming that Paul is the author of 1 Corinthians 14:33b-36, and it is not an interpolation by a later editor, the conundrum becomes reconciling what appears to be an absolute command for silence on the part of women worshippers and Paul's earlier statements about women prophesying in 1 Corinthians 11, a passage that makes clear that Paul did not suppress women speaking in church. Accordingly, all scholars who accept the genuineness of the passage (including complementarians) agree that Paul is not demanding absolute silence of women in worship, but is restricting some kind of disruptive speech leading to disorderly worship. Numerous suggestions have been proposed, and the most plausible focuses on the nature of the speech as in some way disruptive in itself: "chatting in church," "asking questions," and "judging prophets" in a manner that creates public shame. What gives these interpretations their plausibility is that they seek clues within the text itself to provide an answer to the question "what kind of disruptive speech was Paul correcting?" What distinguishes the complementarian attempt to provide an explanation for the disruptive speech is that it goes outside the text to provide an answer based on a prior-assumed hierarchical scheme that is then imposed on the text. Although Paul says nothing in the text about the authority of men over women, about women challenging the authority of men in their speaking, or about women challenging prophecies in a manner that would involve an attempt to teach or exercise illegitimate authority over men, the complementarian approach assumes that this must be the nature of the problem that Paul is addressing in the text, and then reads an interpretation into the text for which there is no warrant.

Initially, the complementarian case seems stronger regarding 1 Timothy 2:11-15 in that contemporary English translations render the text as if it would be a straightforward prohibition of women either teaching or exercising authority over men. A closer examination of the passage casts doubt on this reading. The general context of the Pastoral Epistles indicates that a concern with false teaching and deception is a prevailing theme throughout the letters. Several references to women in these letters indicate that their author was concerned in particular that at least some of this false teaching involved women, either as teachers or as disciples of the false teachers. This context would indicate that Paul was addressing a specific problem, not giving a universal prohibition. Second, a more careful reading of the Greek text indicates that modern English translations are misleading. Comparisons with Paul's use elsewhere as well as the way the verb *epitrepō* is used in the rest of the New Testament indicates that Paul was not giving a timeless imperative, but rather describing a current policy: "I am not permitting." Comparison of the verb *authentein* with its rare uses elsewhere in ancient culture indicates that at the time the Pastoral Epistles were written, the verb did not refer to a neutral exercising of authority, but had the stronger connotation of "domineer," "usurp authority," or "assume authority." Debates between Greek scholars are difficult for non-experts to settle, but there seems to be a strong indication that the passage should more properly be translated something like "I am not permitting women to teach or to domineer over men" or "I am not permitting women to teach so as to assume authority over men."

More important than the grammatical issues is the warrant that Paul provides for his prohibition, based on a summary of the story of Adam and Eve. A crucial issue is whether this passage should be read typologically to provide an example for a point that Paul wants to make, or, rather, whether it provides a timeless warrant for Paul's prohibition. Complementarians argue that Paul is providing such an unconditional warrant.

Historically, there has been a tradition of subordinating women to male hierarchy in church tradition, and advocates appealed to 1 Timothy 2:3-14. However, the appeal was consistently to the second half of the passage; women were held to be subordinate to men because they were considered to be more gullible, less intelligent, more easily deceived, and more subject to temptation than men. The complementarian position may not be genuinely new insofar as it embraces an ontological subordination of women to men, but (at least in its official formulations) it is a new position in that it does not regard this subordination as based in an ontological inferiority or susceptibility to deception, but rather in creation order. In contrast to traditional readings, complementarians focus on the first half of the passage and ignore the second half with its implications for a subordination rooted not merely in creation order, but in the fall and deception: "Adam was not deceived, but the woman was deceived."

If the passage is read typologically, this uncomfortable dilemma is avoided. The writer of 1 Timothy was not making a timeless injunction based on either creation order or on woman's inherent susceptibility to deception, but providing a typological illustration to address a particular local problem. As Eve was deceived, so the women in Ephesus were in danger of being deceived, and consequently should not teach until they were better informed. The concern is almost exactly parallel to another reference to Eve in Paul's writings: "But I am afraid that as the serpent deceived Eve by his cunning thoughts, your thoughts will be led astray from a sincere and pure devotion to Christ" (2 Cor. 11:3).

Finally, this passage provides a warning about hermeneutical carelessness. It is all too tempting to look to isolated verses here and there in the Bible addressing historical situations in different contexts, only to make a leap of application to a contemporary setting without regard to either the immediate context of the passage in its own setting, or to a careful consideration of a very different contemporary setting. The timeless appeal to women's "silence" in 1 Corinthians 14 or to Paul's prohibition of "teaching" or "exercising authority over men" in 1 Timothy 2 seems too easily to yield to just such a temptation.

POSTSCRIPT: WOMEN AND PUBLIC VERSUS PRIVATE SETTINGS

One of the problems with reading 1 Timothy 2:12 as a timeless prohibition of women teaching men is that it seems to stand in blatant contradiction to the New Testament account of Priscilla, wife of Aquilla, who is mentioned, along with her husband, as having taught Apollos in Acts 18:1-3, 24-26. The passage indicates that both she and her husband taught Apollos, and, since her name is mentioned first, she was presumably the primary instructor. Apollos is portrayed as already knowing the Scriptures, and as being "instructed in the way of the Lord," so the assumption is that Priscilla and Aquilla were providing additional knowledge to someone who already had a strong background in basic Christian faith. Priscilla is mentioned as a regular companion of Paul (Rom. 16:3; 1 Cor. 16:19; 2 Tim. 4:19), so she clearly played a significant role in his ministry. If the prohibition of women teaching in 1 Timothy 2:12 is a universal prohibition, then it presumably would have prohibited the teaching of Priscilla as well.

To avoid this difficulty, complementarians regularly make a distinction between private and public ministries of women. Complementarians affirm that women are allowed to engage in public ministry to and to teach other women and children. Women may teach and evangelize unbelievers (including men) in a public setting. However, women may talk with *Christian* men about the Bible and Christian doctrine only in a private context. The sole warrant for this distinction seems to be the reference to Priscilla and Aquila teaching Apollos in Acts 18:26: "[Apollos] began to speak boldly in the synagogue, but when Priscilla and Aquila, heard him, they took him and explained to him the word of God more accurately." Grudem states that the phrase "'they took him' . . . indicates that they waited to speak to him until they could take him aside, out of public view." Grudem denies that the case of Priscilla can provide a warrant for women's teaching, appealing to 1 Corinthians 14:33-36 and 1 Timothy 2:11-15: "[I]t is specifically the situations where the whole church is assembled that Paul restricts governing and teaching activities to men."[91]

However, as noted above, 1 Corinthians 14:33-36 says nothing about women *teaching*. First Timothy 2:11 does mention teaching, but places no restriction on a public context: if read as an absolute prohibition, it would prohibit all teaching of men by women, full stop. Grudem reads the prohibition of teaching from 1 Timothy 2:11 into 1 Corinthians 14:33-36, where no such prohibition exists, to prohibit *teaching* in a context of Christian worship; Grudem reads what is argued above as a restriction on disruptive speech leading to disorderly worship in 1 Corinthians 14:33-36 into 1 Timothy 2:11 in order to argue that the teaching prohibited must be *public* teaching, although no such qualification exists in 1 Timothy 2:11. Grudem takes the isolated verse of Acts 18:26 and reads an historical account of an incident in the life of Priscilla and Aquilla into other parts of the New Testament to provide a prohibition of public teaching that is mentioned neither in 1 Corinthians 14:33-36, in 1 Timothy 2:11, nor in Acts 18:26. Finally, Grudem's reading of the Acts passage itself is problematic. The passage does not say that Priscilla took Apollos aside, but that *both* Priscilla and Aquila took him aside. If the reference to Priscilla implies that women can only teach privately, then the mention of Aquila would necessarily imply the same about men. Witherington's assessment is more to the point: "The fact that this took place in at least semi-privacy is probably not very significant in terms of implication for correct church practice, since there is no indication that Luke was trying to avoid having Priscilla teach Apollos in a worship context."[92]

Catholic Arguments

10

A *Presbytera* Is Not a "Priestess"

Old Testament Priesthood

Previous chapters have focused primarily on Protestant objections against women's ordination, dealing especially with issues of biblical exegesis. The following chapters will address Catholic objections, focusing primarily on issues dealing with sacramental integrity.

Strictly speaking, this chapter should not be necessary. As with a previous chapter addressing non-theological objections to women's ordination, this one will address an objection that is not actually a theological objection.[1] Stated as succinctly as possible, the objection is that an ordained woman would be a "priestess," and the Christian church does not have "priestesses," but "priests." This is an objection that one does not hear among Protestants, since Protestant churches do not refer to their clergy as either "priests" or "priestesses," but as pastors. It is not an objection that is encountered in the theological literature, as most theologians realize that the term "priestess" is offensive, and those who advocate women's ordination are not advocating the ordination of "priestesses," but the ordination of women who will fulfill the same roles as male clergy, who in Protestant churches are referred to as "pastors," and in churches of Catholic tradition (Orthodox, Roman Catholic, many Anglicans) as "priests."

The objection appears primarily in two venues: (1) on the bad-mannered no-holds-barred free-for-all of the internet, where the term is used regularly by those opposed to women's ordination, and (2) in private conversation, where those opposed to women's ordination are referring out of earshot to women clergy, for whom they use the term "priestess." In both cases, the term is used disparagingly, with the conscious realization that the women to whom reference is being made would not use the term to describe themselves, and would find the term offensive. Those who use the term "priestess" are assuming as valid assumptions about women's ordination that those who are in favor of women's ordination would reject, and are addressing arguments that those in favor of women's ordination would not make. Since advocates of women's ordination do not believe that ordained women are "priestesses," to argue against "priestesses" is a classic example of a "red herring" argument. Nonetheless, since the argument does raise issues concerning the continuity between the Old Testament priesthood and New Testament church office, and concerning the differences and similarities between Old Testament priesthood and pagan religions, it provides a helpful introduction to the Catholic discussion.

What is perhaps the first formal use of the argument is found in an essay by C. S. Lewis, "Priestesses in the Church?"[2] As an Anglican, Lewis was objecting in 1948 to the possible ordination of women in the Church of England. In a short span of six pages, Lewis raises many of what will become the standard Catholic objections to women's ordination, particularly issues about language and imagery concerning God as male and the symbolic implications of female clergy, objections that will be addressed in the next few chapters. Most significantly, Lewis uses the term "priestesses" and makes the argument to be addressed in this chapter. The single issue that is at the heart of his essay can be found in a succinct statement: "Goddesses have, of course, been worshipped; many religions have had priestesses. But they are religions quite different in character than Christianity." Lewis goes on to say that the ordination of women "is an argument not in favour of priestesses but against Christianity."[3]

Lewis makes two assumptions: (1) the ordination of women necessarily implies the worship of "goddesses," not of the biblical God; (2) the ordination of women would be equivalent to the ordination of pagan "priestesses," which would, in effect, be the replacement of Christianity with a different religion. Questions of religious imagery or "goddess worship" will not be discussed here; that will come in a later chapter.[4]

Lewis does not specify which practices he associates with "priestesses" in his essay. He assumes that his readers are familiar with them. However, many of those opposed to the ordination of women presume as self-evident that pagan "priestesses" engaged in "cult prostitution," so this is the first issue to be addressed. Briefly expressed, the argument assumes the following: There was in ancient Israel a "sex cult" which was a major focus of attack by the Old Testament Hebrew prophets. This cult included sacred prostitutes, sexual orgies, and initiation rites in which young women offered sexual favors as part of a fertility ritual. This sex cult had its origins in Canaanite worship, was connected with the worship of Baal and Asherah, and was directly connected to goddess worship. One of the main reasons—perhaps the single most important reason—that Israelite religion had only male priests, while pagan religions that worshiped goddesses had female priestesses as well, was that female priestesses were directly associated with cultic prostitution, a practice antithetical to Old Testament religion. To advocate the ordination of women as "priestesses" today is to turn Christianity into a fertility "goddess" religion, with all that implies, including, especially, sexual lasciviousness.[5]

The obvious response to this concern is to ask, "Is it true?" Did pagan priestess cult prostitutes exist? Did Canaanite religion include sexual rites? Is there any evidence for Canaanite initiations that included sexual activity? Is there any historical evidence for the existence of such cult prostitutes? Is there evidence that Canaanite religion included any sexual activity whatsoever? Recent more careful examination of the evidence indicates that the answer is "no." As Tikva Frymer-Kensky notes in her definitive book on the Bible and goddesses, "the whole idea of a sex cult—in Israel or in Canaan—is a chimera, the product of ancient and modern sexual fantasies."[6]

Frymer-Kensky provides an overview of the historical evidence. The belief that Canaanite religion was sexual in nature and included sacred prostitutes was a major assumption of modern historical scholarship, appearing in William Robertson Smith's *Lectures on the Religion of the Semites* (1889) and James George Frazer's *Adonis, Attis and Osiris: Studies in the History of Oriental Religions* (1906). The assumption of sexual license continued with later twentieth century writers such as William Foxwell Albright and Gerhard von Rad. Subsequent scholars simply assume the existence of such a sex cult, and, uncritically cite the references used in earlier sources as evidence.[7]

The historical evidence for religious prostitution derives from a single reference in the classical Greek historian Herodotus, who describes a Babylonian practice connected with the cult of Mylitta (Ishtar) in which young women supposedly "sit in the temple of Aphrodite" and have intercourse with strangers.[8] Scholars point out that Herodotus is talking about Babylon, not Syria or Israel, and that his observations about Babylon are often untrustworthy. As a Greek, he believed in the superiority of Greek culture over that of "barbarians," whom he often accused of cannibalism and sexual license. There are no cuneiform texts that confirm the practice Herodotus describes, and, as Frymer-Kensky points out, "[a]ll the later Roman and Christian allegations of sexual initiation ultimately derive from this one passage in Herodotus."[9]

All evidence for the existence of sacred prostitution in ancient Israel derives from the translation of the word *qedeshah*, which means literally "holy woman" or "tabooed woman." The Old Testament prohibits both *qedeshot* (feminine plural) and *qedeshim* (masculine plural), and they are often associated with local shrines, pillars, and asherah[10], which were regarded as idolatrous and foreign to Hebrew religion.[11]

Modern English translations of the Bible often translate the terms as "female cult prostitute" and "male cult prostitute"; however, there is no historical evidence to indicate that there is anything sexual about their nature. In Ugaritic texts, the *qadesh* is a type of priest; the Babylonian *qadistu* is a kind of priestess. In neither case do the texts indicate any sexual activity in connection with their functions. There are two passages in the Old Testament that have been pointed to as indication of sexual prostitution in connection with the terms. In Genesis 38:16, Tamar disguises herself as a prostitute (*zona*) so that Judah will impregnate her. When he returns to find her again, he asks, "Where is the *qedeshah*?" (v. 22). Frymer-Kensky suggests that prostitutes and *qedeshah* were equally women outside the normal family structure, with no males to protect them, and were thus vulnerable to male sexual approach; but there is no reason to believe based on this passage that sexual activity was an inherent part of the role of the *qedeshah*.[12]

In Hosea 4:14, the terms "prostitute" (*zona*) and *qedeshah* appear in tandem, and many translations translate the latter as "cult prostitute": "[F]or the men themselves go aside with prostitutes, and sacrifice with cult prostitutes" (ESV). However, recent commentators recognize that without further evidence, "it is premature to assume that *qedeshah* is a woman involved in cultic sexual service."[13] There is nothing in the text itself that suggests that *qedeshah* should be translated as "cult prostitute." Frymer-Kensky sums up the evidence succinctly: "There is no native evidence for sexual religious cult activity."[14]

If the existence of "cult prostitutes" in ancient Israel is not based on solid evidence, the same conclusion is now being realized concerning cult prostitution in the New Testament world. The single source most cited as evidence is an ambiguous passage in Strabo (ca. 64 BC–AD 21), who refers to the temple of Aphrodite in Corinth as owning temple slaves and "courtesans" (*hetairai*) dedicated to the goddess. Strabo refers to this not as something contemporary, but as existing long in the past. As with Herodotus, Strabo is regarded as a less than trustworthy source, and the meaning of the passage is unclear. Strabo states that the slaves and courtesans were owned by the temple, but says nothing about cult prostitution taking place on temple grounds. If Strabo was actually describing cult prostitution, he was describing something unique to Corinth in the distant past, something that no longer existed, and was certainly not characteristic of Greek culture in general. In another passage, Strabo refers to cult prostitution in Persia, and cites for his authority the problematic passage from Herodotus referred to above. The only other literary reference is from Athenaeus (AD 200), who refers to *hetairai* in Corinth who participated in public sacrifices to Aphrodite, and to private citizens who vow to "render courtesans (*hetairai*)" to Aphrodite. Again, the passage is ambiguous. Nothing suggests that the "courtesans" were cult prostitutes. Finally, there are contemporary biblical scholars who suggest that cult prostitution in Ephesus lies behind Paul's admonition against women teaching in 1 Timothy 2:11-15. However, there simply is no evidence for cult prostitution in ancient Ephesus. There were priestesses who served the goddess Artemis, but there is no evidence to suggest that there was anything sexual about their roles. The notion of cult prostitution in the pagan Greek culture of New Testament times seems to be as much a figment of modern imagination as the cult prostitution of Old Testament times.[15]

Since the evidence indicates that the orgiastic cult prostitution of ancient culture did not exist, it is necessary to find another explanation for the all-male priesthood of ancient Israel. Why did ancient Israel have only male priests? One suggested answer is that the practice had to do with preserving male authority. As discussed in previous chapters, this is an explanation endorsed by both radical feminists and by hierarchical complementarians, although with diametrically opposite evaluations.

Since Catholic objections to women's ordination are no longer tied to issues of male hierarchy or authority, a different explanation is in order. Two plausible explanations follow. A previous chapter discussed differences between roles of men and women in the Old Testament period rooted in socioeconomic realities.[16] Given that the household was the basic unit of production in ancient societies, and only women gave birth and breastfed children, women's social and economic activities were necessarily limited to activities that kept them close to children. In ancient societies, biological necessity limited women's roles to the domestic sphere, while men worked in the public sphere outside the household because they were never pregnant and were not required to nurse children.

What follows suggests an additional explanation, one largely overlooked by both Protestant complementarians and Catholic sacramentalists in the current discussion, but also connected to women's physical biology. One of the most obvious historical differences between Judaism and Christianity is the way that they deal with what have been called the "ceremonial" or "ritual purity" laws of the Old Testament. Both Jews and Christians endorse as authoritative what Jews call the "Hebrew Bible" and Christians the "Old Testament,"

However, historically, Christians have distinguished between the ritual, civil, and moral laws of the Old Testament in a way that Jews have not. For Christians, those Old Testament laws whose subject matter is moral behavior are considered to be still binding and obligatory, such as the Ten Commandments. The ritual laws of the Old Testament, concerning such matters as temple sacrifice, the distinction between clean and unclean foods, and male circumcision, are no longer binding because they have been "fulfilled" by the sacrifice of Jesus Christ on the cross. Christians do not have a Jewish priesthood because Jesus is our High Priest (Hebrews 7–10). Christians do not have a temple because the church is the temple of the Holy Spirit (1 Cor. 3:16-17). The civil laws of the Old Testament, matters regulating such things as punishment for theft or murder and other kinds of wrongdoing, are not binding in themselves, but the moral principles behind them are binding. This distinction between ritual, moral, and civil law appears as early as Irenaeus of Lyons (ca. 120/130–202/203) in his *Against Heresies* (4.14.3; 4.15.1). In the medieval period, Thomas Aquinas developed the distinction systematically in the *Summa Theologiae*, where he discussed distinctions between different kinds of law. Reformation Christianity preserved the distinction where it appears in such places as the Anglican Thirty-nine Articles, the Lutheran Augsburg Confession, and John Calvin's *Institutes of the Christian Religion*.[17]

In recent decades, the distinction has been challenged as providing too simple an explanation of how law functions in the Old Testament. More recent discussion has focused on the issue of "purity," influenced initially by sociological discussions such as Mary Douglas's *Purity and Danger*.[18] Biblical scholars after Douglas have focused more narrowly on the way that "purity" functions in the Old Testament/Hebrew Bible, tending to distance Old Testament purity from general cultural notions such as "taboo."[19] Scholars sometimes claim that the Old Testament does not distinguish between moral and ritual laws in the manner of the later Christian distinction. On a surface level, this is correct in that both kinds of material appear in the legal material of the Pentateuch, and nowhere does the Biblical text explicitly identify some laws as moral and others as ritual. The distinction is clearly presumed, however, as discussions of "purity" in the Old Testament make clear. What are the characteristics of Old Testament purity?

(1) Old Testament purity makes sense only in the context of holiness or its absence. Holiness belongs first to God, and, by extension, to people, places, and times associated with God.

(2) Ritual purity and moral purity are distinguished. A woman who has recently given birth to a child or who is having her menstrual period is "unclean," or ritually impure, but is not immoral. A man who has a bodily emission is, again, ritually impure, but not evil. A house that has certain kinds of growths (identified as "leprosy") must be destroyed, but the house is not considered to be "evil" or occupied by evil spirits.

(3) Although distinct, similar language is used to describe ritual impurity and moral impurity. Both ritual impurity and moral impurity "defile" or cause "pollution." However, they are dealt with in different ways. Ritual impurity causes "uncleanness" and cleansing takes place through a rite of purification. Moral impurity can only be resolved by repentance, punishment, and/or sacrifice.

(4) Ritual impurity originally seems to have arisen from association with repulsion or loathing: certain kinds of animals (e.g., reptiles, scavengers that eat dead bodies, or insects); bodily emissions; dead bodies. However, neutral things (such as bowls, clothing, or houses) can also become unclean.

(5) The Old Testament law code associates purity and impurity chiefly with reference to the "cult," or temple worship. This applies primarily to priests; a priest who has touched a corpse, who has had sexual relations, or is a leper may not perform priestly functions. However, by extension the purity laws apply to non-priests as well. The ritually impure may not participate in temple worship, eat of sacrificial meals, or participate in Passover.

(6) By extension, language of purity and holiness is also transferred to moral behavior. Idolatry, murder, and sexual misdeeds, in particular, are said to defile or pollute the land itself. However, there is no ceremonial ritual that can purify the land from moral defilement or remove its pollution. Once the land has reached a certain level of moral pollution, God exercises judgment by expelling the inhabitants.[20]

The Book of Leviticus lists the primary categories of clean and unclean things and activities, and shows the close connection between purity and temple worship. Leviticus 7:19-21 stipulates that sacrificial meat may not come into contact with impurity, and that unclean persons may not eat the sacrifice. Leviticus 11 lists unclean animals that may not be eaten: non-ruminant mammals without split hooves; any sea creature without scales (shellfish, etc.); predatory birds and scavengers; most insects. Childbirth results in uncleanness (Lev. 12:1-8), as do bodily discharges (semen and menstruation; Lev. 15:1-33). Finally, skin diseases (leprosy) and even certain "leprous diseases" associated with houses (mildew) are considered "unclean" (13-14). Again, while ritually defiling, none of these conditions is considered to be sinful. The solution for each condition is ritual purification, not repentance.[21]

There is an inherent connection between ritual purity and moral holiness, but they are also clearly distinguished. On the one hand, Israel is called to be a holy people, separate from the nations. There is a link between worship and ethics in that those called to celebrate and participate in God's holiness in worship enter into a realm of sanctified space and time. Certainly this is one of the functions of the Old Testament purity laws and Israel's annual feasts. The purity laws distinguish that which is sacred from that which is profane. Unlike pagan fertility religions, Israel's feasts have nothing to do with guaranteeing the fertility of the annual crops. They are feasts of thanksgiving, and are associated with specific historic events in Israel's history, such as the exodus from Egypt. At the same time, Israel's prophets make clear that ritual purity alone does not guarantee holiness or divine blessing. Sacrifices unaccompanied by moral holiness are worse than useless, and moral perversity will pollute the land, resulting in judgment. It is not fertility rituals or even ritual purity that brings God's blessing or results in God's curse, but moral holiness.[22]

Those opposed to women's ordination sometimes look to the Old Testament, point to the exclusively male Old Testament priesthood, and assume an intrinsic connection to male identity, either in terms of male authority (Protestant complementarians), to the relationship between male symbolism and sacrifice (mentioned above, and to be discussed later), or to unfortunate associations connected with female "priestesses" (discussed above). Those who make the analogy ignore other more plausible reasons for an exclusively male priesthood. First, as noted already, socioeconomic factors in ancient cultures existing until the modern era largely restricted the work of women to the domestic sphere. Second, advocates of male-only ordination miss that the Old Testament priesthood was restrictive in many ways, not simply in reference to gender. Old Testament priests were not only exclusively male, but also exclusively members of the tribe of Levi who could trace their ancestry to Moses' brother Aaron.

Oddly, those who point to an exclusively male Old Testament priesthood ignore what is certainly the most significant and obvious factor excluding women from the priesthood. The Old Testament purity laws, which, again, were primarily connected with temple worship, would have prohibited women from performing priestly functions for several days at least once a month, and for a significant period after childbirth. In addition, many Old Testament temple functions were periodically scheduled (feasts, periodic prayers), and women could not be depended on to be ritually pure on each occasion the function needed to be performed. Tikva Frymer-Kensky's claim that the "religious dimension of sexuality disappears in biblical monotheism" provides the rationale: "The priests, guardians of Israel's ongoing contact with the Holy, had to be particularly careful to keep preserve (sic) the separation between Israel's priestly functions and attributes of any hint of sexuality." One of the purposes of the impurity provisions of Israel's law was to keep both sexual activity and death separate from the sacred realm. Anyone who was ritually impure was not allowed to participate in the rites of the temple.[23] Women did perform certain religious roles during the Old Testament period, but they were generally the kinds of things that one could do at home.[24]

Women were prohibited not only from priestly office, but even from getting too close to the area of sacrifice itself. The Jerusalem temple at the time of Jesus included not only a Court of the Gentiles, beyond which non-Jews were prohibited to enter on threat of death, but also (just inside that) a Court of the Women, halfway between the Court of the Gentiles and the Court of Israel (or court of the men) beyond which women could not enter. Certainly the most plausible reason for excluding women from the Old Testament priesthood, as well as excluding their presence even from too close proximity to the innermost regions of the temple itself, had to do with concerns about ritual purity, not about "goddess worship" or sexual license.

PURITY AND HOLINESS IN THE NEW TESTAMENT

New Testament Christianity was a form of Judaism. Christians affirmed their faith in the God of Israel who had created the world, had made a covenant with Abraham and his descendants, had rescued the people of Israel from slavery in Egypt, and had given the people his law at Mount Sinai. New Testament Christians accepted as authoritative the same Hebrew Scriptures as did Pharisaic Judaism. What distinguished Christians from other Jews was their conviction that the God of Abraham was also the Father of Jesus of Nazareth; that Jesus had brought salvation by being crucified for the sins of the world; that God the Father had raised Jesus from the dead, declaring him to be both Messiah and Son of God; that the Christian church was the gathered community to whom the Father and the risen Son had given the Holy Spirit, who awaited Jesus' return in glory and judgment.

Much Christian biblical interpretation has been concerned to draw a radical distinction between the Old Testament and the New Testament, using such distinctions as those between law and gospel. Historically, there have been Christians who have ventured close to the heresy of Marcionism, denying that the Old Testament and Judaism have anything to do with Christianity, and vice versa. The earliest Christians did not understand Christianity and Judaism to be opposed, however, but understood God's saving work in Jesus Christ to be the fulfillment of the hopes of the Jewish people. The earliest Christians continued to be concerned with both purity and holiness. Markus Bockmuehl points out that ἅγιος (*hagios*) and cognate terms for holiness occur 275 times in the New Testament, that ninety-six of these references are in the Pauline epistles, and that Paul speaks of holiness twice as often as all four gospels put together.[25] One of the key distinctions between Judaism and Christianity, however, was that New Testament writers associated language of purity and holiness exclusively with the moral realm; Christians were not obligated to keep Old Testament purity laws.

There seem to have been two primary reasons for this. The first was the Gentile mission and the admission of Gentiles to the church. Perhaps the single most important issue of controversy in the New Testament church concerned whether Gentile converts needed to be circumcised and keep other Old Testament ritual purity laws. This is the presenting issue in Paul's letter to the Galatians, and led eventually to the Council of Jerusalem (Acts 15), at which it was decided that Gentiles needed to refrain from idol worship and sexual immorality, but did not need to abide by the Old Testament purity laws, including circumcision and dietary laws.[26] Paul's discussion of food in 1 Corinthians 6:12-13, Galatians 2:11-12, and food offered to idols in 1 Corinthians 8:1-13 makes clear that he did not think Old Testament dietary laws were any longer binding. His reference to "sabbaths" (Col. 2:16) indicates that he did not believe that Christians were bound to keep Old Testament feasts.

The second reason had to do with sacrifice and the temple. The Book of Acts makes clear that early Jewish Christians continued to worship in the temple until they were expelled (Acts 2:46; 5:42; 8:1). At the same time, New Testament Christology made temple worship unnecessary if not problematic. The New Testament identifies Jesus as the high priest who has succeeded the Old Testament priesthood, and his death on the cross as the single sacrifice making animal sacrifices no longer necessary (Heb. 7–10). The New Testament identifies the temple no longer with the temple in Jerusalem, but with both Christ and the church (1 Cor. 3:16-17; Eph. 2:19-22). Given the inherent connection between Old Testament purity laws and temple worship, the Christological transformation of sacrifice and temple makes the Old Testament purity laws superfluous.[27]

JESUS AND PURITY

How did Jesus address issues of purity and holiness? Jesus was certainly concerned about the sanctity of Israel and the holiness of the temple. He participated in the temple festivals, and his controversies about the Sabbath should not be understood to mean a rejection of the Sabbath, but a concern for its purpose and sanctity (Mark 2:27; 3:4). At the same time, Jesus' interpretation at the Last Supper of his own death as a sacrifice and a new covenant both fulfills and surpasses the temple sacrificial system (Matt. 26:28; Luke 22:20). Significantly, Jesus predicted the destruction of the temple (Matt. 24:2; Mark 13:2; Luke 21:6), and at his trial was accused of having threatened to destroy the temple and restore it in three days (Matt. 26:61; Mark 14:58). John's Gospel interprets this to be a reference to his own resurrection and the temple of his body (John 2:18-22).

Most significant for this discussion are those stories about Jesus in which he seems to have contravened the purity codes.[28] The gospels contain numerous stories of Jesus' healing of lepers (Mark 1:40-44; Matt. 8:2-4; 10:1, 8; 11:5; Luke 5:12-14; 17:11-19). By touching the lepers in order to cure them, Jesus should have been made ceremonially unclean. In Mark 14:3 and Matthew 26:6, Jesus is said to have eaten at the house of Simon the leper. If Simon was still a leper, Jesus would have been ceremonially unclean. There are also incidents in which Jesus raised the dead (Luke 7:11-17; John 11:1-44). Again, coming into contact with a corpse should have made Jesus ceremonially unclean. Concerning *kosher* food laws, in the story of a conflict between Jesus and the Pharisees about whether his disciples ate with "defiled" hands because they did not follow the "tradition of the elders" about washing before eating, Jesus responded: "Do you not see that whatever goes into a person from outside cannot defile him . . . ? . . . What comes out a person is what defiles him.

For from within out of the heart of man, come evil thoughts. . . . All these evil things come from within, and they defile a person" (Mark 7:14-23). Famously, the Gospel of Mark interpreted this to mean, "Thus he declared all foods clean" (v. 19). Finally, although it happened infrequently, some of Jesus' healings involved Gentiles (Matt. 8:5-13; Luke 7:1-10; John 4:46-54). Though this is a matter of disagreement, some scholars believe that Jews of Jesus' time would have regarded coming into immediate contact with Gentiles or entering their homes as creating ritual impurity.[29]

Significantly, the gospels say nothing about Jesus having gone to the temple to purify himself after having engaged in behavior such as touching lepers or corpses that should have made him ceremonially unclean.[30] The oddness of the Gospels not even mentioning the issue of impurity would seem to imply that in Jesus' healings, rather than himself being contaminated by ritual impurity, contact with Jesus brings about and expands the realm of holiness. Rather than the unclean making Jesus ceremonially impure, Jesus' presence makes the unclean clean. As David deSilva notes:

> The Gospels . . . present Jesus encountering a stream of ritually impure and potentially polluting people, but in encounter their contagion does not defile Jesus; rather his holiness purges their pollutions, renders them clean and integrates them again into the mainstream of Jewish society where they can reclaim their birthright, as it were, among the people of God.[31]

In this light, there are three incidents involving women in Jesus' ministry that directly touch on the issue of ceremonial uncleanness. In the incident of the healing of the Syrophoenician woman (Mark 7:25-30; Matthew 15:21-28), Jesus came into contact not only with a non-Jew, but also with a Canaanite (Matt. 15:22). The Canaanites had been the historical enemies of Israel, dating from the time of the exodus from Egypt and the conquest under Joshua. Rather than being defiled by the woman's presence, Jesus healed her daughter. In the double story of the raising of Jairus' daughter and the healing of a woman with a hemorrhage (Mark 5:21-43), Jesus twice came into contact with women in a manner that should have made him ceremonially impure—touching a corpse, and being touched by a menstruating woman. Rather than being made unclean, Jesus makes the unclean clean—raising the girl from the dead, and healing the woman with a twelve-year hemorrhage. Significantly, unlike the previous incident with the leper, whom Jesus had commanded to have his healing confirmed by a priest, Jesus does not even require the woman to undergo the usual seven-day purification period.[32]

All three of these incidents are theologically significant in that they indicate that in his interaction with women, Jesus overrode the traditional Jewish purity laws concerning impurity; however, the story of the healing of the woman with the hemorrhage is especially significant because of its connection with the one significant reason that Jewish women would have been excluded from full participation in Jewish religious life. If the ordinary Jewish woman would have been ceremonially impure once a month and after child-birth, this woman had been ritually impure and excluded from full participation in Jewish religious life for twelve years. Again, rather than being made ritually impure by coming into contact with this woman, Jesus healed the ritually impure woman and brought her back into the circle of participation in religious life. A central theme of the gospels is therefore that men and women could equally be Jesus' disciples because his presence overcame the distinction between ceremonially pure and impure.[33]

THE NEW TESTAMENT CHURCHES AND RITUAL PURITY

As noted above, issues of ritual purity were an area of contention in the admission of Gentiles into the Christian churches, particularly regarding circumcision and diet. Paul's letter to the Galatians and the Jerusalem council of Acts 15 made it clear that Gentile male converts did not have to become Jews by undergoing circumcision in order to become Christians, and Gentile Christians did not have to adopt a Jewish kosher diet. An obvious question to ask at this point would concern the status of Gentile women converts to Christian faith. Did the New Testament churches continue to uphold the Jewish purity laws regarding women? Surprisingly, the New Testament simply does not discuss this issue. However, it seems clear that the New Testament churches no longer followed Old Testament purity laws in reference to women, and the New Testament's silence is itself a confirmation. Given the specific discussions concerning food and circumcision, if female ritual purity were an issue, surely there would have been at least some mention of the problem. Female purity was not mentioned in the Jerusalem council of Acts 15; it is not mentioned in any of the epistles. The Book of Acts indicates that women such as Lydia were leaders in the Gentile churches, and that churches met in their homes (Acts 16:14-15). Paul's letters make clear that many of the leaders in the Pauline churches were women (Rom. 16:1-7).[34] If female ritual purity were an issue, women church leaders and worshiping in the homes of women would have created a problem.

It would seem that there is a logical parallel between the issues of male circumcision and Old Testament purity laws regarding women. The presenting issue of Paul's letters to the Galatians was whether Gentile male converts needed to be circumcised—an issue of male ritual purity. Paul does not mention issues of women's ritual purity, but the logical principles should be the same. Paul's theological stance concerning both issues is found in Galatians 3:28: "There is neither Jew nor Greek, there is neither slave nor free, there is neither male nor female, for you are all one in Christ Jesus." Those opposed to women's ordination often complain that appeals to Galatians 3:28 are illegitimate in this context because Paul is not discussing the "gender roles" of men and women, but rather their equal access to salvation.

The passage has no bearing whatsoever on the issue of women's ordination, they claim.[35] This objection oversimplifies Paul's argument, however. The crucial issue in Galatians was not simply the equal access of men and women, slaves and free, to salvation, but also the cultural barriers between Jew and Gentile as expressed in the purity code boundary markers of male circumcision and the sharing of meals between Jewish and Gentile Christians. Paul's argument is that equal access to salvation through faith in Christ eliminates the necessity of the Jewish ritual purity boundary markers of circumcision or food purity. It follows of logical necessity that purity codes concerning female uncleanness would also have been one of the purity code boundaries removed by the gospel.

Purity codes concerning women's ritual impurity are the most plausible primary factor that prevented Jewish women from full participation in religious life. Women could not be priests because of ceremonial uncleanness. So Paul's argument in Galatians would indeed be relevant to the issue of women's ordination in the Christian churches. Appeals to Jewish temple practice concerning an exclusively male priesthood should have no relevance in the context of Christian worship since Jesus' transforming presence has overcome purity boundaries that separate not only Jews and Gentiles, but also men and women. Jesus has made the unclean clean, and the impure pure.

CONCLUDING REFLECTIONS

It was suggested at the beginning of this chapter that this chapter should not strictly be necessary. Advocates of the ordination of women to church orders are not asking for the ordination of "priestesses"; opposition to women's ordination because of concern about "priestesses" is a red herring. Nonetheless, given the frequent occurrence of the "priestess" objection, at least at a popular level, the chapter addressed it by looking at priesthood in the Old Testament, particularly the single issue of why the Old Testament priesthood was exclusively male. The common presumption that this had something to do with the opposition to a pagan sex cult involving female "priestesses" is a modern myth fueled by overactive imaginations. There simply is no historical evidence that such a sex cult existed. There were no ancient women "sacred prostitute priestesses."

The only reason for the exclusion of women from Old Testament priesthood actually mentioned in the Old Testament concerns ritual purity connected with temple worship. Only men were priests in the Old Testament because Old Testament purity laws would have made it impossible for women to function as priests on a regular basis. Indeed, women were not only precluded from the priesthood, but also relegated to a completely separate area outside the main temple itself—the Court of the Women.

The discussion concluded by looking at holiness and purity in the New Testament—in Paul's writings, the Jerusalem Council of Acts 15, and the ministry of Jesus. While the New Testament is concerned about moral holiness and purity, the New Testament is also clear that ritual purity is no longer an issue for New Testament Christians. The Old Testament's primary reason for having an exclusively male priesthood is thus irrelevant to the ordination of Christian women to ecclesial office in the church.

One final concern needs to be addressed: the issue of "shaming" and social (rather than "ritual") purity codes that is associated with shaming. A previous chapter discussed the issues of honor and shame at length, specifically in the context of the New Testament.[36] The Mediterranean culture of New Testament times was an "honor/ shame" culture, and Jesus intentionally subverted this culture by redefining honor in terms of servanthood. This subversion of honor culture was picked up by Paul in his notion of cruciform discipleship.[37] For both Jesus and Paul, honor is not found in conventional notions of status, but in following the path of the cross by willingly submitting one's own concerns to those of others.

Issues of honor and shame are not unique to ancient culture. Indeed, as postmodern culture moves more and more away from identifying behavior as "sinful" or "guilt-inducing," it seems to have embraced in its place a stronger focus on shaming. One of the ways in which women in particular are shamed has to do with behavior or clothing that contravenes acceptable sexual, gender, or even fashion standards. The coarse expression used to describe this kind of disapproval is "slut-shaming." It would seem that the correlation between ordination of women to Christian ministry and "priestess" language is just such an example of cultural shaming behavior. Ordained women do not think of themselves as "priestesses," but using the term suggests that such women are engaging in sexually inappropriate behavior; for a woman to be ordained is the social equivalence of cult prostitution. "Priestess" language is a form of shaming by associating the ordination of women with questionable sexual behavior.

Issues of ritual purity are also relevant to the historical reasons for opposition to women's ordination. "Purity codes" can function in a specifically religious context, as did the Old Testament purity codes. However, there can also be sociological purity codes, codes that have to do with the acceptability of certain behaviors within a given culture. A previous chapter addressed the single most significant historical reason for opposition to women's ordination in the church, namely, that women are incapable of being ordained because they were considered to be less intelligent, more easily susceptible to temptation, and a sexual temptation for men.[38] Although not a ritual purity code, such attitudes toward women have functioned historically as a social purity code, excluding women from church office essentially because they were considered to be defiling.

As noted in the beginning of this chapter, such reasons for opposition to women's ordination are not properly theological, yet they need to be addressed. From a theological perspective, the proper Christian response to such objections is to point once again to Jesus' own behavior toward those who were "impure" or "unclean" as well as to the New Testament church's early refusal to endorse purity distinctions between Jews and Gentiles, slave and free, and, yes, men and women. As Paul wrote in response to those who demanded Gentile circumcision: "For freedom Christ has set us free; stand firm therefore, and do not submit again to a yoke of slavery" (Gal. 5:1).

11

Women's Ordination and the Priesthood of Christ

Biblical and Patristic Background

Continuing to address Catholic objections to the ordination of women, this chapter will be the first to examine the definitive *new* Catholic objection to the ordination of women that first appeared in the Congregation for the Doctrine of the Faith's Declaration *Inter Insigniores*, approved by Pope Paul VI. In summary, the objection runs as follows: Women cannot be ordained because, during the celebration of the Eucharist, the presiding priest represents Jesus Christ. During the eucharistic prayer, the priest recites Christ's words (the "words of institution")—"This is my body . . . this is my blood"—and thus makes Christ present by acting as a representative of, or "in the person of" Christ (*in persona Christi*). Because Jesus Christ is a male, only a male priest can exercise this representative function. This chapter will summarize the rise of the objection and examine the relevant biblical and patristic background.

Catholic objections to women's ordination are distinct from the Protestant hierarchical position based on permanent authority of men over women (discussed previously) in that Catholic objections focus not on authority *per se*, but on issues of sacramental and, in particular, eucharistic theology. Catholic objections rest on the following assumptions not usually shared by those referred to above as "Protestants." First, while the priesthood of Christ is unique, ordained clergy in some manner participate in Christ's priesthood. The clergy are not simply members of the congregation who have been delegated to perform a function, but have a distinct ontological status bestowed on them through the laying on of hands in ordination. The clergy are not simply "elders" or representative members of the congregation, but are in some sense, "priests."[1] Second, while the primary duty of ordained clergy is to proclaim the Word and to celebrate the sacraments, the Eucharist has the distinct purpose of making the risen Christ sacramentally or "really" *present* in a way that he is not present in creation in general. The Eucharist is not *simply* a memorial or "nothing more" than a symbol (as in Zwinglianism), but in some sense, it really is or enables participation in the risen humanity of Christ. The consecrated elements of the Eucharist "are" or "become" or "enable participation in" the risen Christ's body and blood. Third, the Eucharist is, in a qualified sense, a sacrifice. Protestant objections at the time of the Reformation to the notion of eucharistic sacrifice as a "repetition" of Christ's sacrifice seem largely based on misunderstanding. No one seems ever to have believed *that*! The patristic and Catholic position is that Christ's sacrifice took place once-and-for-all on the cross of Calvary, and cannot be repeated. Nonetheless, in the celebration of the Eucharist, Christ's once-and-for-all sacrifice is made effectively present or "re-presented." Although Christ's once-and-for-all sacrifice is a past event, its effectiveness is not relegated to the past.

Although using the adjective "Catholic" to describe this position, it is not assumed here that "Catholic" means exclusively *Roman* Catholic. Broadly speaking, Eastern Orthodox Christians, many Anglicans (particularly "Anglo-Catholics"), Lutherans, and some Reformed could embrace the above three points. The third point would be problematic for Lutherans (as well as low-church Anglicans and many Reformed) insofar as Luther rejected the "sacrifice of the mass," but Lutheran affirmation of the "real presence" still makes the Lutheran position fall into the parameters of what is here referred to as "Catholic."[2]

It needs to be emphasized that this is a new argument against women's ordination. The traditional argument was that women cannot be ordained because they are less intelligent, more emotional, and more subject to temptation. Precisely because of this ontological defect, women cannot be ordained and they cannot exercise authority over men. Neither Protestant complementarians nor Catholic sacramentalists any longer hold to this traditional position.

Catholics no longer endorse any hierarchical opposition to women's orders. To the contrary, the modern Roman Catholic church has fully embraced women's equality—including the assumption that women are fully equal to men in exercising leadership and authority. Thus, Pope John Paul II's *Mulieris Dignitatem* adapts what could be called an "egalitarian" interpretation of Paul's exhortation to husbands and wives in Ephesians 6. The "submission" that Paul enjoins to wives is a "mutual submission": "However, whereas in the relationship between Christ and the Church the subjection is only on the part of the Church, in the relationship between husband and wife the 'subjection' is not one-sided but mutual."[3] Sara Butler notes: "Because the contemporary magisterium has abandoned the view that women are unilaterally subject to men, it obviously does not supply this as the reason women cannot be priests."[4]

Accordingly, the Roman Catholic Church embraced a new argument against the ordination of women rooted in sacramental theology. Only a male can be ordained because only a male priest can represent Christ (act *in persona Christi*) in the celebration of the Eucharist. That this position is indeed a new position is evident in that it first appeared in the Congregation for the Doctrine of the Faith's *Inter Insigniores* (*Declaration on the Question of the Admission of Women to the Ministerial Priesthood*) in 1976. In the Declaration, the writers state first "that the bishop or the priest in the exercise of his ministry, does not act in his own name, *in persona propria*: he represents Christ, who acts through him: 'the priest truly acts in the place of Christ.'" The Declaration associates this representative stance particularly with the celebration of the Eucharist and the "words of consecration": "[T]he priest, who alone has the power to perform [the Eucharist], then acts not only through the effective power conferred on him by Christ, but *in persona Christi*, taking the role of Christ, to the point of being his very image, when he pronounces the words of consecration." Finally, the Declaration draws the evident conclusion. Only a male priest can represent Christ in this way because Jesus Christ is a male:

> The same natural resemblance is required for persons as for things: when Christ's role in the Eucharist is to be expressed sacramentally, there would not be this "natural resemblance" which must exist between Christ and his minister if the role of Christ were not taken by a man: in such a case it would be difficult to see in the minister the image of Christ. For Christ himself was and remains a man.[5]

The same position reappears in Pope John Paul II's *Mulieris Dignitatem* and *Pastores Dabo Vobis*. In *Mulieris Dignitatem*, John Paul II stated:

> It is the Eucharist above all that expresses the redemptive act of Christ the Bridegroom towards the Church the Bride. This is clear and unambiguous when the sacramental ministry of the Eucharist, in which the priest acts *"in persona Christi,"* is performed by a man. This explanation confirms the teaching of the Declaration *Inter Insigniores*, published at the behest of Paul VI in response to the question concerning the admission of women to the ministerial priesthood.[6]

Pastores Dabo Vobis refers to the priest as a "sacramental representation of Jesus Christ." Priests "share in the one priesthood of Christ," and they perform their "sacramental actions" *in persona Christi*.[7]

Throughout the 1970s and 1980s, numerous Roman Catholic theologians challenged this new position. However, in *Ordinatio Sacerdotalis* (1994), Pope John Paul II officially closed the discussion:

> Wherefore, in order that all doubt may be removed regarding a matter of great importance, a matter which pertains to the Church's divine constitution itself, in virtue of my ministry of confirming the brethren (cf. Lk 22:32) I declare that the Church

has no authority whatsoever to confer priestly ordination on women and that this judgment is to be definitively held by all the Church's faithful.[8]

On October 28, 1995, the Vatican Congregation for the Doctrine of the Faith issued its *Responsum Ad Propositum Dubium Concerning the Teaching Contained in "Ordinatio Sacerdotalis,"* signed by Cardinal Joseph Ratzinger (later Pope Benedict XVI). It states: "This teaching requires definitive assent, since, founded on the written Word of God, and from the beginning constantly preserved and applied in the Tradition of the Church, it has been set forth infallibly by the ordinary and universal Magisterium."[9]

This effectively silenced the issue of theological discussion for Roman Catholics. This does not mean that the argument of *Inter Insigniores* is a sound argument. It does mean that any Roman Catholic theologian who publicly questions the argument is taking a risk. Since *Ordinatio Sacerdotalis*, the public Roman Catholic discussion largely seems to have dried up. In the words of Sara Butler, "Catholics may no longer regard this as an open question or publicly advocate for a change in Church practice."[10]

After *Inter Insigniores*, non-Roman Catholics (such as Orthodox and Anglo-Catholics) who opposed the ordination of women embraced the new position. For example, in a 1978 essay, Orthodox Bishop Kallistos Ware wrote against women's ordination based on the argument that a priest must be male because the priest is an "icon" of the male Christ:

> Such, then, is the Orthodox understanding of the ministerial priesthood. The priest is an icon of Christ; and since the incarnate Christ became not only man but a male—since, furthermore, in the order of nature the roles of male and female are not interchangeable—it is necessary that the priest should be male. Those Western Christians who do not in fact regard the priest as an icon of Christ are of course free to ordain women as ministers; they are not, however, creating women priests but dispensing with priesthood altogether.[11]

A more recent Anglican document affirms:

> [I]n order to represent the High Priesthood of Christ, . . . sacramental symbolism *is* required—namely, the ordained minister, who visibly carries in his human person the likeness of the Son. . . . There is a "natural resemblance" which must exist between the matter of the sacrament and the thing signified. It is because the priest has to be the sign and image of Christ that only men can be ordained to the priesthood. . . . While it is true that the priest represents the whole Church in the celebration of the Eucharist (acting *in persona ecclesiae*), he does so only because first he represents Christ himself, and acts *in persona Christi*; more specifically, *in persona Christis capitis*, in the person of Christ who is the head of the Church.[12]

In order to address the new Catholic objection to the ordination of women, there will first be a summary of the biblical and historical background to the notion of priesthood and sacrifice.

OLD TESTAMENT PRIESTHOOD

According to the Pentateuch, God established the worship of Israel at Sinai along with the giving of the law. The goal of the exodus from Egypt was to produce a kingdom of priests (Exod. 19:6). Moses received instructions concerning both the building of the tabernacle and the institution of the priesthood when he ascended Mt. Sinai (Exod. 24). The role of the priesthood was twofold: to offer sacrifice and to teach the people concerning God's requirements. One of the main tasks of the priesthood was to distinguish between the holy and the common, the clean and the unclean (Lev. 10:10-11).[13] The priest's role can also be thought of as "mediatorial": the priest represents God to the people in teaching and oracular functions, and the people to God in sacrifice and intercession.[14]

One of the problems in assessing the notion of priesthood in the Old Testament has to do with the limited and isolated nature of its discussion. Instructions concerning the requirements for Israel's worship are limited primarily to Exodus 24–31; 35–40, the book of Leviticus, and Ezekiel 40–48.[15] Despite what must have been its importance in Israel's life, this material is discussed little elsewhere, with the exception of the Psalter. Even within the material that provides instructions for administering Israel's cult, the biblical text provides no theory or explanation for the reasons behind sacrifice and atonement: "[T]he biblical weight falls on the function of sacrifice rather than on a theory of its meaning."[16]

While similar in many respects to the religious practices of the surrounding pagan nations, there are aspects of Israel's temple worship that are unique. Israel's priesthood is understood as functioning only within God's covenant with Israel and God's gracious relation to his people. God provided the sacrifice, and Israel's worship was a response to God's action, not as a means to procure God's favor.[17] Although Israel, like other nations, had festivals that corresponded to the repeated cycles of the agricultural year (Exod. 23; Lev. 23; Deut. 16), the "nature" symbolism of these cyclical festivals was incorporated into the events of Israel's redemptive history: the Passover (Exod. 12; Lev. 23), the Feast of Tabernacles (Lev. 23), and the Day of Atonement (Lev. 16).[18] Israel's worship is thus a "liturgical expression into the history of Israel and her worship of the once-and-for-all events of Exodus and Sinai."[19]

After the exodus, the tabernacle and later the temple provided the exclusive focus for the understanding of "sacred space" in Israel's worship. The temple was the location of the "holy of holies," the place where the ark of the covenant was located, inside of which were the tablets of the Ten Commandments (Exod. 40:20; 1 Kgs 8:9). The holy of holies was the location of God's "glory" where "God's name" dwells (Exod. 40:34-35), and a space where the high priest entered only once a year, on the Day of Atonement (Lev. 16). The Psalms are full of references to the special significance attached to the temple as the physical location of Israel's worship, the presence of God on "Mount Zion" (Ps. 48). At the same time, the temple also became the special object of criticism by Israel's prophets who insisted that the temple provided no absolute guarantee of God's presence (Jer. 7). The Book of Ezekiel describes not only the departure of God's glory from the temple (Ezek. 8:5-6), but also the restoration of a new temple (Ezek. 40–47).[20]

Finally, there is the role of the priest. The Israelite priesthood was hereditary, confined to descendants of Aaron. This restriction of the priesthood seems to have served two primary functions: (1) to provide historical continuity to the Mosaic period; and (2) to maintain ritual purity. Priests were bound by laws of purity, particularly in respect to marriage and to contact with the dead. They could not marry divorcees, prostitutes, or daughters of forbidden sexual unions. Priests were bound by the strict Old Testament dietary laws; they could not have physical blemishes; and they could not participate in Old Testament rituals if they were in any way ritually unclean (Lev. 21–22).[21] It is sometimes asked why the Old Testament restricts the priesthood exclusively to males. As argued in the previous chapter, the most plausible explanation for this restriction has to do with Old Testament ritual purity. Because of ritual purity regulations concerning childbirth and bodily discharges, women would be ritually impure on a regular basis, and so would be unable to perform temple sacrifice.

Before leaving discussion of the Old Testament priesthood, it is important to mention two final selections of passages because of their importance for the later New Testament understanding of Jesus' own priesthood and sacrifice: Genesis 14:18-20, describing Abraham's encounter with Melchizedek and the "suffering servant" passages of Isaiah (41:8-10; 42:1-4; 49:1-7; 50:4-11; 53). Melchizedek was a Canaanite priest of "God Most High" (*El Elyon*) who blessed Abraham. Melchizedek is mentioned again in Psalm 110:4, and, in Hebrews 5-7, is interpreted as a type of Christ. The "suffering servant" of Isaiah is described in language reminiscent of Israel's cult. Christians would later interpret Isaiah 53, with its description of a servant who "was led like a lamb to the slaughter," and who was made an "offering for guilt," as a "passion" text whose typology was fulfilled in the death and resurrection of Jesus Christ.[22]

PRIESTHOOD IN THE NEW TESTAMENT

The New Testament uses the word "priest" (ἱερεύς, *hiereus*) in the following contexts:

First, "priests" refers to Jewish priests who exercise Jewish religious functions. John the Baptist's father Zechariah was a priest to whom the angel Gabriel appeared and announced John's birth while Zechariah was offering sacrifice (Luke 1:8-20). When Jesus healed a leper, he instructed him to go to a priest and make an offering (Luke 5:12-14). In the parable of the Good Samaritan, one of those who passes by the wounded traveler is a priest (Luke 10:29-37).[23]

Priests are often found among Jesus' enemies. They challenged Jesus' authority (Luke 20:1-8). Judas betrayed Jesus to the "chief priests," and when Jesus was arrested, the chief priests played a major role in his condemnation and execution (Mark 14:53-64; 15:10-11; Luke 22). The chief priests and scribes mocked Jesus on the cross (Mark 15:31-32). In Matthew's Gospel, the chief priests used Judas' thirty pieces of silver to buy a field; they set a guard in front of the tomb of Jesus, and bribed the guards to spread the story that Jesus' body had been stolen (Matt. 27:6-10, 62-65; 28:11-15). All four gospels portray the temple priesthood and the Jewish leaders as responsible (along with the Romans) for Jesus' death.[24]

Second, the New Testament portrays Jesus' theological identity using the Old Testament symbolism of priest, sacrifice, and temple.

The gospels portray Jesus as both priest and sacrifice. Jesus' prophetic ministry of teaching and performing miracles has a "priestly" dimension. As noted above, instructing the people of God is a primary priestly function. In speaking of his upcoming death as a "ransom for many" (Mark 10:45; Matt. 20:28), Jesus identified himself with the "suffering servant" whose death was a sacrifice for others.[25]

All three Synoptic Gospels portray the miracle of the multiplication of the loaves and the fishes as anticipating the Last Supper (Mark 6:30-44; Matt. 14:13-21; Luke 9:10-17). Note the verbal parallels: Jesus "took," "blessed," "broke," and "gave." At his Last Supper with his disciples, Jesus used deliberately priestly language, identifying his death as a sacrifice in the "words of institution": "This is my body. . . . This is my blood [of the new covenant]" (Mark 14:22-24; Matt. 26:26-28; Luke 22:19-20). Jesus' language echoed imagery of Old Testament sacrifice, of the "suffering servant," and of Jeremiah's "new covenant" (Jer. 31:31-33).[26]

John's Gospel portrays Jesus as both sacrifice and temple. John the Baptist identifies Jesus as the "lamb of God" (John 1:29). The gospel identifies Jesus' crucifixion as the time when he will draw all people unto him (John 12:32), and the time of his glorification (John 13:31). There are clear eucharistic references in Jesus' invitation in John's Gospel to "eat my flesh and drink my blood" (John 6:51-58). John interprets the incarnation of the Word in Christ as a transference of God's glory dwelling in the temple to now dwelling in Jesus (John 1:14). Jesus' prediction of the destruction and rebuilding of the temple means that Jesus will replace the temple with his own body (John 2:18-22). Jesus' discussion with the Samaritan woman indicates that a time is coming when it will no longer be appropriate to worship either in Jerusalem or Mount Gerizim (the location of the Samaritan temple), but will now "worship in spirit and in truth" (John 4:19-26).[27]

Nowhere in his letters does the apostle Paul refer to Jesus as a "priest." He does, however, identify Jesus with the sacrificial paschal lamb (1 Cor. 5:7). Paul says that God put Christ forward as an expiation/atonement (ἱλαστήριον, hilastērion) "through his blood" (Rom. 3:25). The term hilastērion refers to the Old Testament "mercy seat" or lid that covered the ark in the holy of holies of the Jewish temple. Paul is saying that Jesus' death on the cross is a new "Day of Atonement." Significantly, Paul does not portray God as the recipient of the sacrifice, but as the one who offers sacrifice. Paul does not only portray Christ in sacrificial language, but also through the use of priestly metaphors. Paul writes that the risen Christ sits enthroned at the "right hand of God" and "intercedes for us" (Rom. 8:34).[28]

In his own description of the Last Supper, Paul speaks of Jesus' death in sacrificial terms (1 Cor. 11:23-26). In Paul's recounting of the "words of institution," Jesus speaks of the bread as his "body, which is for you," and of the cup as the "new covenant in my blood." Paul describes the "cup of blessing, which we bless" as a "communion (κοινωνία, koinōnia) in the blood of Christ," and the "bread that we break" as a "communion (koinōnia) in the body of Christ" (1 Cor. 10:16-21).[29]

Paul also uses temple and sacrificial language to refer to the church. Paul speaks of the church as the "body of Christ" (1 Cor. 12:27), and of our physical bodies as "temples" of the Holy Spirit (1 Cor. 6:19-20) because we were "bought with a price," that is, the "price" of Christ's death. Christians are called to present their bodies as a "living sacrifice," which is their "spiritual worship" (Rom. 12:1).[30]

The lengthiest discussion of the priesthood of Christ takes place in the book of Hebrews. Hebrews speaks of Christ as both priest and sacrifice. As "high priest," Jesus has made "expiation/atonement for the sins of the people" (Heb. 2:17). Hebrews both compares and contrasts Christ's sacrifice with that of the Old Testament priesthood. Unlike the Old Testament sacrifice of animals, Jesus died once for all (7:27); rather than sacrificing animals, Jesus offered himself (9:25-26). In contrast to the hereditary priesthood of the Old Testament, Jesus has an "eternal priesthood," after the "order of Melchizedek" (5:6, 10; 6:20). Because Jesus did not sin, he did not need to offer sacrifice for himself, but only for sinners (2:17; 4:15; 10:11-12). Hebrews also portrays Christ's priesthood using temple imagery. The Old Testament tabernacle was only a "shadow" of the true tabernacle, set up by God (8:2-5); the risen Christ has now entered this true tabernacle, where he continually intercedes on our behalf in God's presence (9:23-24). Christ's sacrifice has provided a "new and living way" for those who have faith in Christ to "enter the sanctuary by the blood of Jesus" (10:19-22). As in Paul, Christian life is presented as "sacrificial."

The author of Hebrews writes: "We have an altar from which those who serve the tent have no right to eat." The readers are encouraged: "Through him then let us continually offer up a sacrifice of praise to God, that is, the fruit of lips that acknowledge his name" (13:10, 15).[31]

Third, the New Testament also uses the word "priest" in reference to members of the church. In Romans 15:15-16, Paul refers to his own ministry as "a minister (λειτουργός, leitourgos) of Christ Jesus to the Gentiles in the priestly service (ἱερουργοῦντα, hierourgounta) of the gospel of God, so that the offering (προσφορά, prosphōra) of the Gentiles may be acceptable, sanctified by the Holy Spirit." First Peter speaks of Christ as a "living stone," and of the church as "living stones," "built into a spiritual house, to be a holy priesthood (ἱεράτευμα ἅγιον, hierateuma hagion), to offer spiritual sacrifices acceptable to God through Jesus Christ" (1 Pet. 2:4-5), and states a few verses later: "But you are a chosen race, a royal priesthood (βασίλειον ἱεράτευμα, basileion hierateuma), a holy nation, God's own people, that you may declare the wonderful deeds of him who called you out of darkness into his marvelous light" (2:9).[32]

At the same time, although the passage in 1 Peter speaks in a general way of how all Christians are "priests" (a "priesthood of all believers"), the New Testament never uses the word "priest" to describe those who exercise offices of leadership in the church. In his letters, Paul addresses the "bishops/overseers" (ἐπισκόποι, episkopoi), and "deacons" (διάκονοι, diakonoi) (Phil. 1:1). The Pastoral Epistles speak of "bishops/overseers," "presbyters/elders" (πρεσβύτεροι, presbyteroi), and "deacons" (1 Tim. 3:1-7; Tit. 1:5-9). The Acts of the Apostles refers to "elders/presbyters" and "deacons" (Acts 11:30; 15:2, 4, 6; 16:4; 6:1-6).[33] Setting aside for office seems to have occurred through the "laying on of hands" (1 Tim. 4:14, 5:22; 2 Tim. 1:6). Those who held these offices clearly exercised some sort of leadership, but the New Testament says nothing about what we would call their liturgical functions. The New Testament says nothing about the role of these leaders in baptizing, celebrating the Eucharist, or ordaining others in their succession.[34]

In short, the New Testament emphasizes three aspects of a Christian theology of priesthood and sacrifice: (1) the priesthood and sacrifice of Christ; (2) Christians as a new temple; and (3) the priesthood and sacrifice of all Christians. At the same time, the New Testament does not use the word "priest" to refer to church office, and refers to Christian priesthood and sacrifice "not in acts of ritual and liturgical worship but in the practical, ethical sphere of the lived Christian life."[35]

PRIESTHOOD IN THE EARLY CHURCH

An examination of the writings of the church fathers finds a continuation of the themes noted above: (1) the priesthood and sacrifice of Christ; (2) Christians as a new temple; and (3) the priesthood and sacrifice of all Christians. At the same time, there is not much discussion of these issues. As O'Collins and Jones note, "The first millennium of Christianity provides some but not much explicit teaching about the priesthood of Christ. The references to him as priest are scattered and yield little by way of systematic thought." The primary reason for this seems to have been that, although the Letter to the Hebrews was acknowledged as canonical in the East from the second century, it was not universally accepted in the West until the fourth century.[36]

The first post-New Testament document to deal with a controversy concerning the nature of ministry having to do with priesthood is 1 Clement. Clement refers to Christ three times as the "High Priest," and refers to "approved officers" (δεδοκιμασμένοι, *dedokimasmenoi*) who "offered the sacrifices with innocence and holiness."[37] What Clement meant by "sacrifice" is "unclear."[38] Justin Martyr's *Dialogue with Trypho* speaks of the "sacrifices" the church offers in "the bread of the Eucharist, and also the cup of the Eucharist"; however, the immediate context makes clear that the "sacrifices" to which he refers are "prayers"—"the spiritualized sacrifice of the practical living of Christian life."[39] Justin is clear that it is the "president" who offers "prayers and thanksgivings" at the Eucharist, but this tells us at the most that he had a "positive attitude toward the ministerial office."[40] Irenaeus of Lyons echoes Paul's threefold division of the theology of priesthood and sacrifice: he writes of Christ as the "high Priest," and of the "offering" of his humanity to the Father;[41] Irenaeus refers to the Eucharist as a "pure sacrifice," in which "the Church alone offers this pure oblation to the Creator, offering to Him, with giving of thanks, [the things taken] from His creation."[42] Yet, again, however, as in Justin, the "sacrifice" that is offered seems to be the "spiritualized one of prayers of praise and thanksgiving."[43]

The Alexandrian theologian Origen drew on the imagery of the Old Testament Book of Leviticus rather than on the New Testament book of Hebrews. Origen may well have been the first church father to refer to ordained Christian ministers as "priests." He speaks of Christian priests as imitating their "Teacher" by granting people the forgiveness of sins. Origen states that these priests "have a part in the divine sacrifice through the Eternal Priest, our Lord and Savior Jesus Christ."[44] At the same time, Origen seems to have understand all Christians to participate in Christ's priesthood, so that ordained clergy differ only in function and not in nature from the priesthood that all receive through faith and baptism.[45]

One of Cyprian of Carthage's letters is an important early discussion of the nature of the Eucharist. In the letter, Cyprian views Melchizedek's offering of bread and wine as a foreshadowing of Christ's own offering of his body and blood, which was ritually enacted at the Last Supper: "For who is more a priest of the most high God than our Lord Jesus Christ, who offered a sacrifice to God the Father, and offered that very same thing which Melchizedek had offered, that is, bread and wine, that is, His body and blood?" Cyprian refers to the Eucharist as a "sacrifice" ("for the Lord's passion is the sacrifice which we offer") and to ordained clergy as "priests" who "imitate" what Christ did:

> For if Jesus Christ, our Lord and God, is himself the chief priest of God the Father, and has first offered himself a sacrifice to the Father, and has commanded this to be done in commemoration of himself, certainly that priest (*sacerdos*) truly discharges the office of Christ, who imitates that which Christ did; and he then offers a true and full sacrifice in the Church to God the Father, when he proceeds to offer it according to what he sees Christ himself to have offered.[46]

Might this be the first known example of an *in persona Christi* understanding of eucharistic theology—that during the eucharistic celebration the priest is acting as a representative or icon of Christ? What does Cyprian mean when he suggests that the priest should "imitate" Christ? In the latter part of the letter, he asks: "For to declare the righteousness and the covenant of the Lord, and not to do the same that the Lord did, what else is it than to cast away His words and to despise the Lord's instruction, to commit not earthly, but spiritual thefts and adulteries?" Cyprian concludes in a manner that indicates that the "imitation" referred to is that of spiritual and moral discipleship: "Wherefore, if we wish to walk in the light of Christ, let us not depart from his precepts and monitions, giving thanks that, while he instructs for the future what we ought to do, he pardons for the past wherein we in our simplicity have erred."[47] Of course, it is also possible that by "imitation" Cyprian simply means that the priest, in celebrating the Eucharist, patterns his actions on the New Testament accounts of the Last Supper: "[H]e [the priest] proceeds to offer it according to what he sees Christ Himself to have offered." Whether Cyprian understood "imitation of Christ" to mean either Christian discipleship or basing the pattern of the Eucharist on the New Testament's description of the Last Supper, there is nothing in the passage to indicate that Cyprian believed that the celebrant in his own person is acting as an icon of, *in the place of,* or in the "person of" Christ (*in persona Christi*).[48]

Two last figures are important as contributing to the patristic understanding of priesthood and sacrifice. John Chrysostom delivered thirty-four homilies on the Letter to the Hebrews. In these homilies, Chrysostom says much about Christ's high-priestly role, particularly his role as mediator.[49] Chrysostom explicitly links Christ's priestly sacrifice to the Eucharist, insisting at the same time that the Eucharist is not "another sacrifice," but the "same" as Christ's once-and-for-all sacrifice.[50] Chrysostom emphasizes the *priestly sacrifice of all* Christians, citing Romans 12:1, stating that "each one is himself the Priest" of the offerings of "moderation, temperance, mercifulness, enduring ill-treatment, long-suffering, humbleness of mind."[51]

What seems to be missing from the homilies is any discussion of the priestly nature of ordained ministry.

Finally, Augustine is important for something new he brings to the discussion—that it is the risen Jesus Christ who is the central actor in the sacraments. Augustine regularly uses *sacerdos* in reference to Christ, but rarely applies the term to bishops or presbyters. Against Donatism, Augustine is critical of the notion that "the ordained minister was the source rather than the merely visible mediator of holiness."[52] The efficacy of the sacrament does not depend on the personal holiness of the priest because it is the risen Christ who performs the sacrament, acting through the visible signs of sacramental grace. Augustine was addressing the sacrament of baptism in his debate with the Donatists; it was only later that this principle could be applied to the Eucharist as well.[53]

In summary, the church fathers largely repeat the three key themes of the New Testament writings concerning priesthood and sacrifice: (1) Jesus Christ is both high priest and sacrifice. (2) The authors recognize the sacrificial context of Jesus' Last Supper, and there is, among some at least, the beginnings of a notion of "eucharistic sacrifice"—not that the Eucharist is a "repetition" of Christ's once-and-for-all sacrifice, but that, in the celebration of the Eucharist, the efficacy of Christ's sacrifice is "remembered" in such a way that it is "made present" or re-enacted. In the words of Chrysostom, "it is not another sacrifice . . . but the same."[54] (3) The authors speak of the priesthood of all Christians, which they interpret in spiritual and moral terms; this notion of sacrifice is "not a cultic but rather an ethical idea."[55] (4) The writers assume some kind of relationship between the priesthood of Christ and the priesthood of ordained clergy. When the celebrant presides at the Eucharist, he is presiding over a "sacrificial" action. At the same time, in the earliest examples, the sacrificial action is not understood to be the liturgical rite itself, but the prayer of the celebrant and the community. In later writers like Cyprian and Chrysostom, the Eucharist is itself spoken of as a sacrifice in the sense of a re-presentation of Christ's once-and-for-all sacrifice. With this understanding of eucharistic sacrifice, Cyprian also uses the word "priest" (*sacerdos*) to refer to the celebrant of the Eucharist. At the same time, as made clear in Augustine, the primary celebrant of the sacraments is the risen Christ himself: "It is the one High Priest who now offers the Eucharist for Christians everywhere."[56]

What is missing from the writings of the church fathers is any detailed discussion of this relationship between Christ's priesthood and the priesthood of the ordained clergy. There is one passage in Cyprian that has been appealed to as an early example of an *in persona Christi* theology of ordained ministry, but this is almost certainly a misreading. There is no warrant in the writings of the church fathers for the claim that the church should exclude women from ordination because the priest represents Christ, and only a male can represent Christ. If the reference to "this teaching" in Cardinal Ratzinger's *Responsum Ad Propositum Dubium* is to the teaching of *Inter Insigniores* concerning the priest acting *in persona Christi*, then it is simply not the case that it is "founded on the written Word of God, and from the beginning constantly preserved and applied in the Tradition of the Church." To the contrary, there is no such teaching either in Scripture or in the patristic tradition of the church. To discover the origins of the notion that the priest acts *in persona Christi*, it is necessary to look to the theology of the later medieval period, and particularly to Thomas Aquinas.

12

Women's Ordination and the Priesthood of Christ

In persona Christi

This is the third chapter discussing Catholic objections to the ordination of women and the second to address the argument that women cannot be ordained because only a male priest can represent Christ in the celebration of the Eucharist. Specifically, in presiding at the Eucharist, the priest acts "in the person of Christ" (*in persona Christi*). Since Jesus Christ is a male, only a male can play this representative role. The previous chapter summarized the biblical and historical background to the New Testament notion of priesthood and to the understanding of ordained ministry in the early church, and concluded that there is no evidence that either the New Testament or the patristic church understood ordained clergy to play this representative role, that is, to be acting *in persona Christi*. This chapter locates the sources of this theology in the sacramental theology of the Western Church, specifically as articulated by Thomas Aquinas.

During the early Middle Ages, Latin theologians taught that only the universal Catholic church was able to celebrate the Eucharist. Local churches who were in communion with the one holy Catholic church (*una sancta catholica ecclesia*) were understood to represent the whole church in the eucharistic liturgy. The priest who presided at the Eucharist was understood to represent the whole church when he acted as the liturgical leader of the local church. A key concern in the development of eucharistic doctrine was the problem of the heretical priest. How could a priest represent the whole church if he lacked the faith of the church? The consensus was that the Eucharists of heretical priests were invalid. The author of the *Summa Sententiarum* (probably Otto of Lucca [d. 1146]), held that they were invalid because in the eucharistic prayer the priest says "we offer" (*offerimus*), not "I offer" (*offero*); the priest thus acts *ex persona totius ecclesiae* (in the person of the whole church).[1] In a discussion of the differences between the offering of the congregation and the offering of the priest, Lothar of Signi explained that the priest offers in the person of the whole church: "*offerimus* is said in the plural because the priest sacrifices not only in his own [person] but in the person of the whole church."[2]

Different opinions concerning this ecclesiological status of who does or does not qualify to be a priest led to an "evolving theology of the hierarchical priesthood," along with changes in terminology. Medieval commentaries on the Mass depicted the "priest of the New Covenant" as the fulfillment of Old Testament priesthood as one who offers sacrifice for the people. This description is applied first to Christ, and then to ordained clergy. Beginning in the eleventh and twelfth centuries, figures such as Peter Pictor and Rupert of Dietz began to use the term *similitudo* (likeness) to describe the participation of ordained clergy in Christ's priesthood. In addition, the imagery of drama is introduced and the priest is said to imitate Christ when he recites the words of institution in the Eucharist. Priests are referred to as *vices Christi* (deputies of Christ). The priest is compared to an ambassador of the church to Christ, and of Christ to the church.[3]

THOMAS AQUINAS

As mentioned above, Thomas Aquinas (1225–1274) is the central figure in the development of the notion that, in celebrating the Eucharist, the priest acts "in the person of Christ" (*in persona Christi*), as representing Christ to the church. It is this theology of eucharistic representation that lies behind the recent and modern Catholic objection to the ordination of women to clerical office. If Jesus Christ is a male, then only a male priest/presbyter can represent Christ.

Aquinas's earliest discussion of eucharistic theology does not mention the notion of representation of Christ at all, but follows the earlier notion that the priest acts as representing the church. In Aquinas's earliest venture into a more or less comprehensive theology, his *Commentary* on Peter Lombard's *Sentences*, he claimed that the priest proclaims the eucharistic prayer in the name of the church and represents the church: "He alone [the priest] who consecrates the Eucharist is able to conduct the act of the entire church, which is a sacrament of the universal [or entire] church."[4]

The claim that the priest acts as a representation of Christ first appears in Aquinas' mature theological work, the *Summa Theologiae*. Aquinas's sacramental theology is subordinate to his theology of the incarnation: Jesus Christ is the second person of the Trinity, the Word through whom God created the world, and the Son through whom, as a human being in Jesus Christ, God is restoring a fallen creation, both through the forgiveness of sins and through uniting the church to himself. The humanity of Jesus Christ is the created "instrument" of salvation; the same Holy Spirit through whose power the incarnate Christ was conceived, and through whom he was anointed in his own baptism by John, has been sent by the risen Jesus Christ to be given to the church. The grace of the Holy Spirit is the bond that unites believers to the crucified and risen Christ, bringing about a union not only between individual believers and the Triune God, but also with one another as the mystical body of Christ.[5]

In *ST* 3.60.3, Aquinas argues that a sacrament is a special kind of "sign," and the reality signified in the sacraments is Christ himself, the head of the church, who is the unique and universal principle of the church's sanctification.[6] Sacraments are the risen Christ's "continuing active presence in the world, transforming it through time until the consummation of all things at his coming again in glory."[7] As the incarnate Word Jesus Christ's humanity is the unique instrument of salvation, so the sacraments are created physical instruments through which believing Christians receive the grace of the Holy Spirit to be united to Christ's crucified and risen humanity.[8]

Key to Aquinas's understanding of the manner in which the priest represents Christ is his understanding of worship as rooted in sacramental "character." In *ST* 3.62.5, Aquinas argues that sacraments have a twofold nature: through the sacraments, God both takes away sin and "perfect[s] the soul in things pertaining to divine worship in regard to the Christian religion." In *ST* 3.63.5, 6, Aquinas asserts that the sacraments make possible the grace-filled worship of those who have been sanctified through creating both "holiness of life and consecration for holy actions." This capacity to worship is enabled by the sacramental "character" that Aquinas argues is a "certain participation in the priesthood of Christ":

> [E]ach of the faithful is deputed to receive, or to bestow on others, things pertaining to the worship of God. And this, properly speaking, is the purpose of the sacramental character. Now the whole rite of the Christian religion is derived from Christ's priesthood. Consequently, it is clear that the sacramental character is specially the character of Christ, *to whose character the faithful are likened* (*cuius sacerdotio configurantur fideles secundum sacramentales characteres*) by reason of the sacramental characters, which are nothing else than certain *participations of Christ's priesthood*, flowing from Christ himself (*quaedam participationes sacerdotii Christi, ab ipso Christo derivatae*).[9]

Aquinas here modifies a traditional notion of "character" as a "sign of grace conferred in the sacrament" (*ST* 3.63.3 obj 2) in the light of Hebrews 1:3: "But the eternal character is Christ himself, according to Heb. 1:3, 'who being the brightness of his glory and the figure,' or character, 'of his substance.' It seems, therefore, that the character should properly be attributed to Christ."[10] Thus, for Aquinas, the sacramental character is, in actuality, the character of Christ as the incarnate "image" of God the Father, and *all* baptized Christians are enabled to partake in worship through participation in Christ's priesthood. In *ST* 3.63.6, Aquinas utilizes a distinction between the roles of agent and recipient to argue that sacramental character is uniquely associated with the sacraments of the Eucharist and baptism (as well as confirmation). In the Eucharist, the priest administers a sacrament for others; in baptism, one receives the capacity to receive other sacraments.[11] Crucial for this discussion, however, is the statement that Aquinas makes concerning the sacraments and participation in Christ's priesthood:

> Every sacrament makes the human being a participator in Christ's Priesthood (*per omnia sacramenta fit homo particeps sacerdotii Christi*), from the fact that it confers on him [or her] some effect thereof. But every sacrament does not depute someone to do or receive something pertaining to the worship of the priesthood of Christ: while it is just this that is required for a sacrament to imprint a character.[12]

Thus, *every* sacrament (not simply ordination) enables *all* human beings (not simply ordained males) to participate in Christ's priesthood. Baptism and Eucharist communicate a special character to participate in divine worship; this character is itself a participation in the "character" of Christ, and, while there is a special role for the ordained priest—only a priest can administer the sacraments—both the baptized and ordained clergy *equally* receive the character that enables worship; both the baptized and ordained clergy *equally* participate in the character of Christ's priesthood. Moreover, through sacramental character, both all of the baptized as well as the ordained clergy *resemble* Christ. Thomas identifies sacramental character as the "character of Christ . . . to whose character the faithful are likened" through their participation in Christ's priesthood.[13]

Aquinas's understanding of the role of the priest in celebrating the Eucharist can be summarized as follows: first, Aquinas follows the notion common in his day that the consecration of bread and wine within the eucharistic prayer takes place when the priest recites the words of Jesus that are included in the narrative of the last supper in which bread and wine are identified with Christ's body and blood. Adopting the Aristotelian distinction between form and matter that he had used elsewhere to explain that each sacrament must have both a physical element (the matter) and accompanying words (the form),[14] Aquinas argues that the "matter" of the sacrament consists of the change of the elements of bread and wine, while the "form" consists of the words of institution:

> But in this sacrament the consecration of the matter consists in the miraculous change of the substance, which can only be done by God; hence the minister in performing this sacrament has no other act save the pronouncing of the words. . . . [T]he form of this sacrament implies merely the consecration of the matter, which consists in transubstantiation, as when it is said, "This is my body," or, "This is the cup of my blood."[15]

The words of institution are not only essential to the Eucharist, but Aquinas insists that the recitation of these words alone would be sufficient to the performing of the sacrament. The words alone are sufficient because, in reciting the words, the priest is speaking the very words of Jesus Christ, and thus acting as a representative of, or in the "person" of Christ:

> But the form of this sacrament is pronounced as if Christ were speaking in person (*ex persona ipsius Christi loquentis*), so that it is given to be understood that the minister does nothing in perfecting this sacrament, except to pronounce the words of Christ.
>
> Accordingly it must be held that if the priest were to pronounce only the aforesaid words with the intention of consecrating this sacrament, this sacrament would be valid because the intention would cause these words to be understood as spoken in the person of Christ (*haec verba intelligerentur quasi ex persona Christi prolata*), even though the words were pronounced without those that precede.[16]

This is (almost) the whole of what Aquinas says about the priest acting "in the person of Christ" (*in persona Christi*).[17] As Edward Kilmartin points out, the argument presumes a particular understanding concerning the words of institution and the "moment of consecration," as well as that, by consecrating the eucharistic elements, the priest is enacting a drama in which he plays the role of Jesus Christ at the Last Supper. At the same time, what Aquinas says about the priest acting *in persona Christi* should not be isolated from the rest of his sacramental theology. The eucharistic prayer is the expression of the worship of the entire church, which is made possible by the sacramental character bestowed in baptism—which itself is a participation in Christ's priesthood, enjoyed by all the baptized. The priest performs this role for the whole church because, as Aquinas had written earlier in his *Commentary on the Sentences*, the sacrament is the "sacrament of the universal church." The priest who consecrates the Eucharist thus represents both Christ and the church. While distinguishable, these two functions are inseparable. The priest acts as a minister of Christ, intending to do "what the church does" (*faciendi quod facit ecclesia*).[18] On the basis of their participatory character in Christ's own priesthood, the entire church participates in the eucharistic worship in union with the presiding ordained priest, who proclaims the eucharistic prayer both in the person of the whole church and in the person of Christ.[19]

It is also important to note that Aquinas says nothing about the need for the priest to be male in the context of the priest acting *in persona Christi*.[20] To the contrary, if the priest must be male in order to participate in Christ's priesthood or to resemble Christ, then it would seem to follow that only males can be baptized because Aquinas locates the sacramental character of both baptism and the Eucharist (which makes worship possible) in a participation in the priesthood of Christ, in which he insists *all* baptized people participate. In recent years, some have argued that the priest represents the whole church because he *first* represents Christ.[21] This would seem to reverse the logic of Aquinas's position; it is because they first share in the sacramental character of Christ's priesthood (in which all the baptized participate), and which enables *all* the baptized to resemble Christ, that ordained priests are later (through ordination) enabled to share in the special priestly character that enables them to both participate in Christ's priesthood and resemble Christ as they consecrate the Eucharist.

It is the understanding of the priest as consecrating the Eucharist when he recites the words of institution (and thus acts as a representative of Christ) that comes to dominate eucharistic theology in the Western Roman Catholic Church following Aquinas's formulation, and especially after the Reformation-era Council of Trent.[22] At the same time, despite their rejections of the doctrines of transubstantiation and eucharistic sacrifice strongly endorsed at the Roman Catholic Council of Trent, many Reformation churches still affirmed (at least implicitly) the logic behind the position that followed Aquinas. The Lutheran formularies, for example, explicitly state that ordained pastors "represent the person of Christ, and do not represent their own persons. . . . When they offer the Word of God, when they offer the Sacraments, they offer them in the stead and place of Christ." It is in reciting the words of institution that the pastor celebrates the Lord's Supper.[23] This theology is also at least implicit in those Protestant churches in which the liturgical practice of the Lord's Supper consists of nothing more than the pastor reciting the narrative of the Last Supper.

ORTHODOX RESERVATIONS

As noted in the previous chapter, with the possible exception of a single passage in Cyprian of Carthage, there is in the early church no evidence of any discussion of the relationship between Christ's priesthood and the priesthood of the ordained clergy. More important for the present discussion, there is no evidence whatsoever for a theology in which the priest, in the celebration of the Eucharist, represents or acts "in the person of Christ" when reciting the words of institution. This is a medieval Western development that is first formulated explicitly in the eucharistic theology of Thomas Aquinas. It should perhaps be no surprise then that a conflict arose between Western Catholic and Eastern Orthodox theologians concerning the Eucharist in the first half of the fourteenth century. The controversy concerned the "moment of consecration," but the real issue of disagreement concerned the agent of the consecration—whether it was the priest who acted as representative of Christ when the words of institution were recited, or the Holy Spirit when the *epiclesis* was invoked. The controversy began when Westerners accused the East of adding additional prayers after the words of institution.[24]

The background to the conflict lay in the inclusion of the *epiclesis*, a prayer for the invocation of the Holy Spirit that occurs in Eastern eucharistic prayers following the account of the Last Supper, but was missing from the Western Latin mass. The crucial historical texts are the *Mystagogical Catechesis* of Cyril of Jerusalem (c. 350), the liturgy of Basil the Great (ca. fourth century), and the liturgy of John Chrysostom (398–404). Cyril's *Mystagogical Catechesis* contains a description of the invocation of the Holy Spirit, while the two liturgies both contain prayers in which the Holy Spirit is invoked to "bless and sanctify" the bread and cup that they might become the body and blood of Christ.[25]

The Western scholastic theologians argued that, in commanding the church to "do this in memory of me," it was Christ's intention that the church should celebrate the Eucharist using Jesus Christ's very words, and that the celebrant intended to speak in the name of and in the person of Christ. The Orthodox insisted to the contrary that the words of institution represented a historical account, and that it was necessary to add the *epiclesis*: Christ is made present not through the recitation of the words of institution, but through the prayer of the priest invoking the presence of the Holy Spirit.[26] Despite more recent ecumenical convergence, this fourteenth-century disagreement has continued to be divisive. Orthodox theologian Paul Evdokimov has stated: "It would seem that, in the ecumenical dialogue the question of the epiclesis is as important at present as that of the *Filioque*, since it is above all in the light of the epiclesis that the *Filioque* can be correctly resituated within the whole problem."[27] Some Eastern theologians have strongly objected to the notion that the priest acts *in persona Christi*. Evdokimov wrote:

> For the Latin Church, the *verba substantialia* of the consecration, the institutional words of Christ, are pronounced by the priest *in persona Christi*, which immediately gives them consecratory power. Now, for the Greeks the identification of the priest with Christ, *in persona Christi*, was quite unknown, and strictly unthinkable. Rather, the priest invokes the Holy Spirit precisely in order that the word of Christ *reproduced, cited* by the priest should acquire all the efficacy of the word-act of God.[28]

The disagreement has implications for the question of the ordination of women to clerical orders. Theologically, the disagreement boils down to the question of whether the presiding minister acts in the person of Christ (*in persona Christi*) and thus represents [a male] Christ, or rather, when invoking the Holy Spirit, the presiding minister praying on behalf of the congregation, represents the church and thus acts in the person of the church (*in persona ecclesiae*). One would think that, given their skepticism about an *in persona Christi* ecclesiology, Orthodox theologians would have to search elsewhere for an argument against women's ordination, but, surprisingly, when Orthodox theologians first began to respond to the question of women's ordination, they adopted rather uncritically the new Roman Catholic arguments that at the very least were in tension with Orthodox eucharistic theology. As noted in the previous chapter, Orthodox theologian Kallistos Ware wrote (in an earlier collection of essays against women's ordination): "The priest is an icon of Christ; and since the incarnate Christ became not only man but a male—since, furthermore, in the order of nature the roles of male and female are not interchangeable—it is necessary that the priest should be male."[29]

CRITIQUE AND RESPONSE

What follows will summarize the views of several theologians from different theological traditions in an attempt to address the question: Does the minister (presbyter/priest) who presides at the celebration of the Eucharist represent Christ in the sense that, in speaking the words of institution, the minister acts "in the person of Christ" (*in persona Christi*) in such a manner that the risen Christ speaks his own words through the minister; and, if this is the case, does the fact that Jesus Christ is a male mean that the presiding minister must necessarily be a male?

AN ORTHODOX RESPONSE

As noted above, the Orthodox understanding of eucharistic celebration, with its emphasis on the invocation of the Holy Spirit in the *epiclesis*, is fundamentally different from the Western medieval scholastic understanding that located the moment of consecration at the priest's recital of Christ's words of institution. This difference led to controversy in the fourteenth century, and continues to have repercussions. Two modern Orthodox theologians in particular have reflected on the implications for how the different understandings bear on the question of women's ordination to the priesthood.

Elisabeth Behr-Sigel (1907–2005) was a prominent female Orthodox theologian. At a young age, she converted to Orthodoxy. She was the author of numerous books on Orthodox spirituality, an instructor of theology at St. Sergius Orthodox Theological Institute in Paris, and was involved in numerous ecumenical discussions between Orthodoxy and other churches. Later in her life, she became interested in the role of women in the Orthodox Church, and, particularly, the issue of women's ordination. Her essays on women's ordination have appeared in two books: *The Ministry of Women in the Church* and *The Ordination of Women in the Orthodox Church*.[30] In the preface to the English edition of *The Ministry of Women in the Church*, Thomas Hopko (who certainly did not agree with her views on women's ordination) described Behr-Sigel as "Eastern Orthodoxy's premier woman thinker. . . . Madame Behr-Sigel provides insights to be reckoned with in an intelligent, clear and forthright manner [which] makes her work all the more valuable."[31] In the preface to the French edition, Metropolitan Anthony Bloom wrote: "The Orthodox, and Roman

Catholics, too, must rethink the problem of women in the Scriptures. They must not make hasty statements about her being and work in the work of salvation to which God has called us to be witnesses."[32]

Kallistos Ware (b. 1935) is an English bishop in the Orthodox Church and was Spalding Lecturer of Eastern Orthodox Studies at the University of Oxford from 1966 to 2001. Ware is the author of numerous books on Orthodoxy, and is best known as the author of *The Orthodox Church*.[33] As noted above, Ware was one of the contributors to an early series of essays on the ordination of women entitled *Man, Woman, and Priesthood*, and objected to the ordination of women on the grounds that as an icon of the male Christ, the priest has to be male. By the time that the second edition of the book was published, Bishop Ware had changed his mind, and his new essay "Man, Woman and the Priesthood of Christ" was reproduced in Elisabeth Behr-Sigel's book, *The Ordination of Women in the Orthodox Church*. Ware writes: "Since then my views on this issue have altered. In 1978, I considered the ordination of women priests to be an impossibility. Now I am much more hesitant. . . . What I would plead is that we Orthodox should regard the matter as essentially an open question."[34]

Behr-Sigel notes that the Orthodox Church no longer upholds the traditional historic arguments against the ordination of women. As in the Roman Catholic Church, women are now allowed to play many roles in the church, including that of teaching theology. She writes:

> The idea of the physical and intellectual inferiority of women has been an uncontested axiom for a long time. . . . Today this idea has been discredited, at least in those societies that have been influenced by Christianity. . . . [T]he arguments put forward today against the ordination of women are by and large no longer the same as those used in past centuries. Among contemporary Orthodox theologians, we hardly hear any more arguments based on the inferiority of women and the hierarchy of the sexes . . . or the responsibility of Eve in the Fall.[35]

Behr-Sigel notes that when the issue of women's ordination was first raised, the Orthodox were caught by surprise.[36] At least one early response suggested that the problem had to do with the ritual impurity of women during their monthly biological cycles.[37] Bishop Ware comments on this: "Some maintain that women cannot be priests because they are morally and spiritually inferior to men, and also because they are physically impure during certain times of the month." Ware insists that this simply will not do as a Christian theological argument: "It is abundantly clear from Christ's teaching in the Gospels and from the decisions of the apostolic council in Acts 15 that the Old Testament prohibitions concerning ritual impurity are not applicable within the new covenant of the Church."[38]

Despite some initial stumbling, the Orthodox (in a manner similar to the Roman Catholic Church) finally endorsed two *new* arguments against the ordination of women: one based on the theological symbolism of Christ's masculinity,[39] and the second based on the question: "In what sense does the priest represent Christ? Since Christ is a man, can a woman be empowered to act liturgically as his priestly icon?"[40] In this regard, Ware complains that Orthodox theologians too often take over their arguments wholesale from other Christian traditions: "How hard it is for us Orthodox to speak with our own true voice! ... [A]ll too often we have borrowed our theological categories from the West, sometimes using Roman Catholic arguments (especially when opposing Protestantism), and sometimes using Protestant arguments (especially when opposing Roman Catholicism)."[41] The argument based on Christ's masculinity and the celebration of the Eucharist is one such example: "Orthodox opponents of the ordination of women have often relied, for example, on the papal statement concerning women and the priesthood *Inter Insigniores* ... without enquiring how far the conception of priesthood assumed in this document in fact corresponds to the Orthodox understanding."[42]

Behr-Sigel suggests that the question of women's ordination concerns two very different notions of the church:

> The question of the status of women is thus placed in relation to ecclesiology and more precisely in relation to two conceptions of the Church as they coexist, more or less inside all historical Churches. The one is patriarchal and hierarchical, and the other is conceived and lived essentially as a mystery of communion. This latter is a communion of persons equal in dignity, and indignity, and saved only by grace. At the same time, each person is ineffably unique and called upon to serve God and men according to his or her own vocation and special charisms. These are certainly colored by the person's sex but not determined by it.[43]

Behr-Sigel's and Ware's arguments for a reconsideration of the Orthodox objection against women's ordination are as follows.

(1) As do Roman Catholics, the Orthodox recognize that the word "priest" has three different meanings. First, there is the priesthood of Christ. Ware states: "*One, and one alone is priest*: Jesus Christ, the unique high priest of the new covenant ... is the sole true celebrant of every sacramental act." Second, there is the priesthood of all baptized Christians: "*All are priests*: by virtue of our creation in God's image and likeness, and also by virtue of the renewal of the image through baptism and anointing with chrism (Western 'confirmation'), we are all of us, clergy and laity together, 'a royal priesthood, a holy nation' ... set apart for God's service." Finally, there is the special sense in which the word "priest" is used of ordained clergy: "*Only some are priests*: certain members of the Church are set apart in a more specific way, through prayer and the laying-on of hands, to serve God in the ministerial priesthood."[44]

(2) The distinction between the priesthood common to all Christians and the unique priesthood of the ordained has been crucial to the new Roman Catholic argument. Sara Butler emphasizes that Catholic opposition to women's ordination is rooted in an understanding of ministry not shared by Protestants: "[T]he ministerial priesthood is a distinct gift, different 'essentially and not only in degree' (*essentia, no gradu tantum*) from the common priesthood." The ministry of the ordained is "offered not on the basis of the sacraments of initiation, but on the basis of the sacrament of Holy Orders."[45]

(3) The Orthodox, at least as represented by Behr-Sigel and Ware, do not view the distinction between baptism and ordination as a fundamental warrant for not ordaining women because in celebrating the Eucharist the priest acts as a representative of the entire church. Behr-Sigel draws a close connection between the common priesthood received in baptism and the special priesthood of ordination: "By the fact that all members of the Body of Christ are intimately united to the head of the Body, Jesus, they participate in the priestly life and the sacrificial death of the Redeemer." The close connection has to do with the *public* nature of worship. In worship, the priesthood of the ordained clergy is essentially representative of the common priesthood of all the baptized gathered together:

> The liturgy celebrated by the eucharistic assembly is a *public* act of worship offered to God by all together. The ordained minister together with the faithful celebrates in Christ by the Holy Spirit and in communion with the whole catholic Church of the saints of all times. . . . The consciousness of the royal priesthood of the people of God in no way, however, implies a negation of the special priesthood. . . . It rather situates this priesthood in its proper place: *not above but within the Christian community.* . . . Their priesthood is not different from the priesthood of believers, but they have received a special mission. They are called by God and the sacrament of order is the efficacious sign of this call, *to express and exercise the universal priesthood.* They are the instruments of this priestly and invisible grace of which the total Church, laymen and clerics, men and women, is the depository. . . . They re-present, make present, the unique mediation and the unique mediator [Jesus Christ] for the assembly of the faithful. But those who attend the liturgy are not present as though at a show. . . . [I]n principle, it is always the whole community that implores the grace of being united by the Spirit to him who "offers and is offered."[46]

Ware does want to "preserve a proper line of demarcation between the second [common] and third [ordained] forms of priesthood, between the ontological priesthood of baptism and the ministerial priesthood of order." Concerning the universal priesthood, Ware insists that "man and woman are equally priests, by virtue of the common humanity that they both share."[47] In a statement that initially seems similar to the Roman Catholic position, Ware states: "[T]he ministerial priest derives his priesthood not by delegation from the people but immediately from Christ." Ordination creates a special relationship to the priesthood of Christ in that "in the eucharist, as in all the sacraments, it is Christ who is the true celebrant: the visible officiant acts only in Christ's name and by his power."[48] However, that the priest acts in Christ's name does not mean that the priest possesses any authority or power of his own:

> The sacraments, then, are always actions of Christ, who is made present in our midst by the Holy Spirit. In the strict and proper sense, the sacraments are performed not by the priest but *through* him. . . . The priest at the Divine Liturgy is not "another Christ," and the sacrifice that he offers, *in union with the people*, is not "another" sacrifice, but always the unique and unrepeatable sacrifice of Christ himself.[49]

This notion of the *public* nature of worship, along with the insistence that the priest acts "in union with the people" is a reflection of the Orthodox understanding that, in presiding at the Eucharist, the priest acts *in persona ecclesiae* (in the person of the church). Ware contrasts the Western with the Eastern understanding: "Thus at the consecration in the Roman rite, as commonly interpreted, the priest represents Christ to the people, but at the consecration in the Byzantine rite the priest represents the people to Christ." Ware argues that this is why the East does not adopt the "westward position" at the prayer of consecration: "[I]t is more appropriate for the priest to face eastward, as the people do, for at this point in the service he is standing not on the Godward but on the manward side."[50]

Ware contrasts the Eastern understanding of eucharistic consecration with that of the West: "In the medieval West, as in most Roman Catholic thinking today, the priest is understood as acting *in persona Christi*. [When the priest says the words of institution,] he speaks these words as if he were himself Christ; or rather, at this moment Christ himself is understood to be speaking these words through the priest." In contrast, in the Byzantine rite, throughout the eucharistic prayer, "the celebrant speaks not *in persona Christi* but in *persona ecclesiae*, as the representative not of Christ, but of the Church." The words of institution "form part of the all-embracing narrative of thanksgiving." Ware states: "The priest, acting in union with the people and in their name, thanks God the Father for the blessings of creation, for the saving incarnation, death, and resurrection of Christ, and in particular for the institution of the eucharist; but at no point in all this does he speak as if he were himself Christ." When the priest recites the *epiclesis*, he prays "in union with the people and in their name," addressing God the Father to send down the Holy Spirit to consecrate the elements of bread and wine: "At this crucial moment as throughout the eucharistic prayer, he is not Christ's vicar or icon, but—in union with the people—he stands as a supplicant before God."[51]

Ware is emphatically clear. There are moments in the liturgy in which the priest acts "in Christ's name," for example, when he blesses the people with the sign of the cross, but, Ware insists, "at no point in the actual prayer of consecration does he speak *in persona Christi*." Ware reiterates: "At the most important of all priestly acts, then, the recitation of the eucharistic *anaphora*, according to the Orthodox understanding the celebrant does not serve as an icon of Christ."[52]

Similarly, Behr-Sigel also insists that the priest "is not seen as possessing an independent power"; Rather, the priest always acts on behalf of, and as a representative of, the church:

> He is a priest within, and not above or independently of the Church, which is made up of women as well as men. It is on behalf of the *ecclesia* that, according to the words of the Byzantine *epiclesis*, he prays to the Father to send his "Spirit on us and on the gifts we offer." Elders, *presbyteroi*, or priests are the visible instruments of the invisible priestly grace entrusted to the whole Church, lay persons and priests.[53]

In what sense, then, might the priest "represent" Christ or act as an "icon of Christ"? According to Behr-Sigel and Ware, the priest "lends his hands and voice" to Christ. Behr-Sigel asks:

> What is the meaning of this "representation" of Christ by the priest? According to the Orthodox understanding, the priest is not "another Christ." He is only the instrument that mediates the personal and invisible presence of Christ. . . . Now the priest mediates the action of Christ not by his masculinity but by pronouncing the very words of the Savior over the holy gifts. . . . The priest is thus the spokesman for the eternal Word. He lends his voice to the Word.[54]

As an icon in *this* sense, the priest is not himself "another Christ," but rather points away from himself to Christ:

> [A]n icon is not a lifelike portrait; nor, on the other hand, is the priest an icon in the literal, technical sense of the term. . . . It is as he repeats the words spoken by Christ at the Last Supper, as he repeats the gestures, that the priest points to the invisible spiritual presence—in and by the Holy Spirit—of the one High Priest, Christ.[55]

Ware insists that the Eastern fathers did not understand the relationship between Christ and the priest to lie in any notion of physical resemblance:

> It is obvious that, when St. Theodore the Studite and others term the priest or the bishop an "imitation" or "icon" of Christ, they cannot mean that there is a physical resemblance between the two. The priest does not "represent" Christ because he has a beard or black hair, or because he is about thirty years old. . . . The Fathers never interpreted liturgical typology in such exterior and materialistic terms as that. A painted icon is indeed intended to bear a visible resemblance to its prototype; but the priest is not a painted icon.[56]

Neither the masculinity of Christ's own sex nor of the priest's sex is pertinent in itself. Ware points out that the church fathers had very little to say about the theological significance of Christ's masculinity. The particularity of the incarnation demanded that Jesus Christ had to be born at a specific time and place, and that he had to have a particular sex. He could not have been both male and female, and he was indeed a male. However, according to Ware, the theological significance lies elsewhere: "What matters for [the church fathers] is not the fact that he became male (ανήρ, *vir*) but the fact that he became human (ἄνθρωπος, *homo*)."[57]

The eucharistic prayer of the priest does have representational and symbolic value. Insofar as the priest acts on behalf of the church, he not only speaks Christ's words, but also represents the church as the bride of Christ. As the priest lends his hands and voice to Christ, he also lends his hands and voice to the church. In neither case is the sexuality of the priest a determining factor. Behr-Sigel writes:

> Thus the symbolic mediation consists in the action of the priest and in the words of the divine Word pronounced by him, or rather pronounced "through him" and placed on the bread and the wine. . . . Moreover, the priest lends his voice and suppliant hand to the Church as well, that is, to the Bride, according to the symbolism of marriage. He lends himself to the Christian people whose common priesthood he activates in communion with Christ's unique priesthood. According to Orthodox sacramental theology, the epiclesis is the summit of the eucharistic prayer, and in this invocation of the Spirit, the priest asks that the Holy Spirit be expressly sent "on us" and on the gifts here present. The priest is the voice of the Bride longing for union with the Bridegroom. Here also, and even more so, the symbolism of sex does not determine his role.[58]

What implications might be drawn concerning the question of whether women can be ordained to the presbyterate? Both Behr-Sigel and Ware claim that there are no apparent theological reasons that women cannot be ordained as priests. Granted that, in reciting the words of institution, the priest is a "spokesman for the eternal Word" who "lends his voice to the Word," Behr-Sigel asks: "Can this voice not be a feminine one?" In the celebration of the Eucharist, "the priest not only represents Christ, but by saying 'we,' he also lends his voice to the Church. He pronounces the epiclesis in the name of the gathered assembly, in communion with the universal Church." In the marriage symbolism of the Church that is often used to justify a male priesthood, the church as the people of God is the bride of Christ. What implications can be drawn from this two-fold male and female symbolism of Christ as bridegroom and the church as bride?

> The Church performs the eucharist and believes that Christ is living and present through the Holy Spirit. Christ acts as the one High Priest who both "offers" and "is offered." The ordained minister does not produce the Lord's real presence. . . . [H]e "loans his tongue and his hands" to the Lord but also to his Church which is called to

be the temple of the Holy Spirit. If this is the essence of the Church's faith as witnessed to by the words of the liturgy, is not the maleness of the priest thereby relativized?[59]

Ware asks similar questions: "If the priest represents Christ not through physical characteristics but in an inward and spiritual sense, does the priest necessarily have to be male in order to fulfill this representative role? . . . While affirming, then the character of the ministerial priest as Christ's icon, I do not find that this in itself excludes women from the priesthood."[60] Ware also points to the symbolic imagery of the church as the bride of Christ. If a male priest in invoking the presence of the Holy Spirit in the *epiclesis* can act as a representative of the female bride of Christ, why could not a female priest speak as an "icon" of the male Christ?

> Since the priest in the Divine Liturgy is a living icon of Christ the bridegroom of the Church, does it follow therefore that the priest must always be a man? Can a woman represent the bridegroom? . . . [T]here is no intrinsic absurdity, provided that we make proper allowance for the subtlety and polyvalence of symbols. After all, when we speak of the Church as bride, this implies that there is a sense in which all of us— men and women alike—are feminine in our relationship to God. If men can represent the Church as bride, why cannot women represent Christ as bridegroom?[61]

TWO ROMAN CATHOLIC RESPONSES: THE LOSS OF THE HOLY SPIRIT

Yves Congar (1904–1995) was a French Dominican priest who was made a cardinal in the Roman Catholic Church in 1994. Congar was an active participant during the Second Vatican Council. Much of his later work focuses on the Holy Spirit, whose role he believed had been neglected in much Western theology. In his three-volume work, *I Believe in the Holy Spirit,* Congar sympathizes with the criticism that Roman Catholic theology has tended to substitute the pope, the Virgin Mary and the sacrament of the mass for the Holy Spirit. Much Roman Catholic theology has shown a tendency toward Christomonism, an insistence on the importance of Christ, but "a rather disturbing absence of any reference to the Holy Spirit and the Church." Concerning the Eucharist and Roman Catholic theology, Congar writes: "[T]he part played by the Holy Spirit in the Eucharist . . . has hardly been developed."[62]

In the third volume of *I Believe in the Holy Spirit,* Congar focuses on "theological dialogue between Orthodox Christianity and Roman Catholicism."[63] At the end of Congar's discussion of the disagreements between Eastern Orthodoxy and Roman Catholicism concerning the Eucharist (already discussed above), Congar provides suggestions for reconciliation. An implicit Christomonism is corrected by the notion that the Eucharist should be understood in a Trinitarian framework, and that the role of the Holy Spirit should not be neglected. Congar does not explicitly address the question of women's ordination, but his discussion certainly has implications for it.

Concerning the disagreement about whether the priest acts as a representative of Christ or a representative of the church, Congar writes: "[T]he priest ... represents not only Christ, the sovereign high priest, in whose person he acts, but also the *ecclesia*, the community of Christians, in whose person he acts also. He therefore acts *in persona Christi* and *in persona Ecclesiae*." Neither aspect can be isolated from the other. If one emphasizes Christology (as does Rome), then "the *in persona Ecclesiae* is situated within the *in persona Christi*." If one emphasizes the Holy Spirit (as does Orthodoxy), then "the *in persona Christi* is more easily seen as situated within the *in persona Ecclesiae*."[64]

It is important to understand that the priest does not consecrate the elements by virtue of a power that is "inherent in him" or that is "within his control." The "power" received at ordination is a gift of the Holy Spirit, exercised in communion with the church in the celebration of the Eucharist. This becomes clear in the Eastern rites, where the *epiclesis* is spoken in the plural voice "indicating clearly that the whole community invokes the Spirit." But even in the Latin Roman canon (eucharistic prayer), the words *offerimus* ("we offer") and *rogamus* ("we ask") are prayers addressed in the plural. Congar suggests that exclusive Western emphasis on the words of institution has led to a "devaluation" of the rest of the eucharistic prayer. In consequence, "the sense of the unity of the eucharistic prayer as a whole has been endangered."[65] Western language concerning the priest has also often been misleading: "Statements ... such as *sacerdos alter Christus* ["The priest is another Christ"], have to be understood in their true sense, which is spiritual and functional, not ontological or juridical."[66]

Edward J. Kilmartin (1923–1994), was a Roman Catholic Jesuit priest and liturgical theologian who was Professor of Sacramental Theology at the Weston Jesuit School of Theology, Professor and Director of the doctoral program in Liturgical Studies at the University of Notre Dame, Professor of Liturgical Theology at the Pontifical Oriental Institute in Rome, and Professor at Boston College. He also served as executive secretary of the United States Bishops Conference Committee for Dialogue with the Orthodox Church.

Kilmartin's approach to liturgical theology focused on ecumenical Trinitarian theology and the role of the Holy Spirit in the liturgy. In a manner similar to Congar, Kilmartin believed that Western theology had neglected the role of the Holy Spirit in the liturgy. In particular, he believed that the deficiencies of Western eucharistic theology needed to be corrected in light of more Trinitarian and ecclesiological Eastern and patristic theologies.[67]

Kilmartin distinguished two essentially different eucharistic theologies in traditional Roman Catholic (and modern Western) accounts, on the one hand, and Eastern Orthodox accounts, on the other. In traditional Roman Catholic theology, sanctification of the elements takes place through the personal mission of Christ actualized through his minister acting *in persona Christi* as he speaks the words of institution. Insofar as the priest represents the church, he does so because he first represents Christ who is the head of the church. This Western understanding neglects the role of the Holy Spirit. Since the Holy Spirit is not understood to have a "personal mission" in Western theology, the Holy Spirit is understood to be present either by "appropriation," or as given by Christ. In contrast, in Eastern Orthodox theology, the priest, speaking as a representative of the church (*in persona ecclesiae*), invokes the Holy Spirit in the *epiclesis*, who brings about Christ's presence through his personal mission.[68]

Kilmartin was critical of what he referred to as the "average modern Catholic eucharistic theology," which displayed a "weak integration of the elements that go into the construction of a systematic theology of the Eucharist";[69] this theology was a "product of the Thomistic tradition but certainly not equated with the eucharistic theology of St. Thomas Aquinas."[70] Kilmartin claimed that the "prevailing official Catholic eucharistic theology that [had] its roots . . . in the 12th and 13th centuries no longer does justice to [the] central Christian mystery."[71] It had the following characteristics:

First, this "average Catholic eucharistic theology" has "no grasp of the literary structure and theological dynamic of the Eucharistic Prayer." Modern Catholic theology isolated the "words of institution," formulated as a "moment of consecration." The words of institution are "posed in the air without access to the other elements of the structure."[72] Kilmartin characterized this as the "product of a splinter tradition of the Western Latin Church," which emphasized the Christological dimension to the neglect of ecclesiology and the role of the Holy Spirit and the Trinitarian dimensions of eucharistic theology.[73]

A consequence of the isolation of the words of institution is that the actions of the presiding minister are understood to be those of "enacting a drama" in which the minister plays the part of Christ while the congregation is an audience observing the drama, in contrast to understanding the presiding minister as leading a prayer on behalf of the church as the gathered Christian community.[74]

In consequence, this eucharistic theology isolates the presiding minister from the community of faith. The presiding minister primarily represents Christ, and only represents the church insofar as Christ is head of the church: "[E]cclesiology enters by the back door, or is equivalently absorbed into Christology." This theology also elevates the role of the priest insofar as he is not perceived to be acting with and in the church as one who is also himself a recipient of Christ's presence.[75] In this theology, "the Eucharist appears to be a sacrament celebrated in the Church for the sake of the Church, but not precisely the sacrament of the Church."[76] The classic illustration of this isolation of the presiding minister from the community is the scholastic conundrum of whether an errant priest could consecrate the bread in the shop window of a bakery.[77]

In contrast to the "average Catholic eucharistic theology," Kilmartin proposed the following alternative:

The sacraments must be considered within a salvation-historical, Trinitarian and ecclesial context: God's self-communication has occurred through historical events and persons, but God has uniquely communicated himself to humanity through the mediation of Jesus Christ, the Word become a human being. This divine self-communication has a Trinitarian structure located in the personal missions of both the incarnate Son and the Holy Spirit. The incarnate Word is not only the Father's communication to humanity, but also, in his humanity, the perfect response to the Father, made possible by the special mission of the Holy Spirit, who sanctified the humanity of Jesus Christ. Through the gift of the same Holy Spirit, the church is enabled to participate through faith, hope, and love in what the Father has done in Christ for the world's salvation.[78]

In the liturgical worship of the church, Jesus Christ, who suffered, died, and is now risen and glorified, is personally present to the church.[79] The sacraments are acts of the risen Christ in which "Christ is united to the Church, not identified with the Church." At the same time, the Holy Spirit acts as the "bond of unity" between Christ and the church. "The Holy Spirit, whom Christ possesses in fulness, was sent by him from the Father to form believers into the Church."[80] Thus the notions of Christian worship and celebration of the sacraments presuppose a Trinitarian and ecclesiological structure: "What sacraments manifest and realize is the Church in its deepest being, namely the communion of life between the Father and humankind in Christ through the gift of the Holy Spirit, which entails sharing of life in faith between those who participate in the mystery of the shared Trinitarian life."[81]

This salvation-historical, Trinitarian, and ecclesial structure of worship is shown in the content of the classical eucharistic prayers of the patristic and (particularly) Eastern churches. The classic prayers of both the Eastern and Western churches have a structure of *anamnesis* (remembrance) and *epiclesis* (petition). The narrative of institution forms the center of the prayers, and provides the warrant for the *epiclesis* of the Holy Spirit, the request for the sanctification of the gifts and the communicants. The literary structure is that of a unified prayer to the Father (as Creator and giver of all gifts), in thankful recognition of his action in Christ (*anamnesis*), followed by a petition (*epiclesis*) that the faithfulness of the Father to his people would be expressed through the sanctification of the Holy Spirit, through whom both Christ is brought to the communicants (through the sanctification of bread and wine) and the communicants brought to Christ (request for sanctification of the people).[82]

This salvation-historical, Trinitarian, and ecclesiological structure of worship has the following implications for understanding of the role of the presiding minister of the Christian community who leads in celebrating the Eucharist.

First, the eucharistic prayer is not a drama, but a prayer spoken on behalf of the entire gathered community of the church. In Kilmartin's words, "The Eucharist is not a dramatic representation of what Christ did at the Last Supper. Rather, it is the Eucharistic celebration of the Church, the Body and Bride of Christ."[83] The "words of institution" cannot, then, be separated from the eucharistic prayer as a whole, and the priest is not to be understood as if he were playing the role of Jesus Christ in a drama of the last supper; rather, the words of institution are part of a prayer that the presiding minister is praying on behalf of the gathered church: "Christian liturgy differs from sacred drama not merely because of the mystery content but because the presence of Christ and his saving work takes place through rites which are a form of expression of the faith of the Church."[84]

Second, sacraments exist for the "building up of the Church," and it is the risen Christ himself who is "actively present as head of the Church and high priest of the worship of the earthly Church."[85] Thus, the "eucharistic community enacts its worship *in, with,* and *through* Jesus Christ ... in the sphere of personal communion with Christ, grounded on the one participation in the one Spirit of Christ."[86] "Liturgical actions are, first and foremost, a special form of expression of the faith of the Church."[87] While worship is only possible because the risen Christ is present as the head of the church, the "active subject" of Christian worship is the "concrete eucharistic assembly."[88] According to Kilmartin, "The liturgical community itself is the proper active subject of the sacramental celebrations";[89] the celebration of the Eucharist is "the corporate act of the ecclesial community."[90] Sacraments are thus "acts of the Church as such, not merely acts of the minister of Christ in the Church."[91] Why, then, is ordination necessary? The pastoral office is an "essential structure" of the church, established by the Holy Spirit to build up the local community of faithful Christians. It is exercised through word and deed, through preaching, teaching, charitable service, and through leading communal worship:[92] "Ordination equips the minister to preside at sacraments in which the whole community is the integral subject."[93]

This salvation-historical, Trinitarian ecclesial eucharistic theology has implications for understanding the role of the presiding minister of the entire community who are gathered for worship, and in which the celebrant's role cannot be separated from or considered independently of the gathering of the church in worship. The priest does indeed have a representative role, but the presiding minister acts first as representative of the church's faith, and thus primarily represents the church: "[T]he presiding priest acts as representative of the Church's faith and therefore the faith of the local community." Kilmartin notes that this is evident in the content of the eucharistic prayer, in which "eucharistic worship is an activity of the whole Christ, head and body"[94]: "By expressing the faith of the Church as formulated in the symbolic language and actions of the liturgy, the minister represents the Church, speaking in the name of the believing Bride of Christ."[95] In celebrating the Eucharist, the priest thus acts *in persona ecclesiae*. The priest also represents Christ, but only as first representing the church: "[T]he minister appears to be, in all liturgical activity, the representative of Christ because he represents, in virtue of ordination the community of which Christ is Head. . . . [H]e represents Christ because he represents the Church of which Christ is the Head."[96]

This understanding that the presiding minister represents Christ insofar as he first represents the church has implications for the issue of women's ordination—implications that Kilmartin did not hesitate to endorse. In an early essay considering the nature of "apostolic office," he insisted that "one cannot situate the peculiarity of ordained ministry in the unqualified concept of representation of Christ";[97] rather, "the ordaining minister must function in such a way that his instrumental task is not separated from an ecclesial context. . . . [T]he minister must represent the faith of the Church in order to serve as minister of Christ."[98] Kilmartin emphasized that ecclesial "office directly represents the faith of the Church and only to this extent can represent Christ."[99] It is because "the office bearer represents the Church united in faith and love in his role as leader, [that] he represents Christ."[100] Kilmartin drew the relevant implications concerning women's ordination: "Since the priest directly represents the Church united in faith and love, the old argument against the ordination of women to the priesthood, based on the presupposition that the priest directly represents Christ and so should be male, becomes untenable." Rather, "the representative role of priest seems to demand both male and female office bearers in the proper cultural context: for the priest represents the one Church, in which distinctions of race, class, and sex have been transcended, where all are measured by the one norm: faith in Christ."[101]

In two other essays, Kilmartin focused specifically on the question of women's ordination. In an essay entitled "Bishop and Presbyter as Representatives of the Church and Christ," he addressed the Congregation for the Doctrine of the Faith's Declaration *Inter Insigniores*, the first appearance of the Roman Catholic argument that women cannot be ordained because they do not resemble a male Christ.[102] In his response, Kilmartin refers to the "common" teaching that the priest "denotes Christ's activity" at the "moment of consecration." Kilmartin complains that this teaching "totally neglects the structure of the eucharistic prayers of the East and West as well as the epicletic character of these prayers." To the contrary, he points out that all the activities carried out by priests express the faith of the church. Ordained clergy do act *in persona Christi*, but "they do so since they represent the one Church united in faith and love." In presiding at the Eucharist, "priests represent the whole Church and so connote Christ's activity. They act in the name of the whole Church and so serve as transparency for the grounds of unity and activity of the whole Church: Christ and the Holy Spirit."[103]

Kilmartin makes his point by referring to the structure of the eucharistic prayer, and particularly to the epiclesis. As a whole, the eucharistic prayer "denotes the action of the Church, which, in turns, connotes the activity of Christ." Since, in celebrating the Eucharist, priests "act in the name of the whole Church," and the whole church is composed of both men and women, Kilmartin states that "it is not immediately clear why maleness is required in this ministry to preserve the proper symbolic correspondence."[104]

Kilmartin addressed the issue at greater length in his essay "Full Participation of Women in the Life of the Catholic Church."[105] In this essay, Kilmartin notes that the "current theological arguments raised against the ordination of women to the ministerial priesthood in official Catholic circles are rather weak."[106] He recognizes that the "current official Roman Catholic position" excludes women only from pastoral functions that are "sacerdotal," that is, celebration of the Eucharist, confirmation and penance.[107] The key argument against the ordination of women in modern papal encyclicals "speak[s] of the priest as representative of Christ."[108]

Kilmartin insists that this argument makes the "typical mistake of traditional scholastic theology." It fails to "use the liturgy as a true source of theology."[109] As well, it discusses the representative role of the priest in relation to Christ apart from his role in representing the church, and as a member of the church. According to Kilmartin, the "christomonism" of scholastic theology fails to "articulate the pneumatological and ecclesiological aspects of ordination"; it "lacks a Trinitarian perspective which gives due consideration to the role of the Spirit."[110]

In contrast, in a "more ample christological, pneumatological and ecclesiological theology . . . the priest emerges as directly representing the church united in faith and love and so representing Christ and the Holy Spirit, sources of unity and faith of the church." Given this realization, the traditional argument that the priest directly represents Christ becomes "difficult." Kilmartin writes, "Logically an appeal to the representative function of the priest would seem to support the view that women should be ordained. For the priest must be seen as representing the one church composed of males and females and so the Lord of the church and the Spirit who grounds the unity of faith and love." Furthermore, following the symbolic argument to its logical conclusion "would seem to end with a preference for females, given the traditional role awarded to the Holy Spirit in the liturgical tradition of the ordination rites."[111]

TWO ANGLICAN THEOLOGIANS

Robert Campbell Moberly (1845–1903) was an Anglican theologian who began his career as one of the contributors to the series of essays entitled *Lux Mundi*. He was Regius Professor of Pastoral Theology at the University of Oxford, Canon of Christ Church Cathedral, Oxford, and chaplain to both Queen Victoria and Edward VII. Moberly's book, *Ministerial Priesthood*, attempted to steer a middle course between the two dangers of Catholic "formalism" and Protestant "spiritualism."[112] Formalism tends to think of the priesthood as "mechanical," gives intrinsic efficacy to outward performance, and understands the priest as a "real intermediary" between God and the people. Spiritualism, in contrast, reacts against formalism by depreciating all outward forms and observances.[113]

Moberly was concerned that both the medieval Sarum Rite—which preceded the Anglican *Book of Common Prayer* in England—and the Roman Catholic Council of Trent tended toward formalism. The Sarum Rite contains two ideas concerning ordination: the first has to do with assisting the bishop (which is an ancient understanding of ordination); the second consists of additional ceremonial actions, the point of which is to "offer (eucharistic) sacrifice." What is missing from the Sarum Rite is any notion of service for the people or any notion of self-sacrifice of the people.[114] The Council of Trent closely connects priesthood to eucharistic sacrifice, and insists that the priest is a "mediator and representative between God and man, which is to be reckoned the principal function of priesthood."[115] Trent does insist that the eucharistic sacrifice is "one and the same" with the sacrifice of Calvary, but the word *proprium* (a "proper" sacrifice) tends to give the impression that the eucharistic sacrifice is "independent" and a "sacrifice *per se*." The Reformers reacted against this language because they perceived it as meaning to "offer actual atoning sacrifices" (plural) and that it "constituted a real propitiary mediation between the lay people and their God."[116]

At the same time, Moberly's own position is equally at odds with "spiritualism." In response to the "spiritualist" question whether ordinances (such as sacraments or ordained clergy) are essential to the church's being, Moberly replies that they are not essential to the church's being, but they are essential to the church's life in the sense that insofar as we are commanded by God to use them, we may not dispense with them. God may not be bound to appointed means of grace, but we are.[117]

What then of the priesthood of ordained clergy? Rather than beginning with either the affirmation or denial of eucharistic sacrifice—the dividing issue between Trent and Protestants—Moberly finds his starting point for discussion of Christian ministry in the unity of the church: "The unity which the Church represents is the Unity of God"—understood in a Trinitarian manner. The church is one because God is one. The New Testament presumes that the church is one; Moberly appeals to Christ's

High Priestly Prayer that "they all may be one" (John 17) and Ephesians 4 ("One baptism, one body, one Spirit, . . . one Lord, one faith, one baptism, one God and Father of all").[118] The New Testament model for the unity of the church is the body of Christ, which is a "corporate" unity. Moberly insists that any contrast between a unity of spirit and a unity of body is not scriptural.[119] Accordingly, he is critical of any understanding of the church (and church office) that contrasts the spiritual with the bodily, or that prioritizes the individual apart from the community.[120]

Thus, the church is one because it is the body of Christ and the temple of the Holy Spirit. This applies to the church as a whole, and not to the clergy specifically.[121] What then is the relationship of ordained ministers to the body as a whole? According to Moberly, ordained ministers are not intermediaries. Following Paul's analogy in 1 Corinthians, Moberly suggests that ordained ministers are organs of the body, representative for specific purposes of the power of the life of the body.[122] Moberly states:

> We think, then, of ministry, not as a holy intermediary, wielding powers peculiar and inherent, because it is Spirit-endowed on behalf of those who are not. But Christian ministry is the instrument which represents the whole Spirit-endowed Body of the Church; and yet withal is itself so Spirit-endowed as to have the right and the power to represent instrumentally. The immense exaltation—and requirement—of lay Christianity, which in respect of its own dignity cannot be exaggerated, in no way detracts from the distinctive dignity of the duties which belong to ministerial function, or from the solemn significance of separation to ministry.[123]

Moberly corrects several misconceptions concerning the implications of a representative clergy. First, it does not follow that, because ordained ministers are organs of the whole body, they are dispensable, or that they simply do as individuals what the entire body does together. The ministry represents the whole body; it does not follow that every member of the body is an ordained minister. Similarly, it does not follow from the representative function of the minister that each minister is a priest only in the sense that each member of the congregation is a priest; there is no blurring of universal priesthood and ministerial priesthood.[124]

Moberly also responds to critics of priestly "sacerdotalism" who complain that priestly ministry separates the clergy from the laity. The complaint misses the point of the representative function of ordained ministry; if ordained ministers represent the body, then they are not separate from the body.[125] At the same time, the minister's function is representative, not vicarious. The minister is not more holy than the layperson. The minister simply has been called to a specific representative ministry in the church that the layperson does not fulfill.[126]

Another commonly expressed criticism of sacerdotalism concerns the issue of sacrifice; by offering an "atoning sacrifice," ministerial priesthood is said to create an "intermediary" between God and the laity, creating a "sacerdotal caste."[127] To the contrary, Moberly argues,

> the Christian ministry is not a substituted intermediary—still less an atoning mediator—between God and lay people; but it is rather the representative and organ of the whole body, in the exercise of prerogatives and powers which belong to the body as a whole.... What is duly done by Christian Ministers, it is not so much that *they* do it, in the stead, or for the sake of the whole; but rather that the whole does it by and through them. The Christian priest does not offer an atoning sacrifice on behalf of the Church: it is rather the Church through his act, that not so much "offers an atonement," as "is identified upon earth with the one heavenly offering of the atonement of Christ."[128]

This leads to the issue of sacrifice and eucharistic sacrifice, in particular. Moberly contrasts the sacrifices of the Old Testament, which were figurative, with the sacrifice of Christ, which is the reality: "All priesthood, all sacrifice, is summed up in the Person of Christ."[129] Moberly does not directly address the question of women's ordination, but, as has been seen, the question of the relationship between the ordained priesthood and the sacrifice of Christ has been the crucial concern. In what sense does the priest represent Christ and his sacrifice?[130] Moberly challenges the traditional notion of sacrifice that focuses on death; rather, Christ's entire life was a sacrifice:

> Wherein, then, is Christ a Priest?... [H]ow was this priestly sacrifice offered by Him? Does it mean the moment of Calvary?... His entire life in mortal flesh was a sacrifice, a dying, a crucifying, so that Calvary, however supreme as a culmination, was a culmination of, rather than a contradiction to, what the life before had meant.[131]

This notion that sacrifice has not to do with death *per se*, but with the giving of life is also key to understanding sacrifice in the Old Testament:

> The culminating point of the sacrifice was not in the shedding of the blood, but in the presentation before God, in the holy place, of the blood that had been shed; of the life, that is, which had passed through death, and had been consecrated to God by dying.... It is the life as life, not the death as death; it is ... the life, which is acceptable to God.[132]

Accordingly, it is not Christ's death on Calvary, but the self-offering of his life, and the presentation of that offering to his Father in heaven by the risen and ascended Jesus Christ that constitutes his sacrifice; Christ is thus a "priest for ever."

> He is a Priest for ever, not as it were by a perpetual series of acts of memory, not by multiplied and ever remoter acts of commemoration of a death that is past, but by the eternal presentation of a life which eternally is the "life that died."[133]

Crucial to the notion of self-offering is love, and self-offering of life in love would be the nature of sacrifice even apart from the existence of the sin that led to Christ's death on Calvary. Thus self-offering in love is the essence of Christ's sacrifice.[134] It follows that Old Testament sacrifices are "external and symbolic" only, since the sacrificed animal does not voluntarily give itself in love.[135]

This notion of the "self-offering" of life is crucial to understanding the universal priesthood of the church. The priesthood of the church flows from Christ's priesthood: "[W]hat Christ is, the Church, which is Christ's mystical body, must also be. . . . [T]he Church's priesthood being in its inner truth the priesthood of Christ."[136] If Christ's sacrificial priesthood is found in his self-offering in love, this also must be the nature of the church's priesthood. This priesthood has both an outward and inward element. Outwardly, the church identifies with Christ's priesthood in the Eucharist, "which is the symbolic counterpart in the Church on earth, not simply of Calvary, but of that eternal presentation of Himself in heaven in which Calvary is vitally contained." In the worship of the Eucharist, the church identifies with Christ's self-offering to the Father, and is also transfigured inwardly by the presence of the Holy Spirit to conform itself to his self-offering as Christ is formed within the church through the Spirit of love.[137]

The consequence of this transformation is a priestly orientation to the world outside the church:

> The Church is priestly because her arms are spread out perpetually to succour and intercede for those who need the sacrifice of love. . . . [T]he Church is God's priest in the world and for the world, alike as presenting to God on the world's behalf that homage which the world has not learned to present for itself, and as spending and suffering for God's sake in service to the world.[138]

This notion of priesthood as loving self-offering in response to and a sharing in Christ's own gift of self-offering to the church and the world, is expressed as well in the priestly ordination of the church's ministers. Moberly states:

> The priesthood of the ministry follows as corollary from the priesthood of the Church. . . . If the priesthood of the Church consists ceremonially in her capacity of self-identification, through Eucharistic worship, with the eternal presentation of Christ's atoning sacrifice, and spiritually in her identification of inner life with the spirit of sacrifice which is the spirit of love uttering itself in devoted ministry to others, so it is by necessary consequence with the priesthood of the ministry.[139]

Ordained ministers are priestly because the church is priestly. By ordination, they have been "specialized and empowered to exercise ministerially and organically the prerogatives which are the prerogatives of the body as a whole."[140] The priesthood has a representative function in that ordained ministers "are Priests because they are personally consecrated to be the representatives and active organs of the priesthood of the Church." Ceremonially, they represent the priesthood of the church in the "external enactment of worship and sacrament," but there is also a demanded inwardness of the "spirit of the priestly Church."[141] Eucharistic leadership has its corresponding corollaries: "the bearing of the people on the heart before God; the earnest effort of intercessory entreating; the practical translation of intercession into pastoral life, and anxiety, and pain."[142] Moberly points out that it is this notion of priestly service for the people, but also self-sacrifice of the people, that were emphasized in the ordination and eucharistic rites of the Anglican *Book of Common Prayer*, in contrast to both the medieval Catholic Sarum Rite and the Council of Trent, from which they were completely missing.[143]

Accordingly, the priesthood of the laity and of ordained ministry are not antithetical, but correlative and complementary. One can magnify the ministerial priesthood, and move from there to speak of the dignity and priesthood of the laity; conversely, one can begin with the dignity of the universal priesthood of the laity, and then speak of the manner in which ordained ministers are representative of the universal priesthood. What should not be done is to discredit the notion of ordained priesthood by contrasting it with the priesthood of the body, or, conversely, to discuss ordained priesthood in a manner that isolates it from the priesthood of the laity.[144]

How might Moberly's discussion bear on the issue of the ordination of women? He does not discuss the issue, and, of course, it would be anachronistic to expect him to have done so. However, his discussion of priestly ministry does have bearing on the modern Catholic objections that have been raised against the practice.

First, Moberly does not simply equate the universal priesthood of the laity and the ordained priesthood, and he objects to accounts that do so—so he is not subject to one usual Catholic objection against "Protestant" accounts.[145] At the same time, however, Moberly closely ties together the notions of universal priesthood and ministerial priesthood. He acknowledges that the ministerial priesthood exercises a representative function, but he understands this to mean that the ordained minister represents the church, and that the "ministerial priesthood" is representative of the "universal priesthood" of the church. In terms of the disagreement between Orthodox and Roman Catholics, Moberly would then hold to the position that the priest acts *in persona ecclesiae* (in the person of the church).

At the same time, although Moberly does not speak in so many words of the priest as representing Christ, his understanding of priesthood makes clear that both universal priesthood and ministerial priesthood participate in (and accordingly act as representatives of) Christ's priesthood. Moberly states: "[W]hat Christ is, the Church, which is Christ's mystical body, must also be. . . . If Christ is Priest, the Church is priestly." In the same paragraph, Moberly even states that the relationship between the church's priesthood and Christ's consists in a participation in Christ's person: "[P]riestliness of character is a consequence which outflows upon the Church from the Person of Christ."[146]

Thus one certainly could make the case that Moberly understands the ordained minister to be representing not only the church, but Christ, and thus acting *in persona Christi*. However, Moberly puts himself at odds with the modern Western Catholic argument against women's ordination by placing the significance of Christ's sacrifice and priesthood not in his maleness, but in his self-offering of sacrificial love. And it is through sharing in and imitating Christ's self-sacrificial love that both laity and ordained ministers participate in Christ's sacrifice and act as representatives of Christ. In so doing, Moberly endorses a notion of the "imitation of Christ" that anticipates the theme of "cruciformity" that New Testament scholar Michael J. Gorman understands to be the key to the apostle Paul's spirituality discussed earlier.[147] Of course, although the notion of self-sacrificial love is something that is expected of clergy—and Moberly points to the Ordinal of the *Book of Common Prayer* as emphasizing this—it is not something that is unique only to clergy, as Moberly also points out.[148] And, of course, self-sacrificial love is certainly not exclusive to males.

The Very Reverend Dr. George R. Sumner was principal and Helliwell Professor of World Mission at Wycliffe College, University of Toronto. He was ordained to the priesthood in the Diocese of Western Massachusetts in 1981, and elected bishop of the Episcopal Diocese of Dallas, Texas, in 2015. Sumner's book, *Being Salt: A Theology of the Ordered Church*, is (in a manner similar to Moberly) an attempt to "move beyond the impasse of Catholic and Protestant perceptions." Sumner's task is to "give arguments which appeal to the heart of the Gospel itself to defend orders, traditionally understood, without claiming that such orders are themselves mandated by Scripture." His goal is to "chart an evangelical course leading to the predetermined catholic harbor."[149] In addition, Sumner intends to "subvert" the "common yet unhelpful antinomies in discussions about ordained ministry" that set functional vs. ontological, lay-oriented vs. clerically oriented, and "the priest *in persona Christi* vs. the priest *in persona ecclesiae*."[150]

Sumner states that any understanding of priesthood will have to take into account the three parties of Christ, priest, and people of God, as well as the fourth party to whom the church's mission is addressed: the world.[151] An evangelical understanding of ministry begins first with the gospel, but includes within that an understanding of the nature of the church.[152] In addition, the priesthood cannot be thought of as "over against" or "in competition" with the laity. Ordained ministry exists for the sake of the laity: "It is for the laity, both practically and symbolic, that priests serve in the Church."[153]

Sumner describes the church Christocentrically:

Hidden presently in the Church, Christ speaks His promise, as Word and sacrament, across time and space until He returns. [Sumner's emphasis] . . . Christ is present in the Church . . . [b]ut this presence is always hidden, veiled, for the Church is yet a sinful creature, slothful, disobedient. It not only sits at supper with Him, it also walks along unable to see who walks beside it.[154]

This simultaneity of both the risen Christ's presence to the church but also his hiddenness within that presence is crucial for Sumner's understanding of ordained ministry. Following a current ecumenical consensus, Sumner affirms that the church practice for which the minister is ordained is "presiding at the Eucharist." Both Catholic and Protestant traditions define the nature of ordained ministry in terms of the "liturgy of Word and table." In the Catholic tradition, Thomas Aquinas wrote that the priest is "ordered" to the celebration of the Eucharist; the Lutheran Augsburg Confession insists that the church is present where the Word is rightly preached and the sacraments rightly administered. To understand the nature of the church, in order to understand the purpose of priestly order, it is necessary to look "at what happens in true preaching and right celebrating."[155]

According to Sumner, the ordained minister serves three basic functions. First, he or she "points to the Word." Second, the "priest serves as a sign of the promissory, avowed nature of the Christian life."[156] Concerning this second role—"The Priest as the Sign of the Oath"—Sumner states that the "priest is a symbol of this aspect of hope by which we live. He or she is called to remind the whole Body of the reality of indwelling, of the permanence and durability of that hope."[157] Third, the priest "focuses on the renewing remnant within and for the Church . . . while they remain loyal to the Church in which they are in orders."[158] Concerning this third role—"The Priest as Church in Miniature"—Sumner notes that the "Church is the tension-laden relationship between structure and moments of renewal, the latter represented by missionary or ascetical orders." Priests are both servants of the Church and representatives of its tradition, but also should point to the lordship of Christ and his gracious action.[159]

It is the first role, that of "point[ing] to the Word," that touches most directly on the role of the priest in terms of the "liturgy of Word and table," and it is this first role that is crucial for the Catholic debate about the ordination of women. Unlike Protestant arguments that focus on questions of authority, Catholic objections to women's ordination would likely not object to lay women fulfilling Sumner's second and third functions of ministry.

The starting point of Sumner's argument is Christocentric, and specifically concerns the presence of the risen Lord when the church gathers to worship. Sumner insists that we must take it as "basic" that "Christians address their prayers to a *Person,*

Jesus Christ." This means that "Jesus is alive, that He is an agent in His own right, and that language addressed to Him, must for all its subtleties, be understood in a realist manner. . . . That Jesus risen is present is the starting point for reflection." At least one implication of the risen Christ's presence is significant for questions concerning the role of the priest in leading worship. The church is not Jesus: "It means that who and what Jesus is cannot be so readily absorbed into who and what we are."[160]

When the church gathers to celebrate the Eucharist, it tells the story of this Jesus who is alive, "the story of the saving death and resurrection of Jesus." It is the Jesus whose story is told in the gospels, who is the true prophet, priest, and king. However, Sumner notes, Jesus fulfills these roles in a paradoxical manner:

> He fulfills these offices in the most surprising and counter-intuitive ways. He is proven king as He surrenders all power in obedience to His heavenly Father. He is the true priest even as He Himself is killed. . . . He is the true prophet even as His own disciples sleep and eventually flee. . . . He Himself is king, priest, prophet in disturbing ways that undo the pre-existing orders of rule and sacrifice in the very moment that true rule and sacrifice are established.[161]

This paradoxical nature of the traditional threefold office is reflected in the paradoxical nature of ordained ministry; in presiding at the Eucharist, the priest points away from his or her own identity to the identity of the risen Christ who has died, is risen, and is now present with the church. The office of the priest is symbolic and representative—not, however, in a straightforward manner, but rather in what Sumner identifies as a "counter-symbol." Because only the crucified and risen Jesus Christ is the true prophet, priest and king, the ordained priest can only represent Christ by pointing away from himself or herself (as does John the Baptist in Grunewald's famous triptych) to the crucified and risen Lord:

> The priest who stands at the table and reads that communion prayer, in the service of this surprising Priest and King, in spite of all appearing, reinforces that he or she is neither, all in the service of pointing to Him. And by so doing he or she is proven a fitting symbol of priestly offering . . . He or she is, then, a kind of counter-symbol. . . . And all this is done to the service of the One who is the real and Only Priest, who redefines, fulfills and ends all priesthood in Himself. The minister at the table is a counter-sign that works by its own displacement, by becoming a great finger stretched away from oneself and toward the dying Jesus at the center of the Church's life.[162]

The priest's role is not, then, one of power; rather, the model for the priesthood is that of an "icon," pointing not toward himself or herself, but to the crucified Christ. In terms of symbolism, the priest is first a symbol of the church: "The priest exists to show the Church something *about itself*, to reflect back its proper and necessary nature as a body turned toward Jesus Christ." The priest is then both an icon and not an icon of Christ: "The priest is not an icon of Christ, but rather of the Church as it seeks to attend to, imitate, be the Body of Christ." One could say then, that the or-dained minister represents both Christ and the church. The priest represents Christ not by himself or herself being *another* Christ (an *alter Christus*), but in pointing away from himself or herself to the crucified and risen Lord Jesus Christ, who is the head of the church, which is his body. The priest represents the church insofar as to be the church means to be the body of Christ in a manner that imitates Christ in his own self-effacement. Sumner states in a footnote that "the priest by this account is *in persona ecclesiae* rather than *in persona Christi*, though the element of nuance comes in the fact that the *ecclesia* is defined by its attention to its Lord."[163]

The ordained priesthood is then, by its very nature, paradoxical. In performing the role of the priest, the priest acknowledges his or her own incapacity to play that role. The priest is not Christ, but points to Christ: "The priesthood is by its very nature an ironic office, a role of self-evacuation by which the priest points away . . . toward . . . Jesus Christ risen and present both in the Word the priest truly proclaims and the sacrament he or she rightly observes, for it is, after all, *His* Word, and *His* table."[164] In pointing toward Christ, the priest plays a representative role on the part of the church, for it is the church's own vocation to point away from itself toward the risen Christ who is the source of its own life as it is joined to him as his body:

> The priest is the member of the Church charged with the task of pointing away from himself or herself so as to point toward the One by whom and for whom the Church exists, the risen and present Jesus Christ. He or she serves as a referent to Him. . . . Thus she or he does not have a priestly ministry, so much as a priestward one, a min-istry of redirection, recasting and escort.[165]

Finally, Sumner addresses the question of priestly authority. The priest has au-thority, but again, the model of authority is based on the iconic role of the priest's ministry. Any authority that the priest has is not based on any personal capacity, but is delegated by the crucified and risen Christ, and must be modeled on his own self-effacement. The priest's authority is entirely derivative:

> Authority must be defined with respect to Jesus Christ alone, for He as Word is the divine *auctor* and He has done the decisively saving deed to which the Church is obliged to offer its "Amen." . . . The Church exercises legitimate authority as it points towards its Lord as the body's Head, and so claims a derivative and dependent au-thority.[166]

A REFORMED CONTRIBUTION

Thomas F. Torrance (1913–2007) was an ordained minister in the Church of Scotland (Presbyterian), a world-renowned theologian, and Professor of Christian Dogmatics at New College, Edinburgh. He was the author of numerous books, and one of the translators of Karl Barth's *Church Dogmatics* into English. Torrance was an ecumenical theologian, and was consecrated an honorary Protopresbyter in the Greek Orthodox Patriarchate of Alexandria in 1973. His many publications included works in ecumenical theology, patristic hermeneutics, Trinitarian theology, Christology and the atonement, as well as the relation between theology and modern science. Torrance's contributions to a discussion of ordained ministry and the priesthood occur in several of his ecumenical essays as well as the book *Royal Priesthood*, which was first published as a contribution to discussions between the Church of Scotland and the Church of England concerning ordained ministry and the episcopate.[167]

A central theme of Torrance's theology of worship and the Eucharist is the "vicarious humanity" of Christ and its crucial significance for the church's participation in Christ's priesthood: "[T]he key to the understanding of the Eucharist is to be sought in the *vicarious humanity of Jesus, the priesthood of the incarnate Son*. Eternal God though he was, he condescended to be our brother."[168] Torrance found this theme in the theologies of church fathers such as Athanasius and the Cappadocians, but especially in the anti-Nestorian and anti-Apollinarian theology of Cyril of Alexandria. Cyril understood not only that the church worships through Christ, but that the church worships *with* Christ. In the incarnation, the Son of God assumed not simply a human body, but a complete human nature, including a human mind. During his earthly ministry, Jesus *as human* was anointed with the Holy Spirit and prayed to and worshiped God the Father: "Cyril laid emphasis upon the human agency of Christ fulfilled within the measures of what is truly human, and not least in prayer, worship and adoration of Christ in which he become one with us."[169] After the resurrection and ascension, the risen Jesus Christ permanently retained his human nature, including his human mind, and exercises his priesthood by interceding for the church and by offering worship to God the Father: "Since the Son of God was made priest in that he was made man, without ceasing to be God, he fulfils his priesthood as one who *receives* as well as one who *offers* prayer."[170] Accordingly, the church's worship is a participation in the worship of the risen Christ:

> Jesus Christ ascended to the Father [is] the Mediator of our worship in mind and soul and body in union with him. It is as *our* Priest, with all his human condition in body, mind and soul which he took from us, with his human worship and prayer in which he assimilates our worship and prayer in his name, that he appears in the presence of his Father and fulfils his heavenly ministry as Priest over the House of God.[171]

Torrance believed that there had been an unfortunate loss of this crucial insight of the significance of the human mind of Christ as well as his vicarious humanity as mediator of the church's worship in the subsequent development of Christian understanding and practice of worship after the patristic era. He refers to the work of Roman Catholic liturgist Josef Jungmann's *The Place of Christ in Liturgical Prayer* for documentation.[172] Jungmann pointed out that in the early liturgies of the church, prayers were addressed to God the Father through Christ as the one mediator between God and humanity; later, especially from the medieval period on, prayers were directed to Christ himself. The consequence was that Christ was thrust up into the majesty of the Godhead in a way that diminished and even virtually eliminated the biblical and patristic focus on the high priesthood of Christ and his human mediation of prayer to God the Father. This led to a kind of Christological "monophysitism" (the absorbing of Christ's human nature by his divine nature), or what Torrance referred to as "Apollinarianism in the liturgy": "[T]he humanity and mediatorship of Christ recede more and more into the background and the poor creature at worship is confronted immediately with the overwhelming majesty of God."[173]

Torrance insisted that this loss of Christ's human mediation had disastrous consequences for worship: "[T]he Church's understanding of the Eucharist becomes seriously deficient whenever it loses the biblical and early catholic emphasis upon Christ praying and worshipping as one of us, and yet on our behalf, as an essential part of his vicarious obedience in the flesh."[174] In particular, there arose a demand for other mediators to make up for the human priesthood of Christ: "[A]bove all the Church was thrown back upon itself to provide a priesthood which could stand in for Christ, and even mediate between the sinner and Christ."[175]

Torrance developed a corrective theology of Eucharist and ministry that focused on the unique mediation of Christ's priesthood in his human nature and the church's worship as a participation in Christ's vicarious worship on our behalf. In the second edition of *Royal Priesthood*, Torrance wrote that he was "concerned with . . . the biblical and ancient catholic understanding of the royal priesthood of the Church incorporated into Christ as his Body, and of the priesthood of the ordained ministry of the Church."[176]

Torrance's theology of worship is both Christocentric and Trinitarian. Torrance's Christology includes the themes of incarnation, and the notion of Christ's priesthood as self-offering on our behalf: "The starting point must surely be the Incarnation of the Son in which he took our human nature, healed and sanctified it in himself that he might offer it up to God in and through his own self-consecration and self-presentation to the Father on our behalf."[177]

Torrance's theology of worship is Christocentric, but not Christomonist; in a manner similar to the Orthodox and Catholic theologians already examined in this chapter, Torrance points to the Holy Spirit as the ground of union between the risen Christ and the church:

> It is through this Jesus Christ that we worshippers have access by one Spirit to the Father, and repeat the "Abba, Father" of Christ echoed in us by the Spirit who is imparted to us by Christ. Through his Spirit Christ dwells in the Church which is his body . . . through which he acts as our Mediator, Advocate and Priest, representing us before God.[178]

The church has access to Christ through the Spirit because it is the same Spirit by whom Jesus Christ prayed and lived as a human being during his earthly mission that he has sent to dwell in the church. It is the Spirit who enables the church to participate in God's love embodied in his incarnate Son so that the being of the church is love through participation in Christ.[179] The church's worship is thus a participation in Christ's own worship through the Holy Spirit, grounded in the communal love between the Trinitarian persons: "The communion of the Spirit gives the Church to participate in the concrete embodiment of the Love of God in the Incarnate Son, so that the essential nature and being of the Church as love is its participation in Christ the New Man."[180]

This union between Christ and the church is an "ontological fact" in which the church becomes the body of Christ because it is united to and participates in Jesus Christ's crucified and risen vicarious humanity through the love of the Holy Spirit: "When we speak of the Church as the Body of Christ we are saying that it is given such union with Christ that it becomes a communion filled and overflowing with the divine love."[181] The primary sacrament is Jesus Christ himself, the Son of God who became incarnate and joined himself to our humanity, and joined the church of God to himself as his body: "[T]he sacraments have to be understood as concerned with our *koinonia* or participation in the mystery of Christ and his Church through the *koinonia* or communion of the Holy Spirit." As we are baptized in the name of the Father and of the Son and of the Holy Spirit, God the Father, through the Spirit, unites us to Christ and his faithfulness and obedience to the Father, which becomes the ground of our own faith. Baptism is not an act of our own faith, but an act of God in which "we rely . . . upon Christ alone and his vicarious faithfulness."[182] In the Eucharist, we share in the "whole Christ," through the communion of the Holy Spirit. Insofar as the celebration of the Eucharist is an act of worship, it is the church's sharing in the risen Christ's own worship:

> [T]he mystery of the Eucharist is [to be understood] in terms of our participation through the Spirit in . . . the whole Christ, the incarnate, crucified, risen and ascended Son. . . . It is Christ himself, in his paschal mystery, who constitutes the living content, reality and power of the Eucharist. . . . In so far as the Eucharist is the act of the Church in his name and is also a human rite, it must be understood as an act of prayer, thanksgiving and worship . . . but as act in which through the Spirit we are given to share in the vicarious life, faith, prayer, worship, thanksgiving and offering of Jesus Christ to the Father, for in the final resort it is Jesus Christ himself who is our true worship.[183]

Thus, as Torrance writes,

> Jesus Christ is himself our prayer and worship. We worship God and pray to him as Father only through the mediation of Christ our High Priest . . . we worship and pray to the Father in such a way that it is Christ himself who is the real content of our

worship and prayer: we offer Christ to the Father through our prayers, for in the Spirit the prayer that ascends from us to the Father is a form of the self-offering of Christ himself.[184]

This understanding of worship as the church's sharing or participation in Christ's own worship on our behalf has implications for a theology of ordained ministry. In worship, the church offers nothing of its own, but always prays with Christ. The pattern of the church's worship is that of the pattern of Jesus Christ's own life and ministry as the suffering servant: "The conception of the Suffering Servant is the great characteristic of the Church's ministry, and it is that which above all determines the nature of priesthood in the Church."[185] The church shares in the risen Christ's worship by always pointing away from itself and pointing to Christ, much as John the Baptist points away from himself to the crucified Christ in the famous triptych by Matthias Grunewald.[186]

That the office of ministry consists in pointing away from oneself to Christ is shown first in the significance of the apostolate. Jesus Christ is the primary apostle in that he represents God not only in his ministry, but in his very person. He is God incarnate. To the extent that the apostles represent Christ, they do so in that their own persons "retreat into the background" as they proclaim Christ's message.[187] As do previous authors in this chapter, Torrance distinguishes between the general priesthood of the church and the special priesthood of ordained ministry. The priesthood of all Christians is grounded in baptism, while the ordained priesthood or the presbyterate is oriented toward the celebration of the Eucharist. The "real priesthood" is the priesthood of the entire body of the church, but within the church, there is also a "particular priesthood," whose function it is to minister to the body. Arising from the Eucharist, the "special institutional priesthood," is "a special gift of the ascended Lord for the Church for its mission."[188]

The pattern of this priesthood is the same as that of the priesthood of the church as a whole: an imitation of the "suffering servant" ministry of Christ: "The form of this priesthood in the Church derives from the Form of Christ, the incarnate Son of God, as the Form of the Suffering Servant who came among us not to be served but to serve and give his life as a ransom for many."[189] The ordained ministry is in "no sense an extension of the priestly ministry of Christ or a prolongation of his vicarious work." Ordained priesthood takes a "diaconal form." The priest does not act as a substitute for Christ or in his place:

> It is not [a priestly ministry] in which as celebrants we act in Christ's place so that we substitute for him or displace him; rather is it one in which we serve his vicarious Priesthood, in accordance with the biblical principle "not I but Christ" (Gal. 2.20). What we do in eucharistic thanksgiving is to hold up before God the Lord

Jesus Christ in his atoning sacrifice and take refuge in his presentation of himself, and of us in him, before the Father, for he is both the one who offers and the one who is offered.[190]

This notion of ordained ministry as patterned on the suffering servant ministry of Christ has implications for the issue of women's ordination. Torrance complained that both advocates and opponents of women's ordination suffered from the "serious misunderstanding" that the ordained priesthood was concerned with power, specifically the power of celebrating the Eucharist. To the contrary, the ordained priesthood has to do with "a self-abnegating form of ministry in which it is not the priest but Christ himself who is the real Celebrant—so that like John the Baptist the priest must retreat before the presence of Christ."[191]

Torrance also accused opponents of women's ordination of holding to a faulty Christology. What matters about the incarnation is not that Jesus Christ is male, but that he is a divine person who has assumed a complete human nature:

> Although Jesus was of course physically male, divine nature and human nature, divine being and human being, were perfectly and indivisibly united in his one incarnate Person, and it as the incarnate Person of the Son of God, not as male, that he is our Lord and Saviour. . . . Moreover, the mistaken idea that it is not the priest as *person* but as *male* who can represent Christ, not only involves a form of Nestorian heresy in dividing between the divine and human natures of Christ, but conflicts sharply with the great soteriological principle of the ancient Catholic Church that "what has not been assumed has not been saved."[192]

That is, if what is significant about the incarnation is that Jesus Christ is a male, then the priest who acts *in persona Christi* would have to be representing a *human* male person, since an ordained *human* priest could not represent Christ's *divine* person. However, to assert that Christ has a human *person* would be the heresy of Nestorianism—that Jesus Christ is not the divine person of the Word who has assumed a complete human nature, but a human person who had a special relationship with God.[193] Moreover, if what is significant about the incarnation is that Jesus Christ is male rather than that he is human, then the Word's assumption of a human nature would save only male human beings. Indeed, the focus on Christ's male sexuality makes essential what is actually an *accident* of human nature (in the technical philosophical sense), since human beings come in two sexes, but both are equally human; sexuality is something that merely distinguishes one human being from another, not that which is truly essential, and which all human beings have in common. If Jesus Christ is to save all human beings—male and female—then what is essential about his humanity is that he is human, not that he is male.

238 | Icons of Christ

EVALUATION

The above discussion has focused primarily on questions concerning sacramental theology because the primary Catholic objection to the ordination of women has focused on the eligibility of women to exercise the sacramental role of presiding at the Eucharist. If ordination is oriented toward the preaching of the word and the celebration of the Eucharist, then questions of sacramental theology must be addressed. The crucial questions for a catholic theology of the Eucharist have to do with participation in the priesthood of Christ. What is the relationship between the general priesthood of the church and Christ's priesthood? What is the relation between the special priesthood of ordained ministry and the priesthood of the church? What is the relation between the special priesthood of ordained ministry and the priesthood of Jesus Christ?

The beginning of this chapter makes clear that Thomas Aquinas's theology of priesthood and sacrament was crucial for the rise in the Western church of the notion that the ordained priest participates in Christ's priesthood by acting *in persona Christi* as the ordained minister says the words of institution when celebrating the Eucharist. Given that in Aquinas's earliest discussion of eucharistic theology (in his *Commentary on the Sentences*) he echoed the historic position of the church, that the priest represents the church (acts *in persona ecclesiae*), it might be helpful to ask what accounted for the shift to the new position that the celebrant represents Christ. An overlooked possibility could be that Aquinas was simply looking for symmetry in his account of the sacraments. Given his adoption of the Aristotelian distinction between form and matter as a way of articulating a theology of the sacraments, the assumption that the matter of the sacraments consisted of the physical element, while the form consisted of specific words, leads to the question, "What are the essential words in the celebration of the Eucharist?" If water is the matter of baptism, and the Trinitarian formula constitutes the form, then, given that bread and wine are the matter of the Eucharist, might not the words of institution constitute the form? Aquinas's formula that the priest acts *in persona Christi* would not then reflect so much a concern for the uniqueness of priestly ministry in contrast to the general ministry of the church as a concern for the similarity between the two sacraments of baptism and the Eucharist in sharing both form and matter. This concern for similarity is paralleled by Aquinas' discussion of sacramental character. Both baptism and ordained ministry have in common that they bestow a character that is essential for participation in worship, a character that is a participation in the priesthood of Christ and is common to *all* the baptized. It is not ordained *male* clergy who alone participate in Christ's priesthood and represent Christ, but all baptized Christians, women as well as men.

At the same time, as shown above, the reduction of the form of the Eucharist to the repetition of the words of institution has unfortunate consequences. It leads to an understanding of priestly ministry in which the ordained minister is isolated from the congregation, in which the essential role of the congregation in the worship of the church is neglected, and the priest's role becomes that of enacting a drama, of acting the part of Jesus Christ at the Last Supper. In addition, the resulting eucharistic theology is Christomonist, separating the work of Christ not only from its ecclesial context, but from its salvation-historical and Trinitarian context. The role of the Holy Spirit and the church disappear. This theology also reflects a truncated notion of the eucharistic prayer in which the structure of the prayer that surrounds the words of institution is reduced to something like liturgical window dressing. If all that is really important is the words of institution, then the rest of the liturgy is dispensable—as often became the case in those Protestant churches that, despite their rejection of Roman Catholic doctrines of transubstantiation and eucharistic sacrifice, reduced the celebration of the Lord's Supper to a repetition of the account of the Lord's Supper, and, specifically, to the words of institution.

Within the last generation, mainline Western churches—both Roman Catholic and Protestant (Anglican, Lutheran, Reformed, Presbyterian, Methodist)—have adopted new worship texts including revised eucharistic rites, and these rites are patterned on the earlier eucharistic prayers of the patristic era, reflecting more the traditional eucharistic theologies of the (Eastern) Orthodox churches than the historic postmedieval Western churches. They include eucharistic prayers that reflect the structure of *anamnesis* (remembrance) and *epiclesis* (petition), which frame the account of the words of institution. These prayers include an *epiclesis* as an invocation of the Holy Spirit to descend on the elements of bread and wine in order to enable worshipers to be united to the risen humanity of Christ as they receive his body and blood through consecrated bread and wine, and so become the body of Christ as the church. Similarly, modern eucharistic ecumenical agreements utilize language that corresponds to the viewpoint of the Orthodox and Reformed Churches, and is less at home in traditional Anglo-Catholic, Lutheran or Roman Catholic theologies. They speak of a presence of Christ "through the Spirit."[194] Nevertheless, the *new* Catholic argument against the ordination of women—whether embraced by Roman Catholics, Orthodox, Anglicans or other liturgical church bodies—objects to the ordination of women on the grounds that the priest acts *in persona Christi*, reflecting the later Western medieval position that equates consecration with the ordained minister's pronouncing the words of institution rather than with the church's invoking of the Holy Spirit.

What implications might a more salvation-historical, Trinitarian understanding of eucharistic theology have for the ordination of women?

First of all, the celebration of the Eucharist should not be understood as the isolated act of the ordained minister over against the worshiping community. The eucharistic prayer is not a drama in which the priest acts the role of Christ by reciting the words of institution. Rather, the eucharistic prayer is the *prayer of the church*, in which the gathered community addresses God the Father, reminding him of his saving deeds in creation, the calling of Israel, and the saving incarnation, life, death, and resurrection of Jesus Christ. The words of institution are at the center of this prayer and are a reminder of Christ's promise to the church that he will be present whenever the "church breaks this bread" and "drinks this cup . . . in remembrance of me." In the epiclesis, the Holy Spirit is invoked by the entire church to descend on bread and wine to enable Christ's presence. The ordained minister has a special role, speaking the words of the eucharistic prayer on behalf of the church in a prayer that begins and ends with the words "we" and "us." In praying the words of the eucharistic prayer, the presiding minister represents the church and acts *in persona ecclesiae*.

Is there a sense in which we can also speak of the ordained minister acting in the person of, or as a representative of, Christ? Here is where the theologies of ordained ministry of Moberly, Sumner, and Torrance prove helpful. As Torrance makes clear, the historic church's understanding of worship is that the church's worship is always a participation in the vicarious worship of Christ in his ascended human nature. The church has no worship of its own to offer—not even the worship of a special class of ordained ministers. Rather, the church shares in Christ's priesthood by pointing away from itself to the saving, life, deeds, and resurrection of Jesus Christ. The pattern for the church as a whole is the cruciform pattern of the suffering servant, and this is the pattern of ordained ministry as well.

It helps, as Sumner suggests, to think of the priest as an icon of Christ, but in a specific sense. The apostle Paul writes in 2 Corinthians 4:5-7, "For what we proclaim is not ourselves, but Jesus Christ as Lord, with ourselves as your servants for Jesus' sake. For God, who said, 'Let light shine out of darkness,' has shone in our hearts to give the light of the knowledge of the glory of God in the face of Jesus Christ. But we have this treasure in jars of clay, to show that the surpassing power belongs to God and not to us." The priest is not Christ. The priest is a jar of clay. The priest represents Christ primarily in pointing away from himself or herself and by pointing to Christ. But the priest also represents Christ in that he or she shares in Christ's suffering. Paul continues to write, "We are afflicted in every way, but not crushed, perplexed, but not driven to despair, persecuted, but not forsaken, struck down, but not destroyed, always carrying in the body the death of Jesus, so that the life of Jesus may also be manifested in our bodies" (vv. 8-10). So the priest does represent Christ, but is an icon of Christ who points away from himself or herself and his or her own competence to the competence of the crucified and risen Christ. It is Jesus Christ who saves, not the priest. But the priest also takes up the ministry of Christ after the pattern of Christ as Servant, and that will mean suffering.

The ordained minister thus represents both Christ and the church. As Congar pointed out in the discussion above, if we focus on Christology, then "the *in persona Ecclesiae* is situated within the *in persona Christi*." If we emphasize the Holy Spirit, then "the *in persona Christi* is more easily seen as situated within the *in persona Ecclesiae*."[195] Even here, it is crucial to emphasize what it means to represent or act *in the person* of Christ. A previous chapter discussed the significance of Ephesians 5 within the context of what Michael Gorman has referred to as the apostle Paul's pattern of cruciform spirituality. In Ephesians 5, Paul includes his well-known analogy between marriage and Christ, identifying the church as the bride of Christ. In this passage, Paul makes clear that the submission expected of wives to husbands is the same submission that is expected of all Christians to one another, and the model of behavior expected of all Christians is modeled after Christ's own self-sacrificial giving, as exemplified in the paradigm passage of Philippians 2:5-11, in which Paul identifies the love of Christ with the "self-emptying" (*kenosis*) that prefers others over self, taking on the form of a servant that leads to the cross.

Could a woman lead the church in worship and act *in persona Christi*? One might better ask whether a man could lead the church in worship and act as the church's representative *in persona ecclesiae*? As the priest prays the eucharistic prayer, he or she places the words of the church in his or her own mouth. Modern eucharistic prayers all begin and end with the words "we" and "us," and even in the ancient Latin liturgy, the priest prays in the person of the church insofar as he says "we offer" (*offerimus*), not "I offer" (*offero*). Insofar as the New Testament identifies the church as the bride of Christ (Eph. 5:23-32; Rev. 22:17), it might seem more appropriate to ordain *only* women. Since the church contains both men and women, it is certainly appropriate for a female minister to pray those words on behalf of the church.

However, insofar as Christ's servant ministry is the pattern for all Christians, it is also the pattern for all ministry. Insofar as the role of the ordained minister is to point away from himself or herself and to point instead to Christ, it is not his or her sex that is significant because it is not his or her own person that counts, but the person of Jesus Christ. If a male priest can represent the female bride of Christ, then certainly a female priest can represent Christ himself in that the priestly role of ordained clergy is one of self-abnegation. The model for ordained ministry is that of Jesus Christ's suffering servanthood—the model for all Christian discipleship to which all baptized Christians are called, both men and women. In its worship, the church does not rely on its own identity or accomplishments (including gender or sexuality); the church has nothing of its own to offer; the church's worship is entirely a participation in the worship of the risen Christ, and finds its identity entirely through participating in the *vicarious* humanity of the incarnate, crucified, and risen Christ. As it is for the church, so it is for the ordained minister. The ordained priest represents Christ as did John the Baptist: by pointing away from himself or herself to the crucified and risen Christ.

13

The Argument from Symbolism

God, Priests, Incarnation, and Apostles

The previous chapter addressed the definitive modern Catholic objection to the ordination of women—that a priest/presbyter acts as a representative of Jesus Christ, and that a woman cannot be ordained because a woman cannot represent a male Christ. It focused on the liturgical version of that argument: in celebrating the Eucharist, the priest acts *in persona Christi* (in the person of Christ), and a woman cannot act *in persona Christi*. The next two chapters will address a slightly different version of the argument, based on male and female symbolism. The structure of the argument is the same—that a female priest cannot represent a male Christ—but the focus is on the symbolic dimensions of masculinity and femininity rather than the narrower issue of liturgical celebration.

What is a symbol? In his classic text, *Symbolism and Belief*, Edwyn Bevan defined a symbol as "something presented to the senses or the imagination—usually the senses—which stands for something else." Bevan distinguished between two kinds of symbols: (1) "visible objects or sounds which stand for something of which we already have direct knowledge," and which "are not intended to give us any information about the nature of the thing symbolized, but to remind us of them," and (2) symbols that "purport to give information about the things they symbolize, to convey knowledge of their nature, which those who see or hear the symbols have not had before or have not otherwise." The symbols of the first kind have no resemblance to the thing symbolized; the connection is simply a matter of convention. For example, there is no resemblance between a stop sign and the command to stop, and there is nothing about the word "stop" that is like the action of stopping. The second kind of symbol "purport[s] to give information about the nature of something not otherwise known," and "resemblance is essential."[1] Similarly, Manfred Hauke,

one of the authors who embraces the symbolic argument against women's ordination, refers to a symbol as something that "finds its special expression . . . where two
realities enter into sensibly apprehensible interconnection." Hauke distinguishes a
symbol from an "arbitrarily defined sign" (like a stop sign) in that a symbol is "suited
in advance, by virtue of its inner structure, to entering into certain relationships, for
example, 'sun' and 'light' in relationship to intellectual clarity."[2] Thus, Bevan's first
definition of symbol corresponds to Hauke's definition of "sign," while his second
definition of symbol corresponds to Hauke's definition of "symbol."

The use of symbols is essential to religious language and practice insofar as religions need some visual or linguistic way to refer to non-visible realities. Bevan states
that "in religion things are presented to the senses, or ideas presented to the mind,
which purport, not to call to mind other things within the experience of the wor-
shipper, but to convey to him knowledge of things beyond the range of any human
experience."[3] Anglican apologist C. S. Lewis insisted that Christianity necessarily
uses physical imagery (here called "symbol") to refer to spiritual realities because
"anyone who talks about things that cannot be seen, or touched, or heard of, or the
like, must inevitably talk as *if they could* be seen or touched or heard." According
to Lewis, metaphorical (or symbolic) language is indispensable to Christian faith;
language that says that one of the members of the Trinity "entered the universe" to
become one of its own creatures is every bit as metaphorical (or symbolic) as "he
came down from heaven." The former only substitutes imagery of vertical for hori-
zontal movement.[4]

There has been in the last half century an increased emphasis in theology on the
importance of both symbol and narrative. Roman Catholic theologian Avery Dulles
has written that symbols are "signs imbued with a plenitude or depth of meaning
that surpasses the capacity of conceptual thinking and propositional speech. A symbol . . . is a perceptible sign that evokes a realization of that which surpasses ordinary
objective cognition."[5] According to Dulles, the "Christian religion is a set of relationships with God mediated by the Christian symbols. These symbols are imbedded in
the Bible and in the living tradition of the Christian community."[6] Dulles has suggested "symbolic mediation" as a helpful way to understand the notion of revelation,
which "is always mediated through symbol—that is to say, through an externally
perceived sign that works mysteriously on the human consciousness so as to suggest
more than it can clearly describe or define." Symbol is thus understood to be a third
alternative to either a literalist propositionalism or the noncognitive "experiential-
ism" of much liberal theology. Although God is beyond description and definition,
God's reality is truly communicated through symbol.[7]

At the same time, the field of narrative theology adds a partial corrective to the
theological discussion of symbol. It is the narrative content of the biblical texts that

provides meaning to the symbols, and not vice versa. For example, a fundamental divide in modern theology concerns whether or not the person and work of Jesus Christ are constitutive of a salvation we can find nowhere else, or, rather, whether they are illustrative of some general principle or principles that can be found elsewhere as well. If we take the person and work of Jesus Christ as constitutive of our salvation, we will understand the stories and symbols of the gospels to form our own understandings and to challenge our preconceptions of God, Christ, and the world. So, for example, not only will we find the symbolism of the "Father" language that Jesus used to describe God to be informative, challenging, and even subversive of our own understanding of what it means to be a "father," but we will find that it illuminates and challenges our preconceptions of what it means to be God, and it points in the direction of an ontological relationship between Jesus and his Father grounded in the eternally constitutive Trinitarian relations between Father, Son, and Holy Spirit. Conversely, if we understand the person and work of Jesus to be primarily illustrative of other generally known truths, we will tend to view the symbols and narratives of the gospel as projections of a prior universally available religious experience, and thus correctable in ways that speak more adequately to contemporary religious expression.

Such an illustrative and projectionist understanding of symbol can be found in the writings of liberal Protestant (or Catholic modernist) theologians such as feminist theologian Sallie McFague. McFague has argued that all religious language is fundamentally metaphorical, the projections of human experience to talk about the relation between the divine and the world: "[T]heology . . . is principally an elaboration of a few basic metaphors and models in an attempt to express the claim of Christianity in a powerful, comprehensive, and contemporary way . . . the elaboration of key metaphors and models."[8] In contrast to Dulles' account of "symbolic mediation," McFague believes that what she calls "metaphors" do not actually tell us anything about God's nature, but are simply projections of our limited religious experience. As the writers of Scripture used metaphors (or symbols) that spoke to their own needs, so we are free to use metaphors drawn from our own contemporary experience. McFague believes that many of the metaphors found in Scripture are outmoded because they are hierarchical and oppressive, and we would do better to embrace contemporary metaphors such as Mother, Lover, and Friend, and the earth as "God's body."[9] McFague acknowledges that her understanding of metaphor (or symbol) is projectionist and does not actually tell us anything positive about God. The approach is functional and pragmatic, but some metaphors are more "illuminating" and "fruitful" than others.[10]

In summary, there has been in modern theology a significant emphasis on the value of symbol for communicating religious reality. Symbols that have some resemblance to what they symbolize are distinguished from conventional signs that have no such resemblance. There is a significant division between those theologies that presume that religious symbols provide genuine participatory knowledge of transcendent reality (as in Dulles's notion of "symbolic mediation") and those liberal Protestant (or Catholic modernist) theologies that presume that all such use of symbols (or metaphors) is merely projectionist; they tell us nothing about God, but something about ourselves and our own religious experiences.

SYMBOL AND WOMEN'S ORDINATION

The significance of symbols for religious language and theology has thus been a major theme in much modern theology, including among theologians who affirm women's ordination. What is distinctive about the symbolic argument *against* women's ordination is the claim that the theology and practice of women's ordination is in conflict with key symbols of Christian faith. In an early essay in this discussion entitled "Priestesses in the Church," C. S. Lewis wrote:

> One of the ends for which sex was created was to symbolize for us the hidden things of God. One of the functions of human marriage is to express the nature of the union between Christ and the Church. We have no authority to take the living and semitive figures which God has painted on the canvas of our nature and shift them about as if they were mere geometrical figures.

Lewis asserted that the ordination of women would imply that we might as well pray to God as Mother as Father, that the incarnation might as well have taken a female as a male form, that the second person of the Trinity could as well be called Daughter as Son, and that the Church could be the bridegroom and Christ the bride.[11] Manfred Hauke has written, "[O]fficial priesthood for women would obscure the spiritual nature of the relationship Christ-Church and endanger the Christian image of God."[12] Sara Butler expresses her concerns:

> By challenging the tradition that saw a permanent norm for the ministerial priesthood in Christ's call of men, but not women, as apostles, the objections end up questioning the Lord's intention with respect to the priesthood, the Church's hierarchical constitution, and even its foundation. By calling into question the *sacramental significance* of the complementarity of the sexes, the objections undermine not only the distinction between Christ and his Church . . . but also the biblical revelation that God created humanity male and female. . . . The biblical doctrine that the difference between man and woman is willed by God, and with it the doctrine of Marriage as a sacrament, is thereby put in doubt.[13]

The following is a concise summary of the argument against women's ordination based on symbolism. It is a synthetic and composite summary since variations of the argument are used by different authors representing different Christian traditions;

however, as stated, forms of the argument appear in authors who are broadly "Catholic" in their approach, whether Roman Catholic, Eastern Orthodox, or Anglican.

(1) Throughout Scripture, God is portrayed as male, not as female. This is because maleness symbolizes transcendence. The biblical God is the Creator who creates from nothing, and is distinct from creation. In contrast, goddess religions are religions of immanence which identify deity and the creation; to portray God as female leads to pantheism—as one finds in modern feminist theology.[14]

(2) The Old Testament priesthood was always an exclusively male office; this contrasts with pagan goddess religions, in which fertility religion is accompanied by cultic prostitution (priestesses). In the Hebrew religion, the priest represents God; a male priest represents the biblical God's masculinity.[15]

(3) In the incarnation, the Son of God became incarnate as a male and identified the first person of the Trinity as his Father. That the Son of God became incarnate as a male has theological implications. In the incarnation, the male Jesus (who has no physical human father) represents the male (active transcendent) principle, while his mother Mary represents the (receptive immanent) female principle. Thus, Jesus could only have been male.[16]

(4) Although Jesus could have called anyone to be his apostles, significantly he called only male apostles. Because bishops and priests are successors of the apostles, they must be male as were the original twelve apostles. If Jesus had intended that women could be ordained, he would certainly have called his mother Mary to be an apostle, but he did not. That Mary was not an apostle speaks negatively to the question of whether women can be ordained.[17]

(5) There is an anthropological appeal to sexual symbolism. Roman Catholic author Manfred Hauke is one of the earliest writers to use this argument, and does so at great length. Hauke argues that the symbols of masculinity and femininity transcend culture, and he appeals to precedent in both ancient religions and modern biology, sociology, and psychology.[18] According to Hauke, men are active and external (symbolizing transcendence), while women are receptive and internal (representing immanence): "The dynamics of the male are expansive, outer directed and aimed at overcoming particular sorts of resistance. The dynamics of the female are more adaptive to nature, that is, more strongly adaptive to the demands of the existing situation." Men tend more in the direction of "abstractive reason," while women are "guided more strongly by intuition and feeling."[19] According to Hauke, this male-female symbolism (man as active/external/rational/overcoming/transcendent in contrast to woman as receptive/internal/intuitive/relational/feeling/immanent) is presumed throughout both Scripture and church tradition and is fundamental to the order of creation and redemption found therein (thus the subtitle of Hauke's book).[20]

(6) The apostle Paul's reading of Genesis 1–2 in Romans 5 is significant for Paul's understanding of the male as symbolically normative. Although Eve sinned

first, Paul speaks of Adam (a male) as representative of all humanity (both male and female); Christ (as male) is the second Adam. Since transcendence contains immanence, but immanence cannot contain transcendence, males (as transcendent) can represent both males and females (as Adam and Christ represent all humanity), but females (as exclusively immanent) can represent only females. Accordingly, a male priest can represent both a male Christ (the second Adam) and a female church, but a female priest could represent neither. A woman cannot represent Christ because Christ is male, but neither can a woman represent the church because the church is composed of both males and females, and a woman can represent only females.[21]

(7) In a manner similar to Protestant complementarians, Catholic opponents of women's ordination appeal to Paul's references in 1 Corinthians 11 and Ephesians 5 to Christ as "head" of the church, but rather than reading the argument in terms of male authority (as do Protestant complementarians), they argue rather that male "headship" indicates that only males have a representative (symbolic) role.[22]

(8) Based on symbolic speculation by Roman Catholic theologian Hans Urs von Balthasar, opponents to women's ordination argue for the symbolic roles of the apostle Peter and the Virgin Mary. Peter, as an apostle and the rock on whom Christ builds his church, represents the male principle; Mary, as the virgin mother of Christ, represents the female receptive principle. Peter was called to be an apostle, but Mary was not. As a male apostle, Peter represents the (male) clergy, who are successors of the apostles; in contrast, Mary represents the laity (who are symbolically female) and the church.[23]

(9) The argument from liturgy builds on the marriage analogy found in Ephesians 5. In the Old Testament, God is portrayed as the (male) husband, of which the nation of Israel is the (female) bride. In the New Testament, (the male) Christ is portrayed (symbolically) as both the husband and head of the church, which is his body, and is (symbolically) feminine. The ordained priest (as male) represents both God and (the male) Christ; the laity (as both male and female) represent Mary and the church as the bride of Christ.[24]

(10) Finally, the ordained priest acts as father and head of the congregation (who are his family); as father, the priest must be male.[25]

How shall we respond to these arguments against women's ordination based on symbolism, and, more specifically, the argument that male-female symbolism is inherent to the nature and structure of revelation and Christian faith, that the abandonment of this symbolism would be, in essence, an abandonment of Christian faith, and that the ordination of women would constitute just such an abandonment or reversal of essential Christian symbolism?

As a preliminary response, it is unfortunate that writers such as Hauke identify advocacy of women's ordination exclusively with the position of theologically liberal feminist writers such as Rosemary Radford Ruether, Elisabeth Schüssler Fiorenza, Elizabeth Johnson, Mary Daly, or Letty Russell. This liberal feminist theology tends to share the following characteristics:

First, as noted above, since these feminist theologians tend to believe that religious language is projectionist, they argue (as noted above with McFague) that we are as free to use feminine language in reference to God as masculine; indeed such language is preferable: they speak of the "divine feminine," "God/ess" (Ruether), "She Who Is" (Johnson), God as "mother," or God as "Wisdom/Sophia" (1993 Re-Imagining Conference, Johnson, Schüssler Fiorenza). A statement by post-Christian feminist Mary Daly is frequently cited: "If God is male, then the male is God."[26]

Second, coupled with this female deity language is an accompanying rejection of "dualism" and an embrace of an alternative theology of immanence or "panentheism" in which God and creation are in some sense identified.[27] Hauke sets up this immanentist feminism as the single foil against which he writes his book.

Third, this feminist theology tends to view the Christian Scriptures as oppressive rather than salvific; advocates interpret the text in light of the assumed meaning of symbols as used outside the text rather than reinterpreting the symbols in light of the logic of the text's narrative; thus, it is claimed that the notion of God as "Father" has its origins in a hierarchical patriarchy. The corresponding Roman Catholic equivalent to McFague's projectionist hermeneutic is Schüssler Fiorenza's "hermeneutic of suspicion," which views the biblical writings as containing material that is inherently androcentric and oppressive to women.[28]

Fourth, given its projectionist understanding of symbol, feminist theology tends to think of the person and work of Christ as illustrative rather than constitutive of salvation; its Christology is adoptionist, its notion of atonement is exemplarist, and the historic doctrine of the atonement is dismissed as divine "child abuse." Jesus Christ is not a savior from sin, but an inspiration and example for feminist liberation. Jesus of Nazareth was not the Son of God incarnate, but someone in whom the divine feminine principle of Wisdom/Sophia was especially present. If the relationship between God and creation is understood in a monist or panentheist fashion, then there cannot be anything unique about the incarnation. The difference between Jesus and other human beings can be no more than a matter of degree.[29]

Fifth, there is a loss of the doctrine of the Trinity; if God is not Father, and Jesus is not his eternal Son, then language of God as Father, Son, and Holy Spirit is inherently problematic. The substitution of non-Trinitarian language such as Creator, Redeemer, and Sustainer or Parent, Lover, and Friend points to a unitarian understanding of deity.[30]

Finally, this liberal feminist theology tends to advocate "role-model" theology. As illustrated in Mary Daly's axiom "If God is male, then the male is God," role-model theology presumes that religious communities formulate their understandings of "gods" or "goddesses" to express social values. Since a proper theology expresses proper social values, a theology that is committed to full equality of the sexes will not speak of God using masculine language.[31]

This liberal/modernist "immanentist" feminist theology needs to be distinguished from the biblical and Catholic egalitarian feminism of authors such as (among Catholics and Orthodox) Edward Kilmartin, Kallistos Ware, and Elisabeth Behr-Sigel, and (among Protestants) Ben Witherington III, Alan Padgett, N. T. Wright, Kathryn Greene-McCreight, or the Evangelical organization *Christians for Biblical Equality*.[32]

Kathryn Greene-McCreight uses the expression "biblical feminism" to refer to this alternative position. In contrast to "mainstream feminist" theologians, "biblical feminists" proceed on the basis of a "hermeneutics of trust," in which the Bible is understood to be primarily an "*inspired witness* to the grace of God in Jesus Christ," a witness that is "not fundamentally dangerous but rather life-giving" (emphasis in original). Biblical feminists "attempt to read all of reality through the lens of the biblical narrative, and not vice versa." They take their clues not from the secular Enlightenment and the historically liberal theology that follows in the train of Friedrich Schleiermacher, but from a view of the church as the people of God. For biblical feminists, the main problem to be addressed is not that of sexist oppression, but of human sinfulness and the need for salvation. Where mainstream feminists focus on gaining equal rights for women in the church, biblical feminists ask for an equal opportunity to serve the church.[33]

By ignoring the alternative of an orthodox Catholic and Evangelical argument for women's ordination, Hauke and other opponents portray the discussion in terms of a false dichotomy between a revisionist monist feminism that embraces "goddess" worship and the only orthodox Catholic (or Evangelical) position— one that rejects women's ordination. To preserve the distinction between these two very different groups endorsing women's ordination, the rest of this chapter will use the terms "feminist theology" to refer to the views of "mainstream feminist" immanence theologians and "egalitarianism" to refer to the views of orthodox advocates of women's ordination (Greene-McCreight's "biblical feminists"), whether Catholic or Protestant.

To keep the discussion within reasonable length, the response will cover two chapters. The first will focus on issues of symbolism connected with central creedal doctrines of God and creation, the incarnation, and, in Catholic theology, the closely related issue of the role of the apostles as successors to and representatives of Christ. These are the concerns at the center of the Vatican's rejection of women's ordination. The next chapter will focus on the anthropological concerns rising from the claim that men and women have different symbolic significance—specifically, that men represent transcendence and women represent immanence. These are not the Vatican's reasons for rejecting women's ordination, but they have been important for some Roman Catholic, Orthodox, and Anglican opponents.

IS GOD MALE?

One of the ironic commonalities uniting mainstream feminists and those who argue against women's ordination from concerns about symbolism is a shared commitment to "role model theology." Feminist theologians assume that, since religion functions to construct divine models to be imitated by humans, the metaphor of God as Father must be rejected because it legitimates patriarchy.[34] Conversely, anti-feminists such as Hauke argue that, since God is Father, not only must mainstream feminism be rejected, but the ordination of women must be rejected as well because a woman priest cannot adequately represent a God who is Father or the male Jesus Christ who is the Son of God. Both groups share the common assumption that the God of the Bible is a male whose function is to provide a gender-based model to be emulated; is this assumption correct?

Against role-model theology, it must first be strongly affirmed that the God of the Bible has no sexuality and is thus not a male. Rather, sexuality is part of creation, created by God as a fundamental feature of creation (Gen. 1–2). Human beings as male and female are equally created in the image of God (Gen. 1:27). Throughout Scripture, God is portrayed as other than creation, an otherness which is identified with God's holiness. God is God and not human (Num. 23:19; Hos. 11:9; Is. 31:3; 40:18). Throughout Scripture, there is a consistent diatribe against idolatry, the basic offense of which is worshiping the creature as if it were the Creator (Rom. 1:25). In the covenant with Israel at Sinai, the biblical God speaks explicitly against the danger of identifying the divine with any form of sexuality: "Therefore watch yourselves very carefully. Since you saw no form on the day that the Lord spoke to you at Horeb out of the midst of the fire, beware lest you act corruptly by making a carved image for yourselves, in the form of any figure, the likeness of male or female" (Deut. 4:15-18).[35]

Christian tradition is equally emphatic that God has no sexuality. Athanasius, the great advocate of Nicene orthodoxy, wrote (concerning God's Fatherhood and Christ's eternal Sonship):

> Accordingly, as in saying "offspring," we have no human thoughts, and, though we know God to be a Father, we entertain no material ideas concerning Him, but while we listen to these illustrations and terms, we think suitably of God, for He is not as man, so in like manner, when we hear of "coessential," we ought to transcend all sense . . . so as to know, that not by will, but in truth, is He genuine from the Father,

as Life from Fountain, and Radiance from Light. Else why should we understand "off-spring" and "son," in no corporeal way, while we conceive of "coessential" as after the manner of bodies?[36]

Similarly, Hilary of Poitiers wrote concerning the Trinity: "[T]hat which is Divine and eternal must be one without distinction of sex." The theologian must not derive his or her conceptions of God from preconceptions, but from God's own revelation: "[H]e must not measure the Divine nature by the limitations of his own, but gauge God's assertions concerning Himself by the scale of His own glorious self-revelation."[37]

Later, the medieval Catholic theologian Thomas Aquinas wrote that "it is absolutely true that God is not a body," and "it is impossible that God should be a body."[38] The post-Reformation Anglican Thirty-nine Articles state: "There is but one living and true God, everlasting, without body, parts, or passions; of infinite power, wisdom, and goodness; the Maker, and Preserver of all things both visible and invisible. And in unity of this Godhead there be three Persons, of one substance, power, and eternity; the Father, the Son, and the Holy Ghost."[39] If God has no bodily parts, God has no sexuality, and God is not male. Trinitarian language does not mean that a male God is the Father of a male Son.[40]

Given that the triune God is neither male nor female, any language or imagery used to describe God in sexual terms is necessarily symbolic or metaphorical. At the same time, it should be acknowledged that such biblical imagery is overwhelmingly masculine, including use of the personal pronoun "he." Occasionally, it is suggested (even by more moderate feminists or by Evangelical egalitarians) that this masculine language is not the whole story and that "Scripture also contains a significant amount of feminine imagery for God." Similarly, it is pointed out that, in the wisdom literature of the Old Testament, wisdom, personified as a woman, is portrayed as an attribute of God.[41]

The argument is misleading, however. Roland Frye has pointed out the significant difference between how Scripture uses metaphor and simile in reference to God. A metaphor functions by identifying and naming; a simile functions by comparing two things *as* one to the other, by claiming that one thing resembles another. Scripture applies numerous masculine metaphors to God: in Psalm 23, the author addresses God: "The Lord *is* my shepherd." In the New Testament, the same metaphor is applied to Christ: "I *am* the good shepherd" (John 10:11), "Jesus the great shepherd of the sheep" (Heb. 13:20). In both cases, the metaphor functions as a name or identification: God *is* the shepherd; Jesus *is* the good shepherd.

In contrast, a simile does not identify one thing with another, but notes a comparison between two different things. Isaiah 42:13 states, "The Lord goes out *like* a mighty man, like a man of war he stirs up his zeal." Here God is compared to a warrior, but is not *identified* or named as one. In verse 14, a female simile appears: "now I will cry out *like* a woman in labor; I will gasp and pant." In Isaiah 66:13, God states: "*As* one whom his mother comforts, so I will comfort you; you shall be comforted in Jerusalem." In both cases, God is *compared* to a mother, but *not identified* as a mother. Frye points out that while God is regularly identified or named in Scripture using metaphorical masculine language, figurative female language referring to God uses the comparative language of simile, not metaphor. God is *compared* to a mother, but God is never *addressed* or *named* as mother. Similarly, Frye points out that the wisdom figure of Proverbs is not a "female divinity" or a feminine hypostasis of the Old Testament God (the "Wisdom/Sophia" of feminist theologians), but rather a literary device—the personification of an abstract attribute (the divine wisdom by which God creates the world) in which we treat as a person that which is not actually a person.[42]

Given then that God has no sex, what is to be made of the Bible's dominant use of masculine metaphorical symbolic imagery to describe God? Is the Bible teaching that God is a male after all?

One of the most helpful discussions of the significance of male imagery in the Hebrew Bible (Old Testament) is that of Tikva Frymer-Kensky, in her book *In the Wake of the Goddesses*. According to Frymer-Kensky, the key factor that distinguishes Israel's religion from that of the surrounding cultures (with their worship of both male gods and female goddesses) is Israel's embrace of monotheism. For Israel, the one God absorbed all the powers that were shared among the numerous pagan divinities. There was no more interplay between numerous divine powers because Israel's one God exercised power over all creation, including not only those powers assigned to male gods but also to female goddesses. Israel's God alone was responsible for the weather, fertility of crops, sickness and health, and childbirth. Humankind received more responsibility as well, as human beings now became responsible for the social activities that had formerly been assigned to gods and goddesses; human beings become responsible for knowledge and culture. Institutions that had once been supervised or overseen by goddesses—storage, administration, wisdom-writing, song—were now entirely in the domain of human beings: "They are neither divinely granted nor divinely supervised." Because there is only one God, the biblical God does not have a consort. There is no Hebrew goddess; rather, the nation of Israel itself was personified as a female figure, and Israel (and the city of Zion) are elevated to the role of YHWH's bride. The image of Zion as the beloved bride "expresses a sense of the immanent presence of God and of God's concern for Israel." In the New Testament, this nuptial imagery is taken up and transformed as Christ is identified as the bridegroom and "head" of the church, which is identified as his bride (Eph. 5). Accordingly, Frymer-Kensky claims: "Throughout the Bible, in every aspect of biblical thought human beings gain in prominence in—and because of—the absence of goddesses."[43]

Frymer-Kensky acknowledges that the Bible does indeed portray Israel's God using masculine imagery. YHWH is only referred to by the male pronoun ("he," never "she"). The masculine qualities of God are, however, exclusively "social male-gender characteristics": God is King, Shepherd, and Lord. At the same time, although YHWH takes over the functions of female goddesses, there is no element whatsoever of sexuality or sexual attraction in Israel's understanding of God: "The monotheist God is not sexually a male." God's body parts are described anthropomorphically in the Bible (the "arm of the Lord," the "right hand of God"); however, "God is not imagined below the waist." Frymer-Kensky makes the point repeatedly. Although God is the "husband" of Israel, "God does not behave in sexual ways." She writes: "God is not a sexual male. . . . God is not imagined in erotic terms, and sexuality was simply not part of the divine order. God is not sexed, God does not model sexuality, and God does not bestow sexual power."[44]

If the male imagery of the Bible is never sexualized, what then of the "fatherhood" of God? This masculine metaphor of God as "Father" seems to be the primary problematic concern of feminist theology, and, conversely, Hauke appeals primarily to the "Fatherhood of God" as establishing divine transcendence over against the immanence of feminist theology.[45] Given its significance for the debate, it is important to note that the title of "Father" is applied to God only a handful of times in the Old Testament. In Deuteronomy 32:6 and Malachi 2:10, God is described as the "father" who created Israel. In Isaiah 64:8, God is addressed as "our Father," whose work is compared to a potter: "[W]e are the clay, and you are our potter; we are all the work of your hand." In Jeremiah 31:9, God is described as "a father to Israel," and Ephraim as "my firstborn." In Psalm 103:13, there is a simile in which the Lord shows compassion "as a father" to his children. There are also a handful of passages where God is described as having a special father-son relationship to Israel's king (2 Sam. 7:14; Ps. 2:7, 89:26-28).[46]

The Old Testament uses other metaphors (such as judge, warrior, or king) to refer to God far more frequently than it does "father." The distinctive feature of the "father" metaphor is its personal nature; the Old Testament's use of "father" language points to God's compassion and providential care for both Israel and the king. Certainly God is Creator of the entire universe; however, God is not described as "father" to the universe as a whole, but to Israel or the king.[47]

This rare use of "father" language contrasts with the practice of Israel's neighbors, who regularly referred to their "gods" and "goddesses" as both "father" and "mother." A likely reason for Israel's reluctance to use either "father" or "mother" imagery for God had to do with the Hebrew desire to distinguish their God from pagan deities.

YHWH was to be identified neither with Baal, the god of fertility, nor with El, the "father" of the gods.[48]

The rarity of "Father" language in the Old Testament contrasts with the New Testament, where "Father" is the regular way to refer to God, and where "our Father" is the way in which Christians address God in prayer. The fundamental reason for the difference lies in the example of Jesus, whose practice it was to address God as *Abba* or "my Father," and who understood himself in relationship to the Father as "the Son." In the New Testament, this special relationship that existed between Jesus and his Father becomes the basis for the self-understanding of the church: "Christians came to believe that one comes to the Father through Jesus the Son . . . because Jesus believed he had a special relationship with God the Father."[49] This relationship between Jesus as Son and God as his Father is found throughout the Gospels. In the writings of Paul, the gift of the Holy Spirit to the church after the resurrection of Christ enables Christians to confess Jesus as Lord and to pray to God as Father. For Paul, the distinctive understanding of God as Father comes through a distinctive relationship to Jesus Christ as the crucified and risen Son, in a union with the risen Christ made possible by the Holy Spirit. God cannot be known as Father apart from the Trinitarian relationship between the Father, the Son, and the Holy Spirit.[50]

There are then two primary reasons that the Bible uses masculine imagery in reference to God. The first has to do with monotheism; as Creator of the universe, the one God exercises all of the functions of both male gods and female goddesses in pagan religions, but this "masculine" symbolism is not understood at all in a sexual manner. Second, while there are anticipations of the notion of God as "father" in the Old Testament, it is the portrayal in the New Testament of Jesus Christ as the unique Son of God that leads to the new naming of God as the Father of Jesus Christ, and, by extension, of the church as adopted sons and daughters of the Father.

As noted above, however, there is an additional reason theologians like Hauke give for the masculine imagery of God in the Bible: the notion that God is transcendent over creation: "[F]or a personal transcendent image of God . . . it is the masculine traits that occupy the foreground."[51] The argument is stated concisely in the Anglican Forward in Faith document *Consecrated Women?*:

> What the Hebrew Scriptures so desperately want to convey about God is that he is set apart from the gods. God does not create from within himself; he does not bear and give birth to the creation. . . . From the choices available from human experience, only the term *Father* and the relationship suggested by *Fatherhood* does justice to the action of the God of Israel. It is biological fathers who take the initiative in creating new life. They bring it to being not within, but outside, their own bodies.[52]

There is an initial plausibility to this claim. As noted above, feminist theologians who substitute female imagery for the Bible's dominant male metaphors—

identifying God as "mother" or using "goddess" language—are also immanentist and panentheist; for example, they refer to the earth as "God's body."[53] This contrasts with the New Testament's imagery of the church, not the earth, as the body, not of God, but of Christ. Old Testament scholar Elizabeth Achtemeier suggests that the "basic reason" for the Bible's masculine language is that "the God of the Bible will not let himself be identified with creation. . . . And it is that holiness, that otherness, that transcendence of the Creator, which also distinguishes biblical religion from all others."[54] Both Achtemeier and Frymer-Kensky point to Genesis 1 to indicate the uniqueness of Israel's understanding of the God of creation.[55]

Insofar as feminist theologians advocate monist theologies that identify God (or the goddess) with creation, the criticism is justified.[56] At the same time, however, caution is necessary concerning the simple equation "male = transcendent; female = immanent." The biblical account of creation does indeed emphasize God's transcendence in contrast to theologies of panentheism/immanence.[57] However, it is significant that the Bible does not emphasize male imagery to denote transcendence. The dominant imagery that the Bible uses in emphasizing God's transcendence over creation is either God's word (Gen. 1, Isa. 43:1, 6-7; 45:18-19), divine unity (monotheism; Isa. 43:11; 44:6, 8; 45:18, 22-25; 46:9), the imagery of height itself (Isa. 40:22; 44:24), or a combination of these images. Significantly, Bevan notes that the imagery of height to indicate "transcendence" is not translatable. Any attempt to explain the metaphor uses the metaphor, which simply serves to emphasize the distinction between God and creation.[58] At the same time that the Bible associated God with height—God's throne is in the heavens—God is not identified with the heavens or sky (as in pantheist Stoicism), but rather creates the heavens (Gen. 1:1).[59]

Significantly, the "Father" symbolism of the Bible is not associated with God's creation of or transcendence over the world, but is always used personally and socially: God is not "father" of the world in creation, but is rather the "father" of Israel or the king in the Old Testament, but, more definitively, the Father of Jesus Christ in the New Testament. Jesus teaches his disciples to pray to "our Father in heaven," but, again, the symbolism is personal. The Father is "our Father," not the father of the universe. The Father in heaven is transcendent, but the transcendence is associated with "height" imagery (our Father *in heaven*).

As noted above, the writers of the Scriptures seemed hesitant to use "father" language when speaking of God as Creator, and the reason is certainly as noted. The masculine metaphors applied to God have nothing to do with sexuality, but, more specifically, *any* understanding of God as parent of the universe, whether using *either* female "mother" imagery or male "father" imagery, would *equally* have pantheist implications. Significantly, the church fathers understood the implications of the distinction between "fatherhood" and "sonship" (on the one hand), and creation (on the other) in their formulations of the doctrines of incarnation and the Trinity. Against Arius' heretical claim that the Son is a creature, Athanasius made a fundamental distinction between "begetting" and "creating." If the Son is indeed the Son of the Father, then the Son must be of the same nature (*homoousios*) as the Father.[60] So the Nicene Creed states that the Son is "begotten not made." As noted in the quotations from Athanasius and Hilary above, this Fatherhood of God and the eternal begetting of the Son by the Father is nonsexual. In contrast, God creates the world from nothing (*ex nihilo*). The universe is not a son of God, but a creature.

It would seem then, that Hauke and other critics of feminist theology are correct to emphasize the transcendence of God over against feminist immanence; however, in trying to tie the notion of transcendence to masculine imagery of God as Father, they not only violate Trinitarian logic, but also, in their own way, repeat the error of the feminist theology they intend to criticize. Both masculine "father" language and feminine "mother" imagery would be equally mistaken if used to describe God's creation of the universe, because both would be equally monist. The "Father" imagery of Scripture is personal; it refers to God the Father's relationship to Jesus the Son, not to God's creation of the universe.

Finally, care must be taken to avoid the misuse of masculine metaphors to advance a theology that misses the significance of how the metaphors actually function. So-called "traditional readings" that use the masculine metaphors to legitimate traditional patriarchal structures can be as guilty of misreading the metaphors as the feminist readings that reject the male imagery as oppressive. Both approaches tend to read the narratives as if the metaphor itself provided its own meaning. The error is to focus on the metaphor as such rather than the subject matter that the metaphor intends to illumine. When Christians call God "Father," they are not referring to God as a generic "father" of creation, but as "the Father of our Lord Jesus Christ." Attending to the narrative structure of the biblical texts, one finds that they subvert a patriarchal reading. The God described metaphorically as the husband of Israel does not divorce his unfaithful spouse, but loves her despite her infidelity and attempts to win her back (Hosea). The Father of Jesus Christ "did not spare his Son but gave him up for us all" (Rom. 8:32). The Son who existed in the "form of God," did not abuse his status, but "emptied himself, taking the form of a servant," humbling himself to the death on a cross (Phil. 2). The Spirit incorporates the church into the body of Christ, in which there is neither slave nor free, male nor female (Gal. 3:28). To read these masculine metaphors as "oppressive to women" is to take them out of context, but it would be an equal misreading to read them as endorsing male privilege or hierarchy, or as providing a "role model" for male-only ordination.[61]

A MALE PRIESTHOOD?

Hauke's discussion of priesthood in the Old Testament is, at best, ambiguous. He points out that "women are totally excluded from the offices of priest and Levite."[62] He also acknowledges that there were occasionally women prophets. At the same time, he acknowledges that there may well have been cultural and practical reasons for this exclusion of women from the Old Testament priesthood: patriarchal conditions largely restricted the role of women to house and family with limited participation in public affairs; the domestic and maternal duties of women would often have prevented their participation in temple functions; women would not have been physically strong enough to participate in the sacrificial slaying of large animals; menstruation and child-bearing would often have made women ceremonially unclean and excluded from worship. Hauke also points to the so-called Canaanite fertility cult involving female prostitution by priestesses. The most significant argument he advances is that "a priest is not only a representative of the people but also God's delegate." Significantly, he recognizes that "these facts are not sufficient in themselves to prove that there was an internal necessity for the exclusion of women from Old Testament priestly office."[63]

On the other hand, Hauke makes the following arguments against women priests based on anthropological symbolism. He defines a priest as "a mediator between God and man" who functions as the "representation of the Divinity in relation to man." Insofar as the emphasis is on "transcendence and the active workings of God," it is appropriate to reserve the priesthood for men. The priest also has a "public representation of man in relation to the Divinity," and for this also men are more appropriate, as the male "steps outward" into the presence of God, and by virtue of his "more strongly developed capacities for abstract thought and energetic will" is more able to represent the common interest and lead a religious group in a "not subjective-emotive way."[64]

Negatively, Hauke points to the "clear association of women with divine immanence," and states that "priestesses play a special role in the service of female deities, and particularly of mother goddesses." There is thus an "intimate connection" between the "image of God and that of the priest."[65] He writes: "To the sphere of liturgical symbolism . . . belongs the priest as representative of the community before God and of God vis-à-vis the community."[66]

The issue of women priestesses in the Old Testament has already been addressed.[67] The so-called "Canaanite fertility cult" is a myth, and there were no "sacred prostitutes" in the ancient world. Again, the most plausible reason for the exclusion of women from the Old Testament priesthood is precisely one that Hauke acknowledges here—that Old Testament purity regulations would have prohibited women from participating in temple worship. As noted above, the regular occasions when women would have been ritually impure would have provided sufficient reason for the exclusion of women from Israel's priesthood. At the same time, the situation of the New Testament church is different insofar as Christ's redemption has fulfilled the purpose of Israel's temple rituals so that there are no longer concerns about ritual purity.

More important for the discussion of symbolism is Hauke's claim concerning the representational nature of priesthood, where he relies on general reflections concerning anthropology and symbolism rather than a careful reading of the biblical text. The suggestion that a male priest represents a male divinity while a female priestess represents a female goddess might (or might not) have been correct in polytheistic religions, but any such notion of the priest acting as a representation (in the sense of image) of Israel's God would have been prohibited by the anti-iconic nature of Israel's religion summed up in the second commandment (Exod. 20:4-5). There were no images of Israel's God in the temple, and the priest would not have been thought of as such an image. The priest did indeed act as a representative on the part of God to the people, and of the people to God, but here Hauke and others fail to distinguish between a representative (in the sense of spokesperson or ambassador) and a representation (in the sense of an image or likeness). A spokesperson or ambassador can act as a representative (in the sense of speaking on behalf of) while not acting as a representation (in the sense of bearing a physical resemblance). Priests in the Old Testament were representatives, not representations.[68]

Moreover, any argument from Old Testament priesthood is also a red herring insofar as it addresses the wrong issue. The historic (Western Catholic) understanding of the priesthood is not that the priest represents God (in the divine nature), but rather that the priest represents Christ (acts *in persona Christi*) in his incarnate humanity. That is the issue that needs to be addressed.

A MALE INCARNATION?

As pointed out in previous chapters, the new Catholic argument against the ordination of women first appeared in the document *Inter Insigniores*—the basic argument being that there must be a physical resemblance between the male priest who celebrates the Eucharist and Jesus Christ, who as God incarnate, became human as a male human being. The Declaration recognizes that, as the "firstborn of all humanity, of women as well as men," the unity which Christ established makes no distinction between male and female (Gal. 3:28). "Nevertheless," it continues, "the incarnation of the Word took place according to the male sex: this is indeed a question of fact, and this fact, while not implying any alleged natural superiority of man over woman, cannot be disassociated from the economy of salvation." The symbolism to which the document points is that of "nuptial mystery." In the Old Testament,

God is portrayed as the divine bridegroom to whom Israel is the bride. In the New Testament, Christ is the bridegroom and the church is his bride. As Eve was born from Adam's side, so the church is born from Christ's wounded side. The appeal here is to the imagery of 2 Corinthians 11:2; Ephesians 5:22, 23; John 3:29; Revelation 19:7, 9; Mark 2:19; and Matthew 22:1-14. *Inter Insigniores* sums up the argument by appealing to the symbolism of the Eucharist:

> That is why we can never ignore the fact that Christ is a man. And therefore, unless one is to disregard the importance of this symbolism for the economy of Revelation, it must be admitted that, in actions which demand the character of ordination and in which Christ himself, the author of the Covenant, the Bridegroom, the Head of the Church, is represented, exercising his ministry of salvation—which is in the highest degree the case of the Eucharist—his role (this is the original sense of the word *persona*) must be taken by a man. This does not stem from any personal superiority of the latter in the order of values, but only from a difference of fact on the level of functions and service.[69]

The essential argument here is one of liturgical and eucharistic theology, addressed at length in the previous chapter. Here the key concern has to do with the symbolic significance of the masculinity of Christ. The masculinity of Jesus Christ is the presupposition of the symbolism of the "nuptial mystery," in which Christ is the bridegroom and the church is the bride.

The Anglican Forward in Faith document *Consecrated Women?* states that "[t]o turn the maleness of Christ into . . . a merely trivial detail is . . . seriously to damage the classical doctrine of the Incarnation and of the person of Christ." There could be no incarnation in which the Godhead assumed humanity in a sexually undifferentiated manner. Since, the document claims, God is Father, and Christ "bears his image and likeness," "the only possibility is for the Redeemer to be born as a male, including both sexes (male by virtue of his own humanity; female by virtue of the one from whom that human nature is derived, Mary . . .)."[70] The maleness of Christ generates an entire family of images that are critical to the understanding of redemption: Christ the bridegroom, Christ the High Priest, and Christ the Sacrifice for the sins of the world.[71] The document asks whether God could have become incarnate as a woman: "[W]e believe that the answer must be 'No.'" A divine daughter would have spoken of a "Mother in heaven," and so could not have been the image of the Father.[72]

Hauke also endorses the symbolism of bride-bridegroom imagery as the starting point for his argument: "The Roman declaration on women in the priesthood thus goes to the heart of the symbolism of the sexes when it interprets the mystery of Christ and the Church in terms of the images of bridegroom and bride."[73] Hauke goes beyond this, however, by expressing his Christological argument in terms of an anthropological claim concerning male transcendence and female immanence. He reflects on the three Christological offices of prophet, priest, and king. As teacher, Jesus engages in a public forum, which is more suited to men than women. According to Hauke, women are more effective in small groups and with children. Teaching and miracles are an expression of Jesus' power, "which corresponds to his masculine expansivity." In Jesus' kingly office, he acts as lawgiver and judge, and "bearers of authority are more often men than women." Finally, in his priestly sacrifice on the cross, Jesus represents God toward humanity and the community to God. As God's gift to human beings, Christ manifests "a typically masculine dynamics." As representative of the church, "public worship is marked by the eccentricity of the male."[74]

As with concerns about divine transcendence over against immanentist or panentheist notions of deity, there is much in the above argument with which the Catholic or Evangelical egalitarian would sympathize. Certainly, if the Word as the second person of the Trinity became incarnate, the incarnation would have had to have taken place either as a male or female human being, and Jesus Christ is certainly a male human being—as he was a Jewish male who lived in first-century Judea, was born in Bethlehem to a Jewish maiden named Miriam, had twelve Jewish male apostles, and was crucified by a Roman governor named Pontius Pilate on a hill outside the Jewish city of Jerusalem. Jesus' male humanity is one of the particularities inevitably connected with a redemption in history—what is sometimes called the scandal of particularity. Although there is no sexuality in the Divine Trinity itself, Jesus (as a human male who was born of a virgin mother) is rightly identified as the Son of the God who is his Father, not his mother.

Significantly, the church fathers emphasized Christ's humanness, but said little about his "maleness." According to Orthodox bishop Kallistos Ware:

> What matters for them is not the fact that he became male (ἀνήρ, *vir*) but the fact that he became human (ἄνθρωπος, *homo*). . . . It is indeed true that Christ at his incarnation became a male, but that is not what the creed is concerned to assert. The creed is referring to the salvation of the entire human race, men and women together, and so it says that Christ took the human nature that is common to us all, whether we are male or female.[75]

Along the same lines, in an essay entitled "Can a Male Savior Save Women?" Jay Wesley Richards argues against feminist claims that a male savior cannot save women, and that dividing human nature along sexual lines would come into conflict with Cappadocian Christology. Sexuality is an accidental property of human nature. Every human being is necessarily either a male or a female, but if what is essential about humanity is human nature and not human sexuality, then we can meaningfully assert that the assumption of a human nature by the Logos in the male Jesus enables him to stand in for humanity as a whole. By assuming human nature, the Word does not assume a *male* human nature, but fully assumes human nature *as a* male in such a manner that all human beings (whether male or female) can be saved.[76]

That the Word became incarnate as a man was not necessary, but it was what Thomas Aquinas would have called "fitting."[77] Given that it is not essential or necessary that in the incarnation the Word would have become incarnate as a male human being, why might it have been soteriologically fitting for Jesus Christ to be male? First, this makes sense in terms of the principle of "Christological subversion," what New Testament scholar Michael Gorman has called "cruciformity," or what Alan Padgett has called "Type II submission" (voluntary mutual submission).[78] As Gorman has argued, the kenotic self-emptying of Philippians 2 is the key to understanding Christ's salvific mission. The first-century Mediterranean culture in which Jesus exercised his ministry was an honor/shame culture in which women were already necessarily in submission to men. Only a male Savior could challenge and defeat Mediterranean honor culture by voluntarily undergoing the humiliation of death by crucifixion and then conquering death through resurrection. Only a male Savior could meaningfully teach that salvation comes not through domination, but through voluntarily becoming a servant.

At the same time, the maleness of Jesus Christ allows for typological continuity between the Old Testament and the New Testament as the latter fulfills the former. Given that Jesus Christ is the Word of God incarnate, and God is portrayed using masculine metaphors in the Old Testament, it certainly makes symbolic sense for Jesus to be male. There really is a parallel between the nuptial imagery of YHWH and Israel, and Christ as the bridegroom and the church as his bride. Jesus Christ (as male) typologically fulfills the Old Testament offices of prophet (Moses), priest (Aaron), and king (David). Egalitarians affirm this!

Once again, however, the clue to interpreting properly the metaphors of Scripture is provided by their narrative context. The narrative context of the parallel between the husband/Christ and bride/church symbolic imagery of Ephesians 5:32 is provided by 5:1, where Paul instructs the members of the church to "walk in the way of love, just as Christ loved us and gave himself up for us as a fragrant offering and sacrifice to God," and verse 21, where all are asked to "[s]ubmit to one another out of reverence for Christ." The model enjoined on the church throughout the passage is the pattern of Christ-imitation for all (not men only), which Gorman calls "cruciformity." Jesus Christ is the "head" of the church, which is his body, but he is the head who "loved the church and gave himself up for her" (v. 25). It is the narrative structure of the passage that defines what is meant for Christ to be bridegroom and the church to be bride. To read this passage as if its point was that ordained clergy should be male because Christ is male is to divorce the nuptial symbolism from its textual context to make a theological point that was nowhere in Paul's mind, while simultaneously missing the point that Paul was actually making about the cruciform imitation of Christ that applies to all Christians—women as well as men. The "male-only" ordination argument simply misreads the passage.

Typologically, Christ's three offices of prophet, priest, and king also make sense only if Jesus Christ is a Jewish male because Jesus as antitype fulfills the pattern of three Old Testament Jewish males: Moses, Aaron (or Melchizedek), and David. Again, however, the principle of Christological subversion comes into play as it is the New Testament narratives that give meaning to the typological symbols. As prophet, Jesus claims not to do away with the Mosaic law, but to fulfill it (Matt. 5:17). At the same time, Jesus' fulfillment of the law involves an "eschatological reversal" in which he shows favor to lost sinners rather than those who are considered "righteous." Jesus subverted Jewish distinctions between "clean" and "unclean" by ministering to Gentiles (Mark 7:24-30; Luke 7:1-10), by healing a Samaritan leper (Luke 17:11-19), and by asking for a drink of water from a Samaritan woman (John 4:7-9). He allowed a "sinful" woman to wash his feet (Luke 7:36-50). He refused to condemn a woman caught in adultery (John 8:1-11). Jesus should have been made ceremonially unclean by being touched by a menstruating woman and by touching a dead girl. Instead, he healed the woman and raised the dead girl to life (Mark 5:21-43).[79] Jesus antagonized the religious leaders of his time by healing on the Sabbath (Mark 3:1-16). His claim to forgive sins led to accusations of blasphemy (Mark 2:1-12). After his crucifixion and resurrection, early Christians realized the implications of Jesus' fulfillment of Jewish law by welcoming Gentile members of the church without insisting on male circumcision or kosher diet (Acts 15:22-29).

That Christians believe that Jesus fulfilled the role of Old Testament priesthood is also subversive. Although not of the traditional priestly tribe of Levi, the New Testament proclaims that Jesus is the High Priest (of the order of Melchizedek rather than Aaron) who is simultaneously priest, victim, and temple, and it is through his death on the cross that Jesus fulfilled the Old Testament notion of priestly sacrifice by taking upon himself the sins of humanity.[80]

It is perhaps the office of king in which Christological subversion is most evident. As the notice posted by Pontius Pilate over Jesus' cross makes clear, it is Jesus the crucified peasant who is "king of the Jews." This man who was condemned to death by the religious and political leaders of his time as a religious blasphemer, a law-breaker, and a political pretender, who died in the most humiliating and shameful manner imaginable in his culture, was proclaimed in his resurrection by the God of Israel who was his Father to be the divine judge who pardons rather than condemns the guilty.

Certainly it is symbolically and theologically significant that Jesus Christ was (and is) a male, but significant, among other things, precisely because, through his

264 | Icons of Christ

life and mission, Jesus radically challenged and subverted traditional honor/shame culture, and, with it, male privilege. As with the marriage symbolism of Ephesians, to conclude from the gospel narratives that the crucial point of Jesus' masculinity is to provide a pattern for exclusively male ordination is to misread the texts.

MALE APOSTLES

The fundamental Catholic theological argument against the ordination of women is that a woman cannot preside at the celebration of the Eucharist because a woman cannot represent a male Christ. The argument concerning male apostles is the corresponding historical warrant supplied by Catholic opponents of women's ordination. Male-only ordination is grounded in the example of Jesus who chose only men as apostles. Butler makes the following claims: (1) The fundamental reason that the church does not ordain women is based not on any notion of women's inferiority, but on the "fact" of Jesus' example. (2) Jesus chose twelve male apostles, and no women; in so doing, he expressed his will for the priesthood. (3) Bishops are successors of the apostles, and so, must themselves be males. (4) The unbroken tradition of the church confirms this practice of not ordaining women. She summarizes the argument succinctly:

> This doctrine of priesthood, as we shall see, determines the judgment of the Catholic Church concerning the possibility of ordaining women. The answer to the question "Why?" is bound up with the belief that Holy Orders is a sacrament instituted by Christ, that his intention for the priesthood is known by way of the mission he gave the Twelve, and that this office is passed on in apostolic succession. If the Church does not have the authority to change her tradition regarding this, it is because the ministry is a gift which the Lord "entrusted to the Apostles" and which she is bound to preserve.[81]

Again, she writes: "The fact that Jesus did not choose any women to belong to the Twelve, and that the apostles followed his example by handing on the apostolic charge only to men, was seen to be the fundamental reason."[82] As noted above, the argument first appears in *Inter Insigniores*: "Jesus Christ did not call any women to become part of the Twelve. . . . Even his Mother, who was so closely associated with the mystery of her Son, and whose incomparable role is emphasized by the Gospels of Luke and John, was not invested with the apostolic ministry."[83] Butler is clear that the heart of the argument in *Inter Insigniores* concerns the twelve apostles and their relation to the subsequent church:

> This rather sober, ecclesiastical formulation directs attention to the vocation and symbolism of the Twelve, and its importance for the constitution of the Church. It is by way of Jesus' choice of 12 men that we know his will for the apostolic ministry of bishops and priests. No other appeal is made.[84]

The argument thus stands and falls on the symbolic significance of Jesus having chosen only men to be his apostles. The crucial weakness in the argument lies in a tendency to impose onto the text preconceived assumptions about what the symbols of the Scriptures must mean rather than allowing the narrative structure of the texts to determine the meaning of the symbols. As with the case of Jesus' masculinity, the reason his apostles had to be male is evident from the text itself. Jesus chose *male* apostles for the same reason that he chose *twelve* apostles and *Jewish* apostles. Insofar as Jesus' followers represent the new Israel, Jesus' twelve apostles typologically represent the twelve tribes of Israel, and, specifically, the twelve patriarchs (sons of Jacob/Israel) from whom the nation of Israel was descended. In the new age, Jesus gives his apostles a special role in judging the twelve tribes of Israel (Matt. 19:28; Luke 22:30). The book of Revelation records that the New Jerusalem has twelve gates on which are written the names of the twelve tribes of Israel, and twelve foundations on which are written the names of the twelve apostles of the Lamb (Rev. 21:12-14). Gentile inclusion in the church rests on the foundation of the (Jewish) twelve apostles and on the (Hebrew) prophets (Eph. 2:11, 19-21). At his Last Supper, Jesus is present with his twelve disciples, and reconstitutes the Passover as a meal of bread and wine in which he forms a new covenant. Significantly, it is at this last meal where Jesus pronounces the role of the twelve in judging Israel (Luke 22:14-30; cf. Jer. 31:31-34). The twelve had to be free Jewish males, and not slaves, women or Gentiles in order to fulfill the symbolic function of their typological role.[85]

Inter Insigniores emphasizes that "Jesus Christ did not call any women to become part of the Twelve." Butler asserts that, given Jesus' freedom in breaking from the cultural roles of his time, the way that he freely mingled with women, and his disregard for ritual purity laws, he could have called women apostles if he had wanted to: "If Jesus did not share the prejudices of his contemporaries, it would appear that he 'could have' entrusted the apostolic church to women if he had wished to, but freely chose to do otherwise." She also mentions (with approval?) several times in her book the significance of the fact that Jesus did not call even his mother (the Virgin Mary) to be one of his apostles or to exercise priestly ministry.[86] However, that Jesus was free from the prejudices of his contemporaries does not mean that, in some kind of absolute freedom without regard either to cultural context or Jewish faith, he "could have" entrusted the apostolic ministry to women, any more than he could have called someone who was Chinese or Buddhist to be an apostle. As a reviewer of Butler's book points out, the demand of communication places limits on what one can say. If the twelve apostles were to play the symbolic role that Jesus assigned to them—as representatives of the New Israel and the twelve patriarchs—they had to be twelve free Jewish males.[87]

The question then of why Mary the virgin mother of Jesus was not called to be an apostle is fairly easily answered. As a Jewish woman, Mary could not have fulfilled the typological role fulfilled by the twelve. At the same time, pointing to Mary as a counterexample to women's ordination is rather odd. Mary was not ordained because, apart from her significance as the mother of Jesus, her role in the earthly mission of Jesus and in the later New Testament church seems to have been fairly limited. For instance, she did not play the kind of major role in the ministry of Jesus that was played by the sisters Mary and Martha of Bethany or by Mary Magdalene. After the resurrection of Jesus, Mary is mentioned by name only once in the book of Acts (1:14), and not at all in any of the epistles.[88] Again, women like Lydia (Acts 16:11-15, 40) or Priscilla (Acts 18:2, 18, 26; Rom. 16:3; 1 Cor. 16:19; 2 Tim. 4:19) or the numerous women Paul greets in some of his letters (Rom. 16) seemed to have played more significant roles in the early church than did the Virgin Mary. It would seem that her single vocation in redemptive history was to be the mother of Jesus.

Significantly, Butler recognizes the typological symbolic significance of the twelve, but insists, following *Ordinatio sacerdotalis*, that "the symbolism of the Twelve is not limited to representing the 12 patriarchs of Israel, and that their vocation is not limited to judging the 12 tribes of Israel." Her claim is that those who raise this objection "deny that the Lord's choice of the Twelve . . . reveals his will for the ordained ministry." To the contrary, she writes, "The Church must consult the tradition, and the tradition sees in his example with respect to the Twelve an expression of his will for the ordained ministry."[89]

The argument as Butler sets it out is circular, and thus begs the question of whether Christ's choice of twelve male apostles is an "expression of his will" for an exclusively male ordained ministry. The structure of the argument is as follows:

(1) We know that in the post-New Testament church, the reasons for not ordaining women are theological, not cultural, and are grounded in Christ's will because Christ chose only male apostles.

(2) We know that masculinity is what is important about Christ's choosing the apostles and not simply biblical typology (the number twelve and Jewishness) because in the post-apostolic church, no women were ordained (although Gentiles were).[90]

To express the argument succinctly:

(1) Christ's choosing of male apostles is used to explain the practice of the post-apostolic church, but then (in a circular manner),

(2) The practice of the post-apostolic church is used to explain Christ's choosing of male apostles.

What we can actually affirm with certainty is the following:

(1) The primary reason that Jesus chose only male apostles is the same reason he chose only twelve apostles and only Jewish apostles—the fulfillment of Old Testament typology. Moreover, the twelve apostles had a distinctive role that cannot be repeated. The apostles were companions of and witnesses to the mission of Jesus (Matt. 28:20; Luke 24:44-49; Acts 1:8, 21-22). The apostles were witnesses to Jesus' resurrection (Acts 1:22; 1 Cor. 9:1). After his death, the role of Judas was replaced by Matthias, but after that, there were no more replacements. Bishops and presbyters may be successors to the apostles, but they are not themselves apostles.[91]

(2) We do not know whether the office of bishop and presbyter was based on the office of apostle, and if so, to what extent.[92] We do not know whether the practice of the post-resurrection church concerning presbyters and bishops was based on the masculinity of the apostles because the New Testament never addresses the issue. The argument concerning the ordination of women based on the practice of the New Testament church after the resurrection of Jesus is thus necessarily an argument from silence. No writer of the New Testament ever says "women should be ordained," but neither does any New Testament writer say, "women should not be ordained." We can speculate about the actual practice of the New Testament church, but the data is limited. The New Testament says nothing about the actual practices of sacramental ministry that are so essential for Butler's argument. The New Testament contains no descriptions of how the Eucharist was celebrated and who might have officiated. Because we do not know who presided at the Eucharist, we do not know whether women did so. For the same reason, we do not know whether men did so. The ministerial roles that women practiced in the New Testament church will be discussed in a later chapter.[93]

Moreover, Butler cannot appeal to those New Testament passages used by Protestant complementarians to reject women's ordination because the passages do not have to do with sacramental ministry, but rather with speaking and teaching; Butler is clear that the Roman Catholic Church no longer considers these prohibitions to have anything to do with ordination. Women are allowed to speak and teach in Roman Catholic Churches; they just cannot preside at the Eucharist.[94]

Finally, the understanding of priesthood and sacrifice that is so essential to Butler's argument is anachronistic. The early church did not understand a presbyter to be a priest or to exercise a sacrificial ministry in the sense that Butler imagines. Insofar as presbyterial ministry is "priestly," it is Christ who celebrates and the sacrifice is Christ's, not that of the presider.[95]

In the end, Butler has to appeal to post-biblical tradition to make her argument. What about this tradition, then? Butler points out that the early church did not object to the admission of Gentiles, but did object to the ordination of women.[96] Again, however, in the case of the New Testament, this is an argument from silence. The New Testament neither approves of nor objects to women's ordination because it does not address the issue. After the New Testament, we know that the main reason the tradition rejected women's ordination—which Butler acknowledges in her book—was because women were considered to be ontologically inferior to men, less intelligent, more emotional, and more easily tempted.[97]

Butler is clear that the contemporary Catholic Church does not use this argument, so, in an attempt to save the argument from tradition, Butler appeals to an anti-Montanist work of the fourth-century bishop Epiphanius of Salamis, whom she refers to as the "first undisputed witness of patristic opposition to the priestly ordination of women."[98] Epiphanius does indeed appeal to the fact that Jesus chose only male apostles as a historical warrant against the practice of women's ordination, but his arguments are the unhelpful ones already addressed: (1) that there were no women priests in the Old Testament;[99] (2) that the Virgin Mary was not a priest;[100] and (3) that no woman was an apostle or priest in the New Testament.[101] Butler states concerning Epiphanius: "Epiphanius bears witness, then, to the tradition that God's will regarding the female priesthood is known by means of Christ's choice of the Twelve.... The reason is not their 'subject' status or some unworthiness deriving from their sex; it is a dispensation of the Lord's will."[102] To the contrary, Epiphanius does embrace the "reasons" that Butler would prefer to avoid. There is the appeal to women's ontological inferiority: "Women are unstable, prone to error, and mean-spirited ... so here the devil has seen fit to disgorge ridiculous teaching from the mouths of women."[103] There is also the prohibition of women teaching based on the Pauline passages: "[T]he Word of God does not allow a women 'to speak' in church either, or to 'bear rule over a man.'"[104] Perhaps Epiphanius is not so helpful after all.

The argument against women's ordination based on the masculinity of the apostles is, as noted above, a circular argument: (1) The traditional argument against women's ordination is acknowledged as inadequate insofar as it was based on the presumption of the ontological inferiority of women. Given that the original argument from tradition is insufficient, it becomes necessary to appeal to Scripture, namely the example of the male apostolate. However, (2) the argument from the male apostolate is also insufficient, as Butler acknowledges.[105] Accordingly, (3) it is necessary to appeal beyond Scripture to tradition, and specifically to the rather isolated witness of one fourth-century bishop. However, examination of the writings of this bishop discloses that he has little to offer in terms of actual argument beyond the mere assertion that Christ chose only male apostles (which no one denies), and, unfortunately, embraces the assumptions concerning women's inferiority and prohibition of women's teaching that have already been found insufficient.

CONCLUSION

This chapter has examined a key modern Catholic argument against the ordination of women based on symbolism. The argument is essentially an appeal to masculine imagery found in both Scripture and tradition.

First, it is noted that the dominant symbolic imagery used to portray God in the Scriptures is masculine. Specifically, the God of the Old Testament is a God, not a goddess, who transcends and freely creates the world. God is not mother, and the world is not his body. In the New Testament, God is the Father, not mother, of Jesus Christ.

Second, the Old Testament priesthood was an exclusively male priesthood, and the primary reason for this is that priests are representatives of God. Only a male priest can represent a God who is portrayed using male imagery.

Third, in the incarnation, the Son of God became incarnate as a male Savior who addressed God as his Father, not his mother.

Fourth, Jesus Christ (the male Savior) chose only male apostles to be his witnesses and representatives.

Fifth, insofar as contemporary priests are successors to the male apostles, they must also be males in order that they might function as successors of the male apostles and represent the male Jesus Christ.

In contrast to those mainstream feminist theologians who find this masculine imagery oppressive, those theologians here designated as Catholic and Evangelical egalitarians (whom Greene-McCreight designates as "biblical feminists") would not object to any of the masculine imagery to which the Catholic opponents of women's ordination appeal in this argument. The Bible does indeed portray God using masculine imagery; the Old Testament priesthood was exclusively male; in Jesus Christ, the Son of God did indeed become incarnate as a male human being who addressed God as his Father; Jesus did indeed choose twelve male apostles; and, as successors to the apostles, contemporary clergy are indeed called to be representatives of Christ. None of this is denied. The key issue concerns the symbolic significance of this male imagery.

In the symbolic argument against women's ordination, it seems that the concern to reject the possibility of women's ordination drives the tendency to turn every example of male imagery in the Bible and the Christian tradition to the desired conclusion. This chapter has taken another look at this masculine imagery and specifically asked the question, "How does the narrative context of the biblical texts make sense of the imagery?" rather than assuming that, since we already know the meaning of masculine imagery, and since we already know the meaning of representation, it is a simple task to make a straightforward connection between masculine imagery and a male-only church office.

In each case, the masculine imagery has a function, but it is not the function imagined by the opponents of women's ordination. The God of the Bible is certainly portrayed using masculine imagery, but the purpose of this male symbolism has nothing to do with sexual modeling since God has no sex. Rather, in Israel, the one God takes on all of the tasks of both the pagan male gods and female goddesses. To call God "he" means that God is a "person," not that God is a male.

The Old Testament priesthood was indeed a male-only office, but the primary reason for a male priesthood had to do with the purity codes of the Old Testament law, a law that was fulfilled by Christ and whose purity regulations were abrogated when Gentiles were admitted to the church.

Jesus Christ the Son of God did indeed become incarnate as a male human being. Only as a man could Jesus have fulfilled the Old Testament typological roles of prophet, priest, and king. At the same time, Jesus fulfilled these roles in a manner that was subversive and challenged traditional Mediterranean "shame culture." Jesus fulfilled Old Testament law and promises by transforming them, and by calling both men and women to be his followers and to be servants of one another.

Jesus certainly called only twelve men to be his apostles. Again, only in calling twelve Jewish men could Jesus have both fulfilled and transformed the symbolism of Old Testament typology. That Jesus' twelve apostles were males no more requires that their successors be males than that their successors be Jewish or twelve in number. More specifically, what it means to be a "representative" of Christ has nothing to do with male or female sexuality, and everything to do with what Michael Gorman has called "cruciformity." The pattern of mutual submission to which all of Christ's followers are called means following Jesus Christ in the pattern of his self-emptying in which, rather than holding tightly to his divine prerogatives, the Son of God humbled himself, took on the form of a servant and became obedient "even to death on a cross" (Phil. 2:1-11). To be a representative of Christ means to follow this pattern by taking up our own cross, to become servants of the Triune God, and servants of one another. Both men and women are called to this task. Those who are called to church office have the special task of serving the church in the ministry of Word and Sacrament. For Catholic and Evangelical egalitarians, the ordination of women to the office of Word and Sacrament is not a demand for "equal rights" in the church, but a request for an equal opportunity to serve in the church.

14

The Argument from Symbolism

Transcendence and Immanence

The last several chapters have been addressing Catholic objections to the ordination of women. This chapter is the second that focuses on Catholic objections to women's ordination based on symbolism. The previous chapter dealt with objections based on the doctrines of God and creation, the Old Testament priesthood, the incarnation, and the significance of a male apostolate. This one will discuss objections based on a theory of anthropological symbolism, specifically that men and women have unique symbolic roles based on inherent differences between the sexes: men represent externality, action, rationality, objectivity, and transcendence; women represent internality, receptivity, emotion, subjectivity and immanence.

The most prominent voice in this discussion is that of German theologian Manfred Hauke, whose book *Women in the Priesthood?* was one of the first contributions to the discussion, and is certainly one of the lengthiest. The central argument of Hauke's book is one of anthropological symbolism. As noted in the previous chapter, Hauke insists that masculine and feminine symbolism transcends culture. He appeals to examples from ancient religion, modern biology, sociology, and psychology. The book abounds with statements such as the following:

> The dynamics of the male are expansive, outer directed and aimed at overcoming particular sorts of resistance. The dynamics of the female are more adaptive in nature, that is, more strongly adjusted to the demands of the existing situation. . . . The fact that women are guided more strongly by intuition and feeling also means that they are more open to concrete experience, whereas men always behave more critically. . . . Women are always dependent, in one way or the other, on the leadership of men, but men, without the intuition and assistance of women, are only half human. . . . The superiorities of men, to express things pointedly, lead to a position of authority, but the superiorities of women, to a position of subordination.[1]

According to Hauke, because masculinity is bound up with externality and transcendence, men are symbols of God. In contrast, the "accent of feminine symbolism falls . . . not on the representation of God, but on the depiction of creation . . . women are simultaneously *representative of mankind.*" Hauke states succinctly: "*The basic axis of the symbolism of the sexes* can thus be equated with the relationships *man = God, woman = creation*"—although he insists that this does not imply a lesser valuation of women.[2]

As discussed in the previous chapter, Hauke insists that the "symbolism of the sexes" is "reflected in Christ's entire redemptive work, namely his *masculine* human nature." Jesus' teaching and miracles are "expressions of Jesus' *power*, which corresponds to his masculine expansivity."[3] Hauke recognizes that the gospels describe Jesus in terms of graciousness and mercy, but "Jesus' benevolence can be understood only through his omnipotence."[4] Jesus' masculinity is also of central significance on the cross, where Jesus represents God with respect to humanity, but also the submission of humanity with respect to God. Hauke here appeals to a dynamic between transcendence and immanence he had discussed elsewhere. Transcendence includes immanence, but immanence cannot include transcendence.[5]

If Jesus represents both God and the masculine principle, the Virgin Mary represents the feminine qualities of receptiveness and obedience. Mary is thus "the *representative of creation as creation.*" She also "represents *mankind.*"[6] Most importantly, Mary is the representative of the church: "The Church appears, in the image of Mary, as having feminine traits."[7]

Building on the above reflections about masculine and feminine symbolism, Hauke concludes the following:

The priest represents the Church, but "represents the Church insofar as he first *represents Christ as the head of the Church.*"[8] In contrast to the masculine role of the priest, Hauke writes, every Christian "stands as a receiver before God and thus fulfills the bridal role." Although all Christians can represent the bride, it is appropriate to restrict ordination only to men because only men can realize "an ontological approximation of Christ" in the indelible character of ordination. Because Jesus Christ's "masculine identity" is soteriologically necessary, only a male can represent Christ in church office.[9]

Hauke's book has continued to be influential, not only among some Roman Catholics, but also among some Anglicans opposed to women's ordination.[10] Whether there is direct influence or not, there are also Orthodox arguments against women's ordination that appeal to similar symbolic imagery. What follows will first assess some of these arguments used by theologians of different "Catholic" traditions that presume some version of the anthropological case against women's ordination. Before doing so, it is important to point out an initial problem with Hauke's approach.

Although Hauke and others who take a similar approach are examples of "Catholic" opposition to women's ordination, the approach is inherently problematic in that it is one that the Roman Catholic magisterium has explicitly repudiated. Sara Butler, in what is perhaps the best summary of what is here called the "new Catholic argument" against women's ordination—based on the assumption that the priest acts as a representative of the male Christ—acknowledges that "until quite recently Catholic theologians generally *did* explain the Church's practice, at least in part, by appealing to the difference and the 'hierarchical' ordering of the sexes. They appealed as well to the Pauline texts that prohibited women's public teaching in the Church and their exercise of authority over men (1 Corinthians 14:34; 1 Timothy 2:12)."[11] However, Butler is clear that this is no longer the case. She writes:

> Undoubtedly, how one construes the difference between the sexes, and how much importance one accords to this difference, enters into speculation as to *why* the Lord chose men and not women. But it is imperative to grasp that this is not at the root of the magisterium's judgment. *The complementarity of the sexes does not appear among the "fundamental reasons" given for the Church's tradition.*[12]

Butler's heading for the beginning of this section reads: "The Magisterium's Judgment Is Not Based on a Theory of Christian Anthropology."[13] But such a "theory of Christian anthropology" is almost the entire basis for Hauke's argument. Moreover, fundamental to Hauke's argument is an exegesis of 1 Corinthians 14:33-38 in which he argues that Paul's prohibition against women speaking is the single most important biblical passage to consider in terms of the discussion of women's ordination. Hauke writes: "[T]his ban on speaking . . . together with 1 Timothy 2:11-12, constitutes the most penetrating biblical evidence that can be brought against the ordination of women."[14] And later: "If my interpretation of 1 Corinthians 14 is correct, then it is not difficult to formulate the result: by force of divine law, only a baptized male can validly receive consecration to the priesthood."[15]

Finally, Hauke also interprets Ephesians 5 to teach a hierarchical understanding of marriage, which he believes is crucial to his argument from symbolism:

> Those who reject the "hierarchical structure of marriage" must, if they are consistent, trim back the symbolism of the Christ-Church relationship. . . . For marriage as the most anthropologically central relation, also possesses the strongest powers of symbolic expressiveness for the religious sphere. If there were to be full equality between husband and wife, the relation of Christ to the Church would also be affected analogically.[16]

Hauke was happy to report at the time he wrote: "To my knowledge, such an attempt [i.e., to espouse full equality between husband and wife] has not yet been made."[17] Of course, within a few short years, such an attempt was indeed made—by Pope John Paul II, who, in his apostolic letter *Mulieris Dignitatem*, interpreted Ephesians 5 as teaching a complete equal dignity of man and woman in marriage, and a "mutual submission," not only of the wife to the husband, but of the husband to the wife.[18] It is important to recognize, then, that those "Catholic" opponents of women's ordination who appeal to the kind of anthropological arguments Hauke uses are going against the grain of current Roman Catholic teaching in that the magisterium itself has found these arguments unsatisfactory. In addition, the Vatican no longer endorses the exegetical interpretations of the three controversial Pauline passages that are crucial to Hauke's argument. The Vatican does not base its position concerning the ordination of women on the assumption that women cannot exercise authority over men or teach in an authoritative manner in the church.

ARGUMENTS FOR MALE SYMBOLIC PRIORITY

The proponents of arguments for masculinity as symbolically normative for the representation of humanity appeal to the same passages of Scripture that are central to Protestant complementarian arguments against women's ordination. However, in contrast to the Protestant approach, they do not focus on the passages so much as teaching a hierarchy of command-and-obedience, but rather as indicating normative masculine symbolism.

Orthodox theologian Thomas Hopko discusses the creation stories of Genesis, pointing out that man (*anthrōpos*) is created first, and then woman is created from man's substance: "Man and woman belong together; they cannot be separated." They are man (*anthrōpos*) together, and so humankind is a "communal being." Human beings are created in God's image to know and love and to participate in the eternal knowledge and love of shared between God the Father, Jesus Christ the Son, and the Holy Spirit. God has made this possible in Jesus Christ, who is the new Adam, and the Church, which is the new Eve, personified in Mary, the mother of Christ.[19]

At the same time, Hopko asserts that "a certain priority is given to Adam who has the name of man (*anthrōpos*) even when he is yet alone." Hopko insists that "Adam the man is head of Eve the woman," and appeals to 1 Corinthians 11:3. He also appeals to Romans 5, where Paul describes Jesus as the "new and last Adam." Drawing on the marriage symbolism of Ephesians, Hopko states that "Jesus is Adam, the Church is Eve. Jesus is the Husband, the Church is his wife. Jesus is the bridegroom, the Church is his friend and bride. Jesus is the head, the Church is his body."[20] Hopko moves from this symbolism to an argument against women's ordination:

> As Jesus, the personal image of God the Father, is the head and husband of the Church, which is his body and bride, so the Christian man is the head and husband of his wife, and the presbyter/bishop the head and husband of his church. . . . The fatherhood, headship and husbandhood which belongs to believing men in Christ and the Church cannot be exercised by women, and cannot by exercised without them.

He concludes: "If what I have written here is right and true, women cannot be bishops and priests in the Orthodox view because it is not their divine calling and competence as women."[21]

In a similar manner, the Anglican Forward in Faith document *Consecrated Women?* appeals to Romans 5 and 1 Corinthians 11:3, 12; 15:21-23 to establish the symbolic priority of masculinity:

> [A]s the Scriptures consistently portray Adam as both the created origin of the human race, male and female, and its representative, so Jesus, the new Adam, is simultaneously both head and representative of the new humanity redeemed in him. While the Old Testament texts nowhere use such terms as "headship," *they clearly establish a pattern in which the male can represent the whole human race in a manner in which the female cannot.*[22]

The exegetical claims have already been discussed above. Concerning the figure of Adam in the creation passages of Genesis 1 and 2 as well as the parallel between Adam and Christ in Romans 5, what is significant about both Adam and Christ in both sets of passages is that they are human (ἄνθρωπος, *anthrōpos*), not that they are male. It is interesting to contrast the very different conclusions drawn by Orthodox theologian Elisabeth Behr-Sigel from a reading of the same passage:

> In Romans, St. Paul says, "... the grace of God and the free gift in the grace of that one man [*anthropos*] Jesus Christ abounded for many" (Rm 5:15). In line with the contemporary Jewish interpretation, the whole of Romans 5 uses Adam as a name standing for the whole of humankind and not as a proper name applied to a masculine individual. Adam is the figure of "the one who was to come," Jesus who is designated as the "New Adam" and brings together in his person the new humanity, the new community of which he is both the firstfruits and the head. And that Community is the Church where "there is neither male nor female," where all baptized people, all men and women who through baptism "have put on Christ," and "are all one in Christ Jesus" (Ga 3:28).[23]

Both Hopko and Behr-Sigel agree that Adam is representative of "the whole of humankind" (Behr-Sigel); both affirm Paul's typological parallel between Adam and Christ, recognizing Christ as the "new Adam" and the head of the church. However, Hopko points to the *contrast* between the male Christ and the female Church, and argues that Adam is representative of all humanity because he is *male*; Behr-Sigel points to the *unity* of the church, "in which there is neither male nor female," and argues that Adam is representative, *not* because he is male, but because he is *human*. Ironically, both make their case by appealing to Paul's use of the word *anthrōpos* to designate Adam.

It was argued earlier that in Hebrew *ha'adam* (Adam) simply means "human being." Hopko is misleading in using the ambiguous English word "Man" to claim that "man" was created before "woman," since the English word translated "man" (*ha'adam*) in Genesis 2:7 and following is not the word translated "man" (*'is*) in 2:23. Similarly, nothing in the Adam/Christ typology in Romans 5 suggests that either Adam or Christ are representative because of their sex. That Paul uses ἄνθρωπος (*anthrōpos*, human being) rather than ἀνήρ (*anēr*, male human being) to refer both to Adam and to Christ indicates that what is significant about both is their humanity, not their sexuality. Again, a careful reading of Paul's argument in both 1 Corinthians and Ephesians indicates that he did not understand "head" to mean either hierarchy or authority (as in Protestant complementarianism), but neither is there any indication from the context that it means "symbolic representation" (as in the Catholic symbolic argument). In both Ephesians and 1 Corinthians, Paul corrects conflicts between the sexes in light of "Christological subversion." Paul's emphasis is mutuality and cruciformity, and not male hierarchy or masculine symbolism.

As with the argument from Jesus having chosen male apostles, the arguments for normative masculine symbolic representation are circular and anachronistic. If one already knows ahead of time that the priest *must* be male because he acts *in persona Christi* and that representation demands a masculine physical resemblance, then one might find oneself reading the passages from Genesis, Romans, 1 Corinthians, and Ephesians in that light to suggest a normative male representative function in those passages; but apart from that prior assumption, there is no reason to do so. To read the passages in that sense is to impose a reading on the text rather than to draw out the inherent meaning of the passage.

It is this understanding of Christological representation that is at the core of the symbolic argument against women's ordination. So Hopko writes in a manner that sounds oddly Western (and indeed Roman Catholic) despite coming from the pen of an Orthodox theologian: "[T]he presbyter/bishop performs the good work of oversight and eldership. . . . He presides at worship, *holding the place of the Lord*, repeating his words and imitating his actions. He presents the gifts at the eucharistic offering *in the place of Jesus*, the one great high priest of God's priestly people."[24] It is *this* representative function that Hopko argues demands a parallel between the presbyter/bishop and the role of Christ. As Jesus Christ is the (male) head and husband of the Church, so the presbyter/bishop functions as the (male) husband and head of the local church: "[T]he headship which sacramentally actualizes the headship of Jesus himself may be exercised only by certain men."[25]

Apart from the assumption that the priest must physically resemble Christ in order to preside at the Eucharist, however, there is nothing in Hopko's argument that would require that a presbyter should be male. The roles of "oversight and eldership" of which he first speaks in discussing the office of presbyter/bishop could certainly be exercised by a woman. The words translated "bishop" (ἐπίσκοπος, *episkopos*) and "elder/presbyter" (πρεσβύτερος, *presbyteros*) are simply the Greek words for "overseer" and "old person" with masculine endings; grammatical gender does not determine sex, and there have certainly been women "overseers" and older women of wisdom and experience who could fill these roles. Nevertheless, as Orthodox bishop Kallistos Ware points out, the argument that the priest celebrates the Eucharist as a representative of Christ has never been the Orthodox position; those Orthodox who embrace the *in persona Christi* argument are adopting a Western Roman Catholic position that is at odds with Orthodox sacramental theology.[26]

MALE AND FEMALE SYMBOLISM

What shall be said about the bifurcated sexual symbolism that is key to Hauke's argument and dominates his book? Arguably, Hauke's use of sexual symbolism represents an unbaptized "natural theology" of sexuality, and ignores the principle of "Christological subversion." By "natural theology," what is meant is an *a priori* argument that is derived apart from and prior to a reading of Scripture and in the light of which Scripture is then interpreted. This would contrast to the methodology of "faith seeking understanding" that characterizes the use of reason and philosophy in theologians such as Augustine, Anselm, or Thomas Aquinas. Note that chapters 6–8 of Hauke's book precede his discussion of Scripture, and he establishes his key arguments concerning masculine and female symbolism by appeals to Plato, Aristotle, non-Christian religions (such as Hinduism and the Chinese *I Ching*), secular sociology, and Jungian psychology before any discussion of the Bible, and only then interprets the biblical texts in light of these symbolic gender distinctions between men and women.[27]

Hauke tends to read the Old and New Testaments in light of a transcendence/ immanence schema first drawn from pagan religion and secular psychology and sociology rather than asking the question of how the Old and New Testaments might challenge traditional (and particularly pagan) understandings of the relationship between the sexes. For example, Hauke makes much of pagan distinctions between "sky father gods" and "earth mother goddesses," and of imagery of the "sun" (as masculine) and the "moon" (as feminine), of "sky" (as masculine) and "water," "trees," and "earth" (as feminine). Note, however, that there is no parallel in Hebrew or Christian religion to pagan notions of sky gods or earth mothers because, in the Bible's creation narrative, the one God creates both heaven and earth: in the Bible, heaven and earth are creatures, not divinities, and the one God as Creator transcends both.

Tikva Frymer-Kensky also points to a significant difference between the way pagan religions portray the relationship between the sexes and the way the Bible does. In pagan religions, stories about gods and goddesses provide role models for human men and women; they not only provide "sacred examples," but also "divine warrant" for society's gender structures. In contrast, "[i]n the Bible, ideas about women and gender are conveyed in stories about human women."[28] Despite the differing social roles of men and women (rooted in the biology of childbirth and nurture in a preindustrial society), however, the Bible portrays men and women in remarkably similar ways: "[B]eyond the realities of Israel's social structure, the Bible presents a remarkably unified vision of humankind, for the stories show women as having the same inherent characteristics [as] men."[29] There is one major difference between men and women: some men exercise power, and women (as well as other men) do not—but throughout the Bible, women are portrayed in a manner similar to those men who also have no power. Frymer-Kensky's discussion contains numerous examples of the behavior of women in the Hebrew Bible (Old Testament). She concludes:

> When we survey the biblical record of the goals and strategies of women, a startling fact emerges. There is nothing distinctively "female" about the way that women are portrayed in the Bible, nothing particularly feminine about either their goals or their strategies. The goals of women are the same goals held by the biblical male characters and the authors of the stories. . . . The Bible presents no characteristics of human behavior as "female" or "male," no division of attributes between the poles of "feminine" and "masculine," no hint of distinctions of such polarities as male aggressivity-female receptivity, male innovation-female conservation, male out-thrusting-female containment, male subjecthood-female objecthood, male rationality-female emotionality, male product-female process, male achievement-female bonding, or any of the other polarities by which we are accustomed to think of gender distinctions. As far as the Bible presents humanity, gender is a matter of biology and social roles, it is not a question of basic nature or identity.[30]

In other words, the gender distinctions that are central to what is here called the "argument from symbolism" are simply not present in the Hebrew Bible (Old Testament). The most significant assumption concerning male-female symbolism in the Bible is that women are like men.

When and where, then, did notions of sexually bifurcated male-female symbolism enter Jewish, and later Christian, thought? In a chapter entitled "Gifts of the Greeks," Frymer-Kensky points to a significant change in Jewish thought that took place after the conquest of Alexander the Great in 333 B.C.E. In contrast to the model found in the Hebrew Bible, the Greek social system was "very gender-segregated": "Greek philosophy portrayed females as inherently and essentially different from men, and fundamentally less valued. The male-female distinction was one of the great polarities of the Greek dualistic system." Males represented civilized humanity, while women were "untamed" and "animal-like" and needed to be controlled by men.[31] Greek mythology portrays relationships between men and women as a "battle of the sexes." Misogyny and anti-woman themes are prevalent in Greek literature. Both Plato and Aristotle understand women to be inferior and defective.

The Greeks also glorified pederastic homophilia while reinforcing the separation of the sexes, the limitation of public life to men, and the confinement of women to the domestic sphere.[32]

Jewish writings from the Hellenistic period began to reflect Greek influence. For example, the deuterocanonical Wisdom of Ben Sira (Sirach) states: "Better is the wickedness of a man than a woman who does good; and it is a woman who brings shame and disgrace" (Sir. 42:14, RSV). Sirach blames the fall into sin on Eve rather than Adam: "From a woman sin had its beginning, and because of her we all die" (25:24). Sirach warns men of the dangers of beautiful women, and advises men against their attractions (9:8-9). Later Jewish writings such as the Testaments of the Twelve Patriarchs and the Mishnah forbid men and women to be alone together. In the Talmud, the mere sight of a woman is enough to tempt even the greatest of men. In the Hellenistic period, Jewish women began to be separated and excluded from men, and completely excluded from public life. Women were separated from men in public worship, and discouraged from participation in community prayer. The Hellenistic Jewish philosopher Philo used "male" and "female" as philosophical opposites and developed a "symbolic misogyny" of the sexes. Frymer-Kensky writes: "The rabbinic system represents a dramatic change from the Bible in the conceptualization of women and sex. In place of the Bible's portrayal of women and men as fundamentally similar, the rabbis express a gender-polarized view of humanity."[33]

Frymer-Kensky suggests that the church fathers, as heirs to both the Bible and Hellenism, also embraced this "gender-polarized and negative view of women."[34] Similarly, New Testament scholar Ben Witherington III writes of a retreat from the more egalitarian understanding of the relationship between men and women in the New Testament to a hierarchical view rooted largely in a distrust of female sexuality. What Witherington calls a "deficient view of human sexuality" led to a heightened emphasis on asceticism accompanied by an exalting of celibacy and virginity. Christian marriage came to be seen as a "second best" in comparison to celibacy, and, insofar as they were defined by their sexuality, women fell under suspicion as being temptresses and sources of sin. To the extent that virginity became the highest ideal, women were given only two choices in the church: they could pursue some sort of celibate ministry as deaconesses, virgins, or widows, or they could marry, in which case their role was restricted to that of wife and mother. Witherington summarizes the situation for women in the patristic period:

> Nowhere do we hear of a healthy balance where both one's human sexuality and spiritual gifts are affirmed. Certainly by the fourth century, life in the Church had become a clear either/or proposition with women in ministry being linked to a transcending or abandoning of any affirmation of their sexual identity.[35]

Finally, as discussed in an earlier chapter, Christian theologians as early as Origen blamed women for the fall into sin, considered them to be dangerous sources of male temptation, and to be less intelligent, more subject to emotion, and more easily tempted than men.[36]

In light of the above, it is significant that the bifurcated male-female sexual symbolism that is so central to Hauke's argument finds its roots not in the biblical account of men and women, but in the non-Christian Hellenistic world of Plato, Aristotle, and the Hellenized Judaism of Philo. There is an ironic parallel between this version of symbolic theology and the radical feminist theology that Hauke finds so objectionable. In both cases, there is an appeal outside of the Christian faith for normative ideological principles in the light of which the Christian Scriptures are then reinterpreted. For feminist theology, the principle is "female liberation"; for the anti-women's ordination version of "symbolic" theology, the principle is a sexual bifurcation that is rooted not in Scripture, but in pagan non-Christian understandings of the relation between the sexes.

A TRINITARIAN CORRECTIVE

A previous chapter on the priesthood of Christ noted the tendency of Western eucharistic theologies to be binitarian in focusing (almost) exclusively on the roles of the Father and the Son to the neglect of the Holy Spirit, and Christomonist not only in focusing exclusively on the role of Christ but "Apollinarian" in the sense of focusing exclusively on the deity of Christ to the neglect of his humanity, particularly of his human mind and will. Hauke's theology shares in these characteristics.

Hauke's male-female symbol system plays itself out in a contrast between God (as transcendent) and creation (as immanent), of the male as representing transcendence and the female as representing immanence, of the male as external and the female as internal, of the male as active and the female as receptive, and of the male as substantive and the female as relational. Two key quotes are essential to Hauke's argument:

> "*The basic axis of the symbolism of the sexes* can thus be equated with the relationships *man = God, woman = creation.*"[37]

> "The relations Christ-Mary and Christ-Church are the points on which the symbolism of the sexes turns."[38]

The schema can be illustrated as follows:

Transcendent (Male): God → Christ → Priest

Immanent (Female): Creation → Mary → Church → Laity

Hauke writes: "A personal image of God is always bound up with sexual references."[39] The male is symbolic of transcendence, and thus of God. According to Hauke:

The masculine nature, in particular, is more strongly directed toward mastery of the external world than is that of women. But this task of mastery appears as a specific consequence of being a likeness of God. . . . [J]ust as women represent creation, so, in a special way, man represents God. . . . [M]asculine symbolism is more closely apposite to the personal image of God than is its feminine counterpart. . . . The mother embodies divine immanence, a multirelational embeddedness in the world. God's personality, however, is bound up in a special way with transcendence.[40]

In contrast, Hauke associates immanence, receptivity, and creation with the female:

Receptivity, openness, readiness are the appropriate attitudes in the presence of the Creator. As we have seen, however, this receptivity is, to a higher degree, a characteristic of women. Consequently, the female human being is more likely to be suitably representative of the state of creaturely being before God. Woman is, in a sense, a *likeness of creation.* . . . *As symbolic of human receptivity,* women are simultaneously emblems of deep-rooted, personal, *devotion* to God, for precisely, in receiving, the soul simultaneously engages in a state of highest activity.[41]

Because of their "eccentric symbolism," which is "oriented toward sovereignty and power," Hauke states that men are "not suited to representing adequately this attitude of open receptivity."[42]

TRINITARIAN PERSONALISM AS A CORRECTIVE TO BINARY CONTRAST

The revival of Trinitarian theology and of an associated Trinitarian personalism has been one of the most characteristic developments of the theology of the last few decades. This has been an ecumenical project, shared by Roman Catholics, Orthodox, Protestants, and Anglicans. The Swiss Reformed theologian Karl Barth's Trinitarian theology was the major impetus in this development. In the area of sexuality, Barth advocated a Trinitarian personalism and argued that the creation of humanity in the image of God *as male and female* echoed the Trinitarian relations; to be created as a human being in the image of God means to be inherently oriented toward relation toward other persons as grounded in the inherent relationality of the sexes (man and woman) toward one another.[43]

Hauke's book appeared just prior to the recent Trinitarian revival, and he explicitly repudiates Barth's theology of male-female sexuality as reflective of the Trinitarian relations:

That man must be an essentially relational being because God is in relationship with himself cannot be derived in this way from the biblical text. . . . Barth seems to assume that relationship defines the essence of man in the same way that it grounds the three Persons of the Trinity. . . . [I]f Barth equates the relationship of man and woman with their essences . . . then the independent natures of each are dissolved.[44]

Hauke rather assigns different aspects of personalism to men and to women: Where Trinitarian personalism associates personhood with the relationality common to both men and women, Hauke contrasts the personal nature of men and women. He insists that men are more representative of God's personhood because personhood is primarily *individual*, while women, because they are more *relational*, are less so:

> If the experience of a personal God presupposes the transcendence of the soul and of God himself, then it aligns itself with masculine symbolism. Women, of course, are persons just as much as are men, but their personhood is lived out more strongly through relationships; they are, to a special degree, relational beings. . . . Women are no less persons than are men, but the individual, self-dependent reality of the personal is just symbolized to a lesser degree in women.[45]

To the contrary, a Trinitarian personalism would claim that Hauke's dichotomy between the "individual" and the "relational" is a false contrast. Roman Catholic philosophical theologian W. Norris Clarke, S.J., expresses the point well in the title of his essay "To Be Is to Be Substance in Relation."[46] In a book considering the implications of Trinitarian personalism entitled *Person and Being*, Clarke argues that "drawing upon God's own self-revelation in the doctrine of the Trinity (three Persons within one Divine Being) can here illumine the very nature of being, as well as of God." The doctrine of the Trinity means that the "very inner life of God himself . . . is by its very nature *self-communicative Love*," and that consequently, "self-communication is written into the very heart of all beings, as finite but positive images of their Source."[47]

At the heart of Clarke's argument is that all reality possesses both an "in-itself" and a "towards-the-other" dimension. Within the Triune Divine Being, substantiality and relationality are "primordial" and "necessary" in that God is three persons in one nature. All creatures manifest both relationality and substantiality in that they are all in some sense reflections of the God who is their creative source: "All being, therefore, is, by its very nature as being, *dyadic*, with an 'introverted,' or *in-itself* dimension, as substance, and an 'extraverted,' or *towards-others* dimension, as related through action."[48] In terms of human personhood, Clarke argues that all persons must possess a "self-presence," which enables them to meaningfully say "I" and engage in responsible action, but also a relationality toward the other as "Thou," in which we respond to another self. It is only in relation to others that we can return to our self to achieve self-possession: "Thus, a personalized being must obey the basic dyadic ontological structure of all being, that is, *presence in itself and presence to others*."[49] To be a person, therefore, is "to be-in-communion," and communication between persons entails both giving and receiving. Accordingly, Clarke insists that mutuality is essential to love, and that the "ontological value of receptivity" is "not a defect or inferiority but a positive perfection of being."[50] Self-communication and receptivity are thus "complementary and inseparable sides of the dynamic process of being itself," and Clarke insists that in the Trinity itself, "receptivity is present in the Son and the Spirit at its most intense." The Father is "subsistent Self-communication," while the Son and Spirit are "subsistent Receptivity."[51]

Crucial for the current discussion is that the distinctions between transcendence and immanence, between substance and relationality, between action and receptivity, which Hauke portrays as contrasting characteristics of men and women, and thus crucial to his distinction between masculine and feminine symbolism, should not be understood as contrastive, but rather complementary and dyadic, and as characteristic not of men and women respectively, but of all persons. Communication and personhood are impossible without both transcendence and immanence, action and receptivity, substantiality and relationality being present in both persons in the conversation. These are not male or female characteristics, but simply human and personal characteristics. Hauke's male-female symbolism divides and assigns alternatively to the male and female sexes characteristic of persons as such which intrinsically belong together and which cannot be parceled out, and without which persons would not be persons, but isolated monads.

A TRINITARIAN ACCOUNT OF TRANSCENDENCE AND IMMANENCE

Hauke's theology is binary throughout, with transcendence (equated with masculinity) and immanence (equated with femininity) marking the primary distinction. This binary dichotomy is fundamental not only for his discussion of male and female human beings but for his discussion of the Trinitarian persons as well. As noted above (and in the previous chapter), Hauke points to transcendence as the primary identifying characteristic of both God the Father and God the Son. Hauke certainly acknowledges Jesus Christ's humanity:

> Jesus Christ is *the* representative of God. . . . It is not only in his divinity but also in his human nature that Christ is a likeness and a representative of his Father. . . . Certainly, God's becoming man is the fundamental precondition for our redemption, which Christ effected representatively for women as well as men. . . . Jesus Christ, through his human nature, represented not only men in relation to God but also women. Just as the mother symbol is, in a sense, enclosed within the father symbol, so Jesus, too, embodies "feminine" values, such as kindness and mildness.[52]

However, the emphasis throughout is on Jesus' transcendence and masculinity: "[A]ll of Christ's tasks are inseparably bound up with his masculinely stamped human nature."[53] The humanity of Christ does not play a significant role in Hauke's discussion. What is important about Jesus is that he is God. So Hauke writes: "Thus Jesus' benevolence can be understood only through his omnipotence," and, "The humbling of Jesus can only be understood, however, when in its enduring starting point is kept in view, namely, infinite divine power." Even when Hauke speaks of Jesus as representative of humanity, Hauke says little or nothing about the significance of Jesus' humanity *as* receptive, either to God or humanity: "Whereas Jesus' love appears, with respect to sinners, as mercifulness, it takes on, with respect to his turning toward God, the aspects of *righteousness*."[54]

Despite Hauke's claim to be presenting orthodox Christology, the implicit logic of his position seems to be monophysite or perhaps Apollinarian. Is Jesus Christ omnipotent, possessing "infinite divine power" *as* human? This would seem to be a confusion or conflation of the incarnate Word's divine and human natures. Significantly, Hauke never portrays Jesus Christ as receptive. That is always the role of the church and, particularly, of the church as female (to be discussed below).

Hauke does associate immanence with the mission of the Holy Spirit, the third person of the Trinity. Hauke identifies the Holy Spirit with the "feminine" characteristics of (1) immanence: "God's immanence in nature and grace is thus attributed, in a special way, to the Holy Spirit, because he is himself the intradivine immanence in person"; (2) relationality: "In themselves, the Divine Persons are, of course, substantial relationship. Still, to the Holy Spirit, we can attribute, in a special way, a mode of being that, although sustained by personal identity, is exhaustively constituted in and through relationality. . . . Now 'relationality' is characteristic to a greater degree of women than of men"; and (3) receptivity: "[T]he Holy Spirit is constituted only by receiving. In a certain sense, then, we can therefore, 'designate' him 'as the feminine principle in the divinity. . . . He is, in fact, the divinely receiving.'"[55]

If men resemble the male Christ, Hauke suggests that women resemble the Holy Spirit. He writes, "Woman is, in a certain respect, an image of the Holy Spirit," and: "Thus, we find in the Holy Spirit certain characteristics that can link up with feminine symbolism, such as immanence, relationality, and above all his identity as receptive."[56] Hauke makes a specific connection between the symbolically feminine characteristics of the Holy Spirit and the church as the bride of Christ: "The relation Christ-Spirit corresponds to the relation husband-wife, but also to the relation Christ-Church."[57] Hauke is quick, however, to discourage any conclusions that might be drawn concerning the "feminine" symbolism of the Holy Spirit and women's ordination: "[I]n contrast to a *repraesentatio Christi*, we will hardly encounter an explicit *repraesentatio Spiritus Sanctus*."[58] But, of course, the counterargument would not be that the presiding minister (whether man or woman) represents the Holy Spirit (*repraesentatio Spiritus Sanctus*), but rather that, as offering the eucharistic prayer on behalf of the congregation, the celebrant speaks in the person of the church (*in persona ecclesiae*) and thus represents the church, which, as the bride of Christ, is symbolically feminine.

The binary structure of Hauke's schema can again be laid out (with slight modification):

Transcendent (Male): God the Father → Jesus Christ → Men

Immanent (Female): God the Holy Spirit → Women → Church

What is significantly missing from Hauke's schema and marks it as implicitly monophysite or Apollinarian is the Chalcedonian dimension. A properly Trinitarian and Chalcedonian account of transcendence and immanence could acknowledge what Hauke says about the transcendence of God the Father—given that creation is "attributed" to the Father—and the immanence of the Holy Spirit as the indwelling principle of grace and as the link between the church and the other two Trinitarian persons. What is missing from Hauke's schema is the significance of the incarnation, the hypostatic union, and the full Chalcedonian definition. The hypostatic union means that Jesus Christ is a divine person with two complete natures, one divine and one human. It is thus Jesus Christ (who as God is Creator and as human is creature) who is the perfect meeting place between transcendence and immanence. As the second person of the Trinity, the Word of God is transcendent over all creation; in him, "all things were created . . . all things were created through him and for him . . . and in him all things hold together" (Col. 1:16-17; cf. John 1:1-3). But as human, Jesus Christ is also the "Word made flesh" (John 1:14); in Jesus Christ, "the whole fullness of deity dwells bodily" (Col. 2:9). Although the preincarnate Son existed "in the form of God" (Phil. 2:6), he took on the "form of a servant," existing in "human form" (Phil. 2:6-8). As the Chalcedonian formula states, Jesus Christ is "one and the same Son . . . truly God and truly human . . . of one substance with the Father as regards his Godhead, and at the same time of one substance with us as regards his manhood." Accordingly, a genuinely Trinitarian account of transcendence and immanence would have to modify Hauke's schema in something like the following manner:

Transcendent (Neither Male nor Female): God the Father

Fully Transcendent and Fully Immanent: the incarnate Son of God, Jesus Christ

Immanent: God the Holy Spirit → Church (Both Men and Women)

As God incarnate, Jesus Christ is both fully transcendent and fully immanent. He is active, but also receptive, substantive, and relational. If the Father represents transcendence and the Spirit represents immanence, then the incarnate Son represents both transcendence and immanence. As noted above, the nature of the person is both communicating and receiving—active and receptive. The Son as God incarnate is both God speaking to humanity and humanity responding to God. It is this emphasis on the humanity of Jesus Christ as being representative of humanity in responding to God that is missing in Hauke's binary account.

A CHRISTOCENTRIC AND TRINITARIAN ACCOUNT OF WORSHIP

One of the most important modern discussions of the theology of worship is found in Thomas F. Torrance's essays "The Paschal Mystery of Christ and the Eucharist" and "The Mind of Christ in Worship: The Problem of Apollinarianism in the Liturgy."[59] These essays have already been discussed at some length, and readers are referred there for a full discussion.[60] Two key points are central, however. First, following Cyril of Alexandria, Torrance argued that a key theme for the theology of worship is the "vicarious humanity" of Jesus Christ and its significance for the church's participation in Christ's priesthood: "[T]he key to the understanding of the Eucharist is to be sought in the vicarious humanity of Jesus, the priesthood of the incarnate Son. Eternal God though he was, he condescended to be our brother."[61] A key theme in Cyril's theology was that during his earthly ministry, Jesus as human was anointed with the Holy Spirit and prayed to and worshiped God the Father. After his resurrection and ascension, the risen Jesus Christ permanently retained his human nature, including his human mind, and exercises his priesthood by interceding for the church and by offering worship to God the Father. The church's own worship is a participation in the worship of the risen Christ. Torrance writes:

> Jesus Christ ascended to the Father [is] the Mediator of our worship in mind and soul and body in union with him. It is as our Priest, with all his human condition in body, mind and soul which he took from us, with his human worship and prayer in which he assimilates our worship and prayer in his name, that he appears in the presence of his Father and fulfils his heavenly ministry as Priest over the House of God.[62]

Second, Torrance argued that this centrality of Christ's vicarious humanity had been lost in much of the church's worship after the patristic era, resulting in what he called "Apollinarianism in the liturgy." One of the consequences of this loss was the substitution of various other mediators to make up for the loss of the humanity of Christ: "[T]he Church was thrown back upon itself to provide a priesthood which could stand in for Christ, and even mediate between the sinner and Christ ..."[63]

Paradoxically, although the subject of Hauke's book is the "ordination of women," there is very little in the way of a theology of worship or liturgy in his book. What he does say confirms the concerns raised by Torrance. As noted above, Hauke says very little about the significance of the humanity of Christ, and nothing about the significance of Jesus' human mind and will. In the closest thing to such a discussion, Hauke contrasts Jesus and Mary. Hauke states that Mary exercises faith, but Jesus does not:

> Thus the way for the obedience of the "new Adam" is prepared by the "new Eve." In this, the significance of Mary extends far beyond that of her predecessor. Nowhere in the New Testament does Jesus appear as a believer, because he does not first have to endorse his revelation but proclaims it himself as one who sees. In contrast, the Mother of God is, by virtue of her belief, the first and exemplary Christian.[64]

Hauke associates faith with dependence and receptivity, making it a primarily feminine quality: "Faith is always related to obedience, to subordination. Women, because of their biological constitution, possess in principle a greater readiness for this than do men."[65]

Contrary to Hauke's claim here, there has been considerable recent discussion among New Testament scholars concerning Jesus' exercise of faith, with numerous advocates of the "New Perspective on Paul" arguing that Paul's expression πίστις Χριστοῦ (*pistis Christou*, Gal. 2:16) should be translated as the "faith of Christ" or the "faithfulness of Christ" rather than "faith in Christ." Just as significant would be a passage such as Hebrews 5:7: "In the days of his flesh, Jesus offered up prayers and supplications, with loud cries and tears, to him who was able to save him from death, and he was heard because of his reverence." Nowhere in Hauke's book is there any discussion of the significance of Jesus' own prayer to God or his own anointing *as human* with the Holy Spirit. For Hauke, the significance of Jesus' mediatorial role is consistently that Jesus is on the side of God—that he represents God *to human beings.*

In discussing priesthood, Hauke ascribes to the priest as mediator that which the New Testament ascribes uniquely to Jesus Christ: "A 'priest' in the broadest sense of the world, is a mediator between God and man." Hauke ascribes two functions to the priest: First, the "representation of the Divinity in relation to man. When the emphasis is on transcendence and the active workings of God . . . it seems appropriate to reserve the priesthood for men." Second, the "public representation of man in relation to the Divinity. For this, too, men tend to be more suitable. As the representative of his community, a man steps, so to speak 'outward' into the presence of God."[66] Note that Hauke gives to the human priest the mediating role that the New Testament gives to Jesus Christ. Also, Hauke sees the priest as representing God (in the divine nature) rather than Jesus Christ in his humanity.

As noted in a previous chapter, the Roman Catholic theologian Yves Congar regretted the tendency of Roman Catholic theology to substitute the pope, the Virgin

Mary, and the sacrament of the mass for the Holy Spirit.[67] Certainly Hauke tends to associate Mary particularly with the Holy Spirit, but also ascribes to Mary the role of mediating the Holy Spirit that the New Testament gives to the risen Jesus Christ (John 14:16; 16:7). Hauke writes: "Mary can, therefore, be characterized as 'the most perfect human personal image of the Holy Spirit.' . . . Mary does not replace the Holy Spirit, but mediates him through her intercession."[68] Hauke gives to Mary the role of representative of humanity that Torrance claims patristic theologians such as Cyril gave to the vicarious humanity of Christ. In fact, Hauke specifically denies this representative role to Jesus' humanity. Hauke writes:

> In her receptiveness, Mary is thus, in a special measure, *the representative of creation as creation.* . . . [S]he represents *mankind.* . . . The representation of mankind through Mary . . . is thus precisely not to be identified with the task of Jesus. . . . [T]hus the virginal conception of Jesus implies a priority of woman in the representation of creation and of mankind before God.[69]

It seems clear then that Hauke's binary account is an example of the kind of Apollinarian liturgical theology to which Torrance objects. Hauke says nothing about the role of the vicarious humanity of Jesus Christ in worship, either as receptive or as worshiping on behalf of humanity with his human mind and will. The mediatory role that church fathers such as Cyril applied to the risen Christ, who exercises his priesthood as the crucified, ascended, and risen representative of humanity, Hauke applies to the Virgin Mary instead.

Hauke consistently follows through with his binary male-female symbolism as he explains the roles of the apostle Peter and Mary in the church: "While Peter assumes the role of 'head' of the Church and proclaims the gospel at Pentecost, Mary appears earlier as the 'heart' of those who plead in prayer for the descent of the Holy Spirit."[70] Hauke characterizes the church as Marian (and feminine) in being receptive, while ordained clergy, because they represent Christ, are "intermediaries" or "mediators" who play the masculine Petrine role:

> [T]he Church is Marian in her basic structure and therefore exhibits, in contrast to Christ and his official representatives, typically feminine traits. . . . [A]s members of the Church, the office bearers are, in the first instance, receptively and cooperatively active like all other believers. In their specific representation of Christ, they are also distinct from and in contrast to the Church, but only as "intermediaries" and "instruments." They represent the Lord, from whom they themselves are different.[71]

In contrast to Hauke's binary account of the roles of clergy and laity in the church, a personalistic Trinitarian and Christocentric account of worship takes full account not only of the reciprocity and mutuality of substance and relation as intrinsic to personhood as such, but also of the vicarious humanity of Christ as central to a theology of worship, and would include the following.

In God's own nature, God is neither transcendent nor immanent, but Trinitarian and relational. The divine persons are both active and receptive. God is active (as Father), receptive and active (as Son), and receptive (as the Holy Spirit). To be a person is thus to be both communicating and receiving, active and receptive.

In the act of creation, God has shared the love between the Trinitarian persons with creatures. Created in the image of God, humanity as male and female reflects triune personalism. Both men and women are mutually active and receptive, oriented toward communion first with God and second with one another, and are more alike than different. Both men and women are created in the image of God; God has given the creation mandate equally to women and men (Gen. 1:27-28). The relation between male and female is complementary not in terms of gender roles but in terms of personal relationality. To be male or female is to be oriented toward and in mutual communication with the other. Neither man nor woman is complete without the other.

In terms of the relation between God and creation, the divine persons manifest transcendence and immanence in a Trinitarian manner. Although creation is a task of all three persons of the Trinity, creation (and thus transcendence) is attributed primarily to God the Father. The world is created through the Son of God, who, as the Word Incarnate, is both fully divine and fully human, both Creator (transcendent) and creature (immanent). In the beginning of creation, the Holy Spirit "hovered over the waters" (Gen. 1:2), and, as indwelling the church (immanent), is the link between the church (redeemed creation) and the Triune God (Creator) as the Spirit unites redeemed men and women (creatures) to Christ's risen humanity (creature) through the hypostatic union (Creator). Only Jesus Christ can properly represent God because only Jesus Christ is a divine person with a human nature. In terms of the symbolism of transcendence and immanence, if the Father represents transcendence, and the Spirit represents immanence, then the incarnate Son represents both transcendence and immanence, God speaking to humanity, but also humanity responding to God.

Christian worship is a participation in the risen Jesus Christ's worship through means of his vicarious humanity. Union with the risen Christ through the Holy Spirit is crucial. Christ both acts in the Eucharist, but also acts as worshiping the Father on behalf of the church.

Use of a binary contrasting male-female symbolism to define the nature of worship is an example of the loss of Jesus Christ's vicarious humanity. In Hauke's model, the male Christ represents God, but it is rather the role of the Virgin Mary to take the place of Christ's humanity in representing humanity. Accordingly, the church does not participate in Jesus Christ's vicarious human worship. Rather, Christ *as God* is set over against a human church. For Hauke, the priest as male represents

Christ *as God*, and thus the priest becomes an intermediary. That is, it is the ordained male priest who fulfills Christ's divine function in respect to the church. It is the Virgin Mary as female who represents *receptive* humanity and the church. To the contrary, in a properly Trinitarian and Christocentric theology, it is Jesus Christ in his vicarious humanity who represents both deity and humanity. Thus, the church's Christian worship is participation in the risen Christ's human worship. Our worship (including the priest's) is participatory in the worship of the crucified and risen Christ and points away from anything we might offer to the offering of Jesus Christ on our behalf.

How do ordained clergy and the church represent Christ? The human office holder (presbyter/bishop) does not represent God in the divine nature, but rather represents the incarnate Jesus Christ as an icon pointing away from himself or herself to Jesus Christ's finished work, and sharing in suffering. The ordained priest is not Jesus Christ. The priest is an earthen vessel (2 Cor. 4:7-12). As a baptized member of the redeemed community, the priest represents Christ only because he or she first represents the church of which Jesus Christ is the head.

In terms of the distinctive typological roles of the apostle Peter and Mary the mother of Jesus, if Peter represents the active apostolic role, and Mary represents receptive faith, then both roles are true of the entire church, since activity and receptivity are personal characteristics, not gender characteristics. Activity is not specifically masculine; nor is receptivity distinctively feminine; rather, to be a person is to be both active and receptive. As an apostle, Peter represents Jesus Christ not by being active or by physically resembling the male Jesus Christ, but by feeding Christ's sheep, by following in Jesus' way to the cross, and by pointing away from himself to the crucified and risen Lord Jesus Christ. The Virgin Mary represents the church not in her femininity, not by herself being the perfect response to grace, but by being the *Theotokos*, the human bearer of the God-man who is himself the perfect response to grace—insofar as throughout his earthly ministry, Jesus followed in the leading of the Holy Spirit through whom he was conceived and who anointed Jesus and indwelt him at his baptism in the Jordan River.

Finally, in terms of the symbolically representative role of the clergy, it is important to remember the difference between representation as imitation and the representative as a delegate. An ordained presbyter is a delegate, not an imitator or a mimic. The office holder is not acting a part or playing a role in a play. In worship, the triune God addresses humanity, and humanity responds with praise, thanksgiving, confession, and supplication; as leader of the church's worship, the presbyter speaks both to the church on behalf of the triune God (as a delegate, not an imitator) and responds from the church to God, addressing the church's prayer on its behalf to

God the Father through participation in the vicarious worship of the crucified and risen Jesus Christ in the unity of the Holy Spirit. In doing so, the ordained clergy engage in an activity of communication and communion which is inherently both active and receptive—that is, an activity which is primarily personal, not primarily gendered. Theologically, there is no reason why both women and men should not perform this task.

The Ministry of Women in the New Testament

15

Women's Ministry in the New Testament

Office

Previous chapters have addressed theological objections to the ordination of women, both Protestant and Catholic. The next two chapters will discuss the actual ministry of women in the New Testament. What actual ministerial roles did women exercise during the New Testament period, and what might be the implications for current ecclesial practice? Three issues will be addressed: (1) Did women exercise ministerial office in the New Testament period? (2) How does the New Testament address the question of female bishops, presbyters, and/or deacons? (3) What are the contemporary hermeneutical implications of what the New Testament says about women in office? That is, what should be the church's current practice in light of New Testament material concerning women in office? This chapter will address the first question: Did women exercise ministerial office in the New Testament period?

NEW TESTAMENT OFFICE

Roman Catholic theologian Francis Martin brings a helpful contribution to the discussion of the ministry of women in the New Testament by distinguishing between (1) charisms of service, (2) ministry, and (3) office. A charism of service is a particular endowment given by the Holy Spirit that enables a member of the Christian community to contribute to the life of that community. Examples of charisms of service would be prophecy, teaching, words of wisdom or knowledge, speaking, interpretation of tongues, or helping others (1 Cor. 12:4-11, 28; 14; 1 Pet. 4:11). Ministry refers to divinely enabled activities that build up the Christian community and have a more permanent basis. More permanent ministerial gifts would include leadership, some forms of diaconal service, or itinerant preaching (Rom. 12:7-8; 1 Cor. 12:28). Office refers to a stable ministry that secures the permanence of apostolic teaching over space and time. Office works within the corporeal and historical nature of the church, and must be transmitted through some form of human activity. Office is particularly bound up with "remembering" the apostolic message, particularly the life, death, and resurrection of Jesus. The ministerial gifts that enable a person to exercise office include presiding over the faithful transmission of the gospel through word and sacrament in worship. Office is particularly associated with the ministry of presbyters and bishops.[1]

This is precisely the distinction that needs to be made to address the issue of women's ministry and the ordination of women in the church. No one denies (not even Protestant complementarians) that women exercised what Martin calls "charisms of service" in the New Testament church, and presumably may do so today as well. No one denies that women exercised some forms of more permanent ministry in the New Testament church, and may do so today—what might now be designated as "lay ministries"—although Protestant complementarians and Catholic sacramentalists disagree about what kind of permanent ministries might be allowed to women in the contemporary church. For both Protestant complementarians and Catholic sacramentalists, the prohibition lies in the exercise of office; they disagree in their understanding of ordination to office involving different tasks, whether holding authority and teaching or celebrating of the sacraments.

Given the clear distinction between charisms of service and more permanent ongoing ministries, the crucial difference for the current discussion is between more permanent ministries and "office." Given that some women in the New Testament period exercised more permanent forms of ministry, were any of these positions of office? The question is not as straightforward as it might appear for the following reasons.

First, during the New Testament period, the distinction between charism, ministry, and office is not always clear. Martin writes: "There was a period when the charisms, ministries and offices . . . were not differentiated, though they clearly existed and achieved differentiation and identifiability as the church grew."[2] Prophecy, for example, can be a charism of service, since Paul encourages all to "prophecy" (1 Cor. 14:5-19); when the church comes together, each is to have a "teaching" or "revelation" (1 Cor. 14:26). In distinction, other examples of prophecy seem to imply a kind of ongoing ministry (1 Cor. 14:32, 37; Rom. 12:8; Acts 11:27-28; 15:27-33; 21:9). Finally, "prophet" can also refer to someone who holds an office; that is, exercises some kind of supervisory role in the community (1 Cor. 12:28; Eph. 4:11). Similarly, "teaching" may refer to a transient charismatic gift (1 Cor. 12:8; 14:26), but it also can refer to a more stable permanent ministry (Rom. 12:7; Col. 3:16). In most cases, however, teaching refers to an authoritative function of the transmission of the gospel, an "office." In the Book of Acts, "teaching" is the task of apostles (Acts 2:42; 4:2, 18; 5:21, 25, 28, 42; 13:1; 15:35; 18:11; 20:20; 21:21, 28; 28:31). In the Pastoral Epistles, the term applies to Paul as an apostle (1 Tim. 2:7; 2 Tim. 1:11). In Ephesians 4:11, "teacher" is listed as an office alongside apostle, prophet, evangelist, and shepherd. In a given case, then, it may not be clear whether the description of a particular task or title refers to a charism, a permanent ministry, or an "office."[3]

How then to distinguish between ministry and office? Martin acknowledges: "It is obvious that we are not going to find the reality of office existing in a clearly distinct form in the New Testament"—first, because of "fluidity of language" (the same term can be used in more than one way), and second, because many of the charisms and ministries of the New Testament church were later absorbed by office.[4] Martin suggests two indications of the development of office in the New Testament. First is the assurance with which some New Testament figures teach or exercise authority. The apostle Paul would be a prime example. Second would be the exercise of leadership roles. In Acts, Luke refers to "elders" (presbyters) and "overseers" (bishops). Paul's letters refer to "elders" and "overseers" as well as "deacons." In 1 Thessalonians 5:12, Paul refers to those who "labor among you" and are "over you in the Lord." The Book of Hebrews refers to "leaders" who preach the word and "keep watch over your souls" (Heb. 13:7, 17). At the same time, Martin acknowledges that New Testament terminology for office—apostle, overseer, leader, deacon, prophet, teacher, caretaker, and laborer—is fluid and unfixed.[5]

Second, the New Testament simply does not address some of the characteristics essential to Martin's definition of office. The New Testament says nothing about who presided at the celebration of the Lord's Supper/Eucharist in the first-century church or how the eucharistic service was structured. Concern for faithful historical transmission of the gospel through a formal activity of the church—in the specific manner of second-century and historic Catholic discussions of apostolic succession—is not addressed in the New Testament because the apostles were still alive when the New Testament documents were written.

Finally, except for individuals identified specifically as apostles (either the original twelve, Paul, or James the brother of Jesus) or the rare exceptions such as Timothy and Titus, who are assigned specific pastoral responsibilities (1 Tim. 1:3; 4:11-16; 5:1-25; 6:2, 17-20; 2 Tim. 1:6, 14; 2:2, 14-18; 4:1-4; Titus 1:5-9; 2:1-10, 15; 3:1-2, 10), the New Testament does not unequivocally identify specific individuals as exercising the task of what Martin calls "office." For example, opponents of women's ordination sometimes object that the New Testament nowhere identifies any woman by name as a bishop/overseer or presbyter/elder. However, apart from a single reference in 1 Peter 2:25 to Christ as the "bishop/overseer" of your souls, the New Testament nowhere identifies any man by name with these titles either. Rather, the terms are generally applied to groups, and never to specifically named individuals: presbyters/elders (Acts 11:30; 14:23; 15:2, 4, 6, 22, 23; 21:18; 1 Tim. 4:14; 5:17, 19; Titus 1:5; Jas. 5:14; 1 Pet. 5:1, 5; 2 John 1:1; 3 John 1:2), bishops/ overseers (Acts 20:28; Phil. 1:1; 1 Tim. 3:1, 2; Titus 1:7).[6]

These ambiguities are precisely the problem with Martin's concluding statement concerning the exercise of office by women in the New Testament: "The fact that even at the earliest level, when women were rightfully prominent and influential because of their gifts and services, there is no clear evidence that a woman was ever an office holder, is not an accident of the data, nor a patriarchal reading of it."[7] Given the acknowledged fluidity and ambiguity of the language applied to ministry and office in the New Testament, and, given that, with the exceptions of the apostles as well as Timothy and Titus, to whom roles of "office" are specifically assigned, there is "no clear evidence" that specific men were named as office holders either, the strong conclusion that Martin draws from the evidence concerning women holding office is not warranted.

WOMEN OFFICE HOLDERS IN THE NEW TESTAMENT

Given the above ambiguities, any case that there were women office holders in the New Testament would have to be implied. Nonetheless, a careful examination of the evidence indicates that a strong case can be made that Paul's letter to the Romans mentions three women who not only exercised what Martin calls permanent ministries, but also exercised ministries of church office.

Light can be shed on what Paul says about women in ministry by first looking at what he writes about ministry in general. Although Paul is clear that all members of the church have been given gifts of the Spirit for the common good (1 Cor. 12:7), Paul also acknowledges authority figures in the congregation. In Galatians 6:6, he speaks of local teachers. In 1 Corinthians 12:28, he seems to indicate a hierarchical order: (1) apostles, (2) prophets, (3) teachers, and (4) miracle workers and those with other charismatic gifts. Ben Witherington III points to the following specific ministries in Paul's writings: leader, administrator, or overseer (ἐπίσκοπος, *episkopos*; Rom. 12:8; 1 Cor. 12:28; Phil. 1:1); deacon (διάκονος, *diakonos*; Phil. 1:1); fellow-worker (συνεργός, *synergos*). The leadership pattern in Paul's churches is that of (1) apostles; (2) Paul's "fellow-workers"—traveling companions who had authority over and were involved in several congregations; and (3) local leaders. Those with greater financial resources could provide meeting places, patronage, protection, and lodging, which could lead to a kind of church leadership. At the same time, Paul's approach to leadership was neither based on traditional social distinctions, nor, on the other hand, was it merely pragmatic or democratic. Paul's primary criteria for leadership was that of service in building up the body of Christ. In this way, although Paul did not abolish social distinctions he used them for the benefit of the church, and thus turned normal social categories upside down.[8]

In Romans 16, Paul concludes his letter with a series of greetings that reads something like a letter of recommendation. This would not have been unusual, since there were no methods of modern communication in the ancient world, and letters of recommendation were vital. People would often send letters along with travelers they knew, and, in this case, Paul recommends Phoebe, who was likely the carrier of his letter and whom Paul commends to the church in Rome (Rom. 16:1).[9] Paul names twenty-six people in the letter, the majority of whom seem to be Jewish Christians in Rome. The letter is addressed to the Gentile majority, however, whom Paul is encouraging to welcome these Jewish Christians and include them in fellowship. Paul does not directly greet his friends, co-workers, and relatives whom he mentions in the list. Rather, by asking his Gentile audience to do it for him, Paul is likely hoping to effect some kind of reconciliation between Jewish and Gentile Christians in Rome.[10]

One of the most interesting characteristics of the list is the large number of women Paul mentions. Out of twenty-six persons mentioned, ten (including Phoebe, the letter carrier) are women. In the list, Paul describes women as "deacons," "patrons" or "leaders," "apostles," "co-workers," and "hard workers." As James D. G. Dunn notes, "So far as this list is concerned, Paul attributes leading roles to more women than men in the churches addressed."[11]

A WOMAN DEACON

Paul opens his series of greetings by introducing Phoebe, his letter carrier, to the church in Rome. The following is the author's own extremely literal translation: "I commend to you our sister Phoebe, who is a deacon (οὖσαν διάκονον, *ousan diakonon*) of the church in Cenchrea, so that you may receive her in the Lord worthily of the saints, and may stand by her in whatever thing she may need, for indeed, she has been a patron/leader (προστάτις, *prostatis*) of many and of myself" (Rom. 16:1).

English translations from the mid-twentieth century are misleading.[12] Translation of the key words *diakonos* and *prostatis* is more revealing of translator assumptions about women's roles than illuminating of the passage's meaning. The original NIV translates the passage to describe Phoebe as a "servant," and requests Paul's readers "to give her any help . . . for she has been a great help to many people." The older RSV identifies Phoebe as a "deaconess," but also translates *prostatis* as "helper." The more recent ESV translates *diakonos* as "servant," but includes "deaconess" in a footnote. The ESV more correctly translates *prostatis* as "patron." The more recently revised NIV and the NRSV recognize Phoebe as a "deacon," but translate *prostatis* as "benefactor," which is softer than "patron."

It is correct that *diakonos* can be translated as "servant."[13] In Romans 13:4, the civil ruler is described as the "servant" (*diakonos*) of God. In the story of the wedding feast at Cana, Jesus tells the "servants" (*diakonoi*) to fill the jars with water, which becomes wine (John 2:5, 7, 9). In Romans 15:8, Christ is described as a *diakonos* (servant or minister) to the Jewish people. Whether *diakonos* should be translated "servant" or as referring to a church office depends on context and exegesis. This is an exact parallel with the Greek word *presbyteros* (πρεσβύτερος), which is translated variously. In the Book of Acts, *presbyteroi* sometimes refers to Jewish leaders (Acts 4:5, 8, 23; 6:12), in which case it is translated "elders," and sometimes refers to church office (11:30; 14:23; 15:2, 4, 6, 22-23), and, while often translated "elders," could also be transliterated as "presbyters." In the Pastoral Epistles, *presbyteros* generally refers to those holding church office (1 Tim. 4:14; 5:17, 19; Titus 1:5), but may also refer literally to older men (1 Tim. 5:1), and even (with a feminine ending) to older women (1 Tim. 5:2).

There are several reasons why *diakonos* should be translated as "deacon" rather than "servant" in Romans 16:1 and should be understood as referring to an office. The noun *diakonos* is masculine in gender (not the expected feminine), and if Paul had meant "servant," he would likely have used a verbal form such as "one who serves" (διακονέω, *diakoneō*; Rom. 15:25) or the general term "ministry" (διακονία, *diakonia*; 1 Cor. 16:15). The participle *ousan* (οὖσαν διάκονον, *ousan diakonon*, "being a deacon") would seem to refer to an ongoing ministry. This, combined with the qualifier "of the church in Cenchreae," points to a recognized office in the church. The appropriate context for understanding the term should then be the parallels of Philippians 1:1 and 1 Timothy 3:8, 12. Phoebe should not be called a "deaconess" because the gender of the noun is masculine, and "deaconess" was an office of women church workers that did not exist for another three hundred years.[14] Accordingly, as Dunn notes, "Phoebe is the first recorded 'deacon' in the history of Christianity."[15] Romans 16:1 and possibly 1 Timothy 3:11 are the only two places women are given the title διάκονος in the New Testament.[16] N. T. Wright points out that attempts to make the term mean anything else than "deacon" fail. To translate the word as "servant" merely pushes the problem back a further stage, "since that would either mean that Phoebe was a paid employee of the church (to do what?) or that there was an order of ministry, otherwise unknown, called 'servants.'"[17] As Craig Keener points out, "Most readers would probably assume that meaning [deacon] here if this passage did not refer to a woman and if it were translated the way it normally is in the New Testament."[18]

At the same time that Paul's greetings in Romans indicate that Phoebe was a deacon, the New Testament says little about what the office of deacon entailed. Many Christian churches understand the office of deacon in terms of the seven overseers of tables described in Acts 6; however, the title of *diakonos* is not applied to them, even though the work of both the apostles and the seven is described in terms of service or ministry (διακονία, *diakonia*; Acts 6:1, 2, 4).[19] Keener notes that the term generally means a "minister of the word." Paul applies the term to himself as an apostle of the gospel (1 Cor. 3:5; 2 Cor. 3:6; 6:4; 11:23; Eph. 3:7; Col. 1:23, 25), and also uses it for colleagues in the gospel (Eph. 6:21; Col. 1:7; 4:7; 1 Thess. 3:2; 1 Tim. 4:6).[20] Dunn suggests that it "points more to a recognized ministry . . . or position of responsibility within the congregation," and that the office was "likely a ministry of hospitality."[21]

The second key word used to describe Phoebe is προστάτις (*prostatis*). Against translations of the word as "helper," Dunn insists that the word should be given its "full weight," and that it means "patron," "protector," or, alternatively, "leader" or "ruler." The masculine equivalent of *prostatis* is well known as the role of a wealthy or influential individual as patron. The Latin equivalent is *patronis*. There is a Jewish synagogue inscription from Aphrodisias in the third century of a woman προστάτις of a synagogue.[22]

Other New Testament scholars suggest a meaning of "patron" or "sponsor."[23] In his earlier book, Witherington suggested that Phoebe was in charge of the charitable work of the church. The term likely means "helper" or "protector," referring to personal care or hospitality that Phoebe had provided to Paul and others.[24] In his commentary on Romans, Witherington suggests that *prostatis* refers to a person in charge of some kind of charitable work, which is consistent with being called a deacon. It may also mean helper, protector, or "perhaps even *patroness*." Given that Paul had rejected patronage in Corinth, choosing instead to support himself by tentmaking, his acceptance of it from Phoebe shows that he has great respect for and trust in her.[25] Wright points out that the word "benefactor" means much more than the older NIV translation of "she has been of great help": "[B]enefactors and patrons were a vital part of the culture, and this makes Phoebe someone to be reckoned with socially and financially as well as simply a sister in the Lord and a leader—of whatever sort—in her local church."[26]

Philip Payne focuses rather on the notion that *prostatis* should be understood as "leader," "chief," or "executive office": "Every meaning of every word in the NT related to the word Paul has chosen to describe Phoebe as a 'leader' (προστάτις) that could apply to Rom. 16:2 refers to leadership" (cf. Rom. 12:8). Payne argues that the linguistic evidence strongly favors the normal meaning of the term *prostatis* as "leader": "Since her leadership was in the church it would entail spiritual oversight." Given what Paul teaches about mutual submission, it should not be surprising that Paul includes himself under Phoebe's leadership.[27]

Thus, Paul's readers would have regarded Phoebe as a woman of significance who had used her wealth and influence not only as a leader of the church in Cenchreae, but as Paul's patron and benefactor. Dunn suggests that the terms *diakonos* and *prostatis* may be linked. Phoebe was a "deacon" of the church because of her well-known patronage of foreign visitors, resident Jews, and visiting Christians. Paul recognized himself as the beneficiary of both Phoebe's patronage and her protection. Phoebe was a woman of "some stature," a patron or protector of many, including Paul. She was a deacon and must have used her property and influence in the service of Christians in Cenchreae. She was traveling to Rome on business, and Paul took the opportunity of her travel to write the letter and send it along with the commendation attached.[28]

A WOMAN CO-WORKER AND TEACHER

The first people Paul asks to be greeted in Romans 16 are Prisca and Aquila: "Greet Prisca and Aquila, my co-workers (συνεργούς μου, *synergous mou*) in Christ Jesus, who risked their necks for my life, to whom not only I, but all the churches of the Gentiles, give thanks" (Rom. 16:3-4, author's translation). Both Prisca (Priscilla) and Aquila, and Andronicus and Junia (mentioned later), seem to have been husband and wife "ministry teams." There were places in the Greco-Roman world where only men or women could go, and a couple who ministered together could go places where one or the other could not go alone.[29] From 1 Corinthians 16:19 and Acts 18, it appears that they were some of Paul's closest co-workers, and "two of the most important people in Paul's missionary enterprise."[30] They seem to have been involved in a variety of activities, including providing hospitality for Paul, church planting, teaching, and preaching. They were involved in a variety of churches, including Ephesus, Corinth, and Rome. According to Acts 18:2, they came to Corinth after the Jews were expelled from Rome. Paul lived with them in Corinth, and they worked together because they shared the same trade of tent-making (Acts 18:3). They traveled with Paul from Corinth to Ephesus (Acts 18:18-19), and stayed there for some time (1 Cor. 16:19). When Paul wrote his letter, they were now back in

Rome. Second Timothy 4:19 later places them again in Ephesus.[31] They were likely well-to-do business people who could travel extensively. That they risked their necks for Paul may imply that they attempted to use their social status to protect him. That "all the churches of the Gentiles" are grateful suggests sponsorship, missionary leadership, or teaching.[32] They seem to have regularly used their home as a meeting place for believers. Verse 5 refers to an assembly of Christians who meet in the home of Priscilla and Aquila. It would seem that Christian meetings were held in homes where the household owner or owners were Christians. Paul mentions other house churches in 1 Corinthians 16:19 (Priscilla and Aquila again), Colossians 4.15, and Philemon 2.[33]

Paul always refers to Priscilla as "Prisca." Luke adds the diminutive "Priscilla."[34] Four of the six times, her name comes first, which is "highly unusual in a patriarchal culture." That she is mentioned first may be explained either because she was of higher social status, or because she was more prominent in the church. Linda Belleville points out that when reference to their occupation as tent-makers or to "their house" is mentioned, Aquila's name comes first, but when ministry is mentioned (including the teaching of Apollos), Priscilla's name is first. This would suggest that Priscilla had the dominant ministry and leadership skills.[35]

Paul refers to Priscilla and Aquila as "my co-workers" or "fellow-workers" (συνεργούς μου *synergous mou*). Paul's most frequent term to describe those who helped him in ministry is συνεργός (*synergos*), which he uses more frequently than terms such as apostle, brother, or servant. Paul uses it twelve of the thirteen times it occurs in the New Testament (cf. 3 John 8), and it is never used simply to refer to ordinary Christians (Rom. 16:3, 9, 21; 1 Cor. 3:9; 16:16; 2 Cor. 1:24; 8:23; Phil. 2:25; 4:3; 1 Thess. 3:2; Phlm. 24). A "co-worker" is an associate of Paul who works together with him as commissioned by God in the shared work of mission preaching. In 1 Corinthians 16:16, 18, the Corinthians are asked to submit themselves to all who are συνεργοῦντι (*synergounti*) and κοπιῶντι (*kopiōnti*; those who are "fellow-workers" and "laborers"), so the term implies a leadership position.[36] In Philippians 4:2-3, Paul describes two women (Euodias and Synteches) as "fellow-workers" who "struggled together with me in the gospel." They are ranked alongside Clement (a man), and alongside Paul's other "fellow-worker." They are not simply devout women, then, but fellow ministers of the gospel. Witherington notes, "Paul certainly shows no qualms about having women as co-workers in a wide variety of roles."[37]

In addition to being designated as "co-workers," Priscilla and Aquila were teachers. Acts 18:1-3, 24-26 speaks of Priscilla and Aquila teaching Apollos. By mentioning her first, Luke implies that Priscilla is the primary instructor. "More accurately" means that Priscilla went beyond basic Christian teaching. Apollos already had a basic knowledge of Christian faith, and was "well versed" in Scripture. That the act took place in private is "probably not very significant . . . since there is no indication that Luke was trying to avoid having Priscilla teach Apollos in a worship context."[38] That Priscilla was present in Ephesus at the time the Pastoral Epistles were written (2 Tim. 4:19) is significant in light of the complementarian appeal to the prohibition of women teaching men in 1 Timothy 2:12. The passage cannot mean a permanent prohibition of women teaching men because Priscilla taught Apollos.[39]

A WOMAN APOSTLE

Certainly the most controversial among Paul's greetings in Romans 16 is verse 7: "Greet Andronicus and Junia ('Ιουνίαν, *Iounian*), my relatives (τοὺς συγγενεῖς μου, *tous suggeneis mou*) and fellow-prisoners, who are well-known among the apostles (οἵτινές εἰσιν ἐπίσημοι ἐν τοῖς ἀποστόλοις, *oitines eisin episēmoi ēn tois apostolois*), and who were in Christ before me" (Rom. 16:7, author's translation). Similar to Prisca and Aquila, Andronicus and Junia appear to be another husband-wife ministry team. Despite their non-Jewish names, they were certainly Jewish and perhaps even close relatives of Paul, since Paul identifies them as "relatives" (τοὺς συγγενεῖς μου, *tous suggeneis mou* = "my relatives," "kinsfolk"). They had been in prison with Paul, and, since they were "in Christ" before Paul, they were Christians from an early date. They are a man and a woman, either husband and wife, or possibly brother and sister. Described by Paul as "apostles," they would have been witnesses to the resurrection (1 Cor. 9:1), and had a calling or commission to preach the gospel.[40]

The earliest patristic texts and translations of the Greek presuppose that the passage should be translated as has been done here. That is, Junia is identified as a woman who is also a well-known apostle. Despite demeaning comments he made elsewhere concerning women,[41] John Chrysostom spoke highly of Junia: "To be an apostle is something great. But to be outstanding among the apostles . . . [i]ndeed, how great the wisdom of this woman must have been that she was even deemed worthy of the title of apostle."[42] Commentators from the patristic era onward took Paul to mean that Andronicus and Junia were apostles. The Greek fathers were unanimous in understanding Junia to be a female apostle.[43] The Latin fathers, as well as Latin translations, were also unanimous in recognizing that Junia was a woman who was notable among the apostles.[44] Thus the Latin Vulgate reads: "*Salute Andronicum et Iuniam . . . qui sunt nobiles in apostolis.*" Early English translations, such as the KJV, also follow this pattern: "Salute Andronicus and Junia, my kinsmen, and my fellow-prisoners, who are of note among the apostles, who also were in Christ before me."

Two exceptions have been claimed to this universal patristic consensus. Origen, in Rufinus' Latin translation of his commentary on Romans, refers to Junias (not Junia), as does Epiphanius.[45] In both cases, however, the claim is problematic. The passage in Origen occurs in Rufinus' later Latin translation (not Origen's original Greek text, which no longer exists), and recent critical editions indicate a transcriptional error. "Junias" is a variant in two of three twelfth-century manuscripts, but earlier manuscripts have "Junia." Eldon Jay Epp concludes: "In any event, this alleged exception can be dismissed as carrying little if any weight, and we can be confident that Origen read Rom 16:7 as 'Junia.' . . . [T]here can be no doubt that feminine forms were used by Origen in these passages.'"[46]

The reference in Epiphanius is also irrelevant. Epiphanius wrote that Junias was a man and a bishop, but that the unquestionably female Prisca was a male bishop as well! Moreover, it is unlikely that Epiphanius was actually the author of the cited text. The work was not ascribed to Epiphanius until the ninth century, and in only one existing thirteenth-century manuscript (out of nine). The others do not ascribe it to Epiphanius.[47]

Despite the unanimous consensus during the first millennium of Christianity, the patristic reading passed by the wayside. Two key questions were fundamental in the shift: First, is apostleship restricted by sexual identity? Second, are the two individuals well-known apostles, or merely known to the apostles? The key assumption behind the challenge lies in the assumption that a woman cannot be an apostle. Epp points to an interesting pattern. If the two individuals are identified as apostles, then *Iounian* becomes a man. However, if Junia is instead identified as a woman, then, because a woman could not be an apostle, the ending phrase is translated "well known to the apostles": "[I]t is interesting to observe that, over time, the male 'Junias' and the female 'Junia' each has his or her alternating 'dance partners.'"[48]

The pattern appears in some recent discussions of the passage. Roman Catholic theologian Manfred Hauke acknowledged that Andronicus and Junia are "numbered among the 'apostles' here." He claims however, that the accusative *Iounian* can derive as well from the masculine *Iounianos* (Junianus) as from the female *Iounia* (Junia). However, since women cannot be apostles, "an 'apostle Junia' thus seems to fall into the category of modern myth."[49]

Similarly, Evangelical complementarian Wayne Grudem claims that, in Greek, "this name could be either masculine or feminine," and he appeals to modern translations that identify it as masculine. Grudem eventually acknowledges that the name is probably feminine, but concludes that any reading that Junia is a female apostle "carries little weight against the clear teaching of exclusive male eldership and male apostleship in the rest of the New Testament."[50] The Anglican Forward in Faith document *Consecrated Women?* claims that "we cannot be sure" whether Junia was a man or a woman because "*Iounian* could be the accusative of the masculine noun or it could be that of the feminine *Iounia*." However, they also embrace the predictable pattern: "[T]hose who claim Junia as the first woman apostle stand on shaky ground. The disputed interpretation of one verse in one letter of St Paul can hardly call into question the clear witness of the Pauline corpus taken in its entirety."[51] The pattern is clear; if Junia is an apostle, then Junia must be Junias; if Junia is Junia, and not Junias, then she cannot be an apostle.

Given the unanimous patristic consensus, how did the female Junia become the male Junias? It was only in the medieval period that scribes first introduced the form *Junias*—based on the conviction that a woman could not have been an apostle! Aegidius (or Giles) of Rome (ca. 1243/47–1316) seems to have been the first to have identified Junia(s) as a male in the thirteenth century.[52] Luther's translation of the Bible into German also contributed to the view that Junia was not a woman, but a man named Junias.[53] Beginning in the early twentieth century, lexicographers began to turn the female Junia into the male Junias by changing the accent. In Greek, the only difference between the female Ἰουνίαν and the male Ἰουνιᾶν is between the feminine acute and the masculine circumflex accents. In the earlier uncial texts, there were no accents, and when accents were eventually added, the first editions of the Greek New Testament (e.g., Erasmus's Greek New Testament) printed the female acute rather than the male circumflex accent. The change from a feminine acute to a masculine circumflex first occurred in Nestle's Greek New Testament in 1927, followed by other editions of the Greek New Testament, with the rationale usually given that it would have been unlikely for a woman to be among the apostles.[54] Modern lexicons have assumed that the name is masculine without argument.[55] So Arndt and Gingrich state: "The possibility, fr. a purely lexical point of view, that this is a woman's name . . . is prob. ruled out by the context."[56] But the context says nothing that would indicate it is a man's name!

In modern translations, the shift to "Junias" began with the New Testament of the English Revised Version (1881) and the American Standard Version (1901). Interestingly, Westcott and Hort's contemporaneous Greek New Testament [1881] still had the female Ἰουνίαν. The tendency toward masculine translations continued until around 1970. The RSV, for example, has "Greet Andronicus and Junias, my kinsmen and my fellow prisoners; they are men of note among the apostles, and they were in Christ before me."[57] Richard Bauckham comments: "The history of the matter is a sad story of prejudice making bad translation."[58] In summary, the understanding of *Iounian* as feminine dominated the first millennium of Christianity, but then was arbitrarily changed from female "Junia" to male "Junias" without discussion or justification.[59]

What would be the argument or justification for understanding *Iounian* to be either Junia or Junias, feminine or masculine? *Iunia* is a Latin name, not a Greek one. When translated into Greek, the accent (as noted above) is the only determiner of the gender of the name in Greek: 'Ιουνίαν (acute) or 'Ιουνιᾶν (circumflex). The argument for a masculine name is that *Iunias* would be a shortened form or contraction of *Iunianus*. The problem is that there is "no empirical evidence whatsoever for the abbreviated form *Iunias*." There are no occurrences in any Greek or Latin document of the New Testament period, and no evidence that *Iunianus* has ever been shortened to *Iunias*.[60] Belleville also points out that Greek nicknames were shortened versions of longer names, but Latin nicknames were lengthened, not shortened. Also, when there was a final -i in the stem, it was omitted. The shortened form of Ιουνιανός would then be Ιουνᾶς (*Iounas*), not Ιουνιᾶς (*Iounias*). It was also not Paul's habit to use nicknames. For example, he refers to Prisca, not Priscilla, and Silvanus, not Silas.[61]

What, then, would be the case that *Iounian* is the accusative of the Latin female name Junia? In Roman society, women did not generally have a personal name, but were named after their family. For example, *Gaius Iulius Caesar* is masculine; his daughters were *Iulia Major* and *Iulia Minor* (Julia I and II), with "Iulius" being the *nomen* or family name. *Iunius* is a common Latin nomen; there are many men named "Iunius," and consequently many women named "Iunia." Latin names were transcribed into Greek with Latin masculine endings rendered as Greek names in -ος (-os); Latin feminine names in -a are rendered in -α (-a) or -η (ē). The names Iunius/Iunia would thus be *Iounios/Iounia*. The accusative would be *Iounion/Iounian*. Accordingly, *Iounian* would have to be a woman.[62]

Again, while there are examples of the male name "Iunius" and the female name "Iunia," there is not a single example of the male name "Iunias."[63] As Bauckham points out, the evidence of name usage is the "only argument." There would have to be "overwhelming reasons" to support a masculine reading over a feminine one, but given the wide prevalence of the name "Junia" and the complete lack of evidence for "Junias," the conclusion points to the female name: "We certainly cannot presuppose, as such overwhelming reasons, that there could not have been a woman apostle or that Paul would not have recognized a woman apostle. This would be to beg the question."[64] All the evidence points to Junia being a woman, and there is none whatsoever for the male "Junias." Consequently, in the last few decades, the majority of scholars have come to acknowledge that Junia was indeed a woman.

However, as noted above, there is a predictable pattern to the discussion. For much of twentieth-century New Testament scholarship, it was assumed that, since *Iounian* was an apostle, and a woman could not be an apostle, then "Junias" had to be a man. With the new rising consensus, the shift has turned to the argument that the now-recognized female "Junia" could not have been an apostle. Michael R. Burer and Daniel B. Wallace made the case that, although Junia was indeed a woman, she was not an apostle. Rather, the Greek should be translated not as "outstanding among the apostles," but "well known to the apostles."[65] Burer's and Wallace's article is cited as definitively settling the issue by opponents of women's ordination.[66] The complementarian-leaning ESV translates the passage "Greet Andronicus and Junia, my kinsmen and my fellow prisoners. They are well known to the apostles, and they were in Christ before me." There is no footnote providing even a hint that "to the apostles" might be translated "among the apostles."

Two key distinctions are important for the discussion. Richard S. Cervin's essay (cited above) distinguishes between an "inclusive" meaning (noteworthy *among* the apostles), and an "exclusive" meaning (noted *by* the apostles), and this distinction is followed by later writers.[67] The second crucial issue concerns how to understand the meaning of ἐν (*en*) plus the dative case. Paul wrote ἐπίσημοι ἐν τοῖς ἀποστόλοις (*episēmoi en tois apostolois*). Burer and Wallace suggest that a noun in the genitive case is typically used with comparative adjectives; if Paul had meant that Andronicus and Junia were outstanding "among the apostles," he would have used the genitive— τῶν ἀποστόλων (*tōn apostolōn*). If no comparison is suggested, however, he would have used *en* plus the dative—ἐν τοῖς ἀποστόλοις (*en tois apostolois*).[68]

After a comparative analysis of ancient texts, Burer and Wallace conclude that when a comparison is made, *episēmos* is frequently put in the genitive case. So, in 3 Maccabees 6:1, Eleazar was "prominent among the priests."[69] Also key to their discussion is a distinction between personal and impersonal comparisons. They acknowledge that when used with impersonal nouns, *en* is used comparatively. In Additions to Esther 16:22, a "notable day" is to be observed "among the festivals."[70] Crucial to their discussion is the pseudepigraphal Psalms of Solomon 2:6, which they translate as "they [the Jewish captives] were a spectacle among the Gentiles." Burer and Wallace claim that this passage has "all the elements" for a comparison to Romans 16:7: (1) people as the reference of the adjective "well known," (2) followed by *en* plus the dative plural, and (3) the dative plural referring to people. The first group is not part of the second; that is, the Jewish captives were not Gentiles. "That the parallels discovered conform to our working hypothesis at least gives warrant to seeing Andronicus's and Junia's *fame* as that which was among the apostles." They claim: "[A]lthough the inclusive view is aided in some *impersonal* constructions that involve ἐν plus the dative, every instance of *personal* inclusiveness used a genitive rather than ἐν. On the other hand, every instance of ἐν plus *personal* nouns supported the exclusive view, with *Pss. Sol.* 2.6 providing a very close parallel to Rom 16.7."[71]

The two authors conclude by examining a number of papyri and ancient inscriptions. Although they acknowledge that the data is "not plentiful," they do claim that it points in a single direction: "ἐπίσημος followed by ἐν plus personal datives does not connote membership *within* the group, but simply that one is known *by* the group."[72] They conclude that Romans 16:7 "almost certainly" should be translated "well known to the apostles." Thus, Junia was known to the apostles, but she was not an apostle.[73] Despite this strong claim, they acknowledge that the data is not conclusive; in one case Lucianus "unmistakably" has an inclusive force for ἐν (*en*) plus the dative.[74]

Shortly after its appearance, three New Testament scholars (Richard Bauckham, Linda Belleville, and Eldon Jay Epp), responded critically to Burer's and Wallace's essay.[75] Bauckham claims that "their evidence does not actually support [their] conclusion," and that the essay has "serious defects"; its conclusion is "highly tendentious, even misleading."[76] Belleville writes that their analysis is "problematic in a number of respects."[77] Epp states that "even a cursory examination of [the evidence] presented raised significant doubts about the authors' stated thesis."[78] As noted above, Burer and Wallace claim that "some impersonal constructions" of *en* plus the dative point to an inclusive sense, while "every instance" of personal use plus the genitive is inclusive, and "every instance" of *en* plus the dative is exclusive. However, as Bauckham points out, in each case there is only one text given as an example for each category (Add. Esth. 16:22 [impersonal inclusive]; 3 Macc. 6:1 [personal + genitive]; Pss. Sol. 2:6 [personal + dative]). "One" does not equal "some," and certainly not "every case."[79]

Burer and Wallace make much of Psalms of Solomon 2:6, which is their sole evidence of a "very close parallel" to Romans 16:7. Bauckham and Belleville point out that, unfortunately, Burer and Wallace incompletely and inaccurately cite the passage in claiming that *episēmō* refers to the Jewish captives. A complete citation makes clear that *episēmō* does not refer to the captives at all! Bauckham cites a translation by Sebastian Brock: "Her sons and daughters were in grievous captivity, their neck bears a seal-ring, a mark (*episēmō*) among the nations."[80] Belleville translates the passage: "The sons and daughters (of Jerusalem) were in grievous captivity, their neck *with* a seal, *with* a slave-brand among the Gentiles."[81] *Episēmō* refers then not to "sons and daughters," but to "seal" or "seal-ring." Since the essential element (people used as a referent) is not present at all, the passage is irrelevant to the evidence.[82]

Both Bauckham and Epp also question the distinction Burer and Wallace make between personal and impersonal "inclusive" uses. The five impersonal uses provided by the authors are all inclusive, and three of them (Add. Esth. 16:22; 1 Macc. 11:37, 14:48) have *en* plus the dative.[83] Epp also points out that the single example of an inscription (TAM II west wall. Coll. 2.5) which they treat in detail is translated exclusively in a way that begs the question, since it could as easily be translated inclusively. Belleville argues that all of the Hellenistic inscriptions referred to by Burer and Wallace should actually be translated inclusively, and Epp agrees.[84]

Finally, Witherington points out that when patristic authors use "in" to mean "in the eyes of," they actually include the specific words, or something like them. If Paul had meant that Andronicus and Junia were "known to the apostles," he would not have used *en*, but rather *hypo* or a simple dative form.[85] Against Burer's and Wallace's central thesis, Belleville insists that "[p]rimary usage of ἐν and the plural dative (personal or otherwise) inside and outside the NT (with rare exception) is *inclusive* in/among and not *exclusive* 'to'" (citing Matt. 2:6; Acts 4:34; and 1 Pet. 5:1 as examples.)[86] Belleville concludes: "Despite their assertions to the contrary, [Burer and Wallace] fail to offer one clear biblical or extra-biblical Hellenistic example of an 'exclusive' sense of ἐπίσημος ἐν and a plural noun to mean 'well known to.' The authors themselves admit this early on, but then go on to conclude otherwise."[87] Epp concludes that the three evaluations by Bauckham, Belleville, and himself "should put to rest any notion that [Rom. 16:7] carried the sense of 'well known to/esteemed by the apostles.' Again, it is clear that Andronicus and Junia, in Paul's description, were 'outstanding apostles.'"[88]

Burer responded in 2015 to the criticisms of Bauckham, Belleville, and Epp in a new essay in which he attempts to defend the original essay as well as to introduce new textual evidence to make the case for an exclusive reading of Romans 16:7.[89] Some of the essay repeats claims made earlier. Burer continues to make a distinction between personal and impersonal texts, although Bauckham and Epp had questioned whether these should be considered as "grammatically different."[90] Over against Belleville's and Epp's claims that various Hellenistic inscriptions to which Burer and Wallace had referred should be interpreted inclusively, Burer continues to argue that they are exclusive.

Burer concedes that the initial assessment of Psalms of Solomon 2:6 (the most crucial passage in the earlier discussion) "require[s] some modification." The disagreement concerned whether *episēmō* was used as a noun and referred to a "seal" or "seal-ring" (as claimed by Bauckham and Belleville) or was an adjective referring to the captives. Burer now agrees that *episēmō* was not a reference to persons (the captives), but instead argues that it is an adjective modifying a place, and should be translated "their neck with a seal in a [place] well known to the nations."[91] This would make the text "impersonal," and would violate the earlier claim to complete parallelism.

Of greater significance, Burer introduces thirty-six additional texts that he claims support an exclusive sense for *episēmōs* plus (*en* plus) dative. The majority are not exact parallels, however, as only eleven include *en* plus dative. As noted above, Witherington suggested that if Paul's meaning *were* exclusive, he would have used *hypo* or, as in the majority of Burer's examples, simple dative without *en*. Arguably, at least some of these references that Burer argues are exclusive should be read as inclusive.[92] Burer acknowledges that one new passage that contains *en* plus dative is inclusive, but claims that it is not parallel to Romans 16:7 because it is impersonal.[93]

However, even more significant than the detailed grammatical debates is the unanimous agreement among the patristic interpreters of Romans 16:7 that the text identifies Andronicus and Junia as "among the apostles." Bauckham writes that it is a "major error" to dismiss this evidence. Writers such as John Chrysostom and Origen were native educated Greek speakers: "If Burer and Wallace's conclusion is right, then it is inexplicable that these Greek patristic interpreters would have read the Greek of Romans in the way they did."[94] In his most recent essay, Burer writes that "one could reasonably conclude that Chrysostom misunderstood the Greek text that he was reading," and suggests a parallel to Epiphanius's mistaken assumption that both Junia and Prisca were men.[95] This is not a close parallel, however. Not only Chrysostom, but every patristic commentator who refers to Junia recognizes her as an apostle. In contrast, the Epiphanius reference occurs in one thirteenth-century manuscript, and probably was not written by Epiphanius at all.[96]

Finally, there is the further question of whether it is even plausible to suggest that Paul would have written that Andronicus and Junia were "well known to the apostles." As Philip Payne reminds readers, Paul was "not impressed with name dropping," and "is not the type to encourage status based on: 'even the *apostles* think they are outstanding.'" That someone would be "notable" or "remarkable" among the larger group of apostles makes sense of those being distinguished from a larger group, but not that the apostles had an agreed assessment that certain people were "outstanding."[97]

There is one last escape for those who want to deny that Junia was a woman apostle. As with the case of "deacon," which can also mean "servant," the Greek word translated "apostle" can also mean "messenger"; in a manner similar to the way in which Phoebe was downgraded from a deacon to a "servant" of the church at Cenchreae, so there are those who insist that even if Junia was a woman and an "apostle," this does not mean that Junia held a church office. Grudem claims that "apostle" could just as well mean "messenger": "Since Andronicus and Junia(s) are otherwise unknown as apostles, even if someone wanted to translate 'well known among,' the sense 'well known among the messengers' would be more appropriate."[98] While the ESV does not have a footnote offering "well known among the apostles" as an alternative reading, the footnote to "apostles" does read "or messengers."

The clue to how Paul is using the word "apostle" in this context is determined by how he uses it elsewhere. Paul would not have understood Andronicus and Junia to be among the "twelve apostles," whom Paul refers to as "the twelve" (1 Cor. 15:5). Paul does use the word "apostle" in a nontechnical sense twice (2 Cor. 8:23; Phil. 2:25) to refer to messengers of the church. In these cases, Paul qualifies "apostle(s)" by referring to "apostles of the churches" (2 Cor. 8:23) or to "your apostle" (Phil. 2:25). Paul's unqualified use of "the apostles" would indicate that he is using "apostle" as he does when he refers to himself as an apostle, to refer to an office which is larger than the office of the twelve, but includes those (like himself) to whom the risen Christ had revealed himself in a resurrection appearance, and who had been commissioned to preach the gospel. Given the extent to which Paul defends his apostleship, it is "highly unlikely that he would employ the term 'apostle' loosely when applying it to others."[99] Given that Paul claims that Andronicus and Junia were Christians before he was, it is possible that they were among those whom Paul mentions in 1 Corinthians 15:7 as witnesses of the resurrection.[100] If Andronicus and Junia were Christians before Paul, and "outstanding" among the apostles, they would likely have been members of the early Jerusalem church, and perhaps founders of the Christian community in Rome. Paul does not speak so highly of anyone else he mentions in Roman 16.[101]

OFFICE ONCE MORE

The beginning of this chapter referred to a distinction made by Roman Catholic theologian Francis Martin between charism, ongoing ministry, and office in the New Testament church. While acknowledging that women exercised ministries of both charism and ongoing ministry in the New Testament period, Martin denies that there is any evidence that women ever held church office. To the contrary, examination of the apostle Paul's references to three women who exercised church ministry in connection to the church in Rome indicates that all three exercised some form of church office. Phoebe was both a deacon of the church at Cenchreae and a *prostatis*, a patron of Paul's ministry who exercised some form of church leadership. Priscilla was a "co-worker" of Paul, the term that Paul applies to his closest associates, but also exercised the ministry of a teacher. Finally, Junia was an apostle, a witness to the risen Christ who exercised a ministry of gospel proclamation.

Granted that these women exercised some form of ongoing ministries in the early church, does it follow that these ministries were necessarily examples of church office? Martin claims otherwise. Concerning Phoebe, he writes: "Thus the fact that Phoebe is called a *diakonos* . . . probably means that she is traveling as a representative of her community. . . . Although her influence was great and beneficial, there is no indication that she fulfilled what would later be recognized as an office."[102]

As with Phoebe, Martin denies that there is any reason to suggest that the teaching ministry of either Priscilla or Aquila(!) implies any kind of office:

Given this usage of the term and the fluidity of vocabulary we have already seen, it is possible to say of Prisca (Priscilla) that she, along with her husband, was an outstanding proponent of the gospel, whose authority came from the grace of ministry she received, but not that she held some "official" position in the church at large. . . . [W]e see the prominence and influence of a ministry divinely conferred upon both a woman and a man. They are not, however, presented in a way that would lead one to classify either of them along with the "teachers" mentioned in 1 Corinthians 12:28 and Ephesians 4:1, where the term implies office.[103]

Martin makes a similar claim concerning Junia:

I would conclude . . . that there are strict and loose senses of the term *apostle*. . . . [Paul] uses *apostolos* in both a strict and a loose sense. . . . [C]alling Andronicus and Junia "apostles" in Romans 16:7 may approximate the use in 2 Corinthians 8:23, but it is far from the strong sense implied in Paul's self-designation or in lists such as 1 Corinthians 12:28 and Ephesians 4:11.[104]

Concerning the term "co-worker," applied to Priscilla, he writes: "[Co-workers] seems to be a title [Paul] reserves for those who have generously extended themselves for the sake of the gospel, but nothing more precise can be garnered from it." Martin suggests that those who would conclude from the application of terms such as "co-worker" (or presumably "deacon" or "apostle") to women such as Phoebe that they should be equated to "co-workers" such as Timothy and other leaders (1 Thess. 5:12 and 1 Cor. 16:16) are reading the texts too narrowly: "Such a way of reasoning implies a rigidity of terminology foreign to the New Testament in general and Paul in particular." Martin concludes that while these women had great ministerial gifts, "[t]here is, however, no address to a woman or quality attributed to a woman that would suggest that their leadership was of the type I have described as *office*."[105]

Martin's demurral is based on the fluidity of vocabulary concerning ministry in the New Testament. Prophecy and teaching can be examples of either charism, ongoing ministry, or office. Moreover, one could add that the New Testament terms associated with office are simply ordinary descriptive labels that can have more than one meaning. A *diakonos* could be a "deacon," but might only be a "servant." A *presbyteros* could be a "presbyter," but might just be an "older man." An *episkopos* could be a "bishop," but might only be an "overseer." An *apostolos* could be an "apostle," but might only be a "messenger." A "co-worker" might be an office holder (such as Timothy), but might just be one of Paul's traveling companions.

At the same time, granted the possible flexibility of vocabulary, it will not do simply to assume without argument that the same language applied to both men and women implies office in reference to men, but only "flexible vocabulary" and not office in reference to women. To claim, as Martin does, that no women are addressed or exercised leadership in such a manner as to imply that their ministry was a form of office, and then on that basis to conclude that Paul's applications of titles such as "deacon," "co-worker," and "apostle" to these three women must be examples of flexible vocabulary and does not imply office, begs the question. Paul's description of these women is itself the evidence that these women did hold office. Moreover, as noted at the beginning of this chapter, since there are remarkably few men who are identified by name as holding office in the New Testament either, Martin's criteria would eliminate all but a handful of men from being office holders as well.

The strongest argument that these women exercised office is that Paul speaks of them in exactly the same way that he speaks of men about whom there would be no hesitation to attribute office. Linda Belleville states succinctly: "The language Paul uses for the ministries of these women is that which he uses for his own missionary labors and the labors of other colleagues."[106] It is precisely because of possible ambiguity of vocabulary that it is not simply asserted here that these women held office; rather, the language Paul uses in reference to them is exactly the kind of language he uses in describing men who held office. Phoebe is not simply described as a "servant," but as a *diakonos* (masculine ending) of the church at Cenchreae in a manner parallel to the language applied to deacons in Philippians 1:1 and 1 Timothy 3:8, 12. The term "co-worker" (*synergos*) that Paul applies to Priscilla is used in exactly the same way that he applies it to male co-workers such as Titus (2 Cor. 8:23), Epaphroditus (Phil. 2:25), Clement (Phil. 4:3), Timothy (1 Thess. 3:2), Mark, Aristarchus, Demas, and Luke (Phil. 24), and, finally, Urbanus (Rom. 16:9) in the same chapter in which Paul speaks of Priscilla. Priscilla and Aquila are described as leaders of the church and teachers in exactly the same way that Paul describes his other "co-workers." Moreover, 1 Corinthians 16:16, the passage in which Paul asks his readers to "submit" to his "co-workers," and to which Martin appeals as the kind of office that could not be applied to someone like Priscilla says nothing about the sex of the "co-workers." If the ministry team of Priscilla and Aquila were a male ministry team such as Paul and Barnabas (Acts 15:22), Paul and Silas (Acts 15:40), or Barnabas and Mark (Acts 15:39), it is difficult to imagine that anyone would suggest that their ministries should not be described as "office."

Finally, as argued above, the evidence indicates that Andronicus and Junia were not only a husband-wife ministry team, but also "notable apostles," not simply "messengers." Paul's unqualified use of "the apostles" in reference to them indicates that he places their ministry in the same category as his own; they were witnesses to the risen Christ who had been commissioned to preach the gospel.

This chapter concludes with a quotation from New Testament scholar Ben Witherington III:

Paul's specific commendation of seven of the nine women named in this chapter and his reference to Phoebe's role as a deacon are extremely significant. While contemporary believers divide over ordination of women, women teaching men and the like, this chapter suggests that such objections, in general, would have puzzled Paul. . . . The conclusion then follows that Paul has no problem with women as teachers (Priscilla) or leaders, proclaimers, or missionaries of the Good News.[107]

Did women exercise ministries in the New Testament period that would later be designated as office? The evidence indicates that the answer is "Yes."

16

Women's Ministry in the New Testament

Bishops, Presbyters, Deacons

This is the second of two chapters on women's ministry in the New Testament. The previous chapter addressed the question: (1) "Did women exercise ministerial office in the New Testament period?" This one will address the two additional questions: (2) How does the New Testament address the question of female bishops or presbyters? (3) What are the contemporary hermeneutical implications of what the New Testament says about women in office?

As noted in previous chapters, the New Testament says very little about the actual practices associated with the more permanent ministries of "office." For example, the New Testament nowhere describes the ritual celebration of the Eucharist or indicates who presided at its celebration; nor does the New Testament ever use the word "priest" to refer to those who exercise office, both key concerns in Catholic discussions of ordained ministry. Although the New Testament nowhere identifies by name a woman who exercised the role of presbyter or bishop, it does not mention by name any man with these titles either.

In addition (as also pointed out), the New Testament terminology for office is fluid, and a number of titles are used: "co-worker," "apostle," "deacon," "teacher," "prophet," and "leader." However, after the New Testament period, permanent ministry is particularly associated with the offices of overseer/bishop, elder/presbyter, and deacon. These offices are rarely mentioned in the New Testament. The book of Acts indicates that Paul and Barnabas appointed "elders" (πρεσβύτεροι, *presbyteroi*) "in each church" (Acts 14:23). As Paul concluded his third mission journey before returning to Jerusalem, he addressed the "elders" (πρεσβύτεροι, *presbyteroi*) of the church at Ephesus (Acts 20:17). Paul counsels them to keep watch over the flock over whom the Holy Spirit has made them "overseers" (ἐπίσκοποι, *episkopoi*) in order to shepherd the church of God (v. 28). In chapter 15, Acts mentions "the elders" in conjunction with "the apostles" (Acts 15:4, 6, 22, 23). In Philippians 1:1, Paul greets the "saints in Christ Jesus at Philippi," along with the "overseers and deacons" (ἐπισκόποις καὶ διακόνοις, *episkopois kai diakonois*). This is the only letter in which Paul specifically addresses these office holders by title. Again, there is nothing in these passages to indicate the sex of these office holders, and the only person specifically identified as a deacon by Paul is the female deacon, Phoebe (Rom. 16:1).

The only New Testament description of qualifications for the offices of overseer/bishop, elder/presbyter, and deacon occur in the Pastoral Epistles (1 Tim. 3:1-13; Titus 1:5-9); consequently, these are the crucial passages to examine in order to assess whether the New Testament addresses the question of female bishops or presbyters. Those who are opposed to women's ordination appeal to these passages as crucial for deciding the issue. The Anglican Forward in Faith document *Consecrated Women?* states:

> By the time of the Pastoral Epistles, an ordained ministry with full authority has developed, and with these we see, in some places, the first beginnings of monepiscopacy. We naturally stress the witness of the Scriptures that the ministry of *presbyteroi* and *episkopoi* is male. There is no evidence of, or endorsement for, the exercise of oversight or liturgical leadership by women: the opposite is the case.[1]

In a footnote, the document appeals for biblical support to 1 Corinthians 14:33-36 as "possibly a special prohibition by St Paul of female presidency of the Eucharist,"[2] as well as "1 Timothy 3; Titus 1:5ff., etc."[3] Beyond the mere reference, there is no actual exegesis of either 1 Timothy 3 or Titus 1. That these passages provide warrant for a male-only presbyterate and episcopacy is assumed to be self-evident. The strong statement "the opposite is the case" referring to "no evidence of, or endorsement for, the exercise of oversight or liturgical leadership by women" is, again, simply asserted. There could, of course, be no evidence for the exercise of liturgical leadership by men either, since the New Testament says nothing whatsoever about who presided at liturgical celebration, whether male or female. The previous chapter argued that there is indeed strong evidence that women in the New Testament church held "office," and thus exercised some sort of ecclesial oversight.

On the other hand, the Evangelical complementarian Wayne Grudem does attempt an argument based on the observation that 1 Timothy 3:2 states that the office of overseer "should be filled by someone who is the 'husband of one wife.' . . . It is evident that only a man can be a husband. . . . *anēr* . . . is the Greek term that specifically designates a male human being. This means elders [*sic*] had to be men."[4] Grudem's argument will be addressed below.

JOB DESCRIPTIONS OR MORAL QUALIFICATIONS?

The Pastoral Epistles describe the qualifications for overseers/bishops, elders/presbyters, and deacons in two places. 1 Timothy 3:1-7 addresses qualifications for overseers (or bishops), 3:8-12 discusses deacons, and Titus 1:5-9 includes almost identical language concerning elders (or presbyters), who, in verse 7, are also referred to with the title of "overseer/bishop."

The first thing to be noted is that these are not job descriptions, but moral qualifications for church office. New Testament scholar Ben Witherington III notes that the focus is on "character description." The main function of the passages is "to explain *how* a leader should behave, not *what* the leader's full job description should look like."[5] The character description of the overseer/bishop contrasts five vices which the office holder should avoid with six virtues to pursue, in addition to demanding sexual fidelity in marriage. Paul is likely contrasting the moral behavior of overseers, elders, and male and female deacons with that of false teachers and unruly women described elsewhere in the Pastoral Epistles.[6]

MISLEADING TRANSLATION

So, first, the qualifications for church office in the Pastoral Epistles are moral qualifications, not job descriptions, and not gender qualifications. Second, it is also important to note that the standard English translations of these passages are misleading, giving the impression that Paul is describing specifically male office holders. In describing the office of overseer/bishop, Paul uses the generic τις (*tis*), properly translated as "whoever" or "anyone." Paul affirms that "whoever (τις, *tis*) aspires to the office of bishop (ἐπίσκοπος, *episkopos*) desires a noble task" (1 Tim. 3:1-2, NRSV). The same word is used in Titus 1:6: "If anyone (τίς, *tis*) is blameless/irreproachable. . . ." As Philip Payne asks, "Would Paul encourage women to desire an office, as these words do, if it were prohibited to them?"[7]

Unfortunately, by their introduction of male pronouns where there are none in the original Greek text, modern English translations give the misleading impression that Paul is claiming that church leaders must be male. The complementarian-leaning ESV translation introduces the male pronouns "he" or "his" ten times in 1 Timothy 3:1-7, while even the "inclusive language" translations of the NRSV and the revised NIV have eight and ten masculine pronouns respectively. In actuality, the Greek texts of 1 Timothy 3:1-12 and Titus 1:5-9 do not contain a single male pronoun.[8]

A more literal (but admittedly awkward) translation of 1 Timothy 3:1-6 would read as follows:

> Trustworthy is the saying: Whoever [*tis*] aspires to [the office of] overseer/bishop desires a good work. It is necessary therefore that the overseer/bishop be without

reproach, a "one woman man" [literal translation], temperate, self-controlled, respectable, hospitable, apt at teaching, not an excessive drinker, not violent but gentle, not quarrelsome, not greedy; managing one's own household well, having children in subjection with all gravity—but if someone [*tis*] does not know how to manage one's own family, how would one care for God's church?—not a recent convert, lest being puffed up, one become conceited and fall into the devil's snare.

With the single exception of the three-word expression "one woman man" (to be discussed below), nothing in the passage would indicate that the person being discussed for the office of overseer/bishop would be either a man or a woman.

Also significant are the close parallels between the language that Paul uses to describe the qualifications for the office of overseer/bishop and the language he uses to describe women. The language is so close that it cannot be coincidental. There are numerous verbal or conceptual parallels between overseer requirements and passages regarding women. Almost half of these passages use nearly identical terminology; others use synonymous expressions, while others forbid identical characteristics.[9] The following parallels are based on a chart created by Philip Payne:[10]

OVERSEER DESCRIPTION	STATEMENTS ABOUT WOMEN	PASTORAL EPISTLE ODDS
1 Tim. 3:1 (καλοῦ ἔργου, *kalou ergou* "good work")	5:10 (ἔργοις καλοῖς, *ergois kalois* "good works")	8/14
3:2 (ἀνεπίλημπτον, *anepilēmpton* "irreproachable")	5:7 (ἀνεπίλημπτοι, *anepilēmptoi* "irreproachable")	3/14
3:2 (μιᾶς γυναικὸς ἄνδρα, *mias gunaikos andra* "one woman man")	5:9 (ἑνὸς ἀνδρὸς γυνή, *henos andros gunē* "one man woman")	4/14
3:2 (νηφάλιον, *nēphalion* "temperate")	3:11 (νηφαλίους, *nēphalious* "temperate")	3/14
3:2 (σώφρονα, *sōphrona* "sober")	2:9, 15 (σωφροσύνης, *sōphrosynēs* "sobriety," "propriety")	6/14
3:2 (κόσμιον, *kosmion* "orderly")	2:9 (κοσμίῳ, *kosmiō* "orderly")	2/14
3:4 (σεμνότητος, *semnotētos* "gravity," "respect")	3:11 (σεμνάς, *semnas* "to be grave")	6/14
3:6 (κρίμα, *krima* "judgment" to be avoided)	5:12 (κρίμα, *krima* "judgment" to be avoided)	2/14
3:7 (μαρτυρίαν καλήν, *marturian kalēn* "good witness")	5:10 (καλοῖς μαρτυρουμένη, *kalois marturoumenē* "witnessed" by "good" works)	3/14

The repeated use of such identically phrased language in reference to both the requirements for the office of overseer/bishop and in reference to women cannot be a coincidence. Payne calculates that the thirty-six lines of 1 Timothy explicitly about women (out of a total of 516 lines in the Pastoral Epistles) comes to approximately one-fourteenth of the Pastoral Epistles. The total number of times an expression appears in the Pastoral Epistles divided by fourteen gives the odds of a random distribution in the Pastoral Epistles (the third column above). The probability of a random distribution of all these words and expressions occurring in the thirty-six lines of the Pastoral Epistles explicitly about women is the product of each of the separate odds for the appropriate columns, approximately six in one million.[11] Regardless of the exact mathematical possibilities, the use of so much identical terminology both in the verses describing the requirements for the office of overseer/bishop and in the verses explicitly about women only makes sense if Paul deliberately described women using the identical vocabulary that he had used to describe overseers in 1 Timothy (as well as elders in Titus 1:6-9). Given that this is certainly the case, it cannot be that Paul understood the requirements for the office of overseer to exclude women—since they are the same requirements! Rather, Paul seems deliberately to use identical language to describe the moral qualifications of overseers/bishops and elders and the expectations for women in the church. As noted above, the requirements are moral qualifications and character descriptions, not job descriptions—and they are not gender-specific.

A "ONE WOMAN MAN"

What then about the three-word expression μιᾶς γυναικὸς ἄνδρα (mias gunaikos andra, literally "one woman man") in verse 2, translated variously as "the husband of one wife" (KJV, ESV), "married only once" (NRSV), and "faithful to his wife" (NIV)? Does it mean that office holders have to be male? There is disagreement about the meaning of the phrase "one woman man" and its female equivalent (1 Tim. 5:9). Both Grudem and Payne (who agree on almost nothing else) believe that it is an exclusion of polygamists (and likely adulterers).[12] Witherington suggests that polygamy and polyandry are probably unlikely, since these were rare practices in the Greco-Roman world. The emphasis is on the word "one," not on "man" or "woman."[13] As noted above, the requirements of the office of overseer/bishop are primarily moral requirements: "[T]he strong sense in this passage is on being morally irreproachable. It is therefore far more likely that the phrase in question is dealing with behavior *within* marriage, which is, to say, being sexually faithful to one's own wife, and so not engaging in any sort of extramarital infidelity." A "one woman man" indicates, then, someone who has been exclusively faithful to his wife. The close parallel to 5:9 ("one man woman"), which is nearly identical in language and form, indicates that both passages are dealing with the same issue—sexual fidelity in marriage.[14]

The passage does not imply that the person must necessarily be married and cannot be single. Nor do the following statements about managing one's own household and one's children imply that the overseer/bishop necessarily has children. Paul simply assumes as a matter of course that the person would be married with a family, as would have been normal in first-century Mediterranean culture.[15] John Chrysostom's homily on 1 Timothy 3:2 interprets the passage to mean not that there is a rule that the bishop must have a wife, but that he cannot have more than one.[16] If the passage were to be pressed to imply a strict job description with minimum requirements, then the references to managing a household would mean that all bishops, presbyters, and deacons would need to be married home owners with at least two children old enough to be believers. If these were minimum requirements, then not even Paul, who was single and (since he exercised an itinerant ministry) did not own a home, would have qualified as an overseer or deacon.[17]

The phrase "one woman man" functions, then, as an exclusion (no adulterers), not as a minimum job requirement. Grudem recognizes correctly the exclusionary element when he acknowledges that the passage does not rule out single men as overseers, but he is inconsistent in then insisting that the passage implies that the overseer must necessarily be a male.[18] Payne points out that if the requirement is morally exclusionary, it does not prohibit women any more than the requirement prohibits unmarried men or married men who do not own homes or have children:

> Since "one woman man" is a set phrase that functions as an exclusion, any claim that a single word of it ("man") also functions separately as a requirement must posit a double meaning. This is not warranted by the context. It is bad hermeneutics to isolate a single word ("man") from a set phrase ("one woman man") that functions as an exclusion (of polygamists and probably adulterous husbands) and to elevate that single word to the status of an independent requirement (that all overseers be men).[19]

The exclusion operates exactly in the same way that the parallel requirement in 1 Timothy 5:9 functions concerning widows, as a promotion of exclusive fidelity within marriage. Oddly, Grudem claims that the parallel in 5:9 concerning widows is "is not parallel, but exactly the opposite," because "it assumes that the widow is a woman, and it assumes that the elder is a man!"[20] To the contrary, a parallel that was "exactly the opposite" would read something like "a *many* woman man," that is, an adulterer. Genesis 2:23 makes clear that woman is not *the opposite* of man, but *like* him as his "helper" or partner, "bone of my bones and flesh of my flesh." In both passages in 1 Timothy, the requirement is a moral restriction on both men and women that serves an identical function, the exclusion of adulterers and the promotion of fidelity in marriage.

Grudem makes a parallel argument based on Paul's statement in verse 4 concerning household management: *"[T]he New Testament sees a close relationship between male leadership in the home and male leadership in the church.* Paul says that the candidate for the office of elder must manage his own household well."[21] The Forward in Faith document *Consecrated Women?* makes a similar claim: "The bishop's duty is, as described, to be the *paterfamilias* of God's assembly. . . . There is an obvious, although not explicit, logic here relating this monistic paternal episcopal ministry to the unity of the one *oikos* of the Father. One God, one bishop, one flock of the redeemed."[22] Both confuse Paul's accommodation to the normal social setting of the Mediterranean household with an endorsement of that setting as having a permanently normative status. Witherington points out that it is not surprising that there is significant overlap in what Paul writes about the overseer/bishop with the desirable character traits of nonecclesiastical office holders in the contemporary Mediterranean culture. What is surprising and should be given heavier weight, however, is the way that Paul modifies common norms, and especially sexual norms, within a "christological and apostolic paradigm." In contrast to the ancient Mediterranean shame/honor culture is the focus on servanthood. The overseer, elder, or deacon is called to be humble and serve others, not to domineer over them.[23]

In defending his claim that the passage implies male leadership, Grudem argues that Paul never uses the word προΐστημι (*proistēmi;* 1 Tim. 3:5) to speak of women managing or governing a household.[24] However, as Payne points out, Paul does use the even stronger word οἰκοδεσποτεῖν (*oikodespotein*, "to be house despots") in 1 Timothy 5:14 to describe younger widows who are to marry and manage their homes. Moreover, no New Testament passage explicitly applies *proistēmi* to men, either. In Romans 12:8, the word is used in a list of gifts that could apply to either men or women, and Romans 12:6-8 (like 1 Tim. 3:1-13) contains no specifically male pronouns. On the other hand, the *only* time the noun form is used in the New Testament, it describes a woman, Phoebe, who, in Romans 16:2, is called a προστάτις (*prostatis*)—a "leader" or "patron."[25]

WOMEN DEACONS?

In 1 Timothy 3:8-13, Paul provides a list of the requirements for deacons, which are the same kinds of moral or character requirements as those for overseers/bishops. Like overseers, deacons are to be "grave/honorable/above reproach" (σεμνούς, *semnous;* 3:8; cf. 3:4), not heavy drinkers of wine, not greedy (cf. 3:3). Significantly, as with overseers/bishops, deacons are to be "one woman men" who manage their children and household well (3:12; cf. 3:2, 4). Important for this discussion is 1 Timothy 3:11, a short statement in the middle of the qualifications for deacons, which reads: "Similarly, women (γυναῖκας ὡσαύτως, *gunaikas ōsautōs*) [to be] grave/worthy of respect (σεμνάς, semnas), not slanderers (διαβόλους, diabolous), sober (νηφαλίους, nēphalious), faithful in all things (πιστὰς ἐν πᾶσιν, pistas en pasin)" (author translation). As in 3:8 ("Deacons, likewise . . ."), the verse is introduced by the word "likewise" or "similarly" (ὡσαύτως, ōsautōs). This, along with the immediate context of the verse, indicates that the women discussed have some relationship to the office of deacon. Controversy concerns whether 1 Timothy 3:11 refers to female deacons or to deacons' wives. Predictably, the complementarian-leaning ESV translates the passage: "Their wives likewise . . . ," while the NRSV and the NIV play it safe with the literal "Women likewise . . ." and "In the same way, the women . . ." (in footnotes, the NRSV and the NIV both list "wives of deacons" and "women deacons" as possible translations).

Context and vocabulary indicate "women deacons" as the preferable translation. Witherington points out that, grammatically, the sentence is dependent on 3:2 and the word "must" (δεῖ, dei). As 3:8 with its description of deacons is tied to 3:2 by the word "likewise," so 3:11 is then tied to 3:8 by an additional appearance of the word "likewise." The passage would, then, seem to be a continued discussion of church functionaries—women deacons, not wives of deacons. If it is deacons' wives, it is difficult to imagine Paul not first having made similar comments about overseers' wives.[26]

Payne provides additional grammatical and vocabulary indications that the passage must refer to women deacons. If Paul had intended to refer to "wives of deacons," he would have added an expression such as "of deacons," "their," or "having wives" (cf. 3:4, "having children"). Because deacons had already been referred to, there would have been no additional need to supply the word "deacons" when referring to women. The word "likewise/similarly" would have been sufficient as it exactly parallels "deacons, similarly" in verse 8. Each case of "similarly" indicates a church office provided by moral qualifications. Neither "deacons similarly" nor "women similarly" has a verb, but both rather presuppose the continuation of "it is necessary for . . . to be" (δεῖ . . . εἶναι, dei . . . einai) from verse 2. The parallel verbal vocabulary and structure describing the qualifications for "deacons" and "women" also point to a description of office. Deacons (3:8) and women (deacons) (3:11) are required to be "worthy of respect" (σεμνούς, semnous; σεμνάς, semnas); "not double-tongued" (μὴ διλόγους, dilogous) and "not slanderous" (μὴ διαβόλους, diabolous); "not addicted to much wine" (μὴ οἴνῳ πολλῷ προσέχοντας, mē oinō pollō prosexontas) and "sober" (νηφαλίους, nēphalious); not "fond of dishonest gain" (αἰσχροκερδεῖς, aisxrokerdeis) and "faithful in all things" (πιστὰς ἐν πᾶσιν, pistas en pasin).[27]

Finally, as pointed out in the previous chapter, it is helpful to examine patristic interpretations of a passage, since the church fathers were native speakers of ancient

Greek. As with the case of Phoebe being a deacon and Junia an apostle, so most patristic commentators interpret the passage to be referring to women deacons.[28]

Given, then, that verse 11 almost certainly refers to female deacons, this would also cast light on the expression "one woman man," which appears again in verse 12 describing deacons. If "one woman man" and "managing one's household" as character qualifications for deacons in verse 12 does not exclude the female deacons described in verse 11, then the identical vocabulary used to describe overseers/bishops in 3:2, 4 and elders/presbyters in Titus 1:6 cannot exclude female overseers or elders. We would also know from Rom. 16:1 that the "one woman man" qualification would not exclude female deacons since Phoebe is described as a διάκονος, *diakonos* of the church of Cenchreae.[29]

Some (particularly complementarians), however, will appeal to Paul's prohibition of women teaching or holding authority over men in 1 Timothy 2:12. Would this not exclude women from exercising the office of overseer/bishop or elder/presbyter?[30] Paul's use of the present tense verb form οὐκ ἐπιτρέπω (*ouk epitrepō*, "I am not permitting") indicates that the exclusion is temporary, and is addressing a particular local situation involving false teachers. Paul's prohibition in 1 Timothy 2:12 might have something to do with Paul's not explicitly mentioning women overseers in 1 Timothy 3 in the same way that he had mentioned women deacons, but it would not be a permanent prohibition. If there is a tension in interpretation between 1 Timothy 2:12 and 1 Timothy 3, then 1 Timothy 2:12 should be interpreted in the light of 1 Timothy 3 and Titus 1:6 rather than the reverse. A controverted interpretation of a single verse in 1 Timothy 2:12 should not override the normal meaning of τις (*tis*) ("everyone," "any one") in both 1 Timothy 3:1 and Titus 1:6. Moreover, if 1 Timothy 2:12 overrides the normal meaning of "anyone" to imply a permanent exclusion of women from office in the church, then the silencing of members of the circumcision party in Titus 1:10-11 would imply a similar permanent exclusion.[31]

Finally, returning to a criticism raised in an earlier chapter concerning the problem of "women priestesses," an objection sometimes raised by Catholic opponents of women's ordination is that an ordained woman would be a "priestess," and the Christian church does not have "priestesses," but "priests."[32] However, Paul does not use the language of "priest" (ἱερεύς, *hiereus*) to refer to church office, but overseer/bishop (*episkopos*), elder/presbyter (*presbyteros*), and deacon (*diakonos*). The historical origins of the English word "priest" are as a translation of *presbyteros*, the ordinary Greek word for "elder." Paul does indeed use this word in reference to women in the Pastoral Epistles. In 1 Timothy 5:1, he writes "Do not rebuke an elder/older man (πρεσβυτέρῳ, *presbyterō*), but exhort him as a father, younger men as brothers, and female elders/older women (πρεσβυτέρας, *presbyteras*) as mothers, and younger women as sisters, with all purity." Within this context, Paul is probably not referring to church office, but simply using the ordinary Greek word that would have described older men and older women. However, the point is that the issue of the ordination of women to church office has nothing to do with women "priestesses." An ordained woman would be a female overseer/bishop, a female elder/presbyter (*presbytera*), or a female deacon.

HERMENEUTICS AND THE REGULATIVE PRINCIPLE

What are the contemporary hermeneutical implications of what the New Testament says about women in office? An earlier chapter addressed the issue of hermeneutics, and distinguished it from exegesis.[33] That chapter followed some distinctions introduced by Anglican divine Richard Hooker in his *Laws of Ecclesiastical Polity* over against Puritan objections to Anglican ecclesiology and liturgical practices. Specifically, the Puritans advocated a "regulative" principle of biblical interpretation. Whatever was not specifically commanded in Scripture was prohibited. In contrast, Hooker embraced a permissive hermeneutic for the application of Scripture to contemporary practice. Whatever was not specifically forbidden by Scripture was allowed. Hooker also made helpful distinctions between natural law, revealed law, and positive law. Not all "positive laws" recorded in Scripture have permanent validity for all time and places. The church has the freedom to formulate its own positive law that might differ in its specifics from the positive law contained in Scripture if the church law fulfills the same goal.[34] Finally, Hooker made an extremely important observation concerning merely historical statements in Scripture which cannot simply be presumed to provide permanent warrant for later Christian practice.[35]

How then might Hooker's hermeneutical principles be applied in light of what the New Testament says about church office, and particularly about what Paul wrote in the Pastoral Epistles? There is a danger of a hermeneutical misapplication of historical precedent in Scripture. Both Evangelical complementarian and Catholic objections to women's ordination seem to presume that the first-century church's historical practice concerning what is assumed to be exclusively male exercise of church office provides a permanent warrant for later church practice.

The previous chapter argued that there is good historical warrant for the exercise of church office by women in the New Testament church, and, in this one, that nothing of what Paul writes about the requirements for the offices of overseer/bishop, elder/presbyter, or deacon would exclude women from those offices. Even if mistaken, however—if there were no evidence of women holding office in the New Testament church, and if Paul's requirements for office as described in the Pastoral Epistles indicate that the offices of overseer/bishop, elder/presbyter, and deacon were held only by men when he wrote—this in itself would not provide a necessary warrant for male-only leadership in later church practice.

The hermeneutical danger here is that against which Hooker warned, of confusing a merely historical practice with a warrant—of confusing the descriptive with the prescriptive. In the Pastoral Epistles, Paul was writing in and addressing the social setting of first-century Mediterranean culture. House churches were patterned along the lines of the Mediterranean household, and Paul would have assumed that the householder would be male, have children, and manage his household—although there would have been exceptions, such as Paul himself or "co-workers" of Paul such as Priscilla and Aquila. At the same time, the requirements that Paul lists for the offices of overseer, elder, and deacon are *moral*; he provides no *prescriptive* job descriptions. Paul's concern is that the overseer/elder be a good moral example both to the church and to the surrounding pagan culture, manage the church as well as he manages his own household, and be above reproach or scandal. However, nothing that Paul writes would exclude a woman from fulfilling the same functions. Indeed, that Paul refers to "anyone" (*tis*) when describing those eligible for these offices, uses no specifically male pronouns, and deliberately uses identical moral language to describe what he expects of women in the churches (including women deacons) and what he demands of office-holders, makes clear that there are no distinctive gender requirements for holding church office.

There is nothing, then, in what Paul writes in the Pastoral Epistles concerning the requirements for church office that would provide a *theological* warrant for excluding women from ordination, and, as Richard Hooker argued that the church in his own day had the freedom to use written liturgies, written prayers, lectionaries, liturgical calendars, vestments, sing hymns that were not based on the Psalms, and exchange wedding rings (even though none of these were specifically commanded in Scripture), so the church in our own day, facing a vastly different cultural situation from the household culture of the first-century Mediterranean world, should be willing and indeed eager to ordain as office holders those women who meet the kinds of moral character requirements for office on which Paul insisted in his own day, and in whose lives the church discerns evidence of divine vocation to church ministry.

Conclusion

Whether women should be ordained to church office is an issue of both hermeneutics and doctrinal development. That is, how might the teaching of Scripture and the history of the church's tradition faithfully be appropriated in a very different historical and cultural context from that in which the canonical Scriptures of the Old and New Testaments were written? However, it is also a case of doctrinal amnesia. As documented in an earlier chapter, the historical reason for opposition to women's ordination is located in assumptions concerning ontological inferiority: women could not be ordained because they were considered to be less intelligent than men, emotionally unstable, and more susceptible to temptation.[1]

In the last several centuries, two changes led to the abandonment of the church's historical reason for opposition to women's ordination. First, the rise of modern industrialization produced social and economic changes that meant that women were no longer confined to the domestic sphere, and it became common for women to work outside the home. Second, an expansion of the understanding of Christian liberty beyond freedom from sin to include freedom in one's person (including social and economic freedom) provided theological warrant for the church's endorsement of social movements such as representative democracy, the abolition of slavery, workers' rights, social welfare, racial equality, universal suffrage, and equality of women in the work place.[2] This theological endorsement of social liberty and equality is arguably a genuine development of doctrine.[3]

This notion of social liberty and equality means that in all mainline churches—Catholic, Orthodox, Protestant, and Anglican—women are now recognized as having equal ontological status with men.[4] Accordingly, the church has quietly abandoned the historical reasons for opposition to women's ordination. No historic mainline church now claims that women are less intelligent, more emotionally unstable, or more subject to temptation than men. This recognition of women's equality is something genuinely new, and, along with the notions of social liberty and equality, is also a genuine doctrinal development.

How did the churches respond to this new recognition of women's equality? Some have argued that the new understanding leads logically to the ordination of women. If the historic reason for opposition to the ordination of women no longer pertains, then it follows that women should be ordained. That is the position represented in this book. However, some have responded with *new* arguments against the ordination of women that are not recognized as new, combined with a theological amnesia or forgetfulness of the historical reason for opposition to women's ordination.

Both Protestant and Catholic opponents of women's ordination have put forward arguments that are connected with some traditional function of ordained ministry, whether exercising authority (in the case of Protestants) or presiding over liturgical worship and administering the sacraments (in the case of Catholics). These new arguments represent new theological positions that have been defended as if they were traditional, but are not.

The new Protestant opponents to women's ordination endorse neither the historic position, nor its reasons. Complementarians claim emphatically that their opposition to women exercising authority in the church is not based on any understanding of female intellectual or moral inferiority; rather, subordination of women to men is based on a new notion of different gender "roles" presumably founded in creation, a new theology of male "headship" based on an interpretation of the metaphorical use of the Greek word *kephalē* in two of Paul's epistles to mean "authority over," and then read into the rest of the biblical canon in cases where the word does not actually appear along with a problematic doctrine of ontological subordination within the Trinity. As noted in previous chapters, although earlier Christian tradition would not have done so, Protestant complementarians allow women to teach theology or the Bible in secular universities, just not in the church. Presumably, they allow women to work in secular occupations where they might exercise authority over men. So where the earlier tradition restricted women's authority over men in every sphere, the new complementarian position apparently does so only in the context of the church and the family.[5]

If the historic Catholic tradition rejected women priests, the church did not oppose women's ordination for liturgical or sacramental reasons. Roman Catholic author Sara Butler has appealed to the church father Epiphanius for an argument that women cannot be ordained because Jesus Christ called only male apostles. But Epiphanius did not connect this opposition to liturgical celebration of the sacraments; he did not argue that women cannot preside at the Eucharist because they do not resemble a male Christ or male apostles. Rather, Epiphanius appealed to the usual historical argument; specifically, he claimed that women are foolish and easily tempted.[6]

Both complementarian and sacramental opponents of women's ordination also appeal to Christology, but for different reasons. Women cannot be ordained because they both do and do not resemble Jesus Christ. For Protestant complementarians, (1) males resemble Christ in exercising authority in the same way that a male Christ exercises authority over the female church; (2) females resemble Christ in being subordinate to men in the same way that Jesus Christ the Son of God is subordinate to God the Father. Catholic opponents of women's ordination characterize resembling Christ not in terms of exercising authority or in submission to authority, but in terms of sexual iconography. Only male priests can represent a male Jesus Christ in the celebration of the sacraments based on a literal physical resemblance between the male Christ and the male priest.

Protestant complementarians and Catholic sacramentalists appeal to Scripture to provide support for their positions, but in very different ways. Complementarians point to the creation narratives of Genesis 1 and 2, to Paul's use of the word *kephalē* ("head") to refer to men in relation to women in 1 Corinthians 11 and Ephesians 5, to Paul's injunction that wives submit to their husbands in Ephesians 5, and to two of Paul's injunctions against women speaking in church or teaching men. Catholic traditionalists point to the exclusively male priesthood of the Old Testament and to Jesus having called only male apostles. Previous chapters have addressed these arguments at length, arguing that complementarians misread the passages to which they appeal, and that there are reasons for the Old Testament male priesthood and Jesus having chosen male apostles that have nothing to do with whether women can rightly exercise church office. It was also argued that the narrative structure of the texts of the Old and New Testament provides the interpretive key to interpreting what the Scriptures say about men and women and their relationships, and that these narrative texts engage in a process of Christological subversion that challenges traditional patriarchal notions of masculine hierarchy and privilege.

In addition, it was argued that those who reject women's ordination tend to buttress their arguments with appeals to notions or norms imported from outside the biblical text in the light of which they then interpret the texts, imposing on the texts a "natural theology" of sexuality originating from outside the Scriptures. Certainly the cultural setting and historical background of both the Old and New Testaments is that of all traditional agricultural societies in which some men exercise authority over other men and over all women. Protestant complementarians appeal to this structure as a normative pattern for contemporary relationships between men and women, but they do not acknowledge that the pattern is rooted in preindustrial agricultural socioeconomic structures that were common to all ancient societies, but that no longer exist in postindustrial cultures in which women's tasks are no longer confined to home and hearth for biological reasons (e.g., childrearing and breast-feeding). Complementarians also do not acknowledge the extent to which the New Testament patterns of cruciformity and mutual submission challenge and subvert the first-century Mediterranean honor/shame culture that provided the social setting and cultural justification for this hierarchy.[7]

In contrast, Catholic opponents of women's ordination truly recognize that a shift has taken place. Pope John Paul II's *Theology of the Body* advocates equality in marriage and mutual submission between husbands and wives; at least in theory, women can now exercise any role of authority within the church; they can teach and preach, but they simply cannot preside over the Eucharist or ordain others to preside over the Eucharist. To justify this single exception of liturgical presiden-cy, Catholic opponents also appeal to an extrabiblical norm in light of which the texts are then reinterpreted. The norm in this case is a theology of the Eucharist and priestly ordination that first appeared in the writings of Thomas Aquinas in the thirteenth century—that in presiding at the Eucharist, the priest represents (or acts in the person of) Jesus Christ. However, the modern Catholic position interprets this understanding of priesthood in a manner that Aquinas did not—that the priest must literally resemble Jesus Christ in a physical manner, and that only a male priest can represent a male Christ. This later theology of priesthood as male representation is then read back into Jesus' choice of male apostles to provide the warrant for what is actually a later theology.[8]

Similarly, despite official Catholic rejection of male-female sexual symbolism as normative, at least some Catholic, Orthodox, and Anglican opponents of women's ordination appeal to an understanding of male-female symbolism in which they apply the masculine imagery of God as Father, Jesus Christ as a male, and male apos-tleship to demand a male priesthood; and the female imagery of the Virgin Mary and the church as the bride of Christ to a symbolically female laity—although lay people include both men and women. The claim here is that this appeal to sexual symbolism would itself be a case of "natural theology" that finds its origins not in Scripture, but in Hellenistic, intertestamental and post-New Testament opposition-al understandings of the relationship between male and female, understandings of male-female relationality that are rather contrary to the personalist biblical under-standing of man and woman as relationally oriented to one another because they are equally created in the image of the Triune God.[9]

A question could be raised at this point. If opponents to women's ordination in historic mainline churches now recognize (and indeed affirm) that women are onto-logically equal to men, are not less intelligent, not emotionally unstable, and are not more susceptible to temptation than men, and yet they still have refused to endorse the ordination of women, certainly there must be a reason for this besides logical incoherence. Perhaps the real reasons for opposition to women's ordination are not rooted in inequality after all? Perhaps what have been referred to as "new" reasons for oppositions to women's ordination are not actually new at all, but are rather the church's articulation of the actual (albeit implicit) reasons that it had never ordained women, but simply had never needed to articulate until now because the issue had never before been raised seriously. Something like this is the argument that Sara Butler makes when she distinguishes between the historical "argument" (the ontological inferiority of women) and the church's "fundamental reasons" (Christ's choice of male apostles and the priest as a "sacramental sign" of Christ) for opposition to women's ordination.[10]

In reply, given the theological inadequacy of the new "fundamental reasons" to oppose women's ordination, different explanations for this continuing opposition to women's ordination in spite of recognition of women's equality can be proposed. First, most of those who continue to be opposed to women's ordination have failed to acknowledge that the current arguments against women's ordination really are *new* positions. The beginning of the chapter referred to "doctrinal amnesia" because continuing opponents have not recognized that historic opposition to women's ordination was grounded in claims of ontological inferiority and inequality. Given the collapse of this historic reason for opposition, the affirmation of ontological equality between men and women really is a game-changer. It is not enough to presume that what are really entirely new arguments are simply minor adjustments, or, even more misleading, that they actually are the historic reasons, and that the old position can still hold apart from what actually were the historic reasons.

It also helps to consider how changes actually take place within a tradition, as indicated in standard discussions in the works of philosophers and theologians such as Thomas Kuhn, Michael Polanyi, Bernard Lonergan, Alasdair MacIntyre, and Helmut Thielicke.[11] When confronted by radical changes in a new cultural context—such as the change from preindustrial to industrial culture with an accompanying change from an understanding of male and female inequality based on inferiority to one of ontological equality—there are inevitably three responses: (1) reaction, resistance, opposition, or entrenchment; as much as possible, existing communities or social groups reject the new change. Theologically, this has been the response of "fundamentalism" or "conservativism" to modernity. (2) Assimilation; the "progressive" response is to embrace the new change without question, and modify or even discard any previous understanding to accommodate the new. Theologically, this has been the response of "liberal" Protestantism and Catholic "modernism." (3) Conversion and re-actualization: the adoption of a new intellectual paradigm (Kuhn) that is able to incorporate insights from new knowledge while better explaining what was previously known; conversion to a new intellectual, moral or spiritual horizon

(Lonergan); creative engagement with the new situation in coordination with re-actualization of what was previously affirmed (Lonergan, MacIntyre, Thielicke). This is the approach of "critical orthodoxy."

Reaction is not in all cases simply refusal or resistance, however. As Thomas Kuhn argued in his classic works on "paradigm shifts," a conservative tradition can "accommodate" to change by making minor adjustments to the previous "paradigm" in an effort to maintain the earlier tradition. In Kuhn's example, when it became impossible to fit new astronomical observations into the traditional geocentric model of the universe, traditional astronomers did not abandon the earlier position. Rather, small adjustments were made (the postulation of additional epicycles) to allow the old paradigm to accommodate the new data.

In the same way, the new Protestant complementarian notion of male "headship," of different gender "roles" combined with what really is a new Trinitarian theology of eternal subordination of the Son to the Father, or the slight but unacknowledged alteration by Catholic traditionalists of Thomas Aquinas's *in persona Christi* eucharistic theology to mean a *physical* resemblance between the priest and Christ, appear to be just such minor adjustments (something like theological epicycles) made in the hope of accommodating the newly acknowledged equality of women without having to make any drastic changes in the actual participation of women in the life of the church.

Confirmation of this reading of the situation is found in that opponents of women's ordination read things into the biblical text that actually are not there. Complementarians (1) find in Genesis 1 and 2 a hierarchy of men over women before the fall into sin; (2) interpret Paul's "headship" language to mean authority of men over women; (3) read Paul's language of "mutual submission" in Ephesians 5 to mean a submission of women only to men; and (4) read two notoriously difficult to interpret Pauline restrictions on women's speaking in worship settings and teaching of men as universal and permanent prohibitions rather than as addressing specific historical situations. Catholic opponents of women's ordination read into the biblical texts a symbolism concerning Jesus Christ's masculinity and his choice of male apostles, and draw implications for eucharistic theology that had occurred to no one before the twentieth century.

ARE WOMEN HUMAN?

How ought the church to respond to this genuinely new situation?

First, the full implications of what really is a new understanding of the ontological equality of men and women needs to be taken seriously. Given what really is a new doctrinal development and a rejection by all parties of the historic reason for opposition to women's ordination, minor adjustments are not adequate. The churches need to address the issue of whether they really do consider women to be of equal spiritual worth with men. Readers are pointed not to contemporary writings by feminist theologians but to four essays written decades ago by Anglican mystery writer and lay apologist Dorothy L. Sayers.

In *Are Women Human?* Sayers points out changes that had already taken place as a result of the industrial revolution and their consequences for men's and women's roles in the workforce. In reference to the kinds of domestic work that used to be done by women in preindustrial cultures—spinning, dyeing, weaving, catering, brewing, preserving, pickling, and estate management—Sayers writes:

> Here are the women's jobs—and what has become of them? They are all being handled by men. It is all very well to say that woman's place is in the home—but modern civilization has taken all these pleasant and profitable activities out of the home, where the women looked after them, and handed them over to big industry, to be directed and organised by men at the head of large factories.[12]

Sayers notes the incoherence of insisting that women should continue to restrict their occupations to traditional domestic household functions when the preindustrial household no longer exists:

> It is perfectly idiotic to take away women's traditional occupations and then complain because she looks for new ones. Every woman is a human being—one cannot repeat that too often—and a human being must have occupation, if he or she is not to become a nuisance to the world.[13]

More than half a century ago, Sayers had also pointed out that interpreting differences between men and women in terms of symbolic archetypes is a male rather than female obsession:

> [I]t is very observable that whereas there has been from time immemorial an Enigma of Woman, there is no corresponding Enigma of Man. . . . [T]he entire mystique of sex is, in historic fact, of male invention. The exaltation of virginity, the worship of the dark Eros, the apotheosis of motherhood, are alike the work of man.[14]

Over against the abstractions of sexual archetypes of masculinity and femininity, Sayers offers the corrective of the concrete reality of actual men and women and the concrete good of personalist relationalism:

> [T]he average woman of intelligence is fairly ready to believe in the value of a personal relationship, but the idea of a peculiar *mana* attached to femaleness as such, deriving as it does from primitive fertility-cults and nature-magic, is likely to strike her as either nonsensical or repellent.[15]

The most fundamental characteristic of women in comparison to men is that they are, first and foremost, human, and thus are more like men than they are like anything else:

> But the fundamental thing is that women are more like men than anything else in the world. They are human beings. *Vir* is male and *Femina* is female: but *Homo* is male and female.

> This is the equality claimed and the fact that is persistently evaded and denied. No matter what arguments are used, the discussion is vitiated from the start, because Man is always dealt with as both *Homo* and *Vir*, but Woman only as *Femina*.[16]

Accordingly, many of the stereotypical assumptions about similarities and differences between men and women are simply nonsensical. For example, there is the inscrutable mystery that men presume is at the center of femininity when they ask the perennial question, "What do women want?"[17] Sayers writes:

> I do not know that women, as women, want anything in particular, but as human beings they want, my good men, exactly what you want yourselves: interesting occupation, reasonable freedom for their pleasures, and a sufficient emotional outlet. What form the occupation, the pleasures and the emotion may take, depends entirely upon the individual.[18]

Closely tied to Sayers' insistence on the basic human equality between men and women is another central theme in Sayers' writing, that of a Christian theology of work. Drawing on Genesis 1:26-28, Sayers brings together the notion that humanity is created "in the image of God," that humanity is created "male and female," and what has been called the "cultural mandate"—that humanity is created to exercise stewardship over creation—to argue for a Christian "understanding of work."[19] Sayers states that "work is not, primarily, a thing one does to live, but the thing one lives to do," that "good work" and not profit should be the primary point of work, that one should do work for which one is "fitted by nature," that "[w]e should clamor to be engaged in work that was worth doing, and in which we could take pride." Finally, that work should be viewed as a vocation, and "that every maker and worker is called to serve God in his [or her] profession or trade—not outside it."[20]

How is this notion of work connected with the affirmation that men and women are equally created in the image of God, and that, first and foremost, "women are human"? Sayers acknowledges that there are some practical differences between men and women that make some types of work more suitable for most men than they are for most women: "[T]here is no harm in saying that women, as a class, have smaller bones then men, wear lighter clothing, have more hair on their heads and less on their faces . . . ," but such comparisons only apply for particular cases: "Few women happen to be natural born mechanics; but if there is one, it is useless to try and argue her into being something different."[21] What is important is that the particular job should be done by the particular person who does it best:

> If the women make better office-workers than men, they must have the office work. If any individual woman is able to make a first-class lawyer, doctor, architect or engineer, then she must be allowed to try her hand at it. Once lay down the rule that the

job comes first and you throw that job open to every individual, man or woman, fat or thin, tall or short, ugly or beautiful, who is able to do that job better than the rest of the world.[22]

The point is not that every occupation or interest that used to be done by men should now be done by every woman. As a classics scholar, Sayers points out that not every woman wants to know about Aristotle any more than every man wants to know about Aristotle, "but I, eccentric individual that I am, do want to know about Aristotle, and I submit that there is nothing in my bodily shape or bodily functions which need prevent me from knowing about him."[23]

The implications for a theology of women's ordination should be obvious. The crucial question is whether there are any essential differences between men and women that are significant for exercising church office. Specifically, granted that there are obvious physical and social differences between men and women (only men can be fathers, sons, or brothers; only women can be mothers, daughters, or sisters), do any of these have anything to do with the capacity to speak or teach or exercise authority (Protestant complementarianism) or to preside over worship or celebrate the sacraments (Catholic sacramentalism), or exercise pastoral care for parishioners, that would indicate that certainly not every woman, but women with the specifically necessary callings and gifts could not perform these functions?[24]

Opponents of women's ordination might well respond to the above question in two ways. First, it could be argued, while it is generally the case that those with the requisite skills are best suited for particular kinds of work, ordained ministry is not simply "work," but a vocation, a divine calling to be recognized by the church that must be distinguished from merely secular occupations. Problematic in this claim, however, is the recognition since the Reformation that *all* forms of work, if they are good work, should be considered as "vocations." Sayers herself emphasizes this when she writes that any work worth doing is a vocation: "It is the business of the Church to recognize that the secular vocation, as such, is sacred."[25] But the converse is also true. If the secular vocation is sacred, the sacred vocation is also "good work" and should be done by the person who is most able to do the work well. Given the choice, do opponents of women's ordination really believe that it would be preferable to have a man who preaches poorly, presides at worship in a slovenly manner, and has poor pastoral skills (and the examples of these are far too many) over a woman who preaches well, presides reverently at worship, and exercises compassionate pastoral ministry, simply because he is a man and she a woman?

Second, the opponent of women's ordination could well respond that nothing Sayers writes demands that women ought to pursue ordained ministry. Modern opponents of women's ordination nonetheless insist that they recognize women's lay ministries, and there is nothing to prevent a woman with skills in writing (such as Sayers), preaching, teaching, or pastoral care from fulfilling her vocation in a lay ministry. This argument is probably more credible if coming from Catholic opponents to women's ordination, who (at least in theory) restrict women's ministry only from presiding at liturgical functions; however, it is still question-begging insofar as the very same argument could be made concerning men. It could be said of any man as it is said of women that the pastoral skills that are usually recognized as signs of vocation to ordained ministry could also be exercised in some form of lay ministry. So the question is not whether some (not all) women might pursue ordained ministry rather than some form of lay ministry, but rather whether anyone (male or female) should do so when vocational gifts could always be fulfilled in some kind of lay ministry instead? If one argues that, at least in some particular cases, some men should pursue ordained ministry, then *ipso facto*, the case is the same for some (not all) women.

TOWARD A POSITIVE THEOLOGY OF NON-GENDERED ORDINATION

In much of what has been written in this book, the arguments have been defensive, responding to objections to the ordination of women. What follows will provide a summary of a theological case in favor of the ordination of women, or, more specifically, an argument for a non-gendered approach to ordained ministry. Specifically, what is the purpose of ordained ministry within the church, and what would be the requirements for selecting certain persons for church office, whether men or women?

First, any positive argument that men and women are equally eligible for ordination to church office must say "no" to the "culture wars" of the last few decades, and to non-theological arguments concerning sexuality and its relationship to ordained ministry. A properly biblical and systematic theology of sexuality is not hierarchical (as in complementarianism); neither, however, does it derive its understanding of sexuality from postmodern identity politics. Although certainly affirming an equality between men and women, a biblical and systematic theology of sexuality does not regard male and female sexuality as fluid or interchangeable, as does much contemporary sexual identity politics. Again, only men can be fathers, sons, and brothers; only women can be mothers, daughters, and sisters.

At the same time, an argument for the suitability of the ordination of both men and women is not interested in debates between patriarchy and postmodernity for either upholding or rejecting traditional cultural notions of masculinity and femininity. As Carrie Miles points out, traditional notions of male and female "personality" are rooted in preindustrial divisions of labor between the sexes. In preindustrial agricultural societies, successful males need to be physically strong, ambitious, intelligent, competitive, independent, and aggressive. Those who succeed will be those who subdue and master others. Correspondingly, in preindustrial cultures, women compete not for the best jobs, but for the best husbands. Successful women will be physically attractive, nurturing, good household managers, accommodating, emotionally sensitive, patient, and interested in children. These are, of course, traditional cultural understandings of what makes men masculine and women feminine. They also correspond economically to the descriptions of the consequences of sin for men and women in Genesis 3: the curse on the ground means that there is a scarcity of provisions, and men must work hard in order to survive. Women must turn to their husbands since they are financially dependent, and husbands rule over their wives since, in an agricultural economy, men necessarily have more power in the family relationship. The very thing that makes women valuable—their ability to bear and nurse children—makes them economically dependent on their husbands.[26] Traditional male and female cultural stereotypes also correspond to the reward/punishment structures of traditional honor/shame cultures, a structure which, as argued above, was undermined by the principles of "Christological subversion" and "mutual submission."

In addition, however, insofar as traditional notions of masculinity and femininity are tied to the economics of preindustrial cultures, they are increasingly irrelevant in a postindustrial culture. For most jobs, modern men do not necessarily have to be physically stronger or more aggressive since they are no longer restricted to physical labor to make their livings. Modern women are no longer tied necessarily to work that keeps them physically close to children since modern economic production is no longer home-based. Accordingly, even if it were desirable to maintain traditional stereotypical notions of masculinity and femininity, it would not be possible apart from a return to a preindustrial economy that created the distinctions in the first place, a return which is culturally implausible, and which even traditionalists would likely not desire.

Second, a positive argument for a non-gendered account of ordained ministry should be grounded in a theology that is creational, Christocentric (cruciform), and Trinitarian (redemptive-historical and ecclesial). An egalitarian biblical theology of ordination is founded on a proper reading of (1) the account of the creation of humanity in the image of God as male and female in Genesis 1 and 2; (2) Jesus' teaching on marriage and sexuality, along with his relationship to his female disciples; (3) Paul's egalitarian theology of marriage and sexuality; and (4) the practice and ministry of both men and women in the early church. Consequently, an egalitarian anthropology will be grounded in a Trinitarian Christocentric personalist ontology. In terms of symbolism, such a theology will be rooted in a reciprocal Trinitarian personalism, rather than a "binary" and hierarchical male/female symbolism; a personalist ontology will emphasize that relationality and mutual submission are crucial to what it means to be male or female. (Many of the details of the above argument have been made already in the preceding chapters and will not be repeated at length here.)

RETURNING TO GENESIS

A personalist and relational Christian ontology will begin with a return to God's intentions in creation prior to humanity's fall into sin. There is a correlation between the creation of humanity in the image of God as male and female and Trinitarian personalism; all human beings are created to know and love the Triune God who has created humanity in his image. The relational orientation of men and women toward one another is a reflection of the eternal love between the Triune persons. The creation of human beings as male and female is a reflection of and participation through grace in the perichoretic relations of the Triune persons. Men and women are created to know and love God; but they are also made for one another, for mutuality and relationality, and not for a subordination of one sex to another. To the contrary of complementarian hierarchicalism, the historic subordination of women to men characteristic of all preindustrial cultures is a consequence of the fall into sin, and redemption entails a reversal of this subordination, a return to the equality, mutuality, and reciprocity between men and women intended by God in the original creation. Again, the creation mandate of Genesis 1:28 applies to both men and women, and this certainly has implications for a gender-neutral understanding of ordination to church office because the specific roles of ordained ministry parallel the demands of the creation mandate (or, rather, creation blessing, as Carrie Miles argues).[27]

CHRISTOCENTRICITY

The New Testament expands on the Old Testament by applying to Jesus Christ what Genesis says about the image of God. James 3:9 uses language much like that of Genesis, but other passages in the New Testament speak of Jesus Christ as the Son who is the "image of God" (Col. 1:15), of the "glory of Christ, who is the image of God" (2 Cor. 4:4), as the one who preexisted "in the form of God," but took on the "form of a servant" (Phil. 2:6-7), as the "radiance of the glory of God and the exact imprint of his nature" (Heb. 1:3), and as the typological fulfillment of the "Son of Man" language in Psalm 8, "who was made for a little while lower than the angels" (Heb. 2:5-9; cf. Ps. 8:3-8). As the incarnate Son of God, Jesus Christ is the perfect image of the Father. Also discussed previously, Romans 5 identifies Jesus Christ as the second Adam.[28]

Two passages in particular (already discussed at length) pick up on the male-female imagery of Genesis and apply it either to Jesus Christ and humanity or to Christ and the church (1 Cor. 11:3, 11-12; Eph. 5:21-23), speaking of Christ as the "head of every man" (1 Cor. 11:3) or "head of the church," and the church both as Christ's body and his bride (Eph. 5:23, 32). The church fathers developed this bodily and nuptial imagery to suggest that just as the woman was taken from the side of Adam, so the church as the bride of Christ is taken from Christ's bleeding side on the cross.

Just as in Genesis 1, however, the focus of these two passages is on nurture and reciprocity, not authority. First Corinthians 11 emphasizes that the woman is the "glory of man," and that, just as the woman was originally taken from the man, so now all men come to be through women. The only reference to "authority" in the passage is to the woman's own authority (1 Cor. 11:10). Similarly, Ephesians 5 focuses on the mutual subordination of all Christians to one another, and to the way in which both men and woman resemble Jesus Christ by "walking in love as Christ loved us" (Eph. 5:2; cf. 5:25) and by "submitting to one another out of reverence for Christ" (5:21; cf. 5:33). Also of significance is that neither passage specifically says anything about church office; 1 Cor. 11 is addressing disruptive worship practices; Ephesians 5 addresses worship insofar as all Christians are encouraged to address one another in "hymns and spiritual songs," and the Christian family is to echo this mutual submission of all Christians to one another.[29]

The New Testament insistence that it is Jesus Christ who is the true image of God leads to a modification of Old Testament anthropology. Accordingly, all Christians now image Jesus Christ as disciples who are "in Christ" and in whom Christ dwells, and who participate in Christ—the image of God—as they are joined to the risen Christ through the presence of the indwelling Holy Spirit. Unlike Moses, Christians "beholding the glory of the Lord, are being transformed into the same image from one degree of glory to another" (2 Cor. 3:18).

At the same time, cruciformity is crucial to an understanding of Christian discipleship and how Christians resemble or represent Jesus Christ. Three New Testament passages are crucial in this regard: Philippians 2:5-11 is the "master story" for Paul's account of cruciform spirituality; as Christ "emptied himself" by taking on the form of a servant, so also Christians are to look not to their own interests, but to those of others. Ephesians 5 portrays the mutual submission of all Christians to one another, who "walk in love, as Christ loved us and gave himself up for us, a fragrant offering and sacrifice to God" (Eph. 5:2). Second Corinthians 4 describes the practice of Christian ministry as exemplified by the apostles, of those who carry a treasure in jars of clay, carrying in their bodies the death of Jesus so that Jesus' life is manifest in their bodies (2 Cor. 4:7-12). This model of cruciform spirituality is the correct pattern for the manner in which the ordained minister does or does not represent or resemble Jesus Christ.[30]

Ironically, despite their different ways of insisting that the ordained minister must resemble Christ, both Protestant complementarians and Catholic sacramentalists miss the New Testament's most crucial point regarding resemblance of Christians to Jesus Christ—designated above by the terms "Christological subversion" and "cruciformity." For the New Testament, "resembling Jesus Christ" is consistently expressed in terms of cruciformity. Christians resemble Jesus Christ by pointing away from themselves to the crucified and risen Jesus Christ and by sharing in his suffering. Resemblance to Jesus Christ through cruciform discipleship is expected of all Christians, and it is not gender-specific. All Christians resemble Jesus Christ by following the path of the cross. This is the model that the New Testament sets up for following Christ in Philippians 2:1-11. It is the model of mutual submission demanded of all Christians, men and women, parents and children, masters and servants, in Ephesians 5:1–6:9. It is the model for apostleship in 2 Corinthians 4.

Against complementarianism, the New Testament does not speak of leadership simply in terms of authority of some over others; rather, the New Testament consistently challenges what Alan Padgett has called Type I submission. All Christians are called to represent Jesus Christ in terms of what Padgett calls Type II submission, the mutual submission of voluntarily taking on the role of servants in relation to one another.[31] Neither the Old Testament nor the New Testament specifically rejected Mediterranean social institutions, yet Christological subversion consistently challenges those institutions. Leaders are not told simply to exercise authority or power over subordinates. Rather, as in Ephesians 5, mutual submission is the model of authority expected of all Christians. When Paul uses the word *kephalē* ("head") metaphorically in 1 Corinthians 11 and Ephesians 5, he does not use the metaphor to speak of authority, but rather of mutuality, nurture and self-sacrifice. Cruciformity is also the model provided for apostleship and pastoral leadership in 2 Corinthians 4–6. The church's office holders resemble Jesus Christ as those who carry treasure in clay jars, who proclaim not themselves but Jesus Christ, and who represent Christ by carrying in their bodies the death of Jesus (2 Cor. 4:7-12). This is a resemblance to Jesus Christ that is based neither on authority nor in sexuality.

Against Catholic sacramentalist arguments, how does Paul suggest that the church's apostles resemble Christ? Not in terms of masculine sexual imagery, but rather by pointing away from themselves toward the crucified Jesus Christ, as does John the Baptist in Grunewald's painting. The church's office holders resemble Christ as earthen vessels, and through sharing in Christ's suffering. Nothing in any of this New Testament imagery is gender-specific.

WORD AND SACRAMENT

What are the responsibilities of the ordained minister? Ecumenical consensus points to two main tasks: proclamation of the Word and administration of the sacraments.

Ministry of the Word

Historically, there are four primary ways in which the ordained minister is understood to exercise the ministry of the Word: authority, preaching (and teaching), the power of the keys, and pastoral care.[32]

Complementarians have focused on the exercise of authority as the primary function of the ordained minister, and everything else flows from that. The complementarian argument is that women cannot be ordained ministers because they cannot exercise authority over men, and, in consequence, cannot preach or teach either.

There is no rejection here of the notion of authority as such. Insofar as ordained ministry involves genuine leadership, it necessarily entails a kind of authority, yet an authority re-interpreted through the lenses of cruciformity and Christological subversion. Ordained clergy exercise authority by pointing away from themselves to the crucified Christ.

Recent authors have corrected both an authoritarian permanently hierarchical understanding of authority as well as the postmodern tendency to reject all authority as inherently oppressive.[33] Postmodern culture is distrustful of authority, and in recent decades, much of the mainline church has been trying to downplay that part of the pastor's (or priest's) mission. One of the chief ways in which the twentieth-century church did that was by substituting different understandings of authority for the pastor's authority. The ordained minister was no longer someone who points to Jesus Christ, but a therapist, a social worker, or the Chief Operating Officer of the congregation. At the same time, when people are uncertain about the source of their authority, they become frightened, and they fall back on their own personal authority. There are clergy who have no problem imagining themselves to be representatives of Christ, but the image they prefer is that of Christ enthroned in glory, the *Christos Pantokrator*.

To the contrary, in 1 Peter, the apostle explains the proper type of ministerial leadership: "So I exhort the elders (presbyters) among you, as a fellow elder (presbyter) and a witness of the sufferings of Christ, as well as a partaker in the glory that is going to be revealed: shepherd the flock of God among you, not by way of compulsion, but willingly, as God would have you; not for shameful gain, but eagerly; not lording it over those in your charge, but being examples to the flock. And when the chief Shepherd appears, you will receive the unfading crown of glory" (5:1-4, author translation). The presbyter is asked to *shepherd* the flock as one whose role is modeled on that of the Good Shepherd. The language of suffering ("witness of the sufferings of Christ") is reminiscent of similar language in 2 Corinthians 4:7-12.

Lacking in the passage is any use of such terms as *exousia*, the normal Greek New Testament word for "authority"; to the contrary, the presbyter is specifically forbidden from exercising any domineering top-down authority. In 1 Peter, office-holders are called to exercise authority as did Jesus, who said "[W]hoever would be great among you must be your servant, and whoever would be first among you must be your slave, even as the Son of Man came not to be served but to serve, and to give his life as a ransom for many" (Matt. 20:26-28). Verse 5 does indeed call on those who are younger to "submit" (ὑποτάγητε, *hypotagēte*) to the elders/presbyters (πρεσβυτέροις, *presbyterois*). At the same time, however, the submission is not top-down hierarchical submission (Padgett's "Type I submission"), but the mutual submission of all to each other: "But all of you (πάντες, *pantes*) be subject to one another (ἀλλήλοις, *allēlois*), and be clothed with humility: for God resists the proud, and gives grace to the humble" (modernized KJV).

As the role of the Good Shepherd is to lay down his life for the sheep (John 10:11), so the ordained pastor follows the example of the One Shepherd. That kind of leadership is more difficult than being a social worker or a CEO. It demands more longsuffering than does top-down authority. Ordained clergy cannot act as shepherds unless they love the people they are called to serve, and unless they are willing to suffer. The pastor or priest does not then act on his or her own authority. Pastoral ministry is that of a shepherd who shares in the ministry of the One Shepherd. Any authority that ordained clergy have comes from beyond themselves. It is the authority to share with the Good Shepherd in laying down their lives for the sheep. Obviously, such sacrificial authority is not gender-specific.

The second role of the presbyter is that of preaching or proclaiming the Word. The primary job of the preacher is to communicate the Word of God about Jesus Christ as contained in the Scriptures. The main point of such preaching is, once again, to point to Christ. The pastor's sermons should focus on the Good Shepherd: who Jesus Christ is, and what he did. Who is Jesus? He is the Son of God, the incarnate Word become flesh, the second person of the Trinity. What did Jesus do? He became human, he died for our sins, he rose from the dead, and he is coming again. As noted above, in the incarnation, Jesus Christ models a cruciform pattern of life that is the paradigm for all Christian discipleship. That is the gospel. That is what the pastor is to preach. The good news is about Jesus Christ, his person and work, and that is what the preacher needs to come back to in his or her preaching, over and over. And if he or she does that, he or she will play the same role as does John the

Baptist in Grunewald's painting, and God will speak through his or her words. As the Anglican priest and poet George Herbert wrote:

> Lord, how can man preach thy eternal word?
> He is a brittle crazy glass
> Yet in thy temple thou dost him afford
> This glorious and transcendent place
> To be a window, through thy grace.
> (George Herbert, "The Windows")[34]

Again, to proclaim the word that Jesus Christ has died and is risen is not something gender-specific. To the contrary, the Gospels make clear that it was not men, but rather women, who first came to the empty tomb, who were the first witnesses that the crucified Jesus was no longer dead but risen. In his first sermon in the Book of Acts (2:14-40), the apostle Peter makes clear that this proclamation of the resurrection of Jesus Christ is a fulfillment of a prophecy of the Old Testament prophet Joel. When God pours out his Spirit on all people, sons and daughters will prophecy; God will pour out his Spirit on his servants, both men and women (vv. 17-18).

The next way in which the pastor acts as a shepherd is that of the "power of the keys." The power of the keys is the ordained minister's authority to proclaim Christ's forgiveness to the repentant. Reformation Christians get uncomfortable here, but a reminder is needed that this is an authority that Christ has given to his church (Matt. 16:19; John 20:23). The Anglican Reformer John Jewel stated:

> Moreover, we say that Christ hath given to His ministers power to bind, to loose, to open, to shut. And that the office of loosing consisteth in this point: that the minister should ... offer by the preaching of the Gospel the merits of Christ and full pardon, to such as have lowly and contrite hearts, and do unfeignedly repent themselves, pronouncing unto the same a sure and undoubted forgiveness of their sins, and hope of everlasting salvation.[35]

To be able to pronounce Christ's forgiveness to repentant sinners is not in conflict with the Reformation understanding of justification by faith alone; it is a way of making forgiveness concrete and objective. Again, it is important to remember that the ordained minister does not proclaim forgiveness on the basis of his or her own authority. The pastor is a sinner, just like the person who comes for confession. As the prophet Isaiah says, we are all people of unclean lips, dwelling in the midst of a people of unclean lips (Isa. 6:5). But One greater than a seraph has touched our lips, and he has said, "Your guilt is taken away, and your sin atoned for" (Isa. 6:7). It is because Jesus Christ has forgiven him or her that the presbyter can proclaim that Christ forgives others. In order to do this, clergy need to acknowledge their own sins, and they need to accept Christ's forgiveness.

Finally, there is one last way in which the ordained minister acts as a shepherd of Jesus Christ. The minister is pastor and spiritual director. The words "pastor" and "pastoral" come from the Latin word that means "shepherd." There is a uniquely pastoral dimension to ordained ministry. The traditional exhortations given to clergy at ordination speak to this responsibility. One of the responsibilities of the pastor is to get to know his or her parishioners, to spend time with them, to pray with them, to baptize them, to marry them, to bury them.

ADMINISTRATION OF THE SACRAMENTS

If Protestant accounts of ordained ministry have focused on the pastor's authority and proclamation of the word, Catholic accounts have focused on the role of the presbyter in administering the sacraments, specifically in presiding at the celebration of the Eucharist. As noted previously, Catholic arguments against the ordination of women often focus on the Catholic understanding of church office as a "sacramental priesthood."

A theologically nuanced understanding of ordained ministry does not necessarily see these two models as opposed so much as complementary. The office of the presbyter includes both preaching and proclaiming the Word, but also presiding at the celebration of the Eucharist. At the same time, as with the Protestant understanding of ministry as the proclamation of the Word, so an understanding of ministry that emphasizes ordination as "priesthood" needs to recognize that New Testament office is not simply a repristinating of the Old Testament sacrificial system; rather, as with proclamation of the Word, New Testament priesthood must be redefined Christologically: Jesus Christ is not only the perfect image of God and the Good Shepherd; he is also the One High Priest who not only fulfills, but also transforms Old Testament worship. As Cyril of Alexandria emphasized, the church's worship is not something of its own that the church offers to God, but a participation in the risen Jesus Christ's vicarious worship of the Father through the Holy Spirit.[36]

The teleological end of Christian worship is the church's union with the triune God as the church becomes the body of Christ united to the crucified and risen humanity of Jesus Christ its head through the agency of the Holy Spirit. Sacraments do not have an end in themselves, but exist as means of grace to enable this union between the crucified and risen Christ and the church. As they are united to the crucified and risen Jesus Christ through the Holy Spirit in baptism (Rom. 5), all Christians reflect Christ's image and are conformed to it. So in Thomas Aquinas's discussion of baptismal character, it is Jesus Christ who is the primary "character" or image of God (following Heb. 1:3); all Christians participate in and resemble Christ's character through baptism, and it is this participation in Christ's character through the act of baptism that brings one into the church that enables the priest/

presbyter to represent Christ.[37] In other words, the logic of Aquinas's position is that *in persona ecclesiae* (in the person of the church) precedes *in persona Christi* (in the person of Christ). Or, at least, that representational symbolism is dynamic. All Christians resemble Jesus Christ insofar as Christ is the head of the church; the church represents Christ as sharing in Christ's character through baptism. It is thus through their union with Christ in baptism that Christians are made one with his body, the church, and all Christians represent Christ.

Thus, the way in which the ordained minister acts *in persona Christi* when presiding at the church's worship is neither unique, nor is it based on male sexuality. The eucharistic minister resembles Jesus Christ in first receiving the baptismal character shared by all Christians. It is thus not the Eucharist, but baptism that is the originating sacrament of identification with Christ. In the church's worship at the Eucharist, the presiding minister represents the church as having received the baptismal character that makes worship possible, and thus represents Jesus Christ, the head of the church. In the eucharistic prayer, the celebrant first acts on behalf of the church as its representative (*in persona ecclesiae*). The eucharistic prayer is a prayer—it begins and ends with the words "we"—and, in this prayer, the priest represents Jesus Christ as first representing the church, which is his bride. Thus there is a crucial significance to the *epiclesis* in the eucharistic prayer; in invoking the Holy Spirit to descend on bread and wine to make them the risen Christ's body and blood, and on the gathered people to make them Christ's body, the priest acts as a representative of the church as the body of Christ, and in this manner as a representative of Jesus Christ as the head of this body.

If the church's worship is described using the language of "eucharistic sacrifice," it is necessary to affirm (as do all contemporary ecumenical agreements) that it is Jesus Christ who offers the sacrifice, not the presiding minister. It is Jesus Christ who makes himself present, not the celebrant. Moreover, as the patristic church taught, and as modern ecumenical agreements also emphasize, the Eucharist is not a new sacrifice, but simply the same sacrifice of the cross which is "re-presented." Jesus Christ is not "sacrificed again"; rather, as the risen Jesus Christ becomes truly present through the invocation of the Holy Spirit, so Christ is present in the once-for-all atoning significance of his life, death, and resurrection. The eucharistic sacrifice does not depend, then, on the person of the ordained priest, but on the person of the crucified and risen Jesus Christ. The celebrant does not "offer" anything of him or herself; nor is the priest a "mediator" in the sense of being a substitute for Christ or an *alter Christus*.

In the eucharistic prayer, then, it is Jesus Christ who is the primary celebrant, not the ordained priest. Again, it must be emphasized that the eucharistic prayer is a prayer, not a drama. The presiding minister is praying on behalf of the entire congregation, not acting a drama or playing a role in a play. The "words of institution" recited in the eucharistic prayer are part of this prayer in which the presiding minister prays on behalf of, and acts as a representative of, the gathered community (*in persona ecclesiae*).

Of course, in a manner similar to the proclamation of the Word, the eucharistic minister represents Christ not only to the extent that he or she represents the church as Christ's bride, but also, once again, in terms of cruciformity; in recalling Jesus Christ's atoning sacrifice in the "Words of Institution"—"This is my body given for you; this is my blood shed for you"—the celebrant points away from himself or herself and his or her own adequacies or accomplishments to the complete sufficiency of the Lord Jesus Christ, crucified, risen, and returning in glory to redeem and sanctify the church. It is the crucified and risen Jesus Christ's own sacrifice that is made present in the church's worship, not that of the church's ordained clergy. The worship of the church is also a participation in the risen Christ's own worship on the church's behalf. The structure of the eucharistic prayer makes clear that the presiding minister is praying on behalf of and as a representative of the gathered community of the church; insofar as the church is the bride of Christ (and is thus symbolically feminine), women most appropriately have the capacity to illustrate this by leading the church's prayers, especially the eucharistic prayer.[38]

CONCLUDING REFLECTIONS

What might be the implications of what really is the church's *new* understanding of the equality of men and women, and of a gender-neutral understanding of ordination to church office?

First, a Trinitarian understanding of personhood and a relational and reciprocal understanding of the relationship between men and women means not only that men and women are equals, but that their identity as male and female is established in relation to one another; men and women need one another and should be friends with one another. Thomas Aquinas transformed Aristotle's notion of friendship from the *Nicomachean Ethics* in light of Jesus' statement in John 15:15—"I call you no more servants . . . but friends"—to suggest that charity as the highest theological virtue is friendship with Jesus, and friendship with God. But charity is also friendship with fellow human beings, and grounds Aquinas's understanding of ethics summarized in the Ten Commandments as love of God and love of neighbor.[39] Certainly this has implications for the relationships between men and women in the church.

Karl Barth famously developed his understanding of the relationship between men and women in light of the two creation narratives in Genesis 1 and 2. Genesis 1:27 points to the interpersonal and relational nature of what it means to be created in the image of God; man as male and female indicates that the *imago dei* is fundamentally relational, and that the image of God is a reflection of the triune interpersonal relations of Father, Son, and Holy Spirit. That humanity is male and female means that humanity cannot be humanity alone, but only as male in relation to female and female in relation to male. There is no man or woman as such, but "only concretely masculine and feminine co-existence and co-operation in all things." The creation narrative of Genesis 2 indicates that humanity means "fellow human": "the encounter of man and woman as such is being in encounter and therefore the center of humanity." The basic distinction and connection of I and Thou is thus "coincident with that of male and female."[40] So, for Barth, the image of God is essentially personal and relational, grounded in the Trinitarian relations of love between Father, Son, and Holy Spirit. Barth goes beyond Aquinas in emphasizing that it is precisely the mutual and complementary relationship between humanity as man and woman that is the ontological foundation of the personalistic and relational image of God in human beings.[41]

Second, the centrality of cruciformity as the paradigm for Christian discipleship, combined with Paul's call for mutual submission, and both Paul's and 1 Peter's description of ministry, leads to a transformed understanding of Christian ministry and authority in terms of servanthood and mutual submission rather than top-down exercise of authority of some over others. That is, the New Testament challenges the first-century Mediterranean honor/shame culture exemplified in what Alan Padgett calls "Type I submission," and offers instead the paradigm of mutual submission ("Type II submission"). For the New Testament, to exercise church office means to be a servant to one's fellow servants. Again, there is nothing about mutual submission in love patterned on Christ's cruciform self-sacrifice that is inherently gender-specific.

Third, Paul's coordination of a theology of the Eucharist as participation (or communion) in the body of the crucified and risen Jesus Christ, combined with his imagery of the church as a diverse body of many members, points to hospitality at the core of the church's fellowship (koinonia; Rom. 12:4-5; 1 Cor. 12:12-31). Hospitality means not only welcoming the stranger who is outside the church, but, more specifically, welcoming one's brother or sister inside the church. Neither men nor women can say to the other, "I have no need of you." However, a hierarchical understanding of sexual "gender roles" leads necessarily to an antagonistic relationship between men and women. At least insofar as it comes to the question of the kinds of gifts that would normally indicate a call to ordained ministry, the refusal to ordain women is to say to another member of the body of Christ, "I have no need of you."

A proper understanding of Christian community will lead necessarily to male repentance for failure to recognize the gifts and calling of women within the Christian congregation. It will also mean a willingness to listen to the voices of women in the church. Resistance to women's ordination contributes to the double bind in which women find themselves in the church, in that women are denied the moral authority to speak, they lack the power to speak to the church, they are punished if they speak, and they lack support of the community if they do speak.

But refusing women the freedom to speak to the church is not only to deny them the moral integrity of the word that they need to speak to the church, but also to deny the Christian community the word it may need to hear from women. By denying women ordination, we deny them the ability to use a divinely given gift. But more than the harm done to women by refusing to allow them to speak is the harm done to the church. Denying women the opportunity of ordination means that women cannot speak the Word of God to the church. The church needs to hear the word that women are called to speak.

This will also mean that the church needs to reconsider its theology of vocation to embrace an understanding of vocation based on "Spirit-gifting."[42] It helps here to recognize the difference between two different understandings of vocation, what might be called the difference between "Benedictine" and "Dominican" models of ministry. Benedictines are cloistered monks, and the understanding of vocation among monks tends to assume one does not have a vocation until one proves otherwise. It is only after one has been formed in the cloister that it is considered safe to enter once again into the outside world.

To the contrary, the Dominicans were not cloistered monks, but mendicant preachers, the Order of Preachers. The Dominican model of vocation is thus that of an "apostolate"; Dominicans exist in order to preach for the salvation of souls. This results in an entirely different understanding of vocation. The Dominican understanding of vocation is that if one has the gift of preaching, one *must* preach—one has the vocation to preach.[43]

The church's understanding of vocation to ordained ministry has been too often based on the Benedictine model—the assumption that one does not have a vocation unless one proves otherwise, and in the case of women, the church always presumes otherwise. To the contrary, if particular women (not every woman) demonstrate the gifts in preaching, liturgical celebration, and pastoral skills that would (in the case of men) indicate a calling to ordained ministry, then the church should presume that these women have a call to ordained ministry until proven otherwise. The burden of proof is not on those who would argue for the ordination of women, but on those who would deny it.

Again, the adoption of a "Spirit-gifting" or "Dominican" understanding of vocation makes clear that the purpose of ordained ministry is not that of exercising power over others or of privilege. To the contrary, the point of ordained ministry is one of service. As Katherine-Greene McCreight has pointed out, the focus of orthodox "biblical feminists" in the church is not on gaining equal rights for women in the church, but on asking for an equal opportunity to serve within the church.[44]

Finally, there is one last consideration concerning possible differences between men and women and how this might affect their vocations within the church. What is written in this book has focused primarily on similarities between men and women. As Dorothy L. Sayers emphasized, women are human, and women are more like men than they are like anything else. Of course, there are fundamental biological differences between men and women, and both the complementarity between women and men and many of the social roles that men and women fulfill are rooted in these essentially biological differences—again, only men can be husbands, fathers, sons, and brothers; only women can be mothers, wives, daughters, and sisters.

However, it can still be asked whether there are also psychological differences between men and women that might have relevance to the question of women's ordination. Are men (broadly speaking) more rational and abstract? Are women (broadly speaking) more emotional and relational?[45] Caution is in order here. While such psychological differences may exist *broadly* speaking, there will always be exceptions; despite broad tendencies, some particular women will always be more rational, independent, and abstract in their thinking than some men, while some men will always be more emotional and relational than some women.[46] However, even to recognize such differences (again, broadly speaking) between men and women is not an argument against women's ordination, but for it. The relevant corrective here would again be the apostle Paul's discussion of different gifts within the diversity of the church as the one body of Christ. If there are inherent psychological differences between *some* women and *some* men, this would indicate that those women would exercise pastoral ministry differently than those men, but they would do so in a complementary manner to serve the church in a manner in which those men could not. The church should not refuse the pastoral gifts of women because of possible intellectual, emotional, or psychological differences between women and men. To the contrary, the church *needs* the pastoral gifts of women in order to avoid one-sidedly masculine church leadership.

NOTES

1 PRELIMINARIES

1   George R. Sumner, *Being Salt: A Theology of an Ordered Church* (Eugene, Ore.: Cascade, 2007), 9–10; Thomas F. Torrance, *Royal Priesthood: A Theology of Ordained Ministry*, 2nd ed. (London: T&T Clark, 2003 [1993]), 103. In Reformed or Presbyterian polity, the person who fulfills the ministerial role of Word and Sacrament is sometimes identified as a "teaching elder."

2   Francis Martin, *The Feminist Question: Feminist Theology in the Light of Christian Tradition* (Grand Rapids: Eerdmans, 1994), 90–93, 108–9. What forms such "lay ministries" might take would differ among churches according to their understanding of the ministry of Word and Sacrament. For example, if there are churches in which the pastor alone has the primary responsibility of preaching, "lay preachers" would be a self-contradictory notion. In churches that allow certain laity to preach, there would still be a distinction between the role of pastor and the role of "lay preacher."

3   Donald W. Dayton and Douglas M. Strong, *Rediscovering an Evangelical Heritage: A Tradition and Trajectory of Integrating Piety and Justice*, 2nd ed. (Grand Rapids: Baker Academic, 2014). Whether or not women may have held church office during the New Testament or early patristic period is a distinct issue, not addressed in this introductory chapter.

4   See especially Carrie A. Miles, *The Redemption of Love: Rescuing Marriage and Sexuality from the Economics of a Fallen World* (Grand Rapids: Brazos, 2006).

5   On secularism, see Charles Taylor, *A Secular Age* (Cambridge, Mass.: Harvard University Press, 2007).

6   George Hunsinger, *The Eucharist and Ecumenism: Let Us Keep the Feast* (Cambridge: Cambridge University Press, 2008), 1–18.

2 NON-THEOLOGICAL ARGUMENTS AGAINST THE ORDINATION OF WOMEN

1   James Davison Hunter, *Culture Wars: The Struggle to Define America* (New York: Basic Books, 1991).

2   Episcopal Bishop John Shelby Spong was one of the first to use this imagery. See Spong, *Rescuing the Bible from Fundamentalism: A Bishop Rethinks the Meaning of Scripture* (San Francisco: HarperCollins, 1992).

3   Advocates of "inclusiveness" would include the late Marcus Borg and the feminist theologian Sallie McFague. See Borg, *Meeting Jesus Again for the First Time: The Historical Jesus and the Heart of Contemporary Faith* (San Francisco: HarperSanFrancisco, 1994); idem, *The Heart of Christianity: Rediscovering a Life of Faith* (New York: HarperCollins, 2003); idem, *Speaking Christian: Why Christian Words Have Lost Their Meaning and Power—and How They Can Be Restored* (New York: HarperCollins, 2011); McFague, *Models of God: Theology for an Ecological Nuclear Age* (Philadelphia: Fortress, 1987).

4   Martin Luther King Jr., "Letter from a Birmingham Jail," https://www.africa.upenn .edu/Articles_Gen/Letter_Birmingham.html.

5   For a now-classic Evangelical account, see Donald W. Dayton and Douglas M. Strong, *Rediscovering an Evangelical Heritage: A Tradition and Trajectory of Integrating Piety and Justice*, 2nd ed. (Grand Rapids: Baker Academic, 2014).

6   Martin Luther, "The Freedom of a Christian," in *Career of the Reformer I*, Harold J. Grimm, ed., W. A. Lambert and Harold J. Grimm, trans., vol. 31 of *Luther's Works*, American ed., Jaroslav Pelikan and Helmut T. Lehmann, eds. (Philadelphia: Fortress, 1957), 327–77.

7   Luther, "Against the Murdering, Thieving Hordes of Peasants," in *Christian in Society III*, Robert C. Schultz, ed., Charles M. Jacobs and Robert C. Schultz, trans., vol. 46 of *Luther's Works*, American ed., Jaroslav Pelikan and Helmut T. Lehmann, eds. (Philadelphia: Fortress, 1967), 49–55.

8   John Wesley, "Thoughts upon Slavery," in vol. 11 of *The Works of the Reverend John Wesley, A.M.*, Thomas Jackson, ed. (London: John Mason, 1841), https://docsouth.unc .edu/church/wesley/wesley.html, 56–76.

9   Leo XIII, *Rerum Novarum*, encyclical letter, May 15, 1891, https://w2.vatican.va/ content/leo-xiii/en/encyclicals/documents/hf_l-xiii_enc_15051891_rerum -novarum.html; Pius XI, *Quadragesimo Anno*, encyclical letter, May 15, 1931, https:// w2.vatican.va/content/pius-xi/en/encyclicals/documents/hf_p-xi_enc_19310515 _quadragesimo-anno.html; John XXIII, *Pacem in Terris*, encyclical letter, April 11, 1963, https://w2.vatican.va/content/john-xxiii/en/encyclicals/documents/hf_j-xxiii _enc_11041963_pacem.html; Second Vatican Council, "Pastoral Constitution on the Church, *Gaudium et Spes*," December 7, 1965, http://www.vatican.va/archive/hist _councils/ii_vatican_council/documents/vat-ii_const_19651207_gaudium-et-spes _en.html.

10   *GS*, sec. 9.

11   *GS*, sec. 60.

12   This is not a book about homosexuality or whether the church should bless same-sex unions or gay marriage. Nonetheless, the subject needs to be mentioned because both conservative opponents of and liberal advocates of women's ordination often connect the two subjects. My own views coincide with the argument of New Testament scholar Richard B. Hays in his now classic *The Moral Vision of the New Testament: Community, Cross, New Creation* (New York: HarperCollins, 1996) and those of my colleague

Wesley Hill, *Washed and Waiting: Reflections on Christian Faithfulness and Homosexuality* (Grand Rapids: Zondervan, 2016 [2010]); idem, *Spiritual Friendship: Finding Love in the Church as a Celibate Gay Christian* (Grand Rapids: Brazos, 2015).

13　See especially chapter 13, "The Argument from Symbolism: God, Priests, Incarnation, and Apostles," in this volume.

14　However (as New Testament scholar Philip Payne points out), apart from Jesus Christ himself, who is identified as the "bishop/overseer of your souls" in 1 Pet. 2:25, the New Testament never specifically identifies any man with the title of bishop/overseer or presbyter/elder. Rather, the terms are generally applied to groups and not to specific individuals. Philip B. Payne, *Man and Woman, One in Christ: An Exegetical and Theological Study of Paul's Letters* (Grand Rapids: Zondervan, 2009), 453.

15　See chapter 3, "The Argument 'from Tradition' Is Not the 'Traditional' Argument," in this volume.

16　D. Stephen Long, *The Goodness of God: Theology, the Church, and Social Order* (Grand Rapids: Brazos, 2001), 51, 15–28.

17　Peter Brown, *Augustine of Hippo: A Biography* (Berkeley: University of California Press, 1969 [1967]), 372–75.

18　Kathryn Greene-McCreight, *Feminist Reconstructions of Christian Doctrine: Narrative Analysis and Appraisal* (New York: Oxford University Press, 2000), 36–40. On women's work as Christian vocation, see Dorothy L. Sayers, *Are Women Human?* (Grand Rapids: Eerdmans, 1971); idem, "Why Work?" in *Creed or Chaos?* (Manchester, N.H.: Sophia Institute Press, 1995), 72–78.

3　THE ARGUMENT "FROM TRADITION" IS NOT THE "TRADITIONAL" ARGUMENT

1　Sara Butler, *The Catholic Priesthood and Women: A Guide to the Teaching of the Church* (Chicago: Hillenbrand Books, 2006), viii, 59.

2　So, for example, Francis Martin, *The Feminist Question: Feminist Theology in the Light of Christian Tradition* (Grand Rapids: Eerdmans, 1994).

3　Origen, *Fr. 1 Cor.* 74; text in Claude Jenkins, "Origen on 1 Corinthians," *Journal of Theological Studies* 10, no. 37 (1908–1909): 29–51; cited in Patricia Cox Miller, ed., *Women in Early Christianity: Translations from Greek Texts* (Washington, D.C.: Catholic University of America Press, 2005), 29.

4　Tertullian, *On the Apparel of Women* 1.1 (*ANF* 4:14).

5　John Chrysostom, *The Kind of Women Who Ought to Be Taken as Wives* 4 (PG 51:230); cited in Elizabeth A. Clark, *Women in the Early Church*, Message of the Fathers of the Church 13 (Collegeville, Minn.: Liturgical, 1983), 36–38 (emphasis added).

6　John Chrysostom, *Discourse 4 on Genesis* (PG 54:594); cited in Clark, *Women in the Early Church*, 43–44.

7　John Chrysostom, *On Priesthood* 6.8 (*NPNF* 1/9:78–79).

8　See chapter 5, "Beginning with Genesis," in this volume.

9　Albert the Great, *Quaestiones super de animalibus XV* q. 11, in *Questions Concerning Aristotle's "On Animals,"* Irven M. Resnick and Kenneth F. Kitchell Jr., trans., vol. 9 of

Fathers of the Church Mediaeval Continuation (Washington, D.C.: Catholic University of America Press, 2008), 454–55.

10 Thomas Aquinas, *Summa Theologiae*, John Mortensen and Enrique Alarcón, eds., Laurence Shapcote, O.P., trans. (Lander, Wyo.: The Aquinas Institute for the Study of Sacred Doctrine, 2012), 1.92.3, https://aquinas.cc/la/en/~ST.I.Q92.A3. Subsequent references refer to this edition.

11 Aquinas, *ST* 1.93.6 *ad* 2.

12 Aquinas, *ST* 1.92.1.

13 Aquinas, *ST* suppl. 39. Aquinas ended the *Summa Theologiae* unfinished. The Supplement is the work of later writers, edited and compiled from his earlier *Commentary on the Sentences* of Peter Lombard. Although found at the end of the *Summa*, it actually represents Aquinas's earlier theology.

14 Aquinas, *ST* suppl. 39.

15 Aquinas, *ST* 1.92.1.

16 Noted by John Lee Thompson, *John Calvin and the Daughters of Sarah: Women in Regular and Exceptional Roles in the Exegesis of Calvin, His Predecessors, and His Contemporaries* (Geneva: Librairie Droz, 1992), 107, 108.

17 Augustine, *The Literal Meaning of Genesis*, John Hammond Taylor, S.J., trans. (Mahwah, N.J.: Paulist, 1982), 11.37, 2:171. An overview of "Eve in the History of Exegesis: Arguments for Women's Subordination" can be found in Thompson, *John Calvin and the Daughters of Sarah*, 107–59.

18 John Calvin, *Comm. Gen.* 3:16, in *Commentaries on the First Book of Moses Called Genesis*, John King, trans. (Grand Rapids: Eerdmans, 1948), 1:172, https://ccel.org/ccel/calvin/calcom01/calcom01.ix.i.html; Heinrich Bullinger, *Comm.* 1 Tim. 2:11–15, in *In Omnes Apostolicas Epistolas, Divi Videlicit Pavli, xiiii. et vii. Canonicas, Commentarii Heinrychi Bullingiri* (Zürich: Froschauer, 1537), 2 vols.; cited in Thompson, *John Calvin and the Daughters of Sarah*, 138.

19 Martin Luther, *Lectures on Genesis Chapters 1–5*, Jaroslav Pelikan, ed., George V. Schick, trans., vol. 1 of *Luther's Works*, American ed., Jaroslav Pelikan and Helmut T. Lehmann, eds. (Philadelphia: Fortress, 1958), 115; cited in Theo M. M. A. C. Bell, "Man Is a Microcosmos: Adam and Eve in Luther's Lectures on Genesis (1535–1545)," *Concordia Theological Quarterly* 69, no. 2 (2005): 159–84 (168).

20 Bell suggests that there are ambiguities in Luther's discussion of male and female equality before the fall. For instance, Luther suggests that God gave the law to Adam before the creation of Eve, which would imply that Adam (and not Eve) has a mandate to preach. Adam hears God's word directly, which he then gives to Eve. *Luther's Works* 1:105. Bell points out that there is a "certain tension" between this view and Luther's affirmation elsewhere that the woman could perceive God's word on her own. Bell, "Man Is a Microcosmos," 170.

21 James Boswell, *Boswell's Life of Johnson* (London: Henry Frowede, 1904), 2:309.

22 Richard Hooker, *The Laws of Ecclesiastical Polity* (London: J. M. Dent, 1907), 1:*pref.* 3.13. Subsequent references are to this edition.

23 Hooker, *Laws* 2:5.62.2.

24 Hooker, *Laws* 2:5.43.5.

25 Stephen Sykes, *Unashamed Anglicanism* (Nashville: Abingdon, 1995), 81–98. Sykes notes that Hooker's reference to women's "imbecility" was not a "gratuitous insult, but a standard piece of legal theory" at the time. Idem, *Unashamed Anglicanism*, 86.

26 John Knox, *First Blast of the Trumpet against the Monstrous Regiment of Women*, Edward Arber, ed. (Southgate, London, 1878), 5, https://ccel.org/ccel/knox/blast/blast.iv.i.html.

27 Knox, *First Blast of the Trumpet*, 12.

28 Knox, *First Blast of the Trumpet*, 15.

29 Knox, *First Blast of the Trumpet*, 15.

30 Knox, *First Blast of the Trumpet*, 18.

31 Knox, *First Blast of the Trumpet*, 18.

32 Butler, *Catholic Priesthood and Women*, 8.

33 Butler, *Catholic Priesthood and Women*, 46.

34 Butler, *Catholic Priesthood and Women*, 47.

35 Butler, *Catholic Priesthood and Women*, 26–34.

36 Butler, *Catholic Priesthood and Women*, 50.

37 Butler, *Catholic Priesthood and Women*, 2.

38 Butler, *Catholic Priesthood and Women*, 46–51.

39 Butler, *Catholic Priesthood and Women*, 61, 63.

40 Epiphanius, *Panarion* 7.79.2,3; 3.1. This and subsequent references are to *The "Panarion" of Epiphanius of Salamis: Books II and III*, Frank Williams, trans. (Leiden: Brill, 1994).

41 Epiphanius, *Panarion* 7.79.3–4.

42 Epiphanius, *Panarion* 7.79.1,6.

43 Epiphanius, *Panarion* 7.79.1,7.

44 Epiphanius, *Panarion* 7.79.2,1–2 (emphasis added).

45 Epiphanius, *Panarion* 7.79.2,3.

46 *Didascalia apostolorum*, R. Hugh Connolly, trans. (Oxford: Oxford University Press, 1929), 3.6; cited in Miller, *Women in Early Christianity*, 53.

47 *Apostolic Constitutions* 3.9 (*ANF* 7:429).

48 *Apostolic Constitutions* 3.9 (*ANF* 7:429) (emphasis added).

49 *Apostolic Constitutions* 3.6 (*ANF* 7:427–28).

50 John Piper and Wayne Grudem, eds., *Recovering Biblical Manhood and Womanhood: A Response to Evangelical Feminism* (Wheaton, Ill.: Crossway, 1991). An earlier volume with a similar approach was George W. Knight III, *The Role Relationship of Men and Women: New Testament Teaching* (Philipsburg, N.J.: Presbyterian and Reformed Publishing, 1985 [1977]).

51 Alan G. Padgett, *As Christ Submits to the Church: A Biblical Understanding of Leadership and Mutual Submission* (Grand Rapids: Baker Academic, 2011), 10.

52 It is questionable whether such a subordinationist understanding of the Trinity is orthodox. See chapter 8, "Women in Worship and 'Headship,'" in this volume.

53 Thomas Hopko, "Presbyter/Bishop: A Masculine Ministry," in *Women and the Priesthood*, Thomas Hopko, ed., new ed. (Crestwood, N.Y.: St. Vladimir's Seminary Press, 1999), 139, 140.

54   Hopko, "Presbyter/Bishop," 141.

55   Hopko, "Presbyter/Bishop," 152.

56   "Man's priority and headship in his union of love with woman in no way signifies his superiority over woman, neither ontological nor relational. . . . [The presbyter/bishop] presents the gifts at the eucharistic offering in the place of Jesus, the one great high priest of God's priestly people." Hopko, "Presbyter/Bishop," 144, 156.

57   Ben Witherington III, *Women in the Earliest Churches* (Cambridge: Cambridge University Press, 1988), 205.

58   Epiphanius, *Panarion* 7.79.1,6.

59   For a lengthy example of such a theology, see Manfred Hauke, *Women in the Priesthood? A Systematic Analysis in the Light of the Order of Creation and Redemption*, David Kipp, trans. (San Francisco: Ignatius, 1986).

60   Paul K. Jewett, *Man as Male and Female: A Study in Sexual Relationships from a Theological Point of View* (Grand Rapids: Eerdmans, 1975), 187.

4   HIERARCHY AND HERMENEUTICS

1   John Piper and Wayne Grudem, eds., *Recovering Biblical Manhood and Womanhood: A Response to Evangelical Feminism* (Wheaton, Ill.: Crossway, 1991).

2   Wayne Grudem, *Evangelical Feminism and Biblical Truth: An Analysis of More Than One Hundred Disputed Questions* (Sisters, Ore.: Multnomah, 2004).

3   Grudem, *Systematic Theology: An Introduction to Biblical Doctrine* (Grand Rapids: Zondervan, 1994).

4   Grudem, *Politics for the Bible: A Comprehensive Resource for Understanding Modern Political Issues in Light of Scripture* (Grand Rapids: Zondervan, 2010). Grudem's approach contrasts with that of David Koyzis, who argues in *Political Visions and Illusions: A Survey and Critique of Contemporary Ideologies*, 2nd ed. (Downers Grove, Ill.: InterVarsity, 2019 [2003]), that the embracing of any political ideology by Christians—conservative, liberal, nationalist, democratic, socialist—is a case of idolatry.

5   Wayne Grudem, *Evangelical Feminism: A New Path to Liberalism* (Wheaton, Ill.: Crossway, 2006).

6   Christians for Biblical Equality International, "Endorsements," https://www.cbeinternational.org/endorsement; N. T. Wright, "Women's Service in the Church: The Biblical Basis," September 4, 2004, https://ntwrightpage.com/2016/07/12/womens-service-in-the-church-the-biblical-basis; idem, *Surprised by Scripture* (New York: HarperCollins, 2014), 64–82.

7   Grudem, *Evangelical Feminism and Biblical Truth*, 25, 29.

8   Grudem, *Evangelical Feminism and Biblical Truth*, 44.

9   In discussing 1 Tim. 2:14, Grudem does suggest that one reason that women should not teach or exercise authority over men is that "God gave men, in general, a disposition that is better suited to teaching and governing in the church, a disposition that inclines more to rational logical analysis . . . and God gave women, in general, a disposition that inclines more toward a relational nurturing analysis." However, even in what Grudem recognizes as exceptional cases in which individual women might have capacity for rationality and leadership, the prohibition is universal: "Paul . . . prohibits

all *women* from teaching and governing the assembled congregation, not just those with certain abilities and tendencies." Grudem, *Evangelical Feminism and Biblical Truth*, 72–73. The prohibition cannot then be based on an inherent incapacity in that it applies to all women, both those who are "relational and nurturing," as well as those who might be inclined to "rational logical analysis." The complementarian restriction against women exercising leadership is therefore directed to women simply because they are women, not because of any inherent incapacities.

10 John Paul II, *Mulieris Dignitatem*, apostolic letter, August 15, 1988, https://w2.vatican .va/content/john-paul-ii/en/apost_letters/1988/documents/hf_jp-ii_apl_19880815 _mulieris-dignitatem.html, 24.

11 Sara Butler, *The Catholic Priesthood and Women: A Guide to the Teaching of the Church* (Chicago: Hillenbrand Books, 2006), 34–37.

12 Butler, *Catholic Priesthood and Women*, 30–31, 33.

13 "[M]any people in leadership are deciding that the egalitarian view is just not what the Bible teaches." Grudem, *Evangelical Feminism and Biblical Truth*, 51. "The common denominator in all of this is a persistent undermining of the authority of Scripture in our lives." Idem, *Evangelical Feminism and Biblical Truth*, 261.

14 Contrast the statements of the complementarian "Danvers Statement" (1987) and egalitarian "Men, Women and Biblical Equality" published by Christians for Biblical Equality: "Distinctions in masculine and feminine roles are ordained by God as part of the created order. . . . Adam's headship in marriage was established by God before the fall, and was not a result of sin" (Danvers Statement); "The Bible teaches that the rulership of Adam over Eve resulted from the Fall and was therefore, *not a part of the created order . . .*" (CBE); cited by Grudem, *Evangelical Feminism and Biblical Truth*, 29.

15 Grudem, *Evangelical Feminism and Biblical Truth*, 30–42.

16 Alan G. Padgett, *As Christ Submits to the Church: A Biblical Understanding of Leadership and Mutual Submission* (Grand Rapids: Baker Academic, 2011), 14.

17 Richard Hooker, *The Laws of Ecclesiastical Polity* (London: J. M. Dent, 1907), 1:3.5.1. Subsequent references are to this edition.

18 Ben Witherington III, *The Living Word of God: Rethinking the Theology of the Bible* (Waco, Tex.: Baylor University Press, 2007), 197.

19 Witherington, *Living Word of God*, 169.

20 Richard B. Hays, *The Moral Vision of the New Testament: Community, Cross, New Creation* (New York: HarperCollins, 1996).

21 Ellen F. Davis and Richard B. Hays, eds., *The Art of Reading Scripture* (Grand Rapids: Eerdmans, 2003).

22 James Buckley and David Yeago, eds., *Knowing the Triune God: The Work of the Spirit in the Practices of the Church* (Grand Rapids: Eerdmans, 2001).

23 Brevard Childs, *Biblical Theology of the Old and New Testaments: Theological Reflection on the Christian Bible* (Minneapolis: Fortress, 1992).

24 John Webster, *Holy Scripture: A Dogmatic Sketch* (Cambridge: Cambridge University Press, 2003).

25 N. T. Wright, *Scripture and the Authority of God: How to Read the Bible Today* (New York: HarperCollins, 2013).

5   BEGINNING WITH GENESIS

1   Thomas Aquinas, *ST* 1.1.98.1 *ad* 3.

2   See chapter 3, "The Argument 'from Tradition' Is Not the 'Traditional' Argument," in this volume.

3   Theo M. M. A. C. Bell, "Man Is a Microcosmos: Adam and Eve in Luther's Lectures on Genesis (1535–1545)," *Concordia Theological Quarterly* 69, no. 2 (2005): 159–84.

4   John Chrysostom, *Homilies on 1 Cor.* 26 (*NPNF* 1/12:150–51).

5   For helpful theological discussion of issues raised by modern scientific accounts of human origins, see William T. Cavanaugh and James K. A. Smith, eds., *Evolution and the Fall* (Grand Rapids: Eerdmans, 2017); Oliver D. Crisp, "On Original Sin," *International Journal of Systematic Theology* 17, no. 3 (2016): 252–66.

6   In Hebrew, as in many other languages, there is a clear distinction between the generic name for human being or humanity and the more specific names that correspond to "man" (as male human being) and "woman" (as female human being). In Greek, "humanity" is ἄνθρωπος (*anthrōpos*), "male human being" (man) is ἀνήρ (*anēr*), and "female human being" (woman) is γυνή (*gunē*). In Latin, "humanity" is *homo*, "male human being" is *vir*, and "female human being" is *femina*. Modern English has the peculiarity that it no longer makes these distinctions. In Old English, "humanity" was *man*, "male human being" was *wer*, "female human being" was *wifman*. In modern English, "humanity" continued to be *man*, while "female human being" (*wifman*) became *woman*. However, *wer* disappeared, with the result that "man" came to function for both "human being" in general, but also for "male human being." In time, "man" has come to be understood primarily to mean "male human being," with a consequent crisis over whether English "man" can any longer function inclusively as "human being." When modern English translations translate both the Hebrew *ha'adam* and *'is* as "man," an ambiguity is created that is not in the Hebrew text.

7   Richard S. Hess, "Equality With and Without Innocence," in *Discovering Biblical Equality: Complementarity Without Hierarchy*, Ronald W. Pierce and Rebecca Merrill Groothuis, eds. (Downers Grove, Ill.: InterVarsity, 2004), 80.

8   Karl Barth, "Man and Woman," in *The Doctrine of Creation*, vol. III/4 of *Church Dogmatics*, G. W. Bromiley and T. F. Torrance, eds. (Edinburgh: T&T Clark, 1961), 116–239. Subsequent references to this volume are to *CD* III/4.

9   Phyllis Trible, *God and the Rhetoric of Sexuality* (Philadelphia: Fortress, 1978), 17.

10   Terence E. Fretheim, "Genesis," in vol. 1 of *The New Interpreter's Bible* (Nashville: Abingdon, 1994), 345.

11   Trible, *God and the Rhetoric of Sexuality*, 18, 19; Hess, "Equality With and Without Innocence," 82; Fretheim, "Genesis," 345.

12   Walther Eichrodt, *Theology of the Old Testament*, J. A. Baker, trans., 2 vols. (Philadelphia: Westminster, 1967), 2:126–27; Fretheim, "Genesis," 345–46.

13   Carrie A. Miles, *The Redemption of Love: Rescuing Marriage and Sexuality from the Economics of a Fallen World* (Grand Rapids: Brazos, 2006), 20; Hess, "Equality With and Without Innocence," 80–81; Trible, *God and the Rhetoric of Sexuality*, 19.

14   Hess, "Equality With and Without Innocence," 82–83.

15 Hess, "Equality With and Without Innocence," 83; Trible, *God and the Rhetoric of Sexuality*, 77. This connection is deliberately reflected in the words used with imposition of ashes in the Ash Wednesday service that echo Gen. 3:19: "Remember that you are dust, and to dust you shall return."

16 Trible, *God and the Rhetoric of Sexuality*, 80; Miles, *Redemption of Love*, 21.

17 Hess, "Equality With and Without Innocence," 86; Miles, *Redemption of Love*, 23; Trible, *God and the Rhetoric of Sexuality*, 90.

18 Trible, *God and the Rhetoric of Sexuality*, 96–98.

19 Hess, "Equality With and Without Innocence," 84; Trible, *God and the Rhetoric of Sexuality*, 90.

20 Fretheim, "Genesis," 353; Hess, "Equality With and Without Innocence," 87; Miles, *Redemption of Love*, 26–27.

21 Trible, *God and the Rhetoric of Sexuality*, 98–99.

22 Hess suggests that "the text nowhere states that the man exercised authority over the animals by naming them. Rather, he classified them." Hess, "Equality With and Without Innocence," 87. To the contrary, Trible suggests: "Through the power of naming, the animals are subordinate to the earth creature. They become inferiors, not equals. . . . [T]he repeated emphasis on naming underscores the subordination of the animal world to the earth creature and thus demonstrates the unsuitability of the animals for humanity." Trible, *God and the Rhetoric of Sexuality*, 92.

23 Trible, *God and the Rhetoric of Sexuality*, 99, 100. It is only in Gen. 3:20, when the man "calls his wife's name Eve, because she was the mother of all living," an event that takes place after the fall into sin.

24 Miles, *Redemption of Love*, 26.

25 Hess, "Equality With and Without Innocence," 88; Alan G. Padgett, *As Christ Submits to the Church: A Biblical Understanding of Leadership and Mutual Submission* (Grand Rapids: Baker Academic, 2011), 98.

26 Hess, "Equality With and Without Innocence," 85, 94–95; Miles, *Redemption of Love*, 28; Trible, *God and the Rhetoric of Sexuality*, 103–4.

27 Hess, "Equality With and Without Innocence," 88.

28 Hess, "Equality With and Without Innocence," 93; Trible, *God and the Rhetoric of Sexuality*, 128, 133. An important but subsidiary issue is how to understand the judgment on the woman in relation to childbirth. Several recent commentators suggest that the Hebrew should be translated not as referring to pain in childbirth, but to increased effort in assisting the man in cultivating the land as well as the need to have an increased number of children: "'I will greatly multiply your efforts and your childbearing' . . . makes better sense of its syntax." Hess, "Equality With and Without Innocence," 90–91; Fretheim, "Genesis," 363. Trible notes that the naming formula applied to animals is now applied for the first time to the woman: "Now, in effect, the man reduces the woman to the status of an animal by calling her a name." Trible, *God and the Rhetoric of Sexuality*, 133. This seems to be reading too much into the text. Others simply note that the name "Eve" is connected to the woman's function in the same way that the man's is connected to his. Adam is *ha'adam* because he is taken from and tills the earth

(*ha'adamah*). Eve (*havvah*) is associated with living, alive (*hay*). Hess, "Equality With and Without Innocence," 91.

29 Hess, "Equality With and Without Innocence," 90; Trible, *God and the Rhetoric of Sexuality*, 126.

30 Hess, "Equality With and Without Innocence," 92; Miles, *Redemption of Love*, 34. Significantly, there were those who resisted the use of anesthesia in childbirth when its possibility was first discovered on the grounds that this was an undermining of the divine command.

31 Hess, "Equality With and Without Innocence," 94–95; Fretheim, "Genesis," 363; Trible, *God and the Rhetoric of Sexuality*, 128; Padgett, *As Christ Submits to the Church*, 98–99.

32 Wayne Grudem, *Evangelical Feminism and Biblical Truth: An Analysis of More Than One Hundred Disputed Questions* (Sisters, Ore.: Multnomah, 2004), 30ff. It is significant that Phyllis Trible summarizes a similar list of themes in Genesis 1–3 that are decried by feminists in particular as proclaiming male superiority and male inferiority: a male God creates man and then woman; woman comes out of man; man names woman and has power over her; woman tempts man to disobey, etc. Trible comments: "Although such specifics continue to be cited as support for traditional interpretations of male superiority and female inferiority, not one of them is altogether accurate and most of them are simply not present in the story itself." Trible, *God and the Rhetoric of Sexuality*, 73.

33 Hess, "Equality With and Without Innocence," 85–86.

34 Hess, "Equality With and Without Innocence," 84.

35 Hess, "Equality With and Without Innocence," 90.

36 Grudem, *Evangelical Feminism and Biblical Truth*, 40 (emphasis added).

37 As in the new revised ESV translation, which seems to be influenced by Grudem's complementarian reading; see Claude Mariottini, "Genesis 3:16 and the ESV," October 4, 2016, https://claudemariottini.com/2016/10/04/genesis-316-and-the-esv.

38 Tikva Frymer-Kensky, *In the Wake of the Goddesses: Women, Culture and the Biblical Transformation of Pagan Myth* (New York: Macmillan, 1992), 5.

39 Frymer-Kensky, *In the Wake of the Goddesses*, 188–89.

40 Frymer-Kensky, *In the Wake of the Goddesses*, 83.

41 Frymer-Kensky, *In the Wake of the Goddesses*, 5.

42 Frymer-Kensky, *In the Wake of the Goddesses*, 86, 87, 92, 98, 99.

43 Frymer-Kensky, *In the Wake of the Goddesses*, 105.

44 Frymer-Kensky, *In the Wake of the Goddesses*, 116.

45 Frymer-Kensky, *In the Wake of the Goddesses*, 118.

46 Frymer-Kensky, *In the Wake of the Goddesses*, 120. Old Testament scholar Walther Eichrodt also comments on the way in which Old Testament law concerning women both reflects, but also to some extent modifies a common Near Eastern background. On the one hand, "attention should be drawn to the heightening of the moral sense in that most personal of all the spheres of morality, the relations between the sexes." On the other, "a good deal of the mentality typical of the ancient world still remains." Eichrodt, *Theology of the Old Testament*, 1:80, 80–82.

47 Frymer-Kensky, *In the Wake of the Goddesses*, 121, 140.

48 Frymer-Kensky, *In the Wake of the Goddesses*, 128–29.

49 Frymer-Kensky, *In the Wake of the Goddesses*, 142–43.

50 Frymer-Kensky, *In the Wake of the Goddesses*, 143.

51 Miles, *Redemption of Love*, 36–41.

52 Miles, *Redemption of Love*, 43–46.

53 Miles, *Redemption of Love*, 46.

54 Miles, *Redemption of Love*, 35.

55 Miles, *Redemption of Love*, 54.

56 See "Love in an Age of Wealth," in Miles, *Redemption of Love*, 120–35. Just some of the technological changes that marked the end of the preindustrial household included the flour mill, piped-in water, refrigeration, and efficient stoves; improvements in transportation including the locomotive, the automobile, and the airplane; factory-made cloth and clothing, factory-baked bread, professional medicine and medical care; the use of kerosene, oil and electricity for heating; and professional butchers.

57 Miles, *Redemption of Love*, 54; Frymer-Kensky also notes the consequences that the industrial revolution has created for traditional gender roles. Frymer-Kensky, *In the Wake of the Goddesses*, 216.

58 Miles, *Redemption of Love*, 121–35.

59 Miles, *Redemption of Love*, 13.

60 Frymer-Kensky, *In the Wake of the Goddesses*, 216; Miles, *Redemption of Love*, 14.

61 Frymer-Kensky, *In the Wake of the Goddesses*, 217.

62 Miles, *Redemption of Love*, 209.

6   DISCIPLES OF JESUS

1 Sacred Congregation for the Doctrine of the Faith, *Inter Insigniores*, October 15, 1976, http://www.vatican.va/roman_curia/congregations/cfaith/documents/rc_con_cfaith_doc_19761015_inter-insigniores_en.html.

2 For the Catholic argument, see Sara Butler, *The Catholic Priesthood and Women: A Guide to the Teaching of the Church* (Chicago: Hillenbrand Books, 2006); for the Protestant Trinitarian argument, see Wayne Grudem, *Evangelical Feminism and Biblical Truth: An Analysis of More Than One Hundred Disputed Questions* (Sisters, Ore.: Multnomah, 2004), 45–48, 405–33.

3 Exegetically, Wayne Grudem draws on 1 Cor. 11:3 and Eph. 5:23 (*Evangelical Feminism and Biblical Truth*, 41, 45–46) That either of these passages has anything to do with an eternal subordination of the Son to the Father and the subsequent parallel with male-female relationships is questionable.

4 Richard B. Hays, *The Moral Vision of the New Testament: Community, Cross, New Creation* (New York: HarperCollins, 1996), 208–9.

5 Presuming the opposite is a standard hermeneutical mistake. In the nineteenth century, apologists for slavery appealed to the existence of slavery in the Old Testament, and to Paul's exhortations to slaves to obey their masters in the New Testament as warrant for the justification of Christian slave-holding. See, for example, Philip Schaff, *Slavery and the Bible: A Tract for the Times* (Chambersburg, Pa.: Keifer, 1861).

6 Hays, *Moral Vision of the New Testament*, 73.

7 Hays, *Moral Vision of the New Testament*, 74.

8 Richard Hays uses the expression "eschatological reversal," while the late John Howard Yoder used the expression "revolutionary subordination" to mean much the same thing as what is here called "Christological subversion."

9 With the exception of John's gospel, the following summaries echo Hays, *Moral Vision of the New Testament*, 73–137, although the readings here are characteristic of standard contemporary New Testament commentaries on the gospels.

10 Karl Barth, *The Doctrine of Reconciliation*, vol. IV/2 of *Church Dogmatics*, G. W. Bromiley and T. F. Torrance, eds. (Edinburgh: T&T Clark, 1958), 173. Subsequent references to this volume are to *CD* IV/2.

11 K. Barth, *CD* IV/2, 171.

12 K. Barth, *CD* IV/2, 174–75.

13 K. Barth, *CD* IV/2, 172.

14 K. Barth, *CD* IV/2, 177.

15 "The culture of the first-century world was built on the foundational social values of honor and dishonor." David A. deSilva, *Honor, Patronage, Kinship and Purity: Unlocking New Testament Culture* (Downers Grove, Ill.: InterVarsity, 2000), 23.

16 DeSilva, *Honor, Patronage, Kinship and Purity*, 35.

17 DeSilva, *Honor, Patronage, Kinship and Purity*, 28.

18 Plutarch, *To an Uneducated Ruler* 2, in *Moralia*, Harold North Fowler, trans., LCL (Cambridge, Mass.: Harvard University Press, 1969), 780C (10:57); Philo, *Hypothetica (Apology for the Jews)*, F. H. Colson, trans., LCL (Cambridge, Mass.: Harvard University Press, 1941), 7.3, 7.14 (9:424–25, 432–33); cited in Craig S. Keener, *Paul, Women and Wives: Marriage and Women's Ministry in the Letters of Paul* (Peabody, Mass.: Hendrickson, 2004 [1992]), 165.

19 Ben Witherington III, *Women in the Ministry of Jesus: A Study of Jesus' Attitudes to Women and Their Roles as Reflected in His Earthly Life* (Cambridge: Cambridge University Press, 1984), 4.

20 Plutarch, *The Education of Children*, in *Moralia*, Frank Cole Babbitt, trans., LCL (Cambridge, Mass.: Harvard University Press, 1927), 1.51, 1.8c, 1.9d, 1.14b (1:22–23, 38–39, 44–45, 66–67); cited in Ben Witherington III, *Women in the Earliest Churches* (Cambridge: Cambridge University Press, 1988), 16; Josephus, *Jewish Antiquities*, H. St. J. Thackeray, trans., LCL (Cambridge, Mass.: Harvard University Press, 1930), 4.8.15 (4:580–81); cited in Keener, *Paul, Women and Wives*, 163. For the above description of first-century Jewish and Mediterranean culture, see deSilva, *Honor, Patronage, Kinship and Purity*, 80, 81, 183, 184; Tikva Frymer-Kensky, *In the Wake of the Goddesses: Women, Culture and the Biblical Transformation of Pagan Myth* (New York: Macmillan, 1992), 214; Keener, *Paul, Women and Wives*, 159–67; Witherington, *Women in the Ministry of Jesus*, 1–10; idem, *Women in the Earliest Churches*, 5–23.

21 Keener, *Paul, Women and Wives*, vi–ix.

22 DeSilva, *Honor, Patronage, Kinship and Purity*, 190, 192.

23 I. Howard Marshall, "Mutual Love and Submission in Marriage: Colossians 3:18–19 and Ephesians 5:21–33," in *Discovering Biblical Equality: Complementarity without Hierarchy*, Ronald W. Pierce and Rebecca Merrill Groothuis, eds. (Downers Grove, Ill.: InterVarsity, 2004), 188.

24 DeSilva, *Honor, Patronage, Kinship and Purity*, 29.

25 DeSilva, *Honor, Patronage, Kinship and Purity*, 51.

26 Witherington, *Women in the Ministry of Jesus*, 11.

27 DeSilva, *Honor, Patronage, Kinship and Purity*, 195; N. T. Wright, *Jesus and the Victory of God* (Minneapolis: Fortress, 1996), 430.

28 R. Alan Culpepper, "Luke," in vol. 9 of *The New Interpreter's Bible* (Nashville: Abingdon, 1995), 301; Wright, *Jesus and the Victory of God*, 129.

29 Wright states: "[S]enior members of families never do anything so undignified at the best of times, let alone in order to greet someone who should have remained in self-imposed ignominy." Wright, *Jesus and the Victory of God*, 129.

30 Wright, *Jesus and the Victory of God*, 126.

31 Wright, *Jesus and the Victory of God*, 491.

32 M. Eugene Boring, "Matthew," in vol. 8 of *The New Interpreter's Bible* (Nashville: Abingdon, 1994), 403–4.

33 David Bentley Hart, "God or Nothingness," in *I Am the Lord Your God: Reflections on the Ten Commandments*, Christopher R. Seitz and Carl E. Braaten, eds. (Grand Rapids: Eerdmans, 2005), 64–65.

34 DeSilva, *Honor, Patronage, Kinship and Purity*, 70–71; Carrie A. Miles, *The Redemption of Love: Rescuing Marriage and Sexuality from the Economics of a Fallen World* (Grand Rapids: Brazos, 2006), 70–71; Wright, *Jesus and the Victory of God*, 290–91.

35 Culpepper, "Luke," 229–30.

36 Wright, *Jesus and the Victory of God*, 191–92, 431.

37 Miles, *Redemption of Love*, 78–79.

38 See especially Kenneth Bailey, *Jesus Through Middle Eastern Eyes* (Downers Grove, Ill.: InterVarsity, 2008), 200–216; Witherington, *Women in the Ministry of Jesus*, 57–63; Gail R. O'Day, "John," in vol. 9 of *The New Interpreter's Bible* (Nashville: Abingdon, 1995), 565–73.

39 Bailey, *Jesus Through Middle Eastern Eyes*, 217–26.

40 Witherington, *Women in the Ministry of Jesus*, 71–75; Miles, *Redemption of Love*, 61–62.

41 Witherington, *Women in the Ministry of Jesus*, 25–28; Miles, *Redemption of Love*, 58–59.

42 On Genesis and subordination, again see chapter 5, "Beginning with Genesis," in this volume.

43 For what follows, see Bailey, *Jesus Through Middle Eastern Eyes*, 192–93.

44 Culpepper, "Luke," 232.

45 Witherington, *Women in the Ministry of Jesus*, 101; Culpepper, "Luke," 231; Bailey, *Jesus Through Middle Eastern Eyes*, 193.

46 Witherington, *Women in the Ministry of Jesus*, 101.

47 Culpepper, "Luke," 231.

48 Witherington, *Women in the Ministry of Jesus*, 103.

49 Grudem, *Evangelical Feminism and Biblical Truth*, 163, 164.

50 Witherington, *Women in the Ministry of Jesus*, 118.

51 Alan G. Padgett, *As Christ Submits to the Church: A Biblical Understanding of Leadership and Mutual Submission* (Grand Rapids: Baker Academic, 2011), 38, 59. Grudem and Piper write: "[T]he term always implies a relationship of submission to an authority."

John Piper and Wayne Grudem, *Recovering Biblical Manhood and Womanhood: A Response to Evangelical Feminism* (Wheaton, Ill.: Crossway, 1991), 493n6. Grudem states: "What Paul has in mind is not a vague 'mutual submission' where everybody is considerate and thoughtful of everybody else, but a specific kind of submission to an authority." Grudem, *Evangelical Feminism and Biblical Truth*, 190.

52 Padgett, *As Christ Submits to the Church*, 38–39.

53 Padgett suggests that the model of "mutual submission" originates with Jesus. Padgett, *As Christ Submits to the Church*, 49. Also see Miles, *Redemption of Love*, 72–76.

54 O'Day, "John," 720–28; Miles, *Redemption of Love*, 74–76; Padgett, *As Christ Submits to the Church*, 55–56.

55 Aida Besançon Spencer, "Jesus' Treatment of Women in the Gospels," in *Discovering Biblical Equality*, Pierce and Groothuis, eds., 126–41; Walter L. Liefeld, "The Nature of Authority in the New Testament," in *Discovering Biblical Equality*, Pierce and Groothuis, eds., 254–71.

56 Miles, *Redemption of Love*, 72–76. Padgett states similarly: "Jesus rejects this common, worldly way of thinking about authority as a kind of hierarchy of 'power-over.' Instead, his disciples must be the servants of all. . . . In terms of the life, ministry, and teaching of Jesus, the reason for this utter change of attitude and behavior from man-centered hierarchies of power is absolutely decisive. . . . The way of the cross is directly tied to taking up the role of a servant. Servant leadership is *the* sign of greatness and precedence in the reign and realm of God." Padgett, *As Christ Submits to the Church*, 45, 53.

7 MUTUAL SUBMISSION

1 Wayne Grudem, *Evangelical Feminism and Biblical Truth: An Analysis of More Than One Hundred Disputed Questions* (Sisters, Ore.: Multnomah, 2004), 108–10; George W. Knight III, *The Role Relationship of Men and Women: New Testament Teaching* (Philipsburg, N.J.: Presbyterian and Reformed Publishing, 1985 [1977]).

2 Some exegetes have argued that 1 Cor. 14:35 must be a non-Pauline interpolation because it seems so at odds with the general direction of Paul's theology. Others have appealed to the generally accepted historical-critical position of non-Pauline authorship of the Pastoral Epistles to dismiss 1 Tim. 2:12 as a later falling away from Paul's own more positive attitudes toward women. One of the earliest books in the modern discussion, Paul Jewett's *Man as Male and Female: A Study in Sexual Relationships from a Theological Point of View* (Grand Rapids: Eerdmans, 1975), suggested that Paul was inconsistent, not following through on the radical implications of his theology that men and women are equal in Christ. Karen M. Elliott dismisses 1 Cor. 14:33b-36 as a non-Pauline interpolation, and writes concerning 1 Tim. 2:8-15, "Paul did not write this." She writes concerning the authors of the Pastoral Epistles, "In this instance it would seem they did a poor job of representing Paul's thought." Elliott, *Women in Ministry in the Writings of Paul* (Winona, Minn.: Anselm Academic, 2010), 64–65.

3 Many New Testament scholars assume, for various reasons, that Paul is not the author of Ephesians, but that it is the writing of a later disciple or successor of Paul writing in Paul's name. For the purposes of this chapter, it will be assumed that Paul is the author. Ephesians is one of Paul's more profound letters. If Paul did not write it, one has to posit

an unknown disciple of Paul who was at least as profound as Paul, but who nonetheless wanted to conceal his or her identity. This seems unlikely. Most New Testament scholars note the parallels between Col. 3:18–19 and Eph. 5 and consider Eph. 5 to build on the Colossians material by expanding it. Because it is lengthier and provides more theological warrant than the Colossians passage, only Ephesians will be discussed here. Readers can look to standard treatments such as that of Ben Witherington III's commentary (cited below) to see treatments of both passages.

4   Michael J. Gorman, *Cruciformity: Paul's Narrative Spirituality of the Cross* (Grand Rapids: Eerdmans, 2001), 76.

5   Gorman lists these and other "patterns of cruciformity"; see Gorman, *Cruciformity*, 82.–86.

6   Gorman, *Cruciformity*, 177.

7   Gorman, *Cruciformity*, 160.

8   Alan G. Padgett, *As Christ Submits to the Church: A Biblical Understanding of Leadership and Mutual Submission* (Grand Rapids: Baker Academic, 2011), 46, 48.

9   Padgett, *As Christ Submits to the Church*, 40.

10   Readings along this line would include George W. Knight III, "Husbands and Wives as Analogues of Christ and the Church: Ephesians 5:21–33 and Colossians 3:18–19," in *Recovering Biblical Manhood and Womanhood: A Response to Evangelical Feminism*, John Piper and Wayne Grudem, eds. (Wheaton, Ill.: Crossway, 1991), 165–78; Grudem, *Evangelical Feminism and Biblical Truth*, 188–99. Grudem writes: "Paul explains . . . that wives are to be subject to their husbands (Ephesians 5:22–23), children are to be subject to their parents (Ephesians 6:1–3), and slaves (or bondservants) to be subject to their masters (Ephesians 6:5–8). These relationships are never reversed. . . . [W]hile wives are several times in the New Testament told to be subject to their husbands . . . *husbands are never told to be subject to their wives.*" Idem, *Evangelical Feminism and Biblical Truth*, 189–90 (Grudem's emphasis).

11   Gorman identifies four types of interpretation; see Gorman, *Cruciformity*, 263. Distinguishing between the "love patriarchy" position of someone like the feminist scholar Elizabeth Schüssler Fiorenza and the "revolutionary subordination" position of the late Mennonite theologian John Howard Yoder creates five interpretations.

12   The term *Haustafeln* seems to have originated with Martin Luther. Given its prevalence in standard commentaries, it is odd that "complementarian" authors provide absolutely no discussion of the topic of ancient household codes.

13   Aristotle, *Politics* 1253b, in *The Basic Works of Aristotle*, Richard McKeon, ed. (New York: Random House, 1941). Subsequent references are to this edition.

14   Aristotle, *Politics* 1253b, 1254a.

15   Aristotle, *Politics* 1259b.

16   Aristotle, *Politics* 1260a.

17   Ben Witherington III, *The Letters to Philemon, the Colossians, and the Ephesians: A Socio-Rhetorical Commentary on the Captivity Epistles* (Grand Rapids: Eerdmans, 2007), 320.

18   On how Paul's discussion transforms and undermines the logic of the traditional household codes, see David A. deSilva, *Honor, Patronage, Kinship and Purity: Unlocking New Testament Culture* (Downers Grove, Ill.: InterVarsity, 2000), 229–37; Richard B. Hays,

The Moral Vision of the New Testament: Community, Cross, New Creation (New York: HarperCollins, 1996), 65; Witherington, *Letters to Philemon, the Colossians, and the Ephesians*, 183–88.

19 Witherington, *Letters to Philemon, the Colossians, and the Ephesians*, 184, 314, 323.

20 Hays, *Moral Vision of the New Testament*, 65.

21 Carrie A. Miles, *The Redemption of Love: Rescuing Marriage and Sexuality from the Economics of a Fallen World* (Grand Rapids: Brazos, 2006), 84.

22 John Howard Yoder, *The Politics of Jesus: Vicit Agnus Noster*, 2nd ed. (Grand Rapids: Eerdmans, 1994 [1972]). Appeal to John Howard Yoder is problematic in any discussion of women in the church because of the sexual misconduct that finally marred his career. Despite Yoder's own inconsistency in his personal relationship with women, his exegesis still stands. And, of course, Yoder's personal failings have no bearing on the work of scholars such as deSilva, Hays, Keener, or Witherington. On the Yoder scandal, see, among others, Paul Oppenheimer, "A Theologian's Influence, and Stained Past, Live On," *New York Times*, October 11, 2013, https://www.nytimes.com/2013/10/12/us/john-howard-yoders-dark-past-and-influence-lives-on-for-mennonites.html?pagewanted=all&_r=0.

23 Hays, *Moral Vision of the New Testament*, 65; Witherington, *Letters to Philemon, the Colossians, and the Ephesians*, 320; Yoder, *Politics of Jesus*, 171–72, 175–76.

24 DeSilva, *Honor, Patronage, Kinship and Purity*, 233; Hays, *Moral Vision of the New Testament*, 65; Witherington, *Letters to Philemon, the Colossians, and the Ephesians*, 314, 319; Yoder, *Politics of Jesus*, 177–78.

25 Witherington, *Letters to Philemon, the Colossians, and the Ephesians*, 320.

26 Markus Barth, *Ephesians 4–6*, Anchor Bible 34a (Garden City, N.Y.: Doubleday, 1974), 610–11.

27 Yoder, *Politics of Jesus*, 186.

28 Witherington, *Letters to Philemon, the Colossians, and the Ephesians*, 323.

29 M. Barth, *Ephesians 4–6*, 619.

30 DeSilva, *Honor, Patronage, Kinship and Purity*, 232.

31 Witherington, *Letters to Philemon, the Colossians, and the Ephesians*, 314.

32 Hays, *Moral Vision of the New Testament*, 65 (emphasis original).

33 Craig Keener, *Paul, Women and Wives: Marriage and Women's Ministry in the Letters of Paul* (Peabody, Mass.: Hendrickson, 2004 [1992]), 184.

34 So, for example, Philip Schaff, *Slavery and the Bible: A Tract for the Times* (Chambersburg, Pa.: Keifer, 1861). In this tract, Schaff seemed to hope for an eventual emancipation of slaves, but meanwhile argued for a more humanitarian treatment of slaves. He was opposed to an abolition that gave slaves an immediate freedom for which they were not yet prepared. Until then, he wrote, "We should never ungratefully forget, amidst all the exciting passions, criminations and recriminations of political parties, that in the hands of Providence and under the genial influence of Christianity this American slavery in spite of all its incidental evils and abuses has already accomplished much good. It has been thus far a wholesome training school for the negro from the lowest state of heathenism and barbarism to some degree of Christian civilization, and in its ultimate

result it will no doubt prove an immense blessing to the whole race of Ham." Schaff, *Slavery and the Bible*, 32.

35 Keener, *Paul, Women and Wives*, 186, 205.

36 Witherington, *Letters to Philemon, the Colossians, and the Ephesians*, 317n173.

37 Keener, *Paul, Women and Wives*, 207.

38 Gorman, *Cruciformity*, 265.

39 Gorman's translation; see Gorman, *Cruciformity*, 263–64.

40 Compare this to translations in M. Barth, *Ephesians 4–6*, 554–55, 607, and Gorman, *Cruciformity*, 263–65.

41 Gorman, *Cruciformity*, 265.

42 M. Barth, *Ephesians 4–6*, 610. That mutual subordination is what is being asked for by Paul is recognized by numerous contemporary writers: Witherington, *Letters to Philemon, the Colossians, and the Ephesians*, 316n173, 317n198, 323; Padgett, *As Christ Submits to the Church*, 60; Miles, *Redemption of Love*, 85; I. Howard Marshall, "Mutual Love and Submission in Marriage: Colossians 3:18–19 and Ephesians 5:21–33," in *Discovering Biblical Equality: Complementarity without Hierarchy*, Ronald W. Pierce and Rebecca Merrill Groothuis, eds. (Downers Grove, Ill.: InterVarsity, 2004), 197.

43 Padgett, *As Christ Submits to the Church*, 38–40.

44 Knight, "Husbands and Wives," 167n6. This note is authored by editors Piper and Grudem.

45 Padgett, *As Christ Submits to the Church*, 60–61.

46 Miles, *Redemption of Love*, 86–87; Padgett, *As Christ Submits to the Church*, 60–61.

47 Padgett, *As Christ Submits to the Church*, 62.

48 To the contrary, Grudem writes, "What Paul has in mind is not a vague 'mutual submission' where everybody is considerate and thoughtful of everybody else, but a specific kind of submission to an authority." Referring to Paul's use of what most scholars have called the "household codes," Grudem writes, "In no case is there 'mutual submission'; in each case there is submission to authority and regulated use of that authority." Grudem, *Evangelical Feminism and Biblical Truth*, 190. Against Grudem, the context makes clear that in *every* case there is mutual submission.

49 Gorman, *Cruciformity*, 264–65.

50 Gorman, *Cruciformity*, 265.

51 Gorman, *Cruciformity*, 169, 263; deSilva, *Honor, Patronage, Kinship and Purity*, 232.

52 DeSilva, *Honor, Patronage, Kinship and Purity*, 233.

53 Gordon D. Fee, "Praying and Prophesying in the Assemblies," in *Discovering Biblical Equality*, Pierce and Groothuis, eds., 150–51n28. Fee points out that of the 180 times in which *rosh* is used as a metaphor for "leader," it is translated *kephalē* only six times.

54 Fee, "Praying and Prophesying in the Assemblies," 150, 26.

55 Aristotle, *Politics* 1255b.

56 M. Barth, *Ephesians 4–6*, 617–18.

57 Alan F. Johnson, "A Review of the Scholarly Debate on the Meaning of 'Head' (κεφαλή) in Paul's Writings," *Ashland Theological Journal* 41 (2009): 35–57; Philip B. Payne, *Man*

and Woman, One in Christ: An Exegetical and Theological Study of Paul's Letters (Grand Rapids: Zondervan, 2009), 271–90.

58 M. Barth, *Ephesians 4–6*, 614; Marshall, "Mutual Love and Submission in Marriage," 198–99; Gorman, *Cruciformity*, 265–66; Padgett, *As Christ Submits to the Church*, 67; Witherington, *Letters to Philemon, the Colossians, and the Ephesians*, 328.

59 Miles, *Redemption of Love*, 95.

60 In a recent essay, Richard S. Cervin has cast doubt on whether either "authority over" or "source" are the best interpretations of the *kephalē* metaphor. Cervin rather suggests the notion of "prominence" or "preeminence," understood as "projecting outward or upward," "noticeable or conspicuous," or "widely known, eminent." Richard S. Cervin, "On the Significance of *Kephalē* ('Head'): A Study of the Abuse of One Greek Word," *Priscilla Papers* 30, no. 2 (2016): 10.

Thus the meaning of *kephalē* in the New Testament is a "rather simple head-body metaphor." Just as the head is the topmost part of the human body, *kephalē* as a metaphor has a "physical and vertical orientation." In five of seven New Testament passages (Eph. 1:22-23; 4:15-16; 5:23; Col. 1:18, 2:19), Paul uses *kephalē* (head) and *sōma* (body) together to create a "composite metaphor." Only in 1 Cor. 11:3 and Col. 2:10 does Paul use *kephalē* alone (without *sōma*) as an independent metaphor (16).

Cervin claims that "it is *not* the case that the notions of prominence and authority are intrinsically linked together" (10). Although Christ has authority, the notion of authority is not "*necessarily* explicit" in the metaphor itself (Cervin's emphasis). Thus, in Col. 1:17-18, the head/body metaphor means that Christ occupies the "topmost" or "prominent place" in respect to the church as his body, but any notion of authority must be derived from the context. Again, in Eph. 5:21-24, any notion of "authority" cannot be derived from the word *kephalē* itself, but only from the context of mutual submission (17).

Cervin agrees that at times the *kephalē* metaphor has connotations of "source." In Eph. 4:15-16, Cervin suggests that "source" may be implied, and that the "overall tenor of the passage may speak of Christ as the provider of the body's growth." In Col. 2:18-19, Paul writes of Christ as the "head," from whom the whole body of the church is knit together, and grows with a growth that comes from God. Cervin suggests that "source of life may be an implication derivable solely from the context" (17).

According to Cervin, the notion of "topness" (neither "authority" nor "source") is the key to the interpretation of Eph. 1:20-23. As the head is above the physical body, so Christ is "over" all rule and authority, and he has "put all things under his feet." Christ is preeminent in the sense of "being supreme," but it is not evident that authority should be considered the primary connotation of the metaphor. Cervin also claims that it does not make sense to say that Christ is the "source over" all things in the church (16).

While a valid insight concerning the "height" imagery of the passage—what would "source over" mean?—the head/body metaphor continues with further imagery that certainly includes the *connotation* of "source." In contrast to Christ's enemies, who are "under his feet," the church is described as Christ's body, "the fullness of him who fills everything in every way" (Eph. 1:23). As head of the church, Christ would be the *source* of the church's fullness.

At the conclusion of his essay, Cervin states that "neither 'authority' nor 'source' is the *primary* meaning of the *kephalē* metaphor throughout Paul's writings" (18, Cervin's emphasis). However, it does not seem that Cervin so much rejects recent interpretations of Paul's "head" metaphor as meaning "source," as offers a slight corrective. The *primary* focus of the metaphor may be that of "height," or "topmost," which does not mean "authority," but prominence or preeminence. At the same time, as shown above, Paul accompanies the *kephalē* metaphor with imagery of "nourishment," "life-giving" (Eph. 4:15-16, Col. 2:19), "fullness" (Eph. 1:23), and "beginning" (*archē*, Col. 1:18). While Cervin makes a good case that the *primary* focus of Paul's metaphor is that of "height," and neither "authority" nor "source," in several places, Paul's accompanying imagery points to "source" as a clear connotation of the *kephalē* metaphor.

61 Miles, *Redemption of Love*, 87, 110.

62 Keener, *Paul, Women and Wives*, 146–47.

63 Grudem, *Evangelical Feminism and Biblical Truth*, 214.

64 The notion of "Christological subversion" is crucial for the argument in this chapter, and in chapter 6, "Disciples of Jesus," in this volume.

65 Grudem, *Evangelical Feminism and Biblical Truth*, 340.

66 Keener, *Paul, Women and Wives*, 186; deSilva, *Honor, Patronage, Kinship and Purity*, 237.

67 See chapter 5, "Beginning with Genesis," in this volume. Keener, *Paul, Women and Wives*, 208.

68 Padgett, *As Christ Submits to the Church*, 81–84. See also Peter H. Davids, "A Silent Witness in Marriage: 1 Peter 3:1–7," in *Discovering Biblical Equality*, Pierce and Groothuis, eds., 224–38.

69 Padgett, *As Christ Submits to the Church*, 87 (emphasis original).

70 Grudem, *Evangelical Feminism and Biblical Truth*, 215.

71 See particularly William J. Webb, *Slaves, Women and Homosexuals: Exploring the Hermeneutics of Cultural Analysis* (Downers Grove, Ill.: InterVarsity, 2001); A shorter version of Webb's argument is found in "A Redemptive-Movement Hermeneutic: The Slavery Analogy" and "Gender Equality and Homosexuality," in *Discovering Biblical Equality*, Pierce and Groothuis, eds., 382–413.

72 Grudem, *Evangelical Feminism and Biblical Truth*, 353, 356.

73 For some contemporary examples, see Hays, *Moral Vision of the New Testament*; Kevin Vanhoozer, *The Drama of Scripture: A Canonical Linguistic Approach to Christian Theology* (Louisville: Westminster John Knox, 2005); Ben Witherington III, *The Living Word of God: Rethinking the Theology of the Bible* (Waco, Tex.: Baylor University Press, 2007).

8 WOMEN IN WORSHIP AND "HEADSHIP"

1 Anthony Thiselton, *The First Epistle to the Corinthians*, New International Greek Testament Commentary (Grand Rapids: Eerdmans, 2000), 800.

2 George W. Knight III, *The Role Relationship of Men and Women: New Testament Teaching* (Philipsburg, N.J.: Presbyterian and Reformed Publishing, 1985 [1977]), 20.

3 J. Paul Sampley states that "at least at one level—namely, that in Christ there is no male or female—[Paul] has not fully carried through the social critique that he elsewhere sees implied so completely in his gospel. . . . Paul is himself at a bit of loggerheads as he

tries to honor two very different convictions." Sampley, "The First Letter to the Corin-
thians," in vol. 10 of *The New Interpreter's Bible* (Nashville: Abingdon, 2002), 928, 931.
James D. G. Dunn refers to a "tension in Paul's own thinking." Dunn, *The Theology of
Paul the Apostle* (Grand Rapids: Eerdmans, 1998), 589.

4   Thiselton, *First Epistle to the Corinthians*, 821–23; Alan F. Johnson, *1 Corinthians*, IVP
     New Testament Commentary Series (Downers Grove, Ill.: InterVarsity, 2004), 177–
     201.

5   Craig S. Keener, *Paul, Women and Wives: Marriage and Women's Ministry in the Letters of
     Paul* (Peabody, Mass.: Hendrickson, 2004 [1992]), xiv, 31–39.

6   Alan F. Johnson, "A Review of the Scholarly Debate on the Meaning of 'Head'
     (κεφαλή) in Paul's Writings," *Ashland Theological Journal* 41 (2009): 54 (emphasis
     original).

7   Alan G. Padgett, *As Christ Submits to the Church: A Biblical Understanding of Leadership
     and Mutual Submission* (Grand Rapids: Baker Academic, 2011), 103–24.

8   Many English translations translate these as "servant" or "deaconess" and "helper" with-
     out indication that these terms would be translated differently if referring to males.

9   Kenneth Bailey, *Paul Through Mediterranean Eyes* (Downers Grove, Ill.: InterVarsity,
     2011), 301; Karen M. Elliott, *Women in Ministry in the Writings of Paul* (Winona, Minn.:
     Anselm Academic, 2010), 54–57. See chapter 15, "Women's Ministry in the New Testa-
     ment: Office," in this volume.

10   Bailey, *Paul Through Mediterranean Eyes*, 349, 409.

11   If the former, then the concern could be modesty. A covered head would suggest that
     a woman is sexually unavailable. Public worship would not be a place for women to
     become "objects" of male attention. If the latter, then the emphasis would be on gender
     identity, that is, cultural markers between men and women. Thiselton argues for "head
     covering" (Thiselton, *First Epistle to the Corinthians*, 823–33), as do Bailey (Bailey, *Paul
     Through Mediterranean Eyes*, 301, 305–8) and Gordon D. Fee, *The First Epistle to the
     Corinthians*, rev. ed., New International Commentary on the New Testament (Grand
     Rapids: Eerdmans, 2014 [1987]), 547–49. Johnson, *1 Corinthians*, 189–90, and Philip
     B. Payne, *Man and Woman, One in Christ: An Exegetical and Theological Study of Paul's
     Letters* (Grand Rapids: Zondervan, 2009), 199–207, believe that the passage is about
     whether or not hair was pinned up on top of the head.

12   Thiselton, *First Epistle to the Corinthians*, 828. Thiselton cites Richard Hays's comparison
     to wearing a baseball cap to a formal dinner as "rude and irreverent . . . a breach of eti-
     quette." Richard B. Hays, *First Corinthians*, Interpretation (Louisville: Westminster John
     Knox, 1997), 184.

13   Bailey, *Paul Through Mediterranean Eyes*, 300 (emphasis original).

14   Keener, *Paul, Women and Wives*, 32.

15   Johnson, "Review," 35.

16   Gordon D. Fee, "Praying and Prophesying in the Assemblies," in *Discovering Biblical
     Equality: Complementarity without Hierarchy*, Ronald W. Pierce and Rebecca Merrill
     Groothuis, eds. (Downers Grove, Ill.: InterVarsity, 2004), 149.

17   Thiselton, *First Epistle to the Corinthians*, 812. The most complete accounts of the discussion are probably Thiselton, *First Epistle to the Corinthians*, 812–22, and Johnson, "Review," 38–57.

18   Thiselton, *First Epistle to the Corinthians*, 812–22.

19   The most accessible essays are: "Appendix 1: Does *kephalē* (Head) Mean 'Source' or 'Authority over' in Greek Literature? A Survey of 2,335 Examples," in Knight, *Role Relationship*, 49–80; "Appendix 1: The Meaning of *Kephalē* ('Head'): A Response to Recent Studies," in *Recovering Biblical Manhood and Womanhood: A Response to Evangelical Feminism*, John Piper and Wayne Grudem, eds. (Wheaton, Ill.: Crossway, 1991), 425–68; "Appendix 3: Over Fifty Examples of *Kephalē* ('Head') Meaning 'Authority over/Ruler' in Ancient Literature" and "Appendix 4: The Meaning of κεφαλή ('Head'): An Evaluation of New Evidence, Real and Alleged," in Wayne Grudem, *Evangelical Feminism and Biblical Truth: An Analysis of More Than One Hundred Disputed Questions* (Sisters, Ore.: Multnomah, 2004), 544–99.

20   Johnson refers to Grudem beginning what he calls "the battle of the lexicons." Johnson, "Review," 41. Grudem appeals to six lexicons in Grudem, *Evangelical Feminism and Biblical Truth*, 550–51.

21   Grudem, *Evangelical Feminism and Biblical Truth*, 593.

22   Grudem, *Evangelical Feminism and Biblical Truth*, 544.

23   Grudem states: "Over fifty examples of *kephalē* meaning 'ruler, authority over' have been found . . . but no examples of the meaning of 'source without authority.'" "[T]he general of an army is said to be the 'like the head' in Plutarch . . . the Roman Emperor is called the 'head' of the people . . . the King of Egypt is called 'head' of the nation in Philo." Grudem, *Evangelical Feminism and Biblical Truth*, 202, 205.

24   Knight, *Role Relationship*, 20–23.

25   Thomas R. Schreiner, "Head Coverings, Prophecy and the Trinity," in *Recovering Biblical Manhood and Womanhood*, Piper and Grudem, eds., 128.

26   Schreiner, "Head Coverings, Prophecy and the Trinity," 133.

27   Schreiner, "Head Coverings, Prophecy and the Trinity," 132, 135.

28   Fee, "Praying and Prophesying," 150–51n28. In his commentary, Fee states: "Indeed, these statistics seem to make this a clear case where the exception proves the rule. Grudem's unfortunate failure to note these translational phenomena considerably mars his study." Fee, *First Epistle to the Corinthians*, 555n45; Keener, *Paul, Women and Wives*, 32.

In an unpublished essay, New Testament scholar Philip B. Payne writes: "There is no doubt the LXX translators regarded κεφαλή as the closest Greek equivalent to the Hebrew word for 'head.' They almost always chose κεφαλή to translate literal instances of 'head,' in 226 of 239 instances. The Hebrew word for 'head' conveys 'leader' in the Hebrew Scriptures 171 times. . . . How does the LXX translate these 171 instances? In the vast majority by ἄρχων, 'ruler,' different than the word for 'source,' ἀρχή, which is rarely used in the singular for 'ruler.' Only once does the standard LXX translate 'head' κεφαλή clearly as a metaphor for 'leader,' namely without a preposition best translated 'as head.'" Payne, "Evidence for κεφαλή Meaning 'Source' in Greek Literature and in Paul's Letters" (paper presented at the Annual Meeting of the Evangelical Theological Society, November 16, 2016), 5. (There seems to be a transcriptional error in Fee,

"Praying and Prophesying," 150n28. Fee writes that the LXX translators "almost always eliminate the metaphor altogether and translate it *archē* ['leader']." Fee should have written *archōn*, as noted by Payne. While *archē* can mean "leader," it normally means "source.") Also see Payne, *Man and Woman*, 119. Payne notes that some of the instances that Grudem claims means "leader" actually mean "top," not leader. In Grudem's most recent essay on the topic, he lists a total of fourteen passages from the LXX, but even if he is correct that in all of these passages *kephalē* means "authority," the point remains. In approximately 170 passages where the Hebrew Old Testament uses "head" to mean "authority," the LXX translators chose not to translate "head" meaning "authority" with *kephalē*. Although mentioned regularly by New Testament scholars, I have not been able to find in any of Grudem's several articles on *kephalē* any acknowledgment that such a disparity exists between the Hebrew text and the Greek translation, let alone a recognition of its significance.

29 Payne, *Man and Woman*, 120.

30 Grudem, *Evangelical Feminism and Biblical Truth*, 544–51. Gordon Fee complains that Grudem's "Survey of 2,336 examples" is "considerably misleading." Of the 2,336 examples, only a small percentage are metaphorical. The majority simply refer to the physical "head" of the body. Of the forty-nine metaphorical uses that Grudem claims refer to "authority," twelve are from the New Testament. Since these are the passages at issue, to claim them as evidence is question-begging. Eighteen are from Greek translations of the Old Testament, but these "are the exceptions that prove the rule that this *is not* an ordinary reading for this Greek word." Fee, *First Epistle to the Corinthians*, 554.

31 "'Authority' is not a well-established meaning of κεφαλή. . . . Apart from a few NT lexicons, the vast majority of Greek lexicons list no such meaning." Payne, *Man and Woman*, 121. Payne continues, "Unfortunately, some advocates of male authority have misrepresented the lexical evidence." Idem, *Man and Woman*, 122.

32 "Ashkelon [500 AD] hails Demosth[enes] as his master . . . κεφαλή . . . Demosthenes (384–322 BC) could not have had a position of authority over Zosimus since Demosthenes had died over 800 years earlier." Payne, *Man and Woman*, 122. Payne points to Philo referring to Esau as the "progenitor," the head (κεφαλή) or founder of a clan. This cannot mean "ruler," "since Esau is dead and has no authority over the clan that continues." Philo refers to "the virtuous one" as the "head" (κεφαλή). "In both of these passages from Philo the person called 'head' is not in authority over the group identified but is their source of life." Payne, *Man and Woman*, 125.

33 Fee, "Praying and Prophesying," 150n26.

34 Fee, "Praying and Prophesying," 152n32.

35 Fee, "Praying and Prophesying," 151; Keener, *Paul, Women and Wives*, 34.

36 Bailey, *Paul Through Mediterranean Eyes*, 302.

37 Payne, *Man and Woman*, 123.

38 Galen, *On the Doctrines of Hippocrates and Plato: Edition, Translation and Commentary; Second Part: Books VI–IX*, Philip de Lacy, ed. (Berlin: Akademie-Verlag, 1980), 6.3.21.4 (378–79); *De locis affectis*, in *Claudio Galeni Opera Omnia*, C. G. Kuhn, ed. (Hildesheim: Georg Olms, 1962), 3.12 (202); Philo, *Preliminary Studies*, Loeb

Classical Library, F. H. Colson and G. H. Whitaker, trans. (Cambridge, Mass.: Harvard University Press, 1968 [1932]), 61, 120 (4:488–89, 518–19); *On Rewards and Punishments*, F. H. Colson, trans., LCL (Cambridge, Mass.: Harvard University Press, 1939), 125 (388–89); *Apocalypse of Moses* 19.3, in *The Apocrypha and Pseudepigripha of the Old Testament*, R. H. Charles, ed. (Oxford: Clarendon Press, 1913), 2:146; *Orphic Fragment* 168, in *Orphicorum Fragmenta*, Otto Kern, ed. (Berlin: Weidman, 1963), 2:201. This is a selection among several others cited in Payne, *Man and Woman*, 123–28.

39 Payne, *Man and Woman*, 130; Bailey, *Paul Through Mediterranean Eyes*, 302; Fee, *First Epistle to the Corinthians*, 555–56.

40 Grudem, *Evangelical Feminism and Biblical Truth*, 46.

41 Fee, *First Epistle to the Corinthians*, 556–57; idem, "Praying and Prophesying," 152; Payne points out that when Paul refers to a hierarchical sequence, he lists members in a logical descending order (1 Cor. 12:28). To the contrary, in this list, the members are not listed in a descending order of authority, but chronologically. Payne, *Man and Woman*, 129.

42 Grudem, *Evangelical Feminism and Biblical Truth*, 26n4.

43 See chapter 5, "Beginning with Genesis," in this volume.

44 Fee, *First Epistle to the Corinthians*, 572–73.

45 Fee, "Praying and Prophesying," 152.

46 Schreiner, "Head Coverings, Prophecy and the Trinity," 135.

47 Fee, "Praying and Prophesying," 156; Padgett, *As Christ Submits to the Church*, 112.

48 Fee, *First Epistle to the Corinthians*, 576. In the end, however, Fee admits that this passage is uncertain: "Paul seems to be affirming the 'freedom' of women over their own heads; but what that means in this context remains a mystery."

49 Bailey, *Paul Through Mediterranean Eyes*, 309–11.

50 Payne, *Man and Woman*, 183–87; Bailey, *Paul Through Mediterranean Eyes*, 311–13.

51 Payne, *Man and Woman*, 189.

52 Fee, *First Epistle to the Corinthians*, 579–80; Payne, *Man and Woman*, 191.

53 Fee, *First Epistle to the Corinthians*, 578; Bailey, *Paul Through Mediterranean Eyes*, 308.

54 Payne, *Man and Woman*, 195.

55 Payne, *Man and Woman*, 196; Bailey, *Paul Through Mediterranean Eyes*, 307–9.

56 Payne, *Man and Woman*, 195.

57 Payne, *Man and Woman*, 196; Padgett, *As Christ Submits to the Church*, 71.

58 Payne, *Man and Woman*, 194.

59 Fee, *First Epistle to the Corinthians*, 578–79.

60 Judith M. Gundry-Volf, "Gender and Creation in 1 Corinthians 11:2-16: A Study in Paul's Theological Method," in *Evangelium, Schriftauslegung, Kirche: Festschrift für Peter Stuhlmacher*, Jostein Åna, Scott J. Hafeman, and Ottfried Hofius, eds. (Göttingen, Germany: Vandenhoeck & Ruprecht, 1997), 151–71; Thiselton, *First Epistle to the Corinthians*, 799–848; Johnson, *1 Corinthians*, 177–201.

61 Gundry-Volf, "Gender and Creation," 154–60.

62 Johnson, *1 Corinthians*, 181–82; Gundry-Volf, "Gender and Creation," 161–71; Thiselton, *First Epistle to the Corinthians*, 811, 822.

63 Johnson, *1 Corinthians*, 183.

64 Johnson, *1 Corinthians*, 181–87.

65 Johnson, *1 Corinthians*, 191.

66 Johnson, *1 Corinthians*, 194–95.

67 Johnson, *1 Corinthians*, 195–96.

68 Johnson, *1 Corinthians*, 197.

69 Johnson, *1 Corinthians*, 198.

70 Padgett's position occurs in *As Christ Submits to the Church*, 103–24. An earlier version appeared as "Paul on Women in the Church: The Contradictions of Coiffure in 1 Corinthians 11:12-16," *Journal for the Study of the New Testament* 20 (1984): 69–86. For a position similar to Padgett's, see Lucy Peppiatt, *Unveiling Paul's Women: Making Sense of 1 Corinthians 11:2-16* (Eugene, Ore.: Cascade, 2018).

71 Keener, *Paul, Women and Wives*, 43; Bailey, *Paul Through Mediterranean Eyes*, 306; Payne, *Man and Woman*, 201–2.

72 Padgett, *As Christ Submits to the Church*, 108–9.

73 Padgett, *As Christ Submits to the Church*, 122.

74 Padgett, *As Christ Submits to the Church*, 110–11.

75 Padgett, *As Christ Submits to the Church*, 112.

76 Padgett, *As Christ Submits to the Church*, 124.

77 Payne, *Man and Woman*, 114.

78 Fee, *First Epistle to the Corinthians*, 553.

79 Thiselton, *First Epistle to the Corinthians*, 833.

80 Note that Paul's critique of women who prophesy with their heads "uncovered" presumes that they are engaged in public speaking in church in the same manner as are men. He criticizes the manner in which this occurs, but not the practice itself.

81 Largely drawn from Payne, *Man and Woman*, 197. However, the same points are emphasized by Fee, Bailey, Keener, Johnson, Padgett, and others.

82 "What the Nicene fathers called a subordination of order is another way of saying that they saw a subordination in role, or a subordination in the economic Trinity. . . . It is clear that this subjection to the Father is *after* his earthly ministry, so how anyone can say that there is no hint of difference of order or role within the Trinity is difficult to see." Schreiner, "Head Coverings, Prophecy and the Trinity," 129.

83 Grudem, *Evangelical Feminism and Biblical Truth*, 433.

84 Grudem, *Evangelical Feminism and Biblical Truth*, 407.

85 Grudem, *Evangelical Feminism and Biblical Truth*, 45–46.

86 Grudem, *Evangelical Feminism and Biblical Truth*, 46.

87 Grudem, *Evangelical Feminism and Biblical Truth*, 47 (emphasis original).

88 Grudem's primary critic has been Kevin Giles, in a series of books and articles. See Kevin Giles, "The Subordination of Christ and the Subordination of Women," in *Discovering Biblical Equality*, Pierce and Groothuis, eds., 334–54; idem, *The Trinity and Subordinationism: The Doctrine of God and the Contemporary Gender Debate* (Downers Grove, Ill.: InterVarsity, 2002); idem, *Jesus and the Father: Evangelicals Reinvent the Doctrine of the Trinity* (Grand Rapids: Zondervan, 2006); idem, *The Eternal*

Generation of the Son: Maintaining Orthodoxy in Trinitarian Theology (Downers Grove, Ill.: InterVarsity, 2012).

89 See J. Warren Smith, "The Trinity in the Fourth-Century Fathers"; Lewis Ayres, "Augustine on the Trinity"; Joseph Wawrykow, "Franciscan and Dominican Trinitarian Theology (Thirteenth Century) Bonaventure and Aquinas," in *The Oxford Handbook of the Trinity*, Gilles Emery, O.P., and Matthew Levering, eds. (Oxford: Oxford University Press, 2011), 108–37, 182–96; Gilles Emery, O.P., *The Trinitarian Theology of St. Thomas Aquinas* (Oxford: Oxford University Press, 2007); idem, *The Trinity: An Introduction to Catholic Doctrine on the Triune God*, Matthew Levering, trans. (Washington, D.C.: Catholic University of America Press, 2011)

9 SPEAKING AND TEACHING

1 George W. Knight III, *The Role Relationship of Men and Women: New Testament Teaching* (Philipsburg, N.J.: Presbyterian and Reformed Publishing, 1985 [1977]), 33.

2 Origen, *Fr. 1 Cor.* 74; text in Claude Jenkins, "Origen on 1 Corinthians," *Journal of Theological Studies* 10, no. 37 (1908–1909): 29–51; cited in Patricia Cox Miller, ed., *Women in Early Christianity: Translations from Greek Texts* (Washington, D.C.: Catholic University of America Press, 2005), 29.

3 *Apostolic Constitutions* 3.9.1–4 (*ANF* 7:429).

4 Thomas Aquinas, *Summa Theologiae*, John Mortensen and Enrique Alarcón, eds., Laurence Shapcote, O.P., trans. (Lander, Wyo.: The Aquinas Institute for the Study of Sacred Doctrine, 2012), 1.92.3, suppl. 39, https://aquinas.cc/la/en/~ST.IIISup.Q39 .A1. Subsequent references refer to this edition.

5 Richard Hooker, *The Laws of Ecclesiastical Polity* (London: J. M. Dent, 1907), 2:5.62.2. Subsequent references are to this edition.

6 John Knox, *First Blast of the Trumpet against the Monstrous Regiment of Women*, Edward Arber, ed. (Southgate, London, 1878), https://www.ccel.org/ccel/knox/blast.

7 Complementarians recognize that this must be the case: "The interpretation of 1 Corinthians 14:33b-36 is by no means easy. The rub of the difficulty is that in 1 Corinthians 11:2-16, Paul is quite prepared for women to pray and prophesy, albeit with certain restrictions; but here, a first reading of the text seems to make the silence he enjoins absolute." D. A. Carson, "'Silent in the Churches': On the Role of Women in 1 Corinthians 14:33b-36," in *Recovering Biblical Manhood and Womanhood: A Response to Evangelical Feminism*, John Piper and Wayne Grudem, eds. (Wheaton, Ill.: Crossway, 1991), 140. "The passage never did require complete silence of women, even when Paul wrote it. This is evident because Paul says in 1 Corinthians 11, just three chapters earlier, that women who pray and prophesy should have their heads covered, which assumes that they could pray and prophesy aloud in church services." Wayne Grudem, *Evangelical Feminism and Biblical Truth: An Analysis of More Than One Hundred Disputed Questions* (Sisters, Ore.: Multnomah, 2004), 232.

8 Complementarian Douglas Moo rejects as untenable that Paul meant that all women are inherently susceptible to deception: "[T]here is nothing in the Genesis accounts or in Scripture elsewhere to suggest that Eve's deception is characteristic of women in

general." Moo, "What Does It Mean Not to Teach or Have Authority over Men? 1 Timothy 2:11-16," in *Recovering Biblical Manhood and Womanhood,* Piper and Grudem, eds., 190.

9   Alan F. Johnson, *1 Corinthians,* IVP New Testament Commentary Series (Downers Grove, Ill.: InterVarsity, 2004), 270–71.

10   Scholars who would endorse this conclusion include Gordon D. Fee, *The First Epistle to the Corinthians,* rev. ed., New International Commentary on the New Testament (Grand Rapids: Eerdmans, 2014 [1987]), 788–89; Richard B. Hays, *First Corinthians,* Interpretation (Louisville: Westminster John Knox, 1997), 245–48; Philip B. Payne, *Man and Woman, One in Christ: An Exegetical and Theological Study of Paul's Letters* (Grand Rapids: Zondervan, 2009), 225–67.

11   Fee, *First Epistle to the Corinthians,* 784.

12   Fee, *First Epistle to the Corinthians,* 785.

13   Fee, *First Epistle to the Corinthians,* 780–92. Similar and lengthier arguments appear in Payne, *Man and Woman,* 217–67. Also see Hays, *First Corinthians,* 245–48.

14   Philip B. Payne, "Vaticanus Distigme-obelos Symbols Marking Added Text, Including 1 Corinthians 14.34-35," *New Testament Studies* 63, no. 4 (2017): 604–25.

15   Payne writes, "The obelos was the standard symbol for spurious text in ancient Greek literature."

16   Payne, "Vaticanus," 608–9, 610–11.

17   Payne, "Vaticanus," 610–15, 624–25.

18   Ben Witherington III, *Women in the Earliest Churches* (Cambridge: Cambridge University Press, 1988), 91–92; Anthony Thiselton, *The First Epistle to the Corinthians,* New International Greek Testament Commentary (Grand Rapids: Eerdmans, 2000), 1148–50.

19   A point noted by Johnson, *1 Corinthians,* 272, and Witherington, *Women in the Earliest Churches,* 91.

20   Kenneth Bailey, *Paul Through Mediterranean Eyes* (Downers Grove, Ill.: InterVarsity, 2011), 295–99, 409–10.

21   Witherington, *Women in the Earliest Churches,* 96.

22   The KJV translation assumes that the prepositional phrase, "as in all the churches," belongs with verse 33, not with the beginning of verse 34 (as in the ESV translation). The problem with assuming that "as in all the churches" refers to 34 is that it leads to a redundancy: "As in all the *churches* of the saints, let the women be silent *in the churches.*"

23   Alan G. Padgett, *As Christ Submits to the Church: A Biblical Understanding of Leadership and Mutual Submission* (Grand Rapids: Baker Academic, 2011), 72–73.

24   Bailey describes some of his own experiences in village churches in Egypt, but also refers to John Chrysostom's own reflections on Paul's passage: "Then indeed the women, from such teaching keep silence; but now there is apt to be great noise among them, much clamor and talking, and nowhere so much as in this place [the cathedral]. . . . Thus all is confusion, and they seem not to understand that unless they are quiet, they cannot learn what is useful. For when our discourse [sermon] strains against the talking, and no one minds what is said, what good can it do to them?" John Chrysostom, *Homilies on 1 Tim.* 9 (*NPNF* 1/13:435); cited by Bailey, *Paul Through Mediterranean Eyes,* 414–15.

25   Bailey, *Paul Through Mediterranean Eyes,* 409–17.

26 Craig S. Keener, *Paul, Women and Wives: Marriage and Women's Ministry in the Letters of Paul* (Peabody, Mass.: Hendrickson, 2004 [1992]), 80, 81 (emphasis original). Also see Craig S. Keener, "Learning in the Assemblies: 1 Corinthians 14:34-35," in *Discovering Biblical Equality: Complementarity without Hierarchy*, Ronald W. Pierce and Rebecca Merrill Groothuis, eds. (Downers Grove, Ill.: InterVarsity, 2004), 161–71. Keener's view is also embraced by Johnson, *1 Corinthians*, 274–75; Witherington, *Women in the Earliest Churches*, 103–4, Thiselton, *First Epistle to the Corinthians*, 1156–58.

27 Keener, "Learning in the Assemblies," 165; idem, *Paul, Women and Wives*, 82.

28 Keener, "Learning in the Assemblies," 166; David A. deSilva, *Honor, Patronage, Kinship and Purity: Unlocking New Testament Culture* (Downers Grove, Ill.: InterVarsity, 2000), 34.

29 Keener, *Paul, Women and Wives*, 82–83; idem, "Learning in the Assemblies," 169.

30 Keener, *Paul, Women and Wives*, 85–86; idem, "Learning in the Assemblies," 168; deSilva, *Honor, Patronage, Kinship and Purity*, 35n12.

31 Keener, "Learning in the Assemblies," 171.

32 Grudem, *Evangelical Feminism and Biblical Truth*, 243.

33 Grudem, *Evangelical Feminism and Biblical Truth*, 544–99.

34 Grudem, *Evangelical Feminism and Biblical Truth*, 243.

35 Grudem, *Evangelical Feminism and Biblical Truth*, 233. "Perhaps the greatest weakness of the position is that there is nothing in the text that specifically leads us to suppose that 'judging prophesies' is the particular sort of speech in view." Keener, "Learning in the Assemblies," 163.

36 Witherington, *Women in the Earliest Churches*, 101–4; Thiselton, *First Epistle to the Corinthians*, 1156–62.

37 Witherington, *Women in the Earliest Churches*, 101–3.

38 Witherington, *Women in the Earliest Churches*, 103–4, 259n128.

39 "This passage requires women to be silent with respect to the activity under discussion, which is the judging of prophesies." Grudem, *Evangelical Feminism and Biblical Truth*, 233. "There is nothing in 1 Corinthians that says women were being disruptive." Idem, *Evangelical Feminism and Biblical Truth*, 243.

40 Grudem, *Evangelical Feminism and Biblical Truth*, 230. Grudem insists that "in all the churches" in verse 33b belongs with verse 34; see idem, *Evangelical Feminism and Biblical Truth*, 234.

41 Grudem, *Evangelical Feminism and Biblical Truth*, 234–35.

42 Keener, *Paul, Women and Wives*, 79.

43 Witherington has an extended discussion of the distinction between prophecy and teaching. See Witherington, *Women in the Earliest Churches*, 93–94.

44 "[O]ne view that has *no* support in the context is that Paul's requirement that women be silent just means that they are not allowed to *teach*." Keener, *Paul, Women and Wives*, 79 (emphasis in original).

45 Johnson, *1 Corinthians*, 274, 276; Witherington, *Women in the Earliest Churches*, 102–3.

46 Thiselton, *First Epistle to the Corinthians*, 1153–54.

47 Witherington, *Women in the Earliest Churches*, 104.

48 Moo, "What Does It Mean," 180, 193; Grudem, *Evangelical Feminism and Biblical Truth*, 296. The passage is so crucial to the complementarian case that an entire book has

380 | Notes to Pages 155–159

been written on it: Andreas Köstenberger, Thomas Schreiner, and H. Scott Baldwin, eds., *Women in the Church: An Interpretation and Application of 1 Timothy 2:9-15*, 3rd ed. (Wheaton, Ill.: Crossway, 2016).

49 James D. G. Dunn, "The First and Second Letters to Timothy and the Letter to Titus," in vol. 11 of *The New Interpreter's Bible* (Nashville: Abingdon, 2000), 802. Richard Hays refers to the "lame exoneration of Adam." Richard B. Hays, *The Moral Vision of the New Testament: Community, Cross, New Creation* (New York: HarperCollins, 1996), 67. The quotations from Dunn and Hays are included not because they are notorious "liberal" theologians but because they are not. They are rather two of the foremost critically orthodox New Testament scholars.

50 In Romans, justification by faith is about trust in the work of Jesus Christ. In the Pastorals, the "faith" is a body of truths to be preserved.

51 Dunn, "1 and 2 Timothy," 778–79; Brevard Childs, *The New Testament as Canon: An Introduction* (Philadelphia: Fortress, 1984), 379. There is a similar concern in the Petrine epistles.

52 Padgett, *As Christ Submits to the Church*, 84–89.

53 Payne, *Man and Woman*, 293–94.

54 Payne suggests that Luke might have been Paul's amanuensis; Payne, *Man and Woman*, 292–93.

55 Dunn, "1 and 2 Timothy," 781; Hays, *Moral Vision of the New Testament*, 61; Childs, *New Testament as Canon*, 382–95.

56 Witherington, *Women in the Earliest Churches*, 118; Payne, *Man and Woman*, 295–99. Grudem claims that "no clear proof of women teaching false doctrine at Ephesus has been found either inside the Bible or outside the Bible" (Grudem, *Evangelical Feminism and Biblical Truth*, 282), but this is really to ignore the central concern of all three Pastoral letters. Payne provides numerous parallels between the language that Paul uses of false teachers in the Pastorals and the language he uses to describe the problematic women at Ephesus (Payne, *Man and Woman*, 299–304). Grudem also ignores the significance of Paul's reference to "deception" in 1 Tim. 2:14. Paul is clearly making a connection between Eve's deception and the teaching that he is forbidding. In Titus 1:10–12, he makes a clear connection between "deceivers" and "teaching what they ought not to teach."

57 Keener, *Paul, Women and Wives*, 105.

58 Payne, *Man and Woman*, 311–12; Keener, *Paul, Women and Wives*, 107–8.

59 Moo, "What Does It Mean," 181, 183.

60 Keener, *Paul, Women and Wives*, 107–8; Payne, *Man and Woman*, 311–17; Witherington, *Women in the Earliest Churches*, 120.

61 See chapter 8, "Women in Worship and 'Headship,'" in this volume.

62 Moo, "What Does It Mean," 185 (emphasis original).

63 Grudem, *Evangelical Feminism and Biblical Truth*, 301 (emphasis original).

64 Witherington, *Women in the Earliest Churches*, 120.

65 1 Cor. 7:6, 7, 8, 25, 26, 28, 29, 32, 35, 40; Phil. 4:2.

66 See Payne's detailed discussion, *Man and Woman*, 319–25.

67 The KJV has: "But I suffer not a woman to teach, nor to usurp authority over the man, but to be in silence." Linda Belleville notes that post-World War II translations routinely translate the verb "to have authority over," but lists fifteen translations beginning with the Old Latin where it is translated along the lines of "dominate" or "usurp authority." Belleville, "Teaching and Usurping Authority," in *Discovering Biblical Equality*, Pierce and Groothuis, eds., 209–10.

68 Rom. 9:21; 1 Cor. 6:12; 7:37; 9:4, 12, and elsewhere. See Payne, *Man and Woman*, 375.

69 Grudem, *Evangelical Feminism and Biblical Truth*, 675–702. This originally appeared in the first edition of Köstenberger et al., *Women in the Church*, 269–305.

70 Payne notes that there are only two cases of *authenteō* "unambiguously documented" up to Paul's time (Payne, *Man and Woman*, 361, 385). In a response on his blog to a review of his book, Payne states: "[T]here is not a single instance where it can be demonstrated to mean 'exercise authority' prior to ca AD 370." Payne, "A Critique of Thomas R. Schreiner's Review of *Man and Woman, One in Christ*," August 23, 2010, http://www.pbpayne.com/?p=456. Grudem is thus misleading when he writes, "What should be evident from this chart is that there are no negative examples of the word *authenteō* at or around the time of the New Testament." Grudem, *Evangelical Feminism and Biblical Truth*, 308. Since the vast majority of the usages occur centuries after the New Testament period, they say nothing about the period "at or around the time of the New Testament."

71 Witherington, *Women in the Earliest Churches*, 121. See the detailed discussion in Payne, *Man and Woman*, 361–97, and Belleville, "Teaching and Usurping Authority," 205–23.

72 Grudem, *Evangelical Feminism and Biblical Truth*, 318.

73 Payne, *Man and Woman*, 337–59. Payne lists seven examples showing that *oude* can connect two verbs, one expressing a positive example and one negative. Paul usually understands teaching as something positive, but 1 Tim. 2:12 is clearly prohibiting something negative: "self-assumed authority, which is exactly what the false teachers were doing." Payne concludes: "Understood as a single prohibition, 1 Tim 2:12 conveys, 'I am not permitting a woman to teach and [in combination with this] to assume authority over a man.' The only established category of οὐδέ that makes sense of this passage joins conceptually different expressions to convey a single idea." Payne, *Man and Woman*, 358.

74 Belleville, "Teaching and Usurping Authority," 217–19.

75 Moo, "What Does It Mean," 190.

76 Grudem, *Evangelical Feminism and Biblical Truth*, 287 (emphasis original).

77 Grudem, *Evangelical Feminism and Biblical Truth*, 124.

78 Witherington, *Women in the Earliest Churches*, 122. "The 'for' ('for Eve was created') can be understood either as the reason for the impropriety of Ephesian women's teaching of as an explanation of it." Keener, *Paul, Women and Wives*, 115. "Either the explanatory or the illative use of γάρ, or a mixture of the two, can make good sense in the context of 1 Tim 2:13." Payne, *Man and Woman*, 400. Payne again provides an in-depth discussion of the grammar; see idem, *Man and Woman*, 399–405.

79 Padgett, *As Christ Submits to the Church*, 90–91.

80 Padgett, *As Christ Submits to the Church*, 92–93.

81 Keener, *Paul, Women and Wives*, 116; Witherington, *Women in the Earliest Churches*, 122.

82   Hays, *Moral Vision of the New Testament*, 67.

83   Moo recognizes the problem: "If the issue, then, is deception, it may be that Paul wants to imply that all women, are, like Eve, more susceptible to being deceived than are men, and that this is why they should not be teaching men!" He finds this reading "unlikely": "For one thing, there is nothing in the Genesis accounts in Scripture elsewhere to suggest that Eve's deception is representative of women in general." Moo, "What Does It Mean," 190.

84   Moo, "What Does It Mean," 190.

85   Payne, *Man and Woman*, 409–10.

86   Grudem, *Evangelical Feminism and Biblical Truth*, 287, 296 (emphasis original).

87   Keener, *Paul, Women and Wives*, 115. Grudem complains of a similar suggestion: "This objection removes the reason that Paul does give and replaces it with a reason that Paul does not give. . . . Paul does not mention anything about hearing a command from God or not hearing a command from God. . . . [This suggestion] claims that what Paul says is not a good reason for what Paul commands; and then [it] substitutes a different reason for the one Paul actually gives. Are we free to treat Scripture this way, to change a verse we disagree with into something completely different, and then claim that that is what the verse really says? Is this the kind of treatment of God's Word that we want to allow and endorse in our churches?" Grudem, *Evangelical Feminism and Biblical Truth*, 125. But, of course, Keener's suggestion does no such thing. The key interpretative issue is how to explain the relationship between (1) creation order (Adam was formed first) and (2) the woman's deception (Eve was deceived, not Adam). Grudem affirms the first, but carefully avoids talking about the second. Unless we understand Paul's argument to be that all women are inherently subject to deception because Eve was deceived, and Eve was deceived because Adam was formed first, then it is necessary to posit a different plausible explanation for the connection between the order of creation and deception. Keener's suggestion foots the bill. It is true that Paul does not mention anything explicitly about "hearing a command from God or not hearing a command from God." But neither does Paul mention anything explicitly about male authority over women or different male/female "roles." Both Keener's interpretation and Grudem's are speculative attempts to make sense of something that Paul did write by suggesting plausible scenarios to account for something that Paul did not write, but presumed his readers understood, about the connection between (1) and (2). One cannot solve the problem by focusing exclusively on (1) and simply ignoring (2).

88   See a similar argument in Padgett, *As Christ Submits to the Church*, 94–101.

89   See chapter 4, "Hierarchy and Hermeneutics," in this volume.

90   Hooker, *Laws* 1:3.5.1.

91   Grudem, *Evangelical Feminism and Biblical Truth*, 179.

92   Witherington, *Women in the Earliest Churches*, 154.

10   A *PRESBYTERA* IS NOT A "PRIESTESS"

1   See chapter 2, "Non-theological Arguments against the Ordination of Women," in this volume.

2   C. S. Lewis, "Priestesses in the Church?" in *God in the Dock: Essays on Theology and Ethics*, Walter Hooper, ed. (Grand Rapids: Eerdmans, 1970), 234–39.

3   Lewis, "Priestesses," 237.

4   Some Liberal Protestant and Catholic Modernist feminist theologians have advocated "goddess worship." Many opponents of women's ordination suggest a direct connection between ordination of women and "liberal" Protestant theology. Lewis here claims a direct connection between women's ordination and "goddess worship." That some liberal feminist theologians have advocated "goddess worship" would seem to confirm both the suspicions of Lewis as well as opponents who equate women's ordination with Liberal Protestant theology. However, there is no logical connection between the two positions. Such revisionist feminist theologians should be distinguished from orthodox women clergy, whether Evangelical or Catholic, whose position is more properly identified as "Egalitarianism." Revisionist feminist theologians and egalitarians are no more equivalent than are male Liberal Protestant theologians such as Paul Tillich, Rudolf Bultmann, or Marcus Borg equivalent to critically orthodox theologians such as Karl Barth, Robert Jenson, or N. T. Wright.

5   This is a key argument in the Anglican Forward in Faith document *Consecrated Women?*: "The 'theology' of sacrifice in the Old Testament is complex and many-layered. What is made emphatically clear in the texts is a rejection of the deification of sexual intercourse, as in the fertility cults of Canaan. Those cults had temple prostitution at their heart." Forward in Faith, *Consecrated Women? A Contribution to the Women Bishops Debate*, Jonathan Baker, ed. (Norwich: Canterbury Press, 2004), 49. Significantly, the document does not list any references to substantiate this claim.

6   Tikva Frymer-Kensky, *In the Wake of the Goddesses: Women, Culture and the Biblical Transformation of Pagan Myth* (New York: Macmillan, 1992), 199.

7   William Robertson Smith, *Lectures on the Religion of the Semites* (New York: Appleton, 1889), 455; James George Frazer, *Adonis, Attis and Osiris: Studies in the History of Oriental Religion* (London: Macmillan, 1906), 21–25; William Foxwell Albright, *Archaeology and the Religion of Israel* (Baltimore: Johns Hopkins University Press, 1946), 75–77; Gerhard von Rad, *Old Testament Theology*, D. M. G. Stalker, trans. (New York: Harper & Row, 1962–1965), 2:141–42.

8   Herodotus, *The Histories*, Aubrey de Sélincourt, trans. (London: Penguin, 2003), 1.199 (87–88). Subsequent references are to this edition.

9   Frymer-Kensky, *In the Wake of the Goddesses*, 200.

10 Cult symbols or images associated with the goddess Asherah.

11 Deut. 23:17-18; 1 Kgs. 14:24; 15:12; 22:46; 2 Kgs. 23:7.

12 Frymer-Kensky, *In the Wake of the Goddesses*, 201.

13 Gale A. Yee, "The Book of Hosea," in vol. 7 of *The New Interpreter's Bible* (Nashville: Abingdon, 1996), 241, 202–3.

14 Frymer-Kensky, *In the Wake of the Goddesses*, 200.

15 S. M. Baugh, "Cult Prostitution in New Testament Ephesus: A Reappraisal," *Journal of the Evangelical Theological Society* 42, no. 3 (1999): 443–60. Baugh states: "Hopefully Ephesian cult prostitutes will soon disappear from our literature and from our pulpits,

for these chimera exist only in the minds of people today, not in the past." Idem, "Cult Prostitution," 460.

16 See chapter 5, "Beginning with Genesis," in this volume.

17 Thomas Aquinas, *Summa Theologiae*, John Mortensen and Enrique Alarcón, eds., Laurence Shapcote, O.P., trans. (Lander, Wyo.: The Aquinas Institute for the Study of Sacred Doctrine, 2012), 1.2.99–105, https://aquinas.cc/la/en/~ST.I-II.Q99 (subsequent references refer to this edition); Thirty-nine Articles, art. 7, http://anglicansonline.org/basics/thirty-nine_articles.html; Augsburg Confession, art. 28.59–60, in *The Book of Concord: The Confessions of the Evangelical Lutheran Church*, Robert Kolb and Timothy J. Wengert, eds. (Minneapolis: Fortress, 2000), 100–101; John Calvin, *Institutes of the Christian Religion*, John T. McNeill, ed., Ford Lewis Battles, trans. (Philadelphia: Westminster John Knox, 1960), 4.20.15 (2:1503).

18 Mary Douglas, *Purity and Danger: An Analysis of Concepts of Pollution and Taboo* (London: Routledge, 1966).

19 Markus Bockmuehl, *Jewish Law in Gentile Churches* (Edinburgh: T&T Clark, 2000); "'Keeping It Holy': Old Testament Commandment and New Testament Faith," in *I Am the Lord Your God: Christian Reflections on the Ten Commandments*, Carl E. Braaten and Christopher R. Seitz, eds. (Grand Rapids: Eerdmans, 2005), 95–124; Brevard Childs, "The Role of the Ritual and Purity Laws," in *Old Testament Theology in a Canonical Context* (Philadelphia: Fortress, 1985), 84–91; David A. deSilva, *Honor, Patronage, Kinship and Purity: Unlocking New Testament Culture* (Downers Grove, Ill.: InterVarsity, 2000), 241–315; Jacob Neusner, *The Idea of Purity in Ancient Judaism* (Leiden: Brill, 1973).

20 For the above several points, see Neusner, *Idea of Purity in Ancient Judaism*, 7–31; Bockmuehl, "Keeping It Holy," 103–6.

21 Neusner, *Idea of Purity in Ancient Judaism*, 18–22.

22 See especially Frymer-Kensky, *In the Wake of the Goddesses*, 100–107.

23 Frymer-Kensky, *In the Wake of the Goddesses*, 188–90.

24 Ben Witherington III, *Women in the Ministry of Jesus: A Study of Jesus' Attitudes to Women and Their Roles as Reflected in His Earthly Life* (Cambridge: Cambridge University Press, 1984), 8.

25 Bockmuehl, "Keeping It Holy," 107–8.

26 The one anomaly in the list seems to be abstaining from blood consumption, a Jewish dietary distinctive. This is not mentioned elsewhere in the New Testament.

27 On the New Testament modification of Old Testament purity laws, see deSilva, *Honor, Patronage, Kinship and Purity*, 279–304; Neusner, *Idea of Purity in Ancient Judaism*, 59–60; On the significance of the temple as a dividing issue for Jews and Christians, see N. T. Wright, *The New Testament and the People of God* (Minneapolis: Fortress, 1992), 224–35, 365–66, 409–10, 459–60.

28 DeSilva, *Honor, Patronage, Kinship and Purity*, 280.

29 DeSilva, *Honor, Patronage, Kinship and Purity*, 280–85; Neusner, *Idea of Purity in Ancient Judaism*, 60–62; Wright, *New Testament and the People of God*, 238–40.

30 Neusner, *Idea of Purity in Ancient Judaism*, 60. Jesus does instruct cured lepers to go to priests for purification (Mark 1:44).

31 DeSilva, *Honor, Patronage, Kinship and Purity*, 284–85; Bockmuehl, "Keeping It Holy," 115.

32 Pheme Perkins, "Mark," in vol. 8 of *The New Interpreter's Bible* (Nashville: Abingdon, 1994), 587–88.

33 DeSilva, *Honor, Patronage, Kinship and Purity*, 284–85; Witherington, *Women in the Ministry of Jesus*, 63–66, 71–75.

34 Ben Witherington III, *Women in the Earliest Churches* (Cambridge: Cambridge University Press, 1988), 104–16, 128–57.

35 John Piper and Wayne Grudem, eds., *Recovering Biblical Manhood and Womanhood: A Response to Evangelical Feminism* (Wheaton, Ill.: Crossway, 1991), 71–72.

36 See chapter 6, "Disciples of Jesus," in this volume.

37 See chapter 7, "Mutual Submission," in this volume.

38 See chapter 3, "The Argument 'from Tradition' Is Not the 'Traditional' Argument," in this volume.

11 WOMEN'S ORDINATION AND THE PRIESTHOOD OF CHRIST: BIBLICAL AND PATRISTIC BACKGROUND

1   Sara Butler, *The Catholic Priesthood and Women: A Guide to the Teaching of the Church* (Chicago: Hillenbrand Books, 2006), regards this as a crucial distinctive for the Catholic position: "The ministerial 'priesthood' is different 'in kind' or in essence from common priesthood" (56).

2   Ecumenical progress between Roman Catholics and Lutherans on the question of eucharistic sacrifice was reached as early as 1967: See the Roman Catholic/Lutheran statement on "The Eucharist," October 1, 1967, http://www.usccb.org/beliefs-and -teachings/ecumenical-and-interreligious/ecumenical/lutheran/eucharist.cfm; Anglican and Roman Catholic agreement on eucharistic sacrifice can be found in the "Agreed Statement on Eucharistic Doctrine," in the ARCIC (Anglican-Roman Catholic International Commission) *Final Report*, September 3, 1981, http://www.prounione.urbe.it/ dia-int/arcic/doc/e_arcic_eucharist.html. Further clarification is found in "ARCIC's Clarification of Certain Aspects of the Agreed Statements on Eucharist and Ministry," September 1993, http://www.vatican.va/roman_curia/pontifical_councils/chrstuni/ angl-comm-docs/rc_pc_chrstuni_doc_199309_clarifications-arcici_en.html.

3   John Paul II, *Mulieris Dignitatem*, apostolic letter, August 15, 1988, https://w2.vatican .va/content/john-paul-ii/en/apost_letters/1988/documents/hf_jp-ii_apl_19880815 _mulieris-dignitatem.html.

4   Butler, *Catholic Priesthood and Women*, 47.

5   Sacred Congregation for the Doctrine of the Faith, *Inter Insigniores*, October 15, 1976, http://www.vatican.va/roman_curia/congregations/cfaith/documents/rc_con _cfaith_doc_19761015_inter-insigniores_en.html, 5.

6   John Paul II, *Mulieris Dignitatem* 26.

7   John Paul II, *Pastores Dabo Vobis*, apostolic exhortation, March 15, 1992, https://w2 .vatican.va/content/john-paul-ii/en/apost_exhortations/documents/hf_jp-ii_exh _25031992_pastores-dabo-vobis.html.

8 John Paul II, *Ordinatio Sacerdotalis*, apostolic letter, May 22, 1994, https://w2.vatican .va/content/john-paul-ii/en/apost_letters/1994/documents/hf_jp-ii_apl_19940522 _ordinatio-sacerdotalis.html, 4.

9 Congregation for the Doctrine of the Faith, *Responsum Ad Propositum Dubium Concerning the Teaching Contained in "Ordinatio Sacerdotalis,"* October 28, 1995, http:// www.vatican.va/roman_curia/congregations/cfaith/documents/rc_con_cfaith_doc _19951028_dubium-ordinatio-sac_en.html.

10 Butler, *Catholic Priesthood and Women*, 2. In May 2011, Pope Benedict XVI removed Bishop William Morris of the Roman Catholic Diocese of Toowoomba in Australia from his position, shortly following the release of a pastoral letter by Morris, calling for the discussion of the ordination of married men and women. Nonetheless, serious questions remain concerning whether *Ordinatio Sacerdotalis* meets the formal criteria of papal infallibility for the Roman Catholic Church. Numerous Roman Catholic theologians have insisted that it does not. Representative challenges to its infallibility can be found here: Wijngaards Institute for Catholic Research, "Theologians Assess 'Ordinatio Sacerdotalis,'" http://www.womenpriests.org/teaching/mag_con2.asp#cathol.

11 Kallistos Ware, "Man, Woman, and the Priesthood of Christ," in *Man, Woman, and Priesthood*, Peter Moore, ed. (London: SPCK, 1978), 82, http://www.womenpriests .org/classic/ware.asp. It will be noted in the next chapter that Bishop Ware changed his mind on this question.

12 Forward in Faith, *Consecrated Women? A Contribution to the Women Bishops Debate*, Jonathan Baker, ed. (Norwich: Canterbury Press, 2004), 45–46 (sentences rearranged to indicate logical progression).

13 Brevard Childs, *Old Testament Theology in a Canonical Context* (Philadelphia: Fortress, 1985), 149–50; Walther Eichrodt, *Theology of the Old Testament*, J. A. Baker, trans. (Philadelphia: Westminster, 1967), 1:395–96; Thomas F. Torrance, *Royal Priesthood: A Theology of Ordained Ministry*, 2nd ed. (London: T&T Clark, 2003 [1993]), 3. Also see the discussion on Old Testament sacrifice in Robert J. Daly, S.J., *The Origins of the Christian Doctrine of Sacrifice* (Philadelphia: Fortress, 1978), 11–44, and idem, *Christian Sacrifice: The Judaeo-Christian Background before Origen* (Washington, D.C.: Catholic University of America Press, 1978), 11–136.

14 Gerald O'Collins, S.J., and Michael Keenan Jones, *Jesus Our Priest* (Oxford: Oxford University Press, 2010), 3.

15 Childs, *Old Testament Theology*, 155.

16 Childs, *Old Testament Theology*, 157.

17 Torrance, *Royal Priesthood*, 3.

18 Childs, *Old Testament Theology*, 162–63; Eichrodt, *Theology of the Old Testament*, 119–33.

19 Torrance, *Royal Priesthood*, 4.

20 Childs, *Old Testament Theology*, 163–65.

21 Paul L. Reddit, "Book of Leviticus," in *Dictionary for Theological Interpretation of the Bible*, Kevin J. Vanhoozer et al., eds. (Grand Rapids: Baker Academic, 2005), 447–49.

22 O'Collins and Jones, *Jesus Our Priest*, 2; Torrance, *Royal Priesthood*, 6.

23 O'Collins and Jones, *Jesus Our Priest*, 8–9.

24 O'Collins and Jones, *Jesus Our Priest*, 9–12.

25 O'Collins and Jones, *Jesus Our Priest*, 16–17.

26 O'Collins and Jones, *Jesus Our Priest*, 17–24.

27 O'Collins and Jones, *Jesus Our Priest*, 24–26; Torrance, *Royal Priesthood*, 7.

28 O'Collins and Jones, *Jesus Our Priest*, 27–28, 30–32.

29 O'Collins and Jones, *Jesus Our Priest*, 28–30.

30 O'Collins and Jones, *Jesus Our Priest*, 32–35.

31 O'Collins and Jones, *Jesus Our Priest*, 45–56; Daly, *Origins of the Christian Doctrine of Sacrifice*, 69–76.

32 O'Collins and Jones, *Jesus Our Priest*, 34–37; Daly, *Origins of the Christian Doctrine of Sacrifice*, 65–67.

33 A hoary debate concerns whether or not the offices of bishop and presbyter are distinct in the New Testament, or are simply different names for the same office. For a recent argument that the offices were distinct, see Alistair C. Stewart, *The Original Bishops: Office and Order in the First Christian Communities* (Grand Rapids: Baker Academic, 2014).

34 O'Collins and Jones, *Jesus Our Priest*, 281–84.

35 Daly, *Origins of the Christian Doctrine of Sacrifice*, 82. Daly continues: "[T]he commonly accepted methods of modern scholarship prove beyond reasonable doubt that the primary ethical concept of Christian sacrifice is indeed the one that is operative in the New Testament." Idem, *Origins of the Christian Doctrine of Sacrifice*, 82–83.

36 O'Collins and Jones, *Jesus Our Priest*, 68.

37 1 Clem. 44.4–6, *Early Christian Fathers*, Cyril C. Richardson, trans., Library of Christian Classics (Philadelphia: Westminster, 1953), 64, https://www.ccel.org/ccel/richardson/fathers.vi.i.iii.html.

38 Daly, *Origins of the Christian Doctrine of Sacrifice*, 86; O'Collins and Jones refer to Clement's "ambiguities." O'Collins and Jones, *Jesus Our Priest*, 69.

39 Justin Martyr, *Dialogue with Trypho* 41; "Now, that prayers and giving of thanks, when offered by worthy men, are the only perfect and well-pleasing sacrifices to God, I also admit." Idem, *Dialogue with Trypho* 117:1–3 (ANF 1:257); Daly, *Origins of the Christian Doctrine of Sacrifice*, 90.

40 Justin Martyr, *First Apology* 65 (ANF 1:185); Daly refers to the "meager evidence supplied by Justin." Daly, *Origins of the Christian Doctrine of Sacrifice*, 90.

41 Irenaeus of Lyons, *Against Heresies* 4.18.2; 3.19.3 (ANF 1:485, 449).

42 Irenaeus, *Against Heresies* 4.18.1, 4 (ANF 1:484, 485).

43 Daly, *Origins of the Christian Doctrine of Sacrifice*, 96.

44 The reading is uncertain because we only have Rufinus' Latin translation of Origen's Greek text. The "ministers and priests" are called *ministri* and *sacerdotes*. The latter may be a translation of *hiereis*. Origen, *Homilies on Leviticus 1–16*, Gary Wayne Barkley, trans., Fathers of the Church (Washington, D.C.: Catholic University Press, 1990), 5.3.2; 5.12.9; cited by O'Collins and Jones, *Jesus Our Priest*, 74, 75.

45 O'Collins and Jones, *Jesus Our Priest*, 76; "[W]e must take note how Origen's idea of sacrifice has so little to do with liturgy or ritual." Daly, *Origins of the Christian Doctrine of Sacrifice*, 127.

46 Cyprian of Carthage, *Letter* 63 (62), 17–18 (*ANF* 5:363); O'Collins and Jones, *Jesus Our Priest*, 76–79. Cyprian is the first Latin writer to refer to the presider of the Eucharist as a *sacerdos*; O'Collins and Jones, *Jesus Our Priest*, 78n31.

47 Cyprian, *Letter* 63 (62).18.

48 *Inter Insigniores* cites this letter to affirm that the "priest truly acts in the name of Christ," but the context indicates this a misreading. O'Collins and Jones write: "[T]here is little dispute over Cyprian's call to his episcopal colleagues to walk in the light of Christ, follow him, and to observe his commandments." O'Collins and Jones, *Jesus Our Priest*, 78.

49 John Chrysostom, *Homilies on Heb.* 16.2 (*NPNF* 1/14:443); O'Collins and Jones, *Jesus Our Priest*, 79–80.

50 "What then? do not we offer every day? We offer indeed, but making a remembrance of His death, and this [remembrance] is one and not many. How is it one, and not many? Inasmuch as that [Sacrifice] was once for all offered, [and] carried into the Holy of Holies. This is a figure of that [sacrifice] and this remembrance of that. For we always offer the same, not one sheep now and to-morrow another, but always the same thing: so that the sacrifice is one. And yet by this reasoning, since the offering is made in many places, are there many Christs? but Christ is one everywhere, being complete here and complete there also, one Body. As then while offered in many places, He is one body and not many bodies; so also [He is] one sacrifice. He is our High Priest, who offered the sacrifice that cleanses us. That we offer now also, which was then offered, which cannot be exhausted. This is done in remembrance of what was then done. For (saith He) "do this in remembrance of Me" (Luke 22:19). It is not another sacrifice, as the High Priest, but we offer always the same, or rather we perform a remembrance of a Sacrifice." Chrysostom, *Homilies on Heb.* 17.6 (*NPNF* 1/14:449); O'Collins and Jones, *Jesus Our Priest*, 83.

51 Chrysostom, *Homilies on Heb.* 11.5 (*NPNF* 1/14:419–20); O'Collins and Jones, *Jesus Our Priest*, 81.

52 O'Collins and Jones, *Jesus Our Priest*, 88.

53 Augustine of Hippo, *Homilies on the Gospel of John 1–40*, Edmund Hill, O.P., trans. (Hyde Park, N.Y.: New City Press, 2009), 5.18 (118–19); idem, *In Answer to the Letters of Petilian, the Donatist* 1.5.6 (*NPNF* 1/4:521); O'Collins and Jones, *Jesus Our Priest*, 95–96.

54 Chrysostom, *Homilies on Heb.* 17.6 (*NPNF* 1/14:449).

55 Daly, *Origins of the Christian Doctrine of Sacrifice*, 140.

56 O'Collins and Jones, *Jesus Our Priest*, 104.

12 WOMEN'S ORDINATION AND THE PRIESTHOOD OF CHRIST: *IN PERSONA CHRISTI*

1 Edward Kilmartin, S.J., *The Eucharist in the West: History and Theology* (Collegeville, Minn.: Liturgical, 2004 [1998]), 134–38.

2 "[S]acerdos non tantum in sua, sed in totius Ecclesiae persona sacrificat." Translated and cited in Kilmartin, *Eucharist in the West*, 141–42.

3 Kilmartin, *Eucharist in the West*, 138–39.

4 "Ipse solus [i.e., the priest] potest gerere actus totius Ecclesiae qui consecrat eucharistiam, quae est sacramentum universalis Ecclesiae." *Sentences* 4.24.2 ad 2, in *Commentary on the Sentences* (Latin-English Opera Omnia), Peter Kwasniewksi and Jeremy Holmes, ed., Beth Mortenson, trans. (Steubenville: Emmaus Academic, 2017), bk. 4, d. 14–25, https://aquinas.cc/la/en/~Sent.IV.D24.Q2.A2; cited in Kilmartin, *The Eucharist in the West*, 249. The translation is my own.

5 Liam G. Walsh, "Sacraments," in *The Theology of Thomas Aquinas*, Rik van Nieuwenhove and Joseph Wawrykow, eds. (Notre Dame: University of Notre Dame Press, 2005), 331–32; but also see the numerous other articles in this book as well as standard texts such as Jean-Pierre Torrell, O.P., *Spiritual Master*, vol. 2 of *Saint Thomas Aquinas*, Robert Royal, trans. (Washington, D.C.: Catholic University of America Press, 2003) and Matthew Levering, *Christ's Fulfillment of Torah and Temple: Salvation According to Thomas Aquinas* (Notre Dame: University of Notre Dame Press, 2002).

6 Walsh, "Sacraments," 334–35.

7 Walsh, "Sacraments," 343.

8 Aquinas, *ST* 3.62.3–4. "Now the principal efficient cause of grace is God Himself, in comparison with Whom Christ's humanity is as a united instrument, whereas the sacrament is as a separate instrument. Consequently, the saving power must needs be derived by the sacraments from Christ's Godhead through His humanity." Idem, *Summa Theologiae*, John Mortensen and Enrique Alarcón, eds., Laurence Shapcote, O.P., trans. (Lander, Wyo.: The Aquinas Institute for the Study of Sacred Doctrine, 2012), 3.62.5, https://aquinas.cc/la/en/~ST.III.Q62 (subsequent references refer to this edition); Walsh, "Sacraments," 347.

9 *ST* 3.63.3 (emphasis added); Walsh, "Sacraments," 349, 351; Kilmartin, *Eucharist in the West*, 248.

10 *ST* 3.63.3, *sed contra*.

11 "But it is the sacrament of order that pertains to the sacramental agents: for it is by this sacrament that human beings [*homines*] are deputed to confer sacraments on others: while the sacrament of Baptism pertains to the recipients, since it confers on the human being the power to receive the other sacraments of the Church; whence it is called the 'door of the sacraments.'" *ST* 3.63.6; Walsh, "Sacraments," 351. The English translation here modifies "man" to "human being." Aquinas does not use the Latin *vir*, which means male human being, but *homo*, which means generic "human being."

12 *ST* 3.63.6, *ad* 1.

13 *ST* 3.63.3.

14 *ST* 3.60.6, *ad* 2. In baptism, the "matter" is water and the "form" are the words expressed in the Trinitarian formula "I baptize you in the name of the Father, and of the Son, and of the Holy Spirit."

15 *ST* 3.78.1.

16 *ST* 3.78.1; 3.78.1, *ad* 4.

17 In *ST* 3.82,1 and 3, Aquinas affirms: "Such is the dignity of this sacrament that it is performed only as in the person of Christ (*in persona Christi*)," and "[t]he dispensing of Christ's body belongs to the priest . . . because . . . he consecrates as in the person of Christ (*in persona Christi*)."

18 *ST* 3.60.8; Walsh, "Sacraments," 341–42.

19 Kilmartin, *Eucharist in the West*, 261–63.

20 The authors of Forward in Faith, *Consecrated Women? A Contribution to the Women Bishops Debate*, Jonathan Baker, ed. (Norwich: Canterbury Press, 2004), state: "Thomas understands the priest to be male in terms of the congruity of sacramental signs. There is a 'natural resemblance' which must exist between the matter of the sacrament and the thing signified. It is because the priest has to be the sign and image of Christ that only men can be ordained to the priesthood." Idem, *Consecrated Women?* 46. Aquinas says no such thing. As Roman Catholic author Sara Butler recognizes: "The Scholastic theologians explained the impossibility of admitting women to the priesthood on the basis of sacramental signification, but they did not all relate this explicitly to the representation of Christ as a male. In fact, Saint Thomas did not do so. His interpretation of women's incapacity for ordination involves an appeal both to the Pauline ban and also to a hierarchical understanding of sexual complementarity: a woman cannot signify 'eminence' because she is in a 'state of subjection.'" Sara Butler, *The Catholic Priesthood and Women: A Guide to the Teaching of the Church* (Chicago: Hillenbrand Books, 2006), 81.

The citation of Aquinas provided by the authors of *Consecrated Women* says nothing whatsoever about the priest being male: "For the same reason, the priest also bears Christ's image, in whose person and by whose power he pronounces the words of consecration. . . . And so, in a measure, the priest and victim are one and the same." *ST* 3.83.1 *ad* 3. As noted above, the "image" of Christ which the priest bears is bestowed in the sacramental character of baptism, which is shared in by both men and women.

Aquinas's actual reason for opposition to the ordination of women can be found in his *Commentary on the Sentences*, which was published after his death in a "Supplement" to the *Summa Theologiae*: "Whether the female sex is an impediment to receiving Orders?" Thomas answers that it is: "Accordingly, since it is not possible in the female sex to signify eminence of degree, for a woman is in the state of subjection, it follows that she cannot receive the sacrament of Order." (*ST* suppl. 39.1); thus, Aquinas's own opposition is based on the assumption of an intrinsic ontological subordination of women to men—a position no longer affirmed in current Roman Catholic theology.

21 Butler writes, "The declaration [*Inter Insigniores*] vigorously opposes this reasoning, insisting that the priest acts first *in persona Christi Capitis Ecclesiae*, and only then *in persona Ecclesiae*." Butler, *Catholic Priesthood and Women*, 98–99. *Consecrated Women?* states: "While it is true that the priest represents the whole Church at the celebration of the Eucharist (acting *in persona Ecclesiae*), he does so only because he first represents Christ himself, and acts *in persona Christi*." Forward in Faith, *Consecrated Women?* 46. The authors state that "all who are baptized are the Church by virtue of their baptism. But in order to represent the High Priesthood of Christ, further sacramental symbolism

is required—namely, the ordained ministry, who visibly carries in his human person the likeness of the Son." Idem, *Consecrated Women?* 45. This would seem to be directly contrary to what Aquinas states about the sacramental "character," which all the baptized receive, as a "participation" in the priesthood of Christ.

22 On post-Reformation Roman Catholic eucharistic theology, see especially Robert J. Daly, S.J., "Robert Bellarmine and Post-Tridentine Eucharistic Theology," *Theological Studies* 61, no. 2 (2000): 239–60.

23 "Apology of the Augsburg Confession" 7.28; "Solid Declaration of the Formula of Concord" 7.75; in *The Book of Concord: The Confessions of the Evangelical Lutheran Church*, Robert Kolb and Timothy J. Wengert, eds. (Minneapolis: Fortress, 2000).

24 Yves Congar, *The River of the Water of Life (Rev 22:1) Flows in the East and West*, vol. 3 of *I Believe in the Holy Spirit*, David Smith, trans. (New York: Crossroad, 1997), 228. According to Congar, the first historical witness is Nicholas Cabasilas, *A Commentary on the Divine Liturgy*, J. M. Hussey and P. A. McNulty, trans. (London: SPCK, 1960).

25 Congar, *River of the Water of Life*, 232.

26 Congar, *River of the Water of Life*, 232–33.

27 Paul Evdokimov, *L'Esprit Saint dans la tradition orthodoxe*, Bibliothèque œcuménique 10 (Paris: Cerf, 1969), 101n42; cited by Congar, *River of the Water of Life*, 228.

28 Paul Evdokimov, *Orthodoxy*, Jeremy Hummerstone, trans. (Hyde Park, N.Y.: New City Press, 2011), 256.

29 Kallistos Ware, "Man, Woman, and the Priesthood of Christ," in *Man, Woman, and Priesthood*, Peter Moore, ed. (London: SPCK, 1978), 83, http://www.womenpriests.org/classic/ware.asp.

30 Elisabeth Behr-Sigel, *The Ministry of Women in the Church*, Steven Bigham, trans. (Pasadena, Calif.: Oakwood Publications, 1991); Elisabeth Behr-Sigel and Kallistos Ware, *The Ordination of Women in the Orthodox Church* (Geneva: WCC, 2000).

31 Thomas Hopko, preface to Behr-Sigel, *Ministry of Women in the Church*, ix, xi.

32 Anthony Bloom, preface to Behr-Sigel, *Ministry of Women in the Church*, xiv.

33 Kallistos Ware, *The Orthodox Church: An Introduction to Eastern Christianity*, rev. ed. (New York: Penguin Books, 2015).

34 Kallistos Ware, "Man, Woman and the Priesthood of Christ," in Behr-Sigel and Ware, *Ordination of Women in the Orthodox Church*, 50.

35 Behr-Sigel, *Ministry of Women in the Church*, 14–15, 176.

36 Behr-Sigel and Ware, *Ordination of Women in the Orthodox Church*, 12, 13.

37 In an early response, Nicolas Chitescu argued that "the impure state of women" during their biological cycle would not allow them to "carry out priestly duties." Cited in Behr-Sigel and Ware, *Ordination of Women in the Orthodox Church*, 14.

38 Behr-Sigel and Ware, *Ordination of Women in the Orthodox Church*, 73, 74.

39 The argument from symbolism appears in the essay by Thomas Hopko, "Presbyter/Bishop: A Masculine Ministry," in *Women and the Priesthood*, Thomas Hopko, ed., new ed. (Crestwood, N.Y.: St. Vladimir's Seminary Press, 1999), 139–64.

40 Behr-Sigel and Ware, *Ordination of Women in the Orthodox Church*, 52.

41 Behr-Sigel and Ware, *Ordination of Women in the Orthodox Church*, 49.

42 Behr-Sigel and Ware, *Ordination of Women in the Orthodox Church*, 49–50. Similarly, Behr-Sigel and Ware recognize, "According to an initial interpretation quite common among Orthodox, the argument that the priest is an icon is very close to that of 'natural likeness' in the declaration *Inter Insigniores*." Idem, *Ordination of Women in the Orthodox Church*, 40.

43 Behr-Sigel, *Ministry of Women in the Church*, 16.

44 Behr-Sigel and Ware, *Ordination of Women in the Orthodox Church*, 80 (emphasis original).

45 Butler, *Catholic Priesthood and Women*, 56. Even if we accept this premise of a fundamental distinction between the sacraments of baptism and orders, it does not follow that women cannot receive the sacrament of orders; that would need a distinct argument.

46 Behr-Sigel, *Ministry of Women in the Church*, 140–41 (emphasis original).

47 Behr-Sigel and Ware, *Ordination of Women in the Orthodox Church*, 81.

48 Behr-Sigel and Ware, *Ordination of Women in the Orthodox Church*, 82.

49 Behr-Sigel and Ware, *Ordination of Women in the Orthodox Church*, 83 (emphasis added).

50 Behr-Sigel and Ware, *Ordination of Women in the Orthodox Church*, 85.

51 Behr-Sigel and Ware, *Ordination of Women in the Orthodox Church*, 85.

52 Behr-Sigel and Ware, *Ordination of Women in the Orthodox Church*, 86.

53 Behr-Sigel and Ware, *Ordination of Women in the Orthodox Church*, 41.

54 Behr-Sigel, *Ministry of Women in the Church*, 177–78.

55 Behr-Sigel and Ware, *Ordination of Women in the Orthodox Church*, 41.

56 Behr-Sigel and Ware, *Ordination of Women in the Orthodox Church*, 86.

57 Behr-Sigel and Ware, *Ordination of Women in the Orthodox Church*, 87.

58 Behr-Sigel, *Ministry of Women in the Church*, 22.

59 Behr-Sigel, *Ministry of Women in the Church*, 178–79.

60 Behr-Sigel and Ware, *Ordination of Women in the Orthodox Church*, 86–87.

61 Behr-Sigel and Ware, *Ordination of Women in the Orthodox Church*, 88.

62 Yves Congar, *The Holy Spirit in the "Economy": Revelation and Experience of the Holy Spirit*, vol. 1 of *I Believe in the Holy Spirit*, David Smith, trans. (New York: Crossroad, 1997), 159–62, 160.

63 Congar, *River of the Water of Life*, xiv.

64 Congar, *River of the Water of Life*, 235–36.

65 Congar, *River of the Water of Life*, 238.

66 Congar, *River of the Water of Life*, 236.

67 Kilmartin's views are expressed in *Christian Liturgy: Theology and Practice: Systematic Theology of Liturgy* (Kansas City: Sheed and Ward, 1988) and *Eucharist in the West*, published posthumously, as well as numerous articles.

68 Edward J. Kilmartin, S.J., "Apostolic Office: Sacrament of Christ," *Theological Studies* 36, no. 2 (1975): 243–64; idem, "The Active Role of Christ and the Holy Spirit in the Sanctification of the Eucharistic Elements," *Theological Studies* 45, no. 2 (1984): 225–53; idem, "Sacraments as Liturgy of the Church," *Theological Studies* 50, no. 3 (1989): 527–47; idem,

"The Catholic Tradition of Eucharistic Theology: Towards the Third Millennium," *Theological Studies* 55, no. 3 (1994): 405–55.

69 Kilmartin, "Catholic Tradition of Eucharistic Theology," 441; idem, *Eucharist in the West*, 365.

70 Kilmartin, "Catholic Tradition of Eucharistic Theology," 405.

71 Kilmartin, "Catholic Tradition of Eucharistic Theology," 405.

72 Kilmartin, *Eucharist in the West*, 351–52.

73 Kilmartin, *Eucharist in the West*, 346–48, 368.

74 Kilmartin, "Apostolic Office," 257.

75 Kilmartin, "Sacraments as Liturgy of the Church," 529; idem, "Catholic Tradition of Eucharistic Theology," 439; idem, *Eucharist in the West*, 350.

76 Kilmartin, "Catholic Tradition of Eucharistic Theology," 439.

77 Kilmartin, "Apostolic Office," 260.

78 Kilmartin, *Eucharist in the West*, 356–57.

79 Kilmartin, *Christian Liturgy*, 237, 328; idem, *Eucharist in the West*, 356.

80 Kilmartin, "Sacraments as Liturgy of the Church," 535–36.

81 Kilmartin, "Sacraments as Liturgy of the Church," 527.

82 Kilmartin, "Catholic Eucharistic Theology," 443–44.

83 Kilmartin, *Christian Liturgy*, 338.

84 Kilmartin, "Apostolic Office," 257.

85 Kilmartin, "Sacraments as Liturgy of the Church," 530.

86 Kilmartin, *Eucharist in the West*, 372 (emphasis original). "In the liturgy the creative activity of God is manifested through the explicit response of praise and thanksgiving made by the community for the gift of the Spirit bestowed by the Father through Christ." Idem, *Christian Liturgy*, 367.

87 Kilmartin, "Apostolic Office," 259.

88 Kilmartin, *Eucharist in the West*, 372.

89 Kilmartin, *Christian Liturgy*, 366.

90 Kilmartin, *Eucharist in the West*, 360.

91 Kilmartin, *Christian Liturgy*, 363.

92 Kilmartin, *Eucharist in the West*, 375.

93 Kilmartin, "Sacraments as Liturgy of the Church," 530.

94 Kilmartin, *Eucharist in the West*, 375.

95 Kilmartin, *Christian Liturgy*, 324.

96 Kilmartin, *Christian Liturgy*, 363, 325.

97 Kilmartin, "Apostolic Office," 250.

98 Kilmartin, "Apostolic Office," 252.

99 Kilmartin, "Apostolic Office," 255.

100 Kilmartin, "Apostolic Office," 258.

101 Kilmartin, "Apostolic Office," 263.

102 Edward Kilmartin, S.J., "Bishop and Presbyter as Representatives of the Church and Christ," in *Women Priests: A Catholic Commentary on the Vatican Declaration*, Arlene Swidler and Leonard Swidler, eds. (New York: Paulist, 1977), 295–302, http://www.womenpriests.org/classic/kilmarti.asp.

103 Kilmartin, "Bishop and Presbyter," 299, 297–98.

104 Kilmartin, "Bishop and Presbyter," 298, 299.

105 Edward Kilmartin, S.J., "Full Participation of Women in the Life of the Catholic Church," in *Sexism and Church Law*, James A. Corriden, ed. (New York: Paulist, 1977), 109–35, http://www.womenpriests.org/classic2/kilmarti.asp.

106 Kilmartin, "Full Participation," 128.

107 Kilmartin, "Full Participation," 114.

108 Kilmartin, "Full Participation," 123.

109 Kilmartin, "Full Participation," 123.

110 Kilmartin, "Full Participation," 125.

111 Kilmartin, "Full Participation," 125–26.

112 R. C. Moberly, *Ministerial Priesthood: Chapters on the Rationale of Ministry and the Meaning of Christian Priesthood* (New York: Longmans, Green, 1898).

113 Moberly, *Ministerial Priesthood*, 221–22.

114 Moberly, *Ministerial Priesthood*, 226–28.

115 Moberly, *Ministerial Priesthood*, 230.

116 Moberly, *Ministerial Priesthood*, 232–33.

117 Moberly, *Ministerial Priesthood*, 60–62.

118 Moberly, *Ministerial Priesthood*, 6–8.

119 Moberly, *Ministerial Priesthood*, 19, 31.

120 Moberly, *Ministerial Priesthood*, 43–47.

121 Moberly, *Ministerial Priesthood*, 66.

122 Moberly, *Ministerial Priesthood*, 65, 68.

123 Moberly, *Ministerial Priesthood*, 99.

124 Moberly, *Ministerial Priesthood*, 69–70, 72, 77.

125 Moberly, *Ministerial Priesthood*, 76.

126 Moberly, *Ministerial Priesthood*, 92–96.

127 Moberly, *Ministerial Priesthood*, 240–41.

128 Moberly, *Ministerial Priesthood*, 241–42 (emphasis original).

129 Moberly, *Ministerial Priesthood*, 243.

130 Moberly, *Ministerial Priesthood*, 244.

131 Moberly, *Ministerial Priesthood*, 244.

132 Moberly, *Ministerial Priesthood*, 244–45.

133 Moberly, *Ministerial Priesthood*, 246.

134 Moberly, *Ministerial Priesthood*, 247–48.

135 Moberly, *Ministerial Priesthood*, 250.

136 Moberly, *Ministerial Priesthood*, 251.

137 Moberly, *Ministerial Priesthood*, 254–55.

138 Moberly, *Ministerial Priesthood*, 255–56.

139 Moberly, *Ministerial Priesthood*, 257–58.

140 Moberly, *Ministerial Priesthood*, 258.

141 Moberly, *Ministerial Priesthood*, 259.

142 Moberly, *Ministerial Priesthood*, 261.

143 Moberly, *Ministerial Priesthood*, 286–90.

144 Moberly, *Ministerial Priesthood*, 261–62.

145 Butler, *Catholic Priesthood and Women*, 53–57.

146 Moberly, *Ministerial Priesthood*, 251.

147 Michael J. Gorman, *Cruciformity: Paul's Narrative Spirituality of the Cross* (Grand Rapids: Eerdmans, 2001); also see chapter 7, "Mutual Submission," in this volume.

148 "Now this priestly spirit—I must repeat it once more—is *not* the exclusive possession of the ordained ministry; it is the spirit of the priestly Church." Moberly, *Ministerial Priesthood*, 261.

149 George R. Sumner, *Being Salt: A Theology of an Ordered Church* (Eugene, Ore.: Cascade, 2007), 13–14.

150 Sumner, *Being Salt*, 100.

151 Sumner, *Being Salt*, 101.

152 Sumner, *Being Salt*, 13.

153 Sumner, *Being Salt*, 78.

154 Sumner, *Being Salt*, 83.

155 Sumner, *Being Salt*, 9–10.

156 Sumner, *Being Salt*, 78.

157 Sumner, *Being Salt*, 57.

158 Sumner, *Being Salt*, 78.

159 Sumner, *Being Salt*, 71–72.

160 Sumner, *Being Salt*, 30 (emphasis original).

161 Sumner, *Being Salt*, 24–25.

162 Sumner, *Being Salt*, 25.

163 Sumner, *Being Salt*, 35n9 (emphasis original).

164 Sumner, *Being Salt*, 27.

165 Sumner, *Being Salt*, 34.

166 Sumner, *Being Salt*, 41.

167 See especially Thomas F. Torrance, *Royal Priesthood: A Theology of Ordained Ministry*, 2nd ed. (London: T&T Clark, 2003 [1993]); idem, "The One Baptism Common to Christ and His Church," "The Paschal Mystery of Christ and the Eucharist," and "The Mind of Christ in Worship: The Problem of Apollinarianism in the Liturgy," in *Theology in Reconciliation: Essays towards Evangelical and Catholic Unity in East and West* (Grand Rapids: Eerdmans, 1975), 82–214.

168 Torrance, "Paschal Mystery," 110 (emphasis original).

169 Torrance, "Mind of Christ in Worship," 158–59.

170 Torrance, "Mind of Christ in Worship," 175, 180 (emphasis original).

171 Torrance, "Paschal Mystery," 114 (emphasis original).

172 Josef A. Jungmann, *The Place of Christ in Liturgical Prayer* (Collegeville, Minn.: Liturgical, 1989 [1965]).

173 Torrance, "Mind of Christ in Worship," 142; idem, "Paschal Mystery," 116; *Royal Priesthood*, xi; Jungman, *Place of Christ in Liturgical Prayer*, 239–63.

174 Torrance, "Paschal Mystery," 116–17.

175 Torrance, "Mind of Christ in Worship," 203–4.

176 Torrance, *Royal Priesthood*, xiv.

177 Torrance, "Mind of Christ in Worship," 208.

178 Torrance, "Paschal Mystery," 114.

179 Torrance, "Mind of Christ in Worship," 209; idem, *Royal Priesthood*, 29.

180 Torrance, *Royal Priesthood*, 30.

181 Torrance, *Royal Priesthood*, 29.

182 Torrance, "One Baptism Common to Christ and His Church," 82, 104.

183 Torrance, "Paschal Mystery," 109.

184 Torrance, "Mind of Christ in Worship," 209.

185 Torrance, *Royal Priesthood*, 87.

186 Torrance, "Mind of Christ in Worship," 209; idem, *Royal Priesthood*, 21, 22.

187 Torrance, *Royal Priesthood*, 27, 41.

188 Torrance, *Royal Priesthood*, 74, 77, 81, 97, 103.

189 Torrance, *Royal Priesthood*, xiv.

190 Torrance, *Royal Priesthood*, xv–xvi, xvii, 85, 94.

191 Torrance, *Royal Priesthood*, xi.

192 Torrance, *Royal Priesthood*, xiv.

193 The key theological notions here are *enhypostasia* and *anhypostasia*. Although the incarnate Jesus Christ had a complete human nature with a complete human mind and will, Jesus does not have a human person (*anhypostasia*), because his personal identity (*enhypostasia*) is that of the Word of God, the second person of the Trinity.

194 See especially Kilmartin's essay, "Active Role of Christ."

195 Congar, *River of the Water of Life*, 235–36.

13 THE ARGUMENT FROM SYMBOLISM: GOD, PRIESTS, INCARNATION, AND APOSTLES

1 Edwyn Bevan, *Symbolism and Belief* (Boston: Beacon, 1957 [1938]), 11–13.

2 Manfred Hauke, *Women in the Priesthood? A Systematic Analysis in the Light of the Order of Creation and Redemption*, David Kipp, trans. (San Francisco: Ignatius, 1986), 121–22.

3 Bevan, *Symbolism and Belief*, 14.

4 C. S. Lewis, *Miracles: A Preliminary Study* (New York: Macmillan, 1960 [1947]), 73, 79 (emphasis original).

5 Avery Dulles, *The Craft of Theology: From Symbol to System* (New York: Crossroad, 1992), 18.

6 Dulles, *Craft of Theology*, 19.

7 Avery Dulles, *Models of Revelation* (Garden City, N.Y.: Doubleday, 1983), 131–73.

8 Sallie McFague, *Models of God: Theology for an Ecological Nuclear Age* (Philadelphia: Fortress, 1987), x–xi.

9 McFague, *Models of God*, ix.

10 McFague, *Models of God*, 192–93.

11 C. S. Lewis, "Priestesses in the Church?" in *God in the Dock: Essays on Theology and Ethics*, Walter Hooper, ed. (Grand Rapids: Eerdmans, 1970), 237–38.

12 Hauke, *Women in the Priesthood?* 479.

13 Sara Butler, *The Catholic Priesthood and Women: A Guide to the Teaching of the Church* (Chicago: Hillenbrand Books, 2006), 111 (emphasis added).

14 Hauke, *Women in the Priesthood?* 65–72, 175–90, 216–43; Forward in Faith, *Consecrated Women? A Contribution to the Women Bishops Debate,* Jonathan Baker, ed. (Norwich: Canterbury Press, 2004), 18–19.

15 Hauke, *Women in the Priesthood?* 190–94.

16 Forward in Faith, *Consecrated Women?* 22, 26–29; Hauke, *Women in the Priesthood?* 249–76, 297–325.

17 In the modern discussion, the argument first appears in Sacred Congregation for the Doctrine of the Faith, *Inter Insigniores,* October 15, 1976, http://www.vatican.va/roman_curia/congregations/cfaith/documents/rc_con_cfaith_doc_19761015_inter insigniores_en.html; Butler, *Catholic Priesthood and Women,* 5, 50, 66 70, 72 76, 105; Hauke, *Women in the Priesthood?* 326–39.

18 Hauke, *Women in the Priesthood?* 85–204.

19 Hauke, *Women in the Priesthood?* 90, 92, 94.

20 Butler, *Catholic Priesthood and Women,* 91, appeals to the nuptial imagery of "the husband's initiative and the wife's response as a paradigm of the initiative of divine grace and the human response" as parallel to the ordained priest as the Bridegroom and the "other baptized" as the Bride.

21 Hauke, *Women in the Priesthood?* 175–90; Thomas Hopko, "Presbyter/Bishop: A Masculine Ministry," in *Women and the Priesthood,* Thomas Hopko, ed., new ed. (Crestwood, N.Y.: St. Vladimir's Seminary Press, 1999), 143–47.

22 Butler, *Catholic Priesthood and Women,* 82–92; Forward in Faith, *Consecrated Women?* 29–31; Hopko, "Presbyter/Bishop," 144–45, 157–59.

23 Forward in Faith, *Consecrated Women?* 40–43; Hauke, *Women in the Priesthood?* 318–25; See Hans Urs von Balthasar, *Mary for Today* (San Francisco: Ignatius, 1988); idem, *The Office of Peter and the Structure of the Church* (San Francisco: Ignatius, 1986); idem, *Theo-Drama,* vol. 3: *Dramatic Personae: Persons in Christ* (San Francisco: Ignatius, 1992), 283–360.

24 The imagery appears in Pope John Paul II's *Pastores Dabo Vobis:* "The priest is called to be the living image of Jesus Christ, the spouse of the Church. . . . [I]n virtue of his configuration to Christ, the head and shepherd, the priest stands in this spousal relationship with regard to the community." Idem, *Pastores Dabo Vobis,* apostolic exhortation, March 15, 1992, https://w2.vatican.va/content/john-paul-ii/en/apost_exhortations/documents/hf_jp-ii_exh_25031992_pastores-dabo-vobis.html.; Forward in Faith, *Consecrated Women?* 34–47; Hauke, *Women in the Priesthood?* 330–39; Butler, *Catholic Priesthood and Women,* 78–82, 88–92.

25 Hopko, "Presbyter/Bishop," 156–59, 164.

26 Mary Daly, *Beyond God the Father: Toward a Philosophy of Women's Liberation* (Boston: Beacon, 1985 [1973]), 19. In the first paragraph, Daly writes: "If God in 'his' heaven is a father ruling 'his' people, then it is in the 'nature' of things and according to divine plan and the order of the universe that society be male-dominated." Idem, *Beyond God the Father,* 13. See also Rosemary Radford Ruether, *Sexism and God Talk: Toward a Feminist Theology* (Boston: Beacon, 1993 [1983]); Elizabeth A. Johnson, *She Who Is: The Mystery of God in Feminist Theological Discourse* (New York: Crossroad, 1992);

Elisabeth Schüssler Fiorenza, *Jesus: Miriam's Child, Sophia's Prophet: Critical Issues in Feminist Christology* (New York: Continuum, 2004 [1994]).

27 McFague, *Models of God*, 72, 129.

28 Elisabeth Schüssler Fiorenza, "The Will to Choose or to Reject: Continuing Our Critical Work," in *Feminist Interpretation of the Bible*, Letty Russell, ed. (Philadelphia: Westminster, 1985), 125–36; idem, *Bread Not Stone: The Challenge of Feminist Biblical Interpretation* (Boston: Beacon, 1995).

29 Johnson, *She Who Is*, 150–69; McFague, *Models of God*, 64–65, 145.

30 McFague, *Models of God*, 91, 181.

31 Garrett Green, "The Gender of God and the Theology of Metaphor," in *Speaking the Christian God: The Holy Trinity and the Challenge of Feminism*, Alvin F. Kimel Jr., ed. (Grand Rapids: Eerdmans, 1992), 48.

32 Writing in 1986, Hauke refers to Behr-Sigel in two footnotes, praising, with unintentional irony, the Orthodox as a "bulwark in the defense of the male priesthood." Hauke, *Women in the Priesthood?* 50n17, 193n375. He makes no references to Kilmartin in his text. His discussion of Protestant theologians focuses almost exclusively on liberal Protestant feminists.

33 Kathryn Greene-McCreight, *Feminist Reconstructions of Christian Doctrine: Narrative Analysis and Appraisal* (New York: Oxford University Press, 2000), 36–41 (emphasis original).

34 Green, "Gender of God," 52.

35 Elizabeth Achtemeier, "Exchanging God for 'No Gods': A Discussion of Female Language for God," in *Speaking the Christian God*, Kimel, ed., 4; Roland M. Frye, "Language for God and Feminist Language: Problems and Principles," in *Speaking the Christian God*, Kimel, ed., 20.

36 Athanasius, *De Synodis* 42 (*NPNF* 2/4:472).

37 Hilary of Poitiers, *On the Trinity* 1.4.18 (*NPNF* 2/9:41, 45).

38 Thomas Aquinas, *Summa Theologiae*, John Mortensen and Enrique Alarcón, eds., Laurence Shapcote, O.P., trans. (Lander, Wyo.: The Aquinas Institute for the Study of Sacred Doctrine, 2012), 1.3 art. 1.

39 Thirty-nine Articles, art. 2, http://anglicansonline.org/basics/thirty-nine_articles.html.

40 Addressing the issue of the Son's maleness, it is important to distinguish between the immanent and the economic Trinity, between the Son's eternal generation and his temporal mission, as well as the twofold principle of predication of the *communicatio idiomatum*. One of the implications of the hypostatic union is that the Son is a single divine person with two natures, one divine and one human. Because of the unity of person, two sets of predicates can be attributed to the Son, but the distinction of natures must also be maintained. As divine, the Son is eternal, but as human, the incarnate Son was born in Bethlehem at a particular time. Similarly, it is true that the Son *as divine* has no sexuality because God *as* God has no body; it is also true however that the Son *as human* is male because the Son became incarnate as the human male Jesus Christ.

41 Judy L. Brown, "God, Gender and Biblical Metaphor," in *Discovering Biblical Equality: Complementarity without Hierarchy*, Ronald W. Pierce and Rebecca Merrill Groothuis, eds. (Downers Grove, Ill.: InterVarsity, 2004), 291–93.

42 Frye, "Language for God," 34–43.

43 Tikva Frymer-Kensky, *In the Wake of the Goddesses: Women, Culture and the Biblical Transformation of Pagan Myth* (New York: Macmillan, 1992), 83–117, 168–78.

44 Frymer-Kensky, *In the Wake of the Goddesses*, 188–89.

45 Hauke begins his discussion of the biblical material with the subheading "God as Father." Hauke, *Women in the Priesthood?* 217. For reasons that will become clear, there is actually little in Hauke's discussion concerning "God as Father" until he reaches the New Testament.

46 Ben Witherington III and Laura M. Ice, *The Shadow of the Almighty: Father, Son, and Spirit in Biblical Perspective* (Grand Rapids: Eerdmans, 2002), 1–2.

47 Witherington and Ice, *Shadow of the Almighty*, 2–3.

48 Witherington and Ice, *Shadow of the Almighty*, 2–5.

49 Witherington and Ice, *Shadow of the Almighty*, 20–21.

50 Witherington and Ice, *Shadow of the Almighty*, 19–65; Wesley Hill, *Paul and the Trinity: Persons, Relations, and the Pauline Letters* (Grand Rapids: Eerdmans, 2015).

51 Hauke, *Women in the Priesthood?* 184.

52 Forward in Faith, *Consecrated Women?* 18.

53 McFague, *Models of God*, 69–78.

54 Achtemeier, "Exchanging God," 8.

55 Achtemeier, "Exchanging God," 10; Frymer-Kensky, *In the Wake of the Goddesses*, 93.

56 See also David A. Scott, "Creation as Christ: A Problematic in Some Feminist Theology," and Stephen M. Smith, "Worldview, Language, and Radical Feminism: An Evangelical Appraisal," in *Speaking the Christian God*, Kimel, ed., 237–75.

57 Bevan, *Symbolism and Belief*, 28–81.

58 Bevan, *Symbolism and Belief*, 28, 68.

59 Bevan, *Symbolism and Belief*, 44–48.

60 Athanasius, *Orationes contra Arianos* 2.4–5 (*NPNF* 2/4:350–51).

61 Green, "Gender of God," 59–60.

62 Hauke, *Women in the Priesthood?* 212.

63 Hauke, *Women in the Priesthood?* 209–15.

64 Hauke, *Women in the Priesthood?* 190–91.

65 Hauke, *Women in the Priesthood?* 192.

66 Hauke, *Women in the Priesthood?* 192–94.

67 See chapter 10, "A *Presbytera* Is Not a 'Priestess,'" in this volume.

68 Hugh Montefiore, "The Theology of Priesthood," in *Yes to Women Priests*, Hugh Montefiore, ed. (Essex: Mayhew-McCrimmon, 1978), 3.

69 Sacred Congregation, *Inter Insigniores* 5.

70 Forward in Faith, *Consecrated Women?* 26–27.

71 Forward in Faith, *Consecrated Women?* 28.

72 Forward in Faith, *Consecrated Women?* 27n41.

73 Hauke, *Women in the Priesthood?* 256.

74 Hauke, *Women in the Priesthood?* 257–67.

75 Elisabeth Behr-Sigel and Kallistos Ware, *The Ordination of Women in the Orthodox Church* (Geneva: WCC, 2000), 87.

76 Jay Wesley Richards, "Can a Male Savior Save Women? Gregory of Nazianzus on the Logos' Assumption of Human Nature," *Christian Scholar's Review* 28, no. 1 (1998): 42–57. Significantly, the authors of *Consecrated Women?* quote a letter from E. L. Mascall that states: "It was *male human nature* the Son of God united to his divine person" and that "no *female human nature* was assumed by a divine person." Forward in Faith, *Consecrated Women?* 28. To the contrary, there is no *male* human nature as such. If the Word united a *male* human nature to himself, but no *female* human nature was assumed, then the feminist theologians are correct—a male Savior who assumed a *male* human nature could not save women.

77 Adam Johnson, "A Fuller Account: The Role of 'Fittingness' in Thomas Aquinas' Development of the Doctrine of the Atonement," *International Journal of Systematic Theology* 12, no. 3 (2010): 302–18.

78 Michael J. Gorman, *Cruciformity: Paul's Narrative Spirituality of the Cross* (Grand Rapids: Eerdmans, 2001); Alan G. Padgett, *As Christ Submits to the Church: A Biblical Understanding of Leadership and Mutual Submission* (Grand Rapids: Baker Academic, 2011), 38, 59. See chapter 6, "Disciples of Jesus," and chapter 7, "Mutual Submission," in this volume.

79 See chapter 6, "Disciples of Jesus," in this volume.

80 See chapter 11, "Women's Ordination and the Priesthood of Christ: Biblical and Patristic Background," in this volume.

81 Butler, *Catholic Priesthood and Women*, 3–4, 83.

82 Butler, *Catholic Priesthood and Women*, 50.

83 Sacred Congregation, *Inter Insigniores* 2.

84 Butler, *Catholic Priesthood and Women*, 75–76.

85 Aida Besançon Spencer, "Jesus' Treatment of Women in the Gospels," in *Discovering Biblical Equality*, Pierce and Groothuis, eds., 135–36.

86 Butler, *Catholic Priesthood and Women*, 63, 65, 67; Hauke also finds it significant that Jesus called only male apostles: "That no woman received the apostolic charge is particularly remarkable." Hauke, *Women in the Priesthood?* 333.

87 Robert J. Egan, "Why Not? Scripture, History and Women's Ordination," *Commonweal*, April 3, 2008, https://www.commonwealmagazine.org/why-not-0.

88 Gal. 4:4 states that Christ was "born of a woman," but does not even mention her name.

89 Butler, *Catholic Priesthood and Women*, 68, 94, 95.

90 Hauke also contrasts the role of women with Gentile converts: "[T]here was never any controversy about the pros and cons of admitting Gentile Christians to apostolic office." Hauke, *Women in the Priesthood?* 334. By "apostolic office," Hauke is actually referring to *post-apostolic* office, since none of Jesus' original twelve apostles were Gentiles.

91 Hauke insists that, "since their office remains necessary until Christ's Second Coming, they transferred it, with laying on of hands, to their successors." He insists that the task of an ordinary parish priest celebrating the Eucharist, "distinguishes itself in no way from that of Saint Peter or John." Hauke, *Women in the Priesthood?* 334–35. This misses the significance of the radical distinction between the twelve apostles and contemporary clergy. No "ordinary parish priest" accompanied Jesus during the years of Jesus' earthly ministry, or was a witness to Jesus' resurrection. More significant for this argument, no

modern *Gentile* parish priest could function in the typological role of the twelve necessarily Jewish apostles who typologically represented the new Israel.

92 "There is no evidence in the New Testament that Jesus made any connection between the Twelve and any established offices or continuing roles of leadership in the local communities like elders or overseers." Egan, "Why Not?"

93 See chapter 15, "Women's Ministry in the New Testament: Office," in this volume.

94 Butler recognizes that previous Roman Catholic objections appealed to "Pauline texts that prohibited women's public teaching in the Church and their exercise of authority over men." However, "[b]ecause the contemporary magisterium has abandoned the view that women are unilaterally subject to men, it obviously does not supply this as the reason women cannot be priests." Butler, *Catholic Priesthood and Women*, 46, 47.

95 See chapter 11, "Women's Ordination and the Priesthood of Christ: Biblical and Patristic Background," in this volume.

96 Butler, *Catholic Priesthood and Women*, 103.

97 See chapter 3, "The Argument 'from Tradition' Is Not the 'Traditional' Argument," in this volume.

98 Butler, *Catholic Priesthood and Women*, 61.

99 Epiphanius, *Panarion* 7.79.2,3, in *The "Panarion" of Epiphanius of Salamis: Books II and III*, Frank Williams, trans. (Leiden: Brill, 1994). For a selection of the relevant texts from Epiphanius, see: http://www.womenpriests.org/traditio/epiphan.asp.

100 Epiphanius, *Panarion* 7.79.3,1.

101 Epiphanius, *Panarion* 7.79.3,3–4.

102 Butler, *Catholic Priesthood and Women*, 63.

103 Epiphanius, *Panarion* 79.1,6–7.

104 Epiphanius, *Panarion* 79.3,6.

105 Butler acknowledges, citing *Inter Insigniores*: "In any event, 'a purely historical exegesis of the texts cannot suffice' to establish Christ's will on the matter. The Church must consult the tradition, and the tradition sees in his example with respect to the Twelve an expression of his will for the ordained ministry." Butler, *Catholic Priesthood and Women*, 95.

14 THE ARGUMENT FROM SYMBOLISM: TRANSCENDENCE AND IMMANENCE

1 Manfred Hauke, *Women in the Priesthood? A Systematic Analysis in the Light of the Order of Creation and Redemption*, David Kipp, trans. (San Francisco: Ignatius, 1986), 90, 93, 115.

2 Hauke, *Women in the Priesthood?* 175–97 (emphasis original).

3 Hauke, *Women in the Priesthood?* 258.

4 Hauke, *Women in the Priesthood?* 260.

5 "In transcendence, the immanence of God is always implicit anyway, since transcendence is a concept that is first formed on the basis of God's *relationship* to the world. The concept of immanence is thus, in a certain sense, included in that of transcendence, but the reverse does not apply." Hauke, *Women in the Priesthood?* 143.

6 Hauke, *Women in the Priesthood?* 304 (emphasis original).

7 Hauke, *Women in the Priesthood?* 319.

8   Significantly, a couple of paragraphs later, Hauke states that the priest "effectively repre-sent[s] God," and, in so doing, "also participates in Christ's 'headship.'"

9   Hauke, *Women in the Priesthood?* 334–39. See chapter 12, "Women's Ordination and the Priesthood of Christ: *In persona Christi,*" in this volume. Among other things, I point out in this chapter that Thomas Aquinas affirmed that all Christians (men and women) receive the indelible character of Christ in baptism, and that the character received in ordination builds on this character received in baptism. If a physical resemblance to Christ's masculinity is necessary for the character of ordination, the same would have to be true for baptism as well—in which case women could not be baptized.

10   See the Anglican Forward in Faith document, *Consecrated Women? A Contribution to the Women Bishops Debate,* Jonathan Baker, ed. (Norwich: Canterbury Press, 2004), which cites Hauke several times.

11   Sara Butler, *The Catholic Priesthood and Women: A Guide to the Teaching of the Church* (Chicago: Hillenbrand Books, 2006), 46.

12   Butler, *Catholic Priesthood and Women,* 47 (emphasis added).

13   Butler, *Catholic Priesthood and Women,* 46.

14   Hauke, *Women in the Priesthood?* 364.

15   Hauke, *Women in the Priesthood?* 476.

16   Hauke, *Women in the Priesthood?* 356.

17   Hauke, *Women in the Priesthood?* 356.

18   John Paul II, *Mulieris Dignitatem,* apostolic letter, August 15, 1988, https://w2.vatican .va/content/john-paul-ii/en/apost_letters/1988/documents/hf_jp-ii_apl_19880815 _mulieris-dignitatem.html; Butler, *Catholic Priesthood and Women,* 34–38.

19   Thomas Hopko, "Presbyter/Bishop: A Masculine Ministry," in *Women and the Priest-hood,* Thomas Hopko, ed., new ed. (Crestwood, N.Y.: St. Vladimir's Seminary Press, 1999), 143–44.

20   Hopko, "Presbyter/Bishop," 149. Similarly to Hopko, Hauke states concerning Gene-sis 2: "Initially, it is only the man who appears as the representative of being human." Hauke, *Women in the Priesthood?* 201. Hauke also asserts that "it would be the case of reading modern liberal ideas into the biblical text if one were to assume that, for the Yahwist, any and every part of the subordination of women to men is a consequence of sin." Idem, *Women in the Priesthood?* 202. However, as I point out in chapter 5 in this vol-ume, "Beginning with Genesis," there is no evidence whatsoever for the subordination of woman in the Genesis account before the existence of sin.

21   Hopko, "Presbyter/Bishop," 158–59.

22   Forward in Faith, *Consecrated Women?* 29–30 (emphasis added).

23   Elisabeth Behr-Sigel, *The Ministry of Women in the Church,* Steven Bigham, trans. (Pasa-dena, Calif.: Oakwood Publications, 1991), 56.

24   Hopko, "Presbyter/Bishop," 156 (emphasis added).

25   Hopko, "Presbyter/Bishop," 157.

26   Elisabeth Behr-Sigel and Kallistos Ware, *The Ordination of Women in the Orthodox Church* (Geneva: WCC, 2000), 49–50, 85.

27   Hauke, *Women in the Priesthood?* 85–197.

28 Tikva Frymer-Kensky, *In the Wake of the Goddesses: Women, Culture and the Biblical Transformation of Pagan Myth* (New York: Macmillan, 1992), 118.

29 Frymer-Kensky, *In the Wake of the Goddesses*, 120.

30 Frymer-Kensky, *In the Wake of the Goddesses*, 140, 141.

31 Frymer-Kensky, *In the Wake of the Goddesses*, 203.

32 Frymer-Kensky, *In the Wake of the Goddesses*, 204–5.

33 Frymer-Kensky, *In the Wake of the Goddesses*, 203–12.

34 Frymer-Kensky, *In the Wake of the Goddesses*, 211.

35 Ben Witherington III, *Women in the Earliest Churches* (Cambridge: Cambridge University Press, 1988), 205.

36 See chapter 3, "The Argument 'from Tradition' Is Not the 'Traditional' Argument," in this volume.

37 Hauke, *Women in the Priesthood?* 196 (emphasis original).

38 Hauke, *Women in the Priesthood?* 473.

39 Hauke, *Women in the Priesthood?* 178.

40 Hauke, *Women in the Priesthood?* 200, 179.

41 Hauke, *Women in the Priesthood?* 186, 187 (emphasis original).

42 Hauke, *Women in the Priesthood?* 187.

43 See especially Karl Barth, *Doctrine of Creation*, vol. III/4 of *Church Dogmatics*, G. W. Bromiley and T. F. Torrance, eds. (Edinburgh: T&T Clark, 1961). Subsequent references to this volume are to *CD* III/4.

44 Hauke, *Women in the Priesthood?* 78.

45 Hauke, *Women in the Priesthood?* 178.

46 W. Norris Clarke, S.J., *Explorations in Metaphysics: Being-God-Person* (Notre Dame: University of Notre Dame Press, 1995), 102–22.

47 W. Norris Clarke, S.J., *Person and Being* (Milwaukee: Marquette University Press, 1998 [1993]), 11, 12.

48 Clarke, *Person and Being*, 15–16.

49 Clarke, *Person and Being*, 42, 66, 71 (emphasis original).

50 Clarke, *Person and Being*, 84.

51 Clarke, *Person and Being*, 86, 87.

52 Hauke, *Women in the Priesthood?* 249–50, 267.

53 Hauke, *Women in the Priesthood?* 267.

54 Hauke, *Women in the Priesthood?* 260, 262–63, 265.

55 Hauke, *Women in the Priesthood?* 285, 287, 289 (quoting M. J. Scheeben).

56 Hauke, *Women in the Priesthood?* 291, 296.

57 Hauke, *Women in the Priesthood?* 290.

58 Hauke, *Women in the Priesthood?* 296.

59 Both essays appear in Thomas F. Torrance, *Theology in Reconciliation: Essays towards Evangelical and Catholic Unity in East and West* (Grand Rapids: Eerdmans, 1975), 82–214.

60 See chapter 12, "Women's Ordination and the Priesthood of Christ: *In persona Christi*," in this volume.

61 Thomas F. Torrance, "The Paschal Mystery of Christ and the Eucharist," in *Theology in Reconciliation*, 110.

7(7)
Reason

62 Torrance, "Paschal Mystery," 114.

63 Thomas F. Torrance, "The Mind of Christ in Worship: The Problem of Apollinarianism in the Liturgy," in *Theology in Reconciliation*, 203–4.

64 Hauke, *Women in the Priesthood?* 300.

65 Hauke, *Women in the Priesthood?* 299.

66 Hauke, *Women in the Priesthood?* 190–91.

67 Yves Congar, *The Holy Spirit in the "Economy": Revelation and Experience of the Holy Spirit*, vol. 1 of *I Believe in the Holy Spirit*, David Smith, trans. (New York: Crossroad, 1997), 160, 162.

68 Hauke, *Women in the Priesthood?* 317.

69 Hauke, *Women in the Priesthood?* 304–5.

70 Hauke, *Women in the Priesthood?* 316.

71 Hauke, *Women in the Priesthood?* 324.

15 WOMEN'S MINISTRY IN THE NEW TESTAMENT: OFFICE

1 See Francis Martin, *The Feminist Question: Feminist Theology in the Light of Christian Tradition* (Grand Rapids: Eerdmans, 1994), 90–93, 108–9.

2 Martin, *Feminist Question*, 95.

3 Martin, *Feminist Question*, 95–96.

4 Martin, *Feminist Question*, 109.

5 Martin, *Feminist Question*, 110–12.

6 Philip B. Payne, *Man and Woman, One in Christ: An Exegetical and Theological Study of Paul's Letters* (Grand Rapids: Zondervan, 2009), 453. Payne specifically mentions the lack of specific reference to the names of male overseers (bishops), but the above list shows that this is true of the office of presbyter as well. The two exceptions would be 1 Pet. 5:1, where the writer identifies himself as a "fellow elder," and 2 and 3 John, where the writer identifies himself as "the elder." Assuming (for argument's sake) the traditional authorship of these letters, the apostolic authors Peter and John are identified as "presbyters" but not explicitly named as such.

7 Martin, *Feminist Question*, 113.

8 Ben Witherington III, *Women in the Earliest Churches* (Cambridge: Cambridge University Press, 1988), 107–11.

9 James D. G. Dunn, *Romans 9–16*, Word Biblical Commentary 38b (Waco, Tex.: Word, 1988), 886; N. T. Wright, "Romans," in vol. 10 of *The New Interpreter's Bible* (Nashville: Abingdon, 2002), 761.

10 Ben Witherington III with Darlene Hyatt, *Paul's Letter to the Romans: A Socio-Rhetorical Commentary* (Grand Rapids: Eerdmans, 2004), 376, 379–80.

11 Dunn, *Romans*, 900.

12 Linda Belleville notes that English translations from the 1940s to the 1980s tended to "obscure" Paul's descriptions of these women: "[W]omen can't be leaders, so the language of leadership must be eliminated. Phoebe becomes a 'servant' and Paul's 'helper' (instead of a deacon and Paul's patron . . .)." Linda Belleville, "Women Leaders in the Bible," in *Discovering Biblical Equality: Complementarity without Hierarchy*, Ronald W. Pierce and Rebecca Merrill Groothuis, eds. (Downers Grove, Ill.: InterVarsity, 2004),

116. Craig Keener writes that the RSV "badly translates" *prostatis* as "helper." Craig S. Keener, *Paul, Women and Wives: Marriage and Women's Ministry in the Letters of Paul* (Peabody, Mass.: Hendrickson, 2004 [1992]), 240. Dunn writes that the "unwillingness of commentators to give προστάτις its most natural and obvious sense of 'patron' is most striking." Dunn, *Romans*, 888.

13 As complementarian Wayne Grudem is eager to point out. Grudem recognizes correctly that the key issue has to do with "office": "The question is whether Paul has a church office in view ('deacon') or is simply honoring Phoebe for her service to the church." Grudem, *Evangelical Feminism and Biblical Truth: An Analysis of More Than One Hundred Disputed Questions* (Sisters, Ore.: Multnomah, 2004), 264.

14 Dunn, *Romans*, 886; Payne, *Man and Woman*, 61; Witherington and Hyatt, *Paul's Letter to the Romans*, 382.

15 Dunn, *Romans*, 887.

16 Witherington, *Women in the Earliest Churches*, 113; Pliny speaks of two female slaves who were called *ministrae* in Bithynia. Dunn, *Romans*, 887.

17 Wright, "Romans," 761–62.

18 Keener, *Paul, Women and Wives*, 239. This was noted as long ago as 1917 by B. H. Streeter, who asked, "Why is it that the translators, when interpreting it [*diakonos*] for men, use the word *ministers*, when for women, the word *servant*?" B. H. Streeter and Edith Picton Tuberville, *Woman and the Church* (London: Unwin, 1917), 63; cited by Keener, *Paul, Women and Wives*, 239.

19 Keener, *Paul, Women and Wives*, 238.

20 Keener, *Paul, Women and Wives*, 238–39.

21 Dunn, *Romans*, 886, 887.

22 Dunn, *Romans*, 888.

23 Keener, *Paul, Women and Wives*, 240.

24 Witherington, *Women in the Earliest Churches*, 114.

25 Witherington and Hyatt, *Paul's Letter to the Romans*, 383.

26 Wright, "Romans," 762.

27 Payne, *Man and Woman*, 62–63.

28 Lydia (Acts 17:12) would be another example of such a wealthy patron. Dunn, *Romans*, 889.

29 Witherington and Hyatt, *Paul's Letter to the Romans*, 381.

30 Dunn, *Romans*, 891.

31 Witherington and Hyatt, *Paul's Letter to the Romans*, 385; Witherington, *Women in the Earliest Churches*, 114; Dunn, *Romans*, 891; Payne, *Man and Woman*, 64; Wright, "Romans," 762; Keener, *Paul, Women and Wives*, 240–41.

32 Dunn, *Romans*, 892.

33 Witherington and Hyatt, *Paul's Letter to the Romans*, 386; Dunn, *Romans*, 893.

34 Payne, *Man and Woman*, 64.

35 Witherington and Hyatt, *Paul's Letter to the Romans*, 385; Belleville, "Women Leaders," 122.

36 Witherington, *Women in the Earliest Churches*, 111; Witherington and Hyatt, *Paul's Letter to the Romans*, 385; Dunn, *Romans*, 892.

37 "In light of what we have learned about Paul's συνεργοί, this text strongly suggests that the two women engaged in spreading the gospel with Paul." Witherington, *Women in the Earliest Churches*, 111–12; Witherington and Hyatt, *Paul's Letter to the Romans*, 392–93; Payne, *Man and Woman*, 67.

38 Witherington, *Women in the Earliest Churches*, 154.

39 Grudem dismisses the example of Priscilla as a teacher by distinguishing between public and private teaching, appealing to 1 Tim. 2:12 for warrant, but nothing in 1 Tim. 2:12 makes a distinction between private and public teaching. Grudem, *Evangelical Feminism and Biblical Truth*, 179. See also chapter 9, "Speaking and Teaching," in this volume.

40 Dunn, *Romans*, 894–95; Witherington, *Women in the Earliest Churches*, 115; Witherington and Hyatt, *Paul's Letter to the Romans*, 387; Wright, "Romans," 762.

41 See chapter 3, "The Argument 'from Tradition' Is Not the 'Traditional' Argument," in this volume.

42 John Chrysostom, *Homilies on the Epistle to the Romans* 31 (*NPNF* 1/11:555); cited by Eldon Jay Epp, *Junia: The First Woman Apostle* (Minneapolis: Fortress, 2005), 32.

43 Richard Bauckham, *Gospel Women: Studies of the Named Women in the Gospels* (Grand Rapids: Eerdmans, 2002), 166.

44 Linda Belleville, "'Ιουνιαν . . . ἐπίσημοι ἐν τοῖς ἀποστόλοις: A Re-examination of Romans 16:7 in Light of Primary Source Materials," *New Testament Studies* 51, no. 2 (2005): 231–49 (236).

45 John Piper and Wayne Grudem, eds., *Recovering Biblical Manhood and Womanhood: A Response to Evangelical Feminism* (Wheaton, Ill.: Crossway, 1991), 80; Grudem continues to make this claim in *Evangelical Feminism and Biblical Truth*, 225–26.

46 Epp, *Junia*, 34; Belleville, "'Ιουνιαν," 236.

47 Bauckham, *Gospel Women*, 166–67n242; Belleville, "'Ιουνιαν," 235.

48 Epp, *Junia*, 72.

49 Manfred Hauke, *Women in the Priesthood? A Systematic Analysis in the Light of the Order of Creation and Redemption*, David Kipp, trans. (San Francisco: Ignatius, 1986), 358, 359.

50 Grudem, *Evangelical Feminism and Biblical Truth*, 227.

51 Forward in Faith, *Consecrated Women? A Contribution to the Bishops Debate*, Jonathan Baker, ed. (Norwich: Canterbury Press, 2004), 66.

52 Epp, *Junia*, 35; Bauckham, *Gospel Women*, 167.

53 Epp, *Junia*, 38.

54 Belleville, "'Ιουνιαν," 236–39. Hauke makes the rather embarrassing error of concluding that *Iounian* must be male because the word is masculine in form, with a circumflex accent. Hauke, *Women in the Priesthood?* 359. There would have been no accents when Paul wrote Rom. 16:7!

55 Epp, *Junia*, 58.

56 William Arndt and F. Wilbur Gingrich, *A Greek-English Lexicon of the New Testament and Other Early Christian Literature* (Chicago: University of Chicago Press, 1957), 381.

57 Epp, *Junia*, 65; Bauckham, *Gospel Women*, 167.

58 Bauckham, *Gospel Women*, 166.

59 Epp, *Junia*, 39.

60 Richard S. Cervin, "A Note Regarding the Name 'Junia(s)' in Romans 16.7," *New Testament Studies* 40, no. 3 (1994): 464–70 (464–66); Dunn, *Romans*, 894.

61 Belleville, "Ἰουνιαν," 239, 240. Cf. Hauke, *Women in the Priesthood?* 359. Hauke points to "Silvanus" being shortened to "Silas" as an example of name shortening (Acts 15:40) similar to "Junias," but Belleville points out correctly that Paul himself uses "Silvanus," not "Silas" (2 Cor. 1:19; 1 Thess. 1:1; 2 Thess. 1:1).

62 Cervin, "Note Regarding the Name 'Junia(s)," 467–69.

63 Epp, *Junia*, 33, 34–35, 43; Bauckham, *Gospel Women*, 168; Belleville, "Ἰουνιαν," 240–41.

64 Bauckham, *Gospel Women*, 169; "The assumption that it must be male is a striking indictment of male presumption regarding the character and structure of earliest Christianity." Dunn, *Romans*, 894.

65 Michael H. Burer and Daniel B. Wallace, "Was Junia Really an Apostle? A Reexamination of Rom 16.7," *New Testament Studies* 47, no. 1 (2001): 76–91.

66 Cited by Grudem, *Evangelical Feminism and Biblical Truth*, 224, and Forward in Faith, *Consecrated Women?* 66.

67 Cervin, "Note Regarding the Name 'Junia(s)," 470.

68 Burer and Wallace, "Was Junia Really an Apostle?" 84.

69 Burer and Wallace, "Was Junia Really an Apostle?" 86.

70 Burer and Wallace, "Was Junia Really an Apostle?" 86.

71 Burer and Wallace, "Was Junia Really an Apostle?" 87.

72 Burer and Wallace, "Was Junia Really an Apostle?" 88 (emphasis original).

73 Burer and Wallace, "Was Junia Really an Apostle?" 90.

74 Burer and Wallace, "Was Junia Really an Apostle?" 89.

75 Bauckham, *Gospel Women*, 172–79; Belleville, "Ἰουνιαν," 242–48; Epp, *Junia*, 72–78.

76 Bauckham, *Gospel Women*, 174.

77 Belleville, "Ἰουνιαν," 242.

78 Epp, *Junia*, 73.

79 Bauckham, *Gospel Women*, 174–75.

80 Bauckham, *Gospel Women*, 175–76.

81 Belleville, "Ἰουνιαν," 247.

82 Bauckham, *Gospel Women*, 176.

83 Bauckham, *Gospel Women*, 178; Epp, *Junia*, 74.

84 Belleville, "Ἰουνιαν," 245–46; Epp, *Junia*, 75–76.

85 Witherington and Hyatt, *Paul's Letter to the Romans*, 390.

86 Belleville, "Ἰουνιαν," 243.

87 Belleville, "Ἰουνιαν," 244–45.

88 Epp, *Junia*, 78.

89 Michael H. Burer, "ΕΠΙΣΗΜΟΙ ἘΝ ΤΟΙΣ ἈΠΟΣΤΟΛΟΙΣ in Rom 16:7 as 'Well Known to the Apostles': Further Defense and New Evidence," *Journal of the Evangelical Theological Society* 58, no. 4 (2015): 731–55.

90 Burer, "ΕΠΙΣΗΜΟΙ," 736, 742, 746, 754; Bauckham, *Gospel Women*, 178; Epp, *Junia*, 74.

91 Burer, "ΕΠΙΣΗΜΟΙ," 737–38.

92 Amy Peeler, "Junia/Joanna: Herald of the Good News," in *Vindicating the Vixens: Revisiting Sexualized, Vilified, and Marginalized Women of the Bible*, Sandra Glahn, ed. (Grand Rapids: Kregel Academic, 2017), 283.

93 Burer, "ΕΠΙΣΗΜΟΙ," 754. But again, note Bauckham's and Epp's objections to the personal/impersonal distinction.

94 Bauckham, *Gospel Women*, 179; also Witherington and Hyatt, *Paul's Letter to the Romans*, 390; Epp, *Junia*, 69.

95 Burer, "ΕΠΙΣΗΜΟΙ," 745.

96 Peeler, "Junia/Joanna," 284.

97 Payne, *Man and Woman*, 66n22 (emphasis in original).

98 Grudem, *Evangelical Feminism and Biblical Truth*, 227.

99 Epp, *Junia*, 70; Bauckham, *Gospel Women*, 180; Witherington and Hyatt, *Paul's Letter to the Romans*, 390.

100 Dunn, *Romans*, 895. Another possibility, defended at length by Bauckham, is that Junia was the same person as the "Joanna" mentioned by Luke (Luke 8:3; 24:10). See Bauckham, *Gospel Women*, 181–86.

101 Bauckham, *Gospel Women*, 181.

102 Martin, *Feminist Question*, 100–101.

103 Martin, *Feminist Question*, 106–7.

104 Martin, *Feminist Question*, 100.

105 Martin, *Feminist Question*, 108.

106 Belleville, "Ἰουνιαν," 231.

107 Witherington and Hyatt, *Paul's Letter to the Romans*, 402, 390.

16 WOMEN'S MINISTRY IN THE NEW TESTAMENT: BISHOPS, PRESBYTERS, DEACONS

1 Forward in Faith, *Consecrated Women? A Contribution to the Bishops Debate*, Jonathan Baker, ed. (Norwich: Canterbury Press, 2004), 61.

2 This passage is addressed in chapter 9, "Speaking and Teaching," in this volume. Needless to say, this passage says nothing about "female presidency of the Eucharist" because it says nothing about the Eucharist.

3 Forward in Faith, *Consecrated Women?* 61n105.

4 Wayne Grudem, *Evangelical Feminism and Biblical Truth: An Analysis of More Than One Hundred Disputed Questions* (Sisters, Ore.: Multnomah, 2004), 80. Although Grudem refers to "elders" (presbyters), the text reads *episkopos*, that is "overseer" or "bishop."

5 Ben Witherington III, *Letters and Homilies for Hellenized Christians*, vol. 1: *A Socio-Rhetorical Commentary on Titus, 1–2 Timothy and 1–3 John* (Downers Grove, Ill.: InterVarsity, 2006), 109, 243.

6 Witherington, *Letters and Homilies for Hellenized Christians*, 1:237, 241–42.

7 Philip B. Payne, *Man and Woman, One in Christ: An Exegetical and Theological Study of Paul's Letters* (Grand Rapids: Zondervan, 2009), 448.

8 Payne, *Man and Woman*, 445–48.

9 Payne, *Man and Woman*, 448–49.

10 Payne, *Man and Woman*, 450.

11 Payne, *Man and Woman*, 450–51.

12 Grudem, *Evangelical Feminism and Biblical Truth*, 80; Payne, *Man and Woman*, 445–46.

13 Witherington, *Letters and Homilies for Hellenized Christians*, 1:109.

14 Payne, *Man and Woman*, 451n23.

15 Witherington, *Letters and Homilies for Hellenized Christians*, 1:110, 237.

16 "This he does not lay down as a rule, as if he must not be without one, but as prohibiting his having more than one." John Chrysostom, *Homilies on 1 Tim.* 10 (*NPNF* 1/13:438).

17 Payne, *Man and Woman*, 446.

18 Grudem, *Evangelical Feminism and Biblical Truth*, 80.

19 Payne, *Man and Woman*, 447.

20 Grudem, *Evangelical Feminism and Biblical Truth*, 256.

21 Grudem, *Evangelical Feminism and Biblical Truth*, 80 (emphasis original).

22 Forward in Faith, *Consecrated Women?* 166.

23 Witherington, *Letters and Homilies for Hellenized Christians*, 1:114–15, 236.

24 Grudem, *Evangelical Feminism and Biblical Truth*, 263n107.

25 Payne, *Man and Woman*, 452–53.

26 Witherington, *Letters and Homilies for Hellenized Christians*, 1:241.

27 Payne, *Man and Woman*, 454–59.

28 So, for example, Chrysostom's homily on 1 Tim. 3:8–10: "Some have thought that this is said of women generally, but it is not so, for why should he introduce anything about women to interfere with his subject? He is speaking of those who hold the rank of Deaconesses." Chrysostom, *Homilies on 1 Tim.* 11 (*NPNF* 1/13:441). However, there was no distinction between the office of "deacon" and "deaconess" in the New Testament period. Paul would have been referring to women deacons.

29 Payne, *Man and Woman*, 448.

30 This passage has already been examined at length. See chapter 9, "Speaking and Teaching," in this volume.

31 Payne, *Man and Woman*, 453.

32 See chapter 10, "A *Presbytera* Is Not a 'Priestess,'" in this volume.

33 See chapter 4, "Hierarchy and Hermeneutics," in this volume.

34 Significantly, Hooker considers Paul's instruction to Timothy concerning widows (1 Tim. 5:9) as precisely such an alterable measure in Scripture; Richard Hooker, *The Laws of Ecclesiastical Polity* (London: J. M. Dent, 1907), 1:3.11.8; Stephen Sykes, "Richard Hooker and the Ordination of Women," in *Unashamed Anglicanism* (Nashville: Abingdon, 1995), 93.

35 Hooker, *Laws*, 1:3.5.1.

CONCLUSION

1 See chapter 3, "The Argument 'from Tradition' Is Not the 'Traditional' Argument," in this volume.

2 See chapter 2, "Non-theological Arguments against the Ordination of Women," and chapter 5, "Beginning with Genesis," in this volume.

3 On the notion of development of doctrine, see John Henry Newman's classic work, *An Essay in the Development of Doctrine* (Notre Dame: University of Notre Dame Press,

1994 [1845]), along with the definitive Anglican response by James B. Mozley, *The Theory of Development: A Criticism of Dr. Newman's Essay on the Development of Christian Doctrine* (London: Rivingtons, 1878). Against Newman, Mozley argued for two different senses of the notion of development: (1) a simply explanatory process, in which an idea is said to be developed, but not altered; and (2) a development which is a positive increase in the substance of the thing developed, a fresh formation not contained in or growing out of the original subject matter. Mozley argued that the Nicene formula and the Athanasian Creed were examples of the first notion of development, not the second (144, 146, 149–53). This book argues that the notions of "social liberty and equality" as a development of the notion of Christian liberty, and the ordination of women as a development from the church's affirmation of the ontological equality of women, are developments of the first kind. They do not add something *new* in the sense of something "different," but something *new* in the sense of an explanatory process or drawing out of the logical implications of something inherent in the original subject matter of Christian faith.

4   "Equal" does not mean "identical." Certainly there are clear differences between men and women; only men can be fathers, brothers, and sons; only women can be mothers, sisters, and daughters. Ontological equality in the sense in which it is used here affirms that women are of equal intellectual, moral, and spiritual status with men. Men and women are equally human, and mutually complementary, and mutually created for relationship with one another and with the Triune God as their Creator and Redeemer. More specifically, the notion of equality denies the historical claim that women are less intelligent, emotionally unstable, and more susceptible to temptation than men. Obvious physical differences between men and women mean that there are some tasks for which some men would be more suitable than some women; for example, most men are physically stronger than most women. However, there is nothing intrinsic to the differences between men and women that imply that men and women are not equally suited for most tasks. The specific tasks that would be excluded would obviously be those that are biologically determined. Again, only men can be fathers; only women can be mothers.

5   On the new "complementarian" Protestant argument against women's ordination, see chapter 4, "Hierarchy and Hermeneutics," in this volume.

6   On the new Catholic argument against the ordination of women, see chapter 12, "Women's Ordination and the Priesthood of Christ: *In persona Christi*," in this volume. Sara Butler appeals to Epiphanius in *The Catholic Priesthood and Women: A Guide to the Teaching of the Church* (Chicago: Hillenbrand Books, 2006), 61, 63. Epiphanius's statement can be found in idem, *Panarion* 79.7, 2,3; 3,1, in *The "Panarion" of Epiphanius of Salamis: Books II and III*, Frank Williams, trans. (Leiden: Brill, 1994).

7   On these issues, see especially Carrie A. Miles, *The Redemption of Love: Rescuing Marriage and Sexuality from the Economics of a Fallen World* (Grand Rapids: Brazos, 2006), and David A. deSilva, *Honor, Patronage, Kinship and Purity: Unlocking New Testament Culture* (Downers Grove, Ill.: InterVarsity, 2000).

8 See chapter 12, "Women's Ordination and the Priesthood of Christ: *In persona Christi*," in this volume.

9 See chapter 13, "The Argument from Symbolism: God, Priests, Incarnation, and Apostles," and chapter 14, "The Argument from Symbolism: Transcendence and Immanence," in this volume.

10 Butler, *Catholic Priesthood and Women*, 46–51.

11 Thomas Kuhn, *The Copernican Revolution: Planetary Astronomy in the Development of Western Thought* (Cambridge, Mass.: Harvard University Press, 1992); idem, *The Structure of Scientific Revolutions*, 2nd ed. (Chicago: University of Chicago Press, 1970 [1962]); Michael Polanyi, *Personal Knowledge: Towards a Post-Critical Philosophy* (Chicago: University of Chicago Press, 1962); Bernard Lonergan, *Method in Theology* (Toronto: University of Toronto Press, 1990); Alasdair MacIntyre, *Whose Justice? Which Rationality?* (Notre Dame: University of Notre Dame Press, 1988); idem, *Three Rival Versions of Moral Enquiry: Encyclopaedia, Genealogy, and Tradition* (Notre Dame: University of Notre Dame Press, 1990); Helmut Thielicke, *The Evangelical Faith*, vol. 1: *Prolegomena: The Relation of Theology to Modern Thought Forms*, Geoffrey Bromiley, trans. (Grand Rapids: Eerdmans, 1974).

12 Dorothy L. Sayers, *Are Women Human?* (Grand Rapids: Eerdmans, 1971), 24.

13 Sayers, *Are Women Human?* 25.

14 Dorothy L. Sayers, introduction to *The Divine Comedy of Dante Alighieri, Cantica II: Purgatory*, Dorothy L. Sayers, trans. (New York: Penguin Books, 1980 [1955]), 33.

15 Sayers, introduction, 38.

16 Sayers, *Are Women Human?* 37.

17 That this continues to be a male obsession is evident in the title of the film *What Women Want* (2000), released over fifty years after Sayers' essays.

18 Sayers, *Are Women Human?* 32.

19 See particularly Dorothy L. Sayers, *The Mind of the Maker* (San Francisco: Harper & Row, 1979), and idem, "Why Work?" in *Creed or Chaos?* (Manchester, N.H.: Sophia Institute Press, 1995).

20 Sayers, "Why Work?" 72–78.

21 Sayers, *Are Women Human?* 19, 29.

22 Sayers, *Are Women Human?* 25.

23 Sayers, *Are Women Human?* 21.

24 The question might well be raised: "Where did Sayers herself stand on the question of women's ordination?" to which the answer is that she took an ambiguous stance. In 1948, C. S Lewis wrote Sayers a letter in which he asked her to speak out against the "innovation" of women's ordination by "Chinese Anglicans" (actually Hong Kong; the first Anglican women were ordained in Hong Kong in 1944). Sayers responded that it would be "silly" and "inexpedient" to establish a new barrier between Anglicans and "Catholic Christendom." At the same time, she rejected what would become the new Catholic argument against the ordination of women: "I can never find any logical or strictly theological reason against it. Insofar as the Priest represents Christ, it is obviously more dramatically appropriate that a man should be, so to speak, cast for the part.

But if I were cornered and asked point-blank whether Christ Himself is the representative of male humanity or all humanity, I should be obliged to answer 'of all humanity'; and to cite the authority of St. Augustine that woman is also made in the image of God." In the end, she declined Lewis's invitation: "The most I can do is to keep silence in any place where the daughters of the Philistines might overhear me." The letters are cited in Barbara Reynolds, *Dorothy L. Sayers: Her Life and Soul* (New York: St. Martin's, 1993), 358–59.

25   Sayers, "Why Work?" 76.

26   Miles, *Redemption of Love*, 50–56.

27   Miles *Redemption of Love*, 20.

28   Stephen R. Holmes, "Image of God," in *Dictionary for Theological Interpretation of the Bible*, Kevin J. Vanhoozer et al., eds. (Grand Rapids: Baker Academic, 2005), 318–19.

29   See chapter 7, "Mutual Submission," and chapter 8, "Women in Worship and 'Headship,'" in this volume.

30   See especially Michael J. Gorman, *Cruciformity: Paul's Narrative Spirituality of the Cross* (Grand Rapids: Eerdmans, 2001).

31   Alan G. Padgett, *As Christ Submits to the Church: A Biblical Understanding of Leadership and Mutual Submission* (Grand Rapids: Baker Academic, 2011).

32   Much of what follows is based on a sermon that appeared as William G. Witt, "Icons of Christ: A Sermon Preached at an Ordination," *The Living Church* (September 9, 2012): 16–17, 36–41.

33   Yves R. Simon, *A General Theory of Authority* (Notre Dame: University of Notre Dame Press, 1980 [1962]); Victor Lee Austin, *Up with Authority: Why We Need Authority to Flourish as Human Beings* (New York: T&T Clark, 2010); David T. Koyzis, *We Answer to Another: Authority, Office, and the Image of God* (Eugene, Ore.: Wipf & Stock, 2014).

Much confusion about authority arises insofar as authority is confused with coercion or the oppressive use of power. Rather, power is the ability to get something done. Authority is the delegated responsibility of an individual to act on behalf of a community or group to get something done. An Amish farmer who organizes a barn raising is exercising authority even though no coercion is involved.

34   George Herbert, *The Complete English Works*, Ann Pasternak Slater, ed. (New York: Alfred A. Knopf, 1995), 64–65.

35   John Jewel, *Apology of the Church of England*, John E. Booty, ed. Lady Ann Bacon, trans. (New York: Church Publishing, 2002), 26.

36   On Cyril, see Thomas F. Torrance, "The Mind of Christ in Worship: The Problem of Apollinarianism in the Liturgy," in *Theology in Reconciliation: Essays towards Evangelical and Catholic Unity in East and West* (Grand Rapids: Eerdmans, 1975), 139–214.

37   Thomas Aquinas, *Summa Theologiae*, John Mortensen and Enrique Alarcón, eds., Laurence Shapcote, O.P., trans. (Lander, Wyo.: The Aquinas Institute for the Study of Sacred Doctrine, 2012), 3.62–63. Subsequent references refer to this edition.

38   For the above, see especially Elisabeth Behr-Sigel, *The Ministry of Women in the Church*, Steven Bigham, trans. (Pasadena, Calif.: Oakwood Publications, 1991); Elisabeth Behr-Sigel and Kallistos Ware, *The Ordination of Women in the Orthodox Church* (Geneva: WCC, 2000); Edward Kilmartin, S.J., *Christian Liturgy: Theology and Practice: Systematic*

Theology of Liturgy (Kansas City: Sheed and Ward, 1988); idem, *The Eucharist in the West: History and Theology* (Collegeville, Minn.: Liturgical, 2004 [1998]); George R. Sumner, *Being Salt: A Theology of an Ordered Church* (Eugene, Ore.: Cascade, 2007); Thomas F. Torrance, *Royal Priesthood: A Theology of Ordained Ministry*, 2nd ed. (London: T&T Clark, 2003 [1993]); idem, *Theology in Reconciliation: Essays towards Evangelical and Catholic Unity in East and West* (Grand Rapids: Eerdmans, 1975).

39   Thomas Aquinas, *Summa Contra Gentiles*, Laurence Shapcote, O.P., trans. (Steubenville: Emmaus Academic, 2019), 4.54, https://aquinas.cc/la/en/~SCG4.C54; idem, *ST* 2–2.23.1; Jean-Pierre Torrell, O.P., "Charity as Friendship in St. Thomas Aquinas," in *Christ and Spirituality in St. Thomas Aquinas*, Bernard Blankenhorn, O.P., trans. (Washington, D.C.: Catholic University of America Press, 2011), 45–64.

40   Karl Barth, *The Doctrine of Creation*, vol. III/2 of *Church Dogmatics*, G. W. Bromiley and T. F. Torrance, eds. (Edinburgh: T&T Clark, 1960), 286, 292, 293.

41   Paul K. Jewett's early book *Man as Male and Female: A Study in Sexual Relationships from a Theological Point of View* (Grand Rapids: Eerdmans, 1975), is a development of this theme.

42   Gordon D. Fee, "The Priority of Spirit Gifting for Church Ministry," in *Discovering Biblical Equality: Complementarity without Hierarchy*, Ronald W. Pierce and Rebecca Merrill Groothuis, eds. (Downers Grove, Ill.: InterVarsity, 2004), 241–54.

43   On the difference between the monastic and the Dominican understanding of vocation, see Simon Tugwell, *Ways of Imperfection: An Exploration of Christian Spirituality* (Springfield, Ill.: Templegate, 1985), 138–51; on Dominican spirituality, see idem, *Early Dominicans: Selected Writings* (Mahwah, N.J.: Paulist, 1982); idem, *The Way of the Preacher* (London: Darton, Longman & Todd, 1979). Of course, while there were women Dominicans, there were no female Dominican priests or preachers. The reason for that would have been the traditional one based on female intellectual incapacity.

44   Kathryn Greene-McCreight, *Feminist Reconstructions of Christian Doctrine: Narrative Analysis and Appraisal* (New York: Oxford University Press, 2000), 36–41.

45   For an earlier feminist argument that such differences exist, see Carol Gilligan, *In a Different Voice: Psychological Theory and Women's Development* (Cambridge, Mass.: Harvard University Press, 1993 [1982]).

46   Dorothy L. Sayers was one such an example of a woman who tended to be more rational than emotional, and was thus not "typically female."

BIBLIOGRAPHY

CLASSIC TEXTS

Albert the Great. *Questions Concerning Aristotle's "On Animals."* Irven M. Resnick and Kenneth F. Kitchell Jr., trans. Vol. 9 of Fathers of the Church Mediaeval Continuation. Washington, D.C.: Catholic University of America Press, 2008.

Apostolic Constitutions. In vol. 7 of *Ante-Nicene Fathers.* Alexander Roberts and James Donaldson, eds. Peabody, Mass.: Hendrickson, 1994.

Aquinas, Thomas. *Commentary on the Sentences, Book IV, 14–25* (Latin-English Opera Omnia). Peter Kwasniewksi and Jeremy Holmes, ed. Beth Mortenson, trans. Steubenville: Emmaus Academic, 2017. https://aquinas.cc/la/en/~Sent.IV.

———. *Summa Contra Gentiles.* Laurence Shapcote, O.P., trans. Steubenville: Emmaus Academic, 2019.

———. *Summa Theologiae.* John Mortensen and Enrique Alarcón, eds., Laurence Shapcote, O.P., trans. Lander, Wyo.: The Aquinas Institute for the Study of Sacred Doctrine, 2012. https://aquinas.cc/la/en/~ST.I.S1.

Aristotle. *Politics.* In *The Basic Works of Aristotle.* Richard McKeon, ed. New York: Random House, 1941.

Athanasius. *De Synodis.* In vol. 4 of *Nicene and Post-Nicene Fathers,* Series 2. Philip Schaff and Henry Wace, eds. Peabody, Mass.: Hendrickson, 1994.

———. *Orationes contra Arianos.* In vol. 4 of *Nicene and Post-Nicene Fathers,* Series 2. Philip Schaff and Henry Wace, eds. Peabody, Mass.: Hendrickson, 1994.

Augustine of Hippo. *Homilies on the Gospel of John 1–40.* Edmund Hill, O.P., trans. Hyde Park, New York: New City Press, 2009.

———. *In Answer to the Letters of Petilian, the Donatist.* In vol. 4 of *Nicene and Post-Nicene Fathers,* Series 1. Philip Schaff, ed. Peabody, Mass.: Hendrickson, 1994.

———. *The Literal Meaning of Genesis.* Ancient Christian Writers 41. 2 vols. John Hammond Taylor, S.J., trans. Mahwah, N.J.: Paulist, 1982.

The Book of Concord: The Confessions of the Evangelical Lutheran Church. Robert Kolb and Timothy J. Wengert, eds. Minneapolis: Fortress, 2000.

Boswell, James. *Boswell's Life of Johnson*. 2 vols. London: Henry Frowede, 1904.

Bullinger, Heinrich. *In Omnes Apostolicas Epistolas, Divi Videlicit Pavli, xiiii. et vii. Canonicas, Commentarii Heinrychi Bullingiri*. 2 vols. Zürich: Froschauer, 1537.

Calvin, John. *Commentaries on the First Book of Moses Called Genesis*. John King, trans. Grand Rapids: Eerdmans, 1948. https://ccel.org/ccel/calvin/calcom01/calcom01.i.html.

——. *Institutes of the Christian Religion*. John T. McNeill, ed. Ford Lewis Battles, trans. 2 vols. Philadelphia: Westminster John Knox, 1960.

Charles, R. H., ed. *The Apocrypha and Pseudepigrapha of the Old Testament*. Oxford: Clarendon Press, 1913.

Clement of Rome. "1 Clement." *Early Christian Fathers*. Cyril C. Richardson, trans. Library of Christian Classics. Philadelphia: Westminster, 1953. https://www.ccel.org/ccel/richardson/fathers.vi.i.iii.html.

Cyprian of Carthage. *Letters*. In vol. 5 of *Ante-Nicene Fathers*. Alexander Roberts and James Donaldson, eds. Peabody, Mass.: Hendrickson, 1994.

Didascalia apostolorum. R. Hugh Connolly, trans. Oxford: Oxford University Press, 1929.

Epiphanius. *The "Panarion" of Epiphanius of Salamis: Books II and III*. Frank Williams, trans. Leiden: Brill, 1994.

Frazer, James George. *Adonis, Attis and Osiris: Studies in the History of Oriental Religion*. London: Macmillan, 1906.

Galen. *De locis affectis*. In *Claudio Galeni Opera Omnia*. C. G. Kuhn, ed. Hildesheim: George Olms, 1962.

——. *On the Doctrines of Hippocrates and Plato: Edition, Translation and Commentary; Second Part: Books VI–IX*. Philip de Lacy, ed. Berlin: Akademie-Verlag, 1980.

Herbert, George. *The Complete English Works*. Ann Pasternak Slater, ed. New York: Alfred A. Knopf, 1995.

Herodotus. *The Histories*. Aubrey de Sélincourt, trans. London: Penguin Books, 2003.

Hilary of Poitiers. *On the Trinity*. In vol. 9 of *Nicene and Post-Nicene Fathers*, Series 2. W. Sanday, ed. Peabody, Mass.: Hendrickson, 1994.

Hooker, Richard. *The Laws of Ecclesiastical Polity*. 2 vols. London: J. M. Dent, 1907.

Irenaeus of Lyons. *Against Heresies*. In vol. 1 of *Ante-Nicene Fathers*. Alexander Roberts and James Donaldson, eds. Peabody, Mass.: Hendrickson, 1994.

Jewel, John. *Apology of the Church of England*. John E. Booty, ed. Lady Ann Bacon, trans. New York: Church Publishing, 2002.

John Chrysostom. *Discourse 4 on Genesis* (PG 54:594). In Elizabeth A. Clark, *Women in the Early Church*. Message of the Fathers of the Church 13. Collegeville, Minn.: Liturgical, 1983.

——. *Homilies on the Epistle to the Romans*. In vol. 11 of *Nicene and Post-Nicene Fathers*, Series 1. Philip Schaff, ed. Peabody, Mass.: Hendrickson, 1995.

——. *Homilies on Hebrews*. In vol. 14 of *Nicene and Post-Nicene Fathers*, Series 1. Philip Schaff, ed. Peabody, Mass.: Hendrickson, 1995.

——. *Homilies on 1 Corinthians*. In vol. 12 of *Nicene and Post-Nicene Fathers*, Series 1. Philip Schaff, ed. Peabody, Mass.: Hendrickson, 1995.

————. *Homilies on 1 Timothy*. In vol. 13 of *Nicene and Post-Nicene Fathers*, Series 1. Philip Schaff, ed. Peabody, Mass.: Hendrickson, 1995.

————. *The Kind of Women Who Ought to Be Taken as Wives* (PG 51:230). In vol. 51 of *Patrologia Graeca*. J. P. Migne, ed. 166 vols. Paris, 1857–1886. In Elizabeth A. Clark, *Women in the Early Church*. Message of the Fathers of the Church 13. Collegeville, Minn.: Liturgical, 1983.

————. *On Priesthood*. In vol. 9 of *Nicene and Post-Nicene Fathers*, Series 1. Philip Schaff, ed. Peabody, Mass.: Hendrickson, 1995.

Josephus. *Jewish Antiquities*. The Loeb Classical Library. H. St. J. Thackeray, trans. 9 vols. Cambridge, Mass.: Harvard University Press, 1930.

Justin Martyr. *Dialogue with Trypho*. In vol. 1 of *Ante-Nicene Fathers*. Alexander Roberts and James Donaldson, eds. Peabody, Mass.: Hendrickson, 1994.

————. *First Apology*. In vol. 1 of *Ante-Nicene Fathers*. Alexander Roberts and James Donaldson, eds. Peabody, Mass.: Hendrickson, 1994.

Kern, Otto, ed. *Orphicorum Fragmenta*. Berlin: Weidman, 1963.

Knox, John. *First Blast of the Trumpet against the Monstrous Regiment of Women*. Edward Arber, ed. Southgate, London, 1878. https://www.ccel.org/ccel/knox/blast.

Leo XIII. *Rerum Novarum*. Encyclical letter. May 15, 1891. https://w2.vatican.va/content/leo-xiii/en/encyclicals/documents/hf_l-xiii_enc_15051891_rerum-novarum.html.

Luther, Martin. "Against the Murdering, Thieving Hordes of Peasants." *Christian in Society III*, 49–55. Robert C. Schultz, ed. Charles M. Jacobs and Robert C. Schultz, trans. Vol. 46 of *Luther's Works*, American ed. Jaroslav Pelikan and Helmut T. Lehmann, eds. Philadelphia: Fortress, 1967.

————. "The Freedom of a Christian." *Career of the Reformer I*, 327–77. Harold J. Grimm, ed. W. A. Lambert and Harold J. Grimm, trans. Vol. 31 of *Luther's Works*, American ed. Jaroslav Pelikan and Helmut T. Lehmann, eds. Philadelphia: Fortress, 1957.

————. *Lectures on Genesis Chapters 1–5*. Jaroslav Pelikan, ed. George V. Schick, trans. Vol. 1 of *Luther's Works*, American ed. Jaroslav Pelikan and Helmut T. Lehmann, eds. Philadelphia: Fortress, 1958.

Moberly, R. C. *Ministerial Priesthood: Chapters on the Rationale of Ministry and the Meaning of Christian Priesthood*. New York: Longmans, Green, 1898.

Mozley, James B. *The Theory of Development: A Criticism of Dr. Newman's Essay on the Development of Christian Doctrine*. London: Rivingtons, 1878.

Newman, John Henry. *An Essay in the Development of Doctrine*. Notre Dame: University of Notre Dame Press, 1994 (1845).

Origen. *Fragmenta ex commentariis in epistulam i ad Corinthios*. In Claude Jenkins, "Origen on 1 Corinthians." *Journal of Theological Studies* 10, no. 37 (1908–1909): 29–51.

————. *Homilies on Leviticus 1–16*. Gary Wayne Barkley, trans. Fathers of the Church. Washington, D.C.: Catholic University Press, 1990.

Philo. *Hypothetica (Apology for the Jews)*. The Loeb Classical Library. F. H. Colson, trans. Cambridge, Mass.: Harvard University Press, 1941.

————. *Preliminary Studies*. The Loeb Classical Library. F. H. Colson and G. H. Whitaker, trans. Cambridge, Mass.: Harvard University Press, 1968 (1932).

————. *On Rewards and Punishments*. The Loeb Classical Library. F. H. Colson, trans. Cambridge, Mass.: Harvard University Press, 1939.

Plutarch. *The Education of Children*. In *Moralia*, vol. 1. The Loeb Classical Library. Frank Cole Babbitt, trans. Cambridge, Mass.: Harvard University Press, 1927.

————. *To an Uneducated Ruler*. In *Moralia*, vol. 10. The Loeb Classical Library. Harold North Fowler, trans. Cambridge, Mass.: Harvard University Press, 1969.

Robertson Smith, William. *Lectures on the Religion of the Semites*. New York: Appleton, 1889.

Schaff, Philip. *Slavery and the Bible: A Tract for the Times*. Chambersburg, Pa.: Keifer, 1861.

Tertullian. *On the Apparel of Women*. In vol. 4 of *Ante-Nicene Fathers*. Alexander Roberts and James Donaldson, eds. Peabody, Mass.: Hendrickson, 1994.

Wesley, John. "Thoughts upon Slavery." Vol. 11 of *The Works of the Reverend John Wesley, A.M.* Thomas Jackson, ed. London: John Mason, 1841. https://docsouth.unc.edu/church/wesley/wesley.html.

MODERN TEXTS

Achtemeier, Elizabeth. "Exchanging God for 'No Gods': A Discussion of Female Language for God." In *Speaking the Christian God: The Holy Trinity and the Challenge of Feminism*, 1–16. Alvin F. Kimel Jr., ed. Grand Rapids: Eerdmans, 1992.

Albright, William Foxwell. *Archaeology and the Religion of Israel*. Baltimore: Johns Hopkins University Press, 1946.

Anglican/Roman Catholic Joint Preparatory Commission. "Agreed Statement on Eucharistic Doctrine." *The Final Report*. September 3, 1981. http://www.prounione.urbe.it/dia-int/arcic/doc/e_arcic_eucharist.html.

————. "ARCIC's Clarification of Certain Aspects of the Agreed Statements on Eucharist and Ministry." September 1993. http://www.vatican.va/roman_curia/pontifical_councils/chrstuni/angl-comm-docs/rc_pc_chrstuni_doc_199309_clarifications-arcici_en.html.

Arndt, William, and F. Wilbur Gingrich. *A Greek-English Lexicon of the New Testament and Other Early Christian Literature*. Chicago: University of Chicago Press, 1957.

Austin, Victor Lee. *Up with Authority: Why We Need Authority to Flourish as Human Beings*. New York: T&T Clark, 2010.

Ayres, Lewis. "Augustine on the Trinity." In *The Oxford Handbook of the Trinity*, 123–37. Gilles Emery, O.P., and Matthew Levering, eds. Oxford: Oxford University Press, 2011.

Bailey, Kenneth. *Jesus Through Middle Eastern Eyes*. Downers Grove, Ill.: InterVarsity, 2008.

————. *Paul Through Mediterranean Eyes*. Downers Grove, Ill.: InterVarsity, 2011.

Balthasar, Hans Urs von. *Mary for Today*. San Francisco: Ignatius, 1988.

————. *The Office of Peter and the Structure of the Church*. San Francisco: Ignatius, 1986.

————. *Theo-Drama*. Vol. 3: *Dramatic Personae: Persons in Christ*. San Francisco: Ignatius, 1992.

Barth, Karl. *The Doctrine of Creation*. Vol. III/2 of *Church Dogmatics*. G. W. Bromiley and T. F. Torrance, eds. Edinburgh: T&T Clark, 1960.

————. *The Doctrine of Creation*. Vol. III/4 of *Church Dogmatics*. G. W. Bromiley and T. F. Torrance, eds. Edinburgh: T&T Clark, 1961.

———. *The Doctrine of Reconciliation*. Vol. IV/2 of *Church Dogmatics*. G. W. Bromiley and T. F. Torrance, eds. Edinburgh: T&T Clark, 1958.

Barth, Markus. *Ephesians 4–6*. Anchor Bible 34a. Garden City, N.Y.: Doubleday, 1974.

Bauckham, Richard. *Gospel Women: Studies of the Named Women in the Gospels*. Grand Rapids: Eerdmans, 2002.

Baugh, S. M. "Cult Prostitution in New Testament Ephesus: A Reappraisal." *Journal of the Evangelical Theological Society* 42, no. 3 (1999): 443–60.

Behr-Sigel, Elisabeth. *The Ministry of Women in the Church*. Steven Bigham, trans. Pasadena, Calif.: Oakwood Publications, 1991.

Behr Sigel, Elisabeth, and Kallistos Ware. *The Ordination of Women in the Orthodox Church*. Geneva: WCC, 2000.

Bell, Theo M. M. A. C. "Man Is a Microcosmos: Adam and Eve in Luther's Lectures on Genesis (1535–1545)." *Concordia Theological Quarterly* 69, no. 2 (2005): 159–84.

Belleville, Linda. "Ἰουνιαν … ἐπίσημοι ἐν τοῖς ἀποστόλοις: A Re-examination of Romans 16:7 in Light of Primary Source Materials." *New Testament Studies* 51, no. 2 (2005): 231–49.

———. "Teaching and Usurping Authority." In *Discovering Biblical Equality: Complementarity without Hierarchy*, 205–23. Ronald W. Pierce and Rebecca Merrill Groothuis, eds. Downers Grove, Ill.: InterVarsity, 2004.

———. "Women Leaders in the Bible." In *Discovering Biblical Equality: Complementarity without Hierarchy*, 110–25. Ronald W. Pierce and Rebecca Merrill Groothuis, eds. Downers Grove, Ill.: InterVarsity, 2004.

Bevan, Edwyn. *Symbolism and Belief*. Boston: Beacon, 1957 (1938).

Bockmuehl, Markus. *Jewish Law in Gentile Churches*. Edinburgh: T&T Clark, 2000.

———. "'Keeping It Holy': Old Testament Commandment and New Testament Faith." In *I Am the Lord Your God: Christian Reflections on the Ten Commandments*, 95–124. Carl E. Braaten and Christopher R. Seitz, eds. Grand Rapids: Eerdmans, 2005.

Borg, Marcus J. *The Heart of Christianity: Rediscovering a Life of Faith*. New York: HarperCollins, 2003.

———. *Meeting Jesus Again for the First Time: The Historical Jesus and the Heart of Contemporary Faith*. San Francisco: HarperSanFrancisco, 1994.

———. *Speaking Christian: Why Christian Words Have Lost Their Meaning and Power—and How They Can Be Restored*. New York: HarperCollins, 2011.

Boring, M. Eugene. "Matthew." In vol. 8 of *The New Interpreter's Bible*, 87–505. Nashville: Abingdon, 1994.

Brown, Judy L. "God, Gender and Biblical Metaphor." In *Discovering Biblical Equality: Complementarity without Hierarchy*, 287–300. Ronald W. Pierce and Rebecca Merrill Groothuis, eds. Downers Grove, Ill.: InterVarsity, 2004.

Brown, Peter. *Augustine of Hippo: A Biography*. Berkeley: University of California Press, 1969 (1967).

Buckley, James, and David Yeago, eds. *Knowing the Triune God: The Work of the Spirit in the Practices of the Church*. Grand Rapids: Eerdmans, 2001.

Burer, Michael H. "ΈΠΙΣΗΜΟΙ ΈΝ ΤΟΙΣ ἈΠΟΣΤΟΛΟΙΣ in Rom 16:7 as 'Well Known to the Apostles': Further Defense and New Evidence." *Journal of the Evangelical Theological Society* 58, no. 4 (2015): 731–55.

Burer, Michael H., and Daniel B. Wallace. "Was Junia Really an Apostle? A Re-examination of Rom 16.7." *New Testament Studies* 47, no. 1 (2001): 76–91.

Butler, Sara. *The Catholic Priesthood and Women: A Guide to the Teaching of the Church*. Chicago: Hillenbrand Books, 2006.

Cabasilas, Nicholas. *A Commentary on the Divine Liturgy*. J. M. Hussey and P. A. McNulty, trans. London: SPCK, 1960.

Carson, D. A. "'Silent in the Churches': On the Role of Women in 1 Corinthians 14:33b-36." In *Recovering Biblical Manhood and Womanhood: A Response to Evangelical Feminism*, 140–53. John Piper and Wayne Grudem, eds. Wheaton, Ill.: Crossway, 1991.

Cavanaugh, William T., and James K. A. Smith, eds. *Evolution and the Fall*. Grand Rapids: Eerdmans, 2017.

Cervin, Richard S. "A Note Regarding the Name 'Junia(s)' in Romans 16.7." *New Testament Studies* 40, no. 3 (1994): 464–70.

———. "On the Significance of *Kephalē* ('Head'): A Study of the Abuse of One Greek Word." *Priscilla Papers* 30, no. 2 (2016): 8–20.

Childs, Brevard. *Biblical Theology of the Old and New Testaments: Theological Reflection on the Christian Bible*. Minneapolis: Fortress, 1992.

———. *The New Testament as Canon: An Introduction*. Philadelphia: Fortress, 1984.

———. *Old Testament Theology in a Canonical Context*. Philadelphia: Fortress, 1985.

Clarke, W. Norris, S.J. *Explorations in Metaphysics: Being-God-Person*. Notre Dame: University of Notre Dame Press, 1995.

———. *Person and Being*. Milwaukee: Marquette University Press, 1998 (1993).

Congar, Yves. *The Holy Spirit in the "Economy": Revelation and Experience of the Holy Spirit*. Vol. 1 of *I Believe in the Holy Spirit*. David Smith, trans. New York: Crossroad, 1997.

———. *The River of the Water of Life (Rev 22:1) Flows in the East and West*. Vol. 3 of *I Believe in the Holy Spirit*. David Smith, trans. New York: Crossroad, 1997.

Congregation for the Doctrine of the Faith. *Responsum Ad Propositum Dubium Concerning the Teaching Contained in "Ordinatio Sacerdotalis."* October 28, 1995. http://www.vatican.va/roman_curia/congregations/cfaith/documents/rc_con_cfaith_doc_19951028_dubium-ordinatio-sac_en.html.

Crisp, Oliver D. "On Original Sin." *International Journal of Systematic Theology* 17, no. 3 (2016): 252–66.

Culpepper, R. Alan. "Luke." In vol. 9 of *The New Interpreter's Bible*, 1–490. Nashville: Abingdon, 1995.

Daly, Mary. *Beyond God the Father: Toward a Philosophy of Women's Liberation*. Boston: Beacon, 1985 (1973).

Daly, Robert J., S.J. *Christian Sacrifice: The Judaeo-Christian Background before Origen*. Washington, D.C.: Catholic University of America Press, 1978.

———. *The Origins of the Christian Doctrine of Sacrifice*. Philadelphia: Fortress, 1978.

————. "Robert Bellarmine and Post-Tridentine Eucharistic Theology." *Theological Studies* 61, no. 2 (2000): 239–60.

Davids, Peter H. "A Silent Witness in Marriage: 1 Peter 3:1–7." In *Discovering Biblical Equality: Complementarity without Hierarchy*, 224–38. Ronald W. Pierce and Rebecca Merrill Groothuis, eds. Downers Grove, Ill.: InterVarsity, 2004.

Davis, Ellen F., and Richard B. Hays, eds. *The Art of Reading Scripture*. Grand Rapids: Eerdmans, 2003.

Dayton, Donald W., and Douglas M. Strong. *Rediscovering an Evangelical Heritage: A Tradition and Trajectory of Integrating Piety and Justice*. 2nd ed. Grand Rapids: Baker Academic, 2014.

deSilva, David A. *Honor, Patronage, Kinship and Purity: Unlocking New Testament Culture*. Downers Grove, Ill.: InterVarsity, 2000.

Douglas, Mary. *Purity and Danger: An Analysis of Concepts of Pollution and Taboo*. London: Routledge, 1966.

Dulles, Avery. *The Craft of Theology: From Symbol to System*. New York: Crossroad, 1992.

————. *Models of Revelation*. Garden City, N.Y.: Doubleday, 1983.

Dunn, James D. G. "The First and Second Letters to Timothy and the Letter to Titus." In vol. 11 of *The New Interpreter's Bible*, 773–880. Nashville: Abingdon, 2000.

————. *Romans 9–16*. Word Biblical Commentary 38b. Waco, Tex.: Word, 1988.

————. *The Theology of Paul the Apostle*. Grand Rapids: Eerdmans, 1998.

Egan, Robert J. "Why Not? Scripture, History and Women's Ordination." *Commonweal*, April 3, 2008. https://www.commonwealmagazine.org/why-not-0.

Eichrodt, Walther. *Theology of the Old Testament*. J. A. Baker, trans. 2 vols. Philadelphia: Westminster, 1967.

Elliott, Karen M. *Women in Ministry in the Writings of Paul*. Winona, Minn.: Anselm Academic, 2010.

Emery, Gilles, O.P. *The Trinitarian Theology of St. Thomas Aquinas*. Oxford: Oxford University Press, 2007.

————. *The Trinity: An Introduction to Catholic Doctrine on the Triune God*. Matthew Levering, trans. Washington, D.C.: Catholic University of America Press, 2011.

Epp, Eldon Jay. *Junia: The First Woman Apostle*. Minneapolis: Fortress, 2005.

Evdokimov, Paul. *L'Esprit Saint dans la tradition orthodoxe*. Bibliothèque œcuménique 10. Paris: Cerf, 1969.

————. *Orthodoxy*. Jeremy Hummerstone, trans. Hyde Park, N.Y.: New City Press, 2011.

Fee, Gordon D. *The First Epistle to the Corinthians*. Rev. ed. New International Commentary on the New Testament. Grand Rapids: Eerdmans, 2014 (1987).

————. "Praying and Prophesying in the Assemblies." In *Discovering Biblical Equality: Complementarity without Hierarchy*, 142–60. Ronald W. Pierce and Rebecca Merrill Groothuis, eds. Downers Grove, Ill.: InterVarsity, 2004.

————. "The Priority of Spirit Gifting for Church Ministry." In *Discovering Biblical Equality: Complementarity without Hierarchy*, 241–54. Ronald W. Pierce and Rebecca Merrill Groothuis, eds. Downers Grove, Ill.: InterVarsity, 2004.

Fiorenza, Elisabeth Schüssler. *Bread Not Stone: The Challenge of Feminist Biblical Interpretation*. Boston: Beacon, 1995.

———. *Jesus: Miriam's Child, Sophia's Prophet: Critical Issues in Feminist Christology*. New York: Continuum, 2004 (1994).

———. "The Will to Choose or to Reject: Continuing Our Critical Work." In *Feminist Interpretation of the Bible*. Letty Russell, ed. Philadelphia: Westminster, 1985.

Forward in Faith. *Consecrated Women? A Contribution to the Women Bishops Debate*. Jonathan Baker, ed. Norwich: Canterbury Press, 2004.

Fretheim, Terence E. "Genesis." In vol. 1 of *The New Interpreter's Bible*, 319–674. Nashville: Abingdon, 1994.

Frye, Roland M. "Language for God and Feminist Language: Problems and Principles." In *Speaking the Christian God: The Holy Trinity and the Challenge of Feminism*, 17–43. Alvin F. Kimel Jr., ed. Grand Rapids: Eerdmans, 1992.

Frymer-Kensky, Tikva. *In the Wake of the Goddesses: Women, Culture and the Biblical Transformation of Pagan Myth*. New York: Macmillan, 1992.

Giles, Kevin. *The Eternal Generation of the Son: Maintaining Orthodoxy in Trinitarian Theology*. Downers Grove, Ill.: InterVarsity, 2012.

———. *Jesus and the Father: Evangelicals Reinvent the Doctrine of the Trinity*. Grand Rapids: Zondervan, 2006.

———. "The Subordination of Christ and the Subordination of Women." In *Discovering Biblical Equality: Complementarity without Hierarchy*, 334–54. Ronald W. Pierce and Rebecca Merrill Groothuis, eds. Downers Grove, Ill.: InterVarsity, 2004.

———. *The Trinity and Subordinationism: The Doctrine of God and the Contemporary Gender Debate*. Downers Grove, Ill.: InterVarsity, 2002.

Gilligan, Carol. *In a Different Voice: Psychological Theory and Women's Development*. Cambridge, Mass.: Harvard University Press, 1993 (1982).

Gorman, Michael J. *Cruciformity: Paul's Narrative Spirituality of the Cross*. Grand Rapids: Eerdmans, 2001.

Green, Garrett. "The Gender of God and the Theology of Metaphor." In *Speaking the Christian God: The Holy Trinity and the Challenge of Feminism*, 44–64. Alvin F. Kimel Jr., ed. Grand Rapids: Eerdmans, 1992.

Greene-McCreight, Kathryn. *Feminist Reconstructions of Christian Doctrine: Narrative Analysis and Appraisal*. New York: Oxford University Press, 2000.

Grudem, Wayne. *Evangelical Feminism and Biblical Truth: An Analysis of More Than One Hundred Disputed Questions*. Sisters, Ore.: Multnomah, 2004.

———. *Evangelical Feminism: A New Path to Liberalism*. Wheaton, Ill.: Crossway, 2006.

———. *Politics for the Bible: A Comprehensive Resource for Understanding Modern Political Issues in Light of Scripture*. Grand Rapids: Zondervan, 2010.

———. *Systematic Theology: An Introduction to Biblical Doctrine*. Grand Rapids: Zondervan, 1994.

Gundry-Volf, Judith M. "Gender and Creation in 1 Corinthians 11:2-16: A Study in Paul's Theological Method." In *Evangelium, Schriftauslegung, Kirche: Festschrift für*

Peter Stuhlmacher, 151–71. Jostein Åna, Scott J. Hafeman, and Ottfried Hofius, eds. Göttingen, Germany: Vandenhoeck & Ruprecht, 1997.

Hart, David Bentley. "God or Nothingness." In *I Am the Lord Your God: Reflections on the Ten Commandments*, 55–76. Christopher R. Seitz and Carl E. Braaten, eds. Grand Rapids: Eerdmans, 2005.

Hauke, Manfred. *Women in the Priesthood? A Systematic Analysis in the Light of the Order of Creation and Redemption*. David Kipp, trans. San Francisco: Ignatius, 1986.

Hays, Richard B. *First Corinthians*. Interpretation. Louisville: Westminster John Knox, 1997.

———. *The Moral Vision of the New Testament: Community, Cross, New Creation*. New York: HarperCollins, 1996.

Hess, Richard S. "Equality With and Without Innocence." In *Discovering Biblical Equality: Complementarity Without Hierarchy*, 79–95. Ronald W. Pierce and Rebecca Merrill Groothuis, eds. Downers Grove, Ill.: InterVarsity, 2004.

Hill, Wesley. *Paul and the Trinity: Persons, Relations, and the Pauline Letters*. Grand Rapids: Eerdmans, 2015.

———. *Spiritual Friendship: Finding Love in the Church as a Celibate Gay Christian*. Grand Rapids: Brazos, 2015.

———. *Washed and Waiting: Reflections on Christian Faithfulness and Homosexuality*. Grand Rapids: Zondervan, 2016 (2010).

Holmes, Stephen R. "Image of God." In *Dictionary for Theological Interpretation of the Bible*, 318–19. Kevin J. Vanhoozer et al., eds. Grand Rapids: Baker Academic, 2005.

Hopko, Thomas. "Presbyter/Bishop: A Masculine Ministry." In *Women and the Priesthood*, 139–64. Thomas Hopko, ed. New ed. Crestwood, N.Y.: St. Vladimir's Seminary Press, 1999.

Hunsinger, George. *The Eucharist and Ecumenism: Let Us Keep the Feast*. Cambridge: Cambridge University Press, 2008.

Hunter, James Davison. *Culture Wars: The Struggle to Define America*. New York: Basic Books, 1991.

Jewett, Paul K. *Man as Male and Female: A Study in Sexual Relationships from a Theological Point of View*. Grand Rapids: Eerdmans, 1975.

John XXIII. *Pacem in Terris*. Encyclical letter. April 11, 1963. https://w2.vatican.va/content/john-xxiii/en/encyclicals/documents/hf_j-xxiii_enc_11041963_pacem.html.

John Paul II. *Mulieris Dignitatem*. Apostolic letter. August 15, 1988. https://w2.vatican.va/content/john-paul-ii/en/apost_letters/1988/documents/hf_jp-ii_apl_19880815_mulieris-dignitatem.html.

———. *Ordinatio Sacerdotalis*. Apostolic letter. May 22, 1994. https://w2.vatican.va/content/john-paul-ii/en/apost_letters/1994/documents/hf_jp-ii_apl_19940522_ordinatio-sacerdotalis.html.

———. *Pastores Dabo Vobis*. Apostolic Exhortation. March 15, 1992. https://w2.vatican.va/content/john-paul-ii/en/apost_exhortations/documents/hf_jp-ii_exh_25031992_pastores-dabo-vobis.html.

Johnson, Adam. "A Fuller Account: The Role of 'Fittingness' in Thomas Aquinas' Development of the Doctrine of the Atonement." *International Journal of Systematic Theology* 12,
no. 3 (2010): 302–18.

Johnson, Alan F. *1 Corinthians*. IVP New Testament Commentary Series. Downers Grove,
Ill.: InterVarsity, 2004.

———. "A Review of the Scholarly Debate on the Meaning of 'Head' (κεφαλή) in Paul's
Writings." *Ashland Theological Journal* 41 (2009): 35–57.

Johnson, Elizabeth A. *She Who Is: The Mystery of God in Feminist Theological Discourse*. New
York: Crossroad, 1992.

Jungmann, Josef A. *The Place of Christ in Liturgical Prayer*. Collegeville, Minn.: Liturgical,
1989 (1965).

Keener, Craig S. "Learning in the Assemblies: 1 Corinthians 14:34-35." In *Discovering Biblical Equality: Complementarity without Hierarchy*, 161–71. Ronald W. Pierce and Rebecca
Merrill Groothuis, eds. Downers Grove, Ill.: InterVarsity, 2004.

———. *Paul, Women and Wives: Marriage and Women's Ministry in the Letters of Paul*. Peabody,
Mass.: Hendrickson, 2004 (1992).

Kilmartin, Edward, S.J. "The Active Role of Christ and the Holy Spirit in the Sanctification of
the Eucharistic Elements." *Theological Studies* 45, no. 2 (1984): 225–53.

———. "Apostolic Office: Sacrament of Christ." *Theological Studies* 36, no. 2 (1975): 243–64.

———. "Bishop and Presbyter as Representatives of the Church and Christ." In *Women
Priests: A Catholic Commentary on the Vatican Declaration*, 295–302. Arlene Swidler and
Leonard Swidler, eds. New York: Paulist, 1977. http://www.womenpriests.org/classic/
kilmarti.asp.

———. "The Catholic Tradition of Eucharistic Theology: Towards the Third Millennium."
Theological Studies 55, no. 3 (1994): 405–55.

———. *Christian Liturgy: Theology and Practice: Systematic Theology of Liturgy*. Kansas City:
Sheed and Ward, 1988.

———. *The Eucharist in the West: History and Theology*. Collegeville, Minn.: Liturgical, 2004
(1998).

———. "Full Participation of Women in the Life of the Catholic Church." In *Sexism and
Church Law*, 109–35. James A. Corriden, ed. New York: Paulist, 1977. http://www
.womenpriests.org/classic2/kilmarti.asp.

———. "Sacraments as Liturgy of the Church." *Theological Studies* 50, no. 3 (1989): 527–47.

King Jr., Martin Luther. "Letter from a Birmingham Jail." https://www.africa.upenn.edu/
Articles_Gen/Letter_Birmingham.html.

Knight III, George W. "Husbands and Wives as Analogues of Christ and the Church: Ephesians 5:21–33 and Colossians 3:18–19." In *Recovering Biblical Manhood and Womanhood:
A Response to Evangelical Feminism*, 165–78. John Piper and Wayne Grudem, eds. Wheaton, Ill.: Crossway, 1991.

———. *The Role Relationship of Men and Women: New Testament Teaching*. Philipsburg, N.J.:
Presbyterian and Reformed Publishing, 1985 (1977).

Köstenberger, Andreas, Thomas Schreiner, and H. Scott Baldwin, eds. *Women in the Church: An Interpretation and Application of 1 Timothy 2:9-15.* 3rd ed. Wheaton, Ill.: Crossway, 2016.

Koyzis, David T. *Political Visions and Illusions: A Survey and Critique of Contemporary Ideologies.* 2nd ed. Downers Grove, Ill.: InterVarsity, 2019 (2003).

———. *We Answer to Another: Authority, Office, and the Image of God.* Eugene, Ore.: Wipf & Stock, 2014.

Kuhn, Thomas. *The Copernican Revolution: Planetary Astronomy in the Development of Western Thought.* Cambridge, Mass.: Harvard University Press, 1992.

———. *The Structure of Scientific Revolutions.* 2nd ed. Chicago: University of Chicago Press, 1970 (1962).

Levering, Matthew. *Christ's Fulfillment of Torah and Temple: Salvation According to Thomas Aquinas.* Notre Dame: University of Notre Dame Press, 2002.

Lewis, C. S. *Miracles: A Preliminary Study.* New York: Macmillan, 1960 (1947).

———. "Priestesses in the Church?" In *God in the Dock: Essays on Theology and Ethics,* 234–39. Walter Hooper, ed. Grand Rapids: Eerdmans, 1970.

Liefeld, Walter L. "The Nature of Authority in the New Testament." In *Discovering Biblical Equality: Complementarity without Hierarchy,* 254–71. Ronald W. Pierce and Rebecca Merrill Groothuis, eds. Downers Grove, Ill.: InterVarsity, 2004.

Lonergan, Bernard. *Method in Theology.* Toronto: University of Toronto Press, 1990.

Long, D. Stephen. *The Goodness of God: Theology, the Church, and Social Order.* Grand Rapids: Brazos, 2001.

MacIntyre, Alasdair. *Three Rival Versions of Moral Enquiry: Encyclopaedia, Genealogy, and Tradition.* Notre Dame: University of Notre Dame Press, 1990.

———. *Whose Justice? Which Rationality?* Notre Dame: University of Notre Dame Press, 1988.

Mariottini, Claude. "Genesis 3:16 and the ESV." October 4, 2016. https://claudemariottini .com/2016/10/04/genesis-316-and-the-esv.

Marshall, I. Howard. "Mutual Love and Submission in Marriage: Colossians 3:18–19 and Ephesians 5:21–33." In *Discovering Biblical Equality: Complementarity without Hierarchy,* 186–204. Ronald W. Pierce and Rebecca Merrill Groothuis, eds. Downers Grove, Ill.: InterVarsity, 2004.

Martin, Francis. *The Feminist Question: Feminist Theology in the Light of Christian Tradition.* Grand Rapids: Eerdmans, 1994.

McFague, Sallie. *Models of God: Theology for an Ecological Nuclear Age.* Philadelphia: Fortress, 1987.

Miles, Carrie A. *The Redemption of Love: Rescuing Marriage and Sexuality from the Economics of a Fallen World.* Grand Rapids: Brazos, 2006.

Miller, Patricia Cox, ed. *Women in Early Christianity: Translations from Greek Texts.* Washington, D.C.: Catholic University of America Press, 2005.

Montefiore, Hugh. "The Theology of Priesthood." In *Yes to Women Priests.* Hugh Montefiore, ed. Essex: Mayhew-McCrimmon, 1978.

Moo, Douglas. "What Does It Mean Not to Teach or Have Authority over Men? 1 Timothy 2:11-16." In *Recovering Biblical Manhood and Womanhood: A Response to Evangelical Feminism*, 179–93. John Piper and Wayne Grudem, eds. Wheaton, Ill.: Crossway, 1991.

Neusner, Jacob. *The Idea of Purity in Ancient Judaism*. Leiden: Brill, 1973.

O'Collins, Gerald, S.J., and Michael Keenan Jones. *Jesus Our Priest*. Oxford: Oxford University Press, 2010.

O'Day, Gail R. "John." In vol. 9 of *The New Interpreter's Bible*, 492–865. Nashville: Abingdon, 1995.

Oppenheimer, Paul. "A Theologian's Influence, and Stained Past, Live On." *New York Times*, October 11, 2013. https://www.nytimes.com/2013/10/12/us/john-howard-yoders-dark -past-and-influence-lives-on-for-mennonites.html?pagewanted=all&_r=0.

Padgett, Alan G. *As Christ Submits to the Church: A Biblical Understanding of Leadership and Mutual Submission*. Grand Rapids: Baker Academic, 2011.

———. "Paul on Women in the Church: The Contradictions of Coiffure in 1 Corinthians 11:12-16." *Journal for the Study of the New Testament* 20 (1984): 69–86.

Payne, Philip B. "A Critique of Thomas R. Schreiner's Review of *Man and Woman, One in Christ*." August 23, 2010. http://www.pbpayne.com/?p=456.

———. "Evidence for κεφαλή Meaning 'Source' in Greek Literature and in Paul's Letters." Paper presented at the Annual Meeting of the Evangelical Theological Society, November 16, 2016.

———. *Man and Woman, One in Christ: An Exegetical and Theological Study of Paul's Letters*. Grand Rapids: Zondervan, 2009.

———. "Vaticanus Distigme-obelos Symbols Marking Added Text, Including 1 Corinthians 14.34-35." *New Testament Studies* 63, no. 4 (2017): 604–25.

Peeler, Amy. "Junia/Joanna: Herald of the Good News." In *Vindicating the Vixens: Revisiting Sexualized, Vilified, and Marginalized Women of the Bible*, 273–85. Sandra Glahn, ed. Grand Rapids: Kregel Academic, 2017.

Peppiatt, Lucy. *Unveiling Paul's Women: Making Sense of 1 Corinthians 11:2-16*. Eugene, Ore.: Cascade, 2018.

Perkins, Pheme. "Mark." In vol. 8 of *The New Interpreter's Bible*, 507–733. Nashville: Abingdon, 1994.

Piper, John, and Wayne Grudem, eds. *Recovering Biblical Manhood and Womanhood: A Response to Evangelical Feminism*. Wheaton, Ill.: Crossway, 1991.

Pius XI. *Quadragesimo Anno*. Encyclical letter. May 15, 1931. https://w2.vatican.va/content/ pius-xi/en/encyclicals/documents/hf_p-xi_enc_19310515_quadragesimo-anno.html.

Polanyi, Michael. *Personal Knowledge: Towards a Post-Critical Philosophy*. Chicago: University of Chicago Press, 1962.

Rad, Gerhard von. *Old Testament Theology*. D. M. G. Stalker, trans. 2 vols. New York: Harper & Row, 1962–1965.

Reddit, Paul L. "Book of Leviticus." In *Dictionary for Theological Interpretation of the Bible*, 447–50. Kevin J. Vanhoozer et al., eds. Grand Rapids: Baker Academic, 2005.

Reynolds, Barbara. *Dorothy L. Sayers: Her Life and Soul*. New York: St. Martin's, 1993.

Richards, Jay Wesley. "Can a Male Savior Save Women? Gregory of Nazianzus on the Logos' Assumption of Human Nature." *Christian Scholar's Review* 28, no. 1 (1998): 42–57.

Ruether, Rosemary Radford. *Sexism and God Talk: Toward a Feminist Theology.* Boston: Beacon, 1993 (1983).

Sacred Congregation for the Doctrine of the Faith. *Inter Insigniores.* October 15, 1976. http://www.vatican.va/roman_curia/congregations/cfaith/documents/rc_con_cfaith_doc_19761015_inter-insigniores_en.html.

Sampley, J. Paul. "The First Letter to the Corinthians." In vol. 10 of *The New Interpreter's Bible*, 773–1003. Nashville: Abingdon, 2002.

Sayers, Dorothy L. *Are Women Human?* Grand Rapids. Eerdmans, 1971.

———. Introduction to *The Divine Comedy of Dante Alighieri, Cantica II: Purgatory.* Dorothy L. Sayers, trans. New York: Penguin Books, 1980 (1955).

———. *The Mind of the Maker.* San Francisco: Harper & Row, 1979.

———. "Why Work?" In *Creed or Chaos?* 63–84. Manchester, N.H.: Sophia Institute Press, 1995.

Schreiner, Thomas R. "Head Coverings, Prophecy and the Trinity." In *Recovering Biblical Manhood and Womanhood: A Response to Evangelical Feminism,* 124–39. John Piper and Wayne Grudem, eds. Wheaton, Ill.: Crossway, 1991.

Scott, David A. "Creation as Christ: A Problematic in Some Feminist Theology." In *Speaking the Christian God: The Holy Trinity and the Challenge of Feminism,* 237–57. Alvin F. Kimel Jr., ed. Grand Rapids: Eerdmans, 1992.

Second Vatican Council. "Pastoral Constitution on the Church, *Gaudium et Spes.*" December 7, 1965. http://www.vatican.va/archive/hist_councils/ii_vatican_council/documents/vat-ii_const_19651207_gaudium-et-spes_en.html.

Simon, Yves R. *A General Theory of Authority.* Notre Dame: University of Notre Dame Press, 1980 (1962).

Smith, J. Warren. "The Trinity in the Fourth-Century Fathers." In *The Oxford Handbook of the Trinity,* 109–22. Gilles Emery, O.P., and Matthew Levering, eds. Oxford: Oxford University Press, 2011.

Smith, Stephen M. "Worldview, Language, and Radical Feminism: An Evangelical Appraisal." In *Speaking the Christian God: The Holy Trinity and the Challenge of Feminism,* 258–75. Alvin F. Kimel Jr., ed. Grand Rapids: Eerdmans, 1992.

Spencer, Aida Besançon. "Jesus' Treatment of Women in the Gospels." In *Discovering Biblical Equality: Complementarity without Hierarchy,* 126–41. Ronald W. Pierce and Rebecca Merrill Groothuis, eds. Downers Grove, Ill.: InterVarsity, 2004.

Spong, John Shelby. *Rescuing the Bible from Fundamentalism: A Bishop Rethinks the Meaning of Scripture.* San Francisco: HarperCollins, 1992.

Stewart, Alistair C. *The Original Bishops: Office and Order in the First Christian Communities.* Grand Rapids: Baker Academic, 2014.

Streeter, B. H., and Edith Picton Tuberville. *Woman and the Church.* London: Unwin, 1917.

Sumner, George R. *Being Salt: A Theology of an Ordered Church.* Eugene, Ore.: Cascade, 2007.

Sykes, Stephen. *Unashamed Anglicanism.* Nashville: Abingdon, 1995.

Taylor, Charles. *A Secular Age*. Cambridge, Mass.: Harvard University Press, 2007.

Thielicke, Helmut. *The Evangelical Faith*. Vol. 1: *Prolegomena: The Relation of Theology to Modern Thought Forms*. Geoffrey Bromiley, trans. Grand Rapids: Eerdmans, 1974.

Thiselton, Anthony. *The First Epistle to the Corinthians*. New International Greek Testament Commentary. Grand Rapids: Eerdmans, 2000.

Thompson, John Lee. *John Calvin and the Daughters of Sarah: Women in Regular and Exceptional Roles in the Exegesis of Calvin, His Predecessors, and His Contemporaries*. Geneva: Librairie Droz, 1992.

Torrance, Thomas F. "The Mind of Christ in Worship: The Problem of Apollinarianism in the Liturgy." In *Theology in Reconciliation: Essays towards Evangelical and Catholic Unity in East and West*, 139–214. Grand Rapids: Eerdmans, 1975.

———. "The One Baptism Common to Christ and His Church." In *Theology in Reconciliation: Essays towards Evangelical and Catholic Unity in East and West*, 82–105. Grand Rapids: Eerdmans, 1975.

———. "The Paschal Mystery of Christ and the Eucharist." In *Theology in Reconciliation: Essays towards Evangelical and Catholic Unity in East and West*, 106–38. Grand Rapids: Eerdmans, 1975.

———. *Royal Priesthood: A Theology of Ordained Ministry*. 2nd ed. London: T&T Clark, 2003 (1993).

———. *Theology in Reconciliation: Essays towards Evangelical and Catholic Unity in East and West*. Grand Rapids: Eerdmans, 1975.

Torrell, Jean-Pierre, O.P. "Charity as Friendship in St. Thomas Aquinas." In *Christ and Spirituality in St. Thomas Aquinas*, 45–64. Bernard Blankenhorn, O.P., trans. Washington, D.C.: Catholic University of America Press, 2011.

———. *Spiritual Master*. Vol. 2 of *Saint Thomas Aquinas*. Robert Royal, trans. Washington, D.C.: Catholic University of America Press, 2003.

Trible, Phyllis. *God and the Rhetoric of Sexuality*. Philadelphia: Fortress, 1978.

Tugwell, Simon. *Early Dominicans: Selected Writings*. Mahwah, N.J.: Paulist, 1982.

———. *The Way of the Preacher*. London: Darton, Longman & Todd, 1979.

———. *Ways of Imperfection: An Exploration of Christian Spirituality*. Springfield, Ill.: Templegate, 1985.

United States Conference of Catholic Bishops. "The Eucharist." October 1, 1967. http://www.usccb.org/beliefs-and-teachings/ecumenical-and-interreligious/ecumenical/lutheran/eucharist.cfm.

Vanhoozer, Kevin. *The Drama of Scripture: A Canonical Linguistic Approach to Christian Theology*. Louisville: Westminster John Knox, 2005.

Walsh, Liam G. "Sacraments." *The Theology of Thomas Aquinas*. Rik van Nieuwenhove and Joseph Wawrykow, eds. Notre Dame: University of Notre Dame Press, 2005.

Ware, Kallistos. "Man, Woman, and the Priesthood of Christ." In *Man, Woman, and Priesthood*, 68–90. Peter Moore, ed. London: SPCK, 1978. http://www.womenpriests.org/classic/ware.asp.

———. *The Orthodox Church: An Introduction to Eastern Christianity*. Rev. ed. New York: Penguin Books, 2015.

Wawrykow, Joseph. "Franciscan and Dominican Trinitarian Theology (Thirteenth Century) Bonaventure and Aquinas." In *The Oxford Handbook of the Trinity*. Gilles Emery, O.P., and Matthew Levering, eds. Oxford: Oxford University Press, 2011.

Webb, William J. "Gender Equality and Homosexuality." In *Discovering Biblical Equality: Complementarity without Hierarchy*, 401–13. Ronald W. Pierce and Rebecca Merrill Groothuis, eds. Downers Grove, Ill.: InterVarsity, 2004.

———. "A Redemptive-Movement Hermeneutic: The Slavery Analogy." In *Discovering Biblical Equality: Complementarity without Hierarchy*, 382–400. Ronald W. Pierce and Rebecca Merrill Groothuis, eds. Downers Grove, Ill.: InterVarsity, 2004.

———. *Slaves, Women and Homosexuals: Exploring the Hermeneutics of Cultural Analysis*. Downers Grove, Ill.: InterVarsity, 2001.

Webster, John. *Holy Scripture: A Dogmatic Sketch*. Cambridge: Cambridge University Press, 2003.

Wijngaards Institute for Catholic Research. "Theologians Assess 'Ordinatio Sacerdotalis.'" http://www.womenpriests.org/teaching/mag_con2.asp#cathol.

Witherington III, Ben. *Letters and Homilies for Hellenized Christians*. Vol. 1: *A Socio-Rhetorical Commentary on Titus, 1–2 Timothy and 1–3 John*. Downers Grove, Ill.: InterVarsity, 2006.

———. *The Letters to Philemon, the Colossians, and the Ephesians: A Socio-Rhetorical Commentary on the Captivity Epistles*. Grand Rapids: Eerdmans, 2007.

———. *The Living Word of God: Rethinking the Theology of the Bible*. Waco, Tex.: Baylor University Press, 2007.

———. *Women in the Earliest Churches*. Cambridge: Cambridge University Press, 1988.

———. *Women in the Ministry of Jesus: A Study of Jesus' Attitudes to Women and Their Roles as Reflected in His Earthly Life*. Cambridge: Cambridge University Press, 1984.

Witherington III, Ben, with Darlene Hyatt. *Paul's Letter to the Romans: A Socio-Rhetorical Commentary*. Grand Rapids: Eerdmans, 2004.

Witherington III, Ben, and Laura M. Ice. *The Shadow of the Almighty: Father, Son, and Spirit in Biblical Perspective*. Grand Rapids: Eerdmans, 2002.

Witt, William G. "Icons of Christ: A Sermon Preached at an Ordination." *The Living Church* (September 9, 2012): 16–17, 36–41.

Wright, N. T. *Jesus and the Victory of God*. Minneapolis: Fortress, 1996.

———. *The New Testament and the People of God*. Minneapolis: Fortress, 1992.

———. "Romans." In vol. 10 of *The New Interpreter's Bible*, 393–770. Nashville: Abingdon, 2002.

———. *Scripture and the Authority of God: How to Read the Bible Today*. New York: HarperCollins, 2013.

———. *Surprised by Scripture*. New York: HarperCollins, 2014.

———. "Women's Service in the Church: The Biblical Basis." September 4, 2004. https://ntwrightpage.com/2016/07/12/womens-service-in-the-church-the-biblical-basis.

Yee, Gale A. "The Book of Hosea." In vol. 7 of *The New Interpreter's Bible*, 195–297. Nashville: Abingdon, 1996.

Yoder, John Howard. *The Politics of Jesus: Vicit Agnus Noster*. 2nd ed. Grand Rapids: Eerdmans, 1994 (1972).

INDEX

CPSIA information can be obtained
at www.ICGtesting.com
Printed in the USA
LVHW090003270221
680051LV00002B/147